Huck's Raft

The Belknap Press of Harvard University Press

Cambridge, Massachusetts, and London, England

Huck's Raft

A History of American Childhood

Steven Mintz

First Harvard University Press paperback edition, 2006

Title page illustration: Photograph of Charles Lindbergh
at about age ten, rafting on the Mississippi River near
Little Falls, Minnesota, around 1912. Courtesy of the
Lindbergh Picture Collection, Manuscripts and Archives,
Yale University Library.

Library of Congress Cataloging-in-Publication Data

Mintz, Steven, 1953–
Huck's raft : a history of American childhood / Steven Mintz.
p. cm.
Includes bibliographical references and index.
ISBN 0-674-01508-8 (cloth: alk. paper)
ISBN 0-674-01998-9 (pbk.)
1. Childhood—United States—History.
2. Child rearing—United States—History.
3. Children—United States—Social conditions.
4. United States—Social life and customs.
I. Title.

HQ792.U5M57 2004
305.23′0973—dc22   2004042220

Designed by Gwen Nefsky Frankfeldt

Contents

Preface

FOR MORE THAN three centuries Americans have believed that the younger generation is less respectful and knowledgeable, and more alienated, sexually promiscuous, and violent, than previously. Today adults fear that children are growing up too fast and losing their sense of innocent wonder too early. Prematurely exposed to the pressures, stresses, and responsibilities of adult life, the young mimic adult sophistication, dress inappropriately, and experiment with alcohol, drugs, sex, and tobacco before they are emotionally and psychologically ready.

One of the goals of this book is to strip away the myths, misconceptions, and nostalgia that contribute to this pessimism about the young. There has never been a time when the overwhelming majority of American children were well cared for and their experiences idyllic. Nor has childhood ever been an age of innocence, at least not for most children. Childhood has never been insulated from the pressures and demands of the surrounding society, and each generation of children has had to wrestle with the social, political, and economic constraints of its own historical period. In our own time, the young have had to struggle with high rates of family instability, a deepening disconnection from adults, and the expectation that all children should pursue the same academic path at the same pace, even as the attainment of full adulthood recedes ever further into the future.

The history of children is often treated as a marginal subject, and there is no question that it is especially difficult to write. Children are rarely obvious historical actors. They leave fewer historical sources than adults, and their powerlessness makes them less visible than other social groups. Nevertheless, the history of childhood is inextricably bound up with the broader political and social events in the life of the nation—including colonization, revolution, slavery, industrialization, urbanization, immigration, and war—and children's experience embodies many of the key themes in American history, such as the rise of modern bureaucratic institutions, the growth of a consumer economy, and the elaboration of a welfare state.

Certain themes and patterns of American childhood will emerge in this book. The first is that childhood is not an unchanging biological stage of life but is, rather, a social and cultural construct that has changed radically over time. Every aspect of childhood—including children's household responsibilities, play, schooling, relationships with parents and peers, and paths to adulthood—has been transformed over the past four centuries. Just two hundred years ago there was far less age segregation than there is today and much less concern with organizing experience by chronological age. There was also far less sentimentalizing of children as special beings who were more innocent and vulnerable than adults. This does not mean that adults failed to recognize childhood as a stage of life, with its own special needs and characteristics. Nor does it imply that parents were unconcerned about their children and failed to love them and mourn their deaths. Both the definition and experience of childhood have varied according to changing cultural, demographic, economic, and historical circumstances.

Nor is childhood an uncontested concept. The late twentieth-century culture war—pitting advocates of a "protected" childhood, seeking to shield children from adult realities, against proponents of a "prepared" childhood—is only the most recent in a long series of conflicts over the definition of a proper childhood. These range from a seventeenth-century conflict between Anglican traditionalist, humanistic, and Puritan conceptions of childhood; to heated eighteenth-century debates over infant depravity and patriarchal authority; and turn-of-the-twentieth-century struggles between the notion of a useful childhood, which expected children to act in a way that repaid their parents' sacrifices, and the ideal of a sheltered childhood, free from labor and devoted to play and education.

Another major theme is the diversity of childhood. Childhood, the period from infancy to eighteen, includes girls and boys at very different stages of development. It encompasses a wide variety of classes, ethnic groups, regions, religions, and time periods. During the early seventeenth century demographic, economic, ideological, and religious factors combined to make geographical subcultures the most significant markers of childhood diversity. By the mid-nineteenth century, shifts in cultural and religious values and a highly uneven process of economic development made social class, gender, and race more salient sources of childhood diversity. In recent years social conservatives have tended to fixate on differences in family structure, while political liberals have tended to focus on ethnic, gender, and racial differences. In fact social class is the most significant determinant of children's well-being. While race, gender, and ethnicity exert a powerful influence on children's lives, socioeconomic status is intimately linked to their health care, schooling, and family stability.

This book also traces the shifting power relationships between parents and children, especially parents' increasing psychological investment in their children. The Puritans believed that parents were responsible for their children's spiritual upbringing; contemporary parents hold themselves responsible not only for children's physical well-being but also for their psychological adjustment, personal happiness, and future success. As birthrates fell and increasing numbers of mothers entered the paid workforce, parental anxiety intensified; fears for children's safety escalated, as did concern that they not suffer from boredom or low self-esteem. Above all, middle-class parents worried that their children would be unable to replicate their status position.

Then there is the pattern of recurrent moral panics over children's well-being. Ever since the Pilgrims departed for Plymouth in 1620, fearful that "their posterity would be in danger to degenerate and be corrupted" in the Old World, Americans have experienced repeated panics over the younger generation.[1] Sometimes these panics were indeed about children, such as the worries over polio in the early 1950s. More often, however, children stand in for some other issue, and the panics are more metaphorical than representational, such as the panic over teenage pregnancy, youth violence, and declining academic achievement in the late 1970s and 1980s, which reflected pervasive fears about family breakdown, crime, drugs, and America's declining competitiveness in the world.

Far from regarding children simply as passive creatures, who are the objects of socialization and schooling, and consumers of entertainment and products produced by grownups, this book views children as active agents in the evolution of their society. The following pages will demonstrate that children have participated actively in the major events in American history, that child-adult relations have involved a process of contestation and negotiation, and that children have been creators as well as consumers of culture. The balance between childhood dependence and independence has shifted over time and provides a signifier of childhood experience as well as the adult perception of, and relation to, that experience.

In certain respects, today's children are more autonomous than young people have ever been. They have their own institutions and media, most now have their own rooms, and many teens have their own cars. Contemporary children mature faster physiologically than those in the past and are more knowledgeable about sexuality, drugs, and other adult realities. They are also more fully integrated into the realm of consumer culture at an earlier age. Yet from the vantage point of history, contemporary children's lives are more regimented and constrained than ever before. Contemporary society is extreme in the distinction it draws between the worlds of childhood and youth, on the one hand, and of adulthood, on the other. Far more than previous generations, we have prolonged and intensified children's emotional and psychological dependence. Children are far more resilient, adaptable, and capable than our society typically assumes. We have segregated the young in age-graded institutions, and, as a result, children grow up with little contact with adults apart from their parents and other relatives and childcare professionals. Unlike children in the past, young people today have fewer socially valued ways to contribute to their family's well-being or to participate in community life. By looking back over four centuries of American childhood we can perhaps recover old ways and discover new ways to reconnect children to a broader range of adult mentors and to expand their opportunities to participate in activities that they and society find truly meaningful.

THIS BOOK is a work of synthesis and interpretation, and my debts are recorded in every note. Certain individuals, however, deserve special recognition. My colleagues at the Council on Contemporary Families—including Ashton Applewhite, Stephanie Coontz, Carolyn and Phil Cowan, Frank Furstenberg, John Gillis, Ann Hartman, Roger Lake, Joan Laird, Larry McCallum, Barbara Risman, Virginia Rutter, Pepper Schwartz, Arlene Skolnick, and Judith Stacey—taught me that sanctimonious moralizing offers no solution to the problems confronting today's families. The members of the Society for the History of Childhood and Youth, especially LeRoy Ashby, Peter W. Bardalgio, E. Wayne Carp, Howard Chudacoff, Priscilla Ferguson Clement, Miriam Forman-Brunell, Harvey Graff, Philip Greven, Joseph Hawes, Ray Hiner, Joseph Illick, Wilma King, Kriste Lindemeyer, David I. Macleod, James Marten, Susan Porter, Jacqueline S. Reinier, Eric C. Schneider, and Marie Jenkins Schwartz, have demonstrated that the history of childhood provides a revealing window onto the landscape of historical change. I benefited greatly from participation in seminars led by Theda Skocpol at Harvard University's Center for Research on Politics and Social Organization. I am particularly grateful to David Brion Davis, Linda Gordon, Michael Grossberg, Lesley Herrmann, Ken Lipartito, Sara McNeil, and Laura Oren for their ideas, example, and encouragement. I owe a particular debt to Charles Dellheim and to three extraordinarily helpful outside readers— Gary Cross, Paula S. Fass, and Jan Lewis—whose advice has left an indelible imprint on this book. Joyce Seltzer, an editor without peer, was central in transforming a rough manuscript into a finished work. Words cannot express my gratitude for her time, patience, and counsel.

Above all, I thank my partner, Susan Kellogg, my sons Seth and Sean, and my sisters and parents, who remind me each day that parenting's deepest joy is also its greatest heartbreak: watching one's children head off on their own to experience new worlds we can scarcely imagine.

Huck's Raft

Prologue

NOWHERE is it easier to romanticize childhood than in Hannibal, Missouri. In this small Mississippi riverfront town, where Samuel Clemens lived, off and on, from the age of four until he was seventeen, many enduring American fantasies about childhood come to life. A historical marker stands next to a white picket fence like the one that Tom Sawyer convinced his friends to pay for the privilege of whitewashing for him. Another marks the spot where Huck Finn's cabin allegedly stood. Then there is the window that Huck hurled pebbles at to wake the sleeping Tom. Gazing out across the raging waters of the Mississippi—now, unfortunately, hidden by a floodwall—one can easily imagine the raft excursion that Huck and the fugitive slave Jim took in search of freedom and adventure.

Hannibal occupies a special place in our collective imagination as the setting of two of fiction's most famous depictions of childhood. Our cherished myth about childhood as a bucolic time of freedom, untainted innocence, and self-discovery comes to life in this river town. But beyond the accounts of youthful wonder and small-town innocence, Mark Twain's novels teem with grim and unsettling details about childhood's underside. Huck's father, Pap, was an abusive drunkard who beat his son for learning to read. When we idealize Mark Twain's Hannibal and its eternally youthful residents, we suppress his novels' more sinister aspects.[1]

Clemens' real-life mid-nineteenth-century Hannibal was anything but a haven of stability and security. It was a place where a quarter of the children died before their first birthday, half before their twenty-first.

Clemens himself experienced the death of two siblings. Although he was not physically abused like the fictional Huck, his father was emotionally cold and aloof. There were few open displays of affection in his boyhood home. Only once did he remember seeing his father and mother kiss, and that was at the deathbed of his brother Ben. Nor was his home a haven of economic security. His boyhood ended before his twelfth birthday, when his father's death forced him to take up a series of odd jobs. Before he left home permanently at seventeen, he had already worked as a printer's apprentice; clerked in a grocery store, a bookshop, and a drug store; tried his hand at blacksmithing; and delivered newspapers. Childhood ended early in Clemens' hometown, though full adulthood came no more quickly than it does today.[2]

A series of myths have clouded public thinking about the history of American childhood. One is the myth of a carefree childhood. We cling to a fantasy that once upon a time childhood and youth were years of carefree adventure, despite the fact that for most young people in the past, growing up was anything but easy. Disease, family disruption, and early entry into the world of work were integral parts of family life. The notion of a long childhood, devoted to education and free from adult responsibilities, is a very recent invention, and one that became a reality for a majority of children only after World War II.

Another myth is that of home as a haven and bastion of stability in an ever-changing world. Through much of American history, family stability has been the exception, not the norm. At the beginning of the twentieth century, fully a third of all American children spent at least a portion of their childhood in a single-parent home, and as recently as 1940, one child in ten did not live with either parent—compared with one in twenty-five today.[3]

A third myth is that childhood is the same for all children, a status transcending class, ethnicity, and gender. In fact, every aspect of childhood is shaped by class—as well as by ethnicity, gender, geography, religion, and historical era. We may think of childhood as a biological phenomenon, but it is better understood as a life stage whose contours are shaped by a particular time and place. Childrearing practices, schooling, and the age at which a young person leaves home—all are the products of particular social and cultural circumstances.

A fourth myth is that the United States is a peculiarly child-friendly society, when in actuality Americans are deeply ambivalent about children. Adults envy young people their youth, vitality, and physical attractiveness. But they also resent children's intrusions on their time and resources and frequently fear their passions and drives. Many of the reforms that nominally have been designed to protect and assist the young were also instituted to insulate adults from children.

A final myth, which is perhaps the most difficult to overcome, is a myth of progress, and its inverse, a myth of decline. There is a tendency to conceive of the history of childhood as a story of steps forward over time: of parental engagement replacing emotional distance, of kindness and leniency supplanting strict and stern punishment, of scientific enlightenment superseding superstition and misguided moralism. This progressivism is sometimes seen in reverse, namely that childhood is disappearing: that children are growing up too quickly and losing their innocence, playfulness, and malleability.

The history of American children cannot be forced to fit these facile myths. Rather, it is a story of far-reaching change, with each historical era characterized by strikingly different and diverse childhoods. We might conceive of the history of childhood in terms of three overlapping phases. The first, premodern childhood, which roughly coincides with the colonial era, was a period in which the young were viewed as adults in training. Religious and secular authorities regarded childhood as a time of deficiency and incompleteness, and adults rarely referred to their childhood with nostalgia or fondness. Infants were viewed as unformed and even animalistic because of their inability to speak or stand upright. A parent's duty was to hurry a child toward adult status, especially through early engagement in work responsibilities, both inside the parental home and outside it, as servants and apprentices.

The middle of the eighteenth century saw the emergence of a new set of attitudes, which came to define modern childhood. A growing number of parents began to regard children as innocent, malleable, and fragile creatures who needed to be sheltered from contamination. Childhood was increasingly viewed as a separate stage of life that required special care and institutions to protect it. During the nineteenth century, the growing acceptance of this new ideal among the middle class was evident in the prolonged residence of young people in the parental home, longer periods of formal schooling, and an increasing consciousness about the stages of young people's development, culminating in the "discovery" (or, more accurately, the invention) of adolescence around the turn of the twentieth century.

Universalizing the modern ideal of a sheltered childhood was a highly uneven process and one that has never encompassed all American children. Indeed, it was not until the 1950s that the norms of modern childhood defined the modal experience of young people in the United States. But developments were already under way that would bring modern childhood to an end and replace it with something quite different, a new phase that might be called postmodern childhood. This term refers to the breakdown of dominant norms about the family, gender roles, age, and even reproduction as they were subjected to radical change and revision. Age norms that many considered "natural" were called into question. Even the bedrock biological process of sexual maturation accelerated. Today's children are much more likely than the Baby Boomers to experience their parents' divorce, to have a working mother, to spend significant amounts of time unsupervised by adults, to grow up without siblings, and to hold a job during high school. Adolescent girls are much more likely to have sexual relations during their mid-teens.[4]

Superficially, postmodern childhood resembles premodern childhood. As in the seventeenth century, children are no longer regarded as the binary opposites of adults. Nor are they considered naïve and innocent creatures. Today adults quite rightly assume that even preadolescents are knowledgeable about the realities of the adult world. But unlike premodern children, postmodern children are independent consumers and participants in a separate, semiautonomous youth culture. We still assume that the young are fundamentally different from adults, that they should spend their first eighteen years in the parents' home and devote their time to education in age-graded schools. But it is also clear that basic aspects of the ideal of a protected childhood, in which the young are kept isolated from adult realities, have broken down.[5]

Childhood and adolescence as biological phases of human development have always existed. But the ways in which childhood and adolescence are conceptualized and experienced are social and cultural constructions that have changed dramatically over time. To be sure, certain basic biological facts—such as young people's need for nurturing and training—contribute to continuities in the experience of childhood across the centuries. Nevertheless, these biological facts are inevitably modified by history and mediated by culture.[6]

The pages that follow include accounts of ten- and twelve-year-old indentured servants, apprentices, soldiers, cabin boys, and textile mill operatives. Young people are extraordinarily adaptable, resilient, and capable, much more than contemporary society assumes. Historically the young have been exposed to the stresses of child labor, neglect, and malnutrition. African-American children lived in slavery, history's most extreme form of dehumanization and exploitation, followed by nearly a century of *de jure* and *de facto* discrimination. Past experience places contemporary problems of childhood and adolescence in proper perspective. Americans face

genuine problems today, but nothing that compares to those that past reformers faced and overcame.

No single symbol can encompass the diversity of American childhood,
which includes girls and boys of highly varied class, ethnic, and regional
backgrounds. Nevertheless, the image of Huck's raft offers a particularly
appropriate metaphor for a history of children in America. Since Mark
Twain's novel was published in 1884, Huck Finn has served as a remarkably malleable emblem of childhood. He has been celebrated as a symbol
of youthful resourcefulness and spirited rambunctiousness and decried as
a rowdy and reckless risktaker. One prominent literary critic argued that
Huck's relationship with the fugitive slave Jim embodied a sublimated
homoerotic strain that runs through classic American literature; another
suggested that he was modeled on a black child named Jimmy, whom
Clemens called "the most artless, sociable and exhaustless talker I ever
came across." In our own era of diminishing expectations, Huck has been
interpreted as an abused child—illiterate, homeless, beaten, neglected—
and as a victim of attention deficit hyperactivity disorder (ADHD)—
fidgety, impulsive, disruptive, and easily bored. For over a century, Huck
has served as a lightning rod for popular fantasies and anxieties about
childhood.[7]

The image of Huck's raft encapsulates the modern conception of childhood as a period of peril and freedom; an odyssey of psychological self-
discovery and growth; and a world apart, with its own values, culture,
and psychology. But if Huck's raft represents childhood as a carefree time
of adventure, it also points to another meaning. The precariousness of
Huck's trip down the Mississippi suggests the physical, psychological,
emotional, and socioeconomic challenges of childhood. Much as the raft
is carried by raging currents that Huck can only partly control, so, too,
childhood is inevitably shaped and constrained by society, time, and
circumstances.

chapter one

Children of the Covenant

In the predawn darkness of February 29, 1704, 48 French soldiers and 200 of their Abenaki, Huron, and Iroquois allies attacked the frontier settlement of Deerfield, Massachusetts. The attackers burned the village, killing 48 of the 300 inhabitants, and took 111 captives. For the next eight weeks the captives were forced to march northward 300 miles through the snow to Canada.[1]

Among those taken prisoner were seven-year-old Eunice Williams, who lost two brothers in the attack, her clergyman father, her mother, and two surviving siblings. Along the way, Eunice saw at least twenty of her fellow captives executed, including her mother. In Canada the captives were dispersed, some to live with the French, others with the Indians. Eunice, separated from her father and brothers, was taken to a Kahnawake Mohawk mission village, across from Montreal. Two and a half years later, Eunice's father, the Reverend John Williams, was returned to New England as part of a prisoner exchange. In time, her two siblings were also released. But despite Reverend Williams' relentless pleas and protracted negotiations with the French and the Mohawks, Eunice refused to leave the Kahnawake. She had converted to Catholicism, forgotten the English language, adopted Indian clothing and hairstyle, and did not want to return to Puritan New England. At the age of sixteen she married a Kahnawake Mohawk named François Xavier Arosen, with whom she would live for half a century until his death. Reverend Williams in his quest to regain his daughter traveled to Canada and saw her, but she refused to go home with him. "She is obstinately resolved to live and dye here, and will not so much as give me one pleasant look," he wrote in shocked disbelief.[2]

We do not know why Eunice decided to remain with the Kahnawake, separated from her family and friends, but it seems likely that she found life among the Mohawks more attractive than life among the New England Puritans. The Mohawks were much more indulgent of children, and females, far from being regarded as inferior to males, played an integral role in Mohawk society and politics. Nor was Eunice alone in choosing to remain with her captors. A returned captive named Titus King reported that many young captives decided to become members of their Indian captors' tribes. "In Six months time they Forsake Father & mother, Forgit thir own Land, Refuess to Speak there own toungue & Seeminly be Holley Swollowed up with the Indians," he observed.[3]

Eunice Williams was one of many "white Indians," English colonists who ran away from home or were taken captive by and elected to stay with Native Americans. Benjamin Franklin described the phenomenon in 1753:

> When an Indian Child has been brought up among us, taught our language and habituated to our Customs, yet if he goes to see his relations and makes one Indian Ramble there is no perswading him ever to return. When white persons of either sex have been taken prisoners young by the Indians, and lived awhile among them, tho' ransomed by their Friends, and treated with all imaginable tenderness to prevail with them to stay among the English, yet in a Short time they become disgusted with our manner of life, and the care and pains that are necessary to support it, and take the first good Opportunity of escaping again into the woods, from whence there is no reclaiming them.

A fourteen-year-old named James McCullough, who lived with the Indians for "eight years, four months, and sixteen days," had to be brought back in fetters, his legs tied "under his horse's belly," his arms tied behind his back. Still, he succeeded in escaping, returning to his Indian family. When children were "redeemed" by the English, they often "cried as if they should die when they were presented to us." Treated with great kindness by the Indians (the Deerfield children were carried on sleighs and in Indians' arms or on their backs), and freed of the work obligations imposed on colonial children, many young people found life in captivity preferable to that in New England. Boys hunted, caught fish, and gathered nuts, but were not obliged to do any of the farm chores that colonial boys were required to perform. Girls "planted, tended, and harvested corn," but had no master "to oversee or drive us, so that we could work as leisurely as we pleased."[4]

A Puritan childhood is as alien to twenty-first century Americans as an Indian childhood was to seventeenth-century New Englanders. The

Benjamin West, "The Indians Delivering Up the English Captives to Colonel Bouquet." From *A Love of His Country,* by William Smith (1766). Following France's defeat in the French and Indian War in 1763, British settlers seized Indian land in violation of treaties with local tribes. An Ottawa chief named Pontiac led an alliance of western Indians in rebellion, killing more than 2,000 colonists and seizing dozens of captives. The British sent Colonel Henry Bouquet and 1,500 troops to subdue the Indians. In return for sparing Indian villages, Bouquet demanded the captives' return. Benjamin West shows a white child recoiling from a British soldier, seeking refuge in the arms of his adopted Indian parents. Courtesy of the Virginia Historical Society, Richmond.

Puritans did not sentimentalize childhood; they regarded even newborn infants as potential sinners who contained aggressive and willful impulses that needed to be suppressed. Nor did the Puritans consider childhood a period of relative leisure and playfulness, deserving of indulgence. They considered crawling bestial and play as frivolous and trifling, and self-consciously eliminated the revels and sports that fostered passionate peer relationships in England. In the Puritans' eyes, children were adults in training who needed to be prepared for salvation and inducted into the world of work as early as possible. Nevertheless, it would be a mistake to misrepresent the Puritans as unusually harsh or controlling parents, who lacked an awareness of children's special nature. The Puritans were unique in their preoccupation with childrearing, and wrote a disproportionate share of tracts on the subject. As a struggling minority, their survival depended on ensuring that their children retained their values. They were convinced that molding children through proper childrearing and education was the most effective way to shape an orderly and godly society. Their legacy is a fixation on childhood corruption, child nurture, and schooling that remains undiminished in the United States today.[5]

"Why came you unto this land?" Eleazar Mather asked his congregation in 1671; "was it not mainly with respect to the rising Generation? . . . was it to leave them a rich and wealthy people? was it to leave them Houses, Lands, Livings? Oh, No; but to leave God in the midst of them." Mather was not alone in claiming that the Puritans had migrated to promote their children's well-being. Mary Angier declared that her reason for venturing across the Atlantic was "thinking that if her children might get good it would be worthy my journey." Similarly, Ann Ervington decided to migrate because she feared that "children would curse [their] parents for not getting them to means." When English Puritans during the 1620s and 1630s contemplated migrating to the New World, their primary motives were to protect their children from moral corruption and to promote their spiritual and economic well-being.[6]

During the 1620s and 1630s, more than 14,000 English villagers and artisans fled their country to travel to the shores of New England, where they hoped to establish a stable and moral society free from the disruptive demographic and economic transformations that were unsettling England's social order. In the late sixteenth and early seventeenth centuries England experienced mounting inflation, rapid population growth, and a sharp increase in the proportion of children in the population. A 50 percent decline in real wages between 1500 and 1620 prompted a growing number of rural sons and daughters to leave their impoverished families and villages at a very young age to seek apprenticeships or to find employment as live-in servants or independent wage earners. A resulting problem of youthful vagrancy and delinquency led to authorities' ambitious plans to incarcerate idle and disordered youth in workhouses, conscript them into military service, or transport them overseas. Religious reformers, less troubled by youthful vagrancy and crime, focused on childish mischief-making and youthful vice, especially blasphemy, idleness, disobedience, and Sabbath-breaking. This preoccupation with youthful frivolity, religious indifference, and indolence shaped the Puritan outlook, with its emphasis on piety, self-discipline, hard work, and household discipline. When they finally achieved power, the Puritans were eager to suppress England's traditional youthful culture of Maypole dancing, frolicking, sports, and carnival-like "rituals of misrule" in which young people mocked their elders and expressed their antagonisms toward adult authority ritually and symbolically. The Puritans aggressively proselytized among the young, pressed for an expansion of schooling, and sought to strengthen paternal authority.[7]

Against this background of disruptive social change, radically conflicting conceptions of the nature of childhood had emerged in Tudor and Stuart England. Anglican traditionalists regarded childhood as a repository of virtues that were rapidly disappearing from English society. For them, the supposed innocence, playfulness, and obedience of children served as a symbolic link with their highly idealized conception of a past "Merrie England" characterized by parish unity, a stable and hierarchical social order, and communal celebrations. At the same time, humanistic educators, who invoked the metaphors of "moist wax" and "fair white wool" to describe children, expressed exceptional optimism about children's capacity to learn and adapt. For them, children were malleable, and all depended on the nature of their upbringing and education.[8]

Unlike the early humanists or Anglican traditionalists, who believed that children arrived in the world without personal evil, Puritan sermons and moral tracts portrayed children as riddled by corruption. Even a newborn infant's soul was tainted with original sin—the human waywardness that caused Adam's Fall. In the Reverend Benjamin Wadsworth's words, babies were "filthy, guilty, odious, abominable . . . both by nature and practice." The Puritan minister Cotton Mather described children's innate sinfulness even more bluntly: "Are they *Young?* Yet the *Devil* has been with them already . . . They go astray as soon as they are born. They no longer *step* than they *stray,* they no sooner *lisp* than they *ly.*" For Puritans, the moral reformation of childhood offered the key to establishing a godly society.[9]

The New England Puritans are easily caricatured as an emotionally cold and humorless people who terrorized the young with threats of damnation and hellfire and believed that the chief task of parenthood was to break children's sinful will. In fact the Puritans were among the first groups to reflect seriously and systematically on children's nature and the process of childhood development. For a century, their concern with the nurture of the young led them to monopolize writings for and about children, publish many of the earliest works on childrearing and pedagogy, and dominate the field of children's literature. They were among the first to condemn wetnursing and encourage maternal nursing, and to move beyond literary conceptions that depicted children solely in terms of innocent simplicity or youthful precocity. Perhaps most important, they were the first group to state publicly that entire communities were responsible for children's moral development and to honor that commitment by requiring communities to establish schools and by criminalizing the physical abuse of children.[10]

The Puritan preoccupation with childhood was a product of religious beliefs and social circumstances. As members of a reform movement that sought to purify the Church of England and to elevate English morals and manners, the Puritans were convinced that the key to creating a pious society lay in properly rearing, disciplining, and educating a new generation to higher standards of piety. As a small minority group, the Puritans depended on winning the rising generation's minds and souls in order to prevail in the long term. Migration to New England greatly intensified the Puritans' fixation on childhood as a critical stage for saving souls. Deeply concerned about the survival of the Puritan experiment in a howling wilderness, fearful that their offspring might revert to savagery, the Puritans considered it essential that children retain certain fundamental values, including an awareness of sin.

In New England, the ready availability of land and uniquely healthy living conditions, the product of clean water and a cool climate, resulted in families that were larger, more stable, and more hierarchical than those in England. In rural England, a typical farm had fewer than forty acres, an insufficient amount to divide among a family's children. As a result, children customarily left home in their early teens to work as household servants or agricultural laborers in other households. As the Quaker William Penn observed, English parents "do with their children as they do with their souls, put them out at livery for so much a year." But in New England, distinctive demographic and economic conditions combined with a patriarchal ideology rooted in religion to increase the size of families, intensify paternal controls over the young, and allow parents to keep their children close by. A relatively equal sex ratio and an abundance of land made marriage a virtually universal institution. Because women typically married in their late teens or early twenties, five years earlier than their English counterparts, they bore many more children. On average, women gave birth every two years or so, averaging between seven and nine children, compared with four or five in England. These circumstances allowed the New England Puritans to realize their ideal of a godly family: a patriarchal unit in which a man's authority over his wife, children, and servants was a part of an interlocking chain of authority extending from God to the lowliest creatures.[11]

The patriarchal family was the basic building block of Puritan society, and paternal authority received strong reinforcement from the church and community. Within their households, male household heads exercised unusual authority over family members. They were responsible for leading their household in daily prayers and scripture reading, catechizing their children and servants, and teaching household members to read so that they might study the Bible and learn the "good lawes of the Colony." Childrearing manuals were thus addressed to men, not their wives. They had an obligation to help their sons find a vocation or calling, and a legal right to consent to their children's marriage. Massachusetts Bay Colony and Connecticut underscored the importance of paternal authority by making it a capital offense for youths sixteen or older to curse or strike their father.[12]

The Puritans repudiated many traditional English customs that conflicted with a father's authority, such as godparenthood. The family was a "little commonwealth," the keystone of the social order and a microcosm of the relationships of superiority and subordination that characterized the larger society. Yet even before the first generation of settlers passed away, there was fear that fathers were failing to properly discipline and educate the young. In 1648 the Massachusetts General Court reprimanded fathers for their negligence and ordered that "all masters of families doe once a week (at the least) catechize their children and servants in the grounds and principles of Religion." Connecticut, New Haven, and Plymouth colonies followed suit in 1650, 1655, and 1671 with almost identical injunctions to ensure that "such Children and Servants may [not] be in danger to grow barbarous, rude and stubborn, through ignorance."[13]

Toward the end of the seventeenth century, however, rapid population growth, increasing geographic mobility, and the emergence of a more commercial economy combined to erode patriarchal authority. While many sons continued to live in their parents' household into their twenties, a growing number began to leave home intermittently during their teens to attend school, undertake an apprenticeship, or perform seasonal labor. Some moved permanently to fresh lands in western or northern New England, and an increasing number took their inheritance in the form of education or property instead of waiting to inherit land, further diminishing fathers' economic leverage over their offspring. Meanwhile, daughters as well as sons gained greater independence from parental oversight, and peer relationships grew more important. As young people grew more assertive, adult anxieties rose, provoking the first of many moral panics that would characterize American attitudes toward the young. To ensure proper family government, Massachusetts Bay Colony established a system of tithingmen, who watched over ten or twelve families and reported on stubborn children, unruly servants, and negligent fathers. Churches established youth groups to encourage the young "to avoid those temptations . . . that by Sad Experience we find our Youth to be exposed or inclined to." Dependency was giving way to new forms of youthful assertiveness.[14]

When the *Mayflower* left Plymouth, England, on September 16, 1620, 3 of its 102 passengers were pregnant. Elizabeth Hopkins and Susanna White were seven months pregnant. Mary Norris Allerton was in her second or third month. Their shipboard pregnancies were excruciatingly difficult. During "fierce storms" that lasted for six of the voyage's nine and a half weeks, the passengers were confined between decks while high winds scattered their clothing and supplies. While still at sea, Elizabeth Hopkins delivered a baby boy, named Oceanus after his birthplace. Two weeks later, while the *Mayflower* was anchored off Cape Cod, Susanna White gave birth to another boy, christened Peregrine, a name that means "pilgrim." He lived into his eighties, but Oceanus Hopkins died during the Pilgrims' first winter in Plymouth. Mary Norris Allerton died in childbirth; her baby was stillborn.

Childbirth in colonial New England was a difficult and sometimes life-threatening experience. During the seventeenth century, between 1 and 1.5 percent of births ended in the mother's death, the result of exhaustion, dehydration, infection, hemorrhage, or convulsions. Since the typical mother gave birth to between seven and nine children, her lifetime chances of dying from childbirth ran as high as one in eight. Understandably, many Puritan women regarded childbirth with foreboding, describing it as "that evel hour I loock forward to with dread." Likewise, the death of infants and children was common. The Puritan minister Cotton Mather said that a dead child was "a sight no more surprising than a broken pitcher," and almost all families experienced the loss of at least two or three children. Of the fourteen children Samuel Sewall had with his first wife, only six reached adulthood. In New England's healthiest communities, around 10 percent of children died in their first year, and three of every nine died before reaching their twenty-first birthday. In seaports like Boston or Salem, death rates were two or even three times higher. Epidemics of smallpox, measles, mumps, diphtheria, scarlet fever, and whooping cough were special sources of dread. During a 1677 smallpox epidemic, a fifth of Boston's population, mainly children, died. Cotton Mather saw eight of his fifteen children die before reaching the age of two. "We have our children taken from us," he cried out, "the Desire of our Eyes taken away with a stroke."[15]

According to Puritan doctrine, infants who died unconverted were doomed to eternal torment in hell. Although parents were supposed to accept these deaths with resignation, many could barely contain their grief. Over time the Puritans softened the Calvinist emphasis on infant depravity. By the end of the seventeenth century, a growing number accepted the possibility that baptism washed away a child's sins and protected it from damnation. On the day his son was baptized in 1706, Richard Brown, the minister of Reading, Massachusetts, expressed this hope: "Thou has given him to me, O Lord, and I have given him up to thee, in the ordinance [of baptism] & I pray that thou wouldst take him . . . into covenant with thyselfe, cleanse him with the blood of Jesus from his original uncleanness, and keep him whilst in the world from the evil of it."[16]

A Puritan childhood was enveloped in religion. Within two weeks of birth, a father brought his infant to the meetinghouse to be baptized. At this ceremony, a father renewed his covenant with God and promised him his seed. It was the father's duty to baptize the newborn because "the mother at that time by reason of her travail and delivery is weake, and not in case to have her head much troubled with many cares." It was at the baptismal ceremony that the child's name was announced. Although some parents bestowed common English names on their children, many first-generation Puritans, who had joined the movement after breaking with their parents, underscored this new beginning by choosing names with religious and moral significance. Some drew names from scripture (such as Zachariah) or their English equivalents (like "Thankful"); others chose phrase names (such as "If-Christ-had-not-died-for-thee-thou-hadst-been-damned"). Roger Class and his wife named their children Experience, Waitstill, Preserved, Hopestill, Wait, Thanks, Desire, Unite, and Supply. These names gave tangible expression to the first generation's basic values and religion's importance in their lives.[17]

Many New Englanders relied on the Bible for guidance and inspiration in naming their children. More than 80 percent of seventeenth-century

New Englanders had an Old or New Testament name. But family names were also important, underscoring the significance that New Englanders attached to kinship ties. In contrast to England, where it was common for godparents to name children, parents in New England typically named the first-born son after the father and the first-born daughter after the mother, while later-born children received the names of other kin.[18]

A mixture of religious beliefs and novel circumstances led New England Puritans to reject the English customs of wetnursing and swaddling. Although it was customary for another lactating woman to suckle a newborn child for the first four or five days—out of a belief that the mother's first milk (colostrum) was bad for a child—paid wetnursing was less common in New England than in the Old World. The Puritans were the first sect to condemn wetnursing out of fear that negligent nurses passed on undesirable traits through their milk. The Puritans also believed that newborns nursed by their own mothers were less likely to die in infancy. Cotton Mather was one of many Puritan theologians to criticize wetnursing, arguing that a mother had a religious duty to nurse her children: "You will Suckle your Infant your Self if you can; Be not such an Ostrich as to Decline it, merely because you would be One of the Careless Women, Living at Ease." All this despite the fact that Mather, like most of his class, was wetnursed, as were his children.[19]

There was no single prescribed time for weaning, though it usually took place in the second year of life. Maternal illness, a new pregnancy, conflicting demands on a mother's time, or a child's acquisition of teeth, which could make nursing painful, led a mother to wean her children. For Puritan parents, weaning was a time of considerable anxiety, since children, once weaned, were more susceptible to disease. For this reason, children were rarely weaned in the summer, when disease was especially prevalent. Weaning was an abrupt process, with either the mother or child leaving home for a while to stay with relatives. Once weanlings left the breast for good, they were regarded as children and true family members, referred to by name rather than the appellation "it."[20]

The Puritans regarded childhood as a time of deficiency, associating an infantile inability to walk or talk with animality, and considered it essential to teach children to stand upright and recite scripture as quickly as possible. Both were associated with morality and propriety. To prevent infants from crawling, they dressed young children, regardless of sex, in long robes or petticoats and placed them in wooden go-carts, similar to modern-day walkers. Neck stays kept infants' heads upright, while young girls wore leather corsets to encourage an erect and mature bearing.

Wooden rods were sometimes placed along children's spines to promote proper posture.[21]

In Europe infants were wrapped tightly in swaddling bands to ensure that children's bones grew straight and that they did not get into their parents' way. There is no conclusive evidence that the New England Puritans swaddled children. In New England's larger families, older siblings or servants were assigned to watch infants. Still, many young children experienced accidents that indicate a lack of close supervision. Children suffered burns from candles or open hearths, fell into rivers and wells, ingested poisons, broke bones, swallowed pins, and stuffed nutshells up their noses. Unlike parents today, Puritan parents did not "baby-proof" their homes by screening fireplaces, covering wells, or blocking stairways. Stoically accepting accidents as a fact of life, parents instead stressed safety through obedience and assumed that a child's well-being was best served by teaching a child the skills and rules necessary to function in the adult world.[22]

The Puritans were set apart from other religious sects by their emphasis on household religion. Although the meetinghouse was the place for public worship (the term *church* referred to the congregation's members, not to the physical structure), the household was the place for young people's initial religious and moral instruction. In 1650 the Connecticut General Court gave "Masters of families" responsibility to "once a week at least catechize their children and servants in the grounds and principles of religion." Bible readings, prayers, self-examination, psalm-singing, and family instruction formed the household curriculum designed to lead children and servants to faith.[23]

During the sixteenth and seventeenth centuries, the Puritans wrote twice as many books in English on proper methods of rearing children as all other groups combined. Precisely because of their belief that children were born in sin, parents had to raise them with great care. Among the Puritans' most important legacies are the beliefs that early childhood is life's formative stage, that children are highly malleable and need careful training, and that parents should be preoccupied with children's spiritual well-being. A godly education was to start as early as possible. "Parents," declared one minister, "ought to begin to nurture their children, as soone as they are capable of any instruction." Unlike evangelical Protestants of the eighteenth and nineteenth centuries, the Puritans did not emphasize a sudden, dramatic conversion experience. Rather, children's religious education was a gradual process in which fathers instilled a capacity for grace within their offspring through appeals to their affections and reason. Con-

David, Joanna, and Abigail Mason, by the Freake-Gibbs Painter, 1670.
The children of a Boston baker are dressed like adults. Eight-year-old
David Mason holds a silver-topped cane and gloves, a symbol of high
social status. Joanna holds a fan and red coral necklace, which was
thought to ward off disease. Abigail carries a rose, a symbol of innocence.
Courtesy of the Fine Arts Museums of San Francisco, Gift of Mr. and
Mrs. John D. Rockefeller III, 1979.7.3.

ceiving of children's socialization in religious terms, Puritan parents surrounded their offspring from birth with prayer and psalm-singing. In devout households, scripture readings took place daily and family prayers
were held twice a day. Parents encouraged their children to read "as early
as May be" through recitation of catechisms and Bible stories. Even
young children were taken to Sabbath observances, where sermons might
last six hours.[24]

The emphasis on early moral instruction led the Puritans to view children's play with ambivalence. Puritan children had swings, rode hobbyhorses, and drew on slates. Girls cut out paper dolls with scissors, recited
poetry, and played with dollhouses and cradles. Boys flew kites, sailed toy
boats, constructed wigwams and played at being Indians, collected rocks
and bird eggs, and made pets of squirrels, dogs, and cats. Seventeenth-
century records provide a litany of complaints about children playing ball

or flying kites in the streets, robbing birds' nests and orchards, and throwing stones and snowballs at passersby. Yet the dominant view was that play was a sinful waste of time, "a snare of the Old Deluder, Satan." Samuel Sewall and Cotton Mather complained about their children's "inordinant love of play" and worried about the energies diverted to it. They especially abhorred game-playing on the Sabbath and any games involving cards and dice.[25]

The Puritans did not mistake children for angels. Unlike the Romantics, who associated childhood with purity and innocence, the Puritans adopted a fairly realistic view, emphasizing children's intransigence, willfulness, and obstinacy. They worried that if indolence, selfishness, and willfulness were not overcome in childhood, these traits would dominate adulthood. The Reverend Thomas Cobbett said that too many insolent and unruly children "carry it proudly, disdainfully, and scornfully toward parents," and that their mother and father should require them to bow before them and stand bareheaded in their presence. Nonetheless, most Puritan authorities were highly critical of harsh physical punishments, convinced that corporal discipline only induced resentfulness and rebelliousness in children. Parents were told to avoid excessive severity and always to explain the reasons for a punishment. Ministers said that correction of error should never be inflicted arbitrarily or capriciously, and that parents should never discipline a child in anger. Parents were also advised to avoid the indiscriminate use of verbal or physical chastisement and to adapt correction to the child's age, temperament, understanding, and to the nature of the infraction. As the poet Anne Bradstreet explained, "Diverse children have their different natures; some are like flesh which nothing but salt will keep from putrefecation; some again like tender fruits which are best preserved with sugar: those parents are wise that can fit their nurture according to the Nature."[26]

Puritan parents, relatively isolated in a new and difficult land, were in closer and more constant contact with their children for more years than their counterparts in England. Interacting with them more frequently and intensely, they tried to inculcate religious understandings to encourage internal restraints. Joseph Green recalled that when he "was about 4 or 5 years at most," his "father used to tell me I must be a good boy and must service God, and used to ask me whether I went alone and prayed to God to bless me & to pardon my sins." By building up a child's awareness of sin, parents sought to lead children along the path toward salvation. Children's early consciousness of their mortality and of the severity of divine judgment was considered a particularly useful tool for shaping behavior. John Norris' *Spiritual Counsel* advised the young to "be much in contemplation of the last four thyngs, Heaven, Hell, Death and Judgment. Place yourself frequently on your death beds, in your Coffins, and in your Graves. Act over frequently in your Minds, the solemnity of your own funerals; and entertain your Imaginations with all the lively scenes of Mortality."[27]

As early as possible, children were taught to prepare for death. Ministers admonished children to reflect on death, and their sermons contained graphic descriptions of hell and the horrors of eternal damnation. Cotton Mather offered this advice: "Go into Burying-Place, CHILDREN; you will there see *Graves* as short as your selves. Yea, you may be at *Play* one Hour; *Dead, Dead* the next." With his own family, he seized on opportunities to reinforce this lesson. In one incident, he explained, "I took my little daughter, Katy, into my study, and there I told my child, that I am to die shortly, and she must, when I am dead, remember every thing, that I said unto her." Awareness of death was inculcated by showing young children corpses and hangings. References to death pervaded children's primers. In illustrating the use of the letter "T," the *New England Primer* noted: "Time cuts down all / Both great and small." Far from being a sign of parental insensitivity, exposing children to the idea and reality of death was a way to instill in them an awareness of sin and to encourage them to reflect on divine judgment. At least some Puritan children picked up the message that they needed to recognize their sinfulness and strive for repentance and salvation. Samuel Sewall's daughter Betty "burst out" after dinner "into an amazing cry . . . Her Mother ask'd the reason; she gave none; at last said she was afraid she could goe to Hell, her Sins were not pardon'd."[28]

Even sickness offered practical religious lessons. During the seventeenth century, physicians were unable to diagnose or treat scarcely any diseases, and the Puritans regarded illnesses as divinely administered afflictions. "What are sickness," one Puritan divine explained, "but the Rods wherewith GOD counts His own offending Children?" To cope with their children's illnesses, many Puritan parents, like Increase Mather, turned to religious ritual. In 1676, when his son Samuel "was near to death again about a fortnight agoe, I Fasted & prayed for his Life, & God hath heard me." Others worried that their unrepented sins caused their children's illnesses. When his eldest son Ebenezer accidentally fell into a fire while napping, Samuel Sewall noted that "for his relief I immediately killed a cat and he washed his hands in the blood." Some children considered illnesses providential signs. Recalling a bout with measles in 1714, when he was eleven, Ebenezer Parkman wrote that his illness "set me upon thinking upon what would be the estate of my soul after my Dissolution, which was apprehended by all to be Nigh, often in my mind repeating the Psalmists words Blessed is he whose Transgression is forgiven whose Sin is Covered."[29]

The Puritan family was not only a little church; it was also a little school. During the early seventeenth century it was within the household that Puritan children gained basic literacy. In general, mothers were responsible for teaching their children to read, while fathers taught writing. Puritans regarded education as critical to salvation, calling education "God's ordinary way for the conveyance of his grace." In teaching children to read, Puritan mothers did not divide reading and religion. Children were expected to learn to read by listening to others read aloud and then by memorizing the Lord's Prayer, psalms, hymns, catechisms, and scripture passages. Nathaniel Eaton explained: "My education was in a religious manner from a cradle that I was trained to read Scripture." After his mother's death, John Paine of Plymouth wrote: "She was unto her children all teaching them God's word to read as they were but Small." As in England, parents bought primers, catechisms, and hornbooks to teach their children to read. Households educated not only children but also servants and apprentices. Contracts between masters and apprentices obliged masters to make sure that servants learned how to read. And all imbibed religion along with literacy.[30]

During the seventeenth century, a growing perception that parents were failing to properly educate their children led many communities to transfer instructional responsibilities to schools. In 1647 Massachusetts Bay Colony had ordered every town of fifty families to "appoint one within their own towne to teach all such children as shall resort to him to write and reade." In 1670 the Massachusetts General Court described a "great & generall neglect of instructing & governing the rising generation, both in familyes & churches." By the end of the century, young New Englanders increasingly went to school to learn to write and cipher. This early rise of public schooling has been seen as a Puritan innovation, but it would be a mistake to exaggerate the Puritans' commitment to formal schooling. The Massachusetts school law was not rigidly enforced, and many towns failed to regularly provide teachers. All eight towns required to maintain a grammar school did so, but only a third of the smaller towns required to establish reading and writing schools obeyed the law, and no statute required children to attend school. While Puritan New Englanders had a much higher rate of literacy than the English, this phenomenon primarily reflected the lack of a large population of illiterate laborers rather than the Puritan belief that access to books distinguished Protestantism from the tyranny of Catholic priests.[31]

Formal school terms were often quite brief, sometimes no more than a few months, and literacy was highly gendered. The Puritans were generally content to teach girls only reading, while encouraging boys to learn both reading and writing. Among the early settlers, about 60 percent of the men and 30 percent of the women could sign their own wills. By the end of the colonial period, 90 percent of the males and 50 percent of the females signed their wills. Grammar schools and Latin schools were reserved almost exclusively for boys.[32]

The Salem witch scare provides a glimpse into the world of Puritan girlhood. Early in 1692 eight girls, including the nine-year-old daughter and eleven-year-old niece of Salem Village minister Samuel Parris, attempted to gaze into the future, hoping to catch a glimpse of their husbands. Lacking a crystal ball, they suspended the white of a raw egg in a glass of water. Assisting them was the Reverend Parris' slave, Tituba, whom he had brought to Massachusetts from the West Indies and who captivated the girls with forbidden tales of witchcraft. Rather than seeing an image of her husband-to-be, one of the girls spied "a specter in the likeness of a coffin." Soon afterward a number of the girls were afflicted with unknown "distempers," including garbled speech, odd gestures, and convulsive fits. They went into trances, suffered seizures, spat food, shouted blasphemies, and made strange animal sounds.[33]

To determine whether the girls had been bewitched, Tituba baked a "witch cake" out of rye and the urine of the afflicted girls, which she planned to feed to a dog. But before the experiment was completed, the Reverend Parris caught wind of what was going on. Alarmed, he consulted a local doctor. Unable to diagnose the girls' condition, the physician described their conniptions as the devil's handiwork. With other ministers, Reverend Parris tried unsuccessfully to heal the girls through prayer. Finally the girls were pressed to name their tormentors. In June 1692 a newly created court was convened to try the accused. Because the judges admitted spectral evidence—testimony in which witnesses asserted that they had seen apparitions of the alleged witches doing the work of Satan—convictions were much more easily obtained than in earlier witchcraft cases. In all, more than 150 people from twenty-four towns were eventually accused of witchcraft, 14 women and 5 men were hanged, and another man was crushed to death by stones. Five others died in jail awaiting trial. There is no evidence that the girls who touched off the witch scare were mischiefmaking, play-acting attention seekers. Rather, it seems likely that their convulsions and hallucinations were related to the increasingly precarious status of young women in late seventeenth-century

New England and the drudgery and repressiveness of the life that they faced.[34]

It was not accidental that the girls were trying to divine their marriage prospects. Young women's prospects for marriage were growing increasingly uncertain as a result of a growing shortage of young men. Casualties suffered in a war against the French Canadians and the migration of many young men to western and northern New England and New York in search of land diminished the supply of potential suitors. Several girls, orphans whose inheritances were tied up in litigation, had special reason to worry about their marriage prospects. Without a dowry, they were unlikely to find a husband. Uncertainty is likely to have played a role in the accusations as well as the girls' relative powerlessness in Puritan society. As young female servants, many of the girls occupied the lowest status level in their society. Witchcraft accusations gave them a degree of power that no female of their age would otherwise have.

THE NEW ENGLAND Puritans demarcated the stages of growing up very differently than we do today. The period in which a child was primarily under a mother's care (a stage that early Americans called "infancy") was brief, lasting until the age of six or seven. During this period both boys and girls wore dresses or gowns, a visual symbol of their dependent status. In New England as in the Old World, the end of infancy was marked by a ceremony called breeching, in which a boy began to wear pants. Breeching not only marked the transfer of supervision and control over boys from mothers to fathers; it also signaled an increase in work responsibilities, as boys began to fetch water, tend livestock, and perform other chores, either for their family or as a servant in another household. Although girls did not undergo a symbolic shift in status equivalent to breeching, they also took on increased responsibilities for housework, including spinning, cooking, and gardening.[35]

Infancy was followed by childhood and youth, prolonged transitional periods stretching from seven or eight to the early or mid-twenties. In England these were years when many young people lived, at least temporarily, outside their parental home as servants or apprentices, as their families tried to alleviate crowdedness and surplus labor within the family. Conversely, they might take children in to care for or to replace grown children who had left the household. In New England, fostering out was usually limited to children between the ages of seven and twelve, while older youths generally lived with their parents. Whereas in England servants were highly mobile and frequently changed employers and even towns, most older youths in New England remained under their parents' watchful eyes.[36]

Youth was a period in which young people became sexually and physically mature, acquired adult skills, and gradually gained autonomy from their parents. It was the "chusing time" when the young were to "putt away Childish things" and find a calling or vocation. Laws in Massachusetts in 1643 and 1646 specifically charged "parents and masters" to "breed and bring up their children and apprentices in some honest calling, labor or employment." During youth, boys and girls were to abandon the frivolities of early childhood and to make decisions that would shape their adult lives. "Now you commonly chuse your trade," explained Benjamin Colman in 1720. "Now you chuse your master and your education or occupation. And now you dispose of yourself in marriage ordinarily, place your affections, give away your hearts, look out for some companion of life, whose to be as long as you live." Unlike early childhood, when young children "spend much time in pastime and play, for their bodies are too weak to labour" and their minds "are too shallow" for serious study, youth was a time of heightened seriousness, according to the Puritan divine John Cotton. When his fourteen-year-old son was admitted to Harvard College in 1672, the Reverend Thomas Shepard urged him to "Remember . . . that tho' you have spent your time in the vanity of Childhood; sports and mirth, little minding better things, yet that now, when come to this ripeness of Admission to College, that now God and man expects you to putt away Childish things: now is the time come, wherein you are to be serious, and to learn sobriety, and wisdom."[37]

Choice of a calling was often fraught with tension. In his autobiography, the Boston-born Benjamin Franklin described how he became an apprentice printer. When he was eight, his father sent him to a grammar school to prepare for the ministry. His father could not afford the schooling, and at ten Benjamin was withdrawn and began to assist his father in the manufacture of candles and soap. Bored by dipping wicks into wax, the boy hoped to go to sea, but his father rejected this option. Fearing that Benjamin would run away, as another son already had, the father "took me to walk with him, and see joiners, bricklayers, turners, braziers, etc., at their work, that he might observe my inclination, and endeavor to fix it on some trade or other on land." Finally the elder Franklin decided his son should become a cutler, who would make, repair, or sell knives, and sent him to live with an uncle's son who was practicing that trade. But when the man demanded a fee, Benjamin returned home and was apprenticed to a much older brother, a master printer.[38]

In addition to being a time when a young man chose a vocation, youth was also the stage of life when females and males were expected to prepare for conversion. Young people in seventeenth-century New England carried an enormous psychological burden. They were reminded constantly about their responsibility for perpetuating their society's faith. Many kept diaries for spiritual account-keeping, a Puritan counterpart to the Catholic confessional, and those that survive record intense anxiety about their spiritual state. In these journals, Puritan youths laid out their guilt, anguish, and tortured self-examination. Preoccupation with judgment and the difficulties of salvation mark these personal accounts. The fourteen-year-old Increase Mather wrote that his conscience was stricken by "terrible convictions and awakening" and he plunged into the "extremity of anguish and horror in my soul." Similarly Roger Clap's diary reveals how after he left his apprenticeship and father's family, he meditated on his own sinfulness. Samuel Mather, age twelve, was fearful that he might "belong not unto the election of grace": "Though I am well in my body, yet I question whether my soul doth prosper as my body doth." Other diaries reveal a similar preoccupation with sin and salvation. John Clap had a "thorow conviction of his misery by reason of sin both original and actual" when he was eleven. Priscilla Thornton at eleven declared that "she knew she was made up of all manners of sin." Nathanael Mather at thirteen wrote: "I confess, O Lord, I have fallen from thee by my iniquity, and am by nature a son of hell."[39]

Through the seventeenth century the passage of young New Englanders toward adulthood grew increasingly problematic. Young men, in particular, experienced greater educational and occupational choices and greater privacy. Geographic mobility increased as parents no longer had sufficient land to provide their sons with a farmstead nearby. Youth acquired a new potential for creating tension, ambiguity, and uncertainty in the Puritan community as the young struck off on their own.[40]

Toward the end of the century, Puritan ministers of the second generation developed a new literary form known as the "jeremiad." Named for the Old Testament prophet Jeremiah, who had pointed out the ancient Hebrews' evil ways, the jeremiad was a prolonged lamentation and complaint about the rising generation. Jeremiads foresaw a calamitous future for New England unless young people obeyed God's laws and accepted their parents' faith. In 1657 Ezekiel Rogers spoke out in typical terms: "I find greatest Trouble and Grief about the *Rising Generation. Young People* are stirred here; but they strengthen one another in Evil, by Example, by Counsel." In heated terms, ministers denounced filial disobedience, immodest dress, youthful frolics and dalliances, and masturbation. Cotton Mather, writing anonymously in 1723, was one of the first moralists in the western world to attack adolescent masturbation, condemning the "libidinous practices" of those "who do evil with both hands" and "have the cursed way of procuring a discharge, which the God of nature has ordered to be made in a way which a lawful marriages leads unto." "Self-pollution," he and other Puritan ministers feared, "is consecrating the best of our bodyes to the divell."[41]

Contributing to fears of decline was a recognition that young people were falling away from the founders' faith. As early as the 1660s, Puritan church membership was declining. Fear that young people were not being converted led to enactment of school laws designed to spread proper religious views and to overcome the indifference of many families toward religion and household education. The falling number of conversions also led to adoption of a religious reform, the Half-Way Covenant of 1662, which allowed unconverted children of church members to baptize their own children in church. Although the Half-Way Covenant did not increase church membership, it did increase the potential for more church members in the future.[42]

First-generation New England Puritans upheld strict standards for admission to church membership. Their churches demanded that sons and daughters stand up before the adult male community and testify to an experience of regeneration, that is, of reborn faith. It required great courage to undergo the scrutiny of one's parents and community, and most young people were unwilling to do this before their father's death, when they achieved full adult status. The result was a growing number of young people who were unable to become full communicants. Over time some churches relaxed their restrictive requirements for membership. While most churches still required a full public narration of saving grace, others began to offer the options of a private hearing before the minister and deacons or a written relation to be read by the minister before the congregation. More than a few churches, following the example of the congregations in the Connecticut River Valley, dropped the relation altogether as a condition of full membership.[43]

Males were especially unlikely to testify to an experience of regeneration, and by the late seventeenth century church membership became increasingly feminized, although church leadership remained in the hands of male elders and deacons. By the 1690s women made up 70 percent or more of church members, and the typical household contained a churched wife and an unchurched husband. Cotton Mather believed that young women were more likely than young men to become church members out of fear of dying in childbirth: "The *Curse* both of *Subjection* and of *Child bearing* which the *Female Sex* is doom'd unto, has been turn'd into a

Blessing, by the *Free Grace* of our Most Gracious God." It also seems likely that this was related to the greater geographic mobility of women (who often moved to a new town upon marriage) and their greater isolation from extended kin.[44]

The feminization of New England religion carried profound social and religious consequences. It was apparent in a theological shift away from an emphasis on a vengeful God the Father, demanding obedience and submission to his laws, toward an emphasis on the figure of Christ, protecting his followers. It was also evident in a shift away from a stress on the patriarchal household as the central social institution. No longer able to trust male household heads with properly educating and catechizing their children and servants, New Englanders placed greater emphasis on catechism within churches, on public schools, and on maternal nurture. Ministers increasingly argued that the pious, virtuous mother should assume primary responsibility for educating young children.[45]

For much of the seventeenth century, paternal control over property had strengthened a father's authority over his offspring. In England the practice of primogeniture had restricted the prospects of land to the eldest son, but in New England all sons expected to inherit land. Having far more acres than people, the first settlers in New England fell into a pattern of distributing their estates among all male heirs, with generous portions for their daughters, too. New England fathers used their control over property to influence their children's choice of vocation and decisions about the timing of marriage and the marriage partner. Paternal control over property also ensured that children took care of their parents in their old age. Typically fathers retained legal title to their land until their death, delaying their children's achievement of full adulthood until a relatively late age. Fathers controlled family assets to ensure that their sons labored for them productively and maintained them and their widows in old age. The strength of paternal authority extended to daughters as well. In the seventeenth century, daughters generally married in strict birth order to alleviate the father's fear that if younger daughters married earlier, it would be more difficult for older daughters to find husbands.[46]

By the end of the seventeenth century, however, paternal authority had noticeably weakened. No longer was there sufficient land to sustain its distribution to all heirs. Geographic mobility increased markedly in the last two decades of the seventeenth century, as growing numbers of young people in their mid to late teens or early twenties left home for eastern seaports or commercial towns or newly settled frontier regions to find new opportunities. At the same time, nonagricultural employment expanded, particularly in household manufacturing, shipping, and trade, helping to draw young people off the land. An increase in geographic mobility and occupational opportunities allowed men and women to marry at an earlier age without a father's permission. The patriarchalism so dominant in early New England faded considerably during the early eighteenth century. Rather than wait for their inheritance, sons increasingly bought their portions, and hence their economic independence, from their father or siblings and left to farm on available land on the frontier or to make a new start in other towns. Although parents often aided them in this resettlement process, sons were removed from day-to-day paternal and church supervision, something their seventeenth-century counterparts had rarely managed. As a result, paternal control of marital decisions weakened significantly. During the early eighteenth century a growing number of youth also engaged in sexual activity before marriage. From the late seventeenth through the late eighteenth centuries, the proportion of brides who were pregnant before marriage rose from less than 10 percent to about 30 percent.[47]

Further adding to fears of moral decline was the emergence of a distinctive youth culture. In the early seventeenth century there were few communal recreations for youthful New Englanders. Whereas early modern England offered a range of rituals, festivities, and folk customs for young people who lived in a hierarchical, adult-dominated society, New England did not. The Puritans looked upon early modern England's festive culture with scorn. Not only did these recreational activities violate the Puritan taboo against leisure on the Sabbath; they also were seen as relics of Catholicism or paganism that provided the occasion for sinful drinking, swearing, and fornication. The boisterous, drunken, unruly celebration of Christmas in England, during which young men dressed up in women's clothing and animal skins, drew particular ire. Very few of these folk customs made it to New England. To be sure, bands of young people roamed the streets of Boston on Guy Fawkes Day (November 5), firing guns and destroying fences to get wood for bonfires. Yet although there were isolated instances of Maypole dancing or young people playing tricks on April Fool's day, the Puritans were largely successful in suppressing this traditional English folk culture and reorganizing the year around the Sabbath and fast days. In seventeenth-century New England there were no saints' days, no public celebration of Christmas, no pre-Lenten carnival, no celebration of St. Valentine's Day, and no church ales.[48]

However, as early as the 1660s new kinds of rituals, such as militia training days, had arisen that provided opportunities for young people to congregate. Militias customarily trained eight times a year, and these musters bound young men together and became, as one critic wrote in 1677, "days to meet on, to smoke, to carouse, to swagger and dishonor God with the great bravery." An increase in youthful independence was evident in the proliferating complaints about night-walking, frolicking, company-keeping, carousing, merry-meeting, dancing, and singing. The number of sexual offenses by young people also rose. In one county near Boston there were 250 cases of sexual offenses in the second half of the seventeenth century, most involving youths.[49]

To ensure that young people remained on the side of godliness and morality, a 1672 Massachusetts statute forbade "youth, maids and other persons uncivilly walking in the streets and fields of Saturday and Sunday nights." It was at this time of increasing anxiety over youth that Massachusetts Bay Colony instituted tithingmen as overseers of family government and regulators of youthful behavior. Other measures intended to harness youthful energies ranged from legislation requiring the establishment of schools to the creation of catechism classes and "Associations of Young Folks." Ministers encouraged the formation of young men's societies, where youth could meet regularly to pray, sing psalms, hear sermons, and discuss religious subjects.[50]

As early as the 1720s a growing number of religious leaders adopted a new strategy to instill discipline in the young. This was an evangelism that sought to convert young people in their teens and bring them into church membership. Typically, full church membership came at the same time that an individual passed into full adulthood: the time of betrothal, marriage, economic independence, and the prospects of parenthood. By the 1730s, however, proponents of religious revival were convinced that the best way to protect youth from vice was to promote religious conversion at an early age. Rejecting the older Puritan aversion to youthful conversion, ministers during the Great Awakening, the emotional religious revivals of the 1730s and 1740s, stressed the idea that divine grace could save the young.[51]

A majority of those converted during the Great Awakening were single young men and women; a quarter were in their teens. During the 1740s nearly 50 percent of female converts in New England were under the age of twenty, compared with 26 percent in the previous decade. Many of the young people attracted by the revivals were poor youth from inland market towns and coastal seaports who had suffered dislocation from family households as a result of wars with the Indians and the French and rapid commercialization.[52]

Part of the impulse for the Awakening came from young people themselves. In towns like Milford, Connecticut, as early as 1726 young people "set up private Meetings, which they carried on by praying, reading good

Books, singing, etc. The Meetings were chiefly of the younger Sort of People; of Children about five or six Years of Age, and so upwards to about twenty one, or two." Although the Great Awakening has sometimes been described as a generational conflict, pitting the young who favored it against older opponents who resented the erosion of their authority, there is no correlation between the age and attitudes of ministers. Nevertheless, the Great Awakening did reinforce a trend toward greater youthful autonomy. Over time many young people turned away from the local churches that had sought their membership. Youthful piety increasingly found expression in religious ceremonies that took place outside the established churches, sometimes led by lay preachers. Many churches responded by prohibiting teenage members. The fervor and enthusiasm of the religious revival had drawn youth to it as a possible way to assert an independent identity, but it failed to contain the restless energies and passions of the young.[53]

In 1669, when Richard Mather was on his deathbed, his son asked him if he had any special charge to give to him. The elderly Mather replied: "A special thing which I would commend to you, is care concerning the rising generation in this country, that they be brought under the government of Christ in his church." Early New England was intellectually preoccupied with children and youth because the survival of the community depended upon them. And yet it was hard to keep them within the Puritan fold. Children were ignorant, even animalistic, and easily led astray. Youth was dominated by pride and sensuality, evident in Sabbath-breaking, night revels, blasphemy, fornication, rebellion against family government, and even masturbation. Rising adult concern with youthful sensuality shows up in the court records, especially in prosecutions of fornication and bastardy, which increased dramatically over time.[54]

The Puritan obsession with children and youth was not, however, limited to concern about sin. It also expressed fear for the survival of the Puritan faith. With the death of the first generation of New Englanders, with the rapid decline in conversions relative to population growth, how could the younger generation be nurtured in the faith that had motivated their parents? Freed of the experience of persecution and the struggles of migration, how could the young ensure the survival of the Puritan enterprise? While Puritanism in England originated in part in a generational revolt against the Anglican Church, in New England it seemed necessary to ensure that the younger generation sustained loyalty to their parents' faith. To perpetuate their religion, the Puritans instituted mechanisms for indoctrinating youths, including youth-specific catechisms, covenant-renewal ceremonies in churches and homes, private religious societies, catechetical exercises, lectures, and covenant renewals, in which groups of youths were assembled on the Sabbath to renew their parents' covenants.[55]

No earlier people had ever invested greater responsibilities or higher expectations in their children than did the New England Puritans, but this heavy investment produced intense anxiety. The survival and success of the Puritan enterprise hinged on the willingness of the "rising generation" to maintain their parents' religious beliefs and ideals. The Reverend Eleazer Mather put the point bluntly. "There is no little Expectation concerning you," he declared, "your predecessors . . . [and] all of their expectations under God himself, are in you." Beginning in the 1660s and 1670s, Puritan presses and pulpits produced a stream of jeremiads lamenting the sins of the rising generation and the degeneration of the young from the religion and godliness of their forebears. Young people were made to carry an awesome psychological burden. Morality, religion, indeed the future, depended on them. In secularized form, it is this mixture of hope and fear about the rising generation that remains Puritanism's most lasting legacy.[56]

chapter two

Red, White, and Black
in Colonial America

H**IS BOYHOOD** served as an inspiration for *Kidnapped,* Robert Louis Stevenson's classic tale of abduction, betrayal, and adventure on the high seas. Peter Williamson was just thirteen years old when he was abducted from Scotland, transported to America, and sold into indentured servitude. A tenant farmer's son, Peter had attended school in Aberdeen, where he lived with an aunt. One day in 1743, while playing on an Aberdeen pier, two men who worked for a local magistrate enticed him aboard a ship. Taken into the vessel's hold, he was entertained with music and card-playing, but soon discovered that he was not allowed to leave. After a month of confinement, when seventy other boys had been brought aboard, the vessel set sail for Virginia.[1]

In Aberdeen men hired by local merchants and public officials patrolled the streets, looking for orphans, runaways, and vagrant children. "The trade of carrying off boys to the plantations in America, and selling them there as slaves, was carried on at Aberdeen . . . with amazing effrontery," Peter later wrote. "It was not carried on in secret, or by stealth, but publicly, and by open violence." Many parents refused to allow their children to go into the town for fear that they would be kidnapped.[2]

After nearly three months at sea, Peter's ship ran aground off Cape May, New Jersey. The boys were taken to Philadelphia and sold at public auction. "Thus," Peter later wrote, "we were driven through the country like cattle to a Smithfield market, and exposed to sale in public fairs, as so many beasts." Young Peter was bought for a seven-year term by a planter named Hugh Wilson, who had himself been abducted from Scotland and sent to America. "Commiserating my condition," Peter recalled, "he took care of me, indulged me in going to school, where I went every winter for five years, and made a tolerable proficiency."[3]

Dependency and subordination were common features of life for many children in early America. Elizabeth Sprigs, a young servant in Maryland, ran away from her home in England and financed her passage to the colonies by agreeing to serve a term as an indentured servant. In a 1756 letter to her father, she complained bitterly of mistreatment by her master and begged for forgiveness and clothing:

> What we unfortunate English People suffer here is beyond the probability of you in England to Conceive, let it suffice that I, one of the unhappy Number, am toiling almost Day and Night . . . and then tied up and whipp'd . . . [and have] scarce any thing but Indian Corn and Salt to eat and that even begrudged . . . I beg if you have any Bowels of Compassion left show it by sending me some Relief, Clothing is the principal thing wanting,[4]

Nine-year-old Sally Dawson had no say in her future service. In 1793 her father brought her to the home of Henry and Elizabeth Drinker, a prominent Philadelphia Quaker family. After a fifteen-day trial period, Sally was indentured to an eight-year-term. In exchange for arranging her indenture, Sally's father received a bonding fee; the girl was to receive "meat, drink, lodging and washing," and six months of instruction in the "art, craft, and mystery of housewifery."[5]

In addition to the half-million Africans brought to the colonies in chains, more than half of the 307,000 white migrants who arrived in the colonies between 1700 and 1775—most in their teens or twenties—were unfree. They came as indentured servants or bound or convict laborers and were expected to work four or more years of service before attaining their freedom. Meanwhile many young native-born colonists, like Benjamin Franklin, who was indentured to an older brother as a printer's apprentice when he was twelve, also experienced a period of subordination to a master. The experience of indentured servitude gave words like *liberty* and *tyranny* a visceral meaning for many colonists. It bred a suspicion of arbitrary authority and unchecked power and invigorated the antipatriarchal ideology of the American Revolution.[6]

Colonial childhood varied starkly by class, ethnicity, gender, geographic region, religion, and race. Indian children in the Eastern Woodlands enjoyed a degree of freedom from corporal punishment and household labor that was unimaginable to enslaved children, young indentured servants, or youthful apprentices and household servants. In contrast to New England, where stable, patriarchal households structured young people's lives well into the eighteenth century, childhood in the Chesapeake colonies of Maryland and Virginia and the colonies farther south was characterized by highly unstable families, the prevalence of indentured servitude, and, increasingly, by chattel slavery. Only in the Middle Colonies, especially among the Pennsylvania Quakers, did a pattern of childhood premised on affection and an acceptance of early independence emerge by the mid-eighteenth century. For much of the seventeenth and eighteenth centuries, dependency characterized the lives of most colonial children, and it gave added resonance to the revolutionary struggle for freedom in the 1770s and 1780s. Yet throughout the colonial period indentured servitude and apprenticeship gradually weakened, and as the nation moved toward revolution, new patterns of childhood, emphasizing greater autonomy and youthful assertiveness, had begun to arise for white children throughout the colonies.

David Zeisberger was about eighteen years old when he migrated in 1739 from central Europe to a Moravian community in Georgia. For sixty-two years, from the 1740s to the early nineteenth century, he served as a missionary to the Creek, Iroquois, and Delaware Indians in New England, New York, Pennsylvania, and Ohio. As required by his church, he kept a daily diary, which provides a detailed account of Indian childhood in the Eastern Woodlands. Zeisberger was struck by both the similarities and the marked contrasts between childrearing in his culture and among Native Americans. Like Europeans, the Indian peoples of eastern North America surrounded pregnancy with many taboos to ensure the baby's well-being. Newborns underwent a series of initiation rituals, which Zeisberger considered a mockery of the baptism ceremony (such as rubbing newborns with grease) or circumcision (such as the piercing of an infant's ears or nose). Much as Europeans announced a child's formal name at baptism, Indians conferred a newborn's public name at a formal ceremony (although this public name was not necessarily a personal name but rather a description of the child's place in a clan). Much as Europeans used swaddling cloths to ensure that a child's bones grew straight, the eastern Indians placed infants on cradleboards until their "Bones begin to harden, the Joynts to knit, and the Limbs grow strong."[7]

In his diary Zeisberger noted that the Indian peoples, like Europeans, raised boys and girls very differently, to prepare them for distinct adult roles. Boys, almost as soon as they were able to walk, were trained to hunt "squirrels, birds and even raccoon with their bows and arrow" and to spear fish. Young girls, in contrast, were trained in "cooking, bread-making, planting, making of carrying-girdles and bags, the former used to carry provisions and utensils on their backs while journeying and the latter to hold the provisions." Zeisberger was especially intrigued by the contrasts between European and indigenous childhood. One difference involved breast-feeding of infants. "The native Indian women of every grade always nurse their own children," rather than relying on wetnurses, and nursed their offspring much longer than did European women, for four years or even more. The result was that Indian women in the Eastern Woodlands bore relatively few children—usually just three or four—and were very attached to them. Especially striking was Indian mothers' emotional response to their children's death. Unlike European parents, who were expected to show resignation upon a child's death, Indian mothers responded to children's death with "unfeigned tears, and even for months after their decease will weep at the graves of their departed children."[8]

Zeisberger was surprised by the amount of freedom given to Indian children. Unlike European children, Indian boys were not obligated to perform farm chores, nor were girls expected to spin, sew, or knit. To foster independence and initiative, Native American parents rarely restrained their children. "They follow their own inclinations," he wrote, and "do what they like and no one prevents them." The fact that children ran about nearly naked astonished and appalled Europeans. Girls wore "a little frock" while boys wore "little or nothing" until at the age of five or six "a flap of cloth" was worn around the waist. The lack of confining clothing was one of the ways that the Indian peoples of the Eastern Woodlands inured their children to a harsh environment and instilled the stoicism that they highly valued.[9]

Unlike European parents, who considered physical punishment essential to rearing properly disciplined adults, Indian parents eschewed the use of straps and rods. Even when their children committed serious misdeeds, "they are not punished, being only reproved with gentle words." Threats, coercion, and physical punishment, it was feared, would make children timid and submissive; parents' goal was to foster pride, independence, and courage. They did so by honoring certain rites of passage that demarcated the passage from childbirth to adulthood. Newborn children were dipped in cold water or rubbed in animal oil "to make them strong brave men and hardy hunters." Several months later, newborns underwent a special initiation ceremony, in which a child was given a name from a wealth of family names. Because this was a clan name and not a personal name, many Europeans concluded that the Indians lacked a sense of children as individuals. Among many native peoples, young children also underwent a rite involving the piercing of the nose or earlobes, so that they could wear decorative and symbolic jewelry.[10]

Young women, at the time of first menstruation, underwent a special initiation ceremony that marked their exit from girlhood and their entrance into womanhood and eligibility for marriage. "Generally between the twelfth and sixteenth year," Zeisberger wrote about the Delaware, at the onset of her first menses, a young woman separated herself from her community and stayed in a special menstrual cabin for the menstrual period, where she was cared for by her mother and other older female acquaintances. Her head is covered with a blanket, and "she is given little to eat, but regularly dosed with emetics. She is not allowed to do any work." At the end of her ritual seclusion, she wore special clothing and a veil and was subsequently told that she might marry. For an Indian boy, there were ceremonies to mark his first tooth, first steps, and the killing of his first big game. Young men underwent a "vision quest" that took place between the ages of twelve and fourteen. The boys go "alone in the forest in apprehension and in need." Following a period of fasting and sensory deprivation, a guardian spirit (a *Manitou*) appeared who promised to protect them. "If an Indian has no Manitto," Zeisberger went on, "he considers himself forsaken . . . has no hope of any assistance and is small in his own eyes."[11]

During adolescence some young men (and, in the Carolinas, young women as well) went through a ceremony that involved the symbolic death of childhood and rebirth as an adult. Among the Pokanokets of New England, this rite of passage entailed ingestion of a noxious substance that caused vomiting. In Virginia this special initiation ritual, called *huskanaw,* involved the seclusion of young men for eighteen or twenty weeks and use of a hallucinogenic drug intended to make them forget "they ever have been Boys." In the Carolinas, a much larger number of young people were subjected to huskanaw, which took place every year or two, rather than the decade or two that might separate huskanaws in Virginia. Adolescents were confined in a darkened structure for five or six weeks and were provided with little food. They were given hallucinatory plants that led them to "make the most dismal and hellish Cries, and Howlings, that ever humane Creatures express'd." After their confinement ended, they were not to speak for a month. John Lawson, an English visitor, was told that the ritual "hardens" the young "ever after to the Fatigues of War, Hunting, and all manner of Hardship, which their way of living exposes them to. Besides, they add, that it carries off those infirm weak bodies that would have been only a Burden and Disgrace to their Nation." Through these sets of rituals, youths' childish identity was shed and they were reborn as adults.[12]

Indian cultures served as a mirror that allowed Europeans to perceive the distinctiveness of their own customs. Practices that Europeans had considered to be God-given no longer appeared inevitable and inescapable. If, on the one hand, contact with the Indian peoples reinforced European ethnocentrism, it also freed a few European thinkers, such as Jean-Jacques Rousseau, to contemplate alternative ways of bringing up the young, ways that they regarded as freer and more natural.

Unlike Indian children, who experienced relative freedom in childhood, or children in New England, where an ascetic moralism and stable, patriarchal families, reinforced by the church and community, shaped their experience, family instability and indentured servitude structured childhood in the seventeenth-century Chesapeake colonies of Virginia and Maryland. In New England, migration in family units, a healthful environment, and a balanced sex ratio had encouraged the development of large, hierarchical families, in which patriarchal fathers used their control of land to postpone the independence of sons well into their twenties or early thirties. In the Chesapeake, in stark contrast, where a high mortality rate and a sharply skewed sex ratio inhibited the formation of stable families, especially exploitative forms of servitude shaped the experience of young white colonists.[13]

In the seventeenth-century Chesapeake, male immigrants outnumbered females by four to one. In consequence, young women tended to marry at a very early age, generally in their mid or late teens, while males did not marry until relatively late, often in their late twenties or early thirties. Life in early Virginia and Maryland was deadly and chaotic. In this region's endemic malarial environment, infant and child mortality rates were extremely high, two or even three times the rate in England and New England. The high death rate stunted family size, limiting most parents to four or five children, only two or three of whom survived to maturity. In contrast to New England, where grandparenthood was common and patriarchal fathers dominated decisions about their children's choice of vocation and marriage partner, family life in the seventeenth-century Chesapeake was fragile and precarious. In one Virginia county, over 73 percent of children lost at least one parent before they reached the age of twenty-one, and a third lost both parents. Since adults lived only into their mid-forties, contact between parents and their children was relatively brief. Because of the high death rate, the average marriage lasted just seven years, and as a result the typical household in Virginia or Maryland in the seventeenth century contained orphans, half and stepbrothers and sisters of all ages growing up under the care of an uncle, brother, or friend as a father figure, or an aunt, an elder sister, or a stepmother as the female caretaker.

For many children, a father's death resulted in the breakup of the family. Before remarrying, many widowed mothers pushed their daughters into household servitude and their sons into apprenticeships.[14]

To protect the interests of young heirs, communities took on the responsibilities of caring for children traditionally performed by the family. Kin networks provided support, supervision, and education for orphaned youth. Orphan courts were established to manage properties inherited by youthful minors and to oversee the treatment of orphaned youths bound out to labor until their majorities. That such orphan courts often felt compelled to scrutinize the activities of guardians and masters suggests widespread abuse of the system and of the children dependent on it.[15]

Indentured servitude was the defining experience in the lives of immigrant youth. South of New England, two-thirds of all immigrants arrived in various forms of unfreedom: as indentured servants, apprentices, convicts, or slaves. A prominent example was George Washington's namesake, a member of the Virginia House of Burgesses named George Erskine, who served as Washington's mother's legal guardian. He had been kidnapped as a boy in Wales, and sold as a servant in Virginia. Unlike service in New England or the Old World, where servants were considered additional family members, servants in the Chesapeake were regarded as commodities or chattels who could be bought, sold, leased, and cruelly punished. In a letter written to his parents in 1623, Richard Frethorne, a young indentured servant in Virginia, described his miserable circumstances. His diet consisted of nothing but peas and gruel, and as for his clothing, "I have nothing at all—no, not a shirt to my back but two rags (2), nor clothes but one poor suit, nor but one pair of shoes, but one pair of stockings, but one cap, [and] but two bands [collars]." Indentures in Virginia and Maryland were harsher and far longer than in England, and more than half of all indentured servants died before their term of service expired. Planters could sell a servant's contract (a practice that had become illegal in England), restrict a servant's travel, whip servants, and extend their term of service as a form of punishment. There were instances in which servants received 500 lashes at a time and were beaten with rakes. Female servants were especially vulnerable to sexual exploitation, with a third becoming pregnant before their term of service expired.[16]

After 1640, as profits from tobacco cultivation fell, exploitation of the labor of indentured servants intensified. Planters extended the term of service from four to seven years, and master-servant conflict escalated. Rates of suicide and crime rose, as did the number of runaways. In response, Virginia required servants to carry a pass whenever they traveled in the colony. Servant unrest culminated in Bacon's Rebellion, a power struggle between Virginia's governor and his opponents. Arising out of warfare against neighboring Indians in 1675, Bacon's Rebellion quickly escalated into a wholesale uprising against Virginia's planter elite. During the turmoil, in which Jamestown was burned to the ground, both Virginia's governor and Nathaniel Bacon, the rebellion's leader, promised freedom to servants who joined their cause. Although most of the servants who joined the rebellion were young and the governor's supporters were older, Bacon's Rebellion was not perceived in generational terms. Age consciousness was low in the Chesapeake because most young people lived outside of family unit. Class, not age, defined status in the early Chesapeake region, and Bacon's Rebellion was interpreted as a class struggle.[17]

Bacon's Rebellion hastened the transition away from indentured servitude and its replacement with racial slavery. Even before the rebellion, the supply of youthful indentured servants from England had fallen. The English Civil War of the 1640s depressed England's birthrate, while the Great Fire of London in 1666 created a heightened demand for labor in the English capital. Meanwhile the founding of new colonies, such as Pennsylvania, offered much more attractive alternatives to newcomers than migration to the Chesapeake. Between 1680 and 1720 more-stable family patterns emerged among the Chesapeake's white inhabitants. With the decline of indentured servitude, the sex ratio equalized. Life expectancy rose as the number of native-born children, who had been exposed to New World diseases during infancy, increased. Marriages lasted longer, parent-child ties grew more stable, and kinship networks grew more extensive. Families expanded to seven or eight children, with five or six of these normally reaching adulthood, twice the size achieved by seventeenth-century families. Life expectancy rose to the mid-fifties for adult males, and grandparenthood, a rarity in the seventeenth century, became a central feature of family life by the mid-eighteenth century. Among the region's planter elite, patriarchal family patterns slowly emerged, in which fathers exercised control over their sons' careers and their children's choice of marriage partners. Modeling itself after the English gentry, with its values of leisured sociability, classical education, and gentility, the planter class established families that combined a high degree of formality and rigid sex roles with parental indulgence.[18]

Compared with their counterparts in New England, planter families in the eighteenth-century Chesapeake were much more relaxed about their children's upbringing. There were few work responsibilities for sons under the age of twelve or thirteen, and religious instruction, though advocated by ministers and authors of childrearing manuals, appears to have been largely nonexistent. In the absence of strong religious influences, parents exhibited little concern about instilling a moral code in the young, nurturing their conscience, or preparing them for conversion. Since much of the day-to-day care of planters' children was left in the hands of slaves, parents could coddle and spoil their children. Especially toward the end of the eighteenth century, relations within families grew more openly affectionate. Parents increasingly displayed undisguised fondness for young children, who were regarded as a source of pleasure and diversion. In well-to-do families, infants and small children became the centerpiece of family attention and affection, as childhood was perceived as a distinct stage of life characterized by innocence and delightful "prattling." Whereas the loss of a child in the seventeenth and early eighteenth centuries had produced studied resignation, a death in the family after midcentury tended to unleash powerful anxiety and sorrow among the survivors.[19]

Planters' sons attained independence at a very early age. Although they remained at home until they married, usually in their mid-twenties, planters' sons enjoyed considerable freedom of movement. Usually by their early teens, planters' sons had entered the adult world, serving as messengers between plantations and participating in their fathers' business trips. One traveler in the late eighteenth century commented: "A Virginia youth of 15 years is already such a man as he will be at twice that age. At 15, his father gives him a horse and a Negro, with which he riots about the country, attends every fox-hunt, horserace, and cock-fight, and does nothing else whatever." Although parents and kin organized dances and parties for their offspring, dances, drinking, hunting, sports, and courtship generally took place without close parental supervision. Premarital intercourse seems to have been relatively common, and bridal pregnancy rates rose steadily during the eighteenth century. Between 1749 and 1780 from one-fourth to one-third of all brides in one Virginia parish were pregnant on their wedding day.[20]

Given the relative isolation of farms and plantations, sibling relations were more intense in the Chesapeake than in New England, with young women developing especially close attachments to their brothers. Nevertheless, sibling relations were less egalitarian than in the northern colonies. In about four out of five planter families, the eldest son inherited the home plantation, and younger sons received other land, often unimproved, in outlying areas. Daughters rarely inherited real property. On the few occasions when they did receive landed portions—usually when their were no sons or grandsons—the legacy often contained a reversion clause returning the land at their death, if they died childless, to a nephew or some other male relative. In their letters to their daughters, planter fathers were much more likely than their northern counterparts to stress gender hierarchy. A letter from Thomas Jefferson to his daughter, Martha, typifies the idea that a woman needed to subordinate herself to her husband. "The happiness of your life now depends on the continuing to please a single person," he wrote. A woman's willingness to obey her husband was "the keystone of the arch of matrimonial happiness." In fact there was a growing emphasis on family lineage and family honor. Southern sons were much more likely than their northern counterparts to receive a surname as a first name and to marry among their kin. In one Maryland county the percentage of marriages between cousins and other blood relatives almost tripled from the first third of the eighteenth century to the last third. An elaborate cousinry developed, which offered marital, economic, and, at least among the elite, political opportunities.[21]

Discipline in the Chesapeake colonies was directed toward slaves, not white children. Compared with New England, the problems of adolescence and the rising generation were rare topics of discussion, and there was little outcry about youthful drinking and carousing. Discipline appears to have been very inconsistent in the Chesapeake region, with indulgence and rigorous displays of authority existing side by side. Many observers, especially stepfathers, complained bitterly about the effects of premature independence, which they felt produced undisciplined, dissolute young people. One man described his future stepson as "a young Wilde and dissulute person much given to Company Keeping," who was "letting his estate fall to Ruine and decay for want of Management." But such complaints resulted in few tangible efforts to discipline the young.[22]

The direction of familial change in the Chesapeake colonies was the reverse of that found in New England. In the Chesapeake region, family life grew more stable over time and, among the planter class, more hierarchical and patriarchal. Yet the prevalence of slavery produced patterns of parenting decisively different from those in New England by diverting paternal discipline from children onto slaves. Meanwhile planter families placed far less emphasis on shaping a child's conscience. Despite certain trends toward uniformity over the eighteenth century, regional difference remained a defining feature of colonial childhood.[23]

No colonial children experienced a harsher childhood than those of African descent. Put to work from a very early age, they suffered from exhausting labor, high mortality rates, and frequent separation from family members. The English alone imported 1.5 million Africans into their New

World colonies (including the West Indies) during the eighteenth century, more than three times the number of white immigrants, including a sharply increasing number of enslaved children.[24]

The Dutch West India Company brought the first slaves to New Amsterdam in 1626, eleven young men from the Congo River basin. Since few Europeans were willing to build the forts, houses, and roads of the new colony, or to labor in the fields or run the mills, the Dutch relied heavily on slave labor. By 1664, when the Dutch ceded New Amsterdam to the British, 40 percent of the colony's population consisted of enslaved Africans. While a few Dutch slaves owned land and businesses and attended church services in the Dutch Reformed Church, most worked as laborers, cargo loaders, construction workers, farmers, and sailors. In 1697 the English in New York allowed enslaved Africans—who now made up about 20 percent of the population—to be buried in a desolate six-acre plot of land outside Manhattan's town limits.[25]

Studies of the remains present a harsh picture of childhood in bondage. They reveal very high death rates for both male and female slaves in infancy and between the ages of fifteen and nineteen. Eighteen percent of the skeletons belong to children under the age of two, and most had died within six months of birth. Altogether, more than 40 percent of the remains belonged to children under the age of twelve. Skeletal evidence of malnutrition was common among the enslaved children's remains. One chronicle of slave life indicates that slaves usually ate two quarts of buttermilk mixed with cornmeal and a little bread daily, and received meat just once a month. As a result, anemia was rampant, and enslaved children were extremely vulnerable to infectious disease, especially tuberculosis, cholera, and influenza. Many of the children's skeletons reveal bone breaks that did not heal. In some cases the children's backbones were found jammed into the braincase, probably the result of a stumble or fall while carrying a heavy load upon the head. In other cases, bones were broken during fatal beatings. One child, known only as "Burial 39," died around the age of six. Circular fractures of the neck bones and enlarged muscle attachments in the arms suggest that she or he had to carry extremely heavy burdens. The child also shows evidence of cranial synotosis, a premature closure of the sutures in the skull, possibly as a result of carrying heavy loads on the head. Pitting around the eye orbits suggests how much the child, already weakened from infections, malnourishment, and anemia, suffered from this labor. Yet this child was buried by people who cared deeply. Even though the child was stacked with five other bodies in a cedar coffin, the corpse was wrapped in white linen fastened with a copper shroud pin. In a sign that those in bondage retained strong cultural ties with Africa, the vast majority of bones were buried in simple wooden coffins with their heads to the west. Like those of their West African ancestors, their bodies were aligned so that the deceased were facing in the direction of sunrise.[26]

Ottobah Cugoano was about thirteen years old when he was kidnapped from his home on the Gold Coast in present-day Ghana. He and some eighteen or twenty other boys and girls were playing in a field "when several great ruffians came upon us" with pistols and swords. Distraught after his abduction, young Ottobah refused to eat or drink for several days. The horrors he saw and felt, he later wrote, "cannot well be described; I saw many of my miserable countrymen chained two and two, some handcuffed and some with their hands tied behind." When a slave ship arrived off the coast to take them away to the New World, "it was a most horrible scene; there was nothing to be heard but rattling of chains, smacking of whips, and the groans and cries of our fellow men." Aboard the vessel, there was an aborted attempt at a revolt. "Death," Ottobah wrote, seemed "more preferable than life," and the boys and women, who were not shackled, plotted to "burn and blow up" the ship "and to perish all together in the flames." A woman who was sleeping with a member of the ship's crew betrayed the scheme, resulting in a "cruel bloody scene."[27]

Although most enslaved Africans, especially in the fifteenth, sixteenth, and seventeenth centuries, were in their late teens or early twenties, a growing number were much younger. By the late eighteenth and nineteenth centuries, many were young children. They were acquired in a variety of ways. About half were captured during wars. Others were taken as a result of judicial proceedings or repayment for debt. A fifteen-year-old known only as Eve told the doctor aboard the slave ship *Ruby* that her father had been accused of theft and was forced to give one of his daughters as compensation. A significant number of enslaved African girls served as collateral for a debt, working for a creditor until a debt was paid. If the debt went unpaid, the child might be sold into slavery. That is what happened to Kagne, a ten-year-old from Sierra Leone who was taken on a Portuguese slave ship to Cuba. Any child, regardless of status, was vulnerable to enslavement. Twelve-year-old Salih Bilali, who was born around 1770 to a prominent family in Mali, had studied in an Islamic school before he was abducted in 1782 and taken to Georgia.[28]

Initially most were enslaved along the coast of West or West Central Africa, but over time captives were taken from farther inland, 500 or even 1,000 miles from the Atlantic. Torn from kin and their homeland, the captives felt a deep despair. The Scottish explorer Mungo Park, who traveled to Africa in the late eighteenth century, described one girl's misery following her capture: "Never was a face of serenity more suddenly changed into one of the deepest distress. The terror she manifested in having . . . the rope fastened round her neck, and the sorrow with which she bade adieu to her companions, were truly affecting." Some enslaved children, including Ottobah Cugoano, feared that the Europeans were cannibals who planned to eat them and believed that the wine that the European slave traders drank was blood.[29]

Before being transported to the New World, the captives were placed in pens guarded by dogs. One captive described the conditions they faced:

> The slaves were all put into a pen and placed with our backs to the fire, and ordered not to look about us, and to insure obedience, a man was placed in front with a whip in his hand ready to strike the first who should dare to disobey orders; another man then went round with a hot iron, and branded us the same as they would the head of barrels or any other inanimate goods or merchandise.

During the Middle Passage across the Atlantic, younger children were often left unfettered and allowed to spend more time on deck than older captives. Still, much of their time was spent in the cramped, befouled hold, usually in the crowded steerage section in the vessel's rear, where they had little space to move. Generally each child had a space only five feet by twelve to fourteen inches—a fraction of the space provided to convicts on prison ships or galleys. Rations were sparse: a pint of water a day and two meals consisting of beans or mush.[30]

Revolts erupted on about 10 percent of the slave voyages, and at least one owner warned a captain not to put "too much confidence in the Women nor Children lest they happen to be Instrumental to your being surprised which might be fatall." As many as 40 percent of the captives died during the Middle Passage during the sixteenth century, 15 percent during the seventeenth century, and between 5 and 10 percent in the eighteenth and nineteenth centuries. The main cause of death was dehydration, although epidemic diseases sometimes took large numbers of lives on individual voyages and many suffered from dysentery on arrival, leading some ship captains to plug their anuses with molten lead so that potential buyers would not see their bloody discharge. The cramped, oppressive conditions on shipboard left many captives barely able to stand upright. One child recalled on arriving in Charleston harbor: "I was not able to stand. It was more than a week after I left the ship before I could straighten my limbs."[31]

About 6 percent of the eleven to sixteen million Africans forcibly transported to the Americas were brought to what is now the United States.

Their labor played an indispensable role in the settlement and development of the colonies, as they cleared land, constructed buildings, worked as household servants, tended livestock, and raised foodstuff and staple crops such as tobacco, rice, and indigo. Black slavery developed slowly in colonial America. Though Africans were brought to South Carolina by the Spanish as early as 1526 and imported into Virginia even before 1619, the colonists initially relied primarily on white indentured servants and Indian captives as a source of labor. The status of the first blacks in the colonies was uncertain. Some were permanently unfree; others were treated like white indentured servants; and a few were assigned plots of land remote from their master's homes and were allowed to raise tobacco and other crops and purchase their own freedom. As early as the late 1630s, however, the English colonists began to make a clear distinction between the status of white servants and black slaves. In 1639 Maryland became the first colony to state specifically that baptism as a Christian did not make a slave a free person. Around the same time, the colonists broke with English custom and traced slave status exclusively through the mother. Any child born to a slave woman, regardless of the child's father, was automatically classified as a slave.[32]

During the colonial era it was extremely difficult for enslaved Africans and their descendents to create and sustain families. About three of every five Africans brought in chains to the colonies were male, and on individual farms and plantations the ratios were even more distorted, making it hard for men to find a spouse. In the northern colonies, where many slaves were domestic servants and were forced to live in attics or cellars, it may have been equally difficult to marry. As late as 1730, surviving inventories identify just 6 percent of the slaves in South Carolina as living in individual family units; and even in 1790 the figure was only 30 percent. In the Chesapeake colonies of Maryland and Virginia, the figures were modestly higher. A study of Prince George's County, Maryland, in 1776 concluded that a fifth of the population on smaller farms lived in two-parent families, a third in single-parent families, and 40 percent in no family at all. Especially common in the Chesapeake colonies were "abroad" marriages, where spouses lived on separate plantations and could visit family members only with their masters' permission. One observer in the late 1790s reported that husbands sometimes borrowed horses and traveled "ten to fourteen miles" to visit their families.[33]

Not until the middle of the eighteenth century did sex ratios in Virginia and Maryland equalize, allowing a majority of enslaved Africans and African Americans to form families. Beginning in the 1720s, African Americans in the Chesapeake region became the first slave population in the

New World able to reproduce their own numbers. By the 1760s, slaves in North and South Carolina and Georgia were also able to reproduce naturally. With a more equal sex ratio and greater immunities to New World diseases, American-born slaves had a lower death rate, with a greater number living into adulthood. Masters began to recognize that a "Great Encrease in Children" was a source of wealth, and that slaves with families were likely to be more productive workers. Thus, they encouraged marriage and pregnancy among slaves.[34]

Enslaved children, however, were extremely vulnerable to separation from their parents. Children might be separated as a result of a debt, a sale, an owner's death, or a planter's decision to move or to transfer slaves among his various properties. One eighteenth-century record describes a one-and-a-half-year-old slave named Stephen taken away from his mother. He was one of thousands. Still, slave couples created de facto marriages and sought to raise their children according to their own standards. As Johann Bolzius, a mid-eighteenth-century traveler, remarked, enslaved African Americans "have to take as their wives or husbands whomever their masters give them without ceremonies," but they "love their families dearly and none runs away from the other."[35]

In the eighteenth century it was not uncommon for slaveowners to sell or remove adolescent slaves to a new plantation, since clearing land required physical strength and stamina. During the 1750s Peyton Randolph, a Virginia planter, moved a number of young slaves to a unit a hundred miles from the home plantation. In the early nineteenth century, as the nation expanded west in the wake of the Louisiana Purchase and the War of 1812, about a million slaves, many of them young, were moved from eastern parts of the South into the cotton kingdom of Alabama, Mississippi, Louisiana, and Texas, as well as into Arkansas and Missouri, disrupting parent-child ties.[36]

The French immigrant J. Hector St. John Crèvecoeur contended that slaves "have no time, like us, tenderly to rear their helpless offspring, to nurse them on their knees, to enjoy the delight of being parents. Their paternal fondness is embittered by considering, that if their children live, they must live to be slaves like themselves." He was wrong. Charles Ball, a slave in western Maryland, described a slave mother who carried her child on her back while she toiled because she could not stand to hear the child's cries if left alone. Ball also described a child's funeral, which incorporated African traditions. The "father buried with it, a small bow and several arrows; a little bag of parched meal; a miniature canoe, about a foot long, and a little paddle, (with which he said it would cross the ocean to his own country) . . . and a piece of white muslin, with several curious and strange figures painted on it in blue and red, by which, he said, his relations and countrymen would know the infant to be his son, and would receive it accordingly, on its arrival amongst them." This ceremony underscores the depth of parent-child attachments.[37]

Despite the threat of sale and separation, African-American parents instilled a strong sense of family identity in their children. Fathers purchased or made gifts for their children and passed down craft skills to their sons. To sustain a sense of identity over time, slave parents commonly named their eldest son for fathers and paternal grandfathers. Nothing better illustrates the strength of family ties than the number of runaway ads that describe enslaved children running away to visit a father or a mother. These include ads describing a ten-year-old, a twelve-year-old, and a fourteen-year-old who fled to find their parents. The fragility of the nuclear slave family gave special significance to the extended kinship group. By the mid-eighteenth century, the enslaved had created dense networks of family and surrogate families. Slave children were encouraged to refer to older slaves as "aunt" and "uncle" and to younger slaves as "sister" and "brother." Kin, including aunts, uncles, nephews, nieces, cousins, and in-laws, as well as friends, served as substitute parents in the event of family separation. Together, the bonds of family and the extended kin group sustained African-American children through the travails of slavery.[38]

The Middle Colonies, from New York southward to Delaware, were more pluralistic than any other portion of colonial America. Embracing the principle of religious toleration, this region attracted a diversity of immigrants who spoke a variety of languages. It was here, especially among the Quakers, that patterns of childhood and family life emerged that anticipated those that became common among the middle class during the nineteenth century.[39]

When George Mittelberger, a schoolteacher from the German duchy of Wurttemberg who sailed to Pennsylvania in 1750, departed his ship, he witnessed a shocking scene. To pay for their passage to the New World, many German immigrants sold their children into service "like so many head of cattle" so that "the parents can leave the ship free and unrestrained." Children from five to fifteen years in age were bound out to service until they were twenty-one. Frequently, Mittelberger observed, the parents "do not know where and to what people their children are going." He wrote that it "often happens that such parents and children, after leaving the ship, do not see each other again for many years, perhaps no more in all their lives."[40]

Alongside the indentured children that Mittelberger described, another

De Peyster Boy, with a Dog, attributed to Gerardus Duyckinck I, 1730–1734. Modeled on an eighteenth-century British portrait, the boy's rigid posture, outstretched arm, and calf turned to the side emphasize his high social status. Courtesy of the New-York Historical Society, New York City.

pattern of childhood arose in the Middle Colonies, decisively different from those in New England and the Chesapeake. Especially pronounced among the Quakers, this family pattern was characterized by unusually intense emotional bonding between parents and children, indulgent childrearing, and an acceptance by parents of early youthful independence. In the Middle Colonies, most families lived in small nuclear households isolated from extended kin and free from the community controls found in New England. It was within these private, inward-turning households that new patterns of childhood were pioneered. Today we customarily distinguish between two-parent families, single-parent families, and extended families in which two-parent or single-parent families are augmented by other kin. Three centuries ago, very different conceptions of families prevailed. The gentry family—a unit based on lineage and ownership of a landed estate, passed down from generation to generation through the eldest son—proved difficult to sustain in the American colonies. Even the great landed families of New York and the southern colonies abandoned primogeniture and provided large inheritances to every one of their children. A second kind of family—the farm or artisanal household—was a unit of production that included not only a husband, wife, and their children but also the servants, apprentices, laborers, and other dependents. Common in New England, this was a patriarchal unit in which proprietors and masters exercised direct command over their dependents' labor. A third familial model—the clan—consisted of a group of interrelated families that lived in separate households but interacted socially and economically. Especially in seventeenth-century New England, it was not uncommon for the sons and daughters of one family to marry the children of another. Indeed, whole communities in early New England often consisted of a small number of intermarried families.[41]

It was during the eighteenth century in the Middle Colonies that that a fourth kind of family emerged: the private family, consisting of a father, mother, and children bound together by ties of affection. Not simply a unit of production or a vehicle for transmitting property or craft skills, the private family was an emotional entity and an instrument for shaping children's character. Within the private family, space was restructured; particular areas were set aside for cooking, eating, sitting at ease, and sleeping. The shift toward a privatized family was also apparent in burial practices; rarely did inhabitants of the Middle Colonies bury their dead alongside extended family members. Language, too, reflected the emphasis on the private family. Settlers in the Middle Colonies rejected the custom of referring to distant relatives as aunts, uncles, and cousins. Indeed, the very spelling of the family's surname varied from one household to another.[42]

Favorable circumstances, such as the sheer abundance of arable land, encouraged the development of private families in the Middle Colonies, as did religion. Much more than the Puritans, the Quakers and other religious sectarians in the Middle Colonies sought to keep children isolated from the corruptions of the outside world. The Quakers, in particular, were convinced that the best way to promote children's religious salvation was to maintain "holy conversation" with their parents, who had already learned religious truth. More than any earlier group of English immigrants, the Quakers extolled a family life centered on the affection and companionship between a husband and wife and the love, care, and emotional support of their children. Unlike the Puritans, the Quakers emphasized equality over hierarchy, gentle guidance over strict discipline, and early autonomy for children. Precisely because the Quaker Meeting exercised strong communal control over marriage, parents could afford to be more indulgent. Nor did Quaker fathers govern children through the inheritance system. They generally gave their sons outright gifts of land at the time of marriage without any restrictions or stipulations. Sons of the first settlers received an average of over 200 acres of land, and daughters received the equivalent in cash and goods.[43]

The steady influx of new immigrant families into the Middle Colonies, which slowed the development of dense extended family networks, also encouraged the growth of private families. Unlike New England, where immigration declined after 1640, or the Chesapeake, where most new arrivals came as forced laborers, either as indentured servants or as slaves, the Middle Colonies attracted many non-English immigrants, particularly Germans and Scots-Irish. Many of the first immigrants arrived as single young men or teenagers and usually lived with a master's family. Beginning in the 1730s, however, poor economic conditions in Germany, Scotland, and Ireland led to the migration of entire families, usually consisting of a young married couple with one or two children or an older couple and their teenaged children. Even poor tenant families maintained separate households. Private families were especially common in the growing towns and seaports, like Philadelphia, where few journeymen resided in the homes of their masters and few laboring families took extended kin or nonkin into their homes.[44]

In contrast to New England, where paternal control of land allowed fathers to exert a powerful influence on their sons' lives well into their twenties or even thirties, in the Middle Colonies a large proportion of sons moved away from their parents in their teenage years. Even Quaker parents found it difficult to ensure that their children married within the faith and stayed close by. During the mid-eighteenth century, there was a sharp increase in marriages "out of union" as sons and daughters increasingly took non-Quaker mates. The Middle Colonies served as the prototype for the nineteenth-century middle-class family. In their emphasis on familial privacy and an affectionate relationship between parents and children, as well as the early adoption of birth control, which was practiced among Quaker families during the last quarter of the eighteenth century, families in the Middle Colonies pioneered practices and attitudes that would subsequently spread across the middle class.[45]

During the second half of the eighteenth century, regional variations in childhood narrowed as increasing geographic mobility, new employment opportunities, evangelical religious revivals, and military conflict contributed to greater youthful autonomy. Dwindling land supplies in New England and soil exhaustion of the tobacco lands of the Tidewater and Piedmont encouraged many sons to leave family farms for western lands or fresh starts in towns and cities. As a result, boys got their start in life considerably earlier than before and had more occupational choices. Meanwhile the emotional evangelical religious revivals sweeping through the colonies challenged older forms of authority and allowed youths to assert an independent religious identity much earlier. The Great Awakening of the 1730s and 1740s had pronounced effects on the young, encouraging new childrearing practices, reducing the age of conversion, and promoting a new code of values among many. Evangelical families placed a heavy emphasis on suppressing children's willfulness, shaping their conscience, and disciplining their passions to prepare them for the experience of religious rebirth. The age of religious conversion fell sharply, often into the teen years, and young people in increasing numbers decided independently which churches to join. Especially in the Chesapeake colonies, the religious revivals led many teens to embrace a set of values emphasizing self-restraint, including restraints on drinking and other forms of amusement.[46]

Young men's participation in military combat dramatically altered the experience of adolescent white males. Warfare was common during the mid-eighteenth century. Roughly 30 to 40 percent of adolescent males saw action in warfare in the period from 1740 to 1781, against either the Indians, the French, or the British. Wars drew youth away from their parents' homes and accelerated the process by which young people attained independence and adult status.[47]

Even before the Revolution, a new ideology highly critical of patriarchal authority had begun to circulate throughout the colonies. Much more widely read than political discourses such as John Locke's *Second Treatise on Liberty* were childrearing tracts, like his *Essay Concerning Human Understanding* and Jean-Jacques Rousseau's *Emile*. In widely read works of fiction by Daniel Defoe, Henry Fielding, Samuel Richardson, Laurence Sterne, and numerous lesser-known writers, the patriarchal family came under attack as unduly repressive and incompatible with the spirit of the times. Readers learned that parental example was more effective than coercion in governing children; that the ideal parent sought to cultivate children's natural talents and abilities through love; and that young people had a right to choose an occupation and a spouse free from parental intrusion.[48]

The growing emphasis on youthful independence represented a striking reversal in public attitudes. During the seventeenth century most young colonists, regardless of region and social class, had lived in a state of dependency upon their parents or upon a master and a mistress. Through their control over dowries, inheritance, landed property, and access to training and apprenticeships, fathers and masters determined when young people were able to leave home, marry, and achieve the independence of full adulthood. It is not an accident that the very terms used to describe young people—*boy* and *girl*—were words also applied to servants, regardless of age, since subordination and dependency characterized both the condition of service and the condition of childhood and youth. Nothing symbolized this emphasis on domestic hierarchy better than the practice among young people of uncovering their heads and bowing in the presence of their parents. By the mid-eighteenth century, however, adult control over young people's access to economic independence had diminished, and young people were exercising greater autonomy over their leisure activities and courtship practices. A flood of advice books, philosophical treatises, novels, plays, and poems condemned prolonged submission to paternal rule and defended youthful freedom as a natural right. This antipatriarchal, antiauthoritarian ideology helped to sensitize the colonists to arbitrary British colonial authority. In defending the colonists' struggle for independence from British colonial rule, the radical pamphleteer Thomas Paine drew a pointed analogy to the importance of granting children early autonomy. "Nothing hurts the affections both of parents and children so much," he wrote in *The Crisis* in 1778, "as living too closely connected, and keeping up the distinction too long."[49]

chapter three

Sons and Daughters of Liberty

NOT ALL of those who participated in the American Revolution were grownups. Sybil Luddington, the "female Paul Revere," was just sixteen years old when she roused the local militia in 1777 in an unsuccessful attempt to save Danbury, Connecticut, from a British attack. The eldest of eight children and the daughter of a New York militia officer, she rode more than forty miles from her home in Fredericksburg, New York, to spread the alert.[1]

Joseph Plumb Martin was only fifteen when he joined the Continental Army in 1776. Poor, without prospects for acquiring land, he enlisted as a substitute for a local Connecticut gentlemen, with visions of martial glory in his head. During seven years of service as a private, he experienced all the Revolution's hardships, including the terrible winter at Valley Forge, Pennsylvania, where 2,500 soldiers, a quarter of the Continental Army, died of disease, exposure, and malnutrition. He slept on the wet ground without a blanket, marched shirtless and barefoot, and went days without food except "a little black birch bark." At the battles of Brooklyn, Harlem Heights, White Plains, and Yorktown, he dug trenches, dragged cannons, and faced musket balls and bayonets. He also vented his "spleen at our country and government . . . [and] officers" who refused to support and supply the army properly.[2]

James Forten, also fifteen, served as a powder handler on Stephen Decatur's twenty-two-gun privateer, *Royal Louis*. A free black whose great-grandfather had been one of the first slaves in Pennsylvania to purchase his freedom, Forten had attended a school led by the early Quaker abolitionist Anthony Benezet. In a naval engagement with the British ship *Lawrence,* he was the only survivor at his gun station. On his next voyage, after the British captured his ship, Forten expected to be sold into slavery in the West Indies, but the British captain's son befriended him and persuaded his father to offer the American free passage to England. "No, No!" young Forten replied, "I am here a prisoner for the liberties of my country; I never, NEVER, shall prove a traitor to her interests." The British captain then consigned Forten to the prison ship *Jersey* anchored in New York harbor, where about 11,000 sailors died of disease and malnutrition during three years of the Revolutionary War. Forten spent seven months on the ship before he was set free in a prisoner exchange.[3]

The American Revolution had far-reaching effects on children's lives. Many, like Luddington, Martin, and Forten, were drawn into the conflict. The war disrupted thousands of families, greatly increasing the number of widows, single-parent households, and orphans and forcing the new states to institute radically new approaches to the care of dependent children. The Revolution also ended indentured servitude, weakened apprenticeship, and contributed to the emergence of more companionate and egalitarian relations within individual households. Most important, it popularized an antiauthoritarian ideology highly critical of patriarchal authority, social hierarchy, and deference. In 1799 the British moralist Hannah More described the radical implications of the ideas popularized during the Age of Revolution. "The rights of man have been discussed till we are somewhat wearied with the discussion," she wrote. "To these have been opposed, as the next stage in the process of illumination, the *rights of women.* It follows, according to the natural progression of human things, that the next influx of that irradiation which our enlighteners are pouring in upon us, will illuminate the world with grave descants on the *rights of youth,* the *rights of children,* and *the rights of babies.*" As she understood, the language of liberty and equality could not be confined solely to politics; it inevitably also influenced ideas and behavior in the private realm of family.[4]

The disruptions of the revolutionary era provoked a sharp reaction. In the immediate postrevolutionary period, childhood, for the first time in American history, became the object of political discourse. Convinced that the stability of the new republic depended on a virtuous citizenry, the postrevolutionary generation called for more intensive styles of child-rearing and more prolonged and systematic forms of education. Primary responsibility for instilling republican virtues in children rested with mothers, who required better education to meet this high responsibility.

Thus maternal nurture had to be supplemented with an expanded system of schooling that would not simply transmit skills and knowledge but also shape children's moral character.[5]

The popular image of youth during the era of the American Revolution was formed by the historical novel *Johnny Tremain*. Written by Esther Forbes, and published in 1943 in the midst of World War II, it tells the story of a fictional fourteen-year-old Boston orphan, a talented but arrogant silversmith's apprentice whose life is turned upside down when he injures his hand. In time he becomes a messenger boy on horseback for the Sons of Liberty and meets many of the nation's founders. He later becomes a spy, takes part in the Boston Tea Party, and struggles with loss at the battles of Lexington and Concord. For younger readers, *Johnny Tremain* offers a succinct overview of the events leading up to the Declaration of Independence, and a compelling story of a young boy who learned valuable lessons about pride and overcoming obstacles. Yet the novel only hints at the complex role of young people in the American Revolution.

In a famous 1818 letter John Adams wrote: "The Revolution was effected before the War commenced. The Revolution was in the Minds and Hearts of the People." He proceeded to invoke an analogy repeatedly voiced by patriots: that the colonists, like children, had rights that had to be respected, and that Britain, like an abusive parent, had violated those rights through the exercise of arbitrary authority. As Adams put it:

> The People of America had been educated in an habitual Affection for England as their Mother-Country; and while they thought her a kind and tender Parent (erroneously enough, however, for she never was such a Mother,) no Affection could be more sincere. But when they found her a cruel Beldam [older woman], willing, like Lady Macbeth to "dash their Brains out," it is no Wonder if their filial Affections ceased and were changed into Indignation and horror.

The American Revolution was both the product of and catalyst for far-reaching shifts in ideas, values, and behavior. One of the most significant shifts involved a growing rejection of patriarchal rule.[6]

In describing imperial authority and colonial obligations, American patriots and loyalists invoked metaphors relating to childhood and parenthood. Loyalists said that the colonists, like children, owed gratitude and loyalty to the mother country and risked severe chastisement if they revolted. The patriots, in contrast, used the language of nurture and maturation and called upon the colonies to break free from dependence and subordination. As one patriot proudly declared, "The day of independent manhood has arrived." Both Whigs and Tories likened the British empire to a family, but they drew very different conclusions from this analogy. Invoking the ideas of John Locke and the Scottish philosopher Francis Hutcheson, the patriots argued that parliamentary authority, like a parent's powers over children, was limited and temporary, and that the colonists, no less than children, had a right to independence when they achieved maturity or if their parents abused their power. Tories, framing their argument in more traditional patriarchal terms, argued that force alone could restore respect for British authority, much as a parent might use corporal punishment to correct a rebellious or disobedient child.[7]

The parent-child analogy provided the language through which the patriots defended their rights. In the wake of the Boston Massacre of 1770, in which British soldiers fired on a protesting mob and killed five men and boys, a patriot drew upon the Lockean notion that fatherhood was a trust to explain why the colonists rightfully protested violations of their rights: "We swore allegiance to him as a *King*, not as a *Tyrant*—as a *Protector*, not as a *Destroyer*—as a *Father*, not as a *Murderer*." More than a mere metaphor, the parent-child analogy gave expression to the patriots' sensitivity to dependence and degradation, evident in the restrictions that Britain placed on colonial manufactures and the taxes it imposed on colonial commerce. In *The Crisis*, Thomas Paine asserted the colonies' right to independence. "To know whether it be the interest of this continent to be independent," he declared, "we need only to ask this simple question: Is it the interest of a man to be a boy all his life?" Meanwhile British officials and loyalists also drew upon the parent-child analogy. One Englishman, writing in 1768, likened the colonists to an unruly boy, "growing more *imperious, haughty,* nay *insolent* every day." Loyalists, in stark contrast to the patriots, dwelt on the colonists' deficiencies and weaknesses and their need for protection from a powerful mother country.[8]

The patriots' sensitivity to colonial subjection was connected to a broader cultural movement away from patriarchal ideas about deference. By the second half of the eighteenth century, a combination of pressures— demographic, economic, political, and religious—had eroded earlier assumptions about patriarchal authority. The revolutionary struggle for national independence was, in part, fueled by a desire for personal autonomy, shared by many young men and women in the American colonies. The social history of mid-eighteenth-century America presents a paradox. In certain respects, colonial society was becoming more like English society. The power of royal governors was increasing, social distinctions were hardening, lawyers were paying closer attention to English law, and a more distinct social and political American elite was emerging as a result of the expansion of Atlantic commerce, the growth of tobacco and rice economies, and the sale of land. Yet the eighteenth century also witnessed growing claims of "English liberties" against all forms of subservience, including independence from the arbitrary authority of fathers. Opposition to Parliamentary measures restricting colonial trade and imposing taxes on colonial commerce acquired added resonance because the colonists were already highly sensitive to any exercise of authority that they consid-

In this 1784 engraving, children and youth participate in the 1774 tarring and feathering of John Malcom, a British customs official in Boston. Courtesy of the Library of Congress.

ered arbitrary, demeaning, or constraining of their opportunities to exercise free choice in how to live and work.[9]

Even before the end of the seventeenth century, patriarchal authority had come under fire. Defenders of royal authority, such as Thomas Hobbes and Sir Robert Filmer, compared the relationship between a king and his subjects to that between a patriarchal father and his children. Filmer, the Crown's most extreme advocate, argued that monarchical authority received divine sanction in the Fifth Commandment, which enjoined children to honor their father, and that the English monarchy derived its right to rule from God's grant of authority to Adam. Advocates of parliamentary supremacy and constitutional monarchy, who sought to impose limits on royal power, such as John Locke, rejected Filmer's analogy between the family and the polity. In his *Two Treatises on Government,* Locke repudiated Filmer's belief in the absolute, God-given authority of monarchs and argued that government was a human institution that citizens had the right to modify. Against Filmer's emphasis on patriarchal authority, Locke upheld a theory of natural rights, arguing that the laws of nature endow individuals with certain inalienable rights. Locke contended that a king's power was limited by natural law; that his powers were given to him as a trust for the good of the people; that legitimate government rests on the consent of the governed; and that if a ruler breaks that trust, his powers can be taken away. Whereas Filmer had emphasized the commandment to honor one's father, Locke pointed out that the biblical commandment was to "honor thy father and thy mother." Rejecting the idea that authority had to be strictly hierarchical, Locke suggested that if familial authority could be shared, then governmental power could be shared between the Crown and Parliament. Locke's childrearing philosophy was connected to his political theories. Rejecting the patriarchal emphasis on subordination, Locke instead stressed that childhood was a temporary stage of human development. Parental authority was a trust and duty that rested on children's temporary incapacities and weaknesses. The primary purpose of parenthood was not to impose obedience, but rather to nurture children's powers of reason in order to prepare them to become self-governing adults.[10]

Today Locke is best known for his emphasis on children's malleability and his description of their nature as a blank slate. By this he meant that children's socialization could not be left to nature, but required close adult supervision and a carefully considered plan. A crusty bachelor, Locke offered numerous suggestions for producing independent but self-disciplined children, ranging from daily footbaths in cold water to the use of fables rather than adult books in instruction. Instead of relying on corporal punishment, he favored psychological manipulation of a child's "Love of Credit" and "shame of doing amiss." Ideas somewhat similar to Locke's were widely disseminated in eighteenth-century British America. The Scottish moral philosopher Francis Hutcheson, whose ideas were highly influential in American colleges, emphasized that children had rights that needed to be respected. A child was not simply parents' property, but "a rational agent with rights valid against the parents; tho' they are the natural tutors or curators and have a right to direct the actions, and manage the goods of the child, for its benefit, during its want of proper knowledge."[11]

These new ideas about children were not mere abstractions; they were evident in everyday behavior. One sign of change involved a shift in naming patterns. In the seventeenth century, naming practices emphasized the continuity of a lineage. Parents customarily named older sons and daughters for themselves or grandparents and gave younger children the names of recently deceased siblings. By the mid-eighteenth century, names were increasingly individualized; fewer children were named for grandparents or for brothers or sisters who had recently died. Meanwhile an increasing number of mothers and fathers bestowed middle names on their children, signifying greater appreciation of children's individuality. A similar shift in sensibility was apparent in the tendency of wealthy parents to buy toys and books for children, on the ground that they would help educate their offspring rather than assuming that children's innate qualities would emerge and suffice. At the same time, rituals of subordination that had symbolized paternal authority and familial hierarchy gradually disappeared. By the mid-eighteenth century, children were no longer expected to bow before their parents, ask their blessings each morning, stand during meals, or doff their hats before them.[12]

By the second half of the eighteenth century, respect for hierarchy was becoming difficult to sustain. Colleges had long been among the colonies' most hierarchal institutions. Before enrolling (usually around the age of sixteen), students were required to transcribe the institution's rules. Deportment and language symbolized rank and status. At Yale, freshmen had to remove their hats as a sign of respect whenever they encountered a superior. On stairways or in narrow hallways, freshmen must "stop and give way, leaving the most convenient side." Students were required to address tutors and graduates as "sir" and masters of arts as "Mr." (the new term that served as a substitute for "master"). College customs reinforced the emphasis on hierarchy. "Fagging" required freshman to perform errands for more senior students. This obligation to serve upper classmen led one freshman to exclaim: "A Soph[omore] is absolute and despotic as the great Mogul." Meanwhile college authorities were extremely sensitive to disobedience, slights, improper demeanor, and acts of contempt. Appearing without a hat, making an unseemly gesture, or even signing one's name in "an odd and ludicrous manner" could result in expulsion.[13]

In the middle of the eighteenth century, resistance to arbitrary college rules mounted. The first student rebellions on colonial college campuses took place in the 1740s. One of the earliest occurred at Yale College in 1745, where fierce religious struggles had grown out of the religious revivals of the Great Awakening. When two brothers were expelled, their classmates protested by publishing John Locke's *Essay on Toleration.* In 1759 a letter writer sought to explain the outbreak of student rebellions at Yale College. "Can you wonder, Sir," he wrote to a member of the Connecticut Assembly, "that there has been of late Years, such loud Murmuring and Complaints of the Scholars against the College and Government . . . so frequent Tumults and insurrections? . . . *Oppression will make a wise man mad,* how much more a Company of unwise and giddy Youth." The cause of student rebelliousness seemed self-evident: it was a reaction against arbitrary authority and denial of personal liberty.[14]

Over the next few years, disorders erupted at the College of Rhode Island (later Brown University), King's College (Columbia), Dartmouth College, the College of New Jersey (Princeton), Harvard College, and the College of William and Mary. Some of the issues that sparked revolts, such as quality of food at Harvard, seem trivial, and the worst violence involved stoning the college president's house. Nevertheless, there was little doubt in the eyes of contemporary observers that these protests reflected a fundamental shift in social values. In 1772 John Witherspoon, the president of the College of New Jersey, offered his explanation: "the spirit of liberty" had led students into "outrage and sedition." Similar sentiments were voiced at Harvard. In 1769 the college secretary observed that the students "have imbibed the Spirit of the Times. Their declamations and forensic disputes breathe the Spirit of Liberty. This has always been encouraged, but they have sometimes wrought themselves up to such a pitch of Enthusiasm it has been difficult to keep them within due bounds."[15]

Charity Clarke, a young New York woman whose son, Clement Clarke Moore, wrote the celebrated poem *The Night before Christmas,* was one of many young people politicized by the events leading up to the Revolution. In letters to a cousin, a London lawyer, written between 1768 and 1774, she expressed the growing impulse for independence found among many young patriots. In 1768, a month after British soldiers landed in

Boston to quell disorders produced by the imposition of customs duties on imports, including tea, she warned her cousin that such acts would only generate resistance. "When there is the least show of oppression or invading of liberty," she wrote, "you may depend on our working ourselves to the utmost of our power." The next year she reiterated her warning and announced that she would join "a fighting army of Amazones" who would resist British oppression. "If you English folks won't give us the liberty we ask," she declared, "I will try to gather a number of ladies armed with spinning wheels who shall all learn to weave & keep sheep, and will retire beyond the reach of arbitrary power." In 1774, a year after the Boston Tea Party, she informed her cousin to expect open resistance if British authorities continued to attempt to centralize authority over the colonies. "Though this body is not clad with silken garments," she wrote, "these limbs are armed with strength. The soul is fortified by Virtue, and the love of Liberty is cherished within this Bosom."[16]

It is not accidental that early participants in the Revolutionary cause called themselves "sons" and "daughters" of liberty. The phrase "Sons of Liberty" grew out of the debate on the Stamp Act in Parliament in 1765. Charles Townshend, speaking in support of the act, spoke contemptuously of the American colonists as being "children planted by our care, nourished up by our indulgence . . . and protected by our arms." Isaac Barre, a member of Parliament and friend of the colonists, responded to this condescending remark with outrage, declaring that the Americans were not children but "Sons of Liberty." Sons of Liberty chapters formed in Boston and New York early in 1765. Growing out of the Committees of Correspondence that had been established in Massachusetts, New York, and Rhode Island in 1763 and 1764 to organize public opinion and coordinate patriotic actions against Britain, the Sons of Liberty organizations sought to prevent enforcement of the Stamp Act of 1765.[17]

Young people played an active role in the ferment leading up to the Revolution. Teenage apprentices engaged in many mob actions that preceded the outbreak of war. Girls demonstrated their patriotism by participating in campaigns against the importation of British goods and in the production of homespun cloth. In an entry in her diary in February 1772, Anna Green Winslow, an eleven-year-old schoolgirl in Boston, described herself as "a daughter of liberty." "I chuse to wear as much of our own manufactory as pocible," she added. In 1770 in Boston, more than a hundred "young ladies" signed an agreement to refrain from buying or consuming imported tea. Betsy Foote, a Connecticut farm girl, was one of many young women politicized by Parliament's actions. She recorded that after mending, spinning, milking, and performing various other chores, she carded two pounds of wood and "felt Nationly."[18]

Resistance to British imperial authority escalated rapidly during the 1760s. There were at least 150 riots in the thirteen colonies between 1765 and 1769, and the mobs included many teenage apprentices as well as youthful laborers. "Unruly" apprentices played a key role in the events that culminated in the Boston Massacre, one of the pivotal events on the road to revolution. The train of events began when a sixteen-year-old barber's apprentice named Edward Garrick insulted Hugh White, a soldier of the 29th Regiment on sentry duty in front of Boston's Customs House. The sentry gave the apprentice a knock on the ear with his musket and a jab with his bayonet. The boy ran off and later returned with a sizable and unruly crowd, consisting chiefly of boys and youths. After someone rang the bells in a nearby church, drawing more people into the street, the sentry found himself confronting an angry mob. He stood his ground and called for the main guard. Six men, led by a corporal, responded, with guns unloaded but with fixed bayonets. They were soon joined by the officer on duty, twenty-year-old Captain John Preston.

The crowd soon swelled to almost 400 people, who began pelting the soldiers with snowballs and chunks of ice. The soldiers loaded their guns. Instead of drawing back, the crowd dared the soldiers to fire their weapons, reportedly saying: "Come on you rascals, you bloody backs, you lobster scoundrels, fire if you dare, God damn you, fire and be damned, we know you dare not." The soldiers fired, killing three people outright and mortally wounding two others. Six others were wounded but survived. Among those killed were two teenaged apprentices.[19]

As the conflict between Britain and the patriots grew violent, boys in their early and mid-teens played active roles. James Collins, eleven years old in 1775, served as an informal scout, a "collector of news," who provided information on the location of bands of loyalists. Israel Trask, who was ten in 1775, served in the Continental Army as a messenger and cook alongside his father. Boys as young as twelve served as drummers, spies, and even as soldiers. Others served as sailors on privateers—privately owned ships commissioned to attack British shipping. Although the Continental Congress set sixteen as the minimum age of service, the heavy demand for soldiers led recruiting agents to admit boys below that age. With half the population younger than sixteen, teenagers offered a valuable pool of potential recruits. In a society without reliable birth records, a boy could simply lie about his age or find an adult who would testify that he was sixteen or older. About 10 percent of New Jersey's soldiers were younger than eighteen; 5 percent of Virginia's troops were fourteen or fifteen. Privateers actively sought recruits among disgruntled teenaged apprentices. An officer of the Massachusetts ship *Protector* sang:

> All you that have bad masters,
> And cannot get your due;
> Come, come my brave boys,
> And join with our ship's crew.

Boys who were attending school or working as apprentices or assisting on their parents' farm suddenly found themselves thrust into positions of responsibility. Some enlisted to escape their harsh masters or the drudgery of farm work. Others, like Joseph Plumb Martin, were inspired by fantasies of military glory.[20]

The popular image of American revolutionaries is the citizen soldier modeled on the Minutemen who fought at Lexington and Concord. In fact, apart from officers, most long-term soldiers consisted of the poor, the young, the marginal, and the unfree. For many poor boys, the chief inducement to serve was monetary. Lacking property of their own, many were attracted to service by the promise of cash bounties or land. In Maryland the bounty for enlisting was equal to a quarter of the taxable property of the typical recruit. Peer pressure induced some to enlist. Ebenezer Fox was just twelve years old when the Revolution began. A laborer on a neighbor's farm, he recalled that "almost all of the conversation that came to my ears related to the injustice of England and the tyranny of government." The talk proved contagious. "It is perfectly natural," he wrote, "that the spirit of insubordination that prevailed should spread among the younger members of the community." He and a friend applied "the doctrines that we daily heard, in relation to the oppression of the mother country, to our own circumstances; and thought we were more oppressed than our fathers were . . . and that the time was come, when I should liberate myself from the thralldom of others, and set up a government of my own." On the very night that Paul Revere rode to Concord and Lexington, Fox and a friend fled their apprenticeships to enlist.[21]

Teenaged boys from poorer families were regarded as more expendable than older brothers or more prosperous adults. By 1777 each town had an enlistment quota to fill, and many turned to the poor and the young as a pool of substitutes. The *Connecticut Courant* reported that "the inhabitants were busily employed in recruiting the children and servants of their neighbors, and forbidding their own to engage." Daniel Granger was thirteen years old when he arrived at the camp of the Continental Army near Boston in November 1775 in search of an older brother who was sick.

Daniel wound up sending his brother home and taking his place. When Ebenezer Fox's master was called to serve in the local militia, the boy was chosen to serve as his substitute.[22]

A number of boy soldiers such as Joseph Plumb Martin recorded their experiences in their memoirs. They told of marching across miles of countryside without shoes, of lacking blankets and uniforms, of subsisting on horsemeat. They described fear, battlefield bravery, and, in many cases, disillusionment that stemmed from a lack of public support. "Great men get great praise, little men, nothing. But it always was so and always will be," Martin observed. During the Revolution the young assumed adult responsibilities at an early age. The conflict intensified and accelerated the erosion of social hierarchy and deference. In the northern and middle states the Revolution sharply reduced indentured servitude, precisely because many servants fought in the war and thereby won their freedom. By increasing the mobility of the young and encouraging early independence in thought and action, the Revolution was a powerful destabilizing force.[23]

The Revolution brought many children face-to-face with danger and death. Susan Lyttle was just ten years old in August 1777, about a month before the Continental Army defeated a British Army at the Battle of Saratoga in upstate New York. She and her sister Rebecca went outside their farmhouse after dinner to pull flax that could be spun into thread. "A Hessian soldier with his gun and military clothes came along," Susan later recalled. "He was deserting from the British at Fort Edward and finding his way through the country to New England. Eager to get all the news from him we could, we followed him—conversing with him." At that moment, Susan "heard a crackling among the bushes. A party of Tories were secreted east of the road. They rushed upon the Hessian, took away his gun, pinioned him, and said they should take him back to the camp to be shot for deserting. They also said we girls had got to go with them, too, for we were traitors showing a deserter the road for him to escape." Fortunately for Susan and her sister, a neighbor secured their release.[24]

Girls as well as boys got caught up in the conflict. Observed Abigail Adams: "At every house Women & children making Cartridges, running Bullets, making Wallets, baking Biscuit, crying & bemoaning & at the same time animating their Husbands & Sons to fight for their Liberties, tho' not knowing whether they should ever see them again." As armies occupied towns and cities, hungry troops foraged for supplies in the countryside, and bitter partisan conflict pitted loyalist against patriot militias, families were displaced from their homes and suffered severe property losses. Noncombatants also suffered from spiraling prices and a depreciating currency. More than 25,000 people died in the conflict—over one percent of the entire population—making the Revolution the second costliest war in U.S. history relative to the size of the population. The traumas of war—its unpredictability, disruptions, and upheavals—inflicted a heavy physical and emotional toll on many families and their children.[25]

Civilians quickly found their lives turned upside down. To sustain its 35,000-man army, the British resorted to foraging—taking food, wood, livestock, and other provisions from the civilian population. Soldiers chopped down trees and pulled down fences for firewood. Despite some efforts by British officers to suppress the practice, red-coated soldiers also looted civilians' personal possessions, seizing spinning wheels and wagons, bond certificates, and "Wearing Appararel, Money, Furniture and Bedding." The situation was particularly bad in Connecticut and New Jersey, where officers found it difficult to maintain discipline over their troops. There were documented reports of rape of married women, single women, and teenaged girls. In one of the most horrendous incidents, in December 1776 British troops broke into Abigail Palmer's farmhouse and raped the thirteen-year-old three times. Over the next three days they returned and repeatedly raped the girl; "the said Soldiers" also "Ravished" two neighbors, fifteen-year-old Elisabeth Cain and her sister Sarah, and forced them to go to a British encampment, where they were repeatedly raped until a British officer released the girls. Although British troops appear to have done greater damage to civilian property than did the patriots, American soldiers, too, were frequently forced to live off the land and forage for supplies. General Washington permitted scouting parties to seize enemy stores and supplies, and in 1778 he reported that his soldiers looted "cloth, linens, ribbands, some cases of knives and forks, [and] wine glasses," which they pretended was "the property of tories."[26]

The war produced massive numbers of refugees, many of whom were children. Sieges, retreats, and occupations left many women and children displaced and homeless. During the British occupation of Boston, the civilian population fell from about 15,000 to around 5,500 as people fled to the surrounding countryside. Those who remained were "totally destitute of vegetables, flour and fresh provisions" and were "obliged to feed on horse flesh." When the British seized Newport, Rhode Island, in December 1776, half the city's population fled to the countryside. During Britain's seven-year occupation of New York, Staten Island, and Long Island, thousands of loyalists sought asylum. Between 1776 and 1781 New York City's population increased fivefold, excluding the city's 10,000 British regulars. The results were severe housing and food shortages and outbreaks of such diseases as smallpox, dysentery, and typhus. "Whole Families, once in Affluence, are reduced to Wretchedness and Beggary," the *New York Gazette and Weekly Mercury* reported in 1777.[27]

Since soldiers were paid sporadically during the Revolution, wives had to support their families on their own. The Revolution produced young widows on an unprecedented scale, leaving tens of thousands of children fatherless. Although no accurate statistics exist, it seems plausible that as many as 8,000 to 12,000 women lost their husbands during the conflict, the equivalent of a million women today. These widows faced enormous financial difficulties, and their appeals for relief frequently mention infants and young children. Unlike earlier widows, most of whom were middle-aged or older and had grown children to support them, these widows were much younger and were the sole providers for their families. Traditionally widows had relied for support upon their adult children and upon property that was legally reserved for them. Under the principle of dower, a widow had a legal right to one third of her husband's property. But a system that worked for older women proved inadequate for younger widows with dependent young children. Restrictive dower laws made it difficult for widows to sell their property. Even widows of officers, who were supposed to receive half of their husband's pay for seven years, found it difficult to secure a pension.[28]

Unable to rely on traditional methods of support, these women and their children turned to poor relief, which was quickly overwhelmed by the burden. Many widows' children were auctioned off to families that would accept the lowest amount of money, a system known as public vendue. To deal with the burgeoning numbers of poor people, the nation's first benevolent societies arose, establishing sewing rooms for needy women. Towns also experimented with institutionalized systems of support, including almshouses and workhouses. In Philadelphia one resident in six accepted public relief in 1783; in New York the figure was one family in twelve. Not until 1818 did Congress enact pensions for Revolutionary War veterans and their widows.[29]

In addition to creating unprecedented problems of child welfare, the Revolution also challenged the institution of slavery. In a letter written in 1774, when she was around the age of twenty, Phillis Wheatley, the first published African-American poet, illustrated how the colonial struggle against British imperial authority raised fundamental questions about freedom, equality, and natural rights. "In every human breast," she wrote, "God has implanted a Principle, which we call love of freedom; it is impatient of Oppression and pants for Deliverance." Born most likely in the Senegambia region of West Africa, Wheatley was purchased by the wife of a wealthy Boston tailor when she was no more than eight. Educated in Latin, literature, and philosophy, she published her first poem when she was about seventeen. The next year she was taken to a Boston courthouse where a group of prominent citizens met to determine whether she had written a collection of poems that she and her master claimed as hers. After she answered a series of questions about classical mythology and English literature, the company agreed that she had indeed written the poems.

At the time Phillis Wheatley arrived in Boston in 1761, there were about 230,000 African Americans in the British colonies and 16,000 slaves in New England. The Revolution enabled thousands of enslaved women and children to secure their freedom. In some cases they were emancipated by their owners, like Wheatley, who was freed after her mistress's death in 1774. But in many instances wartime disruptions allowed mothers and their children to flee from bondage. During the Revolution a third of the slaves in Georgia and a quarter in South Carolina freed themselves by running away. Equally important, the Revolution politicized many African Americans, as it did fifteen-year-old James Forten, who would draw on the revolutionary ideology to denounce the contradiction between American ideals of freedom and equality and the base reality of slavery.

Young African Americans played a crucial role on both sides of the conflict. African-American soldiers fought for the patriot cause in every major battle of the Revolution, including the engagements at Concord and Lexington. Cuff Smith, who was born into slavery in Rhode Island in 1769, enlisted in the Continental army in his early teens. Festus Smith, a free black born in Deerfield, Massachusetts, in 1763, also enlisted in the Continental Army as a young teenager, one of 5,000 African Americans who served in the army or navy during the Revolution. Other young African Americans were convinced that the prospects for freedom were greater on the loyalist side. Even before Virginia's royal governor, Lord Dunmore, issued a proclamation promising freedom to slaves who reached the king's forces, a young New Jersey slave named Titus escaped from his owner, a Quaker who had ignored his sect's prohibitions against owning slaves. Renaming himself Colonel Tye, he led guerrilla raids in northern New Jersey. Boston King, a teenage apprentice carpenter in Charleston, South Carolina, who had been born around 1760, was one of 3,000 African Americans whom the British transported to Nova Scotia following the war, where he served as a preacher among the black loyalist refugees. For him, as for thousands of other African-American youth, the Revolution offered a moment of fluidity when they were able to liberate themselves from bondage. Revolutionary ferment temporarily disrupted established patterns of authority, including hierarchies based on race and age.

Many of the nation's founders, who later drafted the Constitution and led the government through its earliest years, were remarkably young when the Revolution began. Alexander Hamilton was only fifteen when friends in the West Indies sent him to New York for schooling. At nineteen, while still a college student, he became a noted pamphleteer; at twenty-one he served with distinction as a captain in an artillery company, and at twenty-two he joined Washington's general staff as a lieutenant-colonel. In 1775 Henry Knox, who became one of Washington's most trusted officers, was twenty-five; James Madison, twenty-four; and James Monroe, just seventeen. To be sure, many of the leading revolutionaries were not young. In 1775 Jefferson was thirty-two, Washington was forty-three, and Franklin sixty-nine. Yet even these men had got their start at a remarkably early age. Franklin, who had become a printer's apprentice at twelve and run away from Boston to Philadelphia at seventeen, became part owner of a print shop when he was twenty-two. Washington, whose formal education lasted just seven or eight years, lost his father when he was eleven. At seventeen he was appointed official surveyor for Culpeper County, Virginia; and by twenty he helped manage his family's plantation and was commissioned as a major in the militia. Jefferson, who lost both parents by the time he was fourteen, entered the College of William and Mary at sixteen. These were young men assuming major adult responsibilities.[30]

Surprisingly few of these men were born into gentility. Hamilton had been born out of wedlock in the West Indies, "the bastard brat of a Scotch pedlar," in John Adams' cutting words. Others, too, had risen far above their father's status. Adams himself was a farmer's son whose two brothers followed in their father's footsteps. Despite growing up in a hierarchical, deferential society in which the theological doctrine of predestination had strong support, these men developed an intense desire for fame. The mid-eighteenth century provided many opportunities for teenagers of ambition and talent to leave a mark on the world. By the time he was fourteen, Hamilton yearned to escape from his "gov'ling" position as a merchant's clerk, and had taken General James Wolfe, who had defeated a French army at the Plains of Abraham in the Seven Years' War, as his model. These ambitious young men developed an almost obsessive concern with honor and reputation. Correct facial expression, posture, and speech were essential parts of the rituals of deference and the code of gentlemanly behavior. As a schoolboy Washington copied rules of behavior in an exercise book that helped him learn how to behave like a gentleman.

Years earlier Franklin had also laid out rules for self-improvement, culminating in the admonition to imitate Jesus and Socrates. For young men whose fathers had died or who, like Franklin, had broken away from their fathers, the lessons of gentility were largely self-taught. The fact that they were self-made gentlemen may have made them especially sensitive to matters of public honor.[31]

In what was still a patronage society, there were a variety of avenues for rapid advancement. In Washington's case, a stepsibling provided a connection to the influential and wealthy Fairfax family, and his stepbrother's death allowed him to inherit Mount Vernon. For Hamilton, the patronage of wealthy benefactors permitted him to leave the British West Indies and attend college in New York City. In retrospect, it is striking how many characteristics the founders shared. Most were born between 1730 and 1760. Few were born into wealthy, aristocratic families. Many of the younger revolutionary leaders served their political apprenticeship in the resistance movement of the 1770s. And many of the founders were the first members of their family to attend college. It was there that many were politicized and introduced to republican ideas.

In the years preceding the Revolution, the colonies' nine colleges underwent a profound transformation. Their curricula and libraries no longer focused exclusively on theology; instead the students encountered a "curriculum of independence," reflecting the naturalistic and humanistic emphases of enlightened thought. The colleges' courses of study increasingly included moral philosophy and ancient and modern history, including the history of the Greek and Roman republics. Students were also exposed to English common law, Enlightenment rationalism, and economic liberalism. A disproportionate number of future leaders attended Princeton, a "nursery for republicanism." There they read the republican writings of classical Greece and Rome, Enlightenment notions of the social contract and of natural rights, and the views of defenders of the Commonwealth experiment of Oliver Cromwell. Through these readings students were introduced to basic republican principles, including the superiority of a republican form of government to anarchy, democracy, or oligarchy; and the notion that a republic's health depended upon civic virtue and was threatened by corruption. Meanwhile, outside classes, students formed militias and established literary societies in which they debated politically charged issues.[32]

It appears that the revolutionaries were indeed younger than their loyalist counterparts. In provincial Massachusetts, rebel leaders averaged fourteen years younger than loyalist leaders. Many of these young men were convinced that their desires for land, families, and career were thwarted

Liberty in the Form of the Goddess of Youth: Giving Support to the Bald Eagle, by Edward Savage, 1796. During the late eighteenth century, youth became a potent symbol of innovation and social change, a notion captured in this image, in which liberty is personified as a young woman. Courtesy of the Worcester (Massachusetts) Art Museum.

by "a government monopolized by elderly men who insisted on deference but proved unwilling to fulfill its obligations." A revolution was essential if they were to fulfill their ambitions.[33]

With the end of the Revolution, many of the nation's founders worried deeply about the survival of republican government, a fear intensified by the spread of a democratic, egalitarian ideology that seemed to threaten all forms of authority. Mercy Otis Warren, who was active in the patriot cause and later became one of the first historians of the Revolution, likened the newly independent states to a restless youth "prematurely emancipated from the authority of a parent." The only contemporary examples of republican government—the Netherlands and Switzerland—were far smaller geographically than the United States and even then had proven unstable. Deeply fearful of untethered liberty, many ministers and moralists turned to maternal nurture and education, regarding them as the key to the success of the new nation's experiment with self-government. Only by implanting a capacity for self-discipline, a respect for authority, and a deep regard for civic virtue in the depths of the individual personality could republican society survive.[34]

The newfound significance of children for the future republic put primary responsibility for securing the social order and preserving republican values on two institutions: the home and the school. Dr. Benjamin Rush, a signer of the Declaration of Independence, expressed the conviction that social stability depended on proper parenting and schooling in particularly ringing terms. "Mothers and school-masters plant the seeds of nearly all the good and evil which exist in our world," he declared. The conspicuous emphasis on the maternal role in shaping children's character was novel. Although mothers had always been responsible for the day-to-day care of young children, earlier childrearing literature had been addressed to fathers as the ultimate caregivers. As late as 1776 the Scottish Presbyterian president of Princeton, John Witherspoon, had begun his volume of childrearing advice with "Dear Sir." But after the Revolution, ministers and other moralists invested mothers with primary responsibility for inculcating republican values and virtue in the young and teaching them to be responsible and patriotic citizens, reflecting a growing recognition of young children's vulnerability, malleability, and educability. The emerging view was that children's character was shaped in their earliest years, when the young were mostly in their mother's care. Samuel Harrison Smith made this point bluntly, insisting that the "virtue or the vice of an individual, the happiness or the misery of a family, the glory or the infamy of a nation, have had their sources in the cradle, over which the prejudices of a nurse or a mother have presided."[35]

Proper childrearing alone, Noah Webster insisted, would not be enough to "make good citizens." Improved schooling was also necessary, and the main purpose of education was, in the words of Benjamin Rush, to "convert men into republican machines." "Knowledge and virtue are the basis and life of a Republic," Samuel Stillman remarked; "therefore, the education of children and youth, should be the first object of the attention of government, and of every class of citizens." Since women were going to play a crucial role in forming children's character, it was essential that they be properly prepared for this task. Noah Webster was one of many who argued that in constructing an educational system the "female sex" must "claim no inconsiderable share of our attention." No longer would it be sufficient for female education to be essentially ornamental. Alongside the study of music, drawing, and dancing, young women needed to study subjects that would enable them as mothers to "implant in the tender mind such sentiments of virtue, propriety, and dignity as are suited to the freedom of our governments." This meant that their education had to include such subjects "history, philosophy, poetry, and the numerous moral essays."[36]

By weakening earlier forms of patriarchal authority, the Revolution enhanced the importance of childrearing and education in ensuring social stability. But the erosion of earlier forms of dependence also left young people, especially young women, more vulnerable to exploitation. Susanna Rowson's *Charlotte Temple,* published in Britain in 1791, was not only the first novel set during the American Revolution; it was also the most popular novel in the United States before Harriet Beecher Stowe's *Uncle Tom's Cabin.* Subtitled *A Tale of Truth,* the novel drew upon the experiences of Charlotte Stanley, the fifteen-year-old daughter of an English clergyman. In 1774 a British army officer, Colonel John Montressor, persuaded Charlotte to elope with him to America, and subsequently impregnated and abandoned her. She died at the age of nineteen and was buried in New York's Trinity churchyard. A cautionary tale intended to warn young women to protect their chastity and beware of the methods unscrupulous men used to seduce them, *Charlotte Temple* was the first of many sentimental novels of the early national period to advocate improved female education to help young women resist seduction. Such admonitions were not confined to works of fiction. During the years immediately following the Revolution there were real-life episodes that sent a similar message. One of the best-known involved Nancy Shippen, the upper-class daughter of a Philadelphia doctor.

Born in 1763, Nancy received the kind of ornamental education in singing, dancing, and fine embroidery that was common among Philadelphia's elite. In her mid-teens a number of young men began to court her. Her favorite was a young French diplomat, but he had only modest economic prospects. Her father, William Shippen, pressured her to marry William Beekman Livingston, a member of one of New York's richest families. Nancy gave in to her father's wishes, prompting the young Frenchman to ask: "For what reason in this free country [must] a lady . . . be married to a man whom she dislikes?" Her marriage was unhappy from the start. Within months she fled with her newborn baby to her parents' house. She later described herself as "a wretched slave—doom'd to be the wife of a Tyrant I hate." In 1791 her husband won a divorce on grounds of her desertion. The lessons of this unhappy experience were self-evident. The author of "A Friend to Family Government" insisted that parents had "no right to act the part of tyrants toward their children," because "the imbecility of youth and infancy does not take away their natural rights." Nancy deserved the right to choose her mate.[37]

The Revolution's most lasting legacy was an ideology emphasizing independence and equal rights—an ideology that was embraced by a growing number of young women as well as young men. Before the Revolution few parents raised their children to be independent adults. Benjamin Franklin underscored this point in ironic terms. He condemned his daughter for wanting to marry a poor but ambitious young printer—someone just like himself. Eliza Wilkinson, a young South Carolina woman who had run her father's plantation during the war and was responsible for demonstrating that indigo could be successfully cultivated in the colony, gave pointed expression to the emphasis on female independence that became a key component of the revolutionary ideology: "I won't have it thought that because we are the weaker sex as to bodily strength . . . we are capable of nothing more than minding the dairy, visiting the poultry houses, and all such domestic concerns; our thoughts can soar aloft, we can form conceptions of things of higher natures; and we have as just a sense of honor, glory, and great actions as these 'Lords of Creation.'"[38]

The Revolution unleashed a new stress on female education. In 1798 Judith Sargent Murray, in a pioneering essay on the equality of the sexes, wrote: "Female academies are everywhere establishing and right pleasant is the appellation to my ear . . . I may be accused of enthusiasm; but such is my confidence in THE SEX that I expect to see our young women forming a new era in female history." At the beginning of the eighteenth century, about two-thirds of adult women in the colonies were unable to write their own name. By the early nineteenth century, two-thirds could. Young women celebrated the new educational opportunities open to them in ringing terms. In 1797, while attending school in Massachusetts, Eliza

Southgate wrote to her parents in Maine: "to think that here I may drink freely of the fountain of knowledge . . . writing, reading, and ciphering . . . French and Dancing . . . Geometry . . . Geography."[39]

At the end of the eighteenth century an elderly congressman, Paine Wingate, expressed dismay at the changes in private life that had occurred as a result of the Revolution. He was displeased at seeing "parents & children . . . as familiar as brothers & sisters." "Fathers, mothers, sons & daughters, young & old, all mix together, & talk & joke alike so that you cannot discover any distinction made or any respect shewn to one more than to another. I am not for keeping up a great distance between Parents & Children, but there is a difference between staring & stark mad." An older world of deference and patriarchal authority had truly been turned upside down.[40]

chapter four

Inventing the Middle-Class Child

Today the passage through childhood and adolescence is highly predictable. Children enter preschool around the age of three or four, enroll in kindergarten at five and first grade at six, enter middle school around eleven or twelve, and graduate from high school at seventeen or eighteen. Two centuries ago the sequence was far less regularized or uniform. Unpredictability was the hallmark of growing up, even for the children of professionals and merchants. By the time Herman Melville had reached the age of twelve, his father, an importer of French dry goods, had gone bankrupt, become insane, and died. Forced to withdraw from school, the author of *Moby-Dick* worked in his uncle's bank, as a clerk in a hat store, as a teacher, a farm laborer, and a cabin boy on a whaling ship—all before the age of twenty. As for Ralph Waldo Emerson, before he was fifteen, he had experienced the death of his brother and his father and had entered Harvard College. And Harriet Beecher Stowe, one of eleven brothers and sisters, was just five years old when her mother died and twelve when she left home to live with an older sister.[1]

Idyllic images of childhood past, in which young people moved seamlessly toward adulthood, are invariably misleading, but for no period is this more mistaken than the early nineteenth century, when the pathways to adulthood were exceedingly uncertain. Especially in their teens, many young people underwent a protracted period of doubt, restlessness, and confusion. New opportunities for employment, schooling, and religious choice were opening up, and rates of geographic mobility were sharply rising, with growing numbers of teenage girls and boys leaving rural farms and villages for larger towns and expanding cities. At few times in American history was adolescence filled with greater uncertainty.[2]

It was, however, at this very moment that modern childhood was invented. Confined at first to the urban middle class, and initially limited to the years from birth to thirteen or fourteen, modern childhood was to be free from labor and devoted to schooling. Urban middle-class mothers assumed exclusive responsibility for childrearing, which they exercised with a growing self-consciousness and sense of responsibility. Middle-class parents sheltered their children from the workplace and economic struggles and kept them in school and the family home longer than in the past. As a result, the stages of middle-class childhood were more carefully delineated, and passage through these stages became more predictable.

This new ideal of a sheltered childhood drew upon several sources. These included the enlightened conception of a child as a blank slate waiting to be shaped by parental and environmental influences; the liberal Protestant ideal that granted children innocent souls and assigned parents the task of turning their redeemable, docile wills toward God; and the evangelical stress on childhood development as proceeding through a series of stages, much as religious conversion required passage through such stages as sanctification and justification. The newest and most influential conception of childhood was a Romantic vision, which viewed children as symbols of purity, spontaneity, and emotional expressiveness, who were free from adult inhibitions and thus required parents who would ensure that their innocence was not corrupted. At a moment when the pre-industrial social order was breaking down, Romantics idealized children as emblems of wholeness and intuitive thinking. Bronson Alcott described the child as "a Type of Divinity." "Herein," he wrote, "is our nature yet despoiled of none of its glory." Rather than a condition to be passed through as rapidly as possible, childhood was a stage of life to be enjoyed and prolonged. Childhood became life's formative stage, a highly plastic period when character and habits were shaped for good or ill. In the poet William Wordsworth's famous line, "The child is father of the man." Biographies and autobiographies gave expression to childhood's heightened significance. Instead of beginning with a genealogy, these volumes now began with an account of a subject's childhood.[3]

The Romantic conception of childhood drew on many earlier sources, from such obscure seventeenth-century English writers as Henry Vaughan and John Earle, who had stressed children's spiritual insight; to John Locke's emphasis on children's malleability; and Jean-Jacques Rousseau's notion that children had not yet been corrupted by social artifice and should be encouraged to express their inner selves. The influence of the

Romantic conception of childhood was apparent in art and parental behavior. Stiffly posed portraits depicting children as miniature adults gave way to more romantic renderings emphasizing children's playfulness and innocence. A profusion of toys and books intended specifically for children highlighted the new focus on, and respect for, the child.[4]

The Romantic vision of childhood encouraged the notion that children needed to be sheltered from adult realities, such as death, profanity, and sexuality, in order to preserve their childish innocence. Ironically, it contributed to a moral severity toward actual children who failed to live up to the Romantic ideal. The new stress on children's fragility, malleability, and corruptibility resulted in the establishment and construction of an array of institutions for children, from Sunday schools and public schools to orphanages, houses of refuge, reform schools, and children's hospitals. Mandatory school attendance laws and child labor restrictions were premised on the idea that children were fragile, innocent, and vulnerable creatures who needed adults' paternalistic protection. Overall, childhood dependency was prolonged, childrearing became a more intensive and self-conscious activity, and schooling was extended. Instead of moving back and forth from their parental home and work experiences outside the home, children resided continuously under the family roof into their late teens or early twenties.[5]

A sharp reduction in the birthrate provided the essential foundation for a new kind of upbringing. At the beginning of the nineteenth century, the typical American mother bore seven to ten children. She had her first child in her early twenties, and gave birth every two years or so until menopause. At the end of the eighteenth century the Quakers became the first group to deliberately limit births, and by 1810 the impulse to control births spread to all parts of the country. Relying primarily upon abstinence, *coitus interruptus,* and the rhythm method, supplemented by abortion (usually chemically induced or a result of trauma to the uterus), parents dramatically reduced the birthrate. The average number of births fell to five per family in 1850 and to just three in 1900. At first mothers increased the spacing between births, but by midcentury parents concentrated childbirths in the early years of marriage. Women who married in the 1820s and 1830s had their last child three or four years earlier than those who wed in the 1780s and 1790s.[6]

In part, the reduced birthrate was a matter of economics, as middle-class parents regarded their children not as sources of labor but as "social capital" requiring substantial investments of time and resources. As a result of rapid changes in manufacturing, transport, and marketing, adults could no longer rely on passing on their farms or shops or imparting their skills to their children, who increasingly needed formal education. No longer economic assets who could be put productively to work, children required expensive investments in the form of education. But the drop in the birthrate also reflected new cultural ideas, including a rejection of the view that women were chattels who should devote their adult lives to an endless cycle of pregnancy and childbirth, and the belief that children needed more care and attention than in the past.

The reduction in the birthrate was not a response to falling death rates. Despite the introduction of smallpox inoculations, which virtually eliminated this disease among the middle and upper classes by the 1820s, infant and child death rates remained high. In urban areas mortality rates

The Westwood Children, by Joshua Johnson, ca. 1807. These boys were the sons of a Baltimore stagecoach builder. Despite differences in their age and size, their dress and hair styles are identical, reflecting the view that children share the same distinctive nature. Courtesy of the National Gallery of Art, Washington, D.C.

Letitia Grace McCurdy, by Joshua Johnson, ca. 1800–1802. The four- or five-year-old girl depicted in this painting wears an unadorned gown, which the postrevolutionary generation associated with republican ideals of simplicity, liberty, and a classless society. Courtesy of the Fine Arts Museums of San Francisco.

actually rose as a result of crowded conditions, poor sanitation, and polluted drinking water. The declining birthrate drastically altered family relations. The colonial family had encompassed a wide age range, with the oldest children two decades older than their youngest siblings. But with fewer children in the family, siblings were closer in age. More than in the past, families were clearly divided into two generations.[7]

Nowhere was the Romantic conception of childhood more starkly evident than in infancy. Artistic renderings of colonial infants had been anything but childlike. With their rigid posture and elongated bodies, infants appeared stiff and doll-like. In part, this reflected the artists' desire to see in infants such adultlike characteristics as an upright posture and a mature bearing. But these images also reflected the way that infants were dressed. Infant girls wore corsets (made out of quilted or corded cloth rather than bones) or had a rod along their spine, giving them a firmer, more mature posture. In the early nineteenth century, in line with a new association of children with sexless innocence, infant girls and boys were dressed identically in loose muslin frocks and gowns, usually white in color, and wore similar androgynous hairstyles.[8]

In contrast to seventeenth-century Puritans, who had regarded young children as dangerously unformed, even animalistic, in their inability to speak and their impulse to crawl, the postrevolutionary generation viewed childhood in much more positive terms. Even orthodox Calvinists and evangelical Protestants came to consider early childhood a stage of life valuable in itself. Childish behavior was increasingly accepted and even admired. Almira Phelps, an educator of girls, wrote in her journal in 1835 that she had not intended to allow her son "to learn to creep." But when her child was between six and nine months, she changed her mind after deciding that crawling was "nature's way." Meanwhile, novels began to include examples of baby talk and treated it as endearing.[9]

The growing appreciation of young children as special beings with their own distinct needs and nature was readily apparent in the appearance of separate nurseries in middle-class homes. Loose, naturally fitting garments replaced the heavy clothing intended to restrict children's movement, especially thumb-sucking. Furniture specifically designed for children, painted in pastel colors and decorated with pictures of animals or figures from nursery rhymes, began to be widely produced. In colonial America, young children had been left by themselves or held on a lap during meals, but in the early nineteenth century high chairs allowed children to sit in a position of prominence at the family dinner table.

Following the War of 1812, pious mothers in the Northeast formed maternal associations to discuss such topics as the most effective methods for taming children's willfulness. At the same time, the nation's first extensive body of advice literature on childrearing appeared, built around the theme of shaping children's character. A growing sense of cultural nationalism convinced Americans that they needed advice that addressed distinctly American problems. Written by ministers, physicians, educators, and other moralists from the Northeast, this literature taught that children were infinitely plastic creatures who needed to be shaped into responsible citizens. A key theme in their writings was that the success of America's republican experiment depended on the ability of parents to implant checks and balances in the moral character of future generations. Instead of regarding children as inherently vicious, the advice literature taught that young children were as pliable as fresh clay and that their well-being depended on developing strong moral character, regular habits, and a capacity for self-control during the first five or six years of life. In a journal in which she recorded her children's early lives, Elizabeth Ellery Sedgwick, the wife of a New York attorney, gave pointed expression to this new view: "At this period, which seems at first glance a blank, impressions are received which are the germs of future character."[10]

As the birthrate fell and such domestic tasks as fabricating cloth, making soap, and brewing beer moved outside the household, middle-class mothers gave their children more concentrated and exclusive care. Intensive mothering became an essential part of middle-class women's self-image and altered the preferred methods of discipline. A paternal emphasis on physical punishment gave way to a new stress on the efficacy of maternal tenderness, patience, and love. Nevertheless, middle-class child-rearing practices spanned a wide spectrum closely linked to theological beliefs. At one pole were religious liberals, who embraced the Romantic emphasis on children's innocence and promise. Lydia Maria Child, a Boston Unitarian, gave pointed expression to this view when she wrote in her *Mother's Book* that children "come to us from heaven with their souls full of innocence and peace . . . under the influence of angels." The liberal style of childrearing emphasized the power of maternal influence—"methods silent and imperceptible," involving moral suasion, tenderness, and guilt. Liberal mothers rejected corporal punishment in favor of psychological techniques intended to cultivate a child's capacity for self-control. These techniques—which included confining children in their room, revoking their privileges, and threatening to withdraw love from them—were intended to strengthen a child's conscience.[11]

At the spectrum's other end were orthodox Calvinists and evangelicals, who stressed the importance of breaking a child's sinful will and instilling respect for divinely instituted authority. Evangelical households emphasized early piety, early discipline, and eliciting an early conversion experience. Religious instruction began in infancy. Martha Laurens Ramsay, a member of a wealthy and influential Charleston, South Carolina, family, taught her children from an early age about "their miserable and corrupted state by nature; that they were born into a world of sin and misery—surrounded with temptations—without the possibility of salvation, but by the grace of God." Around the age of eight or nine, evangelical children were expected to enter a stage of religious anxiety, lying awake at night, pondering salvation and death. A contributor to the *Mother's Magazine* stressed the importance of submission to parental and divine authority: "Every mother is solemnly bound to form in her children the habit of unconditional and instant submission to her authority, as a means of leading them to exercise the same disposition in view of the authority and law of God." In order to instill obedience, evangelical parents were much more willing to use physical punishment than were theological liberals. However, by the 1830s a belief in children's sinful nature had eroded, and even evangelical families emphasized moral suasion by appealing to children's affections rather than to their intellect or to fear.[12]

For all their differences, evangelicals and nonevangelicals shared a conviction that the primary purpose of childrearing was to instill habits of regularity and self-control through techniques emphasizing tenderness, love, and patience. The ability to regulate and channel aggressive impulses, including the ability to apply oneself steadily to a task and follow a regular routine, was regarded as an essential ingredient for future success. Parents reinforced childrearing lessons through a highly moralistic children's literature. At the beginning of the nineteenth century, books created specifically for children were limited to primers, catechisms, grammar books, and battledores, folded sheets of stiff paper containing letters and simple phonics lessons. In 1856 Samuel Goodrich, who wrote and edited 157 books for children, observed: "It is difficult now . . . to conceive of the poverty of books suited to children" during his youth, "except for the New England Primer . . . and some rhymes, embellished with hideous [wood]cuts of Adam's Fall, in which 'we sinned all.'"[13]

Throughout the postrevolutionary era, most children's reading material was intended for their moral or intellectual edification. These included didactic, cautionary tales distributed by the American Sunday School Union; Noah Webster's *Grammatical Institute of the English Language* (known as the "Blue-backed Speller" because of its blue cover); Samuel Goodrich's Peter Parley stories (featuring an elderly man who tells moral tales to children, and who served as the prototype for Uncle Remus); and Jacob Abbott's Rollo tales, "intended to explain and illustrate, in a simple manner, the principles of Christian duty." William McGuffey's six *Readers,* published between 1836 and 1857, epitomized the didacticism and heavy-handed moralism that dominated books for children. They contained such simple moral lessons as "Good boys do not play in a rude way, but take care not to hurt anyone" and "Bad boys lie, and swear, and steal." Postrevolutionary authorities were highly critical of fairy tales and fantasy literature, such as ghost stories, with the exception of those that "impress upon" children's "minds the great truth, that disobedience and deception are very wicked and very dangerous." The perceived brevity of mothers' hold on children encouraged a determination to use children's literature to shape character and deliver moral messages to the young.[14]

A host of gender-specific assumptions about behavior, attitudes, emotional sensibilities, and aspirations pervaded the middle-class home. Gender determined the kind of games children played and the chores they performed, and shaped expectations about their education and likely future. Although boys and girls increasingly attended the same schools, the cultures of boyhood and girlhood were defined in opposition to each other. Boys and girls were assumed to differ in their constitution, stature, temperament, and behavior. Femininity was defined in terms of self-sacrifice and service; masculinity, in terms of aggressiveness and daring.[15]

In sharp contrast to the works of Charles Dickens, which depicted both boys and girls as fragile, vulnerable creatures in need of adult protection, nineteenth-century American boys were considered adventurous, resourceful, and self-reliant. Like Tom Sawyer and Huck Finn, the popular image of boyhood was of someone who was independent, fun-loving, and noble-hearted. In the late nineteenth century, a rash of books portrayed pre–Civil War American boyhood as a period of unmatched freedom and independence. An early nineteenth-century British visitor, Frederick Marryat, recounted an incident that summed up the antebellum attitude toward boyhood. After a young boy disobeyed his father's command, the man called the boy "a sturdy republican," while "smiling at the boy's resolute disobedience."[16]

Boyhood was defined in opposition to the confinement, dependence, and restraint of the domestic realm. Boys were freer to roam than girls, and their chores, such as tending animals or running errands, took place free from adult oversight. Boys' games—such as races, fistfights, sledding and skating, swimming, or ball games—invariably took place outside the home and emphasized physical play, self-assertion, physical prowess, stoicism, and competition. Boys' culture simultaneously challenged the dictates of respectable adulthood and prepared boys for it. It was a world of physicality, dirt, and violence, but also a world in which boys learned to channel aggression and to function in groups. Boyhood stressed aggressiveness, which was expressed through the playing of pranks, the torture of small animals, and competition with friends and rivals. Pranks played on adult authority figures, girls, and each other were an essential element in boys' culture; they provided a way for boys to assert their independence and avenge insults. Loyalty and group activities were important values for boys. Boys, much more than girls or their colonial male counterparts, formed clubs and teams. Various hazing rituals and forms of ridicule, such as name-calling and teasing, helped maintain these groups' boundaries.[17]

Compared with their rural counterparts, urban boys enjoyed more free time, more contact with peers, and greater freedom from adult supervision. Freed from farm chores, boys played in streets or fields. By midcentury, boys were also spending much more time with peers in schools. In contrast to the colonial era, when entry into apprenticeship or work experiences away from home marked the end of childhood and entry into youth, boyhood ended more gradually in the mid-nineteenth century, and the lines of separation between boyhood and youth were defined in psychological rather than social terms. As one youth put it, "Suddenly marbles became a childish game which made knuckles grimy and chapped."[18]

In the early nineteenth century the word *girlhood* acquired a new meaning. It came to refer to a period of relative freedom before entrance into the responsibilities of mature womanhood and motherhood. One of the first figures to use the word in this sense was the French traveler Alexis de Tocqueville, whose classic *Democracy in America* drew a sharp contrast between the American girl and her French counterpart. Whereas French girls were subordinated within their homes and achieved a degree of independence only after marriage, in America a carefree girlhood was followed by a staid motherhood. A young Philadelphia woman's diary captured the abruptness of this transition. It ends with the words: "And now these pages must come to a close, for the romance ends when the heroine marries."[19]

Girlhood in the early nineteenth-century North was filled with paradoxes. On the one hand, young women received unprecedented opportunities for education, work outside the home, and participation in religious, charitable, and reform activities. In the late eighteenth century, sewing, weaving, and clothmaking had occupied enormous amounts of time for teenage women, but the mechanization of textile production abruptly altered young women's work patterns. By the early 1830s making cloth by hand was replaced by factory production. Instead of performing handiwork at home, young women in their teens sought paid employment outside the home, as seamstresses, factory operatives, or school teachers. At the same time, the removal of clothmaking outside of households freed many middle-class girls to continue their education into their teens.[20]

On the other hand, a much more rigid ideology of gender roles also emerged, which drew a sharp distinction between girls and boys in temperament, aptitudes, and abilities. For middle-class girls, lessons in femininity began early. From the age of six or seven, farm girls were initiated into certain gender-specific tasks. They worked alongside their mothers and older sisters, sewing, cooking, washing, and tending the dairy. In towns, too, where middle-class girls were relieved from onerous farm chores, there was a clear-cut sexual division of labor, with girls responsible for making beds and caring for younger brothers and sisters. Even in wealthier families, parents sought to foster proper feminine behavior by encouraging their daughters to knit, sew, and perform fancy needlework. Girls' responsibilities for childcare, sewing, and housework left them much less likely than boys to have time to themselves. Although many young girls engaged in active games, such as jumping rope, previously a boy's game, girls' play, much more than boys', involved assuming adult roles. The toys that girls received from their parents, such as needlebooks and dolls fashioned out of wax and decorated with human hair, were intended to foster femininity and nurturing skills as well as to encourage quiet, solitary play. Whereas portraits show boys with swords, guns, bugles, drums, cannons, tin soldiers, hobbyhorses, and wheelbarrows, girls are pictured with miniature china sets, wax dolls, music boxes, or books.[21]

Adults exhibited an ambiguous attitude toward tomboyish (or what was called "hoyden") behavior. While antebellum literature contained memorable images of silent, sickly girls with limited energy, there were also many images of active, playful, and high-spirited girls who preferred boyish games to domestic chores. Long before Henry James's Daisy Miller, a popular literary image of American girlhood was fearless, innocent, bold, and without guile. Many popular advice writers spoke about girls' need to develop a spirit of independence and self-sufficiency. In 1839 Catharine Maria Sedgwick advised girls to "be sure to be so educated that you can have an independent pursuit, something to occupy your time and interest your affections; then marriage will not be essential to your usefulness, respectability, or happiness." Sentiments like Sedgwick's were echoed by girls themselves. In 1838 thirteen-year-old Ednah Dow Littlehale wrote a friend: "What do I mean by the rights of women! I mean, I mean what I say—we have as good a right to rule men as they have to rule us."[22]

Yet as they grew older, girls were supposed to curb their passionate spirits and channel their energies into more genteel pursuits, such as piano playing. A girl was to divest herself "of the light and airy habiliments of girlhood" and assume "the more staid and dignified mantle of womanhood." Catharine Sedgwick advised girls to refrain from "rowdyism," and William Alcott declared that a girl should not run after she achieved physical maturity. "She must not," he wrote, "after she is old enough to need a brassiere, indulge in 'any form of motion more rapid than walking,' for fear of betraying somewhere below the neck some 'portion of the general system which gives to women her . . . distinctive character.'" In contrast to Tom Sawyer and Huck Finn, who remain eternal boys, girls were expected to grow up and reject childish ways. A teenage girl was to put up her hair and lower her skirt—two key symbols of proper deportment. Frances Willard, the future leader of the Women's Christian Temperance Union, the largest late nineteenth-century women's organization, vividly recorded the day in 1856 that she grew up: "Mother insists that at last I must have my hair 'done up woman-fashion.' She says she can hardly forgive herself for letting me 'run wild' so long. We've had a great time over it all . . . My 'back' hair is twisted up like a corkscrew: I carry eighteen hair-pins; my head aches miserably; my feet are entangled in the skirt of my hateful new gown. I can never jump over a fence again, so long as I live."[23]

Since the essence of femininity was perceived to be purity, it is not surprising that many young women were kept in appalling sexual ignorance. Lydia Maria Child regretted the "want of confidence between mothers and daughters on delicate subjects" and suggested that mothers explain the facts of life to daughters around the age of twelve to "set her mind at rest." The mid-nineteenth-century ideal of a sheltered girlhood stifled many girls' abilities and restricted their opportunities. In 1856 a Boston physician named Harriot K. Hunt linked the roots of hysteria to the restrictions that girls lived under. As she diagnosed one patient's problems: "Mind had been uncultivated—intelligence smothered—aspirations quenched. The result was physical suffering."[24]

Throughout American history the experience of each successive generation of girls has been less continuous than the experience of boys. Rarely was the mother-daughter gap greater than during the early nineteenth century, when young women between the ages of fourteen and twenty-five received wholly new opportunities to attend school and work temporarily outside a home as school teachers or mill workers. For the first time in American history, large numbers of young women experienced a period before marriage when they were not subordinated to a father or husband. The significance of this period of life can be seen vividly in the diary of seventeen-year-old Rachel Van Dyke, the daughter of a prosperous New Brunswick, New Jersey, storekeeper and farmer, who railed against young women who talked of nothing "but dress, amusements, the beaux, and such like nonsense." This period of relative freedom from male authority carried profound psychological implications. Many young women came to view marriage in a new light, as a closing off of freedoms and options enjoyed in girlhood. This led many young women to experience a traumatic "marriage crisis" as they decided whether or not to marry.[25]

Nineteenth-century middle-class culture idealized the bond between sisters and brothers as purer and more innocent than any other social relationships, untouched by sexuality and selfishness. To a society deeply troubled by industrialization and urbanization, the sibling bond, based on a common heritage, signified loyalty, connection, intimacy, selflessness, and continuity over time. As birthrates declined and children remained home longer and more continuously, sibling relationships grew far more emotionally intense than they had been or than they are today. In the early twenty-first century, half of all children do not have a sibling; but in the nineteenth century, same-sex siblings often slept in the same room, frequently in the same bed, and younger children often visited or helped out older children for prolonged periods. Many parents consciously fostered intense sibling bonds, reminding siblings that they had an obligation to look out for one another. Further contributing to the intensity of sibling ties was the relative weakness of institutions that might intrude on such relationships. Middle-class families encouraged children to play with each other or with cousins, and mid-nineteenth-century schools made few efforts to foster peer group identities. The emotional and psychological intensity of sibling ties, however, often produced conflicted relationships. One of Freud's greatest insights was his discovery that Victorian sentimentality about the purity and innocence of the sibling bond masked intense rivalries and inequalities.[26]

The invention of modern childhood represented an effort to contain the precocity and uncertainties that had characterized the process of growing up in the early nineteenth century. In the century's early years, childhood dependence had been brief and ended abruptly. In 1834 Alexis de Tocqueville announced that "in America there is, in truth, no adolescence. At the close of boyhood [the young American] is a man and begins to trace out his own path." At the beginning of the century childhood dependence had been followed by a lengthy, nebulous period of youth, in which young men and women moved back and forth between domestic responsibilities, schooling, and work responsibilities outside the home. Behavior that we would consider precocious was commonplace. When Abraham Lincoln was seven and his family moved across the Ohio River from Kentucky to frontier Indiana, the future president helped build a primitive log cabin and cut down trees so that a crop could be planted. Before he reached the age of sixteen and enrolled at Yale College, Eli Whitney had already opened a nail factory. Francis Lieber, a German-born scholar who taught at a South Carolina college in 1835 and 1836, recorded the details of one young man's life. By the age of twenty-two he had been expelled from college for participating in a duel, shot his adversary in the streets of Charleston, studied law, married and had a child, practiced law, and been elected to the state legislature.[27]

The path to adulthood was far less clearly delineated and much more irregular, haphazard, and episodic than it subsequently became. Many farm children, male and female, worked on their parents' homestead until their twenties; others sought employment away from home during the winter (as clerks or laborers) but returned home during the spring and summer months. Still others served a series of short-term apprenticeships, shifting back and forth between their parents' household and work experiences outside the home. Meanwhile an increasing number of young girls left home temporarily to work in early factories or to attend school, and a growing number of boys and girls left home to seek new opportunities in rapidly expanding cities.[28]

For young women as well as young men, youth was a time of uncertain transitions, when they had to make important decisions about their schooling, their career, and where they would live. As their economic role within the family became more problematic, the teen years became a period of profound religious uncertainty. As they entered adolescence, many young women went through an intensely religious phase, often culminating in an emotional conversion experience. A religious crisis often occurred around the time of first menstruation or when young women began to seek work or training outside the home. Joining a church provided young women with friendship and emotional support at a time when they were experiencing disruptive changes in employment and place of residence. Three of every four converts during the early nineteenth century were young women, usually in their mid or late teens. Intense same-sex friendships also helped many young women, as well as some young men, to cope with the uncertainties of youth. At a time when relations between boys and girls were especially stiff, distant, and formal, such relationships could be intensely physical, involving passionate kissing and hugging.[29]

Middle-class and upwardly aspiring working-class young men also sought stability by forming and joining voluntary associations, ranging from literary clubs and debating societies to religious societies, sports teams, amateur theatrical troupes, and young men's political organizations. These associations included a broad spectrum of ages, from boys as young as ten or twelve to young men in their twenties. Rather than being isolated in a rigidly age-segregated world, as is the case today, youth's world was defined more expansively. Younger boys printed their own newspapers and joined reform organizations, like the Cadets of Temperance, which crusaded against hard liquor. Boys as young as fourteen also joined such political organizations as the Little Giants, to support the Democrats, or the Wide Awakes, to back the Republicans. In his 1838 novel *Homeward Bound,* James Fenimore Cooper described one character's involvement in organizations in arch terms: "From his tenth year up to his twenty-fifth, this gentleman had been either a president, vice-president, manager, or committee man of some philosophical, political or religious expedient to fortify human wisdom."[30]

First emerging in the late eighteenth century, when apprentices formed the earliest self-improvement societies and college students founded the first literary societies, youth organizations were mechanisms for self-improvement and self-education, which prepared young men for adulthood. These organizations allowed young men to participate in the public sphere, trained them in leadership skills, and taught them how to function in organizations. Many societies were inspired by a conviction that the young had a historic responsibility to fulfill the founders' ideals. Indeed, these young men expressed an impulse to match and even surpass the founding generation. "To us belong . . . far higher responsibilities than rested upon our fathers," announced one young man. During the 1830s and 1840s middle-class youths constituted much of the rank and file in Bible associations and temperance and antislavery societies, while their working-class counterparts joined volunteer fire companies, military companies, and the nation's first urban youth gangs (which first appeared in the 1770s).[31]

African-American young men formed their own organizations. George T. Downing founded a literary society in New York when he was fourteen years old. This society refused to celebrate the Fourth of July because "the declaration of Independence was to the colored in America, 'a perfect mockery.'" An editorial in the New York *Colored American* in 1837 declared that "history is replete with evidence" that young men "are important and efficient agents" for "moral reformations or political revolutions."[32]

In stark contrast to young black and white men, young women did not form separate organizations based on age. Although there were a few "Young Ladies'" societies, in general young women participated in organizations that encompassed women irrespective of age, including church societies, reform societies, and a wide range of philanthropic endeavors. For the most part, age-based antebellum organizations were male-only.

After the Civil War, the broadly inclusive young men's associations faded away. Somewhat older men continued to join lodges, fraternal orders, and secret societies, and college students established fraternities. But youth groups formed and run by the young themselves were replaced by adult-organized institutions that adopted the name "Young Men's Associations" or "Mechanics' Institutes." The earliest adult-managed organization for youth, the Young Men's Christian Association, modeled on an identically named English organization, appeared in Boston in 1849. It served as the precursor for other adult-organized institutions, such as the Boy Scouts, which were intended to ease the transition to adulthood but which actually intensified the dependence of teenage boys by encouraging them to defer to the leadership and direction of adults.

Early nineteenth-century foreign travelers and home-grown moralists roundly condemned the precocity of American children, whom they considered filthy, ill-mannered, and disrespectful. European visitors universally agreed that American children were less disciplined than Old World children and had a greater voice in family affairs. The explanation for early nineteenth-century parents' permissiveness was at once cultural and economic. American culture not only had a weaker sense of hierarchy, but in labor-short America, parents were highly dependent on their children's labor, a circumstance that encouraged mild discipline and even parental indulgence. After 1830, however, there were growing efforts to impose order on children, especially urban middle-class children between the ages of seven and thirteen. Tolerance of precocious behavior declined, and there was a growing concern with ensuring children's proper chronological development. Perhaps the most dramatic development was greater systematization of a haphazard system of education.[33]

The emergence of Sunday schools represented one of the first attempts to rein in young people's lives. The first Sunday schools, founded in the 1790s, were targeted at the children of the poor, but by the 1820s these institutions had shifted their attention to middle-class children as antebellum churches increasingly envisioned young people's conversion as a gradual development rather than a sudden emotional experience. Convinced that during childhood a person's "character usually becomes fixed for life, and for the most part for eternity," their founders assigned Sunday schools the weighty responsibility of ensuring that young people developed the strength of character to resist the "flattering allurements" of a world bent on "seduc[ing] them to ruin," as the *American Sunday School Magazine* phrased it in 1825.[34]

Far more important than Sunday schools in structuring young people's lives were public schools, which had the effect of extending childhood dependency into early adolescence. Before the advent of public education in the early 1830s, formal schooling was sporadic and unsystematic. Apprenticeship was a major form of education, supplemented by charity schools for the poor, church schools, informal dame schools in which women took children into their own homes, district schools in smaller towns and villages, Latin schools in larger cities, and private academies for the affluent. A typical classroom could contain as many as eighty students, from "infants but just out of their cradles" to "men who had been enrolled . . . in the militia." Opportunity to attend school was circumscribed, and attendance was erratic. Even free schools required payment of tuition, and many required entering students to be literate, barring youngsters whose parents had not taught them to read.[35]

Few textbooks were available, and learning amounted to monotonous repetition of facts. Students memorized and recited the alphabet, the definition and spelling of words, the rules of grammar, the facts of arithmetic, and lengthy prose passages, often long before they understood them. School buildings were often unpainted and overcrowded and lacked blackboards, maps, desks, playgrounds, and even outhouses. Teachers maintained order primarily through "the liberal application of birch and ferule," in Horace Greeley's words, supplemented by such forms of shaming as requiring unruly pupils to wear a dunce's cap or sit on a fool's stool, which had only one leg. As might be expected, students responded to displays of arbitrary authority and humiliation with frequent mutinies.

The campaign for public schools began in earnest in the 1820s, when religiously motivated reformers, inspired by the school systems in Prussia and the Netherlands, advocated public education as a way to promote opportunity, prevent a hardening of class lines, shape children's character, create a unified civic culture, and instill the values and skills necessary in a rapidly changing society: basic literacy, punctuality, obedience, and self-discipline. Convinced that education would take place most effectively in a homogeneous environment, educators concentrated on children between the ages of six and fourteen, which was considered the optimal time to form young people's character and help them to internalize moral restraints. Meanwhile, fearful that premature intellectual stress damaged young children's minds and bodies, reformers argued that three-, four-, and five-year-olds would be better educated at home than in formal classrooms.[36]

To trim costs, a number of cities, including New York and Philadelphia, experimented with a system devised by Joseph Lancaster, an English Quaker, in which a teacher trained student monitors who conducted classes on their own. The Lancaster system allowed a single teacher to teach a thousand students. But localities quickly discovered that they could expand schooling without a proportionate increase in spending by relying on female teachers, who received half or a third the wages of male schoolteachers. At first many local school boards worried that female teachers could not discipline rowdy schoolchildren, but they came to believe that women, relying on the techniques of moral suasion emphasized in childrearing manuals, were actually more effective in disciplining children. As a woman who taught during the 1840s observed, a male student "who would be constantly plotting mischief against a schoolmaster . . . becomes mild and gentle, considerate and well behaved towards a little woman, simply because she is a little woman, whose gentle voice and lady-like manners have fascinated him." In fact, however, many older boys expressed their disdain for the femininization of education by dropping out of school.[37]

Mid-nineteenth-century public schools followed highly regimented schedules. Individual classrooms contained as many as fifty or sixty students, and despite calls for improved teaching methods that would tap students' imaginations and draw out their potentialities, teachers relied on rote memorization, recitation, and strict discipline. A New York City mayor described a typical school day: "During several daily recitation periods, each of which is from twenty to twenty-five minutes in duration, the children are obliged to stand on the line, perfectly motionless, their bodies erect, their knees and feet together, the tips of their shoes touching the edge of the board in the floor." Innovations in pedagogy were left to private schools.[38]

By the eve of the Civil War, educational reformers in New England, the Middle Atlantic states, and the older parts of the Midwest had succeeded in systematizing the system of education. They persuaded legislatures in Massachusetts and New York to pass the first mandatory school attendance laws. Attendance was expected to be a full-time activity, in which the student adjusted to the school's schedule, not vice versa. As a result, schools tended to prolong middle-class children's dependency by forestalling youths' entry into the world of work.[39]

In the early nineteenth century a fundamental tension emerged between idealizing children and regulating their lives. It is a striking irony that the very period that most intensely celebrated children's innocence and playfulness also witnessed unprecedented efforts to systematize and rationalize children's upbringing. Those who waxed most eloquently about childhood purity, such as the educational reformer Horace Mann and the childrearing expert Lydia Maria Child, were also the strongest proponents of improved methods of childrearing and expanded education. Among the goals of the inventors of modern middle-class childhood were to shape children's character and implant habits of self-control through self-conscious maternal nurture; to shelter children from corruption by keeping them home for longer periods; and to enroll them in age-graded schools with a curriculum emphasizing lessons in industry, regularity, and restraint. Precocity was attacked, and order was imposed on young people's lives.[40]

But there was an even more troubling historical irony at work. The very period that freed middle-class children from work and allowed them to devote their childhood years to education also made the labor of poorer children more essential to their families' well-being than in the past, and greatly increased the exploitation that these children suffered. As we shall see, the growth of industry, the commercialization of agriculture, and the expansion of a market economy widened the gulf between middle-class and laboring children and generated new kinds of child labor that differed radically from the household-based activities that young people had performed in the past. Ultimately, however, it was the Romantic ideal of a sheltered childhood that would inspire reformers to embark on efforts to save dependent, destitute, and working children. The sentimentalization of childhood—the assertion of childhood's importance and its vulnerability to mistreatment—would provide a crucial vantage point for criticizing the abuse of children.

chapter five

Growing Up in Bondage

H ER NAME WAS Celia, and she was just fourteen when Robert Newsom, an aging widower and one of central Missouri's most prosperous slave owners, purchased her. Already the owner of five male slaves, Newsom acquired Celia to serve as a domestic servant, a cook, and a sexual partner. Before he had even returned her to his farm, he raped her. He built her a small cabin near his house and visited her frequently. Over the next five years she bore him two children. When she was about nineteen, Celia became involved with a slave named George and demanded that Newsom end their relationship. When he refused, Celia fatally struck her master with a club and burned his body in her fireplace. In 1855 she was executed for murder. Celia's childhood was brief, her womanhood even briefer.[1]

On the eve of the Civil War, four million southerners were enslaved. Fully half were children under the age of sixteen. Slave owners often ascribed childlike characteristics to slaves; in fact most slaves were children, and they experienced the most extreme version of an unprotected childhood. At a time when the urban middle class was freeing its children from work responsibilities, prolonging and intensifying their family ties, and devoting an increasing number of their years to formal schooling, a slave childhood was a world apart. It was a world of poverty, privation, punishment, and early physical labor. Still, through the strength of their kinship and community ties and the force of their character, enslaved children grappled with the harsh day-to-day realities of slavery, made them more bearable, and ultimately transcended slavery's traumas.[2]

Even worse than slavery's physical severities were its psychological cruelties. Children grew up fearful of family separation. They felt an intense sense of powerlessness and quickly came to recognize that their parents were unable to protect them. Many, like Frederick Douglass, the fugitive slave who became one of the country's best-known abolitionists, felt that slavery's greatest evil was the systematic deprivation of knowledge about one's ancestry, about reading and writing, and even about one's birth date. Slavery, he later wrote, "made my brothers and sisters strangers to me; it converted the mother that bore me into a myth; it shrouded my father in mystery, and left me without an intelligible beginning in the world." Slavery, in his view, had robbed him not only of the attributes of childhood but of certain defining elements of a human identity.[3]

Worse yet, slavery instilled in some children a profound sense of inferiority and shame. Thomas Jones, who spent his childhood in slavery in North Carolina, described his memory of growing up under slavery: "My recollections of early life are associated with poverty, suffering and shame. I was made to feel, in my boyhood's first experience, that I was inferior and degraded, and that I must pass through life in a dependent and suffering condition." Denied an education, constantly reminded of his subordinate status, Jones felt a sense of dishonor. Yet for all of slave childhood's horrors, enslaved boys and girls succeeded in "stealing" a childhood. They devised games that prepared them psychologically for the traumas of whippings and family separation. A surprisingly large number learned how to read and write. Above all, they contributed to their family's well-being by supplementing their families' meager diets and assisting in their parents' work. For all its deprivations, childhood in bondage promoted an early sense of personal responsibility and strong communal loyalties.[4]

Enslaved parents looked forward to their children's births with bittersweet emotions. A fugitive slave named Lunsford Lane reprinted a slave mother's address to her infant child, which read:

> And much I grieve and mourn
> That to so dark a destiny
> My lovely babe I've borne.

Harriet Jacobs, who was sexually exploited under slavery, wrote: "My heart was heavier than it had ever been before when they told me my newborn babe was a girl." Slave fathers, too, voiced this ambivalence. Thomas Jones felt "unspeakable anguish as I looked upon my precious babes, and have thought of the ignorance, degradation, and woe which they must endure as slaves."[5]

One reason for parents' ambivalent feelings was an infant death rate that was twice the rate of that for white infants. Half of all slave newborns weighed less than five and a half pounds, and severely underweight births are associated with respiratory problems, ear infections, developmental problems, and high rates of infant mortality. Fanny Kemble, whose husband owned a large South Carolina plantation, questioned a number of enslaved women about their experience losing children. A slave named Nancy reported that she had lost two of three children. Another named Leah said that three of her six children were dead. Sukey told her that five of her eleven children had died. Sarah had lost five of seven children. Altogether, the nine women Fanny Kemble interviewed suffered twelve miscarriages and lost twenty-nine of fifty-five children in infancy or early childhood. In fact half of all slave children died in infancy or early childhood.[6]

Slaveholders attributed infant deaths to "overlaying" in bed or "suffocation." Sudden Infant Death Syndrome—the still-unexplained sudden death of infants, which remains higher among African Americans than among whites—also contributed to the high death rate. But the main contributors to the high mortality were the heavy physical labor that mothers performed during the late stages of pregnancy, the inadequate nutrition provided to pregnant women and their children, and an unsanitary environment. Even though slave owners recognized that newborns were a potential source of labor and wealth, they failed to take practical steps to reduce infant deaths. Thomas Jefferson observed that "a child raised every 2 years is of more profit than the crop of the best laboring man," but slave masters distrusted slave women's claims of pregnancy and proved unwilling to sacrifice their labor to protect the unborn. Although advice manuals recommended that no pregnant woman engage in "lifting, pulling fodder, or hard work," suspicious masters adopted the view that hard labor made for an easier birth. Some masters actually reduced rations to women nearing full term, convinced that smaller babies were delivered more easily.[7]

Under slavery, infants received a grossly inadequate diet. On a few plantations, "sucklings were allowed to come to [their mothers in the fields] three times a day, for the purpose of nursing." But it was more common for mothers to suckle their babies just once during the day, usually around ten in the morning. The infants were fed cow's milk, thin porridge, "potlicker" (the broth left in a pot after the greens were cooked), a mixture of mush and skimmed milk, or bread mashed into gravy. Not only were these foods unsanitary and unhygienic, but because many African-American infants were lactose intolerant, they were unable to digest them.[8]

The physical conditions in which enslaved children lived also contributed to the high death rate. Many childhood deaths were due to tetanus and lockjaw—which were four times more common among slave children than among their white counterparts—resulting from unsanitary living conditions. Lacking privies, slaves had to urinate and defecate in the cover of nearby bushes. Lacking sanitary disposal of garbage, they were surrounded by decaying food. Chickens, dogs, and pigs lived next to the slave quarters, and in consequence animal feces contaminated the area. Such squalor contributed to high rates of dysentery, typhus, diarrhea, hepatitis, typhoid fever, and intestinal worms.[9]

The fragility of family ties was a hallmark of a slave childhood. Charles Ball, who lived for forty years as a slave in Maryland, South Carolina, and Georgia, was just five years old when he was separated from his mother. Frederick Douglass saw his mother only four or five times during his childhood. Separation from fathers was especially common. At least half of all enslaved children grew up apart from their father, either because he lived on another plantation, had died, or was white and refused to acknowledge his offspring. In interviews conducted by the federal government, 10 percent of former slaves reported that their father was white, and many reported that their master's wives took out their anger by punishing the mulatto children. The Kentucky-born Lewis Clarke, the son of a Scottish weaver and a slave mother, reported that "there are no slaves that are so badly abused as those that are related to some of the [white] women, or the children of their own husband; it seems as though they never could hate these quite bad enough." Moses Roper, who was enslaved in North Carolina, was told that after his birth his mistress used a large stick to beat him.[10]

Even in instances in which marriages were not broken by sale, slave children often grew up apart from their father, seeing him only on weekends or once during the week. On large plantations, one slave father in three had a different owner from his wife and could visit his family only at his master's discretion. On smaller holdings, two fathers in three lived on a separate farm. In addition, many large slaveholders had numerous plantations and frequently shifted slaves, splitting families in the process. Renting out slave fathers was also common.[11]

Slaves were much less likely to grow up in a two-parent household than any other children. About a quarter of enslaved children grew up in a single-parent household (nearly always with their mother). Another tenth grew up apart from both parents; 5 percent of young slaves lived in their owners' homes. Even in two-parent families, children frequently reported that they spent little time with their parents. In the South Carolina lowcountry, wealthy slaveholders took young slaves for weeks or even months at a time into the upcountry during malaria epidemics in order to protect their health and future labor. On these occasions, parents were able to visit their children only on Sundays, if then. A former Alabama slave named Maugan Sheppard said she rarely saw her mother or father "'cept upon a Sunday," since they left for the cotton field before sunup and returned to their cabin after she had already eaten her supper and had fallen asleep. The Reverend James W. C. Pennington, who escaped slavery in Maryland and went on to earn a degree from the University of Heidelberg, called "the want of parental care and attention" slavery's very worst evil. Because his parents had been forced to spend their time in the fields, they "were not able to give any attention to their children during the day. I often suffered much from hunger and other similar causes."[12]

Temporary or permanent family separation was an almost universal experience for slave children by the time they reached their late teens. A study of slave hires in Elizabeth City County, Virginia, between 1782 and 1810 indicates that most children spent at least a year working as a servant in another household. During the mid-1930s, when the federal Works Projects Administration interviewed more than 2,300 former slaves (2 percent of all who were alive at the time), a third of these exslaves reported that they had been separated from their parents by sale or transfer of ownership by the age of sixteen. Family separation was one of enslaved children's most vivid memories. James Green, a Texas slave, recalled the "unlucky star" day when he was separated from his mother. One Friday his mother had turned to him and said, "Jim, you be a good boy." His master then led James away. "Dat was de last time I ever heard my mother speak, or ever see her," he recalled. By the age of ten or twelve, many slave children were forced to live in quarters separate from their families, and in their teens most were sold away from their mothers, fathers, or siblings. As a result of sale or parental death, over half of all slave children had lost a parent by sixteen. Children's songs resonated with the anguish of family separation. As if to prepare themselves for a life filled with insecurity, children would sing:

> Mammy, is Ole' Massa gwin'er sell us tomorrow?
> Yes, my chile.
> Whar he gwin'er sell us?
> Way down South in Georgia.[13]

Nevertheless, through distinctive patterns of coparenting, godparenting, and naming patterns that reinforced kin connections throughout an extended community, parents provided their children with a network of support. Names were an essential vehicle for transmitting a sense of family identity, maintaining links to the African past, and forming links to the wider kinship group. During the seventeenth and eighteenth centuries some masters had imposed classical names, such as Hercules, or place-names, such as London, on slaves, a naming pattern rarely found among white colonists. But most slaves were named by their parents, who often followed the West or Central African practice of "day-naming"–assigning names based on the day of their birth. Common day names included Cudjo, Mingo, and Cuffee. Over time, African day names were Anglicized through blending with similar-sounding English names. Thus Fiba, which meant Friday, became Phoebe.[14]

By the early nineteenth century biblical names became common as growing numbers of slaves converted to Christianity. Yet whether the names had African or Christian roots, enslaved African Americans did not passively accept names assigned by slave owners. Rather, they chose

This photograph depicts an African-American slave family in 1861 or 1862, either in Washington, D.C., or in Hampton, Virginia. The absence of adolescent children is not accidental; more than half of all enslaved African Americans were separated from their families during their teens. Courtesy of the Library of Congress.

names that were deeply meaningful to themselves. Namesaking—naming children after grandparents or other kin—was a common practice. Name exchanges—in which brothers named sons for one another—were also common, underscoring the significance attached to kinship ties. To sustain a sense of family identity, slaves often named their children after parents, grandparents, recently deceased relatives, and other kin. Slaves also passed down family names to their children, usually the name of an ancestor's owner rather than their current owner's. At a time when the proportion of whites naming first-born sons for fathers was sharply declining—from over half in the early eighteenth century to less than a third in 1790—slave families used names to recognize kinship ties.[15]

Slave children had multiple caregivers. Children as young as two or three rocked babies and made sure that they didn't crawl too near the fireplace. In one nursery on a rice plantation, "near each baby sat or played a small boy or girl who had been detailed to care for that especial baby, and at the door of the house sat Maum Judy, or later Kate, the nurse." On larger plantations, one or two adults cared for as many as forty or even seventy young children. One white observer reported that on her plantation a caregiver named Aunt Dinah "told stories, demonstrated how to make animals from potatoes, orange thorns, a few feathers." She also offered lessons in "practical living," teaching slave children how to "'set table' with mats made of the green leaves of the jonquils, cups and saucers of acorns, dishes of hickory hulls and any gay bit of china they could find; and had them bake mud pies in a broken stove." Recognizing the likelihood of family separation, slave parents taught their children to call adult slaves "aunt" or "uncle" and younger slaves "sister" or "brother." In this way, slave culture taught the young that they were members of a broader community in which all slaves had mutual obligations and responsibilities.[16]

Apologists for slavery insisted that slave children were well clothed, well fed, and well cared for. In actuality, deprivation was a basic reality of a slave childhood. Children's clothing was minimal, and it was common to see boys "of about Fourteen and Fifteen years Old" with "their whole nakedness exposed." Few owners distributed shoes to children who did not work in the field, and slave children usually wore shoes only during the coldest months. Most youngsters had to make do with moccasins their fathers fashioned from animal hides or rags wrapped around their feet. Slave owners typically issued children two sets of clothing a year, one for the winter and one for the summer. No underclothes were provided, although leggings might be worn in winter. Young children usually wore a shapeless garment of rough cloth that was called a shirt when worn by boys and a shift, a shimmy, or a dress when worn by girls. Made of plainly woven coarse cotton cloth, these one-piece garments, seamed at the shoulders, fell from the shoulders to below the knees. Booker T. Washington wrote that his shirt felt like "a dozen or more chestnut burrs" rubbing on his skin. But however inexpensive their clothing might be, enslaved African Americans sought to individualize their clothing. Girls' clothing, in particular, was often patterned and colorful.[17]

Slave children were severely underfed, and later recalled that they frequently went hungry. On one large plantation, a planter allotted just thirty pounds of meat a week for 130 children. On most plantations, young children were fed out of a wooden trough, "the same as we see pigs, horses, and cattle gather around troughs today." Annie Burton, who was born into slavery in Clayton, Alabama, in 1858, later recalled: "We children had no supper, and only a little piece of bread or something of the kind in the morning. Our dishes consisted of one wooden bowl, and oyster shells were our spoon. This bowl served for about fifteen children, and often the dogs and the ducks and the peafowl had a dip in it. Sometimes we had buttermilk and bread in our bowl, sometimes greens or bones." Children's meals often consisted of cornmeal mush served with molasses or crumbled bread or peas or buttermilk poured into the tub, which they ate with their hands or seashells.[18]

Even though slave children in the American South were larger than their counterparts in the Caribbean, their growth rates were very slow by modern standards, reflecting an inadequate diet. On average slave children did not reach three feet in height until their fourth birthdays. At that age, they were five inches shorter than a typical child today and about the same height as a child in present-day Bangladesh. At seventeen, slave men were shorter than 96 percent of present-day American men, and slave women were smaller than 80 percent of American women. Children's diet under slavery was monotonous and unvaried, consisting largely of cornmeal, salt pork, and bacon. Only rarely did enslaved children drink milk or eat fresh meat or vegetables. As a result, slave children were small for their age, suffered from vitamin and protein deficiencies, and were victims of such ailments as beriberi, kwashiorkor, and pellagra. Poor nutrition and high rates of infant and child mortality contributed to a very short average life expectancy—just twenty-one or twenty-two years—compared with forty to forty-three years for whites.[19]

To compensate for their meager diets, children ate whatever was available. Jake Maddox, who spent his childhood in slavery in Georgia, removed chicken feet from the garbage and gnawed the bones. Alex McCinney beat some dogs to a biscuit that his master's family had thrown out. But the main way that children supplemented their family's diet was by picking nuts and edible weeds, fishing and hunting, and trapping small game and birds. In this way they greatly enhanced their family's well-being.[20]

Early induction into the labor force was one of slavery's cruelest features. Booker T. Washington recalled that "from the time that I can remember anything, almost every day of my life has been occupied in some kind of labor." Only the very youngest children were exempt from work. Elizabeth Keckley, who was born into slavery in Virginia in 1818 and later served as a seamstress for Mary Todd Lincoln, was put to work at the age of four as caretaker for her owner's baby. Plantation inventories indicate that even extremely young children had a positive valuation. At a time when an adult male slave was valued at $1,000, a slave infant was listed in a plantation inventory at as little as $25, reflecting the high infant death rate, but a three-year-old was valued at $150. When an adult male was priced at $1,500, a twelve-year-old male was valued at $800. The value of even young children reflected the fact that slave owners regarded them as productive assets.[21]

Young children worked in the owner's house until they were old enough to toil in the fields, caring for infants, serving food, polishing furniture, and swatting flies and fanning their master or mistress. Many houseboys and housegirls, as young as three, slept in their master's house, in their owner's room, or in attics or stairwells. Far from making life easier or more comfortable, living in the big house led to increased oversight and discipline. Frederick Douglass described a teenage housegirl, a member of his wife's family, who had her nose and breastbone broken during a beating after she fell asleep and failed to respond to a crying infant in her care.[22]

At five or six, enslaved children served as human scarecrows, frightening crows away from corn stalks, or toiled on trash gangs, hauling water and wood, pulling weeds, sweeping yards, driving cows to pasture, and cutting tree limbs for firewood. They also fed chickens, gathered eggs, milked cows, churned butter, and shelled, peeled, and washed vegetables. They plucked grubs off tobacco plants, and sometimes were forced to swallow those that they missed. On sugar plantations, children tossed cut cane into a cart and unloaded the stalks at the mill. In addition, young children picked burrs out of wool, carded, spun and wove cloth, and raked wheat or corn from the ground, tied it into bundles, and stacked the bundles. At the age of eight Henry Johnson of Virginia carried water for twenty-five or even thirty field hands. Between ten and twelve, youngsters began to wield the hoe themselves, with girls entering fieldwork earlier than boys. Thomas Jefferson had "children till 10. years old to serve as nurses. from 10. to 16. the boys make nails, the girls spin. at age 16. go into the grounds or learn trades."[23]

Many enslaved youngsters looked forward to entry into the workforce as a symbol of their growing maturation. It was only when slave children began to work in the fields full-time around age twelve that they received a full ration of food and adult clothing. The recommended portion of food more than doubled, from just a pound of bacon and half a peck of cornmeal a week to two and a half pounds of bacon and one and a half pecks of meal. Meanwhile young men donned the work shirts, pants, and hats that symbolized a working hand. A small number of boys served apprenticeships as blacksmiths, carpenters, ironworkers, masons, millwrights, and shoemakers, while a similarly small number of girls were trained to spin, weave, make dresses, and cut and dress their mistress's hair. These were often the children of slaves who held skilled positions on a plantation.[24]

As grave as the physical dangers posed by slavery were the psychological: that children would internalize a sense of dependence, inferiority, and subordinate status. Much more than a system of labor exploitation, slavery was a complex set of social relationships in which masters strove to make their property obedient, tractable, and dependent. Slavery placed sharp limits on parental authority and parents' ability to shield children from a master's punishment. For many, the harshest memory from their childhood was seeing their parents being whipped and discovering that they were impotent to do anything about it. Allen Wilson never forgot seeing his mother stripped naked, tied to a tree, and whipped. Josiah Henson, who served as Harriet Beecher Stowe's model for Uncle Tom, never forgot watching his father's punishment: "His right ear had been cut off close to his head, and he had received a hundred lashes on his back. He had beaten the overseer for a brutal assault on my mother, and this was his punishment." When William Wells Brown saw his mother being whipped for failing to be in the fields on time, "the cold chills ran over me, and I wept aloud."[25]

Among the most severe traumas experienced by slave children was learning that their parents were helpless to protect them from abuse. When Jacob Stroyer, who was being trained as a jockey, was regularly beaten, he turned to his father for help. His father told him: "Go back to your work and be a good boy, for I cannot do anything for you." When his mother intervened on Jacob's behalf, she was beaten for her efforts. Caroline Hunter, who lived with her mother and three brothers on a small Virginia farm, experienced a similar sense of powerlessness: "Many a day my ole mamma has stood by an' watched massa beat her chillun 'till dey bled an' she couldn't open her mouf. Dey didn' only beat us, dey useta strap my mamma to a bench or box an' beat her wid a wooden paddle when she was naked."[26]

As they recalled their childhood in bondage, former slaves invariably recollected a moment around puberty when they first confronted the reality of lifelong servitude. A whipping, an abusive epithet, a sudden change in how one was treated by white playmates revealed the full meaning of enslavement. For one former Louisiana slave that defining moment came when her mistress whipped her for saying "to missis, 'My mother sent me.'" She explained that on her plantation "We were not allowed to call our mammies 'mother.' It was too near the way of the white folks." For a Virginia slave known as Charles, the crucial moment came when his white playmates began to treat him as a slave. His master's son vividly recalled that moment. "It is customary in nearly all households in the South for the white and black children connected with each other to play together," he wrote. "The trial . . . comes when the young Negroes who have hitherto been on this democratic footing with the young whites are presently deserted by their . . . companions, who enter upon school-life . . . ceasing to associate with their swarthy comrades any longer, meet them in the future with the air of the master." Charles responded with bitterness and defiance. He set fire to the family's house and was subsequently sold to the Deep South. Francis Black underwent a similar experience. He was playing with his master's son, who called him a "nigger." He quickly replied to his playmate: "I say, I ain't no nigger. He say 'Yes you is, my pa pay $200 for you. He bought you to play with me.'"[27]

For slave children, there were daily reminders of their subordinate status and dependence on their master's will. They were expected to display deference and undergo verbal and physical harassment without responding. One South Carolina slave explained how slave children were taught to greet their owner properly. "The boys were required to bend the body forward with the head down and rest the body on the left foot, and scrape the right foot backwards on the ground while uttering the words, 'howdy Massa and Missie.' The girls were required to use the same words, accompanied with a curtsy." Many children were assigned menial tasks, such as holding their mistress's skirt off the dirt, brushing flies away from her, or picking up her daughter's bonnet, reinforcing a sense of social inferiority.[28]

Play, too, could buttress a sense of subordination. Thomas Jefferson believed that "the whole commerce between master and slave is a perpetual exercise of the most boisterous passions . . . Our children see this, and learn to imitate it." In fact many interracial games reenacted the relationship between masters and slaves, reinforcing the plantation hierarchy and accentuating the divide between white and black children. When the game was wagon, slave children served as mules. "Mounted on his pony," Solomon Northrup wrote, "a master's son often rides into the field with his whip, playing the overseer, greatly to his father's delight." Slave children remembered masters' children speaking with the voice of command: "I've got an account to settle with you; I've let you go about long enough; I'll teach you who's your master; go now God damn you, but I haven't got through with you yet."[29]

A defining element of slave childhood was a tug-of-war between the child's parents and the master and his family for the child's affection and obedience. Slave owners frequently intruded on parental prerogatives in an attempt to produce a loyal, diligent, obedient, and even grateful labor force. Showing kindness to slave children played a critical role in sustaining the masters' conception of themselves as benevolent, paternalistic, truly Christian beings. Slave owners thought of themselves as kind and even munificent, citing such examples as giving slave children candy, extra rations, and presents at Christmas time. Many plantation mistresses took special pride in nursing slave children during illnesses. Masters tried to win children's affection with food and privileges that parents could not give. It was difficult for slave children to resist these attentions and not respond by being grateful.[30]

Many enslaved children found themselves torn between the demands of their owners and the interests of the slave community. Mattie Gilmore, an Alabama slave, was required to report any thefts from the plantation house, which meant betraying the community. Childhood represented a battlefield in which parents and masters competed over who would exercise primary authority over children. Harriet Jacobs described an incident in which her father and her mistress called for her brother at the same time. Willie "finally concluded to go to his mistress. When my father reproved him for it, he said, 'You both called me, and I didn't know which I ought to go to first.' 'You are my child,' replied our father, 'and when I call you, you should come immediately, if you have to pass through fire and water.'" Slave parents strove against all odds to instill a sense of pride in their offspring and to educate them to maneuver through the complexities of slavery. Adeline, who grew up in Arkansas, said that from the time she was a small child, she was told "that it was no disgrace to be a Negro and had it not been for the white folks who brought us over here from Africa as slaves, we would never have been here and would have been much better off."[31]

From a very early age, slave parents taught their children the etiquette of interacting with whites. They were told not to repeat things they heard in the slave quarters. As Elijah P. Marrs, who was born in Shelby County, Kentucky, in 1840, explained: "Mothers were necessarily compelled to be severe on their children to keep them from talking too much. Many a poor mother had been whipped nearly to death on account of their children telling white children things." Children were also reminded that they could never appear "uppity" or impudent or disrespectful. Above all, they had to learn to flatter the egos of whites, by behaving in an obsequious manner or feigning stupidity or gratitude without internalizing a sense of inferiority or losing a sense of self-worth.[32]

Learning how to obey racial etiquette without giving in to it was not easy. A slave had to call even a young child "Young Massa" or "Young Misses." Joseph Sanford's father advised him "to be tractable, and get along with the white people in the best manner I could and not be saucy." One slave mother ordered her son to "git dat hat off dat head and bow your head fo' he git hear!" Amos Gadsden learned to "step aside at all times for white people." Children were told not to stare as whites engaged in conversation, lest they be accused of listening. Learning how to deceive and how to separate one's outward demeanor from one's inner feelings was crucial if a child was to preserve a sense of self-worth. Henry Bibb explained: "The only weapon of self defence that I could use successfully was that of deception." Another ex-slave emphasized the importance of deception, trickery, and role-playing even more bluntly: "Got one mind for the boss to see; got another for what I know is me." Parents advised mulatto children not to inquire about their parentage. Candis Goodwin knew her master to be her father, but learned to respond to questions about his identity by explaining that "tuckey buzzard lay me an de sun hatch me." Renty, a Georgia slave, never asked his mother to name his father because he felt "ashamed to ask her."[33]

Under slavery, stories, song, and folklore were an important source not only of amusement but of edification. Many enslaved parents played on children's fears to keep them out of trouble. One mother recited a chant about the patrollers who roamed the countryside looking for fugitive slaves. Slave children throughout the South learned to fear the characters "Raw Head" and "Bloody Bones." Other tales helped sustain a sense of distinctive identity and collective history. One story that was especially common in the slave quarters told of white slave traders enticing Africans with trinkets and holding them in pens before taking them across the Atlantic. Among the most popular slave folktales were animal trickster stories, like the Brer Rabbit tales, derived from similar African stories, which told of powerless creatures who achieved their will through wit and guile rather than power and authority. Much more than amusing stories, these trickster tales were used to comment on the people around them and convey lessons for everyday living. These stories taught slave children how to function in a white-dominated world and held out the promise that the powerless would eventually triumph over the strong.[34]

Children were not simply slavery's victims; they were also active agents, who managed to resist slavery's dehumanizing pressures. Like children of the Holocaust, enslaved African-American children did not simply play games to escape their misery; instead their games mirrored their surroundings. Games like "Hide the Switch," which concluded with the loser being flogged, and "auction," in which children staged slave auctions, allowed black children to reenact what they saw around them in order to understand and cope with slavery's stresses. Other forms of play instilled a sense of self-worth that was vital in resisting slavery's humiliations. Play taught enslaved children that they were equal or even superior to their white counterparts. "We was stronger and knowed how to play, and the white children's didn't," recalled Felix Heywood of Texas.[35]

To be sure, slave children played with homemade marbles, dolls, jump ropes, and hobbyhorses. They roamed the woods and fields, hunting and trapping small game, fishing, and gathering nuts and berries. Ring games, hopscotch, and ball games were especially popular. In the winter many slave children slid across the ice. But play was also a way to learn adult skills and deal with the insecurities of life in bondage. Many games prepared children for adult roles, such as cooking or caring for babies, or taught values that would be useful in the adult world. Role-playing games were especially popular, as children acted out baptisms, funerals, and weddings, and dressed up like adults. The children on one plantation liked to play conjure man in a game called hoodoo doctor, which gave them a sense of power and agency. Play helped forge a sense of solidarity among enslaved children and allowed them to create a semiautonomous realm, beyond the direct control of their masters.[36]

Children for whom education was forbidden learned to count while playing hide and seek. Other games required children to recite the alphabet. Verbal sparring known as "playing the dozens" sharpened young people's wits. Ring games accompanied by songs and riddles allowed slave children to give expression to feelings that often had to be repressed:

> My old mistress promised me,
> Before she dies she would set me free.
> Now she's dead and gone to hell.
> I hope the devil will burn her well.[37]

Play required a great deal of ingenuity, helping to instill resourcefulness and a sense of independence. In order to play ball, slave children had to make balls out of yarn with a sock as covering. Some play involved petty pilfering, such as taking fruit from orchards or eggs from a henhouse. Games that allowed children to accumulate modest material possessions were common. Slave children used corn kernels as a substitute for playing cards. They also competed for marbles, made of bits of clay. Like free children, slave children enjoyed competition that tested their physical prowess, such as shooting, riding, and fishing. Sometimes children used playtime to help older slaves. Richard Carruthers in Texas was posted by fellow slaves as a lookout. "If I see the overseer comin' from the Big House," he recalled, "I sing a song to warn 'em so they no get whipped."[38]

Masters at times required slaves to participate in brutal sports for their own entertainment. Henry Bibb described masters forcing slaves to take part in bloody wrestling and boxing matches. But it is notable that slave children rarely chose such games on their own; nor did they generally play games that required the elimination of players. Even when they played games similar to dodgeball, slave children did not require the "losers" to leave the game. This may have been a reaction to the possibility that any member of the slave community might be sold and their resistance to losing any member of the community.[39]

Denial of an education was among slavery's most painful traumas. "There is one sin that slavery committed against me, which I will never forgive," James W. C. Pennington declared. "It robbed me of my education." Frederick Douglass agreed. When his mistress learned that he could perform mathematics, she slapped him across his face and said, "If I ever catch you making another figure anywhere I'll cut off your right arm." From this incident, he learned an important lesson: that "Knowledge unfits a child to be a slave." From that moment on, he viewed literacy as "the direct pathway from slavery to freedom."[40]

On the eve of the Civil War the overwhelming majority of the slave population was illiterate, a situation that most southern whites favored. A delegate to the Virginia House of Delegates boasted, "We have as far as possible closed every avenue by which light may enter their minds. If we could extinguish the capacity to see the light our work would be completed." Although a few southern religious leaders believed that it was essential for all Christians, including slaves, to be able to read the Bible, others forcefully disagreed. The editors of the *Presbyterian Herald* asked rhetorically: "Is there any great moral reason why we should incur the tremendous risk of having our wives slaughtered in consequence of our slaves being taught to read incendiary publications?"[41]

Only four states—Georgia, North and South Carolina, and Virginia— had laws on the books from 1830 to 1860 making it illegal to teach slaves to read and write, and even these laws could be circumvented. But throughout the region, a slave who knew how to read or taught others to read risked a flogging or even the amputation of a finger. Titus Byrnes's mistress told him "that if he was caught writing again his right arm would be cut off." When Leonard Black's master caught him with a book, he said, "if I ever knew you to have a book again, I will whip you half to death." He then took the book and burned it. Daniel Dowdy recalled: "The first time you was caught trying to read or write you was whipped with a cow-hide the next time with a cat-o-nine tails and the third time they cut the first jin offen your forefinger."[42]

Nevertheless, on the eve of the Civil War perhaps 5 or even 10 percent of slaves were literate. A few masters and mistresses, such as the southern abolitionists John Fee and Moncure Conway, the diarist Mary Boykin Chesnut, and the pioneering feminist Sarah Grimke, subverted law and custom and taught some slaves to read and write. In some instances such efforts were motivated by a Protestant religiosity that stressed the importance of reading the Bible. But practical considerations more frequently prevailed. A slave who could read or write was a valuable asset who could maintain records, order supplies, and conduct correspondence.

A surprising number of enslaved children taught themselves to read. Frederick Douglass yearned to learn the mysterious skill that he and other African Americans were denied. "The frequent hearing of my mistress reading the Bible aloud," he wrote, "awakened my curiosity in respect to this *mystery* of reading, and roused in me the desire to learn." Steeling his courage, he asked his mistress to teach him, and "in an incredible short time, by her kind assistance, I had mastered the alphabet and could spell words of three or four letters." But many whites feared that literate slaves would question their status, and his master was one of them. He forbade his wife to give young Douglass any further instruction. But "the determination which he expressed to keep me in ignorance only rendered me the more resolute to seek intelligence." By stealth and trickery, Douglass learned to write. He made friends with white boys he met and got them to teach him how to write individual letters and words. Lacking paper and a pen and ink, he practiced writing on a fence or a brick wall or pavement with a lump of chalk.[43]

Learning to read and write under slavery was an arduous process that took tenacity and determination and often extended over several years. Thomas Johnson of Richmond encouraged his young master to spell words and read passages from his spelling book out loud. Richard Parker, who was enslaved in Virginia, scavenged old nails until he had collected enough money to buy a speller. He later gave white children marbles if they taught him a letter or two. John Sella Martin learned to read while working as an errand boy in a Columbus, Georgia, hotel where he listened to white workers wager on the correct spelling of words, while Benjamin Holmes, an apprentice tailor in Charleston, studied signs and the names on doors. After he was told that a slave should not learn to read, Thomas Jones, as a child in North Carolina, went to a shopkeeper and claimed that he had been sent to buy a book for a white child. To prevent their masters from discovering their ability to read, children often had to practice in the woods by the light of a fire.[44]

Learning to write proved even more difficult than learning to read. Especially in rural areas, enslaved children encountered few examples of cursive writing. Noah Davis, who was bound out to a shoemaker, learned to write by copying the letters that he saw his master write in the lining of boots and shoes. Henry Bibb explained that whenever he "got hold of an old letter that had been thrown away, or a piece of white paper, I would save it to write on. I have often gone off in the woods and spent the greater part of the day alone, trying to write myself a pass, by writing on the back of old letters." Frederick Douglass learned by watching ships' carpenters fill out manifests for shipping lumber. For many children, literacy was an act of resistance, which instilled a sense of self-worth and offered psychological freedom. It allowed them to read the Bible for themselves and not depend on the interpretations of white southerners. Also, a slave who could write could forge a pass.[45]

Youth, for African Americans, was a much more uncertain and problematic period than it was for whites. Harriet Jacobs said that mothers of slaves lived "in daily expectation of trouble" once their children became teenagers. It was during the teen years that slave sales peaked. Most girls were sold between the ages of thirteen and twenty, while most boys were sold in their late teens and early twenties.[46]

One reason why slave mothers looked to their children's adolescence with dread was the fear of the sexual exploitation of enslaved teenage girls by whites. Within the slave community there were strong norms around sexuality in the teen years. Although some young slave women gave birth outside wedlock in their teens, the overwhelming majority did not. There was a substantial gap between the time slave women became sexually fertile and when they gave birth to their first child. Even though first menstruation for slave women occurred around the age of fifteen, the average age at which slave women had their first child was nearly twenty-one years. But sexual maturation also increased the likelihood of sexual abuse. Virtually every female slave narrative includes a reference to the threat or reality of sexual exploitation. James H. Hammond, a congressman, governor, and U.S. senator from South Carolina, whose wife bore him eight children, purchased an eighteen-year-old slave named Sally and her infant daughter, Louisa, in 1839. He made Sally his mistress, fathered several children by her, and when the daughter reached the age of twelve fathered several children by her.[47]

Religion helped enslaved youth cope with the insecurities and fears generated by slavery. In early childhood many slave children were introduced to religious teachings. One observer noted that "the Negroes on plantations sometimes appoint one of their number, commonly the old woman who minds the children during the day to teach them to say their prayers, repeat a little catechism, and a few hymns, every evening." One former slave explained how religion helped him deal with family separation: "God started on me when I was a little boy. I used to grieve a lot over my mother. She had been sold away from me and taken a long way off. One evening . . . I was walking along thinking about Mama and crying. Then a voice spoke to me and said 'Blessed art thou.'" Religion taught slave children endurance. In the words of one spiritual: "They crucified my Lord, and He never said a mumbling word."[48]

During their teens many slave youth underwent a protracted period of spiritual anxiety, during which they experienced intense feelings of sinfulness and fears of damnation. Then, without warning, many experienced a vision in which they saw themselves as dead, destined for eternal damnation, before undergoing the liberating experience of acceptance by God and a sense that they had been born again. Josiah Henson was eighteen when he underwent conversion, an experience triggered by the words of a sermon he heard. The preacher had said that "Jesus Christ, the Son of God, tasted death for every man; for the high, for the low, for the rich, for the poor, the bond, the free, the Negro in his chains, the man in gold and diamonds." Henson recalled: "I stood and heard it. It touched my heart and I cried out: 'I wonder if Jesus Christ died for me.'" In addition to religion, conjure, herbalism, ghost lore, witchcraft, and fortune telling flourished in the slave quarters. Many young people, like Frederick Douglass, turned to conjurers for charms or herbs that might help them win another slave's love or protect them from punishment. Through the spirit world, enslaved youth found the determination and resources to withstand the destructive impact of slavery.[49]

The outbreak of the Civil War precipitated new uncertainties in the lives of enslaved children. When the Civil War began in 1861, nine-year-old Booker T. Washington was awakened by his mother, who was "fervently praying that Lincoln and his armies might be successful, and that one day she and her children might be free." Slaves, parents and children alike, followed the progress of the war closely, he observed: "Every success of the Federal armies and every defeat of the Confederate forces was watched with the keenest and most intense interest." In an effort to gather information, a Tennessee child "would go round to the windows and listen to what the white folks would say when they were reading their papers and talking after supper." The war penetrated into every aspect of enslaved children's lives, including their play. Candis Goodwin, a Virginia slave, recalled that black and white children on her plantation would "play Yankee and 'Federates, 'course de whites was always the 'Federates. They'd make us black boys prisoners an' make b'lieve dey was gonna cut our necks off."[50]

As the war dragged on and began to disrupt the plantation system, many slave owners attempted to relocate their slaves into more secure areas, often in Texas. At least 30,000, and perhaps as many as 100,000, slaves—mainly adult males—were moved out of the South Carolina and Georgia lowcountry and Mississippi Valley, with many women and children left behind to shift for themselves. In desperation, a growing number of slave women and children fled to northern lines. A seventy-year-old slave woman took twenty-two children and grandchildren on a flatboat down the Savannah River, finding safety at last on a Union vessel. In an attempt to maintain discipline, many slave owners spread horror stories about advancing Union armies, telling children that "a Yankee was somepin what had one great big horn on the haid and just one eye and dat right in de middle of the breast."[51]

After the Emancipation Proclamation went into effect on January 1, 1863, authorizing the enlistment of black soldiers, thousands of slave men escaped from plantations to serve in the military. Altogether, ex-slaves accounted for about two-thirds of the 180,000 black men who fought in the Union army and the 30,000 who served in the navy. Many slaveholders punished the families of men who enlisted by denying them food and compelling wives and children to do the heavy outdoor labor previously performed by the men. Private William Brooks's wife and children were "required to the same work that he formerly had to do, such as chopping wood, splitting rails &c." Elizabeth Scantling, who was fifteen years old in 1865, said that she was required to plow with "a mule an' a wild un at dat. Sometimes my hands get so cold I jes' cry." Some slave owners evicted wives and children from their homes. Early in 1864 the wife of a recent recruit, who was struggling to care for a two-year-old child, recalled that she had "been severely beaten and driven from home by her master and owner." Her master "told her never to return to him . . . and that he would not support the women." In a poignant letter to her husband, Martha Glover, a Missouri slave, wrote: "Remember all I told you about how they would do me after you left—for they do worse than they ever did & I do not know what will become of me & my poor little children."[52]

In November 1863 aid workers estimated that at least 50,000 slaves, mainly women and children, had fled to refugee camps. They had no shelter except crude tents fashioned out of leaves and branches, "fit for nothing but to protect them from night dews." Lacking bedding, thousands slept on the bare ground; many were "half naked." Delays in distributing rations and a lack of cooking facilities left some starving. "No language," aid workers reported to President Lincoln, "can describe the suffering, destitution and neglect which prevail in some of their 'camps.' The sick and dying are left uncared for, in many instances, and the dead unburied. It would seem, now, that one-half are doomed to die." One Union officer described the suffering in particularly gripping terms: "the suffering from hungar & cold is so great that these wretched people are dying by scores—that sometimes thirty per day die & are carried off by wagon loads, without coffins, & thrown promiscuously, like brutes, into a trench." The plight of fugitive slaves was particularly bleak in the border states, where slavery remained legal. Most Union officials took the position that slave owners were responsible for caring for slaves, and refused to provide food or shelter to fugitives. Not until March 1865 did Congress adopt a joint resolution freeing the wives and children of black soldiers and future recruits.[53]

Slavery's abolition as a legal institution was followed by a protracted struggle to define the meaning of freedom. Childhood quickly became a central battleground in this struggle. Former slave owners viewed black children as a potential source of labor and used apprenticeship laws to force them to work without wages. Any fatherless children or any whose fathers "do not habitually employ their time in some honest industrious occupation" could be bound out as orphans to their former master. In addition, children whose mothers were not legally married might be classified as bastards who could be legally indentured. Children of parents deemed "unfit" could also be indentured without their parents' consent.[54]

Many former slaveholders went to Orphan's Courts and invoked apprenticeship laws to claim the labor of those under the age of twenty-one. Within a month of the end of the Civil War, more than 2,500 African-American children were apprenticed to former slave owners. At the same time, landowners invoked the threat of indenturing children to force adult males to sign labor contracts. A federal official in Maryland's Eastern Shore described the situation there: "In many instances, boys of 12 and 14 years are taken from their parents, under the pretence that they (the parents) are incapable of supporting them, while the younger children are left to be maintained by the parents." He explained that "this is done without obtaining the parent's consent" and that the Maryland courts did not take "any testimony relative to the capability of the parents to support their children." An Army chaplain in Mississippi described a subterfuge that many former slave owners used to circumvent laws that required "apprentices" to be freed at the age of twenty-one: they openly lied about the young person's age. He explained: "Children are almost invariably bound out from two to 12 years younger than they are." He described one case where a former slave named Sam, who was eighteen years old, was described as "6 years & six months old!"[55]

Lacking land, draft animals, and tools, the families of former slaves only had one resource to draw upon, their family's labor. Without their children's labor, these families were invariably forced into economic dependency on their former masters, but federal authorities were reluctant to tamper with apprenticeship. Eager to reduce the number of African Americans eligible for relief, fearful that the unemployed would starve or turn to crime, the Freedman's Bureau sought to restore plantation production as rapidly as possible. The bureau took the official position that "children may be bound to service *with the consent* of their parents only." But in practice the bureau acquiesced in the apprenticeship of thousands of black children. One apprenticeship agreement required a thirteen-year-old to labor ten hours a day on his master's farm and be "respectful in his deportment." He received no salary for his efforts; his compensation took the form of "Board, Clothing, and Medical Attendance." One Freedmen's Bureau agent in 1867 recognized that "the binding out of children seems to the freedmen like putting them back into Slavery." But he was convinced that former masters were better able to care for the "apprentices" and, without appreciating the depths of family ties, claimed that the freedmen, too, simply wanted the children's labor. As he wrote sarcastically: "In every case where I have bound out children, thus far Some Grand Mother or fortieth cousin has come to have them released."[56]

Although many white southerners defended apprenticeship as a way to care for orphans, it was essentially a system of labor exploitation. Most apprentices were of working age, mainly between the ages of ten and thirteen. Most were bound without their parents' consent, received no training, and were held beyond the legal age. One North Carolina woman to whom the bureau indentured six children was a pauper and was in fact hiring the children out. In order to obtain land, some African-American families were forced to apprentice their children. Thomson Baker complained in 1867 that his former owner came to his house and took "my

This 1868 photograph depicts an African-American girl who was responsible for caring for a white infant. Courtesy of the Florida Photographic Collection, Florida State Archives, Tallahassee.

children by force and threten to kill my wife and drew his knife and cut at hir and cut a handerkerf around her neck, and carried one of them home and had it bound out without consent."[57]

The struggle over childhood involved more than labor. There was a deep fear among many southern whites that young African Americans, not socialized under slavery, would refuse to accept a subordinate place in society. This led to widespread efforts to enforce subservice in all aspects of their lives, particularly their education. The state of Alabama spent $22.96 each year on the education of a white child and 98 cents on a black child. Inequities like this led Booker T. Washington to quip that it was too great a compliment to expect black children to learn seven times more easily than a white child. Black schooling typically took place in unpainted one-room structures or in churches or private homes. One Mississippi classroom had between 75 and 100 students. When Mary McLeod Bethune taught in Daytona Beach, Florida, she was forced to use splinters from burnt logs for pencils, and elderberries for ink. In 1899 one white summarized the lessons that the schools were to teach: "*Face the music; avoid social questions;* leave politics alone; continue to be patient; live moral lives; live simply; learn to work and to work intelligently; learn to work faithfully; learn to work hard . . . know that it is a crime for any teacher, white or black, to educate the Negro for positions which are not open to him."[58]

Much of an African-American child's essential education took place outside the classroom, where children experienced repeated indignities and humiliations designed to teach them to accept a subordinate status. When James Robinson boarded a bus in Knoxville early in the twentieth century, he was told: "You damn little darkey, didn't anybody learn you to stay in your place? You get the hell back there and wait till the white people get on the bus." Years later the memory of this incident remained fixed in his memory. "Inwardly, I boiled. It hurt inside, all the way down . . . I wanted to cry but hate wouldn't let me . . . What hurt me most of all was that grown-up Negro men had not dared to speak in behalf of a help-less child."[59]

Scenes of racial violence left an indelible impression in many young African Americans' memories. The theologian Benjamin Mays's earliest memory was witnessing a group of white men, guns drawn, curse his father and force him to bow down before them. "I was not yet five years old," he later wrote, "but I have never forgotten them." The poet Pauli Murray was six when she saw the body of an African-American man who had been murdered because he had walked across a white man's watermelon patch. The novelist Chester Himes remembered seeing his father "crying like a baby" when a white hospital refused to admit his critically injured brother. Even those who didn't witness violence firsthand heard stories of racial slights, verbal and physical abuse, and outright violence. The novelist Richard Wright recalled that he "would stand for hours on the doorsteps of neighbors' houses listening to their talk, learning how a white woman had slapped a black woman, how a white man had killed a black man. It filled me with awe, wonder, and fear."[60]

One essential lesson that Benjamin Mays learned as a child was that "in this perilous world, if a black boy wanted to live a halfway normal life and die a natural death he had to learn early the art of how to get along with white folks." This was a lesson repeated again and again by adults. Zora Neale Hurston's father told her: "Lemme tell you something right now, my young lady; you ain't white." As they watched a catfish thrashing on a creek bank, Charles Holcombe's grandfather told him: "Son, a catfish is a lot like a nigger. As long as he stays in his mudhole he is all right, but when he gits out he is in for a passel of trouble. You 'member dat, and you won't have no trouble wid folks when you grows up." Young African Americans were repeatedly told to bite their tongues and repress their feelings of anger. Richard Wright, who was once beaten because he failed to say "sir" to a white man, wrote: "The safety of my life in the South depended upon how well I concealed from all whites what I felt." When the future jazz musician Louis Armstrong was five years old, he asked his mother about the sign "For Colored Passengers Only."

"Don't ask so many questions!" she replied. "Shut you mouth you little fool."[61]

Many young African Americans underwent rituals of humiliation dramatizing their second-class status. Margaret Walker knew before she was ten "what it was to step off the sidewalk to let a white man pass; otherwise he might knock me off." Ed Brown, who grew up in Georgia before World War I, said, "My motto was, when I was a boy, Don't Meet Nobody. When I seen someboy comin or heard a horse, I'd set outside the road and they'd pass on by . . . Because nine times out of ten you'd be made to dance or to drink some whiskey." Margaret Walker, who grew up in Mississippi, had to climb a fire escape to enter a theater, because there was no entrance for blacks.[62]

For some young African Americans, the only way to cope with humiliation was to hate whites. Martin Luther King Sr. wrote: "my way to protect myself, I thought, was to build around myself an armor made of my hatred of whites . . . To hate those responsible made it bearable, and so I indulged myself and began to despise every white face I saw." Many children grew up with intense feelings of helplessness. William Henry Holtzclaw remembered that he and his siblings "would often cry for food until falling here and there on the floor we would sob ourselves to sleep." Yet if parents emphasized the importance of self-restraint and self-control, they also showed children how to maintain a sense of self-respect and self-worth. "When I was a boy your age," Ely Green's grandfather told him, "I was . . . put on the block and sold with five other brothers and sisters." Pauline Fitzgerald's father told her never to call a white person "marse," because she should not suggest that any white man was her master. "If I ever catch you saying 'Marse' again," he said, "I'll whale the daylights out of you."[63]

If African-American childhood was harsher than whites ever understood, and if it sometimes inflicted scars that lasted a lifetime, it also left black children with a sense of pride, family and communal loyalty, and resistance to injustice. The strengths it transmitted were all the greater because of the obstacles that young African Americans had endured and overcome.

chapter six

Childhood Battles of the Civil War

BORN INTO SLAVERY on the Georgia Sea Islands in 1848, Susie Baker was six when she and a brother began to live with her maternal grandmother in Savannah. At a secret school run by a free black woman, she learned to read and write. For two years, she wrote, "We went every day about nine o'clock, with our books wrapped in paper to prevent the police or white persons from seeing them. We went in, one at a time." Later she received additional instruction from another free black woman, a white playmate, and her grandmother's landlord's son.[1]

In April 1862 an uncle led Susie and his own family to a Sea Island under Union control. Although she was only fourteen, she became a laundress for the 33d U.S. Colored troops, one of the Union Army's first black regiments, and led a day school for forty African-American children and a night school for adults. She also nursed wounded soldiers. At first the wounded and bloody soldiers shocked her, but soon she grew accustomed to the sight. "It seems strange," she later wrote, "how our aversion to suffering is overcome in war. How we are able to see the most sickening sights and instead of turning away, how we hurry to assist in alleviating their pain."[2]

In times of war, age lines blur, new demands are made of the young, and children cannot be insulated from adult realities. The Civil War was no exception. The war brought excitement, but also anxiety and privation. It disrupted families, separated children from their fathers and brothers, and thrust the young into the heated political debates of the times. Unlike later wars in American history, young people were involved

This youth, known only as Taylor, served as a drummer with the 78th Regiment, U.S. Colored Infantry. The 78th Regiment played a crucial role in helping the North maintain control over the Mississippi River and dividing the Confederacy in two. Courtesy of the National Archives, Washington, D.C.

in all aspects of the Civil War, including fighting on the battlefield. William Black, the youngest wounded soldier, was twelve when his left hand and arm were shattered by an exploding shell. An unknown number of soldiers—probably around 5 percent—were under eighteen, and some were as young as ten. Others served as scouts or nurses for the wounded. Yet even those who did not participate in the war itself saw their lives altered by the conflict. During wartime young people had to grow up quickly, assuming the responsibilities of absent relatives. At Atlanta, Gettysburg, and Vicksburg, the young experienced war's harshest realities; yet far from the battlefront, the conflict intruded into children's games, magazines, and schools.[3]

Even after the war ended, its repercussions continued to be felt. Parents grew more protective of their children, and "child protection" became a watchword for reform societies seeking to address such social problems as child abuse and neglect. Children's experience during the Civil War permanently altered a generation of Americans, who in turn transformed American society in the years that followed. For the children of former Confederates, the war's legacy was apparent in the formation of organizations such as the Sons and the Daughters of the Confederacy, which sought to ensure that their parents' sacrifices had not been in vain. Meanwhile the children of former Union soldiers took the lead in promoting hiking, camping, and competitive sports to provide their offspring with a "moral equivalent of war." The experience of children during the Civil War forces us to rethink popular assumptions about children's fragility. It demonstrates young people's resilience, but also the indelible impression that war leaves on children's lives.

"What storeyes I shall have to tell when I get home," sixteen-year-old William Wilbur Edgerton wrote his mother shortly after he joined the 107th New York Volunteer Infantry in 1862. Since the age of twelve, Wilbur had taken on a series of odd jobs: fiddle playing, barrelmaking, blacksmithing, and laboring as a farm hand and a factory worker. When the war broke out, he enlisted, and two months later he fought in the battle of Antietam on the bloodiest day of the Civil War. In a letter to a younger brother he described the experience. "The balls flew around my head like hail stones," he wrote, "and sounded like a swarm of bees." His brother would "have no idea what it is to souldier off in a strange country whare your comrades are a dieing off fast and no noing how soon before your time will come." Unlike a friend who deserted, he declared, "I am no *coward* and I never will *disgrace* the *name* of *Edgerton* by *desertion* or *Sneeking* out of *danger* like some have."[4]

The stories of boys and girls in blue and gray read like fiction. Indeed, their exploits provided the basis for dozens of Civil War novels. Kentucky-born William Horsfall was thirteen when he ran away from home in December 1861 to serve as a drummer in the Union Army's First Kentucky Infantry, and just fourteen when he earned the Congressional Medal of Honor for saving the life of a wounded officer caught between Union and Confederate lines at the battle of Corinth in Mississippi. Pinkus Aylee, who served in a black regiment, was sixteen years old when he rescued a young white soldier who had been wounded and left for dead. Soon afterward both young men were captured and taken to Andersonville, the dreaded Confederate prison camp in Georgia where at least 12,000 of 30,000 Union prisoners died. Aylee was hanged immediately, but the white soldier survived to tell their story. Not all child soldiers were boys. Perhaps 400 women, including seventeen-year-old Mary Scaberry of the 52d Ohio Infantry and nineteen-year-old Rosetta Lyons Wakeman, took on male aliases in order to serve in the Civil War. As a soldier, Wakeman explained, she was able to live as "independent as a hog on the ice."[5]

In 1861 President Lincoln announced that boys under eighteen could enlist only with their parents' consent. The next year he prohibited any enlistment of those under eighteen. But heavy casualties led recruiting officers to look the other way when underaged boys tried to enlist, and thousands participated in the conflict as drummers, messengers, hospital orderlies, and often as full-fledged soldiers. They carried canteens, bandages, and stretchers and assisted surgeons and nurses. Many young soldiers signed up as drummers, who relayed officers' commands, signaling reveille, roll call, company drill, and taps. In the heat of battle, many carried orders or assisted with the wounded; at least a few picked up rifles and participated in the fighting. Their motives for enlisting varied, including patriotism and a desire to escape the boring routine of farm life or an abusive family. A few were jealous of older brothers, and some young northerners were eager to rid the country of slavery. For some young Confederates, there was a desire to repel northern invaders from their soil. One southern boy made his feelings clear with words colored by irony: "I reather die then be com a Slave to the North." Many letters convey a conviction that the hand of providence was at work in this terrible conflict, and that blood needed to be shed if the nation was to fulfill its destiny.[6]

Children employed a variety of ruses to enlist. Ned Hunter assured a recruitment officer in Mississippi that although he was fifteen years old, he "can shoot as straight as any who has signed today." Charles E. Goddard, who was sixteen when he enlisted in the First Minnesota Regiment in late April 1861, simply lied about his age. Fifteen-year-old Elisha Stockwell Jr.

A young "powder monkey" stands next to a 100-pound gun on the U.S.S. *New Hampshire*. Powder monkeys carried explosives on board warships. Courtesy of the Library of Congress.

persuaded a friend's father, a captain in the Union army, to accompany him to the recruiting station. "The Captain got me in by my lying a little, as I told the recruiting officer that I didn't know how old I was but I thought I was eighteen."[7]

Like Henry Fleming, Stephen Crane's farmboy protagonist in *The Red Badge of Courage*, the young soldiers' romantic illusions about military glory evaporated under the harsh realities of combat. They suffered hunger, fatigue, and discomfort, and gradually lost their innocence in combat. Every aspect of soldiering comes alive in their letters and diaries: the stench of spoiled meat, the deafening sound of cannons, the sight of maimed bodies, and the randomness and anonymity of death. Excitement over enlistment swiftly gave way to the boring routines of camp life and marches. Because of a lack of equipment, fifteen-year-old Thomas Galwey and other members of the Eighth Ohio Regiment paraded in civilian clothes and drilled with "wooden guns, wooden swords, and cornstalks." "Day after day and night after night did we tramp along the rough and dusty roads," sixteen-year-old John Delhaney, a Confederate soldier, wrote, "neath the most broiling sun with which the month of August ever afflicted a soldier . . . scarcely stopping to gather the green corn from the fields to serve us for rations."[8]

Homesickness afflicted many young soldiers. John Delhaney described his feelings on his first night in camp: "The strange faces and forms . . . were not calculated to allay my uneasiness of mind or lighten my hearts or its cares." Teased by older soldiers, young soldiers suffered from inadequate food, clothing, and shelter. Charles Nott, a sixteen-year-old New Yorker, said that during the winter months coffee was the only warm food he had. "The pork was frozen and the water in the canteens solid ice, so we had to hold them over the fire when we wanted a drink." On a snowy night he and three other soldiers only had four blankets, "two of them wet and frozen," to cover them.[9]

William Bircher was fifteen when he enlisted as a drummer boy in the Second Veteran Volunteer Infantry in 1861. At first his diary entries recorded his excitement in training with his regiment, but soon his tone grew somber. His regiment fought at the battle of Chickamauga after marching for days without shoes; William had to wrap his bleeding feet in rags torn from his own uniform. The young drummer boy described eating rotten food and drinking putrid water from puddles. He recalled:

After we had been in the field a year or two the call, "Fall in for your hard-tack!" was leisurely responded to by only about a dozen men . . . Hard-tack was very hard. This I attributed to its great age, for there was a common belief among the boys that our hard-tack had been baked long before the beginning of the Christian era. This opinion was based upon the fact that the letters "B.C." were stamped on many, if not, indeed, all the cracker-boxes.[10]

Complaints about provisions appeared in many letters. "Rats are found to be very good for food," a Union boy wrote in his diary, "and every night many are captured and slain." "They are so tame," he observed, "that they hardly think it worth while to get out of our way when we meet them."[11]

The young soldiers' most lasting impressions were of the dead and wounded. Sixteen-year-old John Cockerill, a musician in a Confederate unit at the battle of Shiloh, "passed the corpse of a beautiful boy in gray who lay with his blond curls scattered about his face and his hands folded peacefully across his breast." Cockerill admitted: "At the sight of the poor boy's corpse, I burst into a regular boo-hoo." General Ulysses S. Grant's son never forgot the sights after the siege of Vicksburg in 1863. "Here the scenes were so terrible that I became faint," he wrote, "and making my way to a tree, sat down, the most woebegone twelve-year-old in America." Fifteen-year-old Thomas Galwey of the Eighth Ohio Volunteer Infantry offered a particularly vivid picture of the face of battle: "Lieutenant Delaney is shot . . . Lieutenant Lantry, poor fellow, is annihilated instantly, near me. The top of his head is taken off by a shell. Our company is narrowing more and more . . . Fairchild is bleeding; Campion falls, mortally wounded; Jim Gallagher's head is badly grazed, and he rolls, coiled in a lump, down into a ditch." When the war was over, only 97 of the unit's 990 men mustered out.[12]

War, they quickly discovered, was hell. The boy soldiers described drinking water from creeks stained red with blood, and piling up corpses to make a windbreak for a field surgeon's operating theater. Edward Spangler, a sixteen-year-old Pennsylvania private who suffered a leg wound at Antietam, saw "hundreds of prostrate men with serious wounds of every description." "Many to relieve their suffering were impatient for their turn upon the amputation tables," he noted glumly, "around which were pyramids of severed legs and arms. Many prayed aloud, while others shrieked in the agony and throes of death." Some young soldiers, like Henry Graves, gradually grew desensitized to violence. He wrote that he was able to "look on the carcass of a man with pretty much the feeling as I would do were it a horse or hog." But many others suffered from "soldier's heart," or what later generations would call battle fatigue, shell shock, or post-traumatic stress disorder.[13]

The accounts of young Union prisoners at Confederate prison camps are especially harrowing. Sixteen-year-old Michael Dougherty was shocked by the sight of "different instruments of torture: stocks, thumb screws, barbed iron collars, shackles, ball and chain. Our prison keepers seemed to handle them with familiarity." William Smith, a fifteen-year-old soldier in the 14th Illinois Infantry, was shaken by the physical appearance of prisoners at Andersonville in Georgia, a "great mass of gaunt, unnatural-looking beings, soot-begrimed, and clad in filthy trousers." Ranson J. Powell, who was just thirteen years old and barely four feet tall when he left his home in western Maryland to serve as a drummer with the Union Army's 10th Virginia Regiment, was captured and confined at

Andersonville, where his daily rations consisted of a teaspoon of salt, three tablespoons of beans, and half a pint of unsifted cornmeal, and water came from a nearby creek that also served as the camp's sewer. When fifteen-year-old Billy Bates managed to escape from Andersonville, he weighed just sixty pounds.[14]

The war's impact was not confined to the front lines. Far from the battlefields, the war also intruded upon children's lives. In August 1864 an Atlanta girl wrote in her journal: "I was ten years old today. I did not have a cake. Times are too hard. I hope that by next birthday, we will have peace in our land." Carrie Berry was one of many children whose lives were turned upside down by the war. Despite her youth, she had to care for her pregnant mother and a sickly younger sister. She cooked, cleaned, sewed, and scavenged for nails and lead that she could trade for food. Each night she lived in dread of cannon shells. "One has busted under the dining room which frightened us very much," she wrote. "One passed through the smokehouse and a piece hit the top of the house and fell through." After the Union Army under William Tecumseh Sherman captured the city, new fears arose: "Some mean soldiers set several houses on fire in different parts of town." In her journal she confessed that she "could not go to sleep for fear that they would set our house on fire."[15]

Near the battlefront, children, black and white, witnessed the destruction of farms and villages. Their letters and diaries describe foraging soldiers, exploding shells, burning cities, mangled corpses, and stacks of human limbs. A few gave directions to scouts or nursed the wounded, while others sold gingerbread or buttermilk to soldiers or foraged battlefields for souvenirs. Some were wounded or killed by stray shots or shells. Children near the battle lines grew up rapidly during wartime. "In these few months, my childhood has slipped away from me," wrote Celine Fremaux, a twelve-year-old from Baton Rouge, Louisiana, who was responsible for six younger siblings, including a newborn brother. "Necessity, human obligations, family pride and patriotism had taken entire possession of my little emaciated body." At an early age, children learned to improvise. Evelyn Ward of Blandensfield, Virginia, explained what she did when stores ran out of candy. "We used to cut down the sorghum cane," she recalled, "peel off a joint, and chew the pith." Eight-year-old Annie Marmion, whose father was a physician in Harpers Ferry, West Virginia, remembered that "the great objects in life were to procure something to eat and to keep yourself out of sight by day, and keep your candle light hidden by night; lights of every kind, being regarded as signals to the Rebels, were usually greeted by a volley of guns."[16]

Children near the battle lines were vitally affected by the events surrounding them. Before the battle of Gettysburg, fifteen-year-old Tillie Pierce saw free blacks fleeing the town, fearing reenslavement by the approaching Confederate forces. She described "men and women with bundles as large as old-fashioned feather ticks slung across their backs, almost bearing them to the ground. Children also, carrying their bundles, and striving in vain to keep up." During the battle, many children huddled in cellars while cannons shook their homes' foundation. Fifteen-year-old Albertus McCreary carried buckets of water to the soldiers. Army surgeons transformed Sue Chancellor's house into a makeshift hospital. "They had taken our sitting room as an operating room," she recalled, "and our piano served as an amputating table." Young Jeanie McCreary assisted the nurses and surgeons. "I never thought I could do anything about a wounded man," she wrote following the battle, "but find that I had a bit more nerve than I thought I had." Two weeks after the momentous battle was over, Annie Young wrote a cousin. "I have lived a lifetime in the past few weeks," she said, "and yet, to look back, it seems like some fearful dream. God grant that . . . none I love, may ever pass through such scenes or witness such bloody, fearful sights! Words can give you no conceptions. It was perfect agony."[17]

As the war dragged on, hardship on the southern home front grew intense. In the besieged city of Vicksburg, Mississippi, families sought refuge in cliffside caves. A stray shell left one child, Lucy McCrae, buried under a mass of earth. "The blood was gushing from my nose, eyes, ears, and mouth," she later wrote, "but no bones were broken." Youngsters participated in bread riots in Richmond, Virginia; Montgomery, Alabama; Raleigh, North Carolina; and Columbia, South Carolina. A Richmond girl defended the looting: "We are starving. As soon as enough of us get together we are going to take the bakeries and each of us will take a loaf of bread. That is little enough for the government to give us after it has taken all our men."[18]

For some children far from combat, war was an enthralling adventure. Seven-year old Theodore Roosevelt, a New Yorker who had two uncles in the Confederacy, enjoyed playing "Running the Blockade." When Jeanette Gilder was nine, she ran away to join the Union army. A colonel sent her back home, but she was unrepentant. "I was marched off to bed," the recalled, "but I made a tent of my sheets, and with a broom for a musket, drilled myself till I was so tired that I fell asleep." But for many other boys and girls, the war meant taking on adult responsibilities. Twelve-year-old Marion Drury had "to assume the work and responsibilities of a man because most of the farmhands had gone into the army." Anna Shaw, who was fourteen in 1861, grew up in the wilds of Michigan, and later became an important suffrage leader, took on her father and brothers' jobs. In addition to sewing, cleaning, and caring for boarders, she taught school and cleared fields.[19]

Perhaps the most striking development was the politicization of childhood. Even young children got caught up in the heated political debates of the time. In a school composition that he wrote in 1861, eleven-year-old Edward Bellamy, the author of the utopian novel *Looking Backward,* marveled at how "this great nation gathered determination with God's help to forever crush treason from this continent." Katie Darling Wallace of Glencoe, Virginia, who was also eleven, expressed the opposing viewpoint in her journal in July 1863. "I think our people did right to invade the enemy's country," she wrote. "It is the only way to bring them to their right senses." The ideas and emotions articulated by adults infected children as well.[20]

During wartime the games young people played, the entertainments they enjoyed, and the books and magazines they read were saturated with war imagery. Schoolbooks, which had avoided controversy before the war, became politicized to an astonishing extent. The *Union ABC* began: "A is for America, land of the free." A Confederate textbook asked its readers: "If one Confederate soldier can whip seven Yankees, how many soldiers can whip 49 Yankees?" The *Geographical Reader for the Dixie Children* provided a Confederate perspective on the causes of the war:

> In the year 1860, the Abolitionists became strong enough to elect one of their men for President. Abraham Lincoln was a weak man, and the South believed he would allow laws to be made, which would deprive them of their rights. So the Southern States seceded, and elected Jefferson Davis for their President. This so enraged President Lincoln that he declared war, and has exhausted nearly all the strength of the nation, in a vain attempt to whip the South back into the Union.

In occupied parts of the South, schools became contested terrain, where students, administrators, and parents battled over course content, school activities, and songs. In New Orleans schools, Confederate sympathizers wore mourning ribbons and refused to participate in pro-Union ceremonies.[21]

Children's magazines, which had studiously avoided the slavery issue before the war, incorporated war themes into their stories and poems. Some, such as "The Soldier's Little Boy," a tale about a dying boy whose father was killed at Antietam, prepared the young for the realities of death. A few children actually published their own wartime newspapers. In the fall of 1862 an editorial in one of these papers, the Concord, Massachusetts *Observer,* declared: "War must become the daily vocation of us all."[22]

The martial spirit also infected play. Boys held mock parades, skirmishes, and drills. Boys in Shenagno, Pennsylvania, formed their own military company, elected a thirteen-year-old captain and held weekly drills in a nearby schoolyard. A Virginia mother, Margaret Junkin Preston, wrote that her children's "entire set of plays have reference to a state of war." Her five-year-old son George "gets sticks and hobbles about, saying that he lost a leg at the second battle of Manassass; tells wonderful stories of how he cutt off yankees' heads, bayoneted them, &c." Politics became an integral part of young people's experience. Seventeen-year-old Lizzie H. Corning, who lived in Concord, New Hampshire, listened to political

War Spirit at Home, by Lilly Martin Spencer, 1866. As a mother reads a newspaper while holding an infant on her lap, her children celebrate Ulysses S. Grant's victory at the battle of Vicksburg in 1863 by marching and banging pots. Courtesy of the Newark (New Jersey) Museum.

speeches, went to view battlefield panoramas, and raised money for the troops. Many children collected books for soldiers and participated in fundraising events (know as "sanitary fairs") during the war's last two years to support soldiers' aid societies, soldiers' homes, and hospitals. Northern girls raised money and collected supplies for Union troops by selling handicrafts, foods, and even kisses. Some knitted mittens and rolled bandages for soldiers. Clara Lenroot remembered scraping "away at the linen, making fluffy piles of the soft lint" used to pack soldier's wounds.[23]

Little Women, Louisa May Alcott's tale of four girls growing up in Civil War New England, remains the classic depiction of how middle-class girls were transformed by the war into responsible adults. Its portrait of the headstrong Jo, beautiful Meg, shy Beth, and temperamental Amy, and their struggle to cope with genteel wartime poverty, provided generations with insight into what it was like to grow up during the Civil War, separated from one's father. In real life, too, girls' lives were shaken by war and forced into early maturity. Emma Le Conte, the daughter of a Columbia, South Carolina, chemistry professor, declared that the war left her feeling dreadfully depressed. "It commenced when I was thirteen," she wrote, "and I am now seventeen and no prospect yet of its ending. No pleasure, no enjoyment—nothing . . . but the stern realities of life." Compared with other South Carolina families, hers was doing well when they ate two meals a day, including a dinner consisting of a small piece of beef, some cornbread, potatoes, and hominy. But as the war dragged on, her family's situation deteriorated. Their diet consisted of rancid salt pork and stringy beef. She had to knit her own stockings and wear homespun undergarments. The situation became so stressful that she found herself unable to read. Nevertheless, she remained convinced of the righteousness of the Confederate cause, and rejoiced in President Lincoln's assassination. "Hurrah!" she wrote. "Old Abe has been assassinated! It may be abstractly wrong to be so jubilant, but I just can't help it . . . We have suffered till we feel savage."[24]

Far from weakening family bonds, wartime separation intensified many fathers' commitment to their children. James Garfield, the future president, worried that his daughter would forget him, asked his wife to ensure that her memory of "papa, papa" not fade away. "Have her say it, so that when I come she may know to call me." Joshua Chamberlain, a hero at Gettysburg who later received Robert E. Lee's formal surrender at Appomattox, was much more cautious. "If I return," he wrote, "they will soon relearn to love me. If not, so much is spared them." Soldiers' letters to their wives and children abounded with paternal advice about children's diet, medical care, dress, and education. In an 1862 letter to his son, Confederate Major General Mansfield Lovell expressed pleasure that his son's arithmetical skills were improving: "You do not take to it easily or naturally and for that reason will have to apply yourself more studiously, than you would to anything that you learned without trouble." "Write me as often as you wish," he continued. "It will help to improve you in writing in expressing your thoughts."[25]

Especially striking are the number of soldiers' letters that discuss politics with their children. During the Civil War, soldiers were driven to fight not simply by loyalty to fellow members of their unit or fear of disgracing themselves in the eyes of their community, but by deeply held political and moral beliefs, which they communicated to their children. In an 1864 letter to his daughter Loula, Tobias Gibson, an ardent Confederate, complained that "American ideas of liberty have totally changed" since the Union army of occupation had arrived in Louisiana. "As far as I know the white children are to grow up in ignorance or mix in the same cabin with the Negro with the same Yankee Marm for the teacher!" But many letters were much more personal. Twenty-two-year-old Henry Abbott wrote his five-year-old brother that "when you get mad & begin to cry, it makes the rebel bullets come a good deal nearer to me." Henry was killed in battle in 1864. In a letter to her father, sixteen-year-old Maria Lewis of Ebensburg, Pennsylvania, wrote: "O papy should eny thing happen I know it would kill mammy and when I was sick I was so afraid I would die and not get to see you but I am spared and hope to see you again." Her father, Captain Andrew Lewis of the 40th Pennsylvania Regiment, died on July 2, 1862, near Richmond, Virginia.[26]

In an 1884 address, Oliver Wendell Holmes Jr., who was twenty when the Civil War began, and twice seriously wounded in battle, believed that his generation had "been set apart by its experience. Through our great good fortune, in our youth our hearts were touched with fire." The Civil War had a profound and lasting impact on American culture and society, and the children who grew up during the war learned lessons that they carried into the postwar years. Among many future intellectuals and reformers, the war bred a contempt for softness and sentimentality and a deep distrust of political ideologies. Wartime experience encouraged an emphasis on organization and professionalism that was evident in postwar efforts to care for orphans and the children of the poor. The experience of the Civil War also fueled a search for moral equivalents to war, including an emphasis on competitive sports and the strenuous life, which had a powerful impact on postwar middle-class boyhood. One group, the children of abolitionists, perpetuated prewar idealism by continuing to work for racial justice. These descendants of the original abolitionists took a leading role in postwar efforts to establish schools and colleges for African Americans, the struggle against lynching, and the founding of the National Association for the Advancement of Colored People in 1909.[27]

In the South, defeat nurtured nostalgia for the "Lost Cause" and the social order that children's fathers and older brothers had fought to defend. At the war's end, Emma Le Conte lamented: "For four years there has been throughout this broad land little else than the anguish of anxiety—the misery of dear ones sacrificed—for *nothing!*" But later the view that the war had been a waste gave way to a far different outlook. Edwin H. McCaleb, who became a Confederate officer when he was only seventeen, embodied the attitudes that shaped the white southern response to Reconstruction. He deplored the assassination of President Lincoln but also deeply resented any attempts by the North to promote racial equality. "We would gladly substitute white for slave labor," he wrote in 1865, "but we can never regard the Negro our equal either intellectually or socially."[28]

After northern Republicans seized control of Reconstruction from President Andrew Johnson, denied representatives from the former Confederate states their congressional seats, and wrote the Fourteenth and Fifteenth Amendments to the Constitution, guaranteeing African Americans equal protection of the laws and giving black men the vote, many young southern whites responded with violence. Having endured wartime hardship and a postwar sense of powerlessness, they sought to reassert their white supremacist racial ideology. Organizations such as the Sons of the Confederacy and the United Daughters of the Confederacy, which arose after the war, expressed reverence for the sacrifices of the Civil War generation and took the position that sectional reunion required the North to allow the South's "natural" leaders to solve the region's racial problems without outside interference. Efforts to segregate, disenfranchise, and control the South's black population through legislation and violence were part of the war's legacy to the younger generation, which venerated its Confederate fathers and sought to reassert control over African Americans who had not been raised under slavery.[29]

Perhaps the Civil War's greatest impact on children was on family life. Like the American Revolution, the Civil War produced huge numbers of orphans and impoverished fatherless families. In Boston in 1865 an estimated 6,000 vagrant children lived on the streets; in New York the figure reached 30,000. More than 100 bodies of newborn children were found in empty barrels or in the rivers in New York each month. By the late 1860s charitable societies were caring for more than 12,000 dependent children in New York City alone. To cope with the worsening problem of dependent children, eight states opened institutions to care for dead soldiers' orphans in 1865 and 1866, and a decade after the war, Pennsylvania subsidized the care of more than 8,000 soldiers' orphans. Conditions in these institutions were horrendous. In Illinois's Soldiers' Orphans' Home, which had only two bathrooms and no playground or infirmary, a three-year-old was scalded to death when older children were placed in charge of the baths.[30]

Many fathers returned home to discover that their children did not recognize them. To five-year-old Hamlin Garland, his father seemed like "only a strange man with big eyes and [a] care-worn face." Some men, socialized to a soldier's life, found it difficult to readjust to domesticity. One boy later recalled: "My father brought back from two years' campaigning . . . the temper and habit of a soldier." Noting that "the moments of tenderness were few," he said that he and his siblings soon learned "that the soldier's promise of punishment was swift and precise in its fulfillment."[31]

In a reaction to wartime disruptions, postwar parents strengthened and intensified family bonds. Middle-class parents responded to the war's traumas through an intensified commitment to a protected, prolonged childhood. Parents who had been rushed to adulthood sought to provide their offspring with a sheltered childhood. They not only kept their children home longer than in the past, but also emphasized the idea of insulating children from the harsher realities of adult life. But the war also altered—and diminished—the father's role in the family. While they remained authority figures of last resort, postwar fathers were more disengaged from family life than their antebellum counterparts and more likely to participate in activities outside the home, such as fraternal orders and men's clubs. The war itself may have contributed to this reorientation by intensifying the mother-child dyad even as it drew many men outside the home. For many men, the military had promoted male bonding, while for many women, the experience of managing homes on their home encouraged them to assert new authority over the family in the postwar years.[32]

Laboring Children

LUCY LARCOM, the ninth child in a family of ten, was eleven when she went to work in a Lowell, Massachusetts, textile mill in 1836. Her father, a sea captain, had died a year earlier, and Lucy's mother, a boardinghouse proprietor, was barely able to support the family. Lucy felt "it would be a pleasure to feel that I was not a trouble or burden or expense to anyone," so she and an older sister applied to be mill girls. The mill had one job available; because Lucy was taller than her sister, she received the job.[1]

Initially Lucy enjoyed the sense of independence and peer-group companionship she experienced in the mill. She and half a dozen girls changed the bobbins on the machines every three-quarters of an hour, and spent the rest of the time frolicking amid the machinery, "teasing and talking to the older girls, or entertaining ourselves with games and stories in a corner, or exploring" the mill's mysteries. Soon, however, she felt frustrated by the low pay (two dollars for a week's work), the long hours (from five o'clock in the morning till seven at night, with a half-hour for breakfast and dinner, six days a week), and the abysmal working conditions (the windows nailed shut, the dim light, the dust and fabric fibers that filled the air). Above all, she complained about the lack of educational opportunities, the noise, and routine. "The buzzing and hissing whizzing of the pulleys and rollers and spindles and flyers," she later recalled, "often grew tiresome . . . When you do the same things twenty times—a hundred times a day—it is so dull!" She remained in the mill for ten years, then left for Illinois with a married sister.[2]

Capitalist expansion and growth carried far-reaching consequences for children's lives. For the urban middle class, increasing economic affluence allowed parents to provide an extended, protected childhood; but for the laboring classes, a sheltered childhood was impossible. The demands of a market economy made their children indispensable economic resources, whose labor could be exploited in new ways. Unlike their middle-class counterparts, children in laboring families were expected to repay their parents' sacrifices by contributing to the family economy. These children worked not because their parents were heartless, but because their labor was essential to their family's survival.

The wrenching social and economic changes of the nineteenth century—the explosive growth of cities and industry, the rapid movement into the trans-Mississippi West, the sharp increase in foreign immigration, and the expansion of commercial agriculture and tenant farming—produced patterns of schooling, play, and work that differed dramatically by class, ethnicity, gender, race, and region. Indeed, at no point in American history was childhood as diverse as it was in the mid and late nineteenth century. The experiences of Lucy Larcom and two other girls—Lai Chow and Ann McNabb—offer useful examples. Lai Chow was only twelve years old when she was sold by her family in China and smuggled along with two dozen other young girls in crates marked "dishware" on a vessel bound for San Francisco, where she was forced into prostitution. Ann McNabb, who migrated from Ireland to Philadelphia in the 1860s, worked as a live-in cook. Yet these girls' diverse experiences were the product of interconnected economic developments. The early stages of industrialization generated a voracious demand for child labor at the same time that it disrupted rural household industries, stimulating a massive migration from farms and rural villages in Europe and the eastern United States to rapidly growing cities and factory towns. Growing middle-class affluence created intense demand for domestic servants, most of whom were teenaged or even younger. Meanwhile the growth of an integrated national market propelled hundreds of thousands of migrants—including 400,000 pioneers and more than a quarter-million Chinese immigrants—to the Far West.[3]

Several shared realities cut across the boundaries of class, ethnicity, gender, or region, especially a high incidence of child mortality. As late as 1895, 18 percent of children—one in six—died before their fifth birthday. While mortality was greatest among the poor, most affluent families with five or six children experienced the death of at least one child. Another commonality was heavily gendered expectations for sons and daughters. Girls were much more likely to be sheltered in the house, to take part in housework, and to hand over all their earnings to their parents, while boys were more likely to be encouraged to move into the outside world and explore its possibilities. But regional and especially class differences remained the defining feature of family life, work, schooling, and play in the United States throughout the century. It was not until the mid-twentieth century that educators and self-described "child savers" succeeded in universalizing the middle-class norm of an extended, protected childhood.[4]

During the nineteenth century, only a small minority of children experienced the middle-class ideal of maturation taking place gradually, in carefully calibrated steps, within institutions segregated from adult society. The vast majority of families living in urban working-class neighborhoods, in mill and mining towns, and in the rural Northeast, South, Midwest, and Far West continued to rely heavily on children's labor and earnings. On farms, children as young as five or six pulled weeds and chased birds and cattle away from crops. By the time they reached eight, many tended livestock, milked cows, churned butter, fed chickens, collected eggs, hauled water, scrubbed laundry, and harvested crops. In urban areas, working-class children ran errands, scavenged, participated in street trades, or took part in outwork, forms of manufacturing that took place in the home.

As for schooling, its amount varied starkly by ethnicity, social class, and geographic location. While the amount of grammar school education increased sharply for all groups—with enrollment reaching half of all young people five to nineteen in 1850 and almost 60 percent in 1870—enrollment was much higher in the Northeast, Midwest, and Far West than in the South, where fewer than half of all children attended school as late as 1890. In rural areas the school year was much shorter than elsewhere because of seasonal labor needs. While urban students typically began their education around the age of seven, attended school nine months a year, and completed a year of high school, rural children went to school six months a year for less than five years. Schooling differed not only in length but in content and form. Urban students attended schools with age-graded classrooms, a standardized curriculum, and trained educators, while rural students attended one-room schools containing a wide range of ages with teachers lacking formal preparation. Class and region also heavily influenced the age of school leaving. In increasing numbers, the urban middle class enrolled in high school and remained there until the age of sixteen or seventeen. In contrast, around puberty, farm children went off temporarily to work as hired laborers, while the urban working-class entered regular employment at "apprentice" or "youth" wages.[5]

The settings in which children played varied widely, as did the games they played and the toys they had. By the 1870s middle-class children had a growing number of store-bought, manufactured toys and board games, designed to inculcate moral values and gender norms and prepare boys for future careers. In one popular board game, The Mansion of Happiness, players passed by "Honesty" and "Idleness" before reaching "Happiness." Working-class and farm children, in contrast, played with homemade toys—dolls made from corncobs, balls made from socks, or jacks from corn kernels—and amused themselves not in nurseries or playrooms but in rural fields or city streets. Compared with their urban middle-class counterparts, working-class and farm children enjoyed much less privacy inside the home, but greater freedom from parental oversight outside the home. After 1870 urban middle-class children participated in adult-organized youth groups and team sports, while urban working-class children enjoyed commercial amusements, notably penny arcades, dance halls, and amusement parks.[6]

The expansion of a market economy and the growth of industry had paradoxical effects on children's lives. Middle-class children were excluded from the world of work while the economic value of working-class and farm children expanded and their labor potential became more essential to their family's economic well-being. The earnings of children between the ages of ten and fifteen often amounted to 20 percent of a family's income and spelled the difference between economic well-being and destitution. A teenage son's income frequently exceeded his father's. Accumulating a savings account or purchasing a house required sons and daughters to subordinate their personal wishes to larger family considerations. Key decisions—about the length of schooling or the age of entry into the workforce—were based on family needs rather than individual choice. Among many ethnic groups it was common for daughters to leave school at an early age and enter work so that their brothers could continue their education. It was also customary for a daughter to remain unmarried and to care for younger siblings or aging parents. The cooperative family economy made decisionmaking a by-product of collective needs rather than of individual preferences.

While the Industrial Revolution did not invent child labor, it did make child labor more visible by removing child and teenage workers from domestic settings. The first textile mill in the United States, Samuel Slater's mill in Pawtucket, Rhode Island, which opened in 1790, had a workforce consisting of seven boys and two girls, ages seven to twelve, who operated the factory's seventy-two spindles. Slater soon discovered that children, "constantly employed under the immediate inspection" of a supervisor, could produce three times as much as whole families working without supervision in their own homes. To keep the children alert and awake, Slater whipped them with a leather strap and sprinkled them with water. On Sundays the children attended a special school established by Slater.[7]

During the early phases of industrialization, textile mills and agricultural tool, metal goods, nail, and rubber factories had a ravenous appetite for cheap, tractable teenage laborers. In many mechanized industries, from a quarter to half the workforce was under the age of twenty. Generally child and teenage laborers were hired not by the mill or factory owner, but by a skilled adult worker, who was responsible for their discipline. Child workers were disciplined by ridicule and taunting as well as by physical punishments, including slaps, ear boxing, and whippings.[8]

Even before the rise of the factory system, the significance of child labor had grown. During the late eighteenth century the growth of household industries greatly increased young children's economic value. Merchant capitalists distributed raw materials to individual households, which then manufactured finished goods. Dexter Whittemore, the owner of a country store in rural Fitzwilliam, New Hampshire, distributed palm leaves to local farm families. Family members braided the leaves into hats in exchange for credits on the store's ledgers. For cash-strapped farm families, the opportunity to earn cash was a godsend. The money was used to pay off debts, finance farm improvements, purchase household goods, or send children to school. Domestic industries provided work for thousands of rural children, and the quantity of goods they produced was staggering. In 1809 farm families near Philadelphia produced more than 230,000 yards of cloth for sale, four times the amount produced by the area's textile mills. Massachusetts farm households produced more than 100,000 pairs of shoes—more than all the nation's professional shoemakers combined. After 1820, however, household industries declined and were replaced by manufacturing in city shops and factories.[9]

Apprenticeship, like domestic manufacturing, also diminished. Until the early nineteenth century, apprenticeship was how boys were trained in skilled trades. More than a system of labor, apprenticeship was also a way to deal with potentially disruptive adolescents. Like the system of indentured servitude it resembled, the apprenticeship system provided a foster home for youths in their teens. Compared with its rigidly regulated European counterpart, the American system of apprenticeship was an "anemic institution," providing a much briefer experience. Nevertheless, apprenticeship was a major part of the process of growing up in early America, with apprentices usually living in the master's house under his watchful eye.[10]

Following the American Revolution, however, the apprenticeship system disintegrated as teenagers obtained new opportunities to enter trades. The Revolution itself was partly responsible for the system's demise, as many youths were no longer willing to display the deference that the master-apprentice relationship required. Economic uncertainties contributed as well. Faced by sharp fluctuations in demand for the goods they produced, masters shortened the terms of apprenticeships, preferring simply to hire workers when demand was high. The introduction of labor-saving machinery and an influx of immigrants from Europe accelerated the institution's demise. In trades such as printing, mechanization produced a glut of skilled artisans, and "slop shops" offered employment to young men with a minimum of skills. By the 1850s most apprentices were no more than semiskilled workers or machine tenders. Meanwhile, manuals, printed guides, and lectures and demonstrations at mechanics' institutes allowed young men to learn craft skills on their own without going through a formal apprenticeship.[11]

By the mid-nineteenth century, apprenticeship resembled most other employment relationships. Instead of living in a master's home, apprentices received cash wages and resided in boardinghouses in distinct working-class neighborhoods. The paternalistic view of a master who supervised behavior and provided for an apprentice's welfare was replaced by a new conception of labor as a commodity that could be acquired or disposed of according to the laws of supply and demand. No longer did masters advertise in newspapers for the return of runaway apprentices; instead they simply hired new employees. As the apprenticeship system declined, male teenagers were pushed out of the skilled trades and into unskilled labor. In Newark, New Jersey, the proportion of white males between the ages of fifteen and twenty in the skilled trades fell by over a third, while the proportion who were jobless or in school rose from 7 to 27 percent. In the future, teenage workers would be used primarily as helpers, messengers, or unskilled laborers.[12]

As the close, highly ritualized master-apprenticeship bonds disappeared, advice books, self-help manuals, mechanics' institutes, apprentice libraries, and lyceums proliferated to help young men navigate the difficult transition away from home during the teen years and the increasing choices, opportunities, and possible roadblocks they faced. Apprenticeship's decline also encouraged educational reformers to devise the modern high school as an instrument to fill the void left by the end of this system of labor.[13]

The demise of apprenticeship coincided with a shift in authority relations within the working-class family. In certain respects the apprenticeship system had reinforced paternal power, by giving a father a formal say in a son's career choice. Under common law, a son remained under his father's control until the age of twenty-one. Fathers had a legal right to their sons' earnings and had the power of consent over their sons' decision to leave an apprenticeship and assume a new one. By the mid-nineteenth century, increasing numbers of sons were contesting their father's authority to dictate their choice of a career. At the same time a growing number of the sons of skilled laborers and prosperous commercial farmers, convinced that apprenticeships were no longer a secure route to a promising career, were staying at home longer and attending school beyond the middle elementary grades in order to pick up the skills necessary to become a clerk or a broker. For these young men, ties between parents and children were intensified and prolonged, yet paternal authority was giving way to maternal counseling and peer companionship.[14]

The breakdown of the apprenticeship system produced a class division tied to decisions made at puberty. Especially after the economic panic of 1837, young men either entered a factory between the ages of twelve and fourteen, a choice that doomed them to a life of unskilled or semiskilled labor, or remained in school into their mid-teens before entering a clerkship or another salaried position in their late teens or early twenties. Those who pursued school had the care and shelter of the middle-class home. Those who went to work in factories developed a very different and distinctive urban working-class youth culture. Cash incomes made possible the advent of young "dandies," who patronized theaters and music halls, paraded through city streets in ostentatious dress, and promenaded with young women. Barber shops, boardinghouses, firehouses, saloons, and theaters provided settings where young working-class men could socialize. Prizefights, horse races, and politics played an important role in the new peer culture. In the early 1850s the bitterly nativist Know Nothing political party overwhelming drew its most ardent supporters from these same youths in their teens and twenties.[15]

Many young unskilled laborers and factory operatives spent their free time congregating on street corners, committing petty theft, or seeking entertainment in bowling alleys, tippling shops, gaming houses, and theaters. Seeking a sense of belonging, identity, and excitement, they were particularly likely to join volunteer fire companies that allowed them to don hats, badges, and uniforms, and fight fires at close range, sports teams, or youth gangs, which engaged in the ethnic, racial, and religious rioting that plagued mid-nineteenth-century cities. In the deadliest riot of the nineteenth century, the New York City Draft Riots of 1863, most of those arrested were under twenty-one.[16]

Whatever the gains in personal freedom and flexibility that came with apprenticeship's demise, there were also losses. Apprenticeship had allowed young men to gain self-respect, independence, competence, and maturity while remaining connected to adults who had an obligation to them. It provided a balance between youthful independence and adult mentoring that has since been lost. The initiation rites, parades, and other rituals that signaled a young person's entrance into a particular trade and the world of adulthood were swept away. Instead urban adolescents either attended high school and remained in the parental home or else were cast adrift to make their way as best they could. Some—like the young Samuel Clemens, who arranged informal apprenticeships as a printer and later as a riverboat pilot—gradually found their way to a successful adulthood. But many others did not; caught in the tide of a modern market economy, they became delinquents, joined gangs, or drifted into a life of poverty and unskilled labor, joining America's growing underclass of the chronically unemployed or underemployed.[17]

The same economic developments that transformed the experience of teenage males also drastically altered the lives of young working-class women. For young women, the early stages of the Industrial Revolution increased employment opportunities beyond the traditional options of domestic service and clothesmaking. Young unmarried women made up a majority of the workforce in cotton textile mills and a substantial minority of workers in factories manufacturing ready-made clothing, furs, hats, shoes, and umbrellas. Some, like Lucy Larcom, found the new opportunities exhilarating. Unlike farm work or domestic service, employment in a mill offered female companionship and an independent income. Wages (which could be as little as $1.45 a week) were twice what a young woman could make as a seamstress, tailor, or schoolteacher, and mill girls were able to spend their free time attending lectures, participating in sewing groups and literary improvement circles, and producing their own publications such as the *Lowell Offering*. What made mill work tolerable was the fact that employment was a temporary expedient before marriage. Most worked in the mills fewer than four years and frequently interrupted their stints in the mill for several months at a time with trips back home.[18]

By the 1830s, however, increasing competition caused deteriorating working conditions that drove native-born girls out of the mills. Employers cut wages, lengthened the workday, and required mill workers to tend four looms instead of two. Hannah Borden, a young Fall River, Massachusetts, textile worker, was required to have her looms running at five in the morning. She was given an hour for breakfast and half an hour for lunch. Her workday ended at half past seven, fourteen and a half hours after it had begun. For a six-day work week she received between $2.50 and $3.50. Such labor was destructive of health and well-being. The mill girls militantly protested the wage cuts and worsening work environment. In 1834 and again in 1836, they went on strike. Eleven-year-old Harriet Hanson described her role in the 1836 walkout: "When the day came on which the girls were to turn out . . . the girls in my room stood irresolute, uncertain what to do . . . I, who began to think they would not go out, after all their talk, became impatient, and started on ahead, saying . . . 'I don't care what you do, I am going to turn out whether anyone else does or not.'" As a result of her participation in the strike, Harriet's mother, a widow who ran a boardinghouse in Lowell, was fired. She was told: "You could not prevent the older girls from turning out, but your daughter is a child and her you could control." During the 1840s fewer young native-born women were willing to work in the mills. "Slavers"—long, black wagons that crisscrossed the Vermont and New Hampshire countryside in search of mill hands—arrived empty in Rhode Island and Massachusetts mill towns. Increasingly they were replaced with a new class of permanent factory operatives, immigrant women from Ireland.[19]

More common than factory employment for teenage girls was domestic service. Servants, who had previously been regarded as quasi-family members and been referred to as "help," were now considered paid employees. A servant's life was onerous and burdensome. Live-in servants were on call six and a half or even seven days a week. Their day began at half past four or five in the morning, and their responsibilities included cooking and serving meals, washing up, trimming and filling lamps, cleaning, placing coal and wood in fireplaces and stoves, cleaning, doing laundry, and caring for children. Even though domestic service paid better than factory work and the physical conditions were far superior, young women considered household service the most demeaning form of labor because of the psychological abuse and often the sexual abuse.[20]

In rapidly growing urban areas, many young working-class women took on outwork, manufacturing shoes, clothing, or other household items inside their own home or a boardinghouse. By the 1830s a highly visible group of young women used their earnings to participate in the expanding urban working-class youth culture. The "Bowery gal" challenged Victorian notions of propriety by promenading down city streets wearing flashy clothes. But most urban working-class young women, especially the daughters of skilled workers, eschewed fancy clothes and gave their wages to their parents. They worked at home or stayed in school in a working-class version of domesticity.

In the poorest families, especially those headed by widows or single mothers, children's ability to earn their keep provided the indispensable margin of subsistence. They toted water up stairs, helped out with cooking, cleaning, and laundry, and ran errands. Poor families living in cellars or garrets also depended on children to perform various kinds of outwork. Young children cut and glued boxes, dipped matchsticks, or sewed seams and buttons. They also carried goods back and forth to a shop. Poor children too young for wage work scavenged for wood or coal and scoured the docks for tea, coffee, sugar, flour, and other goods that could be used at home. They hawked newspapers, held horses, blackened boots, and even caught butterflies for canary growers. Poor children participated in the informal economy, selling fruit or matches on street corners and scrub brushes and other household goods door-to-door, or peddling loose cotton, old rope, shreds of canvas and rags, bits of hardware, and bottles and broken glass to junk dealers and to papermakers, foundries, and glassmakers.[21]

Scavenging produced considerable dismay among public authorities, who regarded it as a form of petty theft. Most of the child scavengers came from single-parent homes that depended on their labor and expected children to earn their keep. "Of the children brought before me for pilfering," wrote a police magistrate in 1830, "nine out of ten are those whose fathers are dead, and who live with their mothers, and are employed in this way." When children refused to contribute to the family economy, poorer parents turned to public authorities for help. William Codman's mother placed her son in a New York asylum in 1853 "because he would not work, and she could not support him." Working-class families held a very different view of childhood from the middle class. Far less sentimental in their conception of childhood, they did not believe that parents should make economic sacrifices for their children without reciprocal labor from their offspring.[22]

During the nineteenth century an increasing proportion of working-class children were the daughters and sons of immigrants. Many came from Germany, Ireland, and Scandinavia, pushed from their homelands by famine, political unrest, and the destruction of traditional handicrafts by factory enterprise. In addition, 288,000 Chinese immigrants arrived in the United States between 1854 and 1883. Although most immigrants were adult males, one group—Irish Catholics—included significant numbers of children and teens, many of whom arrived in the United States alone.

Fifteen-year-old Diarmuid O'Donovan Rossa of County Cork was one of the many Irish children to suffer grievously from the potato famine. In

1846 he and a brother dug "over two hundred yards of a piece of a ridge, and all the potatoes I could pick . . . would not fill a skillet. They were no larger than marbles." The *Illustrated London News* described conditions in Diarmuid's county. Whole families subsisted on wild weeds, and "15,000 persons . . . are destitute; of this 5000 are entirely dependent on casual charity . . . The deaths . . . now average 25 daily!!" Altogether around 150,000 people in County Cork died during the famine years 1845–1847, including Diarmuid's father. Evicted from their small farm, Diarmuid's mother, sister, and two brothers emigrated to Philadelphia. Only Diarmuid, now seventeen, remained. "I supposed they thought I was old enough to take care of myself," he later said. His family's departure remained etched in his memory. "The cry of the weeping and wailing of that day rings in my ears still," he recalled.[23]

During the summer of 1845 a "blight of unusual character" devastated Ireland's potato crop, the basic staple in the Irish diet. A few days after potatoes were dug from the ground, they turned into a slimy, decaying, blackish "mass of rottenness." Expert panels, convened to investigate the blight's cause, suggested that it was a result of "static electricity" or the smoke that billowed from railroad locomotives or "mortiferous vapours" rising from underground volcanoes. In fact the cause was a fungus that had traveled from America to Ireland. In 1846 the potato crop was just one-fifth as large as it had been two years earlier. Half a million Irish were evicted from their cottages, and "famine fever"—dysentery, typhus, and infestations of lice—soon spread through the Irish countryside. Observers reported seeing children crying with pain and looking "like skeletons, their features sharpened with hunger and their limbs wasted, so that there was little left but bones, their hands and arms." Masses of bodies were buried without coffins, a few inches below the soil.[24]

Over the next five years, 750,000 Irish died, and approximately a million Irish migrated to the United States. Freighters offered fares as low as $17 to $20 between Liverpool and Boston—fares subsidized by English landlords eager to be rid of the starving peasants. The journey to the United States took five to ten weeks, and conditions aboard the "famine ships" were abominable. Steerage compartments were only about five feet high and contained two tiers of bunks, with each berth holding at least four people. On one vessel, only a pound of meal or bread was allotted as a daily ration for each adult, half a pound for each child under the age of fourteen, and a third of a pound for those under seven years, along with a pint of water. As many as 10 percent of the emigrants perished while still at sea. In 1847, 40,000 (or 20 percent) of those who set out from Ireland died along the way. "If crosses and tombs could be erected on water," wrote the U.S. commissioner for emigration, "the whole route of the emigrant vessels from Europe to America would long since have assumed the appearance of a crowded cemetery."[25]

Lacking the money to move elsewhere, most Irish immigrants remained near the port cities where they landed. Often whole families crowded into a single room. Nativist Protestant reformers stigmatized immigrant family life as disorganized, denouncing the prevalence of drinking, youth gangs, domestic violence, and the number of children institutionalized in almshouses, houses of refuge, and reformatories. In fact the biggest contributor to family instability among Irish immigrants was the high death rate among unskilled Irish Catholic workers. "It is well established," one Irish American noted, "that the average length of life of the emigrant after landing here is six years; and many insist it is much less." Harsh outdoor labor, reported another observer, meant that "a man who labours steadily for 10 to 12 years in America is of very little use afterwards."[26]

Many young people arrived in America by themselves and took whatever jobs were available. Some girls, like Ann McNabb, who migrated to Philadelphia, became live-in household servants, an occupation that native-born girls shunned. As late as 1900, three-fifths of all Irish-born women in the United States were domestic servants. Other young Irish women did piecework in factories or their own apartments, making nine shirts a week for a total of about ninety cents. In the second generation, many became schoolteachers or nurses, while many boys worked as laborers, constructing streets or canals or sewers, or toiling on the docks. Al Smith, the grandson of an Irish immigrant, was born in 1873 in Hell's Kitchen on New York's Lower East Side. He took his first job selling newspapers when he was eleven. After his father's death when he was thirteen, he left school and took a series of jobs, including unloading barrels of fish at New York's Fulton Fish Market, where his days began at three in the morning.[27]

Migration to America profoundly altered Irish families. For the first and second generations of immigrants, the stresses of emigration, poverty, and unskilled labor sometimes resulted in severe family tension and disruption, weakening the role of the father and husband and widening the division between male and female spheres. Widowhood and single-parent female-headed households were much more common in the United States than in Ireland as a result of the high male mortality rate, frequent on-the-job accidents, and desertion. One son whose father deserted his family was the dramatist Eugene O'Neill, and as a result his "family always was ill-fed and poorly-clad." Single-parent families were more common among the Irish than any nineteenth-century ethnic group except African Americans. Migration enhanced sons' economic significance and gave daughters greater responsibilities and independence.[28]

The childhood of Anne Sullivan, the "miracle worker" who gained international renown as Helen Keller's teacher, illustrates the problems of poverty and family instability in extreme form. Born to desperately poor and troubled immigrant parents in 1866, she had a father with a drinking problem and a mother suffering from tuberculosis. At the age of five Anne contracted trachoma, an eye disease associated with filthy living conditions. When she was eight, Anne's mother died. A sister and brother were sent to live with relatives, while Anne remained home to care for her father. When she was ten, her father deserted Anne, and she and her brother were placed in the Massachusetts almshouse at Tewksbury, where her brother died of tuberculosis. Anne's experience underscored the stresses and family tensions that migration imposed on many children of immigrants.[29]

During the nineteenth century, as many families made their livelihoods from mining coal or minerals from the earth as worked in the nation's iron and steel mills. In eastern Pennsylvania alone, mining engaged more than 100,000 families. After his family emigrated from Lithuania to the coalfields near Scranton, Pennsylvania, nine-year-old Joseph Miliauska earned seventy cents for a ten-hour day as a breaker boy, separating coal from the slate and rocks. If his boss caught a boy slipping up and letting slate pass by, Joseph recalled, "you'd get it in the back with a broom."[30]

Coalmining families endured a particularly harsh existence. Employment was grueling, dangerous, and erratic, and annual earnings were extremely low. At the end of the nineteenth century, when one state survey estimated that it took a yearly income of $754 to provide food, clothing, and shelter for a family of five, 60 percent of the adult miners in eastern Pennsylvania anthracite fields earned less than $450. To supplement the father's income, sons entered the mines as soon as they were physically able. Boys as young as nine or ten started out as door boys, driver boys, or breaker boys. Door boys sat for hours in the darkness of the mine to open and shut the doors that permitted the mule-drawn mine cars to pass. Driver boys dumped coal from the cars, after which it descended through processing machines to the breaker boys, who cleaned and inspected it and separated rocks and slate from the coal. Breaker boys covered their mouths with handkerchiefs to keep out the coal dust, but they were forbidden to wear gloves, even in the coldest weather, because doing so impaired their finger movement and sense of touch. "If we were discovered

"Breaker boys," who separated slate and impurities from coal, stand outside a
Pennsylvania coal mine in 1911. Courtesy of the National Archives.

wearing gloves," remembered one breaker boy, "the boss would strike
our knuckles with a long stick he carried." As a result, for the first few
weeks the sulfur on the coal irritated the boys' skin and caused their
fingers to swell, crack open, and bleed, causing a condition called "red
tips." Until their fingers hardened, mothers applied goose grease to their
sons' fingers every night.[31]

The heavy reliance on child labor and wages meant that few boys could
stay in school very long. Most boys had no more than five years of formal
education, and half were out of school by their twelfth birthday. Coalmin-
ers' daughters typically assisted their mothers in such tasks as manufacturing handicrafts or taking in laundry or boarders or gardening. As late
as 1924, over half of West Virginia's mining families planted gardens and
kept cows, pigs, and poultry. "Miners couldn't always depend upon the
mine," one later recalled; "therefore we would have to raise a garden to
make sure we always ate."[32]

Much as industrialization generated enormous demand for unskilled
child labor in mills and mines, and growing middle-class affluence created
a growing hunger for household servants, the commercialization of agriculture made children's farm labor more valuable than ever before. The

lure of commercial agriculture led some 400,000 pioneering families to venture westward to settle in California, Oregon, and the Great Plains. Nancy Kelsey was eighteen years old and already a mother when she migrated westward on the first wagon train to California in 1841. "We were then out of provisions, having killed and eaten all our cattle," she recalled. "I walked barefeeted until my feet were blistered and lived on roasted acorns for two days." This first party of sixty-nine pioneers endured almost inconceivable hardships. They were forced to abandon their wagons and eat their pack animals, "half roasted, dripping with blood."[33]

It took Americans a century and a half to expand as far west as the Appalachian Mountains, a few hundred miles from the Atlantic coast. It took another fifty years to push the frontier to the Mississippi River. By 1830, fewer than 100,000 pioneers had crossed the Mississippi. But during the 1840s, tens of thousands of Americans ventured beyond the Mississippi, and by 1850 they had pushed the edge of settlement to California and the Oregon country of the Pacific Northwest. The journey west was a tremendous test of human endurance. Thirteen-year-old Mary Murphy lost her mother and five other relatives to starvation. "I hope I shall not

On the overland trail, sex and age roles blurred as girls and boys cared for younger children, tended animals, and gathered buffalo chips for fuel. Courtesy of the Denver Public Library.

live long, for I am tired of this troublesome world and want to go to my mother," she wrote. That was in 1847. Murphy was a survivor of the infamous Donner party, which became snowbound in the Sierra Nevada and resorted to cannibalism to survive.[34]

Mary Goble lost her mother, two sisters, and a brother along the overland trail to Utah. Born in Brighton, England, she was twelve years old in 1855 when her parents joined the Church of Latter-Day Saints and decided to sell everything they owned and move to the Great Salt Lake. From Liverpool they made a six-week voyage to Boston with 900 other new Mormons, then traveled by train to Iowa City, where they began the thousand-mile trek to Utah. Along the way, they went days without fresh water and subsisted on gruel made out of a quarter-pound of flour a day. The pioneers covered between fifteen and twenty-five miles each day, but they had departed too late in the summer and were overtaken by severe snowstorms. Once, Mary got lost in the snow, and when she was finally found (at eleven at night) she had suffered such severe frostbite that a doctor had to amputate her toes.[35]

Some 40,000 children faced blizzards, desert heat, massacres and epidemics on the way west between 1841 and 1865. On the overland trail, pioneer children bore responsibilities that were crucial to their families' survival. They cared for livestock, hunted and fished, cooked, stood guard, scouted for camping spots, nursed the sick and injured, and buried the dead. Girls got up before dawn and collected wood and buffalo chips (animal dung used for fuel), hauled water, kindled campfires, kneaded dough, and milked cows. They also tended younger children. On the westward trail, it proved impossible to maintain a rigid age or sexual division of labor. Boys and girls drove or maintained wagons and livestock, stood guard duty, and hunted buffalo and antelope for extra meat. Childhood accidents and diseases were an ever-present danger. Young children fell out of wagons and under wagon wheels.[36]

On the far western frontier, a distinctive form of childhood emerged. A severe shortage of labor blurred age and gender distinctions and invested the young with a great deal of responsibility and autonomy. Today the popular image of a frontier childhood derives, first and foremost, from the eight-volume "Little House on the Prairie" series of books written by Laura Ingalls Wilder in the 1930s and 1940s. Born in 1867 in a log cabin outside Pepin, Wisconsin, sixty miles southeast of Minneapolis, she chronicled a pioneer girlhood in the upper Midwest during the 1870s and 1880s, based on her family's experiences as they moved from Pepin to Burr Oak in northeastern Iowa; Spring Valley and Walnut Grove, Minnesota; and De Smet in Dakota Territory. Altogether her family moved seven times in ten years, with each move creating new problems for the family.[37]

Wilder's tales describe the joys and hardships of a frontier childhood on the midwestern plains—a sister who contracted scarlet fever and was left blind, a grasshopper plague that devoured the family's crops, her father fiddling his daughters to sleep, and receiving Christmas stockings filled with peppermint candy and shiny new pennies. The books helped imprint a number of lasting images of a frontier life in the American imagination: of a sod house, scraped out of the prairie, with a stovepipe running through the hay and reed roof; of prairie fires; of town socials and spelling bees and one-room schoolhouses. Even as a young child Laura, like other frontier children, was expected to help with cleaning, childcare, tending animals, and tending the crop. As she grew older, she served as a maid and waitress in a failing hotel, and sewed shirts in town in order to contribute cash to the family economy. Although she hadn't finished high school, she took her first teaching job at the age of fifteen. Her schoolhouse was a crude shanty, and many of the students were bigger and older than she was.

This one-room schoolhouse on the Great Plains was constructed of strips of sod. Courtesy of the National Archives.

The frontier could not have been settled without children's labor. They provided game and wild plants for their families' tables as well as the fuel to cook their food. They cut hay, herded cattle and sheep, burned brush, gathered eggs, and churned butter. They also broke sod, planted, weeded, and harvested. Farmers on the plains could not afford to delay their offspring's entry into the family workforce. A Kansas father bragged that his two-year-old son could "fetch up cows out of the stock fields, or oxen, carry in stove wood and climb in the corn crib and feed the hogs and go on errands." Improved plows and other farm machinery allowed young sons and daughters to assist with plowing, planting, and harvesting. An Oklahoma father gave each of his children a knife to hack the soil and "make a seed bed for a garden and the first crop of kaffir corn." Fannie Eisele was only ten years old when she began to plow her family's Oklahoma fields, and Helen Brock at fifteen was branding calves and erecting fences.[38]

For children who lived near western mining towns, there were many opportunities to earn spare change. Mary Ronan sold edible weeds in Virginia City for a dollar and a half a bucketful, while Martha Collins and her brother made $800 in a year from the sale of butter, bacon, and wild game. Others earned money by cooking, cleaning, or doing odd jobs. Boys of twelve or thirteen also found regular employment outside the home. William Hedges, the son of a Helena, Montana, attorney, was just thirteen years old when he became head of the town's public library; at the same age Walter Smith of Tellurium, Colorado, was swinging a sledgehammer in mine tunnels.[39]

Touring the Rockies in 1873, an English traveler, Isabella Bird, remarked: "One of the most painful things in the Western States and Territories is the extinction of childhood. I have never seen any children, only debased imitations of men and women, cankered by greed and selfishness, and asserting and gaining complete independence of their parents at ten years old." It was easy to find evidence to substantiate the claim that a sheltered childhood was extinguished on the frontier. A child in Creede, Colorado, began smoking cigarettes at the age of five and took up a pipe at six. A twelve-year-old plowed his family farm. A girl was nine when she broke her first horse; another was ten when she broke the sod on her family's west Texas homestead. William Cody, later Buffalo Bill, was fourteen when he rode for the Pony Express. On the western frontier, precocious behavior was not at all unusual.[40]

In contrast to their urban middle-class counterparts, frontier children were not subjected to close supervision in the vast outdoors. Instead they were encouraged to act independently and to assume essential family responsibilities at an early age. An entry in the diary of a twelve-year-old Helena, Montana, girl underscores the degree to which a frontier childhood could be exposed to adult realities: "At two o'clock in the morning a highway Robber was hung on a large pine tree. After breakfast we went to see him. At ten o'clock preaching, at one o'clock a large auction sale of horses and cattle. At two o'clock Sunday school. At three o'clock a foot race. At seven o'clock preaching. The remainder of the time spent by hundreds of miners in gambling and drinking."[41] Meanwhile, schooling on the plains was sporadic and intermittent. As late as 1910, a fourth of the schools in Montana held classes for no more than four months a year; in rural Arizona the school term averaged just 105 days.[42]

Yet if frontier conditions promoted early independence and adultlike responsibilities, adults nonetheless strove to create the institutions considered essential for a proper childhood. One of the first institutions established was a Sunday school, soon followed by an elementary school. Social life in many frontier communities revolved around spelling matches and school programs. Even gamblers sometimes set up play equipment. Yet however romantic a western childhood may seem in retrospect, to many of the children who grew up on the plains, it was a bleak world characterized by loneliness and privation. As an adult, Hamlin Garland would become one of the country's foremost advocates of local color, an indigenous American literature that provided realistic accounts of specific places. His greatest works of fiction, such as *A Son of the Middle Border*, were unflinching looks at the rigors of pioneer life, based on his childhood memories of hardships, frustration, and toil. He described "main-traveled roads" with "a dull little town at one end and a home of toil at the other." Born in a log cabin near La Crosse, Wisconsin, in 1860, Garland grew up in Wisconsin, Iowa, and the Dakota Territory as his parents participated in the nation's westward expansion. In his books he expressed resentment at his father's decision to move the family to remoter and harsher environments in search of a prosperity that never came. He recalled that at the age of eleven he spent seventy days behind a plow all by himself. "It was lonely work . . . There is a certain pathos in the sight of that small boy tugging and kicking at the stubborn turf in the effort to free his plow. Such misfortunes loom large in a lad's horizon." The life he describes was desolate, lonely, and laborious.[43]

Although a frontier childhood encouraged a youth of self-reliance, inner-directedness, and early independence, many western children experienced youths of withering poverty, dispiriting routine, and personal entrapment. Edna Matthews Clifton hated picking cotton on her family's Texas farm. "Sometimes I would lie down on my sack and want to die," she wrote. "Sometimes they would have to pour water over my head to relieve me." A fifteen-year-old girl on a west Texas ranch wrote: "It is so misirably lonely here. I feel buried alive in this slow vally."[44]

The pioneer families that ventured onto the Great Plains went with a strong spirit of optimism. Unfortunately, high hopes were quickly dashed. Of the 400,000 families that took advantage of the Homestead Act to start a farm, fewer than a third managed to "prove up" the land to which they laid claim. During the late nineteenth century drought, grasshoppers, fire, hail, blizzards, and floods devastated farms from Texas to the Dakotas, leaving many families destitute. A Minnesota girl described her family's plight to the state governor: "We have no money now[,] nothing to sell to get any more clothes with as the grasshoppers destroyed all of our crops what few we had for we have not much land broke yet . . . We . . . almost perish here sometimes with the cold."[45] For many children, the western adventure was a nightmare from which they longed to awaken.

The Industrial Revolution had radical effects on children's experiences. For the middle class, growing affluence allowed parents to provide their children a sheltered childhood, free from work responsibilities and devoted to education and play. For working-class, immigrant, and farm children, the growth of industry and the expansion of commercial agriculture increased parents' dependence on child labor. As a result, two divergent conceptions of childhood emerged. One conception, the useful childhood, was based on the premise that all family members, including children, should contribute to a family's support. Rooted in the experience of farm, artisanal, and frontier families, this idea took on heightened significance in an urban and industrial context, where low wages and frequent bouts of unemployment made children's earnings essential for a family's well-being. As a result, many working-class and immigrant parents expected that their economic sacrifices should be matched by sacrifices and labors from their offspring. The other conception was a protected childhood, sheltered from the stresses and demands of the adult world. First adopted by the rapidly expanding urban middle class, this ideal proved highly attractive to working-class and farm families as well. In the late nineteenth century, a central demand of labor unions was the "family wage," which would allow a male breadwinner to support his family without the economic contributions of his wife and children. Meanwhile, in rural areas, the more prosperous farmers began to substitute hired labor for children's labor whenever possible, and in the urban North, African-American parents struggled to keep their children in school and prolonged their children's education despite economic pressures.[46]

It took a concerted struggle lasting more than half a century to ensure that every child had a right to a childhood free from labor and devoted to education. The drive to universalize a sheltered childhood was the result of a determined political struggle by a broad-based coalition that included educators, physicians, psychologists, union leaders, and pioneering feminists, and it required government action in the form of compulsory education laws and restrictions on child labor. Aided by broader technological developments, these reformers, who adopted the name "child-savers," were responsible for one of the most striking social transformations in American history. They succeeded in creating a pattern of childhood—emphasizing prolonged schooling and residence in the parental home—that transcended class, ethnicity, and region.

chapter eight

Save the Child

AMERICANS first discovered the grim realities of child poverty, juvenile delinquency, and child abuse in the nation's cities. As early as the 1790s, philanthropists and reformers were shocked by the sight of a "multitude of half-naked, dirty and leering children" roaming city streets, sleeping in alleyways, picking pockets, and robbing shops. Young girls stood barefoot on street corners, begging for pennies, while small boys picked through garbage scattered in the streets. "Cunning and adroit," they bore no resemblance to the middle-class ideal of children as icons of innocence. Especially appalling was "the female portion of the youngest class, those who have only seen some eight or twelve summers, [who] are addicted to immoralities of the most loathsome descriptions."[1]

As a result of their parents' death or remarriage, poor children frequently shifted from one household to another and sometimes were left with no home at all. In 1827, shortly after her family migrated from Ireland, the parents of twelve-year-old "M. K." died. She was placed as a servant with a distiller's family, where a hired men "made free" with her twice. John Mulligan was ten when his father died. He, too, was placed out, first with a boatman, then with a tailor and an ironmonger; in 1825, when he was fourteen, he was living on New York City's streets. Twice he was arrested for stealing shoes and once for picking pockets. Expected to earn their keep, poor children scavenged on the street and engaged in petty theft. In 1826 a twelve-year-old girl, known by the initials "S. H. L.," assisted her mother by selling stolen soap, needles, pencils, and almanacs. She also had "learnt the trick of getting money from men, with the promise that she would go with them, and afterwards run away." In 1814 an illiterate fourteen-year-old boy, known by the initials "A. B.," helped support his family by picking pockets and stealing fruit, meat, handkerchiefs, shoes, and hats.[2]

In the eighteenth century, destitute and delinquent children had been absorbed into rural and urban households as servants, farm laborers, or apprentices. But with the decline of household industries, the demise of the apprenticeship system, and the growth of factory enterprise, these households were no longer able to absorb sufficient numbers. Juvenile delinquency seemed out of hand and infanticide rampant. In the middle of the century, as many as 150 infants' bodies were found in New York City each month. Something needed to be done. "Save, oh save from impending ruin the miserable neglected little objects that now infest your streets," an anonymous Baltimore writer pleaded in 1820; "take them under your paternal care, and direct their steps in the path of virtue and honesty." Beginning in the 1790s, philanthropists, who came to be known as child-savers, experimented with new strategies to care for indigent and delinquent children, including the establishment of charity schools, Sunday schools, orphan asylums, houses of refuge, and reformatories.[3]

An underlying ambiguity marked these child-saving efforts. They attempted both to protect children from the dangers of urban society and to protect society from dangerous children. Many child-savers were guilty of paternalism, class and racial bias, xenophobia, and double standards regarding gender. They often confused delinquency and neglect with the realities of life under poverty. Reformers proved far too eager to break up the families of the poor, supposedly for the children's own good, but in reality separating the young from their kin and isolating them in a harsh and repressive environment. Fixated on urban problems, the child-savers neglected rural children, who were frequently confined with adults in county poorhouses. Yet for all their limitations and biases, the child-savers were not merely moralistic "social controllers," propounding punitive solutions to the problems of child welfare. A highly disparate group, they included elite philanthropists, evangelical Protestants, benevolent middle-class women, urban missionaries, penologists, amateur and professional charity and youth workers, attorneys, physicians, educators, and social workers with diverse motives and agendas. Furthermore, there was always a dialectic between the child-savers and the people they wanted to help, with poor children and their parents using child-saving institutions for their own purposes. One must balance the myopia of the reformers with their major achievement: a sustained public commitment to children's welfare. The child-savers pioneered innovative and creative approaches to the problems of childhood that should stand as an inspiration and a rebuke to Americans today.[4]

Child-saving evolved in three overlapping phases, each with its own constituency and distinctive approach. In the first phase, stretching from the 1790s through the 1840s, child-savers created congregate institutions to separate children from the corruptions of the public world and provide them with the order and discipline that their families lacked. The use of congregate institutions remained the dominant approach to child-saving throughout the nineteenth century. Only after a profound demographic shift had taken place, sharply reducing the proportion of the population under the age of fifteen, did alternative approaches supplant institutionalization. Yet even before the Civil War, the limitations of institutionalization were already evident. Urban missionaries and charity workers regarded the Christian home as a superior alternative to institutions and experimented with placing-out systems, foster care, adoption, and "cottage" systems to provide a more homelike environment.[5]

The Civil War sparked a second phase in child-saving as a new generation of reformers invoked the state's police powers to protect children from abuse, exploitation, and neglect. In the name of child protection, child-savers founded quasi-public societies to prevent cruelty to children. They also drew a sharper line between childhood and adulthood by removing children from almshouses, enacting laws to suppress obscene materials that might be viewed by the young, attacking child prostitution, raising the age of consent to sexual intercourse, and prosecuting a new crime, statutory rape. The Progressive era, the period stretching from the 1890s to World War I, marked a third phase in the history of child-saving. Progressive child-savers greatly expanded public responsibility and professional administration of child welfare programs. While their reforms had less impact than their creators anticipated, they set precedents for the programs inaugurated by the New Deal.[6]

Rapid urban growth, immigration, and the breakdown of the apprenticeship system greatly increased the number of dependent children, and institutionalization appeared to be the most cost-effective response. But institutionalization also reflected shifting ideas about childhood. The binding out or public auctioning of poor or orphaned children clashed with the sentimental view of the child as an innocent creature who needed care and nurture. Meanwhile, a heightened emphasis on children's plasticity made them much more promising candidates for reform than adults. Orphan asylums, houses of refuge, and reform schools were to rectify the failures of impoverished families; insulate children from a contaminating social environment; and shape their character by instilling habits of sobriety, industry, and self-discipline. These institutions reflected a humanitarian impulse to rescue children from deprived and abusive conditions and a religious impulse to redeem children from sin. Less positively, institutionalization sought to cut the cost of poor relief, remove poor and unruly children from the streets, and place them out of sight. Child-saving was driven by a mixture of hope and fear—by a utopian faith that crime, pauperism, and class division could be solved by redeeming poor children; and a mounting concern over growing cities, burgeoning gangs of idle and unsupervised youths, and swelling immigrant populations.

The earliest and longest-lasting child-saving institution was the orphan asylum. First established in the early eighteenth century, these institutions did not become widespread until a century later. Most inmates were not true "orphans," who had lost both parents, but half-orphans whose single parents could not earn enough money to care for the child at home. A surprising number came from intact but poor two-parent families, like the future baseball great George Herman "Babe" Ruth.

Nineteenth-century literature was obsessed with orphans. Huck Finn, Tom Sawyer, Susan Warner's Elizabeth Montgomery in *The Wide, Wide World,* and Willa Cather's Jim Burden, the narrator of *My Antonia,* were orphans or half-orphans. So, too, were Horatio Alger's heroes. The literary appeal of orphanhood was partly rooted in the number of young migrants who left relatives behind in search of new opportunities. But in a society in which half of all children lost a parent before the age of twenty, orphanhood was also a fact of life. As late as 1900, 20 to 30 percent of all children lost a parent by age fifteen. The number of orphaned and dependent children increased sharply in the late eighteenth century as a result of Revolutionary upheaval, increases in urban poverty, and cholera and yellow fever epidemics. A father's death almost invariably thrust a working-class family into poverty, and the children were sent to live with relatives, indentured to another family, or placed temporarily in almshouses, where they lived alongside criminals, paupers, prostitutes, and the insane. Some children were auctioned off to the lowest bidder through the public vendue system, sparing local communities the cost of supporting poor youth.[7]

In 1800 there were just six orphan asylums in the United States. But as childhood came to be seen as a vulnerable period demanding special protection, it seemed essential to shelter orphaned or homeless children from an unhealthy environment. By 1850 New York State had nearly 100 orphanages. Established mainly by religious denominations or by private charities, orphan asylums were to provide a carefully controlled environment where children would learn the values of industry, sobriety, and self-

control. The annual report for 1865 of the Baltimore Home of the Friendless expressed a widely held philosophy: "Our enterprise is a hopeful one
. . . The children are brought to us before they are corrupted by their vicious surroundings." Control of children's environment was viewed as the
key to transforming their character. As one authority later boasted, "We
can control the influences that make up the child's life. We can control
what he thinks about, from the time when he gets up in the morning till
he goes to bed at night . . . He never will run with the gang. He never will
be out nights."[8]

Many working-class parents used orphanages as temporary and long-
term shelters. This was, however, an emotionally costly arrangement for
parents and children. Surviving letters from parents to orphan officials are
heart-wrenching. "Please don't let him forget that he's got a mother,"
wrote one mother. "Does he ever ask for me?" asked another. It is difficult
to generalize about the orphanage experience. Some parents considered
orphanages a godsend—"I thank god," wrote one, "that there is such a
place . . . what wood become of children if there was [no] place like that
for them to go to." But many orphan asylums were bleak institutions
where corporal punishment was the rule, hugs and affection were rare,
and bullies terrorized younger children.[9]

Most orphanages were small, with fewer than 50 children, but most inmates lived in large institutions of 500 to 2,000, where children wore uniforms, were forced to walk in single file, were identified by numbers, and
slept in barracklike dormitories with little privacy. Many institutions severely restricted visits by parents and relatives. Still, compared with the
slums where many children had previously lived, the orphanages were
safe and healthy. They also offered vocational training, medical care, and
a reliable if monotonous diet. Many of the practices that we regard as especially harsh were intended to reduce health risks and to prevent immoral influences from entering the institutions.

As early as the 1850s, American orphanages had already acquired their
Dickensian image as drab, regimented facilities, characterized by harsh
discipline, rigid routine, and an absence of emotional care. A term arose
to describe the passivity of children in orphanages: *institutionalism*. Reports of physical and sexual abuse abounded. To address these concerns,
some orphanages adopted a "cottage" style, breaking down larger institutions into smaller homelike units. But as the nineteenth century progressed, the size of the larger institutions increased sharply. In the early
1900s more than 100,000 children resided in some 1,200 orphanages
throughout the United States.[10]

Orphanages remained an important mechanism for caring for dependent children well into the twentieth century, and continued to suffer from problems identified a half century earlier. In 1914 an inspection of twenty-six orphanages run by private charities in New York City reported children "overworked and underfed," beds "alive with vermin," and "antiquated modes of punishment," including shackles and chains. "Try to conceive of a girl being compelled to go to work at a washtub at 5 o'clock in the morning, there to remain until the dinner bell sounded at noon, and have such a brutal procedure styled 'vocational training,'" a commissioner of public charities asked rhetorically.[11]

The great flu epidemic that killed half a million Americans during World War I produced a fresh surge of admissions. During the Great Depression orphanages received their final influx, overwhelming these institutions' finances. The establishment of Aid to Dependent Children, as part of the Social Security Act of 1935, ended an era that had lasted more than a century. Those institutions that survived abandoned the term *orphanage,* instead calling themselves group homes or treatment facilities, and transformed themselves into residential care facilities where children with behavioral or psychiatric problems received treatment.[12]

In the 1990s, however, reports of children mired for years in foster care and the exploding number of babies born addicted to crack cocaine sparked talk of creating large group homes. In 1994 Newt Gingrich, soon to become Speaker of the House of Representatives, suggested that orphanages would be better than having children remain with abusive or neglectful parents. Gingrich, who had himself been born to a single teenage mother who had divorced her abusive husband before her son was born, regarded growing up in a family receiving welfare as tantamount to child abuse. Like the harsher nineteenth-century proponents of orphanages, he regarded these institutions as a way to rescue poor children while punishing their parents.[13]

Alongside the orphan asylum, houses of refuge for delinquent and homeless children arose. In 1823, 450 children were incarcerated in New York's Bridewell and Newgate prisons; their only offense was living on the streets. That year the city's Society for the Prevention of Pauperism called for construction of a house of refuge to serve as an alternative to the prison and the almshouse for vagrant children. New York's first House of Refuge, which admitted its first inmates—six boys and three girls—in 1825, was a semipublic institution managed by private philanthropists but receiving financial support from the municipal and state governments. Located in a fortresslike structure on the city's outskirts, the refuge took in 527 children in its first four years of operation. Most had been arrested for vagrancy or petty theft and would otherwise have been incarcerated in a local jail. Destitution, shifting residences, and the death of caretakers had characterized the lives of children admitted to the refuge. Fifteen-year-old Mary Ann Corbitt lived in at least ten different homes after her mother died when she was ten.[14]

The refuges' regimen emphasized order, discipline, routine, plain food, and regular work. Although their founders insisted that the refuges were "an asylum for friendless and unfortunate children, not a prison for young culprits," their architecture and internal organization resembled a penitentiary's. Children wore badges, slept in large dormitories, labored in group workshops, and ate in silence in a common dining hall. A ringing bell awoke the children at five; after washing and making their bed, the children paraded in the yard, where officials examined their dress and hygiene. The children then attended morning prayers and school until seven, when they received breakfast and began to labor in the refuge's workshops, making nails, finishing shoes, constructing wicker chairs, or washing laundry. After an hour for lunch, they worked until five in the afternoon. After dinner their schooling resumed until eight. Well-behaved youngsters were allowed to take unescorted trips outside the institution. Administrators punished unruly behavior severely, inflicting whippings, placing children in solitary confinement, depriving them of meals, and restraining them in leg irons and handcuffs. Children who wet their beds had their names announced in the dining hall. In 1848 a critic named Elijah Devoe reported: "On parade, at table, at their work, and in school, they are not allowed to converse . . . Restriction and constraint are their most intimate companions."[15]

By the 1840s there was a widespread impression that the refuge experiment had failed. The New York refuge suffered from vandalism, runaways, and arson. In one incident, a youthful inmate murdered a refuge official. To maintain discipline, refuge authorities relied on isolation and corporal punishment, including the cat-o'-nine-tails. Part of the problem was demographic. The refuge founders were interested in taking in younger children who had committed only minor offenses. While they sympathized with the plight of older children, the seriously delinquent were expected to remain in adult jails. But over time, those placed in the refuge were older, more experienced in crime, and less amenable to refuge discipline. The refuge became a warehouse for troublesome children. Instead of regarding the inmates as redeemable, refuge officials embraced explanations of delinquency based on heredity.[16]

During the 1840s, as the number of delinquent and neglected children outstripped the capacity of private benevolent societies, the house of refuge was superseded by a new institution, the reform school. Located in rural areas, these schools sought to remove wayward children from the moral contamination of the city and transform them culturally through a regimen of moral instruction, prayer, and physical labor. Like the refuge, the reform school melded the school, the prison, and the workhouse, but unlike the refuge, the reformatory was a state-run institution, publicly financed and administered. It quickly became clear that reform schools faced the same problems of discipline as refuges. Strict regimentation served to "darken, harden, and embitter" the young people placed in these institutions. An 1859 fire at the Massachusetts State Reform School for Boys in Westborough—just eleven years after the institution opened— underscored the bleak underside of reform-school life. Caused by arson (the work of a disgruntled fifteen-year-old), the fire revealed that three inmates had been in solitary confinement for several months. The three, who had been accused, respectively, of running away, assaulting an institution official, and attempted arson, were manacled to the floor in dark, poorly ventilated cells and fed bread and water.[17]

The impulse to rescue vulnerable victims of exploitation and redeem misguided souls inspired efforts to establish reform schools for young women. The first was the Massachusetts State Industrial School for Girls in Lancaster. Originally, most inmates were accused of vagrancy, running away from home, or staying out all night. Although critics accused the Massachusetts courts of taking Irish Catholic girls away from their families, more than half of the inmates were brought to court by their own parents, who felt incapable of controlling disobedient daughters, many of whom refused to contribute to their family's support. The girls were provided with an education, religious instruction, and training in domestic skills before they were indentured as domestic servants. In practice, much of the training was menial; "these arts," the institution's founders explained, "should include not only the washing of tables and dishes, but the scouring of floors, stairs, windows and walls, and of clothes, and especially of bedclothes, and bedsteads."[18]

Today the prisonlike orphan asylums and reformatories of the early nineteenth century stand as relics of a seemingly more repressive, less enlightened past. But these institutions were inspired, to varying degrees, by a utopian faith that it was possible to solve social problems and reshape human character by removing children from corrupting outside influence and instilling self-control through moral education, work, rigorous discipline, and an orderly environment. As early as the 1850s, it was apparent that the early child-saving institutions had failed to live up to their founders' aspirations. Some of the reasons were insufficient funding, overcrowding, and a shortage of trained caregivers. But their failure also reflected contradictions at the heart of the child-saving impulse. In theory, the institutions were to provide the young with a familial environment and use the same techniques that childrearing manuals prescribed to progressive parents to strengthen their children's moral character, substituting psychological discipline for physical restraint and manipulating guilt, shame, and sympathy to instill a capacity for self-control. Yet for all the talk about moral uplift, these institutions mainly served a custodial function, which became more pronounced over time. Even before the Civil War, these institutions had become human warehouses, where the inmates consisted largely of immigrant children subjected to strict surveillance, regimentation, and corporal punishment.[19]

Alongside the development of new child-saving institutions, the early nineteenth century also witnessed far-reaching revisions of laws affecting children. The conception of children as weak, vulnerable, and defenseless creatures gave rise to three legal principles with profound consequences for the future. One was the "best interests of the child" doctrine, which held that children's welfare should be the preeminent consideration in any judicial decision involving custody. A second principle was the "tender years" doctrine that young children were best left to their mother's care. The third principle was *"parens patriae,"* that courts had the authority to override parents' custody rights. Each of these doctrines gave judges broad discretion to grant custody as they saw fit, allowing them to take into account their perceptions of the parents' fitness. In the realm of judicial discretion, however, decisions could easily reflect various biases based on racial, gender, ethnic, and class prejudice.[20]

A widely publicized legal case of the 1830s and 1840s illustrated these legal changes. For six years Ellen Sears, a wealthy woman from Boston, and her estranged husband, a Swiss count named Paul Daniel Gonzalve Grand d'Hauteville, battled over the custody of their son, Frederick. Since Gonzalve had not physically abused his wife or violated his marriage vow, Ellen had no right to a divorce. In a case that attracted widespread attention from the penny press, her lawyers argued that she deserved custody because mothers were better suited to caring for young children than fathers. In awarding her temporary custody, the Pennsylvania Supreme Court rejected the common law presumption that fathers automatically retained custody unless proven to be unfit. "The reputation of a father may be stainless as crystal," the Court stated in its ruling, "and yet the interest of the child may imperatively demand the denial of the father's right and its continuance with the mother."[21]

In child custody cases, judges used the "best interests of the child" and "tender years" doctrines to undercut paternal claims to guardianship. As early as 1809, a South Carolina father, in the case of *Prather v. Prather,* lost custody of his infant daughter because he had committed adultery. Changes in custody occurred as an incremental result of legal decisions, not as a result of statutory enactments. As late as 1900, only nine states and the District of Columbia had established a mother's statutory right to equal guardianship of children. Nevertheless, most courts took the position that young children belonged with their mothers. For many women, this presumption proved to be a double-edged sword as new notions of "parental fitness" supplanted older assumptions about paternal rights. A woman could receive custody only if she conformed to Victorian notions of propriety and if the court found her character above reproach.[22]

The legal right to institutionalize children without parental consent was established by a 1838 Philadelphia case known as *ex parte Crouse.* Mary Ann Crouse's mother considered her daughter incorrigible and had authorities place her in the Philadelphia House of Refuge. Mary Ann's father challenged the government's right to incarcerate her without his consent. Ruling that the government had the authority to remove children "when [the parents were] unequal to the task of education," the court declared that removal did not require due process. Concluding that "it would be an act of extreme cruelty to release" the girl from the facility, the court refused to inquire into the procedures for commitment, the duration of her incarceration, or the conditions in the school.[23]

New ideas about children's welfare also prompted reconsideration of children born outside marriage. Convinced that it was unfair to visit parents' sins upon their children, legislatures and courts extended limited rights to children born outside wedlock. Common law had regarded an illegitimate child as *filius nullius,* with no legal claims on a parent or relative. The only parental obligation was to provide sufficient financial support to ensure that the child did not become a public charge. But even before the Civil War, courts and legislatures reduced the stigma of illegitimacy by recognizing common law marriages and declaring legitimate the offspring of annulled marriages and of parents who subsequently married. State statutes also gave inheritance rights to illegitimate children who were formally acknowledged by their parents. Meanwhile, to prevent illegitimate children from being separated from their mothers, states allowed poor children to be a charge in their mother's place of residence rather than in their place of birth.[24]

Adoption—the notion that adults should be able to become the legal parents of a child who is not their own biological offspring—was another product of the mid-nineteenth century's commitment to new ideas about childhood. Unlike English common law, which refused to recognize adoption out of fear of undercutting blood relatives' inheritance rights, the American colonies allowed adoption on a limited scale. Many adoptions took place without a formal legal proceeding, and some were established through a will. In the mid-nineteenth century the state legislatures of Mississippi (in 1846) and Texas (in 1850) responded to a growing number of requests for private adoption bills by enacting the first general adoption statutes, which provided for public registration of private adoption agreements. In 1851 Massachusetts adopted the first modern adoption law, requiring judges to determine whether adoptive parents were "of sufficient ability to bring up the child . . . and furnish suitable nurture and education" before issuing a decree. The statute also obliged the child's natural parents or guardian to consent to the adoption in writing. As older notions of parental rights rooted in religion, natural law, and property rights eroded, legal adoption presaged a new conception of parenthood emphasizing affection and stewardship. It also provided an alternative to placement of children in institutions and a way to assist abused and neglected children.[25]

Even before the Civil War, the reaction against institutionalization, apparent in the rise of legal adoption, prompted another influential approach to the care of dependent children: the orphan train, a precursor to foster care. The sight of thousands of New York children supporting themselves as beggars, flower sellers, and prostitutes shocked Charles Loring Brace, a young Connecticut-born minister. Asked to head the New York's Children's Aid Society for a single year, he remained on for more than three decades. To protect destitute children from a pernicious environment, he established lodging houses and reading rooms, and set up industrial missions where children (mainly young girls) received free meals and learned to make clothes. He also developed a more ambitious solution, to find slum children homes on western farms, where they would receive an education and get a chance for a better future. Brace's program drew on a number of precedents: traditional forms of indentured servitude, a new German residential school system for homeless children, and the 1849 example of transplanting city children to farm families pioneered by the Boston Children's Mission. His scheme also drew on faith in the power of a fresh start and an idealized image of life in the West. "The best of all Asylums for the outcast child is the farmer's home," was a Children's Aid Society slogan. Between 1855 and 1875 the society sent an average of 3,000 children westward annually.[26]

Between 1853 and 1929, 200,000 young people, almost all of them white, traveled westward not in Conestoga wagons, but in railroad cars, to be placed with farm families in the Midwest and Far West. Driven by a mixture of charitable and economic motives, the orphan trains were an idealistic attempt to remove poor children from corrupting urban influences; an effort to supply workers to labor-short rural areas; and a way to relieve eastern cities of their "dangerous" classes. Brace embodied these contradictory impulses. Deeply sentimental, he considered poor children redeemable and believed they deserved better childhoods than those available in eastern slums. But his thinking also reflected a deepening hereditarian strain of thought that colored mid-nineteenth-century attitudes toward poverty. He feared that "gemmules" in destitute adults' blood made them unsalvageable. In addition, a $10 train ticket cost far less than the $85 it took to support a child in an orphanage or refuge.

In some instances, children were matched with a specific couple before being sent west. More often, a newspaper announcement appeared before a group's arrival, and prospective parents, who had been screened by county commissioners, applied for them. The selection process, held in a town hall or a railroad station, resembled a slave auction. Those not chosen were put back on the train and taken to the next town. Brace rejected written contracts, fearing they would reduce placing-out to a purely legal and financial arrangement. Because the Children's Aid Society retained

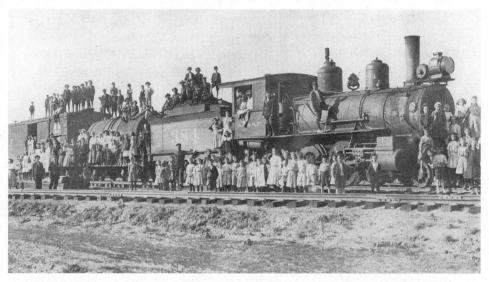

Between 1850 and 1930, at least 200,000 destitute urban children traveled in orphan trains to foster homes, mainly on farms in the Midwest and Far West. Courtesy of the Kansas State Historical Society, Topeka.

legal guardianship, it could reclaim children if families were abusive; conversely, families were free to return the children. In practice, the lack of a formal contract meant that there was no formal legal protection for the child.[27]

There were some notable success stories. Two boys who traveled on the same 1859 train became governors of Alaska and North Dakota respectively. Most boys, however, became farmhands or farmers or mechanics; and most girls were placed as domestic servants, which helps explain why few girls applied to go on the orphan trains. There were many stories of hardship and abuse. Some children were treated more like indentured labor than like sons and daughters. Marguerite Thomson, who was taken to the small farming town of Bertrand, Nebraska, recalled: "I never had enough to eat." She reported that she "never had a glass of milk, the first two years, even though they had cows. They said they had to sell the milk."[28]

Contrary to Brace's contention, most of the children were not parentless waifs: "ragged girls who had nowhere to lay their heads; children driven from drunkards' homes; orphans who slept where they could find a box or a stairway; boys cast out by step-mothers or step-fathers." About one child in five was an orphan or an abandoned child. Another fifth were brought in by parents or relatives during a family crisis only to be retrieved when the crisis had subsided. The single largest group were boys fourteen and older seeking economic opportunity.[29]

Some youths, unhappy with their placement, initiated a move to a new situation. John Fratenburg left his employer after only twenty-four days because the latter refused to pay wages. Maggie Riley left an abusive employer and found employment as a domestic servant with another family. George Higgenbotham could not "learn farming" and took a job in town instead. When fourteen-year-old Peter Hilliard was not allowed to attend Catholic mass, he left his foster family and moved in with an Irish farmer. Nearly 10 percent of children ran away from their foster homes. According to the Children's Aid Society's records, roughly a third of the children remained in contact with their biological families during placement.[30]

As early as the 1870s, complaints mounted that many children were forced aboard the trains without their parents' knowledge or consent. At a Conference of Charities in 1893, an official in one of the receiving states, North Carolina, charged that the so-called orphans were placed with people who "treat them as slaves." Midwesterners claimed that the children's aid societies dumped juvenile delinquents into their states, while many Catholics and Jews regarded the orphan trains as a Protestant scheme to convert their children. At the same time, a new generation of social workers argued that society should try to keep struggling families together.[31]

In 1929 the last orphan train, with three boys aboard, left New York for Sulfur Springs, Texas. Declining demand for farm labor and increasing efforts to preserve families led to the program's demise. But the orphan trains had a profound impact on child welfare in the United States. The children's aid societies were among the first American institutions to use professional case workers instead of volunteers, to maintain case records, and to conduct home visits. They also pioneered foster care, suggesting that it was cheaper and healthier for children than institutionalization.

The orphan train was one expression of a broader revaluation of childhood. Increasingly, children were valued not for the labor they provided, but for emotional reasons. But as children acquired greater sentimental value, they became, for the first time, prey for kidnappers. The first kidnapping for ransom took place in 1874. Four-year-old Charley Ross and his six-year-old brother Walter were abducted outside their affluent Philadelphia home after their abductors promised to buy them firecrackers. Walter was subsequently released, but Charley was not. Twenty-three letters passed between the kidnappers and the boy's frantic father. The police urged him not to pay ransom, fearing that doing so would encourage more abductions, but ultimately he decided to meet the kidnappers' demands. Arrangements to deliver the ransom misfired, and communications from his son's captors ceased. The boy was never found.[32]

After the Civil War a new phase in child-saving arose. The Civil War greatly intensified public concern over children's welfare and convinced reformers that state action was necessary to protect the young. The postbellum years witnessed the first organized efforts to prosecute child abuse, suppress vice targeted at young people, and raise the age at which girls could consent to sexual relations. Child rescue was the movement's watchword.

A single case of abuse ignited a movement to end cruelty to children. Mary Ellen, a foster child, was forced to sleep on an old piece of carpet on the floor and forbidden to play with other children, She had no shoes or stockings, and her body was covered with bruises, whip marks, and burns. In 1874 Etta Angell Wheeler, an urban missionary in New York's Hell's Kitchen slum, heard about the girl's plight and launched a legal battle to free Mary Ellen from her abusive home. Unsuccessful in persuading the police to remove the child from her foster parents, Wheeler turned to Henry Bergh, president of New York's Society for the Prevention of Cruelty to Animals. According to legend, Bergh declared: "The child is an animal. If there is no justice for it as a human being, it shall at least have the right of the cur in the street . . . It shall not be abused." Forty-eight hours later, Mary Ellen and her foster mother were brought before a justice on the New York Supreme Court. Her foster mother was found guilty of assault and battery and was sentenced to a year of hard labor in a penitentiary.[33]

Earlier acts of child abuse had been ignored by the press and public. A few months earlier a thirteen-year-old boy had been beaten to death by his father for "refusing to go after beer without the money to pay for it," but this case aroused no reaction. Several factors made Mary Ellen's case different. Wheeler's husband, a newspaperman, received help from journalists in publicizing the case. Because Mary Ellen had been beaten by someone other than her natural mother, the case did not challenge parents' prerogative to discipline children as they saw fit. Rather, the case involved dereliction on the part of private charities that placed children in foster families without oversight. Above all, Mary Ellen was an attractive girl, and pretty young girls are particularly likely to garner public sympathy.[34]

Over the course of American history, concern about child abuse has been sporadic. Between 1640 and 1680, Puritan Massachusetts adopted the first laws in the western world forbidding "unnatural severity" in disciplining children, but these laws were rarely enforced. Before the Civil War, the temperance movement condemned alcohol on the grounds that it led fathers and husbands to abuse wives and children. As early as 1852, a New England periodical published an article on "The Rights of Children" that spoke of the need to "protect" children from parental "tyranny." But it was not until the 1870s that the first societies to prevent cruelty to children appeared, led by moralistic upper-class reformers, distressed by the rapid growth of cities and the "depraved" habits of the immigrant poor. By 1908 there were fifty-five societies devoted exclusively to protecting children from cruelty.[35]

The cruelty societies did not question parents' right to discipline children with physical punishment. At the organizing meeting of the New York society, Henry Bergh said that although he was anxious "to protect children from undue severity," he himself favored "a good wholesome flogging, which he often found most efficacious." A commitment to family privacy and parental rights led the cruelty societies to focus their attention almost exclusively on impoverished immigrant families and on families headed by single mothers and the unemployed. Relying on threats of prosecution for drunkenness or assault, the societies' preferred solution to abuse was to institutionalize the children by removing them to a city-run institution or a foster home. Working-class children sometimes took advantage of fears about the societies' agents by threatening to report their parents "to the Cruelty."[36]

Although the "Cruelty" was accused of breaking up poor families on flimsy grounds, much of the demand for state intervention came from family members themselves. The societies' most unfortunate effect was to convince the public that constructive steps were being taken against child abuse, when in fact the societies concentrated their energies on child neglect. Although the societies claimed that "the grosser forms of physical cruelty are not so prevalent as they were a few decades ago," the use of corporal punishment remained widespread. A study of autobiographies and letters indicated that three-quarters of the post–Civil War children for whom information was available had been hit with an instrument by their parents in the course of discipline.[37]

Concern with child abuse led to investigation of other abuses, such as "baby-farming," the practice of sending unwanted infants to boarding homes where they were badly neglected or simply allowed to die. "Baby-farms," Elbridge T. Gerry, the head of the Society for the Prevention of Cruelty to Children charged, "are concerns by means of which persons, usually of disreputable character, eke out a living by taking two, or three, or four babies to board . . . They feed them on sour milk, and give them paregoric to keep them quiet, until they die." In fact most baby farms were primitive nurseries for the infants of working mothers. Another abuse that aroused child protectors' concern was the claim that poor parents attempted to profit from their children's death by purchasing life insurance policies for twenty-five cents a week. In reality the insurance payoff, about $17, was only enough to pay for a child's funeral. Although there were a handful of cases in which insurance was indeed a motive in a child's death, what disturbed reformers was the idea that any monetary value should be attached to a child's life, which conflicted with the reformers' notion that a child's value was priceless.[38]

Reformers became especially distressed by the threat that obscene art and literature posed to young people's impressionable minds. Convinced that society's moral health could be enhanced much as sanitary reformers improved nutrition, sanitation, and personal hygiene, the Young Men's Christian Association in 1868 persuaded New York's state legislature to pass a law restricting obscene material. That same year, a British court in the case of *Hicklin v. Queen* ruled that the government might suppress any publication that tended "to deprave and corrupt those whose minds are open to immoral influences, and into whose hands a publication of this sort may fall." The *Hicklin* case allowed a work to be judged obscene on the basis of isolated passages and its potential impact on the "young and inexperienced." This decision encouraged antivice reformers like Anthony Comstock and societies for the suppression of vice to campaign to rid the mails of "Boys' Papers" and other materials that might corrupt youngsters; in 1873 Congress passed the Comstock Act, which made it a crime to distribute obscene materials through the mails. This legislation not only outlawed publications and works of art deemed obscene, but also contraceptive devices or medications.[39]

Child prostitution was a particular source of alarm. In an article published in 1885, William Stead, an English journalist, described how he had purchased a thirteen-year-old girl for five pounds sterling. Stead was convicted and imprisoned (for three months) for kidnapping a minor. Publicity over the case led the British Parliament to raise the age of consent for sexual intercourse from thirteen to sixteen. In 1887 Bessie V. Cushman, an American physician, documented child prostitution in the lumber camps of Michigan's Upper Peninsula. In New York City in the middle of the nineteenth century, an estimated 5 to 10 percent of young women in their teens or early twenties engaged in prostitution for at least a brief period. In the low-wage urban economy with growing numbers of unattached, ill-paid, and unemployed young women workers, prostitution paid twice as much as factory employment. Concern about child prostitution led New York State to raise the age of consent, which was only ten in 1865, to eighteen by 1895. To enforce this new boundary, states relied on statutory rape laws, which working-class families frequently invoked to control their daughters' behavior.[40]

A different form of rescue was apparent in the Florence Crittenton missions. In 1883, after hearing a preacher tell prostitutes, "Go and sin no more," Charles N. Crittenton, who had made a fortune in pharmaceuticals in New York, opened his first home for unwed mothers. By the time of his death in 1909, he had established eighty missions, providing educational, vocational, and welfare services to former prostitutes, indigent immigrants, and victims of venereal disease. Many of the homes also offered infant-care training classes and day nurseries for the children of working women. Strongly opposed to adoption, Crittenton and his successor Dr. Kate Waller Barrett believed that the only way the young women could atone for their sin was by caring for their children. In contrast to the popular image of maternity homes as punitive and coercive, the Crittenton homes apparently encouraged self-respect, self-reliance, and dignity among their clients.[41]

The most far-reaching effort at child protection involved Native American children, as self-proclaimed "Friends of the Indians" launched an ambitious campaign to "Americanize" Indian children and obliterate their tribal identity. Beginning in the late 1870s, the federal government and private religious organizations established dozens of boarding schools to indoctrinate Indian children in Anglo ways. It cost between $6,000 and $10,000 to kill an Indian but only $1,200 to educate a child at a boarding school. Education seemed the cheaper and more constructive approach to assimilating young Indians. Richard H. Pratt, a former army officer, embraced the idea after working with Apache prisoners in St. Augustine, Florida. He believed that removing Indian children from their culture and subjecting them to strict discipline and hard work would lead them to abandon their tribal traditions and assimilate into mainstream society. His famous dictum was "Kill the Indian and save the man." "In Indian civilization I am a baptist," Pratt announced, "because I believe in immersing the Indians in our civilization and, when we get them under, holding them there until they are thoroughly soaked."[42]

In 1879 Congress gave Pratt eighteen students and a barracks at a deserted Army college in Carlisle, Pennsylvania, to try out his ideas. Luther Standing Bear, a young Teton Sioux, later recalled his journey to the school in 1879, just three years after Custer's Last Stand. He remembered being "surrounded by a jeering, unsympathetic people whose only emotions were those of hate and fear" whenever his train stopped at railroad stations. After arriving at Carlisle, he was arbitrarily given the name Luther from a list of names on a blackboard, and his hair was cut short. Students were expected to spend three years at Pratt's school. Between 1879 and 1918 the school educated some 12,000 children from seventy-seven tribes, including a number of African-American as well as Native American students such as the Olympic athlete Jim Thorpe.[43]

Boarding school students, as young as five, were separated from their families, often by hundreds of miles. Indian agents were authorized to withhold rations from families who refused to let their children go. At the schools, students were prohibited from speaking native languages, wearing native dress, or practicing native religions or native dances. Students were pressured to convert to Christianity, and bounties were offered for the return of runaway students, a measure that indicates a substantial resistance to the program. Contagious diseases often swept through the schools; at Carlisle, about one student in ten died. Vocational training in simple crafts was central to the boarding school mission. Students devoted half a day to reading, writing, and arithmetic and the rest of the day to domestic arts for the girls and industrial arts for the boys. Indian girls sewed, set tables, cooked meals, and worked as servants; boys performed manual labor, took part in military drills, and worked as farm laborers.

The schools' psychological impact was even more detrimental than the course of study. Zitkala-Sa, a Dakota girl who later taught at Carlisle and founded and served as president of the National Council of American Indians, was born in 1876 to a Yankton Sioux mother and a white father she never knew. She spent her first twelve years living in a tipi near the Missouri River before being sent to a Quaker-run charity school in Wabash, Indiana, where she was forced to wear tight shoes and a confining dress. She frequently hid under her bed. As an adult she wrote "The Soft-Hearted Sioux," a story of a young man unable to readjust to tribal life after his years in boarding school.[44]

At the turn of the twentieth century, there were 150 boarding schools, most operated directly by the Bureau of Indian Affairs while others were under contract with Christian missionaries. At the schools' peak, in the 1920s, they were educating more than 30,000 Indian children a year. Not until the late 1920s did the government begin to build neighborhood schools on reservations to allow Indian children to attend school closer to home. By the 1960s, as a result of mounting protest from Native Americans, Indian children were no longer forced to attend boarding schools, and by 2002 only four remained. But the impact of the boarding school experience persisted even after the system began to decline. The trauma of early separation from parents and culture, the assumption of Indian inferiority, and the uprooting and alienation at the boarding schools left a lasting imprint on many Native Americans.[45]

A new phase in the history of child welfare arose in the 1890s. Invoking the principles of professionalization, scientific expertise, and rational administration, child-savers of the Progressive era greatly expanded the role of the state and of trained experts in addressing problems of children's health, education, and welfare. But Progressivism's legacy was mixed. While the Progressive commitment to child welfare justified new measures to combat infant and child mortality, increase access to kindergartens and high schools, restrict child labor, and assist single-parent families, it also expanded the definition of the status offenses for which juveniles (but not adults) could be punished, weakened due-process protections for minors accused of wrongdoing, and instituted harsh measures, including sterilization, for children regarded as feeble-minded.[46]

One symbol of a more aggressive approach to youth problems was the George Youth Republic, a prototype for Boys' Town. Founded in 1895 by philanthropist William R. George on 600 acres in Freeville, New York, the republic provided a refuge for delinquent and potentially delinquent adolescents. Convinced that city life quashed many of society's democratic ideals, George sought to implement a self-governing republic in a rural setting, complete with its own currency, workshops, fire department, police force, and system of justice. Disturbed by the segregation of young people from meaningful activities, he viewed self-government as the best way to prepare young people for adult life. With "nothing without labor" as his motto, George expected young people to work for their board, lodging, and pocket money to build up their self-respect and civic spirit. The young residents levied their own taxes and elected their own officials. Theodore Roosevelt called it "a manufactory of citizens," and the republic inspired experiments with student government in public schools.[47]

In the mid-1910s George's republic was struck by scandal, complete with charges of brutality and sexual immorality. It also came under attack from a new generation of psychologically trained child professionals, who decried the republic's unsystematic, unscientific methods and the absence of testing and individualized therapy. Nevertheless, the republic survived, and by the time of George's death in 1936, 3,000 boys and girls, mainly from New York City slums, had lived in the republic.[48]

The Progressive era marked a watershed in the history of child welfare. Progressive-era achievements included reducing infant mortality through aggressive public health measures, establishing playgrounds so that urban children would not have to play in the streets, and providing day nurseries and kindergartens for the children of working mothers. These years also saw enactment of the first effective compulsory school attendance laws, extensive revisions in school curricula, the rapid expansion of the high school, and passage of legislation to regulate the hours and conditions of children's labor.[49]

During the early twentieth century, government's supervisory, regulatory, and caregiving role greatly expanded. Children born out of wedlock received the right to support and inheritance. Beginning with Ohio in 1911, states enacted the first children's codes to provide uniform legal protections for children. At the same time, public agencies assumed functions previously provided by private and religious institutions, and professionally trained female social workers replaced amateur male charity workers and adopted a new approach—casework—to address child welfare. The greatest achievement of the Progressive era was reducing infant and child mortality by more than 50 percent. Public health reform succeeded because it had a measurable goal and relied on scientific principles. The greatest disappointment of the Progressive era was the failure to move children out of almshouses, orphanages, and other large, regimented institutions as the number of institutionalized children rose from

61,000 early in the Progressive era to 205,000 in 1923. Nevertheless, the child-savers did succeed in expanding government's role and reducing the role of private agencies.[50]

In pursuit of child welfare, progressive educators sought to create a child-centered school curriculum. In 1892 Joseph Mayer Rice, a pediatrician, wrote that the typical public school "has been converted into the most dehumanizing institution that I have ever laid eyes upon, each child being treated as if he possessed a memory and the faculty of speech, no individuality, no sensibility and no soul." Teaching emphasized memorization, drill, repetition, and strict discipline. In the early 1870s the Quincy, Massachusetts, school board discovered that while students could read their textbooks, they were unable to read unfamiliar materials. They could recite rules of grammar and mathematical formulas, but could not apply them. Francis W. Parker was hired as the district's new superintendent, and he sought to integrate the ideas of Johann Heinrich Pestalozzi, a Swiss educator who called for learning through direct experience and activities, into the district's curriculum. Parker promptly did away with the textbooks, readers, and spellers and called on teachers to show interest in their students as individuals. He incorporated geography, history, and nature study into the curriculum and taught these subjects through investigation and other forms of active learning. An 1879 state examination showed that the Quincy students surpassed the performance of students in other Massachusetts schools in traditional subjects.[51]

The Progressive era brought dramatic growth to the nation's schools. Between 1870 and 1915 the number of children in school increased from seven to twenty million, and school expenditures jumped even faster, from $63 million to $605 million. By 1918 every state had enacted compulsory education laws, with thirty-one states requiring attendance until the age of sixteen. Progressive educators also had some success in restricting corporal punishment in schools, convincing seven major cities to ban the practice. Meanwhile, Gary, Indiana, pioneered an extended school day that combined academic studies with a wide range of nonacademic activities. Instead of spending just four hours a day at school, students went from nine to five, participating in school assemblies, gym, and vocational training in shop and home economics. Modified versions of the Gary plan were adopted by many cities.[52]

Schooling was extended both in the early years—through the establishment of kindergartens—and in the upper grades—through a massive expansion in high schools. The first kindergarten in the United States was founded in Boston in 1860 by Elizabeth Peabody. Inspired by the nineteenth-century German educator Friedrich Froebel, who emphasized the importance of teaching young children through organized play, the use of the hands and the senses, and nature study, the Transcendentalist educator believed that children's play had intrinsic educational and developmental value. Most early kindergartens were sponsored by wealthy female philanthropists like Pauline Shaw of Boston and Jane Stanford and Phoebe A. Hearst of California, who viewed kindergartens as an adjunct to other charitable endeavors for the poor. Kindergarten teachers in these privately financed institutions spent half their day visiting the homes of their pupils, providing mothers with information about their children's nutritional, hygienic, and moral needs. Kindergarten advocates split about whether the institution was primarily childcare for needy children or a mechanism for promoting all children's emotional and intellectual development. Those who favored making kindergartens available to all children established the first publicly financed kindergarten in St. Louis in 1873; Boston and Philadelphia public schools took over charitable kindergartens in 1888. By 1912 kindergarten enrollment reached 312,000, but even as late as the 1920s, only about 10 percent of five-year-olds attended kindergartens.[53]

High schools grew even more rapidly. It took a century to increase the proportion of young people in high schools from 10 percent (in 1815) to 20 percent (in 1915). It took only another thirteen years to reach half the high school aged population. Between 1890 and 1918 high school attendance soared by over 700 percent, from 200,000 to 1.6 million, while the number of graduates doubled, to 213,000. A new high school opened every day in the first thirty years of the twentieth century.[54]

Progressive educators, led by John Dewey, launched a revolt against drill and rote memorization in favor of a more natural, child-centered education. They called upon teachers to cultivate a respect for diversity and a critical, engaged intelligence that would prepare young people to participate in community affairs. Progressive educators emphasized developmentally appropriate instruction and methods of pedagogy that appealed to all of a child's senses and were tailored to children's individual needs. Ironically, the Progressive era also saw the rise of standardized testing. During World War I the U.S. army used intelligence testing to identify officer candidates. When the war was over, psychometrics, the measurement of psychological variables such as intelligence, became associated with the modern, scientific school system, which used intelligence testing to measure students' academic potential and to guide students into appropriate curricular tracks. Critics argued that intelligence testing threatened democratic ideals. Almost always, racial or ethnic minorities received lower test scores and were tracked into vocational courses of study.[55]

The Progressive educators' ideal of involving children in civic affairs found tangible expression in organizations designed to spread the gospel of cleanliness. In New York City in 1915, 25,000 young people participated in juvenile street cleaning leagues. Wearing buttons inscribed with the slogan "We Are for Clean Streets," boys and girls deposited litter in the city's "red robin" trash cans and reported overflowing trash receptacles, filthy lots, missing street signs, dead animals in roadways, broken curbs, potholes, and blocked fire escapes. They also distributed multilingual circulars calling for civic cleanliness, confronted litterers, visited tenements and businesses, and ridiculed sanitation workers who neglected their duties. The cleanliness campaign sought to check the outbreak of communicable diseases, beautify city streets, and combat the appeal of gangs in order to curb juvenile crime.[56]

Cleanliness was one way to attack the problem of child mortality. At the turn of the century, 20 percent of children died by the age of five, mainly from gastrointestinal, respiratory, and infectious diseases. First recognized as a social problem in the 1850s, child mortality was initially blamed on the unhygienic conditions in crowded cities. During the 1870s pediatricians linked high infant death rates to impure milk, and promoted farm and bottling inspection programs modeled on earlier European efforts. In 1893 Nathan Straus, whose family owned Macy's department store, opened one of the first pure milk stations in the United States, which cut the death rate in New York City's orphan asylum on Randall's Island in half. In 1908 Chicago became the first city in the world to require pasteurization of the city's milk supply. Meanwhile a growing number of physicians and social workers became convinced that the only way to reduce infant mortality was to educate mothers about proper hygiene and nutrition. Milk stations expanded to include medical consultations and education in childcare, while visiting nurses brought instruction into the home. By the early 1910s settlement houses, well-baby clinics, Baby Week campaigns, and home visits by public health nurses sought to educate mothers to raise healthier babies.[57]

The most celebrated achievement of the Progressive era was the establishment of the juvenile court, introduced in Illinois in 1899. In July of that year, eleven-year-old Henry Campbell was brought before Judge Richard S. Tuthill by his own mother, who accused the boy of stealing from her. With his courtroom filled with representatives from the Chicago Women's Club, Judge Tuthill agreed to send Campbell to live with his grandmother in upstate New York, hoping that a rural environment would give the boy a fresh start. In the two years before passage of the Juvenile Court Law, more than 1,700 children were sent to adult jails and prisons. In the first two years after the law passed, only 60 went to jail.[58]

Settlement house worker Jane Addams considered the creation of the juvenile court a landmark in the history of childhood. "There was almost a change in mores when the juvenile court was established," she declared. "The child was brought before the judge with no one to prosecute him and none to defend him . . . The element of conflict was absolutely eliminated and with it all notions of punishment with its curiously belated connotations." But at least part of the juvenile court's appeal was that it promised to reduce the costs of institutionalization. The juvenile court in Denver claimed to save the state $88,000 in eighteen months by reducing institutional commitments.[59]

Based on the idea that young people were less culpable than adults and became delinquent as a result of immaturity, poor parenting, neglect, and poverty, the juvenile courts provided wayward youths with the opportunity to turn their lives around. Functioning as a parent, not a prosecutor, judges had broad leeway to devise alternatives to a prison sentence, such as requiring a youth to attend a vocational school. Judges held informal hearings rather than a trial, talked to the child in a casual manner, and took testimony from trained probation officers and social workers who described the youth's background in detail. The juvenile court handled not only criminal cases but also status offenses that only juveniles could commit, such as underage drinking, running away, and curfew violations, as well as vagrancy, begging, and peddling on the streets. In 1913 half the juvenile arrests in one New York neighborhood were for such offenses as "playing with water pistol . . . shooting craps, snowballing, subway disturbances, and throwing stones."[60]

The juvenile courts had their own distinct language. Unlike the adult courts, cases were begun by petition, not indictment, and judges presided over hearings, rather than trials, and made findings rather than rendering verdicts. The accused were called respondents, not defendants, and were described as offenders rather than criminals. In theory, juvenile courts were supposed to emphasize counseling and treatment over punishment, and rehabilitation over retribution. Court records were kept private, and when a youth reached adulthood, the criminal record disappeared, so that a youth was not stigmatized for life. Instead of being incarcerated, most youthful offenders were handled by a probation system that was supposed to provide a middle ground between incarceration and unsupervised release back into the community. In exchange for this informality, however, juveniles had to give up certain rights to due process, including the right to a trial by jury, the right to an attorney, and the right to confront witnesses. Drawing support from charity reformers and local civic groups, especially middle-class women's organizations, the juvenile courts spread rapidly. By 1925, forty-six states adopted the idea.[61]

The juvenile court's basic components were not as revolutionary as its proponents maintained. As early as the 1870s, several states, including New York, had special judges and separate procedures, including parole systems, for juvenile delinquents. What was new was the conviction that a probation officer, like a trained social worker, would conduct a "complete and thorough" investigation of family conditions, and propose sanctions and treatment that would rehabilitate the youngster, often in the young person's own home. In practice, however, probation staffs were too small to provide anything but superficial services. To trim costs, twenty-one states experimented with voluntary probation officers.[62]

During the century after the juvenile court was founded, the basic assumptions that contributed to its rise eroded as public concern over juvenile crime escalated and faith in the power of the juvenile justice system to rehabilitate wayward youth waned. The defining characteristics of the juvenile justice system—informal procedures, confidentiality, individualized treatment, and probation—gave way to a new emphasis on formal, bureaucratic procedure, rigid sentencing guidelines, and incarceration of violent offenders. At the end of the twentieth century, every state had adopted legislation that made it easier to transfer juveniles to adult courts, hold them in adult jails, and sentence them to adult prisons. Yet even as lawmakers got tough on juvenile crime, it became glaringly apparent that a punitive approach did not serve society well. Incarceration in adult prisons too often transformed youthful offenders into career criminals. Progressive ideals—a recognition of the special developmental characteristics of the young and of the importance of early intervention, individualized treatment, and rehabilitation—stand as a rebuke to the simplistic solutions to juvenile crime favored today.[63]

Eugenicist ideas linking heredity and criminality gained ascendance during the Progressive era. Prompted by *The Jukes,* Richard Dugdale's 1875 study of seven generations of a family of criminals, prostitutes, and paupers, a panic ensued over hereditary criminality and the purported "menace of the feebleminded." To prevent insane or retarded children from reproducing, thousands were confined in sexually segregated institutions beginning in the early twentieth century; by 1964 about 60,000 had been sterilized, a practice upheld as constitutional by the Supreme Court in the 1927 decision of *Buck v. Bell.* Many were institutionalized by hard-pressed parents, who found it difficult to supervise or care for these children. The institutionalization and sterilization of mentally retarded or ill children stands as the most haunting example of the misuse of the concept of child protection.[64]

More positive reforms included the establishment of playgrounds and day nurseries as an alternative to street play for slum children. In 1906 the Boston philanthropist Joseph Lee, the pioneer in physical education Luther Gullick Jr., and the educator Henry Curtis, with encouragement from Jane Addams, Lillian Wald, and Jacob Riis, started the Playground Association of America. Staunch advocates of the value of games and team sports, they argued that supervised playgrounds promoted Americanization, reduced ethnic conflict, and taught children the value of teamwork without undermining competitiveness and initiative. The number of playgrounds rose from fewer than 100 in 1905 to nearly 4,000 in 1917.[65]

To meet working mothers' desperate need for childcare, reformers established day nurseries modeled on the crèches established by France in the early nineteenth century. There was a crying need for childcare. Jane Addams described three children crippled while their mothers were at work: "One had fallen out of a third-story, another had been burned, and the third had a curved spine due to the fact that for three years he had been tied all day long to the leg of the kitchen table." By 1892 there were ninety day nurseries in the nation's cities, including institutions established by African Americans, Catholics, and Jews. Most mothers kept their children in these institutions briefly, in part because the caregiver ratio was extremely poor. In one nursery, a single woman cared for as many as fifty children. Day nurseries quickly acquired an unsavory reputation that retarded the development of daycare in the United States. They were regarded as an unfortunate necessity for families in crisis rather than as an educational institution or as an institutional mechanism to allow mothers to work. Most reformers favored state-funded pensions that would permit mothers to stay home with their children.[66]

A leading goal of Progressive child-savers was to end the institutionalization of dependent children. At the first White House conference on children in 1909, participants agreed that children should be kept in their own families rather than warehoused in huge institutions. Starting with Illinois in 1911, states enacted "mothers' pensions" to allow widows to care for children in their own homes. By 1919, thirty-nine states and the territories of Alaska and Hawaii adopted mothers' pensions. Yet the impact of these measures was insignificant. The amount of aid provided was so small that most eligible mothers had to work to support their families. Because of "local option" provisions, most counties—probably around 60 percent—offered no pensions at all. Eligibility was severely restrictive. Many states excluded African Americans and established "suitable home" provisions for receiving aid, barring divorcees, unmarried mothers, and even women separated from their husbands from receiving pensions. Drinking, smoking, or failure to attend church were grounds for denial of aid.[67]

During the Progressive era the federal government entered the field of child welfare for the first time. In 1912, after a determined campaign by Jane Addams, Lillian Wald, and other college-educated female settlement house and social workers, the federal government established the Children's Bureau to collect and disseminate information on child welfare. Although the agency had no administrative powers, and initially received only a $25,000 appropriation, it compiled data about children's health, labor, and legal status and distributed childrearing advice. Under the leadership of Julia Lathrop and her successor Grace Abbott, it pushed for a federal child labor law.[68]

The bureau advocated a "whole child" philosophy based on the idea that every child had a right to a protected childhood, free from poverty, exploitation, and ill health. To achieve this objective, the agency called for an expansion of juvenile courts, federal support for infant and children's health, and aid to poor families with dependent children. To reduce infant and maternal mortality and improve child health, the bureau lobbied successfully in behalf of the Maternity and Infancy Protection Act (the Sheppard-Towner Act), adopted by Congress in 1921, which provided grants to states to expand visiting nurses' services, especially in rural areas, and to train midwives, nurses, and mothers in maternal and children's health. Before the act expired in 1929, it helped the states (all but three of which participated) distribute twenty-two million educational publications, establish 2,978 prenatal centers, and sponsor three million home visits. More negatively, the bureau supported the sterilization of mentally handicapped girls in the belief that disabilities were transmitted genetically.[69]

Of all the reform campaigns of the Progressive era, the one that attracted the most attention was the crusade against child labor. Many Progressives regarded the movement to abolish child labor as the twentieth-century equivalent of the abolitionist campaign to end slavery. Child labor, they charged, damaged children's health, impeded their education, and imperiled their moral health. *Children in Bondage* (1914), by Edwin Markham, Ben Lindsey, and George Creel, described the two million child laborers, "mangled, mind, body, and soul, and aborted into a maturity robbed of power and promise."[70]

Twelve-year-old Rose Gollup, who emigrated from a small village in western Russia in 1892, was one of those two million children. Her job entailed stitching the sleeve linings of men's coats, breathing "filthy air" and the "cloth dust" twelve hours a day. Her sweatshop was cramped, the width of "two ordinary sized wagons"; dark, with just two gas jets to provide light; and crowded with sixteen employees and four sewing machines. In 1911 Rose and 700 other employees were at work in the Triangle Shirtwaist Factory when a fire broke out, killing 154. With their clothing in flames and the fire doors leading to the stairs locked, many workers leapt off window ledges to their death. "I couldn't stop crying for hours, for days," Rose later wrote. "Afterwards, I used to dream I was falling from a window, screaming . . . Then I would start crying and couldn't stop."[71]

Eleven-year-old Boots McAleenan, another child laborer, was one of dozens of newsboys who went on strike for two weeks after William Randolph Hearst's *New York Journal* and Joseph Pulitzer's *New York World* raised the price they paid for papers. Declared one striker: "Ten cents in the dollar is as much to us as it is to Mr. Hearst . . . We can do more with ten cents than he can with twenty-five." With sales down by 40 percent, the publishers offered a compromise: the price would remain where it is, but the *World* and *Journal* would take back unsold papers at 100 percent refund. Boots and the other newsboys agreed to the terms and returned to the streets.[72]

Several factors accounted for mounting public concern over child labor, including the increasing contrast between middle-class and working-class childhood and organized labor's fear of competition from child workers. Especially significant was the notion that all children, regardless of class, deserved a protected childhood, one devoted to play and education. No one was more effective in arousing public passion over child labor than Lewis Wickes Hine. Hired by the National Child Labor Committee in 1908 to document child labor, he took more than 5,000 photographs of children working in agriculture, canneries, coalmines, factories, mills, and sweatshops, mainly in the South. His photographs revealed the brutal conditions of child labor and the inadequacy of existing child labor laws and awoke the nation's conscience in a way that statistics and reports had failed to accomplish.

Quite selective in their targets, child labor law reformers bitterly opposed child labor in factories, mines, and the street trades, but said little about farm labor, the single largest employer of child labor, since they considered this kind of work valuable in building moral character. Nor did they object to part-time teenage employment in the growing services industries, where teenagers worked as delivery boys, soda jerks, and store

At the turn of the twentieth century, two million children toiled in factories, mills, and mines. The girl in this 1908 photograph had already worked in a North Carolina textile mill for two years when Lewis Wickes Hine took her picture. Courtesy of the National Archives, Washington, D.C.

clerks. In the North, the kinds of child labor that the reformers most objected to were rapidly declining as a result of compulsory education laws, an abundance of inexpensive immigrant labor, and technological innovations (such as the telephone, which reduced the need for messengers). But in the South, the use of child labor in textile mills continued to rise until World War I.[73]

The crusade against child labor drew support from such groups as the National Consumer League, founded in 1890, and the National Child Labor Committee, established in 1904. Trade unions argued that child labor depressed adult wages, while southern advocates of child labor restrictions, like Alexander J. McElvey of the National Child Labor Committee, maintained that having white children work in mills, mines, and factories endangered the "Anglo-Saxon race." Spearheading opposition to any restrictions were southern textile manufacturers, who charged that the National Child Labor Committee was the mouthpiece of New England mill owners, who were out to eliminate their southern competitors. The Catholic church also denounced government interference in the family, partly out of a recognition that poor families desperately needed their children's earnings. Thirty-five states adopted laws restricting child labor in the

1910s, but lax enforcement convinced reformers that federal legislation was necessary.[74]

The first federal child labor law, which would have prohibited children under fourteen from working in factories and mills (but not on farms), was introduced in Congress in 1906. After its defeat, opponents of child labor persuaded Congress to authorize a federal investigation of the working conditions of women and children, which renewed pressure for reform. In 1916 the Keating-Owen bill passed Congress, prohibiting interstate shipment of products from mines employing children under sixteen or factories using children under fourteen. It also barred fourteen- and fifteen-year-olds from working more than eight hours a day, six days a week, or after seven at night. Altogether, the law would have ended child labor for only 150,000 children. Several million other child laborers, notably those who lived on farms, would not have been covered.[75]

Keating-Owen was in effect just 273 days before the Supreme Court, by a five-to-four vote in *Hammer v. Dagenhart* (1918), struck it down, ruling that the federal government had no power to regulate manufacturing in individual states. Four years later the Supreme Court in *Bailey v. Drexel* ruled that a law taxing the profits of corporations utilizing child labor was also unconstitutional. In 1924 Congress passed a constitutional amendment authorizing legislation to restrict child labor. This amendment, which did not prohibit child labor or require Congress to pass any laws, was not ratified by the states. In 1926 the National Association of Manufacturers proposed a minimum age of fourteen for employment as well as restrictions on dangerous work and on work between nine at night and seven in the morning for older children. But the association failed to support any legislation to enact these measures.[76]

In 1892 Kate Douglas Wiggin, the author of the bestselling novel *Rebecca of Sunnybrook Farm,* the story of a rambunctious, rule-breaking ten-year-old orphan, wrote an article for *Scribner's* magazine titled "Children's Rights." In it she drew a distinction between child protection—the child's right to special protection from extreme forms of abuse and neglect—and children's rights—which included an independent legal identity, a degree of autonomy from parents, and the right to a "free, serene, healthy, bread and butter childhood," unburdened by heavy labor. In answer to the question "Who owns the child?" Wiggin answered pointedly: no one. "The parent is simply a divinely appointed guardian," she wrote. Wiggin's notion that children have a right to a proper childhood and that adults have a duty to serve as their stewards remains a challenge to Americans today, who need to duplicate the child-savers' passion, while overcoming their limitations.[77]

Throughout American history, interest in children's welfare has ebbed and flowed. The Progressive era represented a high point. However circumscribed the Progressive reforms might appear in retrospect, they represented an effort, not wholly unsuccessful, to universalize the middle-class ideals of childhood as a period devoted to play and education. Following World War I, public concern over children's issues faded. Contributing to the decline in interest was staunch opposition from the Catholic church to government interference in the family and a hostile Supreme Court, which repeatedly struck down child labor legislation. Equally important, child welfare professionals shifted their focus away from broader political and economic issues and instead focused on psychological maladjustments within individual families. It was not until the Great Depression greatly intensified problems of child welfare that a new phase of reform emerged.[78]

chapter nine

Children under the Magnifying Glass

THE PERIOD from 1865 to 1910 was the golden age of American children's fiction. From the late 1860s—when Horatio Alger's *Ragged Dick*, Louisa May Alcott's *Little Women*, and Thomas Bailey Aldrich's *Story of a Bad Boy* were published—to the early 1900s—when Lucy Maud Montgomery's *Anne of Green Gables*, Booth Tarkington's *Penrod*, Eleanor Porter's *Pollyanna*, and Kate Douglas Wiggin's *Rebecca of Sunnybrook Farm* appeared—a new kind of children's literature arose, fundamentally different from the fiction that preceded it. Unlike postrevolutionary literature, with its wooden characters and simplistic plots, later children's books sought to excite young readers' imagination rather than instruct them or shape their character.[1]

Children's fantasy literature arose during the 1850s. For boys, there were plot-driven adventure stories like Richard Henry Dana's *Two Years before the Mast*. For girls, there were sentimental domestic novels, like Susan Warner's *The Wide, Wide World*, which typically featured a female orphan who must find her way in a threatening world. After the Civil War, imaginative literature proliferated. While there was no American counterpart to the German *Bildungsroman*, a chronicle of a young person's self-discovery, spiritual and emotional development, and growing psychological self-awareness, American children's fiction placed recognizably realistic children at the heart of the narrative and explored the process of growing up. An essay in the December 1865 issue of the *Atlantic Monthly* attributed the sudden outpouring of children's literature to the increasing regimentation of young people's lives. Imaginative literature sustained children's spirits as their lives grew more rigidly structured: "What shall we do with our children? . . . The Slaveholder's Rebellion is put down; but how shall we deal with the never-ceasing revolt of the new generation against the old? And how to keep our Young American under the thumb of his father and mother without breaking his spirit?" In the free-floating world of fiction, children's fantasies of adventure and freedom were realized.[2]

These books allayed children's fears while providing them with fantasies of escape and empowerment. They allowed middle-class children to imagine adventures and challenges no longer attainable in real life. The heroes of many American childhood classics were orphans, like Tom Sawyer, or half-orphans, like Huck Finn. Freed from parental authority, these books' protagonists experience a freedom that is at once exhilarating and terrifying. Many of the books featuring female protagonists, like *Little Women,* also dealt with the challenge of controlling the emotions of anger and envy considered inappropriate for middle-class girls.[3]

Today children's literature is radically separate from adult literature, but after the Civil War this was not the case. Many of the era's greatest authors, including Mark Twain, wrote stories for children, and readers of all ages devoured tales about barefoot rascals and mischiefmakers, exuberant tomboys, and adorable cherubs who redeem curmudgeonly adults. At a time when middle-class children's lives were becoming more regimented, children's books expressed nostalgia for a simpler past and fantasies of youthful freedom. Through literature, children and adults alike got a sense of childhood as adventurous and precarious. But like other golden ages, the golden age of children's literature proved fleeting. Freudian psychoanalysis, with its recognition of childhood sexuality and sibling rivalry, and its conception of children as creatures of unappeasable drives that must be repressed, sublimated, and redirected during the passage to adulthood, made the earlier literature, with its emphasis on childhood innocence and the essential goodness of even the "bad" boy, seem hopelessly naïve and unsophisticated.

Scientific understanding of children's emotional, physical, and sexual development increased markedly at the end of the nineteenth century, giving rise to two developments with far-reaching repercussions for the history of childhood. The first was the advent of scientific childrearing advice; the second was the emergence of the modern concept of adolescence. The heightened awareness of children's developmental stages contributed, in turn, to institutional developments that continue to structure children's experience today: the appearance of the kindergarten; the rapid expansion of the high school; and the proliferation of adult-controlled environments for middle-class girls and boys in their teen years, of which the best known are the Boy Scouts, Boys' Clubs, Camp Fire Girls, and Girl Scouts.

Contributing to the development of scientific information on child-rearing were the high child death rate, the desire to upgrade the maternal role and treat motherhood as a serious vocation, and the sense that the world of white-collar employment required children to be socialized in new ways. A concern with personality development replaced an earlier preoccupation with shaping children's moral character as mothers and childrearing experts expressed a new interest in such psychological traits as shyness, timidity, and bravado. Alongside the emergence of a new science of parenting came an awareness of adolescence as a distinct, conflict-riven stage characterized by intense passions, a penchant for risk-taking, and wildly fluctuating emotions. G. Stanley Hall, the psychologist whose 1904 book on adolescence helped popularize the concept, convinced many parents and educators that young people were growing up too fast, that adolescence needed to be prolonged, and that the early and midteenage years needed to be spent in specialized institutions designed to meet adolescents' special psychological needs. Worried that "our urban-

In this late nineteenth-century elementary classroom in Aspen, Colorado, the girls wear dresses with puffed sleeves and high collars; the boys wear jackets. The formality of the pupils' clothing illustrates the seriousness with which their parents took their schooling. Courtesy of the Denver Public Library.

ized hothouse life . . . tend[s] to ripen everything before its time," Hall argued for institutions where adolescent energies might be sublimated through sports and other age-appropriate activities, and where young people could be shielded from adult pressures and temptations.[4]

One indicator of a shift in outlook was the emergence of pediatrics as a medical specialty. In 1860, when the German-born physician Abraham Jacobi established the country's first clinic for the treatment of children's diseases in New York, 15 to 20 percent of American infants died before their first birthday. Of those who survived to the age of one, another 10 percent were dead before the age of five. By 1880, when the American Medical Association established a section on children's diseases, ten medical schools offered courses in pediatrics and some 700 doctors specialized in treating children's illnesses. No longer were affluent parents or their physicians willing to respond to childhood diseases with resignation. The rise of pediatrics as a distinct specialty was the first sign of a growing interest in "scientizing" childhood.[5]

Charles Darwin inaugurated the scientific study of child development in 1877, when he published "A Biographical Sketch of an Infant," based upon his observations of his son Doddy thirty-seven years earlier. During the infant's first week, the British scientist discovered that his newborn son "was capable of various reflex actions, namely sneezing, hickuping, yawning, stretching, and of course sucking and screaming." "With a naturalist's curiosity and a father's empathy," he tried to determine when his son first exhibited affection, anger, fear, pleasure, shyness, a moral sense, development of language, reaction to his self-image, and a capacity for abstract reasoning. Comparing his child with various primates, Darwin tried to determine which of his son's behaviors were instinctual and which were the product of nurture.[6]

Darwin's sketch inspired the first systematic studies of mental and emotional child development. In September 1880, under the direction of psychologist G. Stanley Hall, four experienced kindergarten teachers interviewed more than 400 children entering Boston's schools. The teachers asked each child 134 questions dealing with animals, astronomy, geography, mathematics, meteorology, and plants. Hall was startled by the children's ignorance. Eighty percent did not know what a beehive was. Fully 90 percent did not know what the ribs were, 65 percent couldn't identify their ankles, and 93 percent did not know that leather came from animals. Hall concluded that teachers could not assume that children came to school with a common fund of basic knowledge.[7]

In the 1880s and 1890s the study of child development was institutionalized as educators, physicians, and psychologists, notably Hall, the president of Clark University, and Earl Barnes, a professor of education at Stanford, gathered empirical information about children's physical growth, psychological development, and sexual maturation. Through questionnaires and close observations of thousands of children, researchers investigated language development, hearing, and eyesight; children's ethical and religious impulses; and their psychological lives, including their ideas about old age, disease, and death. Known as the "Child Study" movement, the scientific study of child development carried profound consequences for the experience of childhood. It identified a series of sharply differentiated developmental stages, each with its own distinctive characteristics and psychology. It isolated certain norms—including norms about weight, size, and cognitive development—that could be applied to children of particular ages. Its standardized norms also altered the way young people were reared by inspiring new kinds of childrearing manuals, written by physicians and psychologists rather than by ministers and moralists, and espousing rational rather than spiritual advice.

The central figure in the scientific study of children was G. Stanley Hall, a student of William James and the recipient of Harvard's first Ph.D. in psychology, who is best remembered today for bringing Sigmund Freud and Carl Jung to the United States in 1909. During the 1880s and 1890s Hall enlisted large numbers of teachers and college-educated mothers to keep detailed records of children's behavior and to participate in regular discussions about child development and children's problems. Through child study, Hall hoped to augment the scientific understanding of child development and awaken the public to children's needs. The first organization formally dedicated to child study was the Society for the Study of Child Nature, founded by mothers in the Ethical Culture movement in New York in 1889, who were especially interested in the toys and punishments appropriate for their children. Three years later the American Association of University Women formed child study groups of its own. By 1897, when the National Congress of Mothers held its first convention, women's clubs and the new parent-teacher associations had also taken up child study activities. Child study appealed primarily to women who were more conservative than those engaged in suffrage agitation or child-saving activities among the poor. Relying on questionnaires drawn up by Hall and others addressing such topics as doll-playing, children's lies, and childhood fears, the groups collected 20,000 questionnaires in 1895.[8]

During the 1910s and 1920s Hall's reliance on data collected by untrained mothers and teachers was dismissed by professional psychologists as amateurish and unscientific. The anthropologist Margaret Mead attacked the movement as well because it emphasized biologically innate stages of development and downplayed the importance of cultural conditioning. The movement, however, contributed much useful knowledge. The anthropologist Franz Boas discovered that children's physical growth occurs in spurts, with wide variations among young people. The studies also detected alarming rates of health problems among schoolchildren, which led to the first eye and hearing tests in schools.[9]

The child study movement promoted the first serious attempts to study children's play, culture, and personal ideals. A particular object of attention was young people's tendency to form cliques, gangs, and clubs. The movement contributed to a new view of juvenile delinquency, which was regarded less as a precursor of criminality than a product of impulsive behavior, misguided instincts, and a faulty environment. The concern with the child's inner life was evident in the movement's emphasis on the importance of children's imagination; for the first time, large numbers of adults took children's impulses, fancies, dreams, and fears seriously. But it was primarily the notion that children develop through clearly differentiated cognitive, emotional, and physiological stages, marked by distinctive psychological and emotional characteristics, that was the movement's lasting legacy.[10]

Heavily influenced by Darwin's theory of evolution, early studies of childhood development embraced the notion of "recapitulation," that the development of each individual mirrors the evolution of the species from savagery to civilization. The child study movement identified a stage of early childhood, a period that should be devoted to free play, healthful exercise, and oral instruction, devoid of premature learning; a succeeding stage suitable for intensive instruction in reading, writing, and arithmetic; and, most important of all, adolescence, a period of psychological and emotional storm and stress that began with puberty and marked a young person's social and sexual maturation. The institutional settings of childhood were radically restructured to meet children's needs in each of these stages. Kindergartens, junior high schools, and new kinds of high schools represented public responses to the new understanding of child development.

In 1897 the *New York Times* published an editorial to mark the founding of the National Congress of Mothers: "Given one generation of children properly born and wisely trained, and what a vast proportion of human ills would disappear from the face of the earth!" In the 1890s there was a growing sense that modern science offered a fresh and correct approach to childrearing, echoing the Progressive era's preoccupation with expertise in other realms. Earlier childrearing manuals had emphasized loose schedules for feeding and toilet training. But in the mid-1890s the most popular advice manuals favored a systematic approach that was strictly regimented, standardized, and rationalized. The child was seen as a small animal with fearsome appetites, who had to be broken in and trained to be a well-adjusted adult, a creature of habit and self-control. To produce a responsible adult, parents needed to impose regular habits, feed and attend infants at appointed times, and refrain from "spoiling" them with unnecessary displays of affection.[11]

The Dr. Spock of his day was L. Emmett Holt, a pediatrician whose *Care and Feeding of Children: A Catechism for the Use of Mothers and Children's Nurses,* published in 1894, served as a guidebook for Benjamin Spock's own mother. Dr. Holt described the child as a "delicately constructed piece of machinery" and recommended a highly regimented approach to parenting, which he considered necessary to ensure children's health. He advised mothers not to pick up babies when they cried, to enforce rigid feeding schedules, and to use stationary cribs instead of rocking cradles. Dr. Holt did not consider breast-feeding necessary. Instead he advocated precise feeding schedules to encourage regular habits, as well as forceful measures to discourage bad ones; he suggested fastening splints to infants' elbows to prevent thumb-sucking. His child was to be forcibly molded into a socially acceptable state.[12]

The dictates of scientific childrearing received their most extreme expression in the writings of the behaviorist psychologist John B. Watson, who believed that the modification of behavior through positive and negative reinforcement was the key to proper childrearing. He claimed that if mothers followed behaviorist principles, they could produce whatever category of child they wanted: "A doctor, lawyer, artist, merchant-chief, and yes, even a beggar-man and thief." Watson insisted that "at three years of age the child's whole emotional life plan has been laid down"; his approach was to mold human behavior by scientific control. He called on mothers to put children on four-hour feeding and sleeping schedules; to begin toilet training no later than the age of six months; to prohibit pacifiers; and, above all, to avoid displays of affection. "When you are tempted to pet your child," he warned, "remember that mother love is a dangerous instrument. An instrument which may inflict a never-healing wound." He placed particular emphasis on the need to suppress thumb-sucking and infantile masturbation, which could be restrained through leather cuffs, aluminum mittens, splints that would keep babies from bending their arms, tape, and bad-tasting ointments placed on babies' fingers and thumbs. It was childrearing by constraint and deprivation.[13]

In the late 1920s there was a sharp reaction against scientific childrearing advice. Freudian theory, with its emphasis on the importance of psychological and emotional nurture, cast an ugly light on Watsonian repressiveness, and affluence made the inner-directed, rigidly self-disciplined adult obsolete. Now the well-adjusted adult was a softer, more easygoing creature, capable of enjoying leisure as well as work. In consequence, the baby began to look less beastly and more justified in its demands. Partly in reaction to Watson's cold-blooded advice, pediatrician Dr. C. Anderson Aldrich in 1936 wrote *Babies Are Human Beings,* which Benjamin Spock would acknowledge in his own manual on baby and childcare.[14]

While the child study movement and the childrearing experts focused their attention almost exclusively on young children, the problems of older boys and girls commanded increasing public attention. Boys seemed less hardy, virile, and manly than their fathers and grandfathers. There was a growing fear that feminine supervision and the comforts of urban life had rendered boys soft and effeminate. Theodore Roosevelt—who had been asthmatic and bespectacled as a boy, before taking up gymnastics, boxing, and shooting—summed up this attitude when he claimed that native-born males were lapsing into "mere animal sloth and ease" and succumbing to a "gradual failure of vitality." Exacerbating fears of emasculation were broader social transformations, such as the closing of the western frontier, the lure of pool halls, and the growth of bureaucratic organization, office work, and age-graded schools, which reduced the opportunities for individual initiative. Urban and industrial life was transforming boys into "flat-chested cigarette smokers with shaky nerves and doubtful vitality."[15]

To cope with the popularly perceived boy problem, youth workers established a number of adult-sponsored youth organizations targeted at middle-class teens, including the boys' department of the Young Men's Christian Association, the Boys' Clubs, and the Boy Scouts, founded in the United States in 1910. For millions of American boys, participation in these organizations would serve as a rite of passage, signaling the transition from boyhood to adolescence. Unlike earlier youth organizations, formed by youths themselves and containing a wide range of ages, these new organizations were adult-directed and targeted at a narrow range of young people.

Temperance organizations and Protestant churches took the lead in sponsoring young people's societies aimed at moral renovation. During the 1870s and 1880s Boys' Brigades and chivalric orders modeled on the court of King Arthur sought to help young men navigate the teen years. Through a program emphasizing character building and "muscular Christianity"—including competitive sports and physical education—these organizations sought to promote an ideal of Christian manliness and counteract the widespread impression that religion was a feminine phenomenon. After the turn of the century, secular organizations, such as the Woodcraft Indians (formed around 1902) and the Boy Scouts, sought to revitalize masculinity through various forms of primitivism, including Indian lore and woodcraft. It was their belief that structured activities supervised by adult men provided the best solution to the boy problem. Many of these organization's founders were deeply uneasy about puberty, adult sexuality, and coeducation, and believed that physical activity would take boys' minds off girls and stave off masturbation. Fears that boys were "overcivilized" and cut off from physical challenges prompted a yearning for a return to the primitive life in the rugged, invigorating wilderness. Deeply fearful of feminine weakness, worried that modern life was emasculating, they wanted to prepare boys for the strenuous life. Emphasis on bodily vigor, outdoor exercise, and other wholesome activities would ensure that boys would not become sissies, itself a new word coined around the turn of the century.

Though modeled on the British Boy Scout movement founded by Robert Baden-Powell, the Boy Scouts of America was fundamentally different. Baden-Powell had formed the Boy Scouts partly in response to British reverses during the Boer War and wanted to prepare British boys for military service. His American counterparts, such as Ernest Thompson Seton, Daniel Carter Beard, and James West, were much more interested in instilling the character traits in boys that would help them succeed in the rapidly shifting occupational world of the middle class by encouraging group bonding and leadership skills. Between 1910 and 1919 the Boy Scouts recruited 300,000 members, almost exclusively from the urban middle class and the sons of skilled workers. Farm boys and working-class youth were too busy or too poor for scouting and Catholics too suspicious of its Protestant Americanism. Though highly successful in recruitment, the Boy Scouts was much less successful in retention. Membership turnover was high, and boys preferred the athletics and camping to the moralizing of scoutmasters. Most boys left the Boy Scouts by the age of fifteen as they became more interested in school sports and girls than in wearing uniforms. As a Salt Lake City Scout executive noted in 1922, "when the girl comes, the Scout goes."[16]

Anxieties about girls echoed the worries about boys. While some parents wanted their daughters to be "young ladies," a class-laden term connoting propriety and rectitude, increasingly adults encouraged them to be "real girls," a phrase signifying wholesome vitality and energy. During the last decades of the nineteenth century, girls acquired growing freedom from societal restraints. The women's bicycle, introduced around 1890,

A Boy Scout troop parades through downtown Denver, Colorado, around 1918. Courtesy of the Denver Public Library.

gave girls greater freedom to move about in public. Late nineteenth-century girls were the first to participate in team sports. In addition to calisthenics and drills, which had been common since the mid-nineteenth century, a growing number participated in field hockey, basketball, croquet, and tennis. As a result of the influence of women physical educators, however, girls' sports were fundamentally different from boys'. Inclusive rather than competitive, they tended to emphasize participation over victory and rhythmic grace over strenuous physical activity. Many girls found elements of boys' culture appealing, such as scouting, with its uniforms and emphasis on outdoor activity. Unlike their British counterparts, who were called Girl Guides, American girls embraced the name Girl Scouts (over strenuous opposition from the Boy Scouts), with its connotations of danger and daring. In contrast to the Boy Scouts, however, neither the Girl Scouts nor the Camp Fire Girls emphasized character building. The Camp Fire Girls' final law, revealingly, was "Be Happy."[17]

Toward the end of the nineteenth century there was a great outpouring of advice manuals, career handbooks, health guides, magazines, stories, and works of fiction featuring the word *girl* in their title. Girls, for the first time, had sufficient money to purchase books and magazines for themselves; those that they bought exposed them to new kinds of social roles and situations about which they could dream. Unlike the obtrusively didactic fiction of the prewar years, the new girls' literature focused on the world outside the home. Decades before the appearance of Nancy Drew, books for girls featured girl detectives, nurses, college girls, and typists. Workplaces were imagined as places of adventure, where young women could assert their independence and prove their mettle, while college was depicted as a place where they could forge strong friendships and exhibit self-sufficiency. Grossly disproportionate to the actual number of women who worked in offices or attended college, these books offered a fantasy world where young women could live free of adult supervision.[18]

One recurrent theme in popular girls' books such as *Anne of Green Gables, Pollyanna,* and *Rebecca of Sunnybrook Farm* was an optimistic young girl's power to redeem adult curmudgeons. Although the word *Pollyanna* has become a synonym for naïve optimism, these literary characters were anything but passive creatures. They consciously deployed their ingenuity and charm to alter adult behavior. Popular girls' books also exposed the bleak underside of family life. Anna Sewall's heartbreaking 1877 tale of animal cruelty, *Black Beauty,* revealed abuse, alcoholism, and family rupture.[19]

During the 1890s the concept of girlhood shifted in two divergent directions. In Charles Dana Gibson's illustrations, the term *girl* is applied to young women in their twenties. The Gibson Girl, with her hourglass figure, upswept hair, and haughty, aristocratic air, personified the spirit of a changing culture. Shapely and self-assured, the Gibson Girl was conscious of her erotic power in ways that Victorian girls were not. "Before her," wrote the *New York World,* "the American girl was vague, nondescript, inchoate." Slim and athletic, she played golf and tennis, rode bicycles, and provided a new model of how postadolescent women were to carry themselves.[20]

At the same time, a juvenilized image of girlhood also took shape as the expansive late nineteenth-century category of girlhood was subdivided and sequenced. Early twentieth-century girls' books, such as those written by "Carolyn Keene," were of interest exclusively to girls younger than their mid-teens, much as girls' organizations, such as the Girl Scouts and the Camp Fire Girls, appealed mainly to early adolescents. Meanwhile, well before World War I, the word *flapper* entered the language, referring not to the bobbed hair, short-skirted young woman but, initially, to the boy-conscious, flirtatious teenage girl. The boundaries separating school-girls from older adolescents were hardening, with schoolgirls regarded as children and adolescence acquiring heightened sexual overtones.[21]

At the beginning of the twentieth century the term *adolescence* came into popular use to describe the turbulent period between puberty and physical maturity. In 1904, in a book titled *Adolescence: Its Psychology and Its Relations to Physiology, Anthropology, Sociology, Sex, Crime, Religion and Education,* G. Stanley Hall described adolescence as a distinct, conflict-ridden stage of development. Brought on by rapid physical, mental, and emotional growth, sexual maturation, and an impulse to separate from parents, adolescence was a "new birth," a phase of emotional upheaval and fluctuating emotions marked by contradictory tendencies toward hyperactivity and inertness, selfishness and altruism, bravado and a sense of worthlessness. Adolescence, in Hall's view, was a biological stage, not a cultural construct. Environment could exacerbate adolescent upheavals, but their roots lay in intrinsic biological forces that accompanied puberty. He asserted that behavior that might be diagnosed as insane in adults was perfectly normal in an adolescent.[22]

The word *adolescence* comes from the Latin *adolescentia,* a term frequently used in medieval discussions of the stages of life. Yet the word did not acquire widespread usage or associations with puberty, generational conflict, identity formation, and psychological volatility until the early twentieth century.[23] Far from inventing the concept single-handedly, Hall systematized earlier ideas about youth that could be traced at least as far back as Rousseau's *Emile:* that the onset of puberty brought on a stormy period of strong fluctuating passions. There can be no doubt, however, that his conception of adolescence—as a time of passion, energy, and emotional instability—was a product of specific cultural and social circumstances. In part, it was a response to late nineteenth-century fears of overcivilization, emasculation, and degeneration. It was also related to changing patterns of middle-class family life. By the beginning of the twentieth century, larger numbers of young people were living at home and remaining in school through their mid-teens. The term *adolescence* provided a handle that urban middle-class parents used to understand the special difficulties they faced in raising teenage daughters and sons. Hall's conception of adolescence was highly gendered, and was much more closely associated with male than with female behavior. The kinds of behaviors that Hall linked with adolescence—such as "storm and stress" and assertions of independence—were associated mainly with masculinity.[24]

Hall believed that adolescence should be prolonged. During this psychologically turbulent period, adolescents needed to be protected from premature adulthood and insulated from contact with older youths who might lead them astray. Adolescents needed to be separated from the world of adults, except for those who would guide and nurture them through the upheavals of adolescence and prepare them for a responsible adulthood. Hall considered adolescence so important to the development of healthy adulthood that any attempt to cut it short would carry dire psychological consequences. In retrospect, it is clear that adolescence is at once a stage of social, psychological, cognitive, and physiological development and a structural status imposed on youth. Psychologists, educators, and youth workers invoked biology and psychology to promote their own middle-class notions of a proper adolescence. Convinced that adolescence was a period of emotional instability and vulnerability, the architects of modern adolescence argued that the best way to promote a healthy adjustment to adulthood was to give adolescents time to mature in carefully controlled, adult-monitored environments, such as the high school, and adult-directed extracurricular activities. Work, they were convinced, was not a proper solution to the problems of adolescence, since it exposed the young prematurely to the stresses and corruptions of the adult world. Rather, it was the high school that was to provide a suitably secure, adult-supervised environment. But if adolescent status was an adult invention and a product of shifts in demography, economics, and institutional arrangements, adolescent culture was largely the creation of young people themselves, who created a distinctive high school culture centering on sports, dating, and the peer group.[25]

As late as 1920, only 16 percent of seventeen-year-olds—less than one in six—graduated from high school. Already, however, high school attendance had become a normative experience among the children of the professional and business classes. Between 1880 and 1900 the number of public high schools increased 750 percent. As the high school student body grew larger and more diverse, intense controversy erupted over the curriculum. Leading college educators wanted high schools to maintain a classical academic curriculum that would prepare students for post-secondary study. This view found its most influential expression in the 1893 report by a Committee of Ten, chaired by Harvard President Charles Eliot, which argued that all students should study the same core subjects but that they should also have an opportunity to take a limited number of elective courses that would address their individual needs. To ensure that students were properly prepared for college, the committee insisted that all students study core courses a specific number of hours each week for a prescribed number of years.[26]

Public school educators disagreed, and called for a highly differentiated high school curriculum, with tracks appropriate to students' abilities and career goals. They believed that the high school should be adapted to the distinct needs of adolescents, not the goal of college admission, thus beginning a gulf in purpose between high schools and colleges that persists to this day. The highly influential 1918 report, *The Cardinal Principles of Secondary Education,* emphasized vocational and practical education for the majority of high school students, along with civics education, health education, and a basic command of reading, writing, and mathematics. To place students in the appropriate track, high schools, beginning in the 1920s, instituted intelligence tests premised on the idea that each person has a fixed intelligence quotient that should determine her or his course of study.[27]

In addition to providing practical vocational training, public school educators believed that high school should serve as an agency of socialization. High schools were to provide "the worthy use of leisure" and "the general social training of the child" by offering a wide range of extracurricular activities, including music and drama clubs, speech and debating societies, sports, and student government. A key issue was whether these activities would be student- or teacher-supervised. By the second decade of the twentieth century, the answer was clear: Schools had assigned faculty advisers to every extracurricular activity.[28]

Sports was the first bastion to succumb to teacher control. Partly at the request of students themselves, high school administrators took over the organization of high school sports teams. Recruitment of athletes had grown so competitive and corrupt that many students felt that only the organization of sports by school officials could clean up athletics. But the drift to adult control was not confined to sports. Debate, too, became a school-organized activity, and as early as 1911 observers complained that high school debate coaches were writing their students' speeches. Perhaps the most contentious conflicts involved high school fraternities and sororities. After the turn of the century, high schools embarked on a prolonged, concerted, and ultimately successful campaign to prohibit these organizations.[29]

Why did the autonomous student organizations of the mid and late nineteenth century disappear, and why did students submit to administrative control of their activities? One reason was that the schools offered better facilities and coaching than students could provide for themselves. But it also reflected a shift in students' self-perception. As high schools grew more important as placement agencies and assumed a more all-encompassing role in middle-class lives, students began to see themselves as juveniles and became more and more acquiescent. It seemed appropriate that adults who knew better should organize their leisure as well as their academic activities.[30]

The history of middle-class childhood can be seen as a story of progress, a Rousseauian tale of middle-class children lavished with more maternal attention, freed from early labor, given extended time to play and mature, and offered the opportunity to pursue extended education and to take part in new institutions, such as the Boy Scouts, the Girl Scouts, and the Camp Fire Girls, designed to meet their needs for recreation and sociability. But in fact the story is much more problematic. The association of the very young with fragility and vulnerability, and of older children with immaturity and psychological volatility, resulted in the denial of many opportunities for young people to associate with adults other than their parents and teachers and to demonstrate their growing maturity and competence. Yet if the contours of young people's lives were increasingly imposed by adults, the content would be largely shaped by young people themselves. Within the boundaries set by schools and adult-sponsored organizations, the young created cultures of their own, in which they would strive, only partly successfully, to assert an independent identity and a sense of competence.

chapter ten

New to the Promised Land

THE PROGRESSIVE ERA'S preoccupation with child welfare was inextricably connected with an influx of immigrants unequaled in American history. In the quarter-century before World War I, eighteen million immigrants entered the United States, mainly from southern and eastern Europe. By 1920 immigrants and their children formed between half and three-quarters of the population of Boston, Cleveland, Milwaukee, San Francisco, and St. Louis. Tens of thousands of immigrant children, many of Catholic or Jewish background, were set adrift in a new culture without the aid of parents to support them. Confronting a new language and novel customs as well as the stresses of poverty, they struggled to make their way in a new and challenging social environment.

Mary Antin was thirteen years old in 1894 when she, her mother, and two siblings migrated from Polotzk in the Pale of Russia to the slums of Boston to join her father, who had arrived three years earlier. Her description of her experiences, *The Promised Land,* published in 1912, is the classic account of the Jewish-American immigrant experience and a prototype for the entire genre of immigrant autobiographies. Mary viewed migration to the United States as a second birth and a liberation from Old World constraints. She was free from both the oppressions of czarist Russia and the restrictions of religious orthodoxy. As a symbol of their Americanization she and her siblings quickly shed their "despised immigrant clothing" and their "impossible Hebrew names."[1]

A seemingly naïve sense of hopefulness pervades her memoirs. Mary saw opportunity all around her. The school, where "no application [was] made, no questions asked," and there were "no examinations, rulings, exclusions; no machinations, no fees," offered a doorway to advancement. The "dazzlingly beautiful palace called a 'department store,'" where her family "exchanged our hateful homemade European costumes," was an agency of assimilation and upward mobility. She even marveled at the streetlights in her slum neighborhood, which provided light all night long, freeing her from having to carry a lantern. Mary celebrated cultural assimilation, and was preoccupied with acquiring English, shedding her accent, and dressing, speaking, and eating like an American. For Mary, the United States was truly the promised land.[2]

It is jarring to read *The Promised Land* today, when so much value is attached to the cultures that the immigrants shed. Later writers, who regarded the second and third generations as vacuous and materialistic, were much more conscious of the Faustian bargain that immigrants struck in order to become Americans. But *The Promised Land* itself contained bleak undertones that reveal the price of Americanization. Mary's home life disintegrated as she grew older and became more fully American. Her father, unable to master English, grew increasingly bitter. She not only had to earn money to help her family pay the rent; she had to parent her own parents.

The challenges that Mary's family faced were not unique. During the late nineteenth century, eastern European Jews found it ever harder to survive as petty traders or artisans in Russia. Facing mounting population pressures, competition from factory industry, and rising waves of anti-semitism, a third of all eastern European Jews migrated to the United States. With no homeland to return to, migration was not confined to adult men. Nor were daughters passive followers of pathways pioneered by their fathers. Like Irish daughters before them, large numbers of single young Jewish women migrated on their own. For many immigrant children, migration proved to be highly disruptive. Early in the twentieth century, Jewish charities identified 100,000 cases of desertion, meaning that a quarter of Jewish fathers deserted their families in the new land. In an attempt to locate these men, the *Jewish Daily Forward* ran a column, complete with photographs, called "The Gallery of Missing Husbands."[3]

As a self-described nation of immigrants, Americans are especially prone to romanticizing the immigrant family as a symbol of strength and cultural continuity. Viewed through the eyes of early twentieth-century immigrant children, however, it is clear that movement from one society to another was accompanied by intense feelings of psychological dislocation and marginality. Within immigrant households, generational roles were inverted, since the young found it easier to learn a new language and to pick up new customs than did their parents. Immigrant children not only became wage earners, but served as guides who helped their parents adjust to American customs and fashions, and as cultural intermediaries who had to negotiate with landlords, school officials, and others. Many immigrant families were beset by severe strains as parents and children clashed over religion, language, children's names, and dress. Americanization was a particularly divisive issue for immigrant daughters, who frequently quarreled with their parents about control over their paychecks, socializing with boys, and attendance at commercial, mixed-sex amusements. For many first-generation immigrant children, the lure of assimilation proved extremely strong, and this collided with their parents' desire to maintain older traditions and ensure that their offspring contributed to the family economy.

Thirteen-year-old Jack Moy and his mother sailed to the United States from China in 1927 and spent a month in the Angel Island detention center in San Francisco Bay separated from each other. Concerned about the entry of Chinese immigrants with false documentation, immigration officials asked embarrassingly personal questions, such as whether Jack's mother had bound feet, how many water buffalo his village had, or "who occupies the house on the fifth lot of your row in your native village." Discrepancies in an answer would result in deportation to China, a prospect that terrified the newcomers. Immigration officials noted every identifying mark, including scars, boils, and moles, on all immigrants before letting them enter the country.[4]

Whether they arrived at Castle Garden or Ellis Island, the receiving stations in New York; Galveston, Texas; or Angel Island, immigrant children shared certain problems. Their new land was not paved with gold. Poor housing; crowded, dirty neighborhoods; precarious economic conditions; a hostile reception from the native born; poorly prepared teachers and crowded classrooms; and child labor cut across ethnic lines. The premature death of children was especially common in immigrant families. In Buffalo in 1900 only about six of every ten Italian and Polish children survived childhood. Overcrowding was rampant in immigrant neighborhoods. In one three-room Russian-Jewish apartment, the parents shared their bedroom "with two, three, or even four of their younger children," while the older children slept in the kitchen on cots or on the floor, and two or more lodgers slept in the front room. In a three-room Philadelphia house, sixteen immigrants slept in two rooms each measuring eight by ten by seven feet.[5]

Psychological and emotional strains posed a special burden. Many immigrant children felt themselves caught between two worlds. Their im-

Japanese families await interrogation by immigration officials at the Angel Island immigration center in San Francisco Bay. Courtesy of the National Archives, Washington, D.C.

poverished homes seemed another world from what they discovered beyond them. Maria Ganz, a Jewish immigrant from Galicia in southern Poland, was just five years old when she took her first ride uptown, out of New York's Lower East Side. Along Fifth Avenue she saw "gorgeous carriages . . . and inside surely princes and princesses." "All the splendors I had seen" made her realize how "miserable our home was."[6]

It was in school that immigrant children confronted the new culture most intensely. Leonard Covello, who was born in southern Italy in 1887 and arrived in East Harlem in 1896, was placed in a "soup school" run by a Protestant mission. He sat in class, "trying to memorize words written on the blackboard, words which had absolutely no meaning to me because the teacher had never explained them." At the turn of the century, immigrant children made up a substantial majority of the students in the nation's largest cities. In New York City in 1905 as many as 125 children were admitted to one school in a single day, resulting in classes of 60 or even 70. Space was in such short supply that a hospital ship was deployed as a school. Many schools operated on two four-hour shifts.[7]

School classrooms frequently became sites of cultural conflict between immigrant pupils and native-born teachers, who attached little value to cultural diversity and sought to transform immigrant children into "little citizens" by forbidding them to speak their native language. Viewing schools as instruments of physical and moral uplift, educators emphasized American traditions and history. In addition to requiring students to recite lessons in arithmetic, spelling, grammar, and geography aloud, teachers inspected children's fingernails and their heads for lice, and lectured their students on "nail brushes, hair ribbons, shoe polish, pins, buttons, and other means to grace." In New York City schools, Jewish students were sometimes punished by having their mouths washed out with nonkosher soap.[8]

It is a myth that immigrant parents were, on the whole, indifferent or hostile toward schooling. Some parents, to be sure, did not want to make their children "better than you are." Parents who had recently arrived from rural, peasant backgrounds were particularly likely to discount the value of education. But it was family income, size, and children's birth order that best predicted how long a child remained in school. Immigrant families needed to balance their income and labor needs with their children's education. Many poorer families made the rational calculation that the child could best contribute to the family economy by going to work at an early age. Younger immigrant children were as likely as their native-born white peers to be enrolled in elementary school, but relatively few immigrant children attended high school. Less than a third of German children and a quarter of Italian children enrolled in secondary school, compared with 60 percent of native-born children, since older children's income was often essential for a family's survival. A typical adult male breadwinner was unemployed for an average of three months a year, and children had to fill this gap. As one immigrant father in St. Louis put it, "a family's wealth depends on the number of hands it has."[9]

Some groups subordinated their children's education to the goal of maximizing family income and acquiring property. Italian immigrants were especially likely to view their sojourn in America as temporary and thus felt pressed to make money quickly. Between 1907 and 1911, for every 100 Italians who arrived in the United States, 73 returned to the old country. It was their children's desire to remain in the United States that ultimately led many southern and eastern European immigrant families to settle here permanently. Other groups, notably Jewish immigrants from Russia, Poland, and Austria-Hungary, had no homeland to return to and planned to settle in the United States permanently, and thus kept their children in school longer. But while Jews used public schools to a greater extent than any other immigrant group, poverty prevented most Jewish children in the first or even the second generation from going beyond grade school.[10]

Among native-born whites and older immigrant groups—such as the Irish, Swedes, and Germans—girls were more likely to attend high school than boys. Among Russian and Polish-born Jews, southern Italians, and Poles, boys predominated. Jewish immigrants placed a premium on school attendance for boys, while first-generation southern Italian immigrants were particularly averse to sending girls to school. Catholic Slavic and Polish immigrants were particularly likely to regard public schooling as a threat to their religious and cultural values, and a substantial minority turned to parochial schools to shelter their children from the impact of Americanization. In Chicago, half the Catholic school-age population attended parochial schools, with separate parish schools for Irish, German, Polish, French, Bohemian, Ukrainian, and Lithuanian immigrants, allowing these ethnic groups to preserve their distinctive traditions. It was only in the 1920s that a more centralized parochial system, with common texts and curricula, emerged.[11]

During the nineteenth century some immigrant groups, notably Germans, had persuaded local communities to authorize tax-supported native-language schools. But by the early twentieth century most urban school systems sought to educate children in English as rapidly as possible and discouraged the use of native languages. Most immigrant children were assigned to a separate "English-immersion" class for five or six months before being moved into a class appropriate for their age. Immigrant children who could not speak English found schools to be an especially threatening and frustrating environment, with absenteeism reaching 60 percent or more in Chicago. Dropout rates were also extremely high. It took enormous determination and discipline for a child to manage the novelty of language, customs, school, and neighborhood alone. Some failed, but many succeeded.[12]

Settlement houses helped immigrant children to assimilate. Modeled after Toynbee Hall, a British charity established in an impoverished part of London in 1884, settlement houses were the most important social service agencies in slum neighborhoods. By 1918 there were 400 across the country. Before there were public libraries, kindergartens, adult evening classes, or community centers, settlement houses provided childcare, recreation, and adult education in immigrant neighborhoods. They taught immigrants English and "modern" forms of childrearing, cooking, and hygiene. They also offered limited job training, including classes in sewing and dressmaking. Unlike the more extreme Americanizers who wanted immigrants to immediately renounce their language, culture, and ethnic identity, settlement house workers, in order to attract clients, were accepting of ethnic cultures.[13]

The settlement houses were run largely by young college-educated women who had middle-class upbringings but felt called to work for the social welfare of less privileged people. Hull House founder Jane Addams, who spoke of the "snare of preparation"—prolonged schooling that seemed purposeless—rebelled against the demands of domesticity and felt called to serve the poor. These pioneering social workers combined a deep concern for the poor with a paternalistic impulse to teach immigrants to adopt scientific ideas about infant care, diet, and hygiene. As one put it, "These strangers from across the water must be taught to discard un-American habits and conventions, to accept new ideals." Immigrants and settlement house workers frequently clashed over such issues as the use of midwives in childbirth, nursing on demand, prolonged lactation, and the use of swaddling clothes and pacifiers—practices that immigrant mothers favored and many settlement workers opposed. The radical Emma Goldman denounced the settlement house movement for seeking to teach "the poor to eat with a fork," but many settlement workers overcame their class bias and worked closely with the immigrant community to alleviate its ills.[14]

The workplace, like the school and the settlement house, was an important site of cultural adjustment for immigrant children. Children's labor was grueling and unlike anything they had experienced before. The example of twelve-year-old Rose Gollup, who emigrated from a small village in western Russia to New York in 1892, underscores the work responsibilities that many immigrant children assumed. She lived with her father in a rented room on the Lower East Side, saving money to bring over her mother and younger brothers and sisters. One day her father told her he had found work for her in a garment shop where he knew the presser. "I lay awake long that night," she later recalled. "I was eager to begin life on my own responsibility but was also afraid." Her new boss asked her to demonstrate her skills. "All at once the thought came," she wrote, "If I don't do this coat quickly and well he will send me away at once." By the end of the first day, she discovered that she could do almost as much work as older women, and that they despised her for her ability, decrying that "snip of a girl coming and taking the very bread out of our mouth." Her chair had no back, and after a fourteen-hour day her neck was stiff and her back aching. For her labors she was paid $3 a week.[15]

Sweatshop discipline was harsh. Child laborers were charged for needles and thread and even the electricity they used. They were fined a half-day's pay if they were fifteen minutes late, and charged for a whole length of cloth if they spoiled a portion. They were even fined for singing and humming. To prevent the workers from leaving, doors were often locked in garment shops. After Rose was laid off from the garment factory, an agent placed her as a domestic servant. Rose regarded domestic service as especially demeaning. She found it hard to eat at the table with her employer's family, where she compared the "soup, meat, [and] potatoes" served at their meals with the bread and sugar-sweetened water that her family ate. As a servant, Rose had to wash and iron clothes, scrub floors, scale fish, clean fowl, and run errands to the nearby store. While her employers had beds, she was expected to throw two quilts over chairs at the end of a day's work. After two months she quit domestic service, saying to herself, "I would rather work in a shop." There, though she might be put upon by a demanding boss, at least she could go home at the end of the day and did not have to tolerate the obvious inequities that made domestic service such a trial.[16]

Most immigrant families depended on children's labor, whether this involved childcare, shopping, cooking, scavenging in the streets, or paid work inside or outside the home. Low wages made income pooling necessary. A federal study found that only 20 percent of Jewish immigrant fathers in seven major cities could support their families on their earnings. Immigrant families expected children to sacrifice their individual inclinations for the family's sake. A survey of Polish immigrants in 1911 found that the children of unskilled workers contributed 46 percent of their family's income and the children of skilled workers 35 percent.[17]

Among Russian-born Jewish girls under the age of sixteen, about 30 percent worked, mainly outside the home. Italian-born girls, in contrast, labored inside the home, making artificial flowers or sewing coats and trousers. Young children transported bundles of clothing and boxes of flowers back and forth from contractors to their homes, performed childcare, and scavenged wood and coal in the streets, a practice that resulted in the largest number of children's arrests. But work was not mere drudgery. For many young immigrants, work connected them to a world outside their family and ethnic community. It also offered them the money they needed to enjoy the pleasures of their new land.[18]

Immigrant parents held a very different view of childhood from the native-born middle class. Just as parents had a responsibility to support their children, their offspring had a reciprocal obligation to contribute to their household's economic well-being. Many immigrant parents considered American-born children, who were supported but not expected to reciprocate, as mere juveniles. Their children, in contrast, were "a little more advanced—not babies like they are here." Many immigrant children, in turn, wanted to be active contributors to the family economy. Jennie Matyras, the oldest daughter in a Russian-Jewish family, said: "My ambition in life was to get to be a good worker because being the oldest daughter, it was my job to do the dressmaking for the family."[19]

The challenge of cultural adjustment was as difficult, for many immigrant children, as adapting to the workplace. Rose Gollup was shocked to discover that many immigrant adults abandoned Jewish traditions in this new country. "The first thing men do in America," she observed, "is cut their beards and the first thing the women do is to leave off their wigs." When she arrived at Castle Garden she scarcely recognized her father, who had trimmed his beard and forelocks. Later she was aghast to realize that he carried money and bought her fruit on the Sabbath. Soon, however, she too became Americanized, and urged her mother to go without the traditional kerchief worn by married Orthodox Jewish women. Rose went from being a resisting traditionalist to an enthusiastic Americanizer in the course of her first year in the United States.[20]

Rose became briefly engaged to a young Jewish grocer from Broome Street in a courtship that involved a mixture of Old and New World traditions. She met the young man after her mother asked her to make a purchase at the store where he worked. She learned about her parents' intentions when they announced that the young man and his uncle would be paying a visit to their apartment. As a dutiful daughter, Rose accepted the engagement. But she did not believe she should marry someone she did not love, nor could she accept the traditional view that love would follow marriage. She found that books meant almost nothing to her husband-to-be, and she had no interest in becoming an assistant in her future husband's store. Unable to imagine herself happy in the marriage, she broke off the engagement. Rose was moved by the New World conception that one should marry someone one loved rather than follow one's parents' wishes. In the failed engagement we see the triumph of New World expectations over those of the old country.[21]

For many immigrant children, becoming American involved the rejection of older identities and adopting distinctively American styles and consumer products. Dress and personal appearance were critical symbols of Americanization. For eastern European Jews and southern Italians, everyday clothing had been practical and plain in the old country. After marriage, Jewish women were expected to cover their hair by wearing a *sheitel,* or wig. In the United States, many Jewish women rejected this custom. "My mother never wore a wig," said one immigrant. "She was modern." Wearing ready-made clothing was one of the first markers of Americanization. Few things were more painful than to be labeled a "greenhorn," an unsophisticated foreigner. Leonard Covello, an Italian immigrant, was proud that even if he couldn't speak English, he still looked "to all outward appearances" like "an American." Many young immigrants were struck by the emphasis that Americans placed on the head and the feet—elaborate hairdos, fancy plumed hats (instead of head-scarves or wigs), and shoes (rather than work boots)—and by the stress on slimness. Shawls were discarded and replaced by store-bought dresses. Flamboyant dress—or what was called "putting on the style"—often became a source of tension between parents and children. Turn-of-the-century young immigrants exhibited little nostalgia for the clothing of the Old World. They wanted to fit in, not stand out, and leave the limitations of tradition behind them.[22]

Leisure activities, even more than clothing, were crucial symbols of Americanization. One immigrant child remembered being asked by her mother: "What does it mean when everybody says, 'Let's have fun'?" For the children of immigrants, fun meant new forms of commercial entertainment: candy stores, ice cream parlors and soda shops, nickelodeons, and, later, movie theaters. For many young immigrants, leisure was associated with freedom, romance, and the joys of consumption.[23]

Immigrant children's rapid acculturation frequently resulted in parent-child tensions. In the pages of the *Jewish Daily Forward,* a mother complained about her daughter's behavior. "During the first few years she was here without us she became a regular Yankee," the mother wrote, "and forgot how to talk Yiddish." The mother continued: "She does not like me to light the Sabbath candles, to observe the Sabbath. When I light the candles, she blows them out." Especially shocking was her daughter's lack of deference. "Once I saw her standing on the stoop with a boy." Her mother "asked her when she would come up," but her daughter didn't reply, and later "she screamed at me because I called her by her Jewish name." A New York City social worker observed a similar phenomenon. "The child attends the public school, and within a few months may come to despise that which he formerly held sacred. He sees no further use of Hebrew and laughs at his father for his pride in the knowledge of it."[24]

In the New World, family and age hierarchies were frequently inverted as immigrant children served as translators, interpreters, and cultural mediators. An Italian doctor observed: "The majority of adult Italians do not read any language, either Italian or English. On the other hand, most of the children read English, but few read Italian." Young immigrants became agents of acculturation. Often the first members of their family to learn English, children served as brokers with landlords, employers, and shopkeepers. The young also demanded changes in cultural practices they considered shamefully backward. Severe generational tensions often resulted from this inversion of family hierarchies.[25]

Hilda Satt Polacheck, a young Jewish immigrant from Poland, was determined to become a real American. Her mother was disappointed by her new country, never learned to speak English, and retreated into a religious piety that distanced her from her daughter. Hull House, the Chicago settlement house, became Hilda's second home and Jane Addams her surrogate mother. After her father's death, Polacheck went to work in a factory to support her family. Although her formal education ended when she was thirteen, she began to teach English to new immigrants at Hull House. Hilda Satt willingly Americanized her name when she entered the German Jewish Training School and took evening classes at Hull House, where she eventually taught Shakespeare and Dickens, but nothing about her Polish or Yiddish culture.[26]

The bitterest fights involved control over language, money, and leisure time. Language was a particular source of contention. One Jewish child remembered her mother declaring: "This is a Yiddish house and no Gentile languages are going to be spoken here." Jerre Mangione's sister sometime spoke English in her sleep; her mother forgave her because "she could not be responsible for her unconscious thoughts." Family battles frequently erupted over how much of children's wages had to be turned over their parents, and whether daughters would be allowed unchaperoned out of their parents' house. Some immigrant children, like Amalia Morandi, willingly handed their unopened pay envelopes to their parents. "I wouldn't dare open it up," she said, as a symbol of respect. But others refused. Abraham Bisno explained: "While the majority of them turned their money over to the family chest, there was quite a significant minority who would themselves be holders of their earnings, pay regular board to their families, and either save or spend money for themselves . . . They acquired the *right to a personality* which they had not ever possessed in the old country." One immigrant explained why he treated his children harshly: "If you don't keep control over them from the time they are little, you would never get their wages when they are grown up."[27]

Generational tensions were especially intense for daughters as they sought to break free from cultural and religious restraints. Immigrant parents were much more restrictive of daughters than of sons. Many immigrant fathers jealously guarded their daughters, restricted educational opportunities to sons, and limited female employment to unskilled labor in the home or in all-female environments. Immigrant parents expected daughters to turn over their earnings and delay marriage to contribute to the household. Coming out of a patriarchal tradition that privileged sons, many young women resented the expectation to subordinate their own freedom and education for their brothers' benefit. Grace Grimaldi's sister told her father "that she wouldn't let him prevent her from educating herself." Because her father needed his daughter's wages, he was forced to compromise.[28]

Many young immigrant women rejected the rigid gender separation that was a key component of Old World life and embraced the coeducational world of dating and commercial leisure. Young Jewish women, who had been confined to a separate place in the synagogue and denied a religious education in eastern Europe, were particularly eager to attend schools, movies, and dance halls. Daughters found ways to evade their parents' controls. Some immigrant parents turned to the police to buttress their authority over their daughters. Fearing the loss of daughters' wages

Between 1910 and 1920 at least 219,000 Mexican immigrants entered the United States, doubling the Hispanic population in Arizona, New Mexico, and Texas, and quadrupling California's. In this 1913 photograph, children account for most of the refugees fleeing revolutionary unrest, crossing the Rio Grande River into Brownsville, Texas. Courtesy of the Robert Runyon Collection, Center for American History, University of Texas.

and of their moral respectability, immigrant parents sometimes invoked newly enacted statutory rape laws to regulate their daughters' behavior.[29]

Becoming American was more complicated than just learning the language, embracing the customs and conventions of the new land, and losing accents and changing Old World habits and clothing. There was great tension over how much had to be sacrificed on the road to Americanization. In *The Rise of David Levinsky*, the 1917 immigrant classic by Abraham Cahan, the protagonist progressively breaks his religious, political, and family ties to achieve business success. Becoming American entailed costs as well as gains. It still does, although today sustaining older cultural traditions has become somewhat easier.

When Lucy Robbins Lang arrived in the United States at the turn of the century, her Aunt Chaye insisted that she and other family members drink a dose of castor oil to "purge Europe from [their] systems." Immigration, for many newly arrived children, entailed fitting in. Greenhorns had to transform themselves from outsiders and embrace the conventions of their new country. With today's higher valuation of multiculturalism, immigrant children find it somewhat easier to retain elements of their home culture. In a mobile, interconnected world, immigrants can not only retain ties to their home society but also consider that society part of their global community. Immigrant children can pick and choose which aspects of America they will adopt and which they will reject. In a 1996 novel, *Mona in the Promised Land*, written by Gish Jen (a second-generation Chinese-American whose birth name was Lillian), one sister decides to become Jewish like her school friends while another decides to devote her life to studying China. Unlike their turn-of-the-century counterparts who struggled to lose their accents and abandon Old World clothing and customs, today's immigrant children feel a greater ambivalence toward mainstream American culture. This is especially true of immigrant children of color, who do not easily fit into this country's bifurcated racial system. The new immigrant children reflect much more self-consciously on the costs and gains that come with migration—the mixture of shame and pride that they feel about their heritage and Old World customs and the difficulties and frustrations that come with adapting to a new culture.[30]

chapter eleven

Revolt of Modern Youth

IT WAS THE first of many crimes of the century. In 1924 two teenage heirs to great wealth abducted and murdered a fourteen-year-old neighbor. Outside Chicago's elite Harvard School for Boys, eighteen-year-old Richard Loeb and nineteen-year-old Nathan Leopold lured Bobby Franks into a rented car. As they drove away, one of the kidnappers fractured the schoolboy's skull with a chisel, then allowed him to bleed to death. To hinder identification, the murderers sprinkled acid over the body before dumping it in a remote culvert. This thrill killing was a vicious and senseless act, intended to demonstrate the superiority of the abductors' intellect. "The killing was an experiment," Leopold later told his defense counsel. "It is just as easy to justify such a death as it is to justify an entomologist in killing a beetle on a pin." Yet despite their arrogance and lack of remorse, the perpetrators were spared the death penalty.[1]

Leopold and Loeb were inseparable friends, academically precocious and socially well connected. Both boys had completed high school at fifteen. Dickie Loeb, the son of a retired Sears vice-president, had an I.Q. of 160 and had graduated from the University of Michigan at seventeen. "Babe" Leopold, whose father was a millionaire box manufacturer, was a University of Chicago graduate fluent in fourteen languages. The two inhabited an elaborate fantasy world. Convinced that they were Nietzschean supermen above ordinary standards of morality, they had thrown bricks through car windshields, started small fires, and engaged in petty theft before deciding to commit the perfect murder.

Their defense attorney, Clarence Darrow, persuaded a judge to spare their lives by getting four psychiatrists to explain how his privileged clients had developed the impulse to kill. The expert witnesses depicted the crime as a reaction to loveless childhoods, sexual abuse by an overly controlling governess, feelings of physical inferiority, trauma over a mother's death, and pressures for extreme academic overachievement. One psychologist described a homosexual relationship between the two, although his testimony was not reported by the press.[2]

Before the 1920s, explanations of juvenile violence emphasized deficiency and deprivation. Juvenile delinquents were assumed to be subnormal in intelligence, neglected by their families, and deprived of education. But the case of Leopold and Loeb suggested that any child, regardless of background, could suffer from a psychological disorder. Explained a juvenile court judge: "Let no parent flatter himself that the Leopold-Loeb case has no lesson for him . . . It is more than the story of a murder. It is the story of modern youth, of modern parents, of modern economic and social conditions, and of modern education." Many observers agreed that the Leopold and Loeb case embodied in extreme form "the story of modern youth": the weakening of parental authority, the growth of peer attachments, and the decline of traditional morality.[3]

Early twentieth-century parents sensed that they were living in a new era, fundamentally different from the one preceding it. Self-conscious modernity was the defining characteristic of this era. Every aspect of childhood was transformed. Instead of clothing infants in white gowns, a symbol of asexual innocence, baby girls began to be dressed in white and baby boys in blue. In another symbol of gender difference, boys started to wear pants and have their hair trimmed at two or three, three or four years earlier than in the past. Meanwhile a new commercial children's culture appeared, as store-bought toys replaced their homemade predecessors and children's book series proliferated. But the development that dominated public attention was the impression that the young were far more independent and less deferential than their predecessors. As a result of cars, telephones, and the movies, the young had broken away from the world of adults and established their own customs, such as dating, which were regulated by the peer group and not adults. This was the revolt of modern youth.[4]

A sociological study of Muncie, Indiana, a manufacturing town of 38,000, forty miles northeast of Indianapolis, underscored the changes taking place in young lives. Muncie's mothers were flabbergasted by their children's insolence. Fourteen-year-olds called them old-fashioned and said they were cruel when they wouldn't let them stay at a dance until eleven. Times had certainly changed. The town's adults had grown up on

farms and had attended just eight years of school. Their parents had expected them to spend their free time plowing fields, weeding gardens,
tending chickens, toting water, and churning butter. Their children, in
contrast, grew up listening to the radio, going to movies, driving cars, and
attending high school. The parents' mothers and fathers had assumed that
their children would comply with their demands, and most did; but by the
mid-1920s the younger generation had grown much more assertive. Parents and adolescents clashed over church attendance, curfews, dress, time
spent with members of the opposite sex, and use of the family car. Especially disturbing to parents were teenage smoking and petting parties,
"machine riding to other towns at night with dates," and the number of
times their children went out on school nights.[5]

In certain respects, Muncie's young people remained staunchly conservative. Less than a third of high school students believed that the theory
of evolution offered a more accurate account of humanity's origins than
the Bible. Ninety percent of the boys and 97 percent of the girls believed
that Christianity was the one true religion and that all people should convert to it. But in behavior, the worlds of adults and the young had drifted
far apart. Muncie's parents complained about "the diminishing place of
the home in the life of the child," the "sophistication" of young people's
"social life," and the "aggressiveness" of teenage girls. Their children
spent too much time on the telephone, and cars provided them with excessive amounts of privacy; a judge called autos "houses of prostitution on
wheels." Girls' growing freedom evoked alarm. "Girls aren't so modest
nowadays," said one resident. "We can't get our boys decent when girls
dress that way." Said another: "Girls are far more aggressive today. They
call boys up to try to make dates with them, as they never could have
when I was a girl." No longer was leisure time devoted to family activities. Instead parents and children spent a significant amount of time apart.
Adolescents spent half their evenings outside the family home.[6]

During the half-century between 1880 and 1930, parent-child relations
underwent a profound transformation. Middle-class family life grew more
democratic, affectionate, and child-centered, and the school and the peer
group became more significant in young people's lives. Bronislaw
Malinowski told a story that underscored the shift. He and his five-year-
old daughter argued, but despite his best efforts, the Polish-born anthropologist was unable to sway her opinion. The girl brought the argument
"to an abrupt conclusion by announcing: 'Daddy, what an ass you are.'"
Malinowski "tried to imagine what would have happened had I thus addressed my father some forty years ago. I shuddered and sighed."
Malinowski's story struck a responsive chord among American parents,

whose domestic authority had diminished while they envied their children's newfound freedom of expression. As sociologist Ernest Burgess put it, "In speech, in manner, and in attitude, boys and girls still in the teen age show heedless disregard for convention; a contempt for the advice of their elders, or worse yet, a smug indifference to it."[7]

By the 1920s families were less important in transmitting status and social position than schools and jobs. As a result, the family became a more private institution, a development reinforced by a rapid decline in family size, which made strict discipline less necessary than in the past. Early twentieth-century families contained, on average, just three children, half the number in 1850, allowing more self-expression for each family member. But there was a decrease in the physical interdependence of family members. Middle-class children were freer to take part in activities with peers, who played a growing role in shaping tastes, regulating behavior, and serving as a source of approval. "The time has passed when parents supervised the morals of their children," the *North American Review* announced in 1913.[8]

A commercial children's culture was a powerful force for change. Today toys like Teddy bears, Lincoln Logs, and Raggedy-Ann dolls evoke images of innocence and nostalgia for simpler times. But these toys were actually an early twentieth-century invention, reflecting new ideas about childhood and the emergence of a modern consumer economy. Cuddly, store-bought stuffed animals were given to infants and toddlers as a way of allaying their anxieties at the moment when they began to sleep by themselves in their own room. The first Teddy bear received its name from an event in 1902. President Theodore Roosevelt, in Mississippi to settle a border dispute with Louisiana, went hunting and, after nine fruitless days, was told that his dogs had cornered a bear in a clearing. Finding a baby bear tied to a tree, he refused to kill the defenseless cub, an incident illustrated in a newspaper cartoon. Morris and Rose Michtrom, candy store owners in Brooklyn, honored the president's gesture by manufacturing a stuffed toy, which they called "Teddy's Bear." Much more than a plaything, the Teddy bear became a source of emotional comfort for small children, an archetypal psychological bodyguard that helped the young to sleep through the night and deal with their frustrations and anxieties.[9]

Children received few store-bought presents before the early twentieth century. Earlier girls and boys had handmade rag dolls, which both sexes used as "action figures," but store-bought dolls were a rarity. Fragile and expensive, most were imported from Europe and made of unglazed porcelain or wax. In 1836, eight-year-old Susan Blunt of Merrimack, New Hampshire, a blacksmith's daughter, had received a wax doll with glass eyes and real hair, the only purchased doll she ever had. "One day," she wrote regretfully, "I went to look at it and it was ruined. The sun had shown in so hot that it had melted the wax to my great greef." Dolls were so delicate and costly that the Sears catalog sold various replacement parts, including heads and body parts.[10]

Most playthings—marbles, kites, skates, jump ropes, hoops, and balls—were meant for group play. Modern manufactured toys implied a solitariness that was not a part of childhood before the twentieth century. By 1903—the year that Crayola introduced the first affordable, multicolored crayons—toy production had advanced so rapidly that manufacturers held the first annual toy fair to promote their products. Initially, store-bought toys were marketed to parents rather than children, as a way to teach the young adult values and skills. Toys for boys centered on science, technology, transportation, construction, and combat and hunting. Jack-knives, popguns, air rifles, and BB guns were especially popular. The first modern construction toy, Crandall's Building Blocks, had appeared in 1867, but demand for construction toys took off only after the marketing of Erector Sets in 1913 and Lincoln Logs three years later. Toys for girls emphasized homemaking, child nurture, and the rituals of domestic life. Tea sets, doll houses, and dolls were intended to socialize girls to become housewives and mothers.[11]

At first toys remained relatively static, with the same dolls, stuffed animals, construction sets, and train sets appearing year after year. Store-bought toys continued to prepare children for adulthood or, like western outfits, drew upon America's past for models of adventure and heroics. But in the late 1920s toys began to be marketed directly to children. The chubby-cheeked, pot-bellied Patsy, the first doll with an extensive wardrobe, accessories, and companions, was introduced in 1928. Also in 1928, an entrepreneur named Donald Duncan purchased a small Mexican-American-owned yo-yo company in Los Angeles and promoted the toy nationwide—transforming yo-yos into the first children's fad, a toy that children felt they had to have. During the Great Depression toy companies appealed to children with an outpouring of fantasy and novelty toys. The toy industry's revenues fell by nearly half between 1929 and 1933, from $336 million to $181 million, and toy manufacturers responded with tie-ins to movies and cartoons, introducing celebrity-inspired toys, including Mickey Mouse watches, Shirley Temple dolls, and Buck Rogers pistols.

The emphasis on fantasy and adventure could be seen even earlier in book series targeted at young readers. First came the gadget-loving Tom Swift, whose first adventure novel, *Tom Swift and His Motorcycle,* appeared in 1910. In 1913 the Bobbsey Twins arrived, two sets of mystery-solving twins, the dark-haired eight-year-olds Bert and Nan and the fair-haired four-year-olds Flossie and Freddie. They were followed in 1927 by the Hardy Boys—Frank and Joe, the teenage sons of a celebrated detective—and in 1930 by the spirited, blue-eyed, roadster-driving sixteen-year-old sleuth Nancy Drew. Like toys, book series for children were the product of a transformation in the consumer economy. Decades before Goosebumps, the Baby-Sitters Club, Sweet Valley High, or Harry Potter, the young were initiated into reading by book series produced by a syndicate founded in 1905 by Edward Stratemeyer. The son of German immigrants and an admirer of Horatio Alger, Jr., Stratemeyer mass-produced books for specific groups of young readers much as Henry Ford mass-produced cars. He provided book outlines to freelance ghostwriters who were paid $75 to $100 a book and wrote under such pseudonyms as Victor Appleton, Franklin W. Dixon, and Carolyn Keene. By the time of his death in 1930, Stratemeyer had created almost a hundred different series of books that sold for between 40 and 60 cents. Highly formulaic and contrived, each volume contained approximately twenty-five chapters, all of which ended with a cliffhanger. The novels contained no murders, guns, or kisses, and no epithets stronger than "Jumping willigers!" But their very predictability proved highly appealing to young readers. Children's literature, like children's toys, provided a simulacrum of reality for increasingly structured lives.[12]

Book series for children were not entirely new. Alongside Louisa May Alcott, a host of lesser-known writers such as John Frost, Elijah Kellogg, and Oliver Optic (William T. Adams) had produced book series. But Stratemeyer's were different: his characters did not grow up; his books emphasized action and adventure, omitting any hint of introspection or character development. As in the Frank Merriwell books, which first appeared in 1896 and featured a Yale-educated star athlete, problems are solved as much by brain power as by physical prowess. In the fantasy world of fiction, young readers, whose everyday lives were increasingly confined to schools, could envision a world in which they solved mysteries and undertook fantastic adventures.

Adults regarded children's toys and literature as much more than mere playthings or pastimes. They were intended to meet children's psychological needs, which loomed increasingly large in adults' minds. In 1938 Lois Barclay Murphy, a child psychologist, drove her family from New York to California. As they approached the Kansas border, her six-year-old daughter, Midge, demanded that the family avoid the state, because she did not want to be blown away like Dorothy in *The Wizard of Oz*. "Since we could not truthfully guarantee that there would be no tornado in Kansas," the mother wrote, "and since it seemed a minor concession to make to a strong-minded child whom we respected, we changed the plan and drove through Nebraska." It is unlikely that earlier parents would have attached such weight to a child's fears. But during the 1920s and 1930s there was a heightened recognition of children's anxieties, phobias, and emotional needs. In ever-increasing numbers, mothers turned to psychologists for expert advice. By the mid-1930s, half of all middle-class mothers reported that they subscribed to a magazine on childcare, and most mothers said they read at least five books or pamphlets on the subject each year.[13]

It was during the 1920s that middle-class parents began to turn to psychologists for help in dealing with such problems as sibling rivalry, bedwetting, moodiness, rebelliousness, and sleeping problems. During that decade, knowledge about children's psychological needs increased substantially. In 1922 Arnold Gesell, a student of G. Stanley Hall and the founder in 1911 of Yale's Child Study Center, developed the first school readiness test, based on his theory that children develop in comprehensible patterns but at different rates. The test allowed educators to evaluate children's social skills, language development, motor skills, and adaptive behavior. Subsequently Gesell and his colleagues Frances L. Ilg and Louise Bates Ames demonstrated that at around two and a half years children became inflexible and rigid, popularizing the concept of the "terrible twos." They also showed that inattention, hyperactivity, and impulsivity were characteristic of a normal child under seven years of age, and that mischievousness was an expression of children's natural desire to be active.

A key figure in funding and disseminating research on child psychology was Lawrence K. Frank, associate director of the Laura Spelman Rockefeller Memorial and author of a popular advice column in the *New York Times*. Frank not only promoted the development of child guidance clinics to treat juvenile delinquents and "problem" children; he came up with the idea for *Parents' Magazine*. Through his advice columns, Frank helped popularize the notion that juvenile delinquents were children who had been neglected, maltreated, and subjected to intolerable brutality, requiring psychiatric care rather than punishment. He also drew on psychological research to show that childish behavior that appeared to be evil, naughty, or impertinent was often symptomatic of psychological confusions or conflicts, or responses to situations and demands beyond the child's capacities.[14]

The psychologizing of childrearing raised parental anxieties considerably. It suggested that parenting was a skill that had to be learned and

that improper parenting could have disastrous psychological consequences. Above all, child psychologists tended to blame almost all of children's misconduct on faulty mothering. During the 1930s and 1940s child
psychologist David M. Levy, drawing in part upon studies of children in
orphanages, developed the concepts of maternal deprivation and overprotective mothers as explanations for children's psychological problems.[15]

In addition to raising parental anxieties, the psychologizing of childhood convinced a growing number of mothers and fathers that professional therapy offered the best hope of taming troublesome behavior.
Many young people behaved in "defiantly modern" and "self consciously
different" ways, spending more time with friends and staying out late on
school nights. Parents like the mother of a girl named Eleanor turned to
psychologists for help. "Is it right," she asked in 1925, for her daughter
"to go out with Tom, Dick, and Harry automobiling to roadhouses and
getting home at two or three o'clock in the morning?" Another parent felt
equally confused and upset. Her fifteen-year-old daughter refused to remove her makeup, in violation of school rules. In desperation, this mother
and many others turned to child guidance clinics for help.[16]

The child guidance clinic, the forerunner of modern mental health clinics and child counseling centers, originated as an adjunct to the expanding
juvenile court system. The most famous, the Judge Baker Guidance Clinic,
was founded in Boston in 1917. Initially most referrals involved urban
immigrant and working-class youngsters charged with delinquency, truancy, theft, shoplifting, and, for girls, sex delinquency. Most offenses were
trivial, such as begging, selling fruit on the street without a license, playing ball on Sunday, and petty theft. Rejecting monocausal explanations of
delinquency (such as feeblemindedness, heredity, or mental defect), the
child guidance centers identified a variety of contributing factors—environmental, familial, and psychological—including poverty, bad companions, an unstable home environment, and the temptations of saloons,
dance halls, and unaffordable goods found in shop windows. Especially
worrisome was poor parenting: "For every problem child is a problem
parent" was the way one expert put it. Discarding the notion that troublesome children were inherently wicked, the guidance clinic's psychiatrists
and social workers argued that they suffered from behavioral and personality problems that could be solved through counseling. Recommendations included advising the family to move to a new neighborhood,
sending the child to a summer camp, and, in extreme cases, institutionalization.[17]

During the 1920s middle-class parents—upset by sons and daughters
who tried their patience, defied their authority, and rejected their values—

turned to the clinics for advice. No longer was generational rebellion confined to the children of immigrants. In a rapidly changing society, where many middle-class adolescents clashed with parents over curfews, dating, dress, and appropriate forms of entertainment and leisure activities, mothers and fathers turned to professionals for expert guidance and assistance. Meanwhile, behavior considered unnoteworthy in the past, such as sibling rivalry, came to be viewed as psychologically problematic. Among the problems parents brought to the clinics were eating and sleeping disorders, nail-biting, bedwetting, phobias, sibling rivalry, and temper tantrums. Other concerns included school failure, running away, and disobedient, defiant, impertinent, and rebellious behavior. The advice parents received emphasized conflict avoidance and adaptation to the realities of modern life. It was normal, parents learned, for the young to have a "desire for emancipation." As the Judge Baker staff told the parents of Phoebe Campbell, "over-restriction" was "much more dangerous than anything she would get into if they allowed her more liberty." The child guidance clinics both reflected and contributed to escalating parental concern about children's psychological and emotional well-being, and convinced many parents that youthful misbehavior could best be addressed through proper psychological treatment, avoidance of conflict, and personality adjustment.[18]

One area that demanded greater intervention involved sexuality. At the beginning of the twentieth century, many children grew up in an environment of extreme sexual ignorance, superstition, and fear. Girls were particularly poorly prepared for the physical and psychological changes that accompanied sexual maturity. Sixty percent of young women in a Boston high school reported that they were totally unprepared for menstruation. One woman recalled that although her mother had told her the basic facts of menstruation, she had also "taught her that such things were not talked about [and] also not thought of." A study of forty-three women who had been born before 1890 found that only six had discussed sex with their mothers before marriage.[19]

Sexual ignorance was not confined to girls. The early twentieth century was preoccupied with adolescent masturbation. No stronger condemnation of the practice appeared than in the Boy Scouts handbook, which told boys: "In the body of every boy who has reached his teens, the Creator of the Universe has sown a very important fluid . . . Any habit . . . that causes this fluid to be discharged from the body tends to weaken his strength . . . and . . . fastens upon him habits which later in life can be broken only with great difficulty." Reformers known as "social hygienists" called for sex education in schools, not to teach students the details of human reproduction, but to preach abstinence from masturbation and premarital sex. By 1922 about half the secondary schools in the United States offered instruction in social hygiene.[20]

As a high school student, Alfred Kinsey, born in 1894, was a loner and a misfit. Bookish, religiously devout, a bird-watcher and collector of butterflies, he was considered a "Momma's boy." In his hometown of South Orange, New Jersey, high school boys were expected to play team sports, and every boy in his 1912 high school graduating class played varsity sports except Kinsey. The high school itself was a jockocracy. Kinsey was selected the "brightest" and "most respectable" boy in his class, but it was athletes who dominated senior class offices and led most high school clubs. In South Orange in the 1910s, boys' lives centered on competitive sports, the main way in which boys forged bonds with each other and established their status. Local adults shared this preoccupation with athletic prowess. Convinced that sports built character, sublimated sexual impulses, and was the most effective way "to impress upon our lads the noblest lessons of real manhood," South Orange's school superintendent introduced team sports shortly after he arrived in South Orange at the beginning of the century.[21]

As a sixteen-year-old high school junior, Kinsey joined the Boy Scouts, and in 1913 he became one of the first seventy-seven Eagle Scouts in the United States. But this achievement did not bring him status as a "real boy." Uniforms might impress preadolescents, but they seemed childish to older boys, who chided Kinsey as a goody-goody. Even in affluent suburbs like South Orange, middle-class boys took part in activities detested by parents: playing pool, smoking cigarettes, and going to the movies on dates. In Kinsey's own school, they challenged adult authority by smuggling flasks of liquor into a high school dance and breaking the school's dress code. Kinsey's parents enforced a very different moral code, forbidding him to drink, smoke, and date, and instilling a deeply rooted sense of guilt about his sexual impulses. One incident that took place while Kinsey served as a young camp counselor illustrates how deeply he had internalized his parents' moral code. When a camper confessed to masturbating, Kinsey responded by admitting that he shared this problem. He then knelt down by the boy's cot and prayed to God to relieve him of this terrible vice.[22]

Many adults worried that boys were becoming "feminized" as mothers and female teachers dominated their early upbringing and fathers became little more than parenting assistants. The personality traits valued in the home were not those that won approval in the peer group, nor were they values conducive to adulthood success. The late nineteenth-century emphasis on vigilant self-control championed by such figures as John Harvey Kellogg, whose cold cereals were intended to curb masturbation, gave way, in the early twentieth century, to an emphasis on the need for boys to assert masculinity through sports and other physical activities. Boys who were perceived as weak, timid, or effeminate were teased, tormented, and taunted with humiliating names like "sissy" and "pussyfoot." Advertisers exploited boys' anxieties about their masculinity. Self-help books proliferated, such as *How to Get Strong and How to Stay So* (1879) and *The Virile Powers of Superb Manhood* (1900), written by Bernard Macfadden, an early bodybuilder and inventor of the peniscope, a glass tube with a vacuum pump engineered to enlarge the penis. "Let me make you a new man in just 15 minutes a day," Charles Atlas told generations of young males. "I rebuild skinny rundown weaklings—fellows so embarrassed by their second-rate physical condition that they always hang back, let others walk off with the best jobs, the prettiest girls, the most fun and popularity."[23]

Worries about their sons' masculinity led a number of parents to consult child guidance clinics. John Montgomery's parents took him to a clinic because he lacked ambition and exhibited "nervousness, carelessness and [a] tendency to dawdle." Psychologists and social workers in the 1920s and 1930s drew upon a growing scholarly literature on masculinity and femininity. By 1933 there were already 249 studies of sex differences in children, most of which posited sharp gender differences in attitudes, aptitudes, and behavior. One study concluded that boys demonstrated "reliably greater *interest* than girls in health, safety, money study, recreation and civil affairs," while girls were more interested in "etiquette, personal attractiveness and getting along with other people." In 1936 psychologists Lewis M. Terman and Catherine Cox Miles created the Attitude-Interest Analysis Test to measure children's masculinity and femininity and their likelihood of acquiring an appropriate gender identity. Like other early students of sex role differences, they considered masculinity and femininity opposite poles on a single continuum, and their test exaggerated gender differences. Of particular concern to child guidance professionals were authoritarian or emotionally absent fathers and controlling and overly directive, indulgent, protective, or possessive mothers, family configurations that they linked to effeminacy in boys.[24]

At the same time that anxieties about boyhood rose, distinctly modern patterns of girlhood behavior emerged. In 1890 thirteen-year-old Mary Anderson Boit complained in her diary: "We can not do anything in this house[;] as soon as we start to have any fun we are stopped . . . It seems as though we are kept in a glass case. " A few months later, after her mother sent her to her room for being "ungrateful & rude," the thirteen-year-old wrote: "I said I had not been rude since spring but had been trying not to be & she would not believe me." The diaries and letters of girls and young women in the early twentieth century have a recognizably modern tone. The deference that distinguished earlier references to mothers disappeared, and girls expressed their feelings and desires for independence far more openly than in the past. When her mother would not let her go to an eighth-grade graduation party in 1916, an eighth-grader exclaimed: "Mother says I can't go with any boy! It isn't the *boy* that I want to go for but all the other girls are going with them and I don't want to be the *only one* . . . left out . . . Maybe fourteen is too young but I don't care."[25]

Some authorities resisted the growth in girls' independence, arguing that their physiology unfitted them for strenuous physical and intellectual activities. Dr. Edward Clarke, a professor at Harvard Medical School, warned that "both muscular and brain labor must be remitted enough to yield sufficient force for the work of [menstruation]." But such arguments met with mounting resistance. If American girls were "pale and weak," one proponent of an active girlhood wrote, this phenomenon was due to lack of exercise. Dr. Mary Putnam Jacobi won Harvard's 1876 Boylston Prize for an essay titled "The Question of Rest for Women during Menstruation," in which she argued on the basis of an investigation of 246 young women that exercise during schooling reduced menstrual pain.[26]

In the 1910s, movie serials such as *The Perils of Pauline, The Exploits of Elaine,* and *The Hazards of Helen* featured athletic, adventurous girls, who rejected ladylike behavior and stay-at-home femininity. In their personal lives, girls consciously rejected Victorian assumptions about gender in favor of distinctly "modern" forms of behavior. Discarding older notions of propriety, they adopted new hairstyles and forms of dress, bobbing their hair, powdering and rouging their faces, and abandoning long skirts and shirtwaist blouses in favor of shorter skirts, sleeveless tops, and sheer silk stockings. With its emphasis on short hair and a slender appearance, the new look struck many as boyish, sparking fears of "masculinization." The most striking development was smoking, which numerous young women regarded as a symbol of modernity, sophistication, and generational independence.[27]

Young women defended the new styles as more comfortable and less constraining than the restrictive fashions and elaborate hairstyles of the past, but the new look imposed its own demands. Girls might no longer wear crinolines or corsets, but they were very interested in the body's shape and appearance. Slenderness and a clear complexion were the defining characteristics of the new ideal of beauty, and the 1920s brought

In this 1927 photograph, high school girls learn about auto mechanics. Courtesy of the Library of Congress.

an unprecedented emphasis on dieting. Sixteen-year-old Margaret Gorman, who became the first Miss America in 1921 and whose measurements were 30-25-32, embodied the new emphasis on thinness. Women's magazines recommended a multitude of diets, including diets emphasizing grapefruit or other foods. Fifteen-year-old Yvonne Blue, who later married psychologist B. F. Skinner, started to diet in 1926. "I'm so tired of being fat," she complained to her diary, as she described clashes with her mother about calorie counting. Girls also began to agonize about their complexion, a concern that was related to the declining frequency of scarring diseases like smallpox and the arrival of mirrors in middle-class bathrooms. During the 1920s a commercial industry of skin cream, acne treatment, and sanitary-pad products shamelessly exploited young people's growing anxieties over their personal appearance. Young women became increasingly aware of themselves as physical objects who were evaluated according to their appearance.[28]

Girls expressed a growing desire to lead a modern life. Just as modern young women did not wear frumpy and constricting clothes, they did they did did not sit at home or accept a gender-segregated world. A 1911 article in *The Independent* observed that modern daughters preferred going out on the town to "dying of asphyxiation at home." Modern femininity was associated not with innocence, modesty, and reserve, but with spunk, vivacity, and exuberance. Young women showed a new enthusiasm for outdoor exercise—especially swimming, tennis, gymnastics, field hockey, and bicycling. Adamant that their lives were going to be different from their mothers', they insisted on the right to go out at night and to dress in new ways. A frequent theme in women's fiction was intense mother-daughter conflict. In her popular semiautobiographical 1916 novel, *Mary Olivier,* May Sinclair wrote: "Ever since I began to grow up I felt there was something about Mamma that would kill me if I let it." It was Mary's "true self"—"the thing she can't see and touch and get at"—that her mother despised. Yet while fiction emphasized estrangement and hostility, letters and diaries illustrate a more complex pattern combining intimacy and tension. Many mothers encouraged greater freedom for their daughters and regarded their emancipation as fulfillment of their own aspirations.[29]

Youthful independence became a cultural obsession for early twentieth-century parents and children. The prophet of the early twentieth-century cult of youth was Randolph Bourne, a fiercely independent intellectual and brilliant political essayist who extolled cultural diversity and condemned American involvement in World War I. Equally important, Bourne issued the "Declaration of Independence" of American youth in a series of essays that he wrote as a college undergraduate. These essays, published between 1909 and 1911, harshly condemned the middle-class family as a repressive institution that chilled the passions of the young and turned them into robots, replicating their parents' hollow lives. His attacks on the older generation, his declaration of generational revolt, and his celebration of youth's vision, which, he said, "is always the truest," made Bourne "the flying wedge of the younger generation," in literary critic Van Wyck Brooks's words.[30]

As a result of a messy forceps delivery and spinal tuberculosis, Bourne was left with a partially paralyzed face, a mouth permanently askew, and a twisted frame. His ideas about the disabled influenced his view of the place of the young in modern America. Like the disabled, the young felt superfluous, cut off from real life in a modern wasteland. They had internalized unconscious feelings of inadequacy, and felt alienated from their elders, who had no relevant knowledge to pass on. Youth, in his view, represented "the incarnation of reason pitted against the rigidity of tradition." Youth welcomed experiment, while their elders feared innovation. The young were a cultural avant-garde, "ever laying the foundation for the future." Bourne admonished young people to live "contemporaneously," to dodge the pressures for conformity, break free from tradition

During World War I teenage girls took on jobs, like carrying ice, previously reserved for men. Courtesy of the National Archives, Washington, D.C.

and outmoded authority, and refashion America in a modern image. "No wonder the older generation fears and distrusts the younger," he proclaimed. "Youth is the avenging Nemesis on its trail."[31]

The radicalism of early twentieth-century youth was not political, but cultural and behavioral, as young people defined new behavior patterns and social values. Nowhere was this more evident than in the invention of dating. In a 1919 novel titled *Betty Bell,* Fannie Kilbourne described a new practice of cross-sex socializing among high school students. The teenaged Betty received phone calls inviting her to high school dances, the movies, and ice cream shops. Asked out by a member of the school's football team, she wanted to be seen and envied by her peers. When Kilbourne wrote her novel, dating was a new phenomenon. The term itself originated within Chicago's working class in the 1890s and was introduced into the middle class by George Ade, a Chicago journalist.[32]

During the nineteenth century, boys and girls had socialized together, taking strolls, attending dances, and participating in sleigh rides and other outdoor activities. Some went further. In a diary she kept during the late 1860s, Antha Warren, a nineteen-year-old school teacher in St. Albans,

Vermont, placed an asterisk whenever she and her suitor kissed. After one of his visits, she wrote: "Too many * to count." But dating differed dramatically from earlier forms of socializing. It not only took place away from home; it usually involved some form of commercial amusement paid for by the male. It was unchaperoned and not subject to a parental veto. It was not exclusive (the phrase "going steady" appeared only around the late 1930s) and existed independently of the courtship process. It remained the chief form of adolescent heterosexual recreation until the 1970s, when it was replaced with "hooking up" and "hanging out" in mixed-sex groups.[33]

Compared with the earlier and formal process of courting, dating was much more casual. It permitted young females and males to interact without proclaiming an intention to marry. Dating also provided acceptable ways to demonstrate physical intimacy. It allowed a girl to have erotic interaction—petting and necking—without endangering herself with an unwanted or out-of-wedlock child. Petting could mean kisses or fondling, but it stopped short of intercourse; although parents equated petting with fornication, teenagers did not, and their peer group still accepted and respected them. Through gossip, teasing, and labeling, the peer group regulated dating, including how much sexual intimacy was permissible. But as the sociologist Willard Waller observed in his influential 1937 study of the "Rating and Dating Complex," dating involved something more than casual cross-sex socializing; it was part of the adolescents' status system. Whom and how many people one dated determined one's popularity. Successful dating was a measure of a person's social skills and physical attractiveness. It was a defining element in a new youth culture that worshipped popularity and fitting in.[34]

Gender asymmetry was one of dating's defining features. A young man initiated the date: he asked a girl out; paid for the date; and sought, indeed expected, physical intimacy in exchange. As one boy complained, he "gave a girl a good time but when I ask for a kiss she refuses. Don't I deserve at least one?" he asked rhetorically. A 1933 government pamphlet described dating as a "wholesome" abandonment of "Victorian" conventions, but it is clear in retrospect that dating established a new double standard in which a young woman was responsible for imposing limits on the young man's sexual demands.[35]

As a dating system evolved, new terminology appeared. The word *crush* described an infatuation, while the word *love* acquired more transitory and less serious connotations. Degrees of commitment were also conveyed through language. "Going out" represented the lowest level of seriousness. During the 1920s the words *girlfriend* and *boyfriend* gained their modern connotations, and by the 1930s the expression *going steady* had entered the popular vocabulary. More tangible symbols of deepening commitment included pinning a girl or giving her a letter sweater earned in a varsity sport.[36]

Dating was a product of the spread of commercial amusements, a weakening of parental authority, and, above all, a generation that consciously defined itself against its elders. It began in urban areas and only gradually made its way into rural parts of the country. Because the dating system placed a premium on money, working-class youth were less likely to date. Young women appear to have been largely responsible for the rise of dating. In their book *The Revolt of Modern Youth* (1925), the juvenile court judge Ben B. Lindsey and coauthor Wainwright Evans concluded that "generally, she sets the pace, whatever it is to be, and he dances to her piping." Through dating, young women succeeded in modifying young men's behavior. Dating encouraged boys to display patterns of emotional intimacy that had long been valued by girls' culture. During the 1910s fewer boys had their first sexual experience with prostitutes, and their premarital sexual experiences and those of girls grew increasingly similar.[37]

Modern adolescence grew up hand in hand with the rise of modern commercial amusements. Amusement parks, ice cream shops, and, above all, movie theaters provided spaces where new patterns of behavior, like dating, emerged. The movies also helped reshape values and behavior. A sixteen-year-old girl explained the movies' significance in blunt terms. "No wonder girls of older days, before the movies, were so modest and bashful. They never saw Clara Bow and William Haines . . . If we did not see such examples in the movies, where would we get the idea of being 'hot'? We wouldn't." "Movies," another young woman told an interviewer, "are a liberal education in the art of making love." It was at the movies that she learned "how two screen lovers manage their arms when they are embracing." Movies not only provided models of behavior; they shaped ideals of beauty. A young African-American woman compared her appearance with Clara Bow's. "After seeing her picture," she said, "I immediately went home to take stock of my personal charms before my vanity mirror and after carefully surveying myself from all angles I turned away with a sigh, thinking that I may as well want to be Mr. Lon Chaney."[38]

Some Progressive-era reformers praised movies as a benign alternative to dance halls and city streets and thought they could serve a valuable educational function. Others viewed nickelodeons and movie theaters as breeding grounds of delinquency and sexual promiscuity. Settlement

House founder Jane Addams called the nickelodeon "a house of dreams" and described how, after seeing a Western, a nine-year-old and a thirteen-year-old boy bought a lariat and a gun and ambushed a milkman, nearly killing him. In 1907 the *Chicago Tribune* threw its editorial weight against the movies, declaring that they were "without a redeeming feature to warrant their existence . . . ministering to the lowest passions of childhood." That year Chicago established the nation's first censorship board, to protect its youthful population "against the evil influence of obscene and immoral representations."[39]

In the late 1920s social scientists conducted the first serious studies of movies' effects on children. With support from the Payne Fund, a private foundation that financed research on children, nineteen psychologists and sociologists from seven universities investigated film's impact on children's conduct, attitudes, and emotions. The researchers wanted to know the extent to which the movies' unique features—the darkness of the theater and the intense emotionality and hypnotic quality of the images—influenced children's sleep patterns, their school work, moral standards, delinquency, and ideas about race and world affairs. The project's funders had their own agenda: to demonstrate that the movies "constituted a serious menace to public and private morals." The studies were sober, if methodologically flawed, attempts to understand the movies' impact. The researchers found that children attended movies more frequently than adults and that even very young children attended movies unchaperoned. They also discovered, on the basis of a content analysis of 1,500 films, that virtually no movies were produced exclusively for children, identifying just one such film in 1930. The investigators found that children had an impressive ability to recall information from the movies; that moviegoing influenced children's attitudes toward race, ethnicity, and crime; that films featuring violence or horror interfered with children's sleep; and that frequent moviegoers performed worse in school than their classmates. A summary volume, titled *Our Movie-Made Children*, provided a misleading but popular digest of the studies' findings. The volume, which went through seven printings between 1933 and 1935, asserted that the movies fueled cravings for an easy life and wild parties and contributed significantly to juvenile delinquency.[40]

Other authorities agreed that the movies left an indelible and negative effect on youthful behavior. A leading neurologist, Frederick Peterson, claimed that violent movie scenes had "an effect very similar to shellshock such as soldiers received in war." Seen once, cinematic violence caused no harm, "but repeating the stimulation often amounts to emotional debauch . . . sowing the seeds in the system for future neuroses and psychoses." In a study of an all-white midwestern community, where almost no child had seen a Negro, a University of Chicago professor found that screening of *The Birth of a Nation* caused racial prejudice to spread like a weed. Interviews with children intensified adult concerns about the impact of movies. A boy convicted of robbery claimed that the "luxuries showed in the movies . . . made me want to possess them"; another said that he got his ideas about stealing "from watching pictures where the hero never worked but seemed always to have lots of money to spend." Over half of a group of truants and boys with behavior problems said that gangster pictures made them want to follow their example. Auto thieves claimed that the movies had shown them "how to jimmy a door or window," "how to use a glass cutter and master key," and "the scientific way of pulling jobs—leave no fingerprints or telltale marks."[41]

Of particular concern to adults was the impact of the movies on young people's sexual ideas. One girl reported that she learned that movie stars kissed with their eyes closed, that romance is something that happens quickly, and added: "I kiss and pet much more than I would otherwise." A high school girl stated that "the only benefit I ever got from the movies was in learning to love and a knowledge of sex. When I was about twelve years old I started browsing around and I remember I used to advantage my knowledge of how to love, to be loved, and how to respond." The movies, according to the Payne Studies, were powerful instruments of cultural modernization that helped explain the far-reaching transformations taking place in young people's lives. Like later moralists, their focus was on the mass media rather than on the broader institutional changes—such as the expansion of an age-segregated realm of youth, cut off from the world of adulthood—that were at the heart of the emergence of a modern youth culture.[42]

In 1911 Cornelia A. P. Comer, a Harvard professor's wife, published "A Letter to the Rising Generation" in the *Atlantic Monthly*. The younger generation, she grumbled, couldn't spell, and its English was "slipshod." Today's youth were selfish, discourteous, lazy, and self-indulgent. Lacking respect for their elders or for common decency, the young were hedonistic, "shallow, amusement-seeking creatures," whose tastes had been "formed by the colored supplements of the Sunday paper" and "the moving-picture shows." The boys were feeble, flippant, and "soft" intellectually, spiritually, and physically. Even worse were the girls, who were brash, loud, and promiscuous with young men.[43]

Randolph Bourne responded to this indictment by acknowledging its truth. Young people couldn't care less about proper English or outmoded standards of propriety. The revolt of the young against the conventions of their parents' world reflected a fundamental generational rupture in experience and attitudes. "The modern child," Bourne explained, "from the age of ten is almost his own 'boss.'" A healthy camaraderie had emerged among girls and boys. Kept at home and in school longer than previous generations, the young chafed under the tutelage of adults, "nominal though it is." Fearful of "being swallowed up in the routine of a big corporation," the young hungered for pleasure, gaiety, and intense experience.[44]

Bourne was not alone in thinking about society in terms of generational conflict. In Europe social theorists like Karl Mannheim, Antonio Gramsci, and José Ortega y Gasset popularized the notion that society was divided into distinct generations. In their view, age cohorts—which shared a common experience and consciousness—were units of analysis as significant as economic class. But Bourne went further. He argued that generational conflict was the engine of cultural transformation. With words that anticipated the cult of youth of the 1960s, he argued that it was the young who were "ever laying the foundations for the future." Insisting that "very few people get any really new experience after they are twenty-five," he announced that youth had a special mission: to overturn the outmoded values of a staid culture and remake a stale and static world.[45]

chapter twelve

Coming of Age in the Great Depression

Theirs were the most famous multiple births ever. In 1934 a French-speaking couple in northern Ontario gave birth to five identical baby girls. Annette, Cecile, Emilie, Marie, and Yvonne Dionne were thought to be the first quintuplets to survive infancy. Their combined weight at birth was just fourteen pounds, five ounces; they had to be fed with eye-droppers. The Dionne quintuplets quickly became the object of public adulation, with opinion polls finding them more popular than Shirley Temple. Hollywood made three movies about them: *The Country Doctor, Reunion,* and *Five of a Kind.*

Desperate for money to support their family, the parents, who already had five children, agreed that the quints could be displayed in Chicago in exchange for $200 a week. The Ontario government responded by declaring the parents unfit to rear the sisters, and placed them under a doctor's care. To protect the children from germs and kidnappers, the government constructed a hospital and nursery. Ontario also built a highway to accommodate the five million visitors who came to view the quints through the one-way glass that surrounded their playground. Their father opened a souvenir shop near the facility, and an uncle opened a gas station with five pumps, one named for each quint. Tourism related to the quintuplets reportedly brought $500 million to northern Ontario.[1]

As a result of fertility drugs, multiple births have grown increasingly common. But when the Dionne quints were born, such births were rare. At a time when many couples were postponing marriage and childbirth because of economic constraints—and just two years after the headline-blaring kidnapping of the baby of aviator Charles Lindbergh and Anne Morrow—the Dionne quints were a symbol of hope. The odds of giving birth to quintuplets without fertility drugs were one in fifty-seven million, making the quints a modern medical miracle. In retrospect, however, the story of the Dionne sisters carries a more ambiguous meaning. The quints were two years old before they met their older siblings; only once over a five-year period were the girls allowed to leave "Quintland." Not only were the sisters robbed of a normal upbringing, which was probably inevitable given that they were the first surviving quintuplets; their story demonstrates how easy it is to commercially exploit the public's sentimentalization of childhood and deprive children of fundamental emotional and psychological needs in the name of helping them.

Adults dominate our memories of the Great Depression. Our most vivid images of Depression hardship show haggard men standing in breadlines or selling apples on street corners and exhausted women and men crowding into aging Model T's, heading from the Dust Bowl to California's fruit farms. In fact children were the Depression's most vulnerable victims, both economically and psychologically. When a teacher told a young girl to go home to eat, the child replied, "I can't. This is my sister's day to eat." During the worst years of the Depression one child in five in New York City suffered from malnutrition. In coalmining regions of Illinois, Kentucky, Ohio, Pennsylvania, and West Virginia, the figure was nine in ten. Thousands of schools cut their hours or closed their doors, depriving a million school-aged children of access to an education. Teens suffered the highest jobless rate of any age group, as private businesses preferred to hire adult males. In 1933, when the economy hit rock bottom, only one of every ten or fifteen high school graduates could find work, and as late as 1938, over half of all sixteen- and seventeen-year-olds were out of work and out of school. Meanwhile a quarter-million children became drifters, taking to the roads and rails in search of jobs that didn't exist.[2]

There were widespread fears that the Depression had ignited a youth crisis. Books with such titles as *The Lost Generation* (1936) and *Youth—Millions Too Many* (1940) underscored the depths of the nation's youth problems. America's young were "discouraged, disgusted, sullen and bitter," and many worried that they, like their counterparts in Germany and Italy, were highly vulnerable to the lure of demagogues. As one observer warned in 1931, "When a boy has walked the streets for weeks in search of employment; has slept in parks and has lived only by means of soup kitchens and hand-outs on the way, he is a very likely subject for anyone who might preach a doctrine of revolution or revolt against existing conditions." Anxiety over this youth crisis led the country to reject a key tenet of American political life. The Depression toppled the notion that children's welfare could be left to individual families, private charities, and local and state governments. It created a consensus that the federal government had a responsibility to promote children's well-being. Debate still rages over how successful Franklin D. Roosevelt's New Deal programs were in dealing with the nation's youth problems, but there can be no doubt that the New Deal marked the first time that the federal government intervened in children's lives on a significant scale. To aid the nation's children, the New Deal launched the nation's first free school lunch programs, opened hundreds of free nursery schools, and established the nation's first federally funded work-study programs. Federal aid to education through the Federal Emergency Relief Administration prevented thousands of schools from closing their doors. Through the National Youth Administration and the Civilian Conservation Corps (CCC), the federal government provided employment to over seven million young people. The New Deal's most important innovation was Aid to Dependent Children (later called Aid to Families with Dependent Children),

A boy hops a freight train in Dubuque, Iowa, in 1940. Courtesy of the Library of Congress.

which provided financial assistance to the families of children who lacked a wage-earning parent.[3]

In addition to expanding the federal presence in children's lives, the Depression marked a watershed in childhood experience in several other ways. The economic crisis of the 1930s not only ended child labor; it ultimately made high school attendance a modal experience for adolescents. The Great Depression also led financially hard-pressed marketers and manufacturers to target children as independent consumers. The young became a market for comic books (the first featured Superman), movie serials (starring superheroes like Batman), children's radio shows (such as "The Lone Ranger"), and new kinds of children's toys (including Shirley Temple dolls and Mickey Mouse watches). By the end of the decade a new age category, the teenager, had emerged, personified in the movies by Mickey Rooney, Judy Garland, and Lana Turner. One of the Depression's lasting legacies was nationalizing and commercializing childhood.

The Great Depression left an indelible mark on children's lives. Russell Baker was just five years old when his thirty-three-year-old father died after entering an acute diabetic coma. Russell, his mother, and two sisters were left with an aging Model T Ford, a few dollars of insurance money, and several pieces of Sears, Roebuck furniture. Having no way of making a living and no prospects for the future, Russell's family left their home in rural Morrisonville, Virginia, and moved in with a younger uncle in Belleville, New Jersey, a commuter town on the outskirts of Newark. But before she packed up the family's meager belongings, Russell's mother did something that haunted him for the rest of his life. To lessen her family's burden, she gave up her dimpled, blond-haired, ten-month-old baby, Audrey, to a childless aunt and uncle's care.[4]

A few Americans believed that the Depression had a salutary effect on the family. One writer claimed that the economic crisis encouraged family members to turn "toward each other with greater, more intelligent interdependence." The Depression sharply curtailed activities outside the home and forced family members to pool their resources and find comfort in each other. Divorce rates declined, and popular magazines championed this time of family "comradeship, understanding, affection, sympathy, facilitation, accommodation, integration [and] cooperation." Families turned to new board games like Monopoly and gathered together in the evening to listen to the radio. As a Muncie, Indiana, newspaper editorialized, "Many a family that has lost its car has found its soul."[5]

But most observers agreed that the Depression had a destructive impact on family life. Unemployment, part-time work, reduced pay, and the demands of needy relatives tore at the fabric of family life, devastating many men's self-esteem and undermining family members' self-respect. In Cleveland in 1935, a fifteen-year-old whose father had been out of work for five years wrote: "I just can't stand anymore to look at the crying & thinking my parents do." Divorces declined for the simple reason that fewer could afford them; but desertions soared. By 1940 more than 1.5 million married women lived apart from their husbands. Family disintegration was evident in a 50 percent increase in placements of children in custodial institutions during the Depression's first two years. For the first time in American history, the birthrate dropped below the replacement level; Americans had nearly three million fewer babies during the 1930s than they would have had at the 1929 rate.[6]

In Arkansas some families found shelter in caves; in Oakland, California, whole families inhabited sewer pipes. In St. Louis children and adults dug through garbage dumps for rotten food; in Harlan County, Kentucky, families subsisted on dandelions and blackberries. During 1932, the Depression's worst year, 28 percent of the nation's households, containing thirty-four million men, women, and children, did not have a single employed wage earner. But even those fortunate enough to hold jobs suffered drastic pay cuts and reductions in hours. Only one company in ten did not reduce wages, and by mid-1932, three-quarters of the nation's workers were on part-time schedules.[7]

Pooling family incomes provided a buffer against loss of work. The Depression thrust adult responsibilities upon the young. Especially in the poorest families, sons were expected to earn money at odd jobs, while their daughters took on household tasks so that their mothers could work outside the home. Part-time jobs—running errands, mowing lawns, babysitting, shining shoes, carting groceries, and returning soda bottles for two cents apiece—supplemented their family's income. A Los Angeles family subsisted on a teenage daughter's earnings as a five-and-ten-cent-store clerk. Russell Baker was forced to go to work at the tender age of eight. In Oakland, California, half of all teenage boys and a quarter of all teenage girls took up part-time jobs.[8]

The Depression had adverse effects not only on family income but also on family relations. For many children, the Depression meant a declining standard of living, heightened family tension, inconsistent parental discipline, and an unemployed father. Many children experienced severe psychological stress, insecurity, deprivation, and intense feelings of shame. Parents became more irritable, marital conflict increased, and parents disciplined their children more arbitrarily. The impact of family conflict may have been worst for young children, since they were not insulated by the buffer of peers or jobs outside the home.[9]

Thousands of young people, desperate for help and a sympathetic ear, wrote letters to First Lady Eleanor Roosevelt. Their letters described their families' hardships and revealed the humiliation and impotence they felt. An eighth-grader from Salida, Colorado, told the first lady that her family was so poor that "every week we go to bed one or two days without anything to eat." An African-American girl from Old Saybrook, Connecticut, asked Mrs. Roosevelt to try to find a job for her unemployed father: "You don't know what it would mean to me if you would do it for me." Many poor children said they were ridiculed for their poverty. A ten-year-old from Mason, Wisconsin, wrote that after Christmas vacation, "all the children" at her school "talk about how many presents Santa has brought them and I felt so bad because I had nothing to say." Two girls from Lackawanna, New York, explained that they were "mocked and scorned and left out of many social activities" because they didn't have a bicycle. A lack of decent clothing was a particular source of shame. In the winter of 1936 a thirteen-year-old girl from Arkansas asked Mrs. Roosevelt if she could spare "some of your old soiled dresses if you have any. I am a poor girl who has to stay out of school on account of dresses, and slips, and a coat." At her school, a fourteen-year-old from Dows, Iowa, explained, "the kids at school all make fun of you if you can't dress fine." A fifteen-year-old from Port Morris, New Jersey, whose father had been jobless for two years, wrote: "I have no money and no means of getting any . . . How I wish I could have at least a coat." These letters provide a moving and disquieting record of the Depression's impact on the young, from their family roles to their schooling.[10]

During the early years of the Depression, economic hardship forced many schools to cut their hours and even close their doors. Terms were abbreviated in one of every four American cities, and 20,000 schools were shuttered. For 175,000 children during the 1933–34 school term, schools did not open at all. Schools in Dayton, Ohio, were open just three days a week, and more than 300 Arkansas schools were shut for ten months or more. In Arkansas and Mississippi, fewer than 5 percent of black youths of high school age were in school. A fourteen-year-old on the Great Plains described what it felt like to be deprived of an education: "With the school closed (I feel like crying every time I see it with the doors and windows boarded up) I'll be too old before I am ready to go to high school. Do you think that you could get on without a school or even a set of books?"[11]

By the decade's end, however, school enrollment had reached an all-time high. As adult unemployment mounted, there was a growing consensus that children had to be removed from the labor force and put in the classroom. Local school boards and state legislatures raised the minimum age for leaving school to sixteen. From 1930 to 1932, high school enrollment jumped 17 percent, and over the next two years enrollment rose another 10 percent. By 1939 three-quarters of fourteen- to seventeen-year-olds were high school students, and by 1940 half the nation's seventeen-year-olds were high school graduates—twice as many as in 1929. The expansion of high school enrollments carried profound consequences for the future: it institutionalized the teen years as a distinct stage of life. Although the term *teenager* did not enter the vocabulary until the early 1940s, the phenomenon was apparent by the late 1930s.[12]

The economic crisis of the 1930s brought previously ignored inequities in educational opportunity to public attention. Mississippi spent just $20.13 per child in 1935–36, less than a sixth of New York's $134.13. Clinch Valley, Tennessee, did not get a high school until 1937—a "small, four-room building constructed of undressed, unpainted pine boards," with thirty-five desks for the eighty-three students. Racial discrimination was pronounced. In 1930 just 11 percent of black teenagers were in high school, and almost 300 counties in fourteen states provided no high schools for black students. Black schools in the South were open just 146 days a year, compared with 182 days for white schools. The curriculum was also circumscribed. In 1935 a journalist reported that a black teacher was allowed to "teach the art of planting . . . how to build a house or repair steps, but she may not teach either children or adults how to keep a receipt or how to compute their earnings."[13]

Depression hardship was particularly acute in the South, where three-quarters of the black population lived. In Macon County, Alabama, the lives of children were little more than a step removed from slavery. Their diet consisted almost entirely of salt pork, hominy grits, cornbread, and molasses, with red meat, fresh vegetables, fruit, and even milk almost unknown luxuries. Their homes had dirt floors and no windows or screens; three-quarters had no sewage disposal. Economic exploitation, social isolation, and poverty shaped young people's lives. Schooling was brief—most dropped out at fourteen—and even very young children were expected to work. Macon County spent thirteen times as much on the education of a white child as upon a black child, and many children could not attend school at all because they lacked shoes. Several children had to walk fourteen miles to school daily.[14]

Conditions were equally distressed in the North. In Chicago most black families resided in apartments euphemistically called "kitchenettes," six-room apartments that had been subdivided into six separate units. Yet some still experienced the normal pleasures and pains of adolescence. In a diary that she kept in 1931, fifteen-year-old Hattie Lee Cochran provides a window into black teenage life. Born in Daleville in the Mississippi's "Cotton Belt," Hattie Lee moved with her family to Cleveland, Ohio, when she was still an infant, where her father found work in a food processing plant.[15]

In some ways, her diary reads like any adolescent's. She stayed up until two on Saturday night. She went to the beauty parlor, attended high school basketball games, read *True Confessions* magazines, enjoyed movies and carnivals, and listened to popular songs like "Minnie the Moocher." She took pleasure in car rides with friends and wore a boy's class ring. "What a pleasant life this is," she exclaimed. Her diary entries sound familiar decades later. She referred to a teacher as a "big Sap." After a friend "tried to act mad all day," she noted in her diary: "Ho. Hum." She hung out at a nearby barbeque stand, sometimes remaining there for hours. But as the year progressed, and the Depression intruded more and more upon her life, references to fun and leisure became fewer. After an older brother's wife gave birth to their third child, Hattie had to care for the couple's two older daughters. She worked outside the home and frequently cooked dinner for her own family. "What a life this is," she sighed in frustration.[16]

Compared with many African Americans, Hattie was fortunate. Her family had a car and a radio, and her father had a job. In Cleveland in 1931, more than half of all African-American adults were unemployed, and fewer than one black family in four owned a radio. North and South, African Americans faced the Depression's full fury. A year after the stock market crash, 70 percent of African-American adults were jobless in Charleston and 75 percent in Memphis. In Chicago black families had an average annual income of $728 in the middle of the decade, less than half the $1,580 earned by native-born white families.[17]

Mexican-American children, too, faced severe hardship. In Crystal City, in Texas' Rio Grande Valley, the average annual family income was $506 at a time when authorities considered a subsistence income to range from $2,000 to $2,500. Less than one Mexican-American child in five completed five years of school. Transience and family separation were characteristics of early twentieth-century Mexican-American life. Many lived in isolated mining towns; rural communities called *colonias,* near agricultural or railroad work camps; or segregated urban neighborhoods, called *barrios,* near factories or packinghouses. Most families supported themselves through migratory farm labor, in which children toiled alongside their parents, or through piecework in canneries or railroad construction work, earning just $1 or $1.25 a day.[18]

Even before the stock market collapse, intense pressure, spearheaded by the American Federation of Labor and municipal governments, sought to reduce Mexican immigration. Opposition from local chambers of commerce, economic development associations, and state farm bureaus stymied efforts to impose an immigration quota, but in 1930 the Bureau of Immigration (forerunner of the Immigration and Naturalization Service) rounded up immigrants and naturalized citizens and shipped them back to Mexico. The average cost of repatriating a family was $71.14, including food and transportation, a fifth the cost of providing relief. During the Depression, 82,400 *repatriados* were involuntarily deported to Mexico, and more than 300,000 others, many of them American citizens by birth, were forced to leave because of the threat of unemployment, deportation, or loss of relief payments. Texas' Mexican-born population fell by a third. Los Angeles, too, lost a third of its Mexican population. In Los Angeles, a schoolgirl wept as she was forced to leave Belmont High School and board a southbound train. The lone Mexican-American student at Occidental College sang a painful farewell song, "Las Golondrinas" (literally, "The Swallows," but metaphorically a reference to homelessness and displacement) to serenade departing Mexicans.[19]

In such precarious circumstances, many young people took to the road. In 1931, nine black teenagers, ages thirteen to nineteen, hopped on a freight train passing through Alabama. North of the small town of Scottsboro, they got into a fight with some white youths. When the train stopped, police were waiting. Two white females—Ruby Bates, seventeen, and Victoria Price, twenty-one—got off and accused the black youths of brutally raping them. The accused teenagers—the barely literate sons of sharecroppers—were taken to Scottsboro to stand trial. Their lawyer, a real estate salesman, advised them to plead guilty. All declared their innocence. During the 1930s the Scottsboro case became a symbol of racial injustice and a rallying cry for civil rights activists. During the next two decades there would be sixteen trials, and the defendants would spend between six and nineteen years in prison, even though one of the women recanted her claim. One defendant was tried, convicted, and sentenced to death three times. The case led to two landmark Supreme Court decisions: one overturning a conviction based on inadequate defense and another declaring all-white juries unconstitutional.[20]

The Scottsboro boys were among a quarter of a million youths who went "on the bum." Out of school, jobless, and homeless, these young nomads offered a frightening premonition of the future: of young people susceptible to radical appeals of all persuasions. This adolescent army evoked comparisons with the *bezprizorni,* the Russian street children left homeless as a result of the civil strife and famine that followed the 1917 revolution. A special section in the *New York Times* in October 1932 described "A Tragic Aftermath of the Days of Prosperity: The Army of Homeless Boys Now Roaming the Country." A soup kitchen in Yuma, Arizona, fed 7,500 boys and girls between November 1, 1931, and March 15, 1932. In one community center in Los Angeles, the 623 boys who applied for shelter in a five-month period came from forty-five states and the District of Columbia. Girls as well as boys took to the rails. A survey conducted over three days in January 1933 identified 256,000 homeless Americans, of whom 11,323 were female, with 35 to 40 percent under the age of twenty-one.[21]

The Depression nomads were not the first boys and girls to adopt the hobo life. The novelist Jack London was just fifteen years old when he began riding the rails in 1891. But there was nothing romantic about tramp life during the Great Depression. "There comes a day when the boys are alone and hungry, and their clothes are ragged and torn; breadlines have just denied them food, relief stations an opportunity to work for clothes. A man of God at a mission has kicked them into the street. A brakie [railroad brakeman] has chased them from the yards." On the rails, youthful enthusiasm and eagerness quickly gave way to despair.[22]

In 1932 Thomas Minehan, a graduate student in sociology, dressed himself in tattered clothing and began to interview the homeless. He discovered that "many were not youths, but boys. And some were girls—children really—dressed in overalls or army breeches and boys' coats or sweaters." For more than a year he lived among America's ragtag army of wandering children. He asked the boy and girl tramps many questions: "How did they live? What did they eat? Where did they sleep? How did they get clothing? What did they do all day?" By the time he completed his research, Minehan had interviewed more than 500 boys and girls in six states. Nine of the girls had prostituted themselves for bread. Boys explained that when they needed shoes, they had simply stolen them. Destitution, family troubles, and wanderlust were the main reasons young people left their homes. Some took to the road to spare their parents the burden of feeding another mouth. Others were told to fend for themselves. Jim Mitchell was sixteen years old when he learned that his father had lost his job. He left a note on his pillow saying, "I'll write."[23]

For children riding the rails, the euphoria of freedom gave way to hunger, homesickness, and loneliness. Many suffered from malnutrition and lived in squalor. Robert Mitchum, who would play tough guys and cynics in such movies as *Cape Fear,* was sixteen when he left his home in Bridgeport, Connecticut. He rode the rails, supporting himself as a coalminer, deckhand, ditchdigger, and professional boxer, lasting twenty-seven fights. In Savannah, Georgia, he was placed on a chain gang, escaping after six days in captivity. Director William Wellman's 1933 drama *Wild Boys of the Road* painted a bleak picture of the lives of young people leading a hand-to-mouth existence. One of the train hoppers slips and loses a leg; a girl is sexually assaulted. Such images were realistic. The nomads were beaten by brutal railroad police called bulls. They had to learn to beg or steal food and clothing. One boy worked all day in a wheat field only to be paid 15 cents. A traveler recalled a pair of girls who "received 30 or 40 men and boys in a boxcar, some men doubling back on the line." When the girls quit, they had earned a total of 70 cents in nickels and dimes.[24]

Homeless children riding the rails became a defining symbol of youth in crisis. Their example inspired the federal government to inaugurate a host of federal policies to assist the young. "I have moments of real terror," Eleanor Roosevelt wrote in 1934, "when I think we may be losing this generation. We have got to bring these young people into the active life of the community and make them feel that they are necessary." Unlike the Hoover administration, which did little to assist the young, Franklin D. Roosevelt's New Deal program from its earliest days adopted specific measures to address the youth crisis. The Civilian Conservation Corps, established in 1933, hired young men to work in reforestation, park, and soil conservation projects. Before it closed in 1941, it assisted 2.6 million young men between eighteen and twenty-five. The Federal Emergency Relief Administration, set up in 1933, funded teacher salaries in poor states, preventing 4,000 schools from closing; its college aid program provided 75,000 work-study jobs to keep college students in school. It also set up transient camps for 54,000 young people "bumming" their way across the country. In 1934 the National Recovery Act prohibited employment of children under the age of sixteen. After the Supreme Court struck down the NRA, the Fair Labor Standards Act of 1938 reaffirmed the prohibition on child labor. Other New Deal programs funded a free school lunch program for 500,000 students daily in 10,000 schools throughout the country; financed construction of 1,600 nursery schools in rural areas, in crowded city districts, in lumber camps, and in mining districts; and paid 70 percent of the construction cost of new schools.[25]

Two programs established in 1935 carried special significance for young people's lives. In addition to offering retirement benefits to the elderly and unemployment compensation, the Social Security Act provided aid to the disabled, for maternity care, public health work, vocational rehabilitation, and, most important of all, Aid to Dependent Children

(ADC). ADC replaced the mothers' pensions of the Progressive era, which had provided aid to "deserving" single mothers and their children at home rather than removing the children to institutions. Unlike the mothers' pensions, ADC was available in all counties in all states. But like the mothers' pensions, ADC provided inadequate support and included a "morals" test for benefits. Inadequately funded, especially in comparison with the far more generous programs for old age and unemployment, ADC was implemented in ways that were demeaning and punitive, including unannounced visits by state welfare officials seeking to determine whether there was an adult male present (which would cancel the payment). Still, it marked a crucial first step toward the creation of a safety net for children.[26]

The other major New Deal program providing assistance to the young was the National Youth Administration (NYA), established by executive order as part of the Works Progress Administration (WPA). During the mid-1930s, 40 percent of young people between the ages of sixteen and twenty-four were neither gainfully employed nor in school. Some 80,000 college students dropped out of college in 1932–33, making this the only peacetime period in the twentieth century when American college enrollments declined. The NYA was intended to address these problems by providing work-study jobs for both high school and college students and job training and employment for out-of-school youth. For the first time, the federal government assumed a role in helping idle youth make the transition from adolescence into the adult job market. NYA participants constructed roads, schools, community centers, and public parks and playgrounds. They served as hospital and nursery school aides and worked in libraries, youth centers, and school lunchrooms. Young men learned carpentry and automobile repair; young women, typing, sewing, stenography, and bookkeeping. Unlike the participants in the CCC, they wore no uniforms and no insignia. College and out-of-school participants typically worked six days a month for less than $16, while high school students received $6 a month. NYA alumni included the guitarist Chet Atkins, the architect of the Nashville Sound; and Ralph Shapey, the avant-garde composer, who conducted the Philadelphia National Youth Administration Symphony Orchestra before he graduated from high school. Altogether the NYA helped close to five million young people from 1935 to 1943.[27]

At first the NYA concentrated on providing jobs for unemployed youth. It soon expanded its mission to providing work-study jobs for high school and college students, establishing job training programs, and supporting residential centers for rural youth. Some critics denounced the NYA, comparing its program for organizing, indoctrinating, and regimenting the young to Nazi youth organizations in Germany. NYA officials, to the contrary, envisioned the youth agency as a mechanism for educating disaffected youth about democracy and preventing them from falling under the sway of demagogues; they saw it as a vehicle for inculcating middle-class values in the poor. The program's major goals were to prepare young people to function effectively in a modern society, to provide adult supervision to idle youth, to inculcate a work ethic, and to teach the poor the value of money. Rural girls learned to shampoo their hair, apply makeup, and dress in middle-class styles, while their immigrant counterparts were taught to prepare American-style meals. Participants in rural residential centers moved back and forth between the agency's center and their homes so that "they constantly see contrasts in diets, cleanliness, and household management." The most radical of the New Deal programs, the NYA sought to raise the skills and aspirations of the poor.[28]

During its first two and a half years the NYA employed half a million young people who were out of school and out of work. Most were in their late teens and came from very large families, usually with more than seven members. The NYA was the New Deal's most equitable program in terms of gender and race. Over 45 percent of aid recipients were female, and the NYA provided about 13 percent of its high school jobs and 14 percent of the out-of-school jobs to nonwhites. Targeting its efforts at rural youth, black and brown as well as white, the NYA represented the first federal effort to racially integrate education. Nevertheless, the NYA, like other New Deal programs, was wholly inadequate to the Depression's scale. It never employed more than a sixth of the nation's jobless youth at any one time, and most NYA participants graduated not into private-sector jobs but into other government relief programs, like the WPA. In Virginia, only 5,000 of 180,000 unemployed youth received aid. Of 400,000 black youths between fourteen and sixteen on relief rolls, only 19,000 were on the NYA lists. Still, the program did help many high school students remain in school and provided practical, if narrow, training in home economics and industrial arts to unemployed youths.[29]

The crises and challenges of the Great Depression gave rise to the first mass youth movements in American history. In 1936 the American Youth Congress, a coalition of student groups, issued a Declaration of Rights of American Youth, which proclaimed: "We want to work, to produce, to build, but millions of us are forced to be idle . . . We refuse to be the lost generation." The next year the Youth Congress staged a march on Washington, demanding that Congress provide needy students with jobs paying $15 a month. Although this demand went unfulfilled, young people's lobbying prevented Congress from cutting the NYA's budget.[30]

A tenant farm family's shack in Caroline County, Virginia, in 1941. Courtesy of the Library of Congress.

The youth movement of the 1930s provided a historical precedent for the student movement of the 1960s. Led largely by Socialists and Communists, the student movement of the 1930s surfaced in response to two issues: Depression-era unemployment and the mounting international tensions that resulted in World War II. Student organizations—including the American Student Union and the American Youth Congress—called for federal student aid, government jobs for low-income and unemployed youth, and an end to racial discrimination. Veterans of the 1930s student movement included labor union leaders Walter and Victor Reuther, the author and editor Irving Howe, the sociologist Daniel Bell, the writer Saul Bellow, the historian Richard Hofstadter, the sociologist Seymour Martin Lipset, the literary critic Leslie Fiedler, the film critic Pauline Kael, and the journalist Eric Sevareid. All would later distinguish themselves as intellectual and social critics and contributors to a liberal democracy.[31]

The Depression touched off an unprecedented wave of student activism. During the 1920s the student left was limited to the 2,000-member Socialist-led League for Industrial Democracy, an offshoot of the Intercollegiate Socialist Society, founded in 1905 by Upton Sinclair. But during the

Depression many new student groups appeared, such as the Communist-led National Student League, founded in 1931. The two leading student organizations were the American Youth Congress and the American Student Union. The AYC, a loose coalition of youth groups, was organized in 1934 by a twenty-three-year-old writer, Viola Ilma, who had been inspired by European youth movements. The AYC claimed to represent 4.5 million American youths from affiliated organizations ranging from the Young Communist League to the Young Women's Christian Association. The AYC succeeded in winning support from Eleanor Roosevelt, who invited AYC leaders to tea at the White House. The ASU, which emerged in 1935 from a merger between the Socialist-led Student League for Industrial Democracy and the Communist-led National Student League, claimed a membership of 20,000. While local chapters attacked segregation, the national organization sponsored "peace strikes," which attracted hundreds of thousands of college students, including 175,000 in 1935. Though initially isolationist in foreign affairs, the ASU's leadership grew increasingly alarmed by the growing threat from Germany and Italy and, in the late 1930s, emphasized collective security against fascism. In 1939, however, the ASU tore itself apart when the organization's Communist leaders endorsed the Nazi-Soviet Non-Aggression Pact.[32]

Economic hardship, fear of war, and the influence of parents and teachers inspired many to join the student movement. Pacifist sentiment led thousands of students to participate in antiwar rallies. After students at Oxford University took a pledge not to fight "for King and country" in 1933, American student organizations circulated a similar pledge. A poll of college students found that 39 percent said that they would "refuse to support the government of the United States in any war that it might undertake." The rise of fascism in Europe, economic strains, and the increasing visibility of racism at home politicized youth in a new and personal way. Many began to realize how much their lives were shaped by politics at home and abroad.[33]

Many student leaders came from working-class and immigrant backgrounds and were disgusted by the frivolous atmosphere at colleges and high schools. Rather than centering on fraternities, athletics, and socializing, they felt that academic life should focus on political issues. A sampling of student activists found that many attributed their radicalism to their family background. One ASU leader said that his father "was one of the student leaders in pre-revolutionary Russia [who] . . . carried on a great deal of educational work among the peasants," and that "he left Russia because he did not believe in compulsory military training." He concluded: "It is interesting to see that youth of a previous generation fought the same issues that we are fighting now." Some student leaders, such as Nancy Bedford Jones, an activist in the Student League for Industrial Democracy, revolted against what they regarded as their parents' political complacency, while others, like Alice Dodge, the daughter of liberal Republicans, felt that only through political activity could they fulfill their parents' reformist aspirations.[34]

Despite superficial similarities to the 1960s student movement, the 1930s organizations differed in important respects. Student activists of the 1930s did not exhibit the generational antagonism that characterized their 1960s counterparts. Far from distrusting anyone over thirty, the student protesters of the 1930s dressed in suits and skirts, and their leaders rejected the idea that there were distinctive "youth problems." Their problems were war and peace, poverty and prosperity. Nevertheless, the student movement of the 1930s altered campus culture. High school and college newspapers became much more political than in the 1920s, as did student leadership. A 1936 *New York Times* student survey observed: "Nowhere is the new liberalism more apparent than in the 1936-style campus leader . . . He is no longer the star athlete, [or] the 'smooth' prom man . . . His stigmata are more apt to be brains, a good grasp of student and national problems and frequently leadership in the peace movement." Student radicalism peaked in 1936 and 1937. On July 4, 1936, the AYC's "Declaration of the Rights of American Youth" called for "full educational opportunities, steady employment at adequate wages, security in time of need, civil rights, religious freedom, and peace." In February 1937, student organizations held one of the first marches on Washington, a "Youth Pilgrimage for Jobs and Education," to demand a work-study job for every needy student. But as world tensions escalated in 1938 and 1939, and Communist leaders in student organizations defended the Nazi-Soviet Pact, the student movement of the 1930s splintered on the shoals of world crises and impending war.[35]

WHILE OLDER youth became more serious about domestic and international politics, American commercial culture became preoccupied with entertaining the young. Comic books were one of the first products directly marketed to young people. The first comic book carried a picture on its cover of Superman brandishing a car over his head. By its seventh issue, comics featuring the Man of Steel were selling half a million copies a month. During the late 1930s a new breed of caped comic-book superheroes appeared, defying Kryptonite and bullets. Beginning with Superman and his meek-mannered alter ego Clark Kent in 1937, created by Cleveland high school students Jerry Siegel and Joe Shuster, a train of superheroes followed, including Batman, the Human Torch, the Green Lantern, Captain America, and, in 1941, Wonder Woman, "fighting fearlessly for down-trodden women and children in a man-made world." Correcting injustice and defeating evildoers, superheroes served as symbols of empowerment and national pride for powerless Depression-era adolescents.

The comic book was a product of the Depression. In 1933 two salesmen at Eastern Color Printing Company persuaded their employer to reprint Sunday comics as pulp magazines. At first the printing company distributed the magazines to companies that gave them away. It began to sell them after discovering that young readers were willing to pay for cheap fantasy-filled magazines. For children of immigrants, it was reassuring to discover that Superman himself was an immigrant. At a time of mounting international tensions, superheroes fought not just crime, but also alien villains. By showing that hidden powers lurked behind shy appearances, the comic books of the Great Depression provided reassurance to anxious young people.[36]

Hollywood also targeted the youth audience with growing intensity. Two very different gangs of kids—the Dead End Kids and the Little Rascals—became enormously popular during the 1930s. One was a gang of incipient criminals who emulated a neighborhood gangster; the other consisted of cute and rambunctious preadolescents. Both spoke to the public's fears, hopes, and fantasies. In 1935, in a play titled *Dead End*, Sidney Kingsley explored the troubled lives of the poor who lived close by the affluent Manhattan enclave of Sutton Place. A gang of tough, fast-talking juvenile delinquents stole the show. Wayward children with nothing to do—"sneering, spitting, and shaking their fists"—the Dead End kids spend their days hanging out on the docks, mocking their wealthy neighbors, stealing, and engaging in various kinds of mischief. Neglected and misguided, lacking any hopes for the future, the boys nevertheless showed signs of inner goodness. They were, in the title of one of their movies, "angels with dirty faces." The Dead End Kids, later known as the East Side Kids and still later as the Bowery Boys, eventually appeared in eighty-seven films with titles like *They Made Me a Criminal*. During the 1940s their films were transformed into slapstick comedies, but in their early films the Dead End kids illustrated how poverty and neglect might drive adolescents who inhabited society's lower depths into a life of crime.

The Little Rascals were the urban offspring of Tom Sawyer and Huck Finn. Cute, crude, spunky, and mischievous, they inhabited a kids-only world in which adults rarely intruded except for comic relief. Their Our Gang comedies chronicled the pranks and antics of a ragtag gang of prepubescent boys; their adversaries, the bullies Woim and Butch; and the girls they sparred with. In 221 ten- and twenty-minute features, the kids wreaked havoc. Each was a stereotype: the fat kid, the freckle-faced side-kick, and the cherubic little girl. As they grew older, they were replaced by younger performers who fitted the original characters. There was Joe, the chubby kid with the beanie; Pineapple, with an Afro hairdo; the skinny, freckle-faced Speck; and Alfalfa, the cowlicked kid with the screechy voice, ears that stuck out, a bow tie, ankle-length pants, and missing front teeth. Today the ethnic humor and the racial and gender stereotypes are disquieting; but from the 1920s through the 1950s, the images of normal children scheming and fighting on screen entranced young audiences. Their appeal lay in the kids' unfeigned spontaneity, their freedom from parental supervision and adult inhibitions and constraints, and their awkward attempts to act like grownups.

Children in Depression-era films took many forms; there were heartwarming infants, wide-eyed waifs hungering for a family and a home, resourceful orphans, winsome cherubs, and savvy street urchins. Children brought innocence, energy, optimism, and cartoon cuteness to the screen. Unlike in post–World War II films, however, the mystery and otherness of childhood were rarely depicted. It was not until the 1950s that audiences saw depraved children—anticipated in *Mildred Pierce* in 1945, then realized in *The Bad Seed* (1956)—and not until the 1970s that we saw self-absorbed rich kids, in *Harold and Maude* (1971); children as emotional footballs, in *Kramer v. Kramer* (1979); or the disappearance of childhood innocence, exemplified by Louis Malle's *Pretty Baby* (1978). Few American films before the 1960s explored the complexity of children's emotional life or tried to see the world through children's eyes; but many, like the Our Gang comedies, depicted children's antics, energies, and everyday experiences.

Hollywood in the 1920s and especially the 1930s was filled with underage stars. There was Jackie Coogan, who was six when he starred with Charlie Chaplin in *The Kid* in 1921 as a streetwise orphan; Baby Peggy Montgomery (Diana Serra Cary), who was signed to a $1.5 million contract at the age of four and served as the inspiration for *What Ever Happened to Baby Jane?*; the "Kleen Teens," Deanna Durbin, Judy Garland, Roddy McDowell, Dickie Moore, Mickey Rooney, and Jane Withers, who provided models of teenage innocence and exuberance; and the most popular child star of all, Shirley Temple. She was America's little darling, tap dancing and singing through the Depression in fifty shorts and features by the time she was eighteen. Beginning with *Little Miss Marker*, released in 1934, when she was five, she became one of Depression America's most popular stars, topping the box office every year from 1935 to 1938. Part of her attraction was her cuteness, charm, dimpled cheeks, and bouncing curls. She was adults' ideal girl—athletic, flirtatious, independent, even-tempered, but also adorable and infectiously optimistic. She was undeniably talented: she could sing, dance, act, and melt the heart of the grouchiest sourpuss. Escapist fantasy, too, was part of her appeal. Lacking a mother in almost all her movies, she was free from domestic constraints. She danced with millionaires, slid down ropes made of bedsheets, and stowed away on a slow boat from China. As Franklin D. Roosevelt observed in 1933: "It is a splendid thing that for just 15 cents an American can go to a movie and look at the smiling face of a baby and forget his troubles." But Temple's appeal went well beyond escapism. In many films she served as a "spiritual healer" who resolved family disputes, bridged class differences, and restored adults' confidence in themselves. Oblivious to class and racial differences, she moved easily between poor and wealthy homes without ever being greedy or envious. While some of her films seem racially insensitive today, her characters were always unaware of race. As the critic Graham Greene noted at the time, she often portrayed a miniature adult, dressed up in pants or even kilts, dispensing moral advice to older characters.[37]

Shirley Temple wasn't the first child star. The very first was four-year old Cordelia Howard, who played Little Eva in a stage version of *Uncle Tom's Cabin* in 1853. The first cinematic child stars were Little Billy Jacobs, who appeared with Charlie Chaplin in *Kid Auto Races at Venice* in 1914 and with Colleen Moore in *Little Orphan Annie* in 1918; and Kenneth Casey, "the Vitagraph Boy." But without a doubt the most popular was the girl with fifty-six curls who was mass-produced for her adoring public in the form of the Shirley Temple doll. She boosted the spirits of a nation in crisis, gladdening hearts with her cheering innocence and exuberance. She held out the promise that children held the solution to the nation's problems, reinforcing society's intensifying sentimentalization of childhood.

By the end of the 1930s, popular culture and marketers had identified a distinct age group, the teenager. Along with his costars Judy Garland and Lana Turner, Mickey Rooney, the number-one box office star from 1939 to 1941, served as the model for the modern middle-class Kleen Teen. Beginning with *A Family Affair* (1937), MGM released sixteen films in his low-budget Andy Hardy series. With its lighthearted focus on family problems and teenage romance, the series provided a prototype for television family situation comedies, but it also played a critical role in shaping and reinforcing cultural stereotypes about middle-class teenagers and teenage culture. Rooney's cheery and exuberant portrayal of the middle-class teenager's crushes, infatuations, and humorous and embarrassing mishaps provided the caricature that the troubled, misunderstood, and alienated teen characters of 1950s films rebelled against.

The decade that began with Dead End kids and boxcar nomads ended with a widespread perception of a lighthearted teenage world of ice cream shops and high school dances in idealized small towns across America. The emergence of the teenager as a popular and public figure was the product of two major developments: the growth of the high school and the emergence of a distinct teenage commercial market. Earlier in the twentieth century, only a fifth of young people in their mid-teens were in high school; 60 to 65 percent were wage earners, and the rest were working at home or in the street trades. But by 1936 more than half the nation's seventeen-year-olds were high school students. By removing working-class youngsters from the labor force and making high school a largely universal experience, the Depression had inadvertently created teenagers as a common and ubiquitous presence.[38]

The first published use of the word *teenager* occurred in September 1941, when a columnist in *Popular Science Monthly* remarked about a young person: "I never knew teen-agers could be so serious." The nomenclature was quickly picked up, and the category took on diverse attributes. "They live in a jolly world of gangs, games, movies, and music," *Life* magazine reported in 1941. "They speak a curious lingo . . . adore chocolate milkshakes . . . wear moccasins everywhere . . . and drive like bats out of hell." In December 1941, the month of the Japanese attack on Pearl Harbor, MLJ Comics introduced Archie, a carrot-topped, gap-toothed, bow-tie-clad teenager in loud checked trousers, who provided a popular caricature of the middle-class male teenager. Assigned by his publisher to develop an All-American teenaged character along the lines of Andy Hardy, twenty-one-year-old cartoonist Bob Montana created the fictional town of Riverdale, home to Archie Andrews and his high school friends, based on his own experiences during the 1930s at high school in Haverhill, Massachusetts. There was the sweet blonde ponytailed Betty; her romantic rival, the sultry, spoiled Veronica; the hapless, hamburger-hungry Jughead; the dumb jock Moose; and the handsome but conceited Reggie. At its height during World War II, the Archie comic sold six million copies a month. In the comic-book world of superheroes, the awkward, indecisive, goofy teenager Archie seemed out of place. His comics dealt not with crime and violence, but with teenage boys and girls and their conflicts, gripes, and insecurities. Archie comics embodied the classic world of middle-class teens: Pop Tate's Chok'lit Shoppe, a wheezing old red jalopy, saddle shoes, checked knickers, letter sweaters, malt shops, chaste kisses, a teenage love triangle, and the jitterbug.[39]

At first the gulf between teen and adult culture remained narrow. Bobby-soxers—as teenage girls were called after their white ankle-length socks—and adults shared the same popular culture. Both adored the big-band sound of Glen Miller and Benny Goodman, though the adults listened while the teens danced. However, within a few years teen culture would sever its ties with the adult world as marketers began to discover teens' purchasing power and distinctive needs and styles. Within a decade and a half, Andy Hardy, the apple-cheeked small-town boy sipping sodas at the corner candy store, gave way to a new cultural stereotype: the bored, restless, volatile teenager who combined a child's emotions with an adult's passions and was estranged from parents and other authority figures. The Andy Hardy movies were replaced by teenpics with titles like *Young and Wild, The Cool and the Crazy,* and *High School Confidential,* targeted exclusively at a teenage audience.[40]

In recent years the concept of the teenager that arose in the late 1930s has grown increasingly obsolete. During the 1930s, 1940s, and 1950s, young people typically attained full-adult status in their late teens or early or mid-twenties, either by entering military service or an adult career, or by marrying and having children, thereby giving the teen years great significance both as a brief interlude before adulthood and as a crucial time of decision. After 1960, however, entry into full adulthood began to be delayed as a rapidly growing proportion of young people enrolled in college and postponed entry into adult careers until their late twenties or early thirties. As a result, the freedom and lack of adulthood responsibilities that characterized the teen years have been extended for another decade. Yet the popular conception of the teenage years—as a moratorium during which the young were free to explore before committing themselves to marriage or a career—and our cultural expectations of teenagers—as angst-ridden, rebellious, and reckless risk-takers—has remained unchanged. Society has continued to segregate teens in an institution—the high school—which is supposed to cater to their psychological, physiological, emotional, and intellectual needs, but which, in practice, many find juvenilizing and lacking in intellectual stimulation. As the stage of youth became increasingly prolonged, and adulthood more distant, the high school and the culture that surrounded it seemed more and more outdated in its strictures, athletic culture, regimentation, and lack of opportunity for teens to demonstrate their growing competency and maturity.

chapter thirteen

Mobilizing Children for World War II

O N SUNDAY MORNING, December 7, 1941, six-year-old Dorinda Makanaonalani was eating a breakfast of bananas and papayas when she heard the sound of low-flying planes, followed almost immediately by loud explosions. Her family lived on a sliver of land that jutted into Hawai'i's Pearl Harbor. As her father bolted from the kitchen table into the front yard, Dorinda ran after him and saw planes bearing the orange-red emblem of the Rising Sun flying over her house. The planes flew so low that she could see the goggles that covered the pilots' eyes. She watched as incendiary bullets hit her house, setting her kitchen on fire. "Everywhere we looked," she later recalled, "there was smoke and fire . . . It seemed as if the water was on fire from the burning oil." To escape the line of fire, Dorinda's father drove his family into the sugarcane fields above the harbor, where they hid among the tall cane stalks.[1]

Morris Broussard was eight years old when the Japanese attacked Pearl Harbor, five minutes from his Oahu home. His father saw the planes first. Assuming that this was a military exercise, Morris and his twin brothers went outside to watch the maneuvers and wave to the pilots, who were flying no higher than the telephone poles. Police ordered the boys home, where they watched soldiers install a 50-caliber machine gun and a bank of sandbags in their front yard. Morris's mother, a nurse, left for the hospital, where she remained for three days. When classes resumed at his school, the third-grader had to wear a gas mask strapped around his shoulders.[2]

December 7, 1941, was as much a watershed in the lives of young

Americans as it was for their elders. Whether they lived in Hawai'i or on the mainland, children's lives were transformed. World War II disrupted families, sending sixteen million fathers, sons, and brothers into the military. It also set families in motion, pulling them off farms, out of small towns, and packing them into large urban areas. It drew millions of married women into the paid workforce, reduced school attendance, enhanced young people's freedom and work responsibilities, and greatly intensified adult concerns about juvenile delinquency and premarital sexuality. Above all, it politicized the lives of the young; it altered the rhymes they repeated, the cartoons and movies they watched, and the songs they heard, and instilled an intense nationalism that persisted into the postwar years.

Half a century later, children vividly recalled the moment they learned about the attack on Pearl Harbor. Fourteen-year-old David Davis remembered an unseasonably warm December day in Hamburg, New York. After jogging in preparation for spring sports, he entered his house to find his mother and father huddled around the radio. Parents' reactions ranged from despair to rage. Some cried; others cursed. Most were simply scared, afraid that the national security that they had always taken for granted was now put in question and that their homes and nation had suddenly become vulnerable. It was a moment their children would long remember.[3]

Although young people were unable to grasp fully the significance of the attack on Pearl Harbor and the ensuing war, their lives were shaped and altered by it. Children shared adults' anxiety about fathers and brothers overseas and experienced pain and grief when the family learned they would not be coming home. Prolonged separation from husbands, fathers, and brothers produced profound shifts in family roles. The widespread employment of teenagers during the war to fill in for men on the fighting front drastically altered their perception of themselves and their place in the family. For many young people, World War II was the formative experience of their lives. A shared sense of danger and privation instilled a strong sense of patriotism. At the same time, wartime conditions imposed severe emotional and psychological stresses, and the effects could still be seen decades later.[4]

In 1943 Deborah Gorham, age six, was beset by severe fears after her father, an American pilot, enlisted in the Royal Canadian Air Force. She remembered seeing *The Canterville Ghost,* a movie about a comic ghost who could walk through walls. For months she was terrified that a ghost would slip through her home's brick walls and attack her. Worried about Deborah's psychological well-being, her mother described these recurrent anxiety attacks in a letter to her husband. "That child loves you too much for her own good," he mother said. "She gets up at two or three in the morning and comes in fully awake to ask how you are, when you are coming home, are you in danger."[5]

Jonathan Yardley remembered air-raid drills in which grammar school children were escorted home, through suburban woods and back roads, by high school students. "On one unforgettable summer morning," he later wrote, "from the rocks on Marblehead Neck, we watched through binoculars an attack by Navy planes (out of Salem Willows) on a German submarine, which had been trapped on the surface while attacking a Halifax-bound convoy." Others remembered being herded out of classrooms and into school corridors to wait out an air-raid drill sitting on the floor and singing songs. James Roosevelt, the president's son, had his two-year-old boy shout "booooom" whenever he heard an explosion at a nearby naval base. That way, the father wrote, "the child thinks he is creating the explosion, and is quite delighted every time he hears one."[6]

The surprise attack on Pearl Harbor, a San Francisco psychiatrist claimed, "acted as a source of sudden and unexpected danger" for the nation's children. The public response to the attack intensified children's anxiety. New York and Washington fingerprinted children and gave them I.D. tags. Blackouts and air-raid drills contributed to a sense of insecurity and vulnerability. As newspapers and radio told of bombs and battles in Europe, few families did not personally know someone serving overseas. In nearly one family out of five, a father or a brother served in the military during the war. Although it was not until 1944 that *Life* magazine published a photograph of a dead American G.I., children could not be shielded from wartime realities. There were no grief counselors during World War II; children were left to deal with their anxieties largely on their own.[7]

World War II left an indelible mark on the nation's families. Whereas the number of marriages and births declined during World War I, the number accelerated during World War II, continuing a trend that began in the late 1930s. Between 1940 and 1946, three million more Americans married than could have been expected if marriage rates had remained at prewar levels. The rush to the altar was accompanied by a baby boom. For two decades preceding the war, the birthrate, like the marriage rate, had declined. But in 1943 the birthrate reached its highest levels in twenty years. During the 1930s America's population increased by only three million people; during the war it grew by 6.5 million. The postwar baby boom actually began with this wartime surge in births.[8]

The war also stirred an unprecedented tide of family migration. Sixteen million men and women left home for military service, and another 15.3 million civilians moved from town to town to work in defense industries or to follow uniformed husbands and fathers from one military base to another. Laura Briggs, the daughter of a Jerome, Idaho, farmer, was eleven years old when her father decided to sell everything, including the linoleum on the farmhouse floor, pack the family's black 1941 Chevy, and move to Long Beach, California, to work in a defense plant. He was convinced that there was "big money" to be made manufacturing armaments. And so there was. Families not only moved frequently during the war years, but they moved to radically different environments. There was rapid growth in coastal cities in the West and South, the centers of the nation's armaments industries and debarkation points for the armed forces. At the same time the Northeast and the Great Plains lost population. Boston lost 150,000 inhabitants, Pittsburgh 200,000, and the New York City area 800,000. The most dramatic losses were in the Dakotas, Kentucky, Minnesota, and Tennessee as hundreds of thousands of families moved to California, Illinois, Michigan, Oregon, and Washington State.[9]

Wartime migration created severe problems of adjustment. Housing was in short supply, educational and health care facilities were overburdened, and childcare facilities were sorely inadequate. Housing presented the most immediate problem, with 98 percent of all cities reporting a shortage of single-family homes and 90 percent an insufficient number of apartments. Migrating families crowded into squalid trailer camps, shantytowns, and "foxhole houses"—excavated basements covered with tarpaper roofs. A million and a half families shared apartments with relatives, friends, or strangers. The housing shortage was nationwide in scope. In Leeville, Louisiana, young mothers paid $50 a month to live in converted chicken coops and barns. Finding an apartment that would accept children was particularly difficult. Barbara DeNike was forced to place her children temporarily in a Catholic orphanage while she looked for another place to live. Exclaimed one apartment hunter: "[Landlords] got all these rules: no children, no dogs, no cats . . . Why I know one family that lived in a hotel room for two months—couldn't rent a thing—and had to board their kids out." Congestion and overcrowding were the order of the day. "It is not unusual," one observer noted, "to find children of all ages, including adolescents, either occupying the bedroom of the parents or sleeping together where no provision can be made for various sexes or age groups."[10]

For African-American families housing problems were especially acute. Some 700,000 African Americans moved from the rural South seeking jobs in defense industries. Restricted housing covenants kept black families "virtual prisoners" in racial ghettos, the *New York Times* reported. In Baltimore, families were crowded ten persons to an apartment. The housing shortage was the fuse that set off violent racial conflagrations. The worst race riot erupted in Detroit in 1942, after black families sought to enter a housing project set aside for them and a white mob, seeking the housing for itself, resisted. Violence sparked by this incident left forty people dead. Other racial violence provoked by the scarcity of adequate housing struck Mobile, Alabama; Beaumont, Texas; and Harlem.[11]

Growing up in wartime involved disruptions and stress, but also early opportunities to contribute to the family and assert one's independence. In a letter to General Douglas MacArthur, Joan Dooley, a twelve-year-old Girl Scout in Wichita, Kansas, wrote that she was doing her "bit by taking care of small children so that the parents may work in war factories." She and her friends ran "errands for people" and bought a war stamp every time they had a quarter. Nancy Jacobson, also twelve, had to take the place of two brothers serving in the navy. "I was taught to milk cows," she recalled. "I also learned how to drive a team of horses . . . Dad bought a John Deere tractor, and I learned to handle that." By planting a Victory garden, raising chickens, cutting back on nonessential items, and finding substitutes for goods in short supply, children assisted their families in making do during the war.[12]

Children, regardless of age, were expected to contribute to the nation's defense. A booklet published in 1943, called *Your Children in Wartime*, told girls and boys: "you are enlisted for the duration of the war as citizen soldiers. This is a total war, nobody is left out, and that counts you in, of course." Wartime children considered themselves valuable contributors to the nation's defense. They collected scrap metal, rubber, tin cans, and bundles of old newspapers. They sold War Bonds and Victory Stamps and distributed government pamphlets about civil defense, price controls, and rationing. Girls knitted socks, mittens, scarves, and sweaters. Many young people experienced pride in their involvement in the war effort: "From scrap drives to ration books to War Bonds, opportunities for us to become personally involved in the nation's struggle were everywhere; individually and collectively, they encouraged us in the conviction that we could be useful—that the scrap metal we rounded up in our little red wagons soon enough would be used to make bombers or tanks that would hasten the nation toward its inevitable victory."[13]

It was teenagers whose lives were transformed most drastically by the war. The war created a huge demand for labor, which was met by women, racial minorities, and adolescents. In increasing numbers, teenage boys and girls joined the labor force and insisted on adult rights. Four times as many fourteen- and fifteen-year-olds were working in 1945 as in 1941. The ready availability of jobs gave many young people unprecedented amounts of spending money and the autonomy that came with an independent income.

While children in increasing numbers joined the labor force, fewer went to school. In 1942 alone, more than 2,000 schools failed to open, partly because of a teacher and classroom shortage, but also because young people were turning away from education. In Arkansas, 10,000 children, and in Mobile, Alabama, 3,000 children, were without schools. In the Detroit area the school day for most children was cut to three hours. While the number of teenagers who worked rose by 1.9 million, the number attending school fell by 1.25 million.[14]

To permit children and teenagers to fulfill the labor needs of a nation at war, child labor statutes were relaxed. Various states permitted fourteen- and fifteen-year-olds to work at night or at such tasks as peeling shrimp or packaging fresh fruits and vegetables. In Delaware children as young as fourteen could work until midnight delivering milk. Florida permitted fourteen-year-olds to work during school hours and allowed twelve-year-olds to take afterschool jobs. In some states no age restrictions were placed on work in agriculture. Manpower was at a premium, and young people were a valuable resource.[15]

Inevitably wartime exigencies and demands on families led to a relaxation of social restraints on the young. One serviceman's wife voiced a common concern, that the war made it much more difficult to discipline children. Her husband was overseas, and "the kids don't seem to mind as much as they did when he was home." Reports of teenage vice filled the newspapers. In New York City in 1943 a seventeen-year-old was convicted of running a prostitution ring comprised of thirty girls ages twelve to fifteen. At big-city bus stations, teenage "knacky-whacky" or "V" girls flirted with soldiers. Frequent movement from one community to another, the prolonged absence of fathers, the assumption of increased responsibilities, and a weakening of parental discipline unsettled the lives of the young. These factors contributed to a sharp rise in wartime rates of premarital pregnancy, illegitimacy, and venereal disease.[16]

During the war years, popular magazines featured graphic depictions of the wartime plight of youth. The *Saturday Evening Post* described nine young children chained to trailers in a southern California trailer camp while their parents labored, as well as four children locked in their mother's automobile while she worked the graveyard shift. There were widespread reports of youth violence, such as the ruthless murder of a New York City schoolteacher by zoot-suited teenagers in 1942 and the more than 500 gangs in the city, fighting with brass knuckles, blackjacks, broken bottles, ice picks, and guns made out of four-inch pieces of pipe. Most disturbing of all were reports of abusive child labor, including the story of an eleven-year-old girl suffering a heart attack while performing farm labor, a fifteen-year-old boy dying from burns suffered while cleaning a food vat, and a sixteen-year-old boy losing an arm after catching it in a centrifugal dryer.[17]

Such events do not give a typical picture of life for the young during World War II, yet they were common enough to alarm the public. Children lived in a society shaken and disrupted by war. Many were growing up in homes without fathers and with working mothers. Frequent migration subjected children to extreme social and psychological dislocation. School attendance and child labor laws had been relaxed, and wartime excitement and stress were widespread. It is not surprising that most observers believed that the war had intensified the challenge of rearing responsible and well-adjusted young people.

Leading authorities on child psychology feared that the war desensitized children to violence, undermined their respect for authority, and led to parental neglect. Although it is uncertain whether juvenile delinquency or parental neglect were greater problems in the United States in the 1940s than in the 1930s, there is a mass of evidence indicating that social workers, psychologists, and public leaders were deeply troubled by the war's impact on the young. Of particular concern was the influx of mothers into the labor force and its deleterious effect on children. Public attitudes toward married women working were characterized by deep ambivalence. On the one hand, women were repeatedly told by the federal government that victory could not be achieved without their entry into the labor force. On the other, the federal government declared: "Now, as in peacetime, a mother's primary duty is to her home and children." Despite official pronouncements discouraging mothers from working, economic necessity led nearly 1.5 million mothers of children under ten to enter the labor force during the war. The overwhelming majority were members of families with incomes below the national average, who said that their primary motive for working was financial. Guidance counselors, child psychologists, and physicians feared that working mothers gave their offspring inadequate attention, and linked an array of social and psychological problems to maternal neglect, including truancy, sleeping and eating disorders, thumb-sucking, bedwetting, and "slower mental development, social ineptness, weakened initiative, and . . . [an inability] to form satisfactory relationships."[18]

Working mothers were able to make only haphazard arrangements for childcare. Although most left their children in the care of grandparents or neighbors, some children inevitably had to fend for themselves. Newspaper reports called them "8-hour orphans" or "latch-key" children, and experts predicted harmful social consequences from such abandonment. But public childcare facilities were woefully inadequate. At the beginning of the war the Federal War Manpower Commission took the position that mothers with young children should not seek work until childless women had been employed. In 1942, under the Lanham Act, the federal government allowed public works funds to be used for childcare in war-disrupted areas and made all mothers eligible regardless of income. By the end of 1943 the federal government had financed approximately 2,000 centers, serving 58,682 children. At its peak, in mid-1944, after the federal program began to accept children under the age of two, it served about 110,000 children. Federally financed extended-school programs provided afterschool care for between 100,000 and 300,000 children.[19]

Despite the pressing need for childcare, wartime nurseries remained underutilized, because many mothers opposed institutionalized care. Numerous wartime childcare centers were overcrowded, ill equipped, and poorly located. One wartime nursery near Baltimore was initially housed in a pair of trailers. After the trailers were found to violate public health standards, the children were moved into a room in an administration building, where they shared a single bathroom with the building's employees. Many centers were located in churches and private residences, often lacking outdoor space for sports and play. The high fees that war nurseries charged further limited the use of public childcare. Daily fees typically ranged from fifty to seventy-five cents, or nearly a quarter of a day's wages, discouraging many poorer parents from making use of the centers. Most families stayed with informal solutions to problems of childcare. One grandmother called World War II the "grandmother's war," because "the father goes off to war . . . mother goes to the factory to go to work, which is a very patriotic, important thing to do; the kids stay with grandmother."[20]

Compared with the efforts made by our wartime allies, the U.S. government did little to assist families to cope with wartime stresses. The United States lagged far behind Britain, where the government constructed central kitchens, public nurseries, and rural retreats for working mothers and their children, and required employers to give working mothers an afternoon off each week to conduct family shopping. Nevertheless, there were some genuine advances during the war, especially in the areas of infant mortality and child nutrition. Contributing to the improvements were wartime prosperity, migration to urban areas with better health care systems, and the Emergency Maternity and Infant Care program, which provided free maternity care for the wives of military personnel and health care for their infants during their first year of life. By mid-1944 the EMIC program provided assistance to one in every six or seven births.[21]

Public anxiety over women's ability to cope with the family in the absence of a father focused not only on maternal neglect but on its mirror image, maternal oversolicitousness. Americans were shocked by the number of men—over five million—who were rejected for military service on the basis of physical or psychological deficiencies. Three million men were classified as emotionally unstable, and authorities blamed this outcome on overprotective mothers who had shielded their sons from life's realities for too long. Dr. Edward A. Strecker, a psychiatric consultant to the Army and Navy, accused "America's traditional sweet, doting, self-sacrificing mom" of having "failed in the elementary mother function of weaning offspring emotionally as well as physically." Philip Wylie, author of the 1942 bestseller *A Generation of Vipers,* attributed boys' psychological and emotional immaturity to a dominant, overly protective mother and a passive or absent father. Solely responsible for their children's care, mothers and their "smotherlove" were increasingly regarded as the roots of psychological dysfunction.[22]

The specter of Nazism intensified concern about the war's impact on parenting. Many experts believed that Nazism was a product of Germany's patriarchal and hierarchical family structure. Some mental health experts argued that German fathers had implanted in their children "the authoritarian attitude, the belittling of women, and the cult of aggressive masculinity" that furnished fertile soil for the growth of National Socialism. Others blamed German mothers for creating an "authoritarian personality" by placing too much emphasis on obedience and exercising overly strict discipline during early childhood. If analysts agreed that repressive discipline had led to a totalitarian state, there was also a consensus that America's "democratic" family posed problems of its own. Lacking clearly defined roles or status hierarchy, the formlessness of the American family meant that many homes were riven by intense emotional tensions deriving from weak fathers, domineering mothers, and bickering children. The results of an upbringing in such an unstructured domestic environment were reflected in high rates of psychological maladjustment and immaturity—the symptoms ranging from extreme passivity and introversion to intense hostility and competitiveness. And, more often than not, when psychologists, social workers, and family counselors assessed blame, they tended to point an accusing finger not at unsettled wartime conditions but at individual mothers. In the end, mothers, separated from spouses and buffeted by wartime stresses, were viewed as the cause of their children's problems.[23]

In response to the weakening of families, schools took on greater responsibility for maintaining the health, well-being, and patriotism of children. Each morning children were expected to salute the flag as a symbol of their patriotism. At the time, sixteen states had laws requiring students to salute the flag. For some children, this ritual conflicted with their religious faith. Jehovah's Witnesses believed that saluting the flag violated the biblical prohibition against worshipping "graven images." Some children of Jehovah's Witnesses stood silently while their classmates recited the Pledge of Allegiance. Others recited an alternative pledge: "I respect the flag of the United States and acknowledge it as a symbol of freedom and justice to all. I pledge allegiance and obedience to all the laws of the United States that are consistent with God's law, as set forth in the Bible." But some refused to salute the flag, and their refusal sometimes resulted in legal action against their parents. In one instance a judge in Port Angeles, Washington, removed three children who were Jehovah's Witnesses from their parents' custody because they refused to salute the flag. In 1940 the Supreme Court ruled by eight to one that children could be compelled to salute the flag regardless of their religious convictions.

Three years later, after the United States had entered the war, the Supreme Court reversed itself in a six-to-three decision. West Virginia required students to salute the flag with a stiff-armed salute, which organizations such as the Parent-Teachers Association, the Boy Scouts and Girl Scouts, and the Red Cross considered "too much like Hitler's." Students who refused to salute the flag, for whatever reason, were expelled, and their parents were liable to be jailed and fined. In the case of *West Virginia State Board of Education v. Barnette,* the Court ruled that children could not be punished for refusing to salute the flag. Justice Robert H. Jackson wrote that no Americans could be forced to demonstrate their allegiance to "what shall be orthodox in politics, nationalism, religion, or other matters of opinion." This was true for children as well as adults. In his opinion, issued on Flag Day in 1942, Justice Jackson stated that compulsion was not a legitimate way to foster love of country in children, and contradicted our self-image as a nation fighting for democratic values. In an important precedent for the principle of children's rights, the right of children to exercise their religious freedom outweighed any benefits that came from forcing children to recite words contrary to their religious beliefs.[24]

During the war schools acquired heightened ideological significance as instruments for building a more democratic society. As one writer stated in the *School Review,* "To construct a common American culture and to lessen hatred and group prejudice in America, we have to rely chiefly on the schools." Schools embraced a number of rituals to foster patriotism and unity. Each school day typically began with the Pledge of Allegiance. Many schools staged patriotic pageants and plays; organized collection drives for waste paper, scrap metal, and other useful items; planted Victory Gardens in schoolyards; and instilled democratic principles. Some of the most lasting lessons did not come out of textbooks. One child recalled the principal and a man in uniform coming into a classroom and escorting his teacher out of the room to inform her of her husband's death in combat.[25]

Young people's education in patriotism was not confined to the classroom. The mass media also played a crucial role in teaching children why the country was fighting. Wartime comic books, cartoons, and movies were much more than mere entertainment; they served an educational and ideological function. Many comics were filled with subhuman depictions of the Japanese, and carried titles like *The Terror of the Slimy Japs, The Slant Eye of Satan,* and *Funeral for Yellow Dogs.* But it would be a mistake to conclude that comic books simply reinforced prejudice. Many worked to liberalize attitudes toward women and racial and ethnic minorities, part of the broader effort to portray World War II as a "people's war," in which diverse groups were pulling together in a common cause. Combat films such as *Air Force, Wake Island,* and *Destination Tokyo* focused on a small group that served as a microcosm of the American melting pot. *Objective, Burma!,* for example, included a Hennessy, a Miggleori, and a Neguesco. The characters' names demonstrated that this was a democratic war, which drew upon every segment of society.[26]

Like the comics, cartoons, movies, and radio shows enjoyed by children sent the message that World War II was a total war, involving the home front as well as the battlefront. Cartoons were intended to evoke boos for the enemy and catcalls along with laughter. Even Donald Duck and Mickey Mouse went to war, with Donald exhorting audiences to shout "Heil!" in the Führer's face in *A Nightmare in Nutziland.* Highly propagandistic, cartoons had titles like *Bugs Bunny Nips the Nips.* Many celebrated home-front sacrifice. As Donald Duck learns in one cartoon, "Your country needs taxes to beat the Axis!" Cartoons, like comic books, contained many racial stereotypes. Adolf Hitler was drawn as a goose-stepping duck, a pig, or a devil, and Emperor Hirohito and Mussolini as monkeys. Many popular radio programs and movies aimed at a younger audience featured spies and saboteurs or villains who threatened the mainland United States, and called for the forces of the good and patriotic to defeat them.[27]

Comic violence was the mainstay of cartoons and comic books, but violence also penetrated children's play and the mass media. A picture essay in *Life* magazine in March 1942 showed children in Long Island wearing tin helmets and hiding under the dining room table as they played a game called "air raid shelter." During the war years, war games dominated children's play. Unlike today's simulated, impersonal video games, play during the war years involved the active imitation of events overseas, with children engaging in commando raids and bombing raids across backyards. During the war the photographs and newsreels that young people saw grew increasingly graphic. The young saw wounded and dead soldiers in unprecedented numbers. Their need to act out the tragic woundings and deaths they saw depicted and to survive their simulated war games was great. It is not surprising that few were willing to play the enemy.[28]

It was during World War II that a distinctive teen culture began to dominate the public's attention. December 30, 1942, saw the birth of the screaming teenage "bobby-soxer." That day, New York's Paramount Theater featured a standard wartime program combining a patriotic movie—*Star-Spangled Rhythm,* with Bing Crosby—followed by a live stage show. The lead performers were Benny Goodman and his band, pianist Jess Stacyck, and the BG Sextet. As an "extra added attraction," a scrawny singer from Hoboken, New Jersey, named Frank Sinatra also appeared. When Sinatra began to sing, young women in the audience went into a frenzy of shrieking, squealing, and swooning. "What the hell was that?" Goodman asked. The newspapers called it "Sinatratrauma" and "Sinatramania." Sinatra's press agent, George Evans, had paid a number of young women $5 to scream when the singer appeared on stage. But the reaction was far more emotional than anything the agent could have promoted. The audience shrieked and cried and rushed the stage. Some fainted. When Sinatra appeared again at the Paramount in October 1944, the response was even greater. On Columbus Day, a school holiday, an estimated 30,000 teenage fans lined up along 43d Street to see the singer. *Time* magazine declared: "Not since the days of Rudolph Valentino has American womanhood made such unabashed love to an entertainer."[29]

The twenty-seven-year-old Sinatra was America's first teen heartthrob. With his oversized bow tie, his baby blue eyes, and his slender, 130-pound physique, he seemed like someone who needed to be loved. "It was the war years, and there was a great loneliness," Sinatra later explained. "I was the boy on every corner, the boy who'd gone off to war." But the audience's reaction signaled much more: a revolution in American popular culture. Teenagers had emerged as a force driving popular culture and

Teenagers stand next to a jukebox in Richwood, West Virginia, in 1942. Courtesy of the Library of Congress.

defining popular tastes, and teenage fans had become a new cultural and commercial category. Young girls from ten to twenty were willing to wait hours to buy tickets to see their heartthrob and records to hear him. The number of Sinatra fans would soon be in the millions, a force to contend with.[30]

In adjusting to wartime conditions, American youth developed a more autonomous sense of identity. Subject to public demands and criticisms, American adolescents began to assert themselves and create distinctive teenage subcultures with their own garb, hairstyles, dances, language, and values. Teenage boys, particularly in poorer communities, showed their disdain for social conventions by donning zoot suits, modeled on the garb worn by Depression-era gangsters. Zoot suits featured loosely cut coats with wide padded shoulders and pants flaring below the waist but tapered at the ankles. Combined with a wide-brimmed hat, a skin-tight T-shirt, and a ducktail haircut, such a uniform upset many adults, with its aggressive flamboyance and ostentation in time of war. Kleen Teens—their middle-class counterparts—developed a style of their own. Middle-class boys swung yo-yos, participated in bull sessions, congregated around juke-boxes in public places, and sported penny loafers and blue jeans. Bobby-soxers held slumber parties, read new magazines like *Mademoiselle* and *Seventeen* that catered to their tastes, swooned and shrieked over Sinatra, and learned the lindy hop.[31]

Before the war, adolescents were referred to as "youngsters" and were expected to share the outlooks and assumptions of their parents as well as to subordinate their desires to them. Whether in response to the threats of the adult world's war or the stress of family disruption, adolescents took on a new and distinctive social identity, independent of their parents'. Wartime jobs for teenagers enabled them to buy their own magazines, purchase records, attend movies, and wear clothing targeted exclusively at a teenage market. Young people adopted their own dance styles, like the jitterbug, and generated their own customs, status symbols, and fads. More and more, their recreation took place outside the home, away from the family. Much more than in the past, the peer group and the products of popular culture began to rival parents as influences on their behavior and aspirations.[32]

Parents grew more conscious than ever before that teenagers had "been liberated from adult control." With four out of five high school boys serving in the army after graduation, teen life seemed like a brief interlude before adult responsibilities intruded. Across the country recreation centers, sponsored by companies like Coca-Cola and Royal Crown Cola, sprang up. By the end of the war, more than 3,000 Boogie Barns and Jive Hives contained jukeboxes, dance floors, and Ping-Pong tables. Teenagers flocked to these places in droves as havens from family, war, and the future.[33]

As teenagers assumed their own identity and tastes, they were identified as a lucrative commercial market. "Teena"—the prototypical teenage girl—"has money of her own to spend . . . and what her allowance and pin-money earnings won't buy, her parents can be counted on to supply. For our girl Teena won't take no for an answer." With these words, an appeal by *Seventeen* magazine to advertisers, teenagers emerged as a market category. Two people were critical to the creation of this distinct market. One was a grandmother. Helen Valentine, the promotions manager of *Mademoiselle,* founded *Seventeen* magazine after noticing that there was no magazine to promote teen fashions. *Seventeen*'s first issue in September 1944 sold 400,000 copies in two days. Within a year it had a circulation of a million and soon carried more advertising than any other magazine. To attract advertisers, *Seventeen* conducted its "Life with Teena" market survey. It pointed out that teenage girls not only had a substantial discretionary income, but that they wanted to fit in, to "look, act and be just like the girl next door . . . For Teena and her teenmates come in bunches . . . Sell one and the chances are you'll sell them all." The other was Eugene Gilbert, a nineteen-year-old shoe salesman who in 1945 came up with the idea that "stores and manufacturers were losing a lot of money because they were blind" to teenagers' "tastes and habits." He founded Gil-Bert Teenage Services, a consulting firm, to provide systematic market research on teenagers and to advise businesses how to sell goods to teens. Within a year he had 300 "poll takers" providing information about teens' interests and wants. With clients including Maybelline cosmetics, Quaker Oats, and United Airlines, *Time* magazine called him "the Bobby-Soxers' Gallup," referring to opinion pollster George Gallup. "Our salient discovery," he wrote, "is that within the past decade teenagers have become a separate and distinct group in our society." Gilbert convinced businesses that teens were impulsive buyers preoccupied with the here and now and that his youthful poll takers could persuade teens to try their products and make them fashionable.[34]

During the war teens turned away from performers who appealed to adults—like the Glenn Miller orchestra—to performers of their own, showing their taste for novelty over familiarity and for style over sentiment. And teen culture began to exert a powerful impact on adults themselves. As the writer Diana West has noted, the discovery of the distinct teen market during World War II marked "the advent of a brand-new, heretofore unseen, emphasis on—indeed, domination of—the teen experience in mainstream popular culture."[35]

The middle-class teen culture that emerged during the war was a mainstream phenomenon. Unlike the zoot-suit-clad black hipster (like Malcolm Little, who would later become Malcolm X) or Latino *pachuco*, Kleen Teens, wearing bobbysox or penny loafers, were regarded by adults with a mixture of condescension and bemusement. The division of teens between insiders and outsiders reflected much broader splits within wartime culture. Popular culture remembers World War II as a period of national unity, when ethnic and racial divisions were set aside in the struggle to defeat the Axis powers. But the war years were a period of intense stress that found expression in ethnic and racial conflict. In 1943 alone, 242 race riots took place in forty-seven cities. Ethnic tension penetrated into children's culture. Antisemitism peaked during the war, and many Jewish children, like ten-year-old Philip Roth, remembered gangs on the Jersey shore hollering "Kikes! Dirty Jews!" Some children's rhymes were anything but amusing. One went:

Red, white and blue,
Your father is a Jew,
Your mother is Japanese,
And so are you!

The internment of Japanese Americans was the most extreme example of wartime prejudice.[36]

Tsuguo Ikeda kept a diary when he was seventeen years old. In some ways it was quite ordinary. It recorded the latest songs he had heard, his attempts to find a date for a dance, and his mom's complaints when he came home late. But his life was anything but typical. He and his family were interned in the Minidoka Relocation Camp in southeastern Idaho, "a vast stretch of sage brush stubble and shifting, swirling sands—a dreary, forbidding, flat expense of wilderness." Alongside his description of everyday life, his diary recorded his loneliness, the hard work he was assigned (toiling in a sugarbeet field), and his anxiety about whether he and his family would ever get out of the camp.[37]

No group of children was more deeply affected by the war than those who were Japanese Americans. Ten weeks after the Japanese attack on Pearl Harbor, President Franklin D. Roosevelt signed Executive Order 9066, which authorized the secretary of war to designate areas "from which any or all persons may be excluded." Under this order, more than 120,000 Japanese Americans—two-thirds of them U.S. citizens—were removed from their homes in California, Oregon, Washington, and Arizona and herded into ten desolate relocation camps, ringed by barbed wire and guard towers, with search lights and machine guns. Any individual who had one Japanese great-grandparent was liable to internment. The victims of racial prejudice, war hysteria, and economic jealousies, Japanese Americans suffered a gross violation of their civil liberties. In a poem, one child, Itsuko Taniguchi, described the dislocation she felt on the day that her family was evacuated from their home:

Leaving our friends
And my tree that bends
Away to the land
With lots of sand.[38]

For Japanese Americans, internment meant severe economic hardship, physical dislocation, and a sharp reordering of family roles. Some families were given as little as forty-eight hours to dispose of their homes, businesses, farms, and personal property, which were sold for a fraction of their worth. The internees were allowed to take only what they could carry, so families were forced to leave pets behind. Children with serious

A young boy stands near a soldier during the evacuation of Japanese families from Bainbridge Island, Washington, in 1942. Courtesy of the Library of Congress.

disabilities were barred from the camps. Mary Tsukamoto's son, Toyoki, who was blind and mentally retarded, was taken away by a social worker and died within a month. Japanese Americans remained in the camps for an average of 900 days.[39]

The camps' barracks were built of tarpaper over pine boards. When the pine dried, the floorboards separated, allowing dust to blow through. The buildings were uninsulated, and wintertime temperatures sometimes fell to 30 degrees below zero. The "apartments" consisted of a single drafty room, averaging sixteen by twenty feet, shared by an entire family. Nine members of Marge Tanwaki's extended family lived in one room in the Amache Relocation Center in southeastern Colorado. Furnishings were limited to cots, blankets, and a lightbulb. One young Japanese American described conditions in his family's camp: "The apartments, as the Army calls them, are stables . . . mud is everywhere . . . We have absolutely no fresh meat, vegetables, or butter. Mealtime queues extend for blocks; standing in a rainswept line, feet in the mud, for scant portions of canned wieners and boiled potatoes, hash . . . or beans . . . and stale bread." The internees slept on cotton sacks stuffed with hay and fashioned furniture out of discarded crates. They used communal latrines, washed clothes by hand, and ate meals in a mess hall. Phones were forbidden, and there were no stores. Food poisoning, measles, and pneumonia were rampant.[40]

Life in the camps was highly regimented. Kinya Noguchi, who was interned as a child in the Tule Lake camp in northern California along with 18,788 other evacuees, recalled the routine. At seven in the morning a siren blast announced breakfast. Families rushed "to the wash basin to beat the other groups" and then rushed to the mess hall. Work began at eight for adults, and school started at half past eight or nine for children. At Tanforan Assembly Center in San Bruno, California, which held 8,000 internees, a siren announced roll call at half past six each evening. Children had to race to the barracks, where inspectors made sure that each family member was present. Said one young girl, "when the siren rings I get so scared that I sometimes scream."[41]

The internees' biggest complaints were the lack of privacy and of proper schools. Toilets, showers, and dining facilities were communal, precluding family privacy. Dining ceased to be a private family ritual, and strict parental control over children loosened. Children attended makeshift schools, lacking books, blackboards, and desks; many students had to sit on the floor. At one camp, physics was taught in a laundry room because it was the only available space with running water. Family separation was common. After Isao Fujimoto's sister caught measles in the Heart Mountain internment camp near Cody, Wyoming, she was placed in quarantine. While his mother cared for her, the other children, ages ten months to eight years, had to fend for themselves. Internment inverted traditional roles and relationships in Japanese-American families. Men and women, regardless of age, worked at interchangeable jobs paying $12 to $19 a month. In the camps, influence shifted away from the older generation, the Issei, who had been born abroad, to the younger generation, the Nisei, who had been born in the United States. A disproportionate share of those who were released early from the camps were from the younger generation.[42]

Ethnic tensions during the war were not confined to Japanese Americans. In Los Angeles, tensions sparked by an incident known as Sleepy Lagoon flared around Mexican-American youth. An eastside Los Angeles reservoir, Sleepy Lagoon was also a swimming hole and recreation center for Mexican Americans, who were forbidden to swim at the city's segregated public pools. In 1942 it became a synonym for injustice and racial hatred. On August 1, 1942, a party attended by Mexican-American youth at Sleepy Lagoon turned violent. Fighting broke out, and a young man, José Díaz, was beaten to death.[43]

The early 1940s in Los Angeles was the era of the *pachuco*, Latino youth who favored the long coats, wide pants, and watch chains of the zoot suit. Pachucos embraced a style that was bold and defiant, adopting padded-shouldered suits, wide-brimmed hats, triple-soled shoes, ducktailed hairstyles, and a distinctive lingo—*Calo*—drawn from gangsters and jazz musicians. Their female counterparts—*pachuquitas*—also challenged the norms of middle-class respectability. They wore short tight skirts, sheer blouses, dark red lipstick, and black mascara. This represented one of the first times that youths—African American as well as Latino—explicitly and self-consciously used style as a form of rebellion. They wanted to be noticed, and so they were.[44]

The Los Angeles press did a series of articles on pachuco gangs. As public outrage grew, sheriff's officials conducted a sweep through the city's barrios, arresting more than 600 young men in the Sleepy Lagoon case. A grand jury indicted 24 for murder, making the court proceedings one of the largest mass trials in American history. The defendants were referred to in the press as "The Sleepy Lagooners" and then simply as "goons." Only two of the defendants had attorneys, and openly biased testimony was admitted into the trial record. One sheriff's department expert testified that "total disregard for human life has always been universal throughout the Americas among the Indian population. And this Mexican element feels . . . a desire . . . to kill, or at least draw blood." Twelve defendants were found guilty of conspiring to murder Díaz; five others were convicted of assault. Two years passed before an appeals court overturned all the convictions and severely reprimanded the presiding judge for displaying prejudice toward the defendants.[45]

At the end of the Sleepy Lagoon trial, a public campaign against Mexican-American youth intensified. Over a two-week period in May and June 1943, police stood by while several thousand servicemen and civilians beat up young Mexican Americans, stripping them of their draped jackets and pegged pants. Mexican, Filipino, and African-American boys as young as twelve or thirteen were "pushed into the streets, and beaten with sadistic frenzy." The riots ended only after senior military officials declared Los Angeles off-limits to military personnel. The Los Angeles City Council followed by banning zoot suits in the city. For younger Mexican Americans, the Sleepy Lagoon trial and the Zoot Suit riots became symbols of injustice and ethnic hatred. Those events marked the starting point of the modern Mexican-American struggle for equal justice.[46]

The war in Europe ended on May 8, 1945, and the war in the Pacific, on August 14. The United States had emerged victorious, but the war's end produced severe pangs of readjustment. For Deborah Gorham, her father's return from war in December 1944 was anything but happy. "I remember the acute anticipation and joy I felt, and then the let-down, when he was abrupt and unfriendly to me, and appeared far more interested in my year-old sister, whom he had never seen before." She had "remembered a flawless prewar Dad." But her father had "returned a deeply troubled, angry man. And he remembered an exuberant 5 year-old not a shy, gangly 7 year-old." Deborah was not alone in her dismay. Many wartime children found readjustment painful. One adult recalled her father's return as highly disruptive. She and her mother "were a tight, tough unit." "In some way," she continued, "I resented my father's return to the family. Everything changed." Estrangement and problems with alcohol were not infrequent as families tried to readjust after the war. Fathers thought that their children had grown spoiled in their absence, while children considered their fathers excessively strict, "nervous," or "intolerant."[47]

For the most part, families had to deal with problems of postwar readjustment without government assistance. World War II greatly expanded federal involvement in children's health and well-being, but with the war's end, government initiatives like the Emergency Maternity and Infant Care Act, which had provided health services for hundreds of thousands of military families, and the Lanham Act, which had funded childcare for a half-million children, were terminated. For many families, the tensions produced by separation and war proved unmanageable, and the strains were reflected in a startling upsurge in the nation's divorce rate. Between 1940 and 1944 the divorce rate rose from 16 per 100 marriages to 27 per 100. By 1950 a million G.I.'s had been divorced.[48]

The impact of the war upon children was memorialized in fiction. Two great novels dealing with childhood appeared during World War II: William Saroyan's *The Human Comedy* and Betty Smith's *A Tree Grows in Brooklyn*. Superficially the stories could not be more different: one focused on the experience of boys, the other on a girl; one was set during World War II, the other before World War I. Yet they treated a common theme: children coming to grips with death, hunger, and human hatred.

In 1942, when the outcome of the war was most uncertain, Saroyan wrote a screenplay for MGM that he subsequently reworked into a novel. Deeply sentimental, it tells the story of wartime life in a small California town through the experiences of a widowed mother, her daughter, Bess, and her three sons: Marcus, a G.I. who goes off to a war from which he won't return; fourteen-year-old Homer; and four-year-old Ulysses. It is a coming-of-age story, but unlike many that followed, *The Human Comedy* is not about sexual maturation or initiation, but about psychological and emotional growth. It follows the younger brothers as they gradually escape the fantasy world of childhood and become aware of the imperfections, sorrows, and tragedies of the adult world.

Homer has to grow up quickly after his older brother leaves home. In order to help his family financially, he takes a job delivering telegrams to the families of sons who have died in combat. Ulysses, his intensely curious younger brother, who personifies wide-eyed childhood curiosity and innocence, undergoes a personal odyssey of his own that culminates in his discovery of death. Highly discursive in style, *The Human Comedy* touches on many of the disruptive elements of home-front life, including the father's absence, family separation, the widespread employment of teenagers, ethnic and racial conflict, and the weakening of parental supervision and controls over youthful sexuality. Saroyan's great insight was that the war forced young people to mature rapidly and confront the world's sadnesses even as they sought to obey the novel's injunction: "Be happy. Be happy."

A Tree Grows in Brooklyn sold 300,000 copies in the first six weeks after it was published in 1943. Set in Brooklyn's Williamsburg slums between 1902 and 1919, it tells the story of an earnest fourteen-year-old, Francie Nolan; her streetwise preteen brother, Neeley; her resourceful mother, Katie; and her loving father, Johnny, who is drinking himself to death and whose inability to hold a steady job has condemned the family to a life of poverty. Like *The Human Comedy, A Tree Grows in Brooklyn* is a highly sentimental coming-of-age story, and, like Saroyan's novel, it describes children growing up quickly as they confront the world's cruelties. Family need forces Francie to leave school to get a job, to nurture her family, to confront a would-be rapist, and to continue to grow tall and straight like the tree in her backyard. Francie's resilience wins out and prevents her from being permanently scarred by her environment.

The war left an indelible impression on the lives and beliefs of the children who lived through it. Far from fading over time, the war's impact persisted into adulthood. The experience led many young Americans to see themselves as members of a common generation, different from those who preceded or succeeded them. They remembered the war as an elevating time—demanding and stressful, but also inspiring—a period of privation and sacrifice, but also of high ideals and purpose, when the United States and all Americans stood proud. For many young people, participation in the war effort instilled a sense of self-worth, autonomy, and initiative that they carried with them in the years ahead. But perhaps the war's most important legacy was the one that Saroyan described in *The Human Comedy*. Young people had grown aware of life's sorrows. For many young Americans, the war exacted a high toll. At least 183,000 children lost fathers, and many more lost siblings, relatives, or neighbors. Wartime separations and losses led many Americans to place a heavy emphasis on family life in the postwar years.[49]

chapter fourteen

In Pursuit of the Perfect Childhood

For AMERICANS of a certain age, the answer to the question "What time is it?" will always be the same: "It's Howdy Doody time." Baby boomers share many references from their childhood, from afterschool TV shows like *Howdy Doody* and *The Mickey Mouse Club* to toys like Mr. Potato Head and Slinkeys. Half a century later, memories of postwar childhood still make many baby boomers sigh. But nostalgia for the 1950s is highly seductive; it inevitably sanitizes the past and projects us into a world that never existed.[1]

It is easy to understand why many middle-class baby boomers look back fondly on their postwar childhood. The postwar era was a period of rapidly rising real incomes, when the after-inflation weekly earnings of factory workers increased 50 percent, and millions of Americans moved from urban apartments to suburban ranch-style houses. But the era's greatest appeal is that it seems a much more innocent and child-friendly time: a time of open spaces, of brand-new neighborhoods, Good Humor ice cream trucks, 25-cent movies, and amusement parks, long since replaced by shopping malls and strip shopping centers. Consumer culture seemed more innocent then, with shiny silver cap guns embossed with the name of the Lone Ranger, "cigarettes" made of chocolate, and cereal premiums that included bracelets and plastic tanks that fired plastic shells. Even the child-oriented convenience foods evoke nostalgia—Sugar Frosted Flakes (introduced in 1951), Sugar Smacks (in 1953), Tater Tots (in 1958), and Jiffy Pop, the stovetop popcorn (also in 1958). For aging baby boomers, the postwar period stands out as the golden age of American childhood. It serves as the yardstick against which all subsequent changes in childhood are measured.

Yet it is a mistake to look at the postwar era through rose-colored glasses. In fact nearly a third of postwar children grew up near or below the poverty line. The years between World War II and the turbulence of the 1960s are often regarded as a sterile period of quiescence and conformity, but beneath the warmth of the era were intense currents of anxiety. Sociologists like Kingsley Davis and psychologists like Theodore Lidz blamed the growing isolation of the nuclear family and the smothering intensity of the mother-child bond for a host of ills in children, including schizophrenia and sex-role confusion.[2]

To understand postwar childhood, it is essential to recognize that the period's family patterns—a high birthrate, a stable divorce rate, and a low number of mothers in the workforce—were a historical aberration, out of line with long-term historical trends. The era's child-centered character represented a reaction against Depression hardships, wartime upheavals, and Cold War insecurities. The postwar era also represented a period of far-reaching social transformations whose significance would become apparent during the 1960s. It was during the 1950s that teen culture assumed its modern form and that the civil rights movement's activist assault on school segregation got underway.

On January 19, 1953, forty-four million Americans watched Lucy Ricardo give birth to Little Ricky, in one of the most widely viewed broadcasts in television history. That year nearly four million American children were born, more than in any previous year. Between 1946 and 1964 American women bore more than seventy-five million infants, compared with barely fifty million in the preceding nineteen years. At its peak, the birthrate averaged 3.6 babies per woman, nearly double the rate in the 1930s.[3]

After fifteen years of economic privation and war, the surge in birthrates came as no surprise. Between 1940 and 1950 the sharpest increases in fertility occurred among women over thirty-five, who had postponed marriage and childbearing during the Depression and war years. But unlike in Britain, France, and Germany, where the boom quickly subsided, the American rate continued to climb. Not until 1965 did the annual rate drop below four million, a mark not reached again until 1989. Contributing to the ongoing boom were an increase in the proportion of women marrying, a decline in the number of childless and one-child marriages, and a sharp drop in the age of first marriage. For parents whose own childhoods were scarred by war and insecurity, the impulse to marry, bear children, and provide them with a protected childhood was intense.

Childlessness became a sign of maladjustment and parenthood a symbol of maturity and success. "Children," said one single woman in 1955, "give life a new meaning, a new focal point, a new frame of reference, a new perspective." Childless couples became objects of pity.[4]

Parents who had had to mature quickly during the Depression and war didn't want their children to be similarly deprived of childhood pleasures. Middle-class mothers served as full-time camp counselors, leisure coordinators, and chauffeurs. The sociologist William H. Whyte described postwar America as a filiarchy, a society dominated by the young. "It is the children who set the basic design," he wrote in 1956; "their friendships are translated into the mother's friendships, and these, in turn, to the family's."[5]

The sheer size of the baby boom forced the economy to regear itself to feed, clothe, educate, and house the rising generation. Nearly every major U.S. metropolitan area saw its outlying areas spawn versions of Levittown, the planned community with 17,000 homes built in a Long Island, New York, potato field beginning in 1947. Of thirteen million homes constructed in the decade after World War II, eleven million were erected in new suburban developments. Two-thirds of Levittown men said they had moved to the suburbs to spend more time with their children, and 70 percent of these men said they had fulfilled this objective. Nationwide, 80 percent of adults said they had moved to the suburbs "for the kids."[6]

The growth of the suburbs greatly contributed to the image of the 1950s as a child-centered decade. Within the booming suburbs, there were two sharply defined age groups: adults of childbearing age and youngsters under the age of fifteen. Suburbia was a world of families and young children, with few old people and surprisingly few adolescents. Usually living some distance from relatives, suburban families were more isolated, intense, and inward-turning than their urban counterparts.[7]

In an increasingly commercialized, child-centered environment, parents and grandparents spent more money on children than ever before. Toy sales soared from $84 million in 1940 to $1.25 billion two decades later. For very young children, there were new games like Candyland (introduced in 1949) and Yahtzee (1956). For somewhat older children, there were Mr. Potato Head (1952), a package of noses, ears, and mustaches that kids could stick onto real vegetables; and Silly Putty (1950), a combination of boric acid and silicone oil, a gooey compound that bounced on the floor and copied images from comic books and newspapers onto sheets of paper. Many postwar toys sought to socialize boys and girls into proper gender roles. During the Cold War years, toy soldiers and mock weapons were particularly popular among boys. Girls' dolls evolved from baby dolls to nurture to fashion-model dolls, emphasizing hair styling and wardrobes.[8]

Toymakers quickly discovered that the baby-boom market was highly susceptible to fads. Because they watched the same television programs, children everywhere were quickly exposed to the same faddish products. During the Davy Crockett craze of 1955, ten million coonskin hats were sold. Three years later, Arthur Melin and Richard Knerr heard that Australian children used a bamboo ring for exercise. They fashioned a ring of their own and called it a Hula-Hoop. Within four months they sold twenty-five million. The most popular toy of the postwar era was Barbie, the first mass-marketed adult-looking doll.[9]

Contributing to the child-centered mood of the 1950s was anxiety over the scourge of childhood: polio. Terror gripped baby boomers' parents every summer as epidemics of polio left thousands of children in braces, wheelchairs, or iron lungs. Whenever an epidemic struck, movie theaters were abandoned, swimming pools deserted, and summer camps disbanded. Before the early 1950s, polio was a relatively rare viral disease, although in 1916, 6,000 children died of it. After World War II the number of cases skyrocketed, reaching 60,000 in 1952. The culprit, ironically, was modern sanitation. Earlier, poor sanitary conditions exposed children to the disease during infancy, when paralysis was rare. But improved hygiene meant that children were exposed to the disease in later years, when they were most vulnerable to paralysis. In 1952 Jonas Salk of the University of Pittsburgh developed the first polio vaccine, the product of years of research by the March of Dimes, the charity founded by Franklin Roosevelt in 1937. A "killed-virus" vaccine, it sought to prompt the body's immune system to destroy a live polio virus by first exposing it to a "killed" one. In 1954, 1.8 million American schoolchildren participated as test subjects in the largest field trial in history. Anxious parents eagerly volunteered their children, and many protested when their health district was excluded from the test. The successful field trial led to vaccine production by six drug companies. A mistake by one of the companies, which led 204 children and adults to contract polio, resulting in 11 deaths, nearly destroyed confidence in the Salk vaccine. Yet over the next decade, vaccines cut the number of cases of polio from 135 cases per million to 26.[10]

The triumph over polio instilled a lasting faith in the power of medical research to eradicate children's diseases. No group benefited more from medical advances during and after World War II than children. Sulfa drugs, penicillin, insulin, immunization against whooping cough and diphtheria, new treatments against tetanus, and fluoride against tooth decay helped to alleviate many traditional scourges of childhood.[11]

As threats of childhood disease diminished, public attention to childrearing mounted, as did anxiety that faulty childrearing could produce enduring problems. Childrearing authorities of the postwar era called for more relaxed methods, informing parents that a "child should be understood rather than managed." In 1956 *Newsweek* magazine reported: "The new Freudians charged that the old-fashioned, strait jacket type of upbringing was turning out neurotics. Discipline of this nature, they said, tended to 'scar the child's psyche.'" The most famous childrearing expert was white-bearded Benjamin Spock, six feet, four inches tall, who became a father figure to many parents and their children during the 1950s, and who preached a softer, more compassionate approach to bringing up baby.[12]

In 1946 Pocket Books had published Dr. Spock's 25-cent paperback, *The Common Sense Book of Baby and Child Care.* "Trust yourself," the book began. "You know more than you think you do." In the first six months it sold 750,000 copies. For anxious parents, this book was filled with practical and reassuring advice. "Spitting and vomiting are common," begins one section. It is "natural for a baby around one to take a bite out of his parent's cheek." Unlike Calvinists, who considered children the fruit of original sin, or behaviorists, who told mothers to "never hug and kiss" their children, Dr. Spock urged parents to trust their instincts, talk to and play with their infants, and shower them with love. Instead of serving as guards imposing rigid feeding schedules, parents should recognize that their child was essentially good at heart. "He isn't a schemer. He needs love," he wrote. "Your baby is born to be a reasonable, friendly human being."

Spock succeeded in translating Sigmund Freud's ideas about children's psychic development into nonthreatening language that any parent could understand. To deprive a baby of a bottle or a breast too early, or to insist that a child follow a rigid feeding schedule, Spock explained, "robs him of some of his positive feelings for life." He warned parents about the dangers of overpressuring children about toilet training: "If his mother is trying to make him feel naughty about soiling himself with the movement, he may come to dread all kinds of dirtiness . . . If this worrisomeness is deeply implanted at an early age, it's apt to turn him into a fussy finicky person—the kind who's afraid to enjoy himself or try anything new, the kind who is unhappy unless everything is just so." Dr. Spock's greatest talent was to make Freudian concepts—such as the latency period, Oedipal conflict, castration anxiety, and penis envy—seem like common sense. A "boy of 3½ will declare that he is going to marry his mother when he grows up . . . The little girl is about to feel the same way about her father," he explained in straightforward language. Similarly, "if a boy around the age of 3 sees a girl undressed, it may strike him as queer that she hasn't got a penis like his." He went on to explain that if the child doesn't get a "satisfactory answer right away, he may jump to the conclusion that some accident has happened to her" and fear that the same thing "might happen to me, too!" He described bedwetting, reliance on a bottle, thumb-sucking, and a fuzzy blanket as regressive substitutes for a mother during a time of stress.

Despite Spock's admonition to mothers to trust their instincts, maternal anxiety over childrearing intensified during the postwar era. Many mothers found Dr. Spock's view that childrearing was easy and that babies' dispositions were naturally pleasant extremely frustrating. Nor did many accept his vision of managing babies without strict discipline. Dr. Spock's insistence that babies' crying was simply a way to express their needs made many mothers feel all the more frustrated when they were unable to satisfy those needs.[13]

Postwar childrearing was viewed as the key to producing not simply a healthy, happy child, but also psychologically well-adjusted adults and a harmonious democratic society. As one expert put it, "The poorly adjusted child tends to become the ill-adjusted partner in marriage. The parent who is maladjusted in marriage finds it difficult or impossible to be a good parent." In an influential 1947 book titled *Modern Women: The Lost Sex,* Marynia Farnham and Ferdinand Lundburg argued that "the spawning ground for most neurosis in Western civilization is the home. The basis for it is laid in childhood."[14]

Raising sociable, secure, and adaptable children, who were "more cooperative, more consensus-oriented, more group conscious," became a virtual obsession in postwar childrearing literature. "The disturbed, hostile, and rebellious child," warned one expert, "is a danger to himself and to the community, and a poor risk as a future citizen." A *Washington Post* editorial underlined the ideological significance attached to proper childrearing:

> The free child finds himself greatly outnumbered by the hordes of the regimented. As he grows up he will find himself one of the relatively small brigade that must uphold mental enlightenment and human freedom against ruthless primitive masses seeking the slavery of the spirit. To do this, he must be given "the strength of ten" through his emotional stability, maturity, self-discipline, and creativeness.[15]

Although the childrearing techniques of the postwar era are commonly labeled "permissive," childrearing was not nearly as indulgent as later commentators assumed. For one thing, no generation in American history was less likely to be breast-fed. Whereas nearly two-thirds of infants discharged from the hospital had been breast-fed in 1946, this figure fell to 37 percent in 1956 and just 27 percent in 1966. Of the mothers who did breast-feed, the duration was generally short, with only 3 percent nursing for as long as seven months. Nor were parents especially permissive in terms of infantile sexuality or toilet training. The overwhelming majority of parents regarded masturbation as undesirable and attempted to stop it, while nearly half of all children began toilet training before they were nine months old. Concluded a team of sociologists studying one postwar suburb: "Despite the prevalent view that too early and too severe toilet training may be traumatic for the child, many a . . . mother, given the setting of her immaculate home, is virtually compelled to focus attention upon this training."[16]

Childrearing practices heavily emphasized gender distinctions. In articles like "Raise Your Girl to be a Wife" and "How to Raise Better Husbands," childrearing experts urged parents to respond promptly to signs of "sissiness" in boys and masculine behavior in girls. Sissylike behavior not only led to harassment from other boys, but might "make him an indecisive and ineffectual person, and at worst may even lead to homosexuality or impotence," while tomboyish behavior might lead girls to "give up their femininity." Most parents reinforced gender norms. As one study concluded: "The boy or girl whose performance . . . [shoveling walks, washing the car, dusting furniture, fixing light cords, and making beds] does not follow the traditional pattern can still expect censure in many homes."[17]

In an age of conformity, postwar mothers were not overly ambitious about academic progress for their children. Rather than wanting their children to be outstanding, they wanted their children to be normal and average—congenial and well adjusted. In an age when fitting in was the desired goal, parents were happy to have their children be like the others rather than conspicuous.[18]

Anxiety over psychologically unbalanced mothering soared after World War II, permeating popular culture. Advertisements for the movie *Rebel without a Cause* underscored this concern. The boy came from a good family, but was sullen, surly, and tortured. "What makes him tick . . . like a bomb?" advertisements asked. The answer: a weak-willed, apron-wearing father and an overbearing mother. Alfred Hitchcock's *Psycho,* based on Robert Bloch's 1959 novel about a deranged mama's boy, similarly emphasized the dangers of bad mothering. It drew on the real-life story of Ed Gein of Plainfield, Wisconsin, whose mother-fixation purportedly transformed him into a sexually repressed murderer of women. Popular culture warned mothers that repressiveness or improperly handled sexual development could induce nymphomania, frigidity, and homosexuality in their children.[19]

A basic premise of the psychoanalytically oriented childrearing advice of the postwar era was that a mother's relationship with her children was the key to their psychological and emotional development. To this there was a corollary: any mistake in mothering could scar a child permanently. Rigorous toilet training could foster an authoritarian personality. Harsh scoldings, rigid scheduling, and overly involved mothers could have deleterious psychological consequences. The "furtive guilt and anxiety laid up in early childhood" by overprotective mothers, who tied their children to their apron strings, induced promiscuity, masturbation, homosexuality, and frigidity. Even excessive concerns for safety could warp a child psychologically. It was "much better that they suffer for a month of inconvenience of a broken limb than that they suffer for life from undeveloped physical powers and immature personalities."[20]

The Cold War emphasis on conformity, sociability, patriotism, and religiosity colored postwar middle-class childhood. Although the decade of the 1950s is considered especially family oriented, the most important development was the growing influence of extrafamilial institutions in socialization. Schools, churches, television, and the commercial marketplace fostered separate worlds of childhood and youth in which certain cultural references and experiences were shared by peer groups, and from which parents, and even older siblings, were excluded.[21]

Middle-class parents turned to a wide range of extrafamilial institutions to ensure that their children grew up well adjusted and sociable. The postwar era was the golden age of scouting, with enrollment in the Cub Scouts soaring from 766,635 in 1949 to 2.5 million a decade later, and the Girl Scouts and Brownies growing from 1.8 million to four million. Attendance at summer camps also rocketed upward, as a way both to promote social skills and to defuse the intensity of the highly privatized, inward-turning middle-class family. The economic prosperity of the postwar era smoothed the path to separate summer vacations for children. Sunday school participation also rose as a postwar religious revival brought a sharp increase in membership in mainstream religious denominations. F.B.I. director J. Edgar Hoover warned that "out of 8,000 delinquent children, only 42 attended Sunday school regularly."[22]

In the context of the Cold War, there was an intense concern with instilling toughness and competitiveness in boys. Ron Kovic's autobiography, *Born on the Fourth of July*, described how his upbringing in suburban Massapequa, Long Island, led him to despise softness and sensitivity. The eldest son of an A&P manager and his sternly devout Catholic wife, Ron was brought up to believe in certain platitudes about patriotism, family, anticommunism, and manliness. Hollywood's glamorous but unrealistic war movies filled him with visions of glory and heroism in battle, which he mimicked in mock battles with his childhood friends. In later life, after he had graduated from the Boy Scouts and high school athletics to the Marines, he felt betrayed by the John Wayne movies he had watched as a boy, when he returned from Vietnam in a wheelchair, paralyzed from the chest down.

During the Cold War there was a symbolic connection between the struggle with the Soviet Union and the battles boys acted out at recess and in backyards. The television shows boys watched reinforced a simplistic view of life as a struggle between good and evil. Of the top twenty-five prime-time shows in the 1959–60 season, eleven were about cowboys. In an era marked by anxiety over masculinity and intense hostility toward homosexuality, boy culture emphasized toughness and aggression, which found expression in competitive athletics and the cult of the automobile. Boys wanted to win on the sports field and be big and bold on the road.[23]

The middle-class girl culture of the 1950s has often been criticized as the inverse of boy culture: passive and obsessed with physical appearance. In fact many of the role models that middle-class girls embraced during the decade were assertive and self-confident, and one can see the roots of mid-1960s feminism planted in the increasingly autonomous and self-assured girl culture of the 1950s. Shirley Owens, Addie Harris, Beverly Lee, and Doris Coley were just sixteen and seventeen years old when they formed a singing group, The Poquellos, at New Jersey's Passaic High School in 1958. A teacher who overheard them vocalizing in the school's gym persuaded them to enter the school's talent contest. The song they wrote for the occasion contained these lyrics:

> Well I kissed him on a Thursday (oooooo)
> And he didn't come Friday (oooooo)
> When he showed up Saturday (oooooo)
> I said "Bye bye baby"

Rather than a fantasy of endless love, this was a song with undertones of female toughness, shrewdness, and independence. A classmate introduced them to her mother, Florence Greenberg, who owned a small recording company and convinced the group to change their name to the Shirelles.

Perhaps the most popular of the girl groups of the late 1950s and early 1960s, the Shirelles sang of selfless devotion in songs like "Soldier Boy," but also suggested a more skeptical outlook in songs such as "Will You Still Love Me Tomorrow?"[24]

Contemporary critics, struck by the vagueness of girls' occupational plans and their general lack of interest in jobs that required commitment, subjected postwar girl culture to withering criticism. Sociologist Jessie Bernard said that the numerous magazines aimed at teenage girls reveal "the major positive—fun and popularity—and negative—overweight or underweight and adolescent acne—values of its readers." Many girls, it was widely believed, held unrealistic attitudes toward sex, colored by heavily romanticized notions of true love. In the early 1950s, eighty love comics appeared each month, and the song lyrics most popular among girls emphasized wishing, dreaming, and longing for love. Worst of all, many girls considered intellectualism and popularity mutually exclusive. As one girl recalled years later, "When I was in eighth grade I lived in trepidation lest I be cited as class bookworm."[25]

In contrast to postwar boy culture, which stressed physical competition, construction, and rough-and-tumble play, girl culture seemingly centered on love, doll play, relationships, hairdressing, and grooming. It tended to be an indoor culture, unlike boys' outdoor culture. But this sex-segregated culture was also a female-centered culture. *Life* magazine in 1948 described a new fad that would quickly become a basic aspect of girls' social lives: the slumber party, at which girls would gather to talk about all the things that mattered most to them through the night. Even comic books were sharply sex segregated. While boys read war comics and horror comics like *Tales from the Crypt,* girls read romance comics and comics about Wonder Woman and Polly Pigtails. Older girls, too, had their own magazines. Modeled on adult true love and women's magazines, these periodicals regularly included confessional letters and advice about sex, reputation, proper behavior, and dating, as well as features about teen idols.[26]

The postwar girl culture, however, was not merely a matter of sex-role stereotyping. Girls used doll playing for much more than training in the emotional and practical skills of mothering: it was also a way of placing female experience at the center, rather than on the periphery, of life. While superficially girls' play was more passive than boys', it also contained a wealth of imaginative action and fantasy. It was more individualistic, spontaneous, and freer of structure or rules than boys' play, and instilled a conviction in many girls that they were fully equal to, if not superior to, boys. Increasingly critical of male-chauvinist attitudes and conduct, many girls dreaded becoming like their own mothers, whose lives they associated with subordination to their husbands, drudgery, and isolation. As one wrote, "the emptiness of her life appalls me; her helplessness and dependence on my father frightens me."[27]

By the late 1950s magazines, movies, music, and television produced a female culture that cultivated a highly self-conscious sense of girls' importance. Girls learned that they were members of a new, privileged generation whose destiny was more open and exciting than that of their mothers'. On television, Lucille Ball, Audrey Meadows, Imogene Coca, and Gracie Allen played women who refused to stay in their assigned place. By the early 1960s they were succeeded by perky tomboyish teens and preteens on such shows as *Gidget* and *The Patty Duke Show*.[28]

Popular music disseminated diverse and contradictory messages about girlhood. The late 1950s saw the rise of the Girl Group. Along with songs about selfless devotion, masochistic self-sacrifice, and fantasies of true love (such as "He's So Fine," "I Will Follow Him," and "Johnny Angel"), they also sang about male manipulation and fecklessness (such as "Sweet Talking Guy"). With their spike heels, thick eyeliner, and beehive hairdos, groups like the Ronettes did not conform to conventional middle-class images of femininity and offered glimpses of a life outside the world of domesticity. With their warnings about two-timing boys who refused to treat girls right, these defiant singers offered protofeminist messages about female independence and assertiveness. Meanwhile, the new kinds of dances that appeared following Chubby Checker's 1960 hit "The Twist" no longer required a girl to follow a boy's lead. Instead, her dancing moves—her shimmies and thrusts—were at the center of these dances.[29]

During the late 1940s the proportion of teenagers in the American population reached an all-time low. Nevertheless, this cohort created the script of modern teenage life. While the word *teenager* had first appeared during World War II, it was the postwar period that elaborated distinct teenage language, styles, and music. Unlike the term *adolescence*, the word *teenager* implied a distinct culture rather than a state of hormonal transition. The teen culture of the 1950s conjures up a host of nostalgic images of letterman jackets, juke joints, malt shops, drive-ins, sock hops, double dates, and "parking" at secluded spots. But this teen world was a product of specific demographic, economic, and institutional developments: nearly universal high school attendance, suburbanization, early entrance into adulthood, and a degree of affluence that allowed teens to become an autonomous market segment. The growth of high school attendance meant that most teens, for the first time, shared a common experience and could create an autonomous culture, free from adult oversight.[30]

High school life was strongly shaped by the fact that most young people could expect to achieve the markers of adulthood—marriage, entry into an adult job, and establishment of an independent home—by their early twenties. Early entry into adulthood gave high school experiences an intensity that has since disappeared. Since most teens could expect to be married by their early twenties, dating took on special significance and became a major source of public anxiety. In 1955 *Picture Week* magazine ran the headline: "Petting: No. 1 Problem." *People Weekly* asked: "When Is Going Steady Immoral?"[31]

At a time when abortion was illegal and unsafe and few teens had access to reliable forms of birth control—and when girls who got pregnant were often forced out of school and had their children's birth records stamped "Illegitimate"—sexuality was a particular source of anxiety. Teen sexuality was governed by a double standard. Boys were expected to initiate and girls to decide what was appropriate. Girls had to negotiate how to remain popular while preserving their reputation. "The boy is expected to ask for as much as possible," reported anthropologist Margaret Mead; "the girl to yield as little as possible." The dating system made sex adversarial. As one boy put it, "When a boy takes a girl out and spends $1.20 on her (like I did the other night) he expects a little petting in return (which I didn't get)." Meanwhile, girls were told that if they lost their virginity, they also lost their value to boys. "Few boys want to get stuck with a tramp," one dating book announced.[32]

Girls received a great deal of advice about how to handle sex. In a column titled "What to Tell Your Teen-Age Daughter about Sex," *Cosmopolitan* offered mothers detailed guidance. When your daughter says, "All the boys say there is nothing to do after a party but pet," reply: "Trivial sex experience may dull your capacity for truly great love . . . The more you pet, the more your body clamors for closer union." Question: "Boys say they don't want their wives to be virgins anymore." Answer: "The sex act is often painful at first and not pleasurable at all . . . Therefore if you have intercourse at an early age you may be frightened and disgusted by it—and never marry." The *Ladies' Home Journal* described "The Perfect Good-Night Kiss": "Ten seconds—not too hard, not too long."[33]

At a time when the average age of marriage for women was twenty, going steady mimicked and served as preparation for marriage. A boy would give his steady a class ring, a letter sweater, or an I.D. bracelet as a symbol of commitment. Adults described going steady as "stupid, silly, juvenile, nonsensical, time-wasting . . . [and] dangerous," but it provided security to teenagers and served as a testing ground for their future intimate relationships.[34]

While teens socialized at school, they also learned. The baby boom placed intense pressure on schools. In 1952, 50,000 new classrooms were built, and average daily attendance rose by two million. To meet the demand, school systems started double sessions and set up 78,000 makeshift classrooms in churches and vacant stores. Teachers had as many as forty-five students in a class. Parents, who joined parent-teacher groups in record numbers (PTA membership doubled to eight million), demanded new school construction. But it took a 184-pound Soviet satellite to precipitate a radical reconsideration of the nature and extent of American education. No more than a primitive radio beacon transmitting meaningless beeps, Sputnik prompted "a sense of foreboding" in the nation's capital. Rear Admiral Rawson Bennett called Sputnik a "hunk of iron almost anybody could launch"—but most observers disagreed. *Life* magazine compared the Soviet success to the first shots at Lexington and Concord.[35]

Sputnik inspired such words as *beatnik,* coined in 1958, as well as the later *peacenik* and *refusenik.* But the starlike symbol of national shame more importantly inspired science fairs and language labs and provoked nationwide soul-searching about the state of public education. The director of the American Institute of Physics, Elmer Hutchisson, proclaimed that the American way of life was "doomed to rapid extinction" if the nation's youth weren't properly taught the importance of science. President Dwight Eisenhower and Congress responded by allocating the first $1 billion in direct federal aid to public education to recruit and train teachers and raise the standards of science, mathematics, and foreign-language instruction.[36]

The post-Sputnik effort to raise academic standards represented a reaction against educational innovations of the preceding decade. To meet the needs of students who did not plan to go to college, high schools in the 1940s offered an increasing number of practical courses to provide preparation for future vocations. "Life-adjustment" courses, including instruction in health, marriage, and family life, were supposed to promote students' social and emotional development. This emphasis on practical preparation for the workplace and adult responsibilities had received a ringing endorsement in a 1944 publication by the National Educational Association. Rejecting the idea of a uniform curriculum emphasizing core academic subjects, the report insisted that "there is no aristocracy of 'subjects.'" "Mathematics and mechanics, art and agriculture, history and homemaking are all peers," the report insisted. A guiding premise of the

A student at a high school in Jacksonville, Florida, demonstrates his science fair project in 1959, two years after the Soviet Union launched Sputnik, the first artificial satellite. Courtesy of the Florida Photographic Collection, Florida State Archives, Tallahassee.

so-called life-adjustment movement, spelled out in the 1945 Prosser Resolution (named for Charles A. Prosser, a leading proponent of vocational education), was that only about 20 percent of American high school students were college material. Another 20 percent should be prepared for the skilled trades, while the remaining 60 percent should receive a more general education to prepare them for everyday life and work.[37]

Even before Sputnik's launch, however, critics of "progressive" education had condemned the shift in focus away from academics. In his influential 1953 book, *Educational Wasteland,* the historian Arthur Bestor argued that educational frills had supplanted academics, with the result that students had to be taught in college what they should have learned in high school. Sociologist James S. Coleman maintained that an anti-intellectual student culture flourished in the nation's high schools, disparaging serious learning, while the philosopher Hannah Arendt warned in 1958 that academic standards "of the average American school lag . . . far behind the average standards in . . . Europe." Popular culture echoed such criticisms. A former New York City teacher, Evan Hunter, fictionalized his experiences in a 1953 book, *Blackboard Jungle,* which was made into a landmark film starring Glenn Ford and Sidney Poitier. The first film to feature a rock-and-roll song, *Blackboard Jungle* also introduced the term *daddy-o* and popularized the image of urban toughs wearing black leather jackets and T-shirts with rolled-up sleeves, and painted an unsettling portrait of urban vocational schools, filled with alienated students and apathetic teachers.[38]

Sputnik intensified the finger-pointing as the country came to the shocked realization that it was no longer the world's leader in science and mathematics. In a multipart series on the "Crisis in Education," *Life* magazine compared an American eleventh-grader from a leading public school with a tenth-grader in the Soviet Union. While Chicago's Stephen Lapekas was reading Robert Louis Stevenson's *Kidnapped,* Moscow's Alexei Kutzkov had studied English as a foreign language and completed works by Shakespeare and George Bernard Shaw. For the American, *Life* noted that "getting educated seldom seems too serious," but for the Russian, high grades were "literally more important than anything else in his life." *Life* concluded that "U.S. high school students are . . . ignorant of things [elementary] school students would have known a generation ago." Admiral Hyman Rickover echoed this sentiment when he wrote in 1959: "In the American comprehensive school the pupil finds a display of courses resembling the variegated dishes in a cafeteria. . . . No wonder he often gorges himself on sweets instead of taking solid meat that must be chewed."[39]

The panicked response to Sputnik resulted in a number of ill-thought-through attempts at miracle cures. The entire Hagerstown, Maryland, school system was wired for closed-circuit television. A four-engine aircraft circled over a six-state area, beaming prepackaged lessons to hundreds of midwestern schools. But the crisis also had positive effects. To arouse student learning, educators increasingly embraced active participatory learning, including collaborative and individual projects and field trips, and introduced subject-area specialists in science and mathematics into many schools. The National Defense Education Act of 1958 provided grants for summer institutes to train teachers in math, science, and foreign languages. The National Science Foundation invested more than $100 million in innovative curricula such as the "New Math."

One of the most consequential responses to Sputnik was a report written by James B. Conant, Harvard's former president. Titled *The American High School Today,* it sold an astonishing 170,000 copies in five months after its publication in 1959. Conant rejected the European idea of segregating university-bound students in separate institutions for the academically gifted. Instead he called for "comprehensive" high schools that would include academic, business courses, and vocational training, and the elimination of small high schools with fewer than 100 graduating seniors. He argued that these schools would promote interaction across class lines and increase the quality and range of available courses of study. As a result of the Conant report, more than 100,000 small high schools closed, and the size of the average high school increased 300 percent, with many urban high schools ballooning to over 3,000 students.

To address the anonymity of very large schools and promote a democratic spirit, Conant called for homerooms where vocational and academic students would mix. Democracy was also to be enhanced through student government and extracurricular activities. Conant viewed the comprehensive school in the United States as "a great engine of democracy," and a unifying and integrating force in a highly diverse society. But Conant was also convinced that only about 15 to 20 percent of students were capable of mastering a college-prep curriculum and that educators needed to resist "unreasonable parental pressure" to place unqualified students in academic classes. He called for a broad array of elective courses to meet the needs of students who were not going to college, including general education, vocational, and commercial programs. Ability testing, tracking, and a differentiated curriculum lay at the heart of Conant's recommendations.[40]

Conant, a proponent of college admissions testing, played a critical role in the creation of the Educational Testing Service in 1947, which replaced college entrance essay examinations with a standardized multiple-choice test of verbal and mathematical skills. As president of Harvard, Conant wanted to attract students on the basis of merit and ability rather than wealth and social standing. Henry Chauncey, an assistant dean at Harvard, convinced him that machine-graded testing offered a way to measure applicants' academic aptitude. A few liberal educators, including W. Allison Davis and Robert J. Havighurst, argued that the Scholastic Aptitude Test measured social and economic advantage rather than mental ability, but their complaints went unheard. By 1967, when the University of California began to require applicants to take the Scholastic Aptitude

Test (SAT), the college entrance examination had become a rite of passage for college-bound juniors and seniors.[41]

Another reform that grew out of Conant's efforts was the replacement of junior high schools with middle schools. The junior high school, a product of the 1920s, sought to separate preadolescents from younger children and high school students. In practice, Conant argued, junior high school students mimicked the worst features of high school students, especially their obsessions with sports and socializing, while teachers were dissatisfied that they were not teaching in a high school. Educators responded by creating the middle school for students in the fifth through the eighth grades. Unlike the junior high, the middle school was supposed to be more child focused, with flexible scheduling, collaborative teams of teachers, and emphasis on intramural athletics. By 1965 there were about 500 middle schools.[42]

In succeeding years the limitations of the reforms that grew out of Conant's recommendations became increasingly clear. Large high schools proved to be too big and impersonal and fostered alienation and anomie. Tracking, ability grouping, and aptitude testing, which were supposed to broaden opportunity, favored students from upper-middle-class backgrounds and hardened ethnic and social divisions within schools. Meanwhile middle schools turned out to differ little from the junior high schools they replaced. Far from transforming schools into truly democratic institutions, these reforms instilled resentment among students over the paternalism, regimentation, and inflexibility of the modern public school.

Nostalgia may paint the 1950s as a more placid time, but it was an era of anxiety. "Let's Face It," read the cover of *Newsweek* in 1956, "Our Teenagers Are out of Control." Many youths, the magazine reported, "got their fun" by "torturing helpless old men and horsewhipping girls they waylaid in public parks." Newspaper readers learned about twenty-five Washington, D.C., girls, ages thirteen to seventeen, who formed a shoplifting club; and a seven- and nine-year-old from Arkansas who robbed a filling station. The chief of child research at the National Institute of Mental Health warned parents that "no one can tell if a child will turn out to be a delinquent five years later. Some children," he explained, "prepare for delinquency pleasantly and quietly." Haunted by the specter of Hitler youth, many postwar experts feared that the United States was breeding its own homegrown fascists. Robert Lindner, whose nonfiction book *Rebel without a Cause* furnished the title of the most famous 1950s youth film, claimed that "almost every symptom that delineates the psychopath clinically is to be found increasingly in the contemporary adolescent." Respondents to a Gallup poll asking why "teenagers are getting out of hand" placed the blame squarely on poor parenting: parents were "not strict enough," did not "provide a proper home life," had "too many outside interests," were "too indulgent," and gave their children "too much money"; and mothers worked when they were "needed at home." Other observers blamed overcrowded schools, broken homes, the decline of religion, and a lack of proper adult role models.[43]

Comic books, which sold 100 million copies a month, were a particular source of alarm. Two Oklahoma fifth-graders who stole an airplane claimed that they had learned how to fly from comic books. Four boys accused of forming a theft ring said they had been inspired by comic books. When an eight-year-old in Pawnee, Illinois, hanged himself, authorities attributed his deed to ideas he had picked up in comic books. A single issue of one comic contained ten guillotinings, seven stabbings, six shootings, a drowning, and one fatal shove from a ladder. Comics had come a long way from the original Superman, Wonder Woman, and Archie.[44]

Los Angeles responded by passing an ordinance prohibiting the sale of comic books dealing with murder, burglary, kidnapping, arson, or assault with deadly weapons. In Decatur, Illinois, and in Spencer, West Virginia, students and teachers built bonfires of comic books, while the Boy Scouts launched a project to confiscate comic books on the grounds that they spread polio bacteria. A congressional subcommittee headed by Senator Estes Kefauver (D–Tenn.) investigated links between comic books and juvenile delinquency. By 1954, thirteen states passed legislation regulating the production and sale of comic books.[45]

In that same year psychiatrist Frederic Wertham published a book titled *The Seduction of the Innocent,* blaming juvenile delinquency on comic books. A liberal who objected to the racist (mainly anti-Asian) stereotypes that pervaded comic books, Wertham considered Superman a fascist vigilante and argued that "a generation is being desensitized by these literal horror images." Claiming that comic books were filled with homoerotic imagery, he accused comic-book publishers of making "violence, sadism, and crime attractive" and exploiting children's fears of physical inadequacy. He insisted that "comic book reading was a distinct factor of every single delinquent or disturbed child" he ever studied. To avoid government legislation, the comic-book industry formed the Comic Magazines Association of America and required a stamp of approval on every comic book, ensuring that the contents were "wholesome, entertaining, and educational." Specific injunctions in the self-censorship code stated: "We must not chop limbs off characters. The same goes for putting people's eyes out."[46]

The 1950s was a period of outward optimism but inward anxiety and fear. Apart from comic books, another source of concern was "suicide on wheels," drag racing. In 1949 *Life* magazine's cover reported a new youth-related crisis: "The Hot-Rod Problem." Illustrated with pictures "of teen-age death and disaster," it described "chicken races," in which racers drove without holding the steering wheel. It also detailed other teen games, such as "rotation," in which passengers and driver exchanged positions without slowing below sixty, and lying down in the street, daring drivers to run them over. The scariest ploy, "Pedestrian Polo," involved slamming a moving car's door into a pedestrian. "Just brush 'em, don't hit 'em," was the slogan.[47]

We may recall the 1950s as a time of unlocked doors and stable nuclear families, but the decade of Ozzie and Harriet was also a period of intense anxiety over juvenile delinquency and gangs. Senator Robert C. Hendrickson sounded the alarm in 1954. "Not even the Communist conspiracy," he declared, "could devise a more effective way to demoralize, disrupt, confuse and destroy our future citizens than apathy on the part of adult Americans to the scourge known as juvenile delinquency." Between 1948 and 1954 the number of youths appearing before juvenile courts increased 58 percent, with sex offenses up 37 percent. In just three years— 1948 to 1951—auto theft jumped 61 percent; breaking and entering, 15 percent; and robbery, 25 percent. Yale psychologist Irving Sarnoff termed this wave of juvenile crime "a running sore on the full belly of the American way of life."[48]

Whether juvenile delinquency was actually increasing remains unclear, but there is no question that heightened attention was paid to juvenile crime and that teen arrests were climbing, reflecting increased law enforcement and broadened definitions of criminal behavior. The panic over juvenile delinquency reflected fears about changes in young people's lives as well as rapid change in the broader society. In speech and appearance, teens seemed increasingly alien as a growing number of middle-class teens adopted values, fashions, and speech associated with the lower and working classes. *Juvenile delinquency* became an umbrella term referring to everything from duck-tail haircuts to murder; but it was gangs that aroused the most heated concern. The term was applied broadly, to street-corner loungers, neighborhood clubs, and packs of roving teens; but in the popular imagination, the word conjured up images of a world of switchblades, zip guns, and schoolyard rumbles, where groups of working-class youth, bearing names like "Vampires," "Dragons," and "Egyptian Kings," defended turf and avenged real and imagined slights.[49]

For more than a century and a half, lower- and working-class teens had turned to gangs as a way to assert their manliness and to police ethnic boundaries. In 1807 the trustees of the African Methodist Episcopal Zion Church in lower Manhattan pleaded with the New York City Council to do something about gangs of white, working-class youths who harassed their worshippers on Sundays. Gang membership was a normal part of growing up for early twentieth-century urban boys. A Jewish teacher in New York recalled his experience as a gang member: "When I was a youngster . . . a common sight was a street battle between the Jewish and Irish boys . . . One day the Irish boys would raid 'our' territory, turning over pushcarts, breaking store windows and beating up every Jew in sight. Another day saw 'our' side retaliating on Irish home grounds."[50]

The number of gangs in big cities like New York exploded from the mid-1940s to the mid-1960s. Gang conflicts became more racially charged and violent as ice picks, knives, and homemade guns replaced sticks, stones, and bottles. Movies like *Blackboard Jungle* blamed gangs on wartime upheavals. "They were six years old in the last war," the script said. "Father in the army. Mother in a defense plant. No home life. No church life. No place to go. They form street gangs . . . Gang leaders take the place of parents." In fact gangs served tangible functions, providing lower-class and working-class adolescents with a sense of identity, camaraderie, and a sense of manliness unavailable in school or the job market. However, too often, conflict between gangs erupted into hostile and destructive warfare that led to loss of life.[51]

In New York City the adolescent homicide rate doubled after World War II as postwar slum clearance and migration from the rural South and Puerto Rico ignited battles over playgrounds, parks, and neighborhoods. For many working-class youths, who were alienated from school and their own families and were qualified for only the most menial jobs as manufacturing employment declined, gang membership offered a way to win prestige, power, and adulation from girls. Claude Brown, whose own family moved to New York in the mid-1940s, described the impulses that drove his friends into gangs: "The children of these disillusioned colored pioneers inherited the total lot of their parents—the disappointments, the anger. To add to their misery, they had little hope of deliverance. For where does one run to when he's already in the promised land?"[52]

During the late 1950s, government and private social service agencies launched a panoply of programs to reduce the allure of gangs. The most influential, Mobilization for Youth, which provided job training and job placement services, served as a prototype for President Lyndon Johnson's War on Poverty. Proponents of youth programs argued that delinquency stemmed from "the lack of congruence between the aspirations of youth and opportunities open to them." In 1961 the federal government began to provide grants to programs to control delinquency under the Juvenile Delinquency and Youth Control Act.[53]

The troubling image of the leather-jacketed gang member was only one of a pastiche of postwar media stereotypes of young people. Images of boys ran from Timmy, the highly responsible adopted orphan caretaker of *Lassie,* to the cute but naughty Beaver Cleaver on *Leave It to Beaver,* the mischievous Dennis the Menace, and the moody and alienated James Dean and Sal Mineo. Media images of girls ranged from Lucy van Pelt, the neurotic *Peanuts* girl introduced in 1950, to Rhoda, the eight-year-old liar, cheat, arsonist, and murderer in the 1956 film *The Bad Seed;* the pert and perky Sandra Dee; and the adorable "kittens" and "princesses" on television situation comedies. The 1950s marked the first time that all the mass media specifically targeted youth as a distinct audience. In addition to a flourishing industry of children's books, the movies, the music industry, and the new medium of television directed their attention toward the young. But the new focus on the young, especially on teens, evoked anxiety among many middle-class adults, who struggled to control the multiplicity of media messages being transmitted. They were particularly fearful that their children were adopting the form and substance of working-class alienation in their music, dress, slang, and attitudes.[54]

During the 1950s children's books achieved a popularity unmatched since the late nineteenth century. In the 1930s studies revealed that hundreds of thousands of American children were unable to read effectively. To address this problem, Arthur Gates, a professor at Columbia University's Teachers College, and William S. Gray, dean of the University of Chicago College of Education, developed the "whole word" model for teaching reading, in which children learned to recognize entire words and their meanings at a glance. Gates and Gray insisted that this approach was superior to phonics, in which young people learn to recognize individual letters and pronounce their sounds. Gray wrote a series of readers for the educational publisher Scott Foresman using the whole-word method, featuring the characters Dick and Jane and their dog, Spot. Used in 85 percent of U.S. schools at the height of their popularity in the early 1950s, the Dick and Jane readers did raise students' literacy, but not enough to satisfy critics.[55]

When Rudolf Flesch's 1955 volume *Why Johnny Can't Read* was reissued after Sputnik's launch, it became an instant bestseller. Flesch, an authority on literacy, advocated teaching reading by the sounds of letters, or phonics, rather than by whole words. His book claimed that the refusal to use proven phonics methods "is gradually destroying democracy in this country; it returns to the upper middle class the privileges that public education was supposed to distribute evenly." Concerns over reading and math skills soared as pressure was put on educators and schools.[56]

William Spaulding, director of Houghton Mifflin's Educational Division, thought he knew "why Johnny can't read." It was because books like *Fun with Dick and Jane* failed to interest children. He wanted a "whole word" book appropriate for six- and seven-year-olds that children would find amusing, using no more than 225 words. Dr. Seuss, whose real name was Theodore Seuss Geisel, took up the challenge. He looked at the list of words and decided that the first two words on the list that rhymed would be the basis for the book's title. "I found 'cat' and then I found 'hat,'" he later recalled. "That's genius, you see!" *The Cat in the Hat* became the bestselling children's book of the second half of the twentieth century. Later, when publisher Bennett Cerf challenged him to write a book limited to fifty words, Dr. Seuss wrote *Green Eggs and Ham.*

Of the ten bestselling children's books of the twentieth century, Dr. Seuss wrote four: *The Cat in the Hat,* published in 1957; *Green Eggs and Ham* and *One Fish, Two Fish, Red Fish, Blue Fish,* which appeared in 1960; and *Hop on Pop,* published in 1963. The books' appeal lay in what Dr. Seuss called the "logical insanity" of the child's world. His whimsical books, with their emphasis on repetition and rhyme and stress on nonsense, fantasy, and mischief, captivated children. In contrast to Dick and Jane, who always behaved properly, Dr. Seuss's characters misbehaved and refused to obey rules. His books substituted wordplay and humor for a traditional narrative, but they also dealt with serious themes. *How the Grinch Stole Christmas* (1957) criticized the commercialization of Christmas; *Horton Hears a Who!* (1954) condemned narrow-mindedness; and *Yertle the Turtle* (1958) disapproved of selfish ambition. Dr. Seuss's success revealed the huge market for picture books for young children.

Alongside the lighthearted toddler-oriented writings of Dr. Seuss, a new kind of teen's magazine appeared. *Mad,* founded in 1952, served as the opening wedge in a children's culture stressing resistance and subversion. In 1961 an ex–brigadier general denounced *Mad* as "the most insidious Communist propaganda in the United States today." *Mad* parodied magazines *(Bitter Homes and Gardens),* movies *(Seven Itchy Years),* television *(The Ed Suvillan Show),* and comic books *(Superduperman* and *Bat Boy and Rubin). Mad* was filled with sarcasm, parody, and scathing irreverence; *Mad*'s movie spoofs, Cold War satires ("Spy vs. Spy"), and fold-ins were informed by an anarchist sensibility. *Mad* skewered television, advertising, middle-class consumerism, politics, and adult hypocrisy. The magazine's cover boy was the goofy-faced, freckled, gap-toothed, bat-eared, carrot-headed Alfred E. Neuman, whose loopy motto was "What, Me Worry?" In a decade that reeked of blandness (such as Patty Paige singing "How Much Is That Doggie in the Window?") and piety (Norman Vincent Peale's *The Power of Positive Thinking*), *Mad* offered an alternative perspective. But for all of its attacks on authority figures and other sacred cows, the magazine generally avoided the most explosive issue of the era, civil rights.[57]

The postwar era was the classic period for the treatment of adolescence in fiction. There was Frankie Adams in Carson McCullers' classic 1946 novel, *A Member of the Wedding*, which chronicles the coming-of-age of a young southern girl, who feels invisible and unheard and is struggling to understand her emerging feelings of womanhood. There was John Grimes, in James Baldwin's 1953 novel, *Go Tell It on the Mountain*, a fourteen-year-old African-American youth who must confront his religious doubts, sexual confusions, and recognition that he can never realize his dream of being at home in a white world. Then there was Holden Caulfield, the embodiment of the sullen, self-absorbed adolescent, angst-ridden and alienated. Sensitive, troubled, and confused, he was the prototypical prematurely cynical teenager, as portrayed by the brooding Marlon Brando, James Dean, and Elvis Presley. Sixteen years old, he rails against the phoniness of the adult world. His casual talk and brooding but nonchalant style touches a nerve. Asked by a former teacher about his future, he replies: "'Oh, I feel some concern for my future, all right. Sure I do.' I thought about it for a minute. 'But not too much, I guess.'" Traumatized by his younger brother's death from leukemia, he trusts no one except his ten-year-old sister, Phoebe. Lacking any desire to grow up, he contrasts the superficiality and hypocrisy of adults with the innocence and honesty of childhood.[58]

During the postwar era the adolescent became the archetypal figure for the moral and sexual confusions of the age. Unlike earlier writers, like Booth Tarkington, who had treated adolescents with bemused condescension, postwar writers took the problems of adolescence much more seriously. Instead of focusing on puppy love or adolescent self-consciousness, postwar writers focused on weightier subjects, such as adolescents' sexual initiation or juvenile delinquency *(Amboy Dukes)* or a girl's sadistic pleasure in her sexual power over men *(East of Eden)*. Lesbianism *(The Wayward Ones)*, homosexuality *(Compulsion)*, and rape *(Entry E)* become important subjects in the novels of adolescence. Increasingly authors dwelt on the notion that initiation into maturity involved a loss of innocence, through sexual experience or a death of a person or animal for which the youngster might or might not be responsible. Rather than symbolizing immature innocence, adolescents stood out as symbols of self-conscious introspection, estrangement, and confusion.[59]

Of all the forces for change in postwar children's lives, television worried adults most. Newspapers and magazines were filled with frightening stories of children mimicking acts that they had seen on television: a seven-year-old who added ground glass to his family's stew; a thirteen-year-old who stabbed her mother with a kitchen knife; a sixteen-year-old babysitter who strangled a sleeping child to death. In 1945 only 5,000 American households had televisions; in 1960 seven of every eight families had a TV set. Critics likened TV to a narcotic that induced lethargy in children and to a Pied Piper that led young people away from their parents. Many feared that television induced a premature sophistication in the young, cut into their reading and study time, and made dinnertime less of a family occasion by encouraging families to eat with the television on.[60]

In 1961 the first influential book-length study appeared. *Television in the Lives of Our Children* reported that by sixth grade children spent almost as much time watching television as they did in school and that they watched the same programs as adults. The study speculated that television contributed to premature aging by encouraging children to grow up too fast and produced a passive, passionless generation, children who "have no sense of values, no feeling of wonder, no sustained interest." The sexism of children's television, however, went virtually unnoticed. Female characters were grossly underrepresented, especially in children's cartoons, and they were confined largely to family roles.[61]

Television broadcasting produced a shared children's culture unprecedented in history, one that stretched across all social classes and regions. For millions of baby boomers, Nancy Claster, affectionately known as Miss Nancy on *Romper Room*, was their first teacher. Assisted by her helpers Mr. Doobee and Mr. Don'tbee, she introduced preschoolers to their ABC's, arithmetic, and manners, and taught them health lessons, songs, and games. "Do-Bee a milk drinker," young viewers were told. "Don't-Bee a nasty tongue." *Captain Kangaroo*, which debuted in 1955, amused toddlers with Mr. Greenjeans, Grandfather Clock, and the puppet friends Mr. Moose and Bunny Rabbit. The captain also interspersed jazz and classical music with puppetry. Family sitcoms such as *The Adventures of Ozzie and Harriet, Father Knows Best,* and *Leave It to Beaver* showed children what middle-class families were supposed to be like. They were part of a concerted effort to combat the deepening disengagement of fathers from family life. Not an accurate portrait of postwar fatherhood,

Ward Cleaver in *Leave It to Beaver* represented a fantasy of a caring father in a modern family.[62]

Meanwhile the film industry, suffering a drastic drop in attendance as a result of television, antitrust decisions that stripped the studios of their theaters, and the imposition of tariffs and import restrictions by foreign countries, pursued the youth market with vigor. In cinematic portrayals of teenagers, amused condescension gradually gave way to anxiety and bewilderment. The "Kleen Teens" of the 1930s and 1940s were supplanted by sensitive, directionless teens and leather-jacketed rebels, protesting the sterility of American life.

Many teens viewed these movies while sitting in the privacy of their cars at drive-ins. Originally envisioned as places where whole families could watch a movie in the comfort of their own car and not have to worry about babysitters or disturbing other moviegoers, drive-ins quickly became a teen haven. In 1950 there were fewer than 500 drive-ins in the country, but by 1957 there were ten times as many, and by 1959 there were as many drive-ins as traditional theaters. The family car became a means of escape for the teenaged son and daughter and the drive-in their alternate living room.[63]

Troubled adolescents became a focus of many of the most influential films of the 1950s. Family melodramas of the decade abounded with Oedipal problems and sibling rivalry. They pictured adult culture as blind to the problems of youth and portrayed teenagers as searching for genuine family love, warmth, and security. Those who chose delinquency did so because of despair over the seeming rejection of their parents. At least sixty movies portrayed youth as alienated or depraved, wearing a leather jacket, a T-shirt with rolled-up sleeves, jeans, and a dangling cigarette, and had titles like *Date Bait* ("Too young to know. Too wild to care. Too eager to say I will!"); *Live Fast, Die Young* ("The sin-steeped story of today's beat generation"); *High School Hellcats* ("What must a good girl say to 'belong'?"); *On the Loose* ("School-girl by day, thrill-seeker by night"); and *The Violators* ("Too young to know better . . . Too hard to care"). The most famous, *Rebel without a Cause,* was advertised with the catchphrase "He's got a chip on *both* his shoulders!" *Rebel without a Cause* incorporated all the teen flick stereotypes: a pack taunting and baiting a loner, ostracized kids bonding with one another, and parents unable to say or do anything right. Derided as exploitation films, "teenpics" metaphorically addressed adolescent anxieties. Pictures in which a couple necking in a parked car was interrupted by the creature from the Black Lagoon offered not only an opportunity for hugging in fright, but also a message about the dangers of unrestrained sexuality. Adolescents whose bodies were changing could appreciate the feelings of the teenage were- wolf, the incredible shrinking man, and the fifty-foot woman.[64]

The end of the 1950s saw a sharp reaction against the teen genre, with its emphasis on reckless, rebellious, and troubled teens. Signaled by the box-office success of clean-cut teen idol Pat Boone in 1957 in *Bernardine* and *April Love,* the shift in tone was unmistakable when Disney's *The Shaggy Dog* became 1959's second most popular film. The rise of seven- teen-year-old Sandra Dee to stardom in *Tammy and the Bachelor* and *Gidget* underscored the movement away from the classic 1950s teenpic. A 1959 poll named Sandra Dee as "the Number One Star of Tomorrow."[65]

The 1950s are routinely denigrated as a decade of chrome and confor- mity, of gray-flannel organization men and cultural stodginess, in which the most heated front-page controversies concerned issues like "going steady." Photographs of the period—showing boys with military-style crew cuts and girls in pageboys or ponytails wearing pearls—reinforce this image of an orderly and stable era. Yet change was bubbling beneath the surface, and the twentieth century's midpoint bristled with develop- ments that changed American society irretrievably. Youth culture and the civil rights movement would come to full flower in the 1960s, but their emergence was already evident in the 1950s.

In the spring of 1954, when the nation's top record was Perry Como's "Wanted" and the top album was the soundtrack from *The Glenn Miller Story,* a new musical style was germinating. Bill Haley and the Comets cut "Rock around the Clock," Elvis Presley held his first recording session at Sun Records, and Alan Freed became a disc jockey at WINS in New York. Chuck Berry, Bo Diddley, Little Richard, and the Platters were beginning to break the radio color barrier. Rock and roll provided a vehicle through which urban, rural, and suburban youths declared their independence from parental standards and expressed their desire for pleasure. When the first rock-and-roll concert took place at Cleveland Arena on March 21, 1952, some 30,000 teens packed a building that could seat only 10,000, while 15,000 others waited outside. Rock and roll spoke to the alienation and boredom of teenagers in newly built suburbs. The new music exuded sexuality; indeed, *rock and roll* was a slang term in certain black commu- nities referring to sexual intercourse.[66]

Musically, rock and roll was a style of popular music marked by guitar- based instrumentation, blues-based composition, electronic amplification, high volume, and danceability. In contrast to jazz, which depended upon brass instruments, rock and roll emphasized the electric guitar and drums. During the 1950s it became the soundtrack of the lives of those between twelve and twenty-one. Much of the new youth music of the 1950s self-consciously celebrated the teenage years. Groups like Frankie Lymon and the Teenagers embraced the word *teenagers*, and many songs, like Mark Dinning's "Teen Angel" and Dion and the Belmonts' "Teenager in Love," had the word *teen* in their title.[67]

What made this new music possible was the movement of southerners, black and white, to the cities of the Upper South and the North during and after the war. This movement brought diverse musical traditions together and forged a new sound out of the propulsive beat of rhythm and blues and the twang of country and western. As radio's comedy and variety programming shifted to TV, network radio went into a steep decline, and radio stations began to play more youth-oriented music than in the past. A doubling of the number of radio stations between 1945 and 1950 encouraged an emphasis on music, especially the Top 40 format (named for the forty record slots in jukeboxes), transforming disc jockeys into celebrities. Meanwhile technological innovations, such as the introduction of the light, durable, and inexpensive 45-rpm record by RCA Victor in 1948, made it easy for teens to create their own music collections, while the invention of the transistor in 1947 led to the development of portable transistor radios and an explosion in the number of car radios, from six million in 1946 to forty million in 1959. Television helped transform teen culture into a national culture. In 1957 Dick Clark persuaded ABC to include *American Bandstand* in its network lineup. Running Monday to Friday from three to half-past four Eastern Time, the show not only spotlighted new forms of dancing; it also showcased many African-American recording artists and remained one of television's only integrated programs until the mid-1960s. Television's most popular dance show, it brought rock and roll and the latest fashions in dance and dress to millions of teenagers.[68]

But rock and roll generated extraordinary anger. F.B.I. director J. Edgar Hoover called it "a corrupting impulse," and in Hartford, Connecticut, Dr. Francis J. Braceland described rock and roll as "a communicable disease, with music appealing to adolescent insecurity and driving teenagers to do outlandish things." Between 1955 and 1958 there were numerous crusades to ban rock and roll from the airwaves. Meanwhile, executives with the major record companies sought to smooth the jagged edges of rock and roll. Sexually explicit songs were "covered"—rewritten and rerecorded by white performers. The major record companies publicized a series of "kleen" teen idols, beginning with Tommy Sands in 1957.[69]

Within five years the first phase in the history of rock and roll was over: Elvis Presley was inducted into the army, Buddy Holly and Ritchie Valens died in a plane crash, and Chuck Berry was jailed on charges of transporting a minor across interstate lines for immoral purposes. Meanwhile Alan Freed was fired in the midst of a payola scandal, Little Richard's religious conversion led him to stop performing, and Jerry Lee Lewis was in disgrace following his marriage to a thirteen-year-old cousin. Despite these shocks, youth music was not completely absorbed into mainstream culture. By the end of the decade a new phase in the history of rock and roll had begun, with the rise of the Girl Groups, the Motown sound, and surfer music.[70]

More than half a century after its advent, rock and roll remains the distinctive and dominant form of youthful musical expression. Its persistence is not an accident. Rock and roll emerged as a solution to the psychological and emotional frustrations of the teenager. Prolonged schooling, delayed marriage, and postponed entry into adult careers made rock culture increasingly appealing as a visceral form of cultural rebellion. It offered an expressive outlet for all the pent-up energy, sexuality, and individualism that teens experienced. Indeed, now that the category of youth extends far beyond the teenage years, encompassing both children as young as eight and young adults into their late twenties and early thirties, the appeal of rock and roll has broadened even as its forms have fragmented.[71]

Predominant in the emergence of rock and roll, African Americans remained largely invisible in mainstream popular culture. The African American writer Michelle Wallace, who was born in 1950, saw few images of blacks on television and the movies or in comic books and popular magazines: "I . . . grew up watching a television on which I rarely saw a black face, reading Archie and Veronica comics, Oz and Nancy Drew stories and *Seventeen* magazine, in which 'race' was unmentionable." No longer, however, could the country's racial problem be repressed. For many young African Americans, it was a death in the Mississippi Delta that energized their commitment to the civil rights struggle.[72]

His friends called him "Bobo." Emmett Till had suffered from polio and was left with a slight speech impediment. He was just fourteen years old in the summer of 1955, when he and seven relatives and family friends went to visit kinfolk in Money, Mississippi. A Delta town of about 200, Money was located alongside the tracks of the Illinois Central Railroad, which had carried African Americans, like Till's own family, from the South to Chicago. His mother thought he would be safer in Money than in Chicago. Before he boarded his southbound train, she reminded him of Mississippi's racial etiquette: that he should say, "Yes, sir," "No, sir," not look whites straight in the eye, and not talk to them unless spoken to. Despite her warnings, Till found himself in the wrong place at the wrong time. A white woman store clerk in Money claimed, at various times, that the youth had called her "baby," whistled at her, or spit out his bubble gum in her direction. Around two in the morning on Sunday, August 28, the woman's husband and brother came to Till's great-uncle's unpainted cottonfield cabin and dragged the fourteen-year-old out of bed. Three days after he was abducted, his neck was found tied to a seventy-five-pound cotton gin fan dumped in the Tallahatchie River fifteen miles up-river from Money. His face was unrecognizable: an eye was gouged out, an ear torn off, and his skull bashed in. Emmitt Till's mother insisted that the body be brought to Chicago for burial and ordered an open-casket funeral so that the public could see what had been done to her son.[73]

Federal authorities showed no interest in intervening in or even investigating the case. At the trial in 1957, Till's great-uncle, Moses Wright, courageously identified the abductors in open court. But barely an hour after they began deliberating, the jurors returned their not-guilty verdicts. The brutality of the murder of a child aroused African Americans in a way that no previous act of violence had. Coming months after the Supreme Court's landmark *Brown v. Board of Education* decision, declaring segregation in public schools unconstitutional, the murder set the stage for the signal Montgomery bus boycott three months later.[74]

In *Coming of Age in Mississippi,* Anne Moody, who was fifteen years old at the time, described the killing's impact on her life. "Before Emmett Till's murder," she wrote, "I had known the fear of hunger, hell, and the Devil. But now there was a new fear known to me—the fear of being killed just because I was black. This was the worst of my fears." The eldest of nine Mississippi children, she went on:

> I was fifteen years old when I began to hate people. I hated the white men who murdered Emmett Till and I hated all the other whites who were responsible for the countless murders . . .
> But I also hated Negroes. I hated them for not standing up and doing something about the murders. In fact, I think I had a stronger resentment toward Negroes for letting the whites kill them than toward the whites.[75]

Emmett Till's murder underscored blacks' vulnerability, victimization, and powerlessness, which could no longer be tolerated by younger African Americans.

African-American children would stand at the forefront of the civil rights struggle of the 1950s, when school desegregation and integration of public transportation became major battlefields. In 1849 Massachusetts' Supreme Judicial Court ruled that the city of Boston had done nothing improper when it required five-year-old Sarah Roberts to walk past white elementary schools and attend an all-black segregated school. It rejected the argument made by the abolitionist and U.S. Senator Charles Sumner and African-American attorney Robert Morris that segregated schooling "brand[s] a whole race with the stigma of inferiority and degradation." In 1950, 101 years after the Roberts case, Oliver Brown, a railroad worker, filed suit against the Board of Education in Topeka, Kansas. His daughter, eight-year-old Linda, was a third-grader at all-black Monroe Elementary School. To reach her school she had to walk half a mile through a railroad switchyard to catch a bus, even though an all-white elementary school was only seven blocks away. Topeka's white lawyers argued that Monroe Elementary School was architecturally identical with Topeka's white schools and that the black schools had more teachers with master's degrees. Brown's attorney argued that even if the facilities were equal, the very fact of racial discrimination was detrimental to African-American children. At the time that Mr. Brown sued the Topeka school board, similar cases were filed in Delaware, South Carolina, Virginia, and Washington, D.C. In all but the Delaware case, lower courts had ruled that segregation in public schools was permissible as long as the separate facilities were equal. The Supreme Court consolidated the cases.[76]

Thurgood Marshall and the NAACP Legal Defense Fund used sociological evidence to show that segregation harmed black children's self-esteem. During the 1940s the psychologist Kenneth Clark had studied racial preferences among a group of black children and discovered that most black children ascribed positive characteristics to white dolls and negative characteristics to darker dolls. "It was clear," he concluded, "that American racism imposed a tremendous burden of deep feelings of inferiority in the early stages of personality development in black children."[77]

On May 17, 1954, a unanimous Supreme Court handed down its decision. It ruled that segregated schools were inherently unequal. The court stressed that the badge of inferiority stamped on minority children by segregation hindered their full development no matter how equal the facilities. The isolation of African-American children "generates a feeling of inferiority as to their status in the community that may affect their hearts and minds in a way unlikely ever to be undone," wrote Chief Justice Earl Warren. "We conclude that in the field of public education the doctrine of 'separate but equal' has no place." To win a nine-to-nothing vote on the case, and the moral authority that a unanimous decision would carry, Chief Justice Warren agreed in a 1955 decision that schools be desegregated with "all deliberate speed." This contradictory expression called for gradual desegregation. At the time, seventeen states had segregated school systems, and 99 percent of black students in the South attended all-black schools.

Young people played a critical role in desegregating schools and transportation facilities. Nine months before Rosa Parks, a forty-two-year-old black seamstress, refused to surrender her seat on a Montgomery, Alabama, bus to a white passenger, fifteen-year-old Claudette Colvin had been dragged off a bus and arrested for the same thing. Around four in the afternoon on Friday, March 2, 1955, the eleventh-grader boarded a city bus across the street from the Dexter Avenue Baptist Church and took a seat near the emergency exit, toward the middle of the bus. In Montgomery, the ten seats in the front of the bus were reserved for whites, and the ten in the rear were designated for blacks. The sixteen seats in the middle could go to black riders unless white passengers wanted them. Blacks and whites could not sit in the same row. When more white passengers boarded the bus, the driver told Claudette to move to the rear. A black high schooler shouted: "The only thing she's got to do is stay black and die." Claudette recalled her feelings at the time: "If it had been for an old lady, I would have got up, but it wasn't. I was sitting on the last seat that they said you could sit in. I didn't get up, because I didn't feel like I was breaking the law."[78]

Sitting next to her was a pregnant African-American woman, who said "that she had paid her fare and that she didn't feel like standing." A police officer boarded the bus and turned to the black men sitting behind the pregnant woman and said, "If any of you are not gentlemen enough to give a lady a seat, you should be put in jail yourself." One man stood and gave her his seat. When Claudette refused to move, the officer pulled her off the bus and charged her with assault and battery as well as violating the city and state segregation laws. At her trial, Claudette was found guilty and released on indefinite probation in her guardian's care.

Although she was the first person arrested for protesting segregation on Montgomery's buses, her name has remained obscure. Montgomery's black leaders were looking for a symbol around which to organize antisegregation protests and decided that Claudette was not appropriate. She had grown up in King Hill, Montgomery's poorest section, an area of railyards, stockyards, junkyards, and unpaved streets, in a house without indoor plumbing. Raised by a great-aunt who worked as a maid and a great-uncle who mowed lawns, Claudette had a rebellious streak. Her teachers had threatened to expel her from school for wearing her hair in plaits. The summer after her arrest, Claudette became pregnant, and E. D. Nixon, the black businessman who drafted the plan to protest segregated buses, feared that her pregnancy might discredit the cause. Nevertheless, it was a child who had led the way in challenging segregated transportation and provided the example for adults to follow.

The first major confrontation between states' rights and the Supreme Court's school desegregation decision took place in Little Rock, Arkansas, in 1957. Seventy-five black students applied to attend Little Rock's Central High School, and eighteen were chosen. By Labor Day, only nine were still willing to serve as foot soldiers in freedom's march. Little Rock seemed an unlikely place for a civil rights confrontation. Its largest newspapers were generally supportive of desegregation, and the city had already desegregated its public library and bus system. Arkansas's governor, Orval Faubus, owed his reelection in 1956 to black voters. But responding to polls showing that 85 percent of the state's residents opposed school integration, the governor directed the Arkansas National Guard to bar the nine teenagers from enrolling in all-white Central High. Built at a cost of $1.5 million, the school was, at the time of its construction in 1927, the largest and most expensive high school in the United States. In contrast, Horace Mann, the city's black high school, had been built for $300,000 and had no athletic fields.

For three weeks the National Guard, under orders from the governor, prevented the nine students from entering the school. President Eisenhower privately pressed Faubus to comply with the court order. When he refused to budge, the president federalized the Arkansas National Guard and sent in 1,000 paratroopers from the Army's 101st Airborne Division to escort the students into the school.

Elizabeth Eckford, one of the nine black students, encountered an angry white mob hurling racial epithets. "Someone ought to lynch her! Anybody got any rope?" "Go back to your own kind!" she was told, followed by the chant "Two, four, six, eight—we don't want to integrate." Why did she persist? "Part of it was pure stubbornness," she explained, and part a sacrifice for her community. When fifteen-year-old Terrance Roberts was confronted by a boy carrying a baseball bat, he tried to hold his head up high and look the other boy in the eyes. "He came up and he half raised the bat and he said, 'Nigger, if you weren't so skinny . . .' . . . I thought to myself then, 'I'm probably over the worst of it.'"[79]

The Little Rock nine were placed in separate homerooms and were forced to use separate restrooms and drinking fountains. Prohibited from participating in any of the school's clubs or teams, the nine were ostracized and physically harassed, shoved against lockers, tripped down stairways, and taunted by their classmates. One was struck in the head by a lock. Not all the African-American students were able to turn the other cheek. Minniejean Brown was expelled for dumping a bowl of chili on a classmate's head when he persisted in calling her racist names as she tried to eat lunch. The remaining students were greeted the next day by a sign that said, "One down, eight more to go."[80]

"Most of the white students didn't bother us," Elizabeth Eckford recalled; "they just pretended we didn't exist. But there was this small group of white students that bothered us every day. They would call us names, trip us in the hallways, and push us down the steps, without fear of being reprimanded by the teachers or the principal." She went on: "We couldn't fight back . . . It was up to us to make integration a success, and if you think about it that way, then you realize that when you believe in something, even if you're afraid, you'll find a way to accomplish your goals."[81]

Only one of the Little Rock nine graduated from Central High. Ernest Green received his diploma in dead silence. In the fall of 1958 Governor Faubus shut down the public high schools to prevent further integration, and the schools did not reopen for a year. The lessons of Little Rock were clear: integration would not come easily, and it would be African-American children—like six-year-old Ruby Bridges—who had to stand on

Delois Huntley integrates Alexander Graham Junior High School in Charlotte, North Carolina, in September 1957. Courtesy of the Public Library of Charlotte and Mecklenburg County, North Carolina.

the front lines. In 1960 Ruby integrated William Frantz School in New Orleans by herself. Day after day, white adults shouted epithets as federal marshals escorted her to school. In the midst of the screaming mob, Ruby knelt down and prayed for her attackers. Because almost all white parents had withdrawn their children, the school was largely empty except for a single teacher, who taught Ruby in an otherwise vacant classroom. Six years after the landmark *Brown v. Board of Education* decision, just forty-nine southern school districts had desegregated, and only one percent of black schoolchildren in the eleven states of the old Confederacy attended public school with white classmates. Only the activism of the next decade would alter these bleak facts.[82]

For many Americans the 1950s represent the ideal of a child-centered society, a time when children could count on a full-time mother and didn't have to worry about divorce. In the face of nostalgia, we need to recall that the stereotypical 1950s childhood was confined to a minority of children, and that it was a product of a constellation of circumstances unlikely ever to return. In a reaction to Depression hardships, wartime stress, and Cold War anxieties, middle-class parents placed more emphasis on marriage, parenthood, and childhood than ever before. Rapidly rising adult male incomes combined with low inflation, low housing prices, and relatively low economic aspirations to allow middle-class and many working-class families to subsist on one income and to have a full-time mother for young children.

Yet the seeds of social change were already germinating. Early marriages during the 1950s contributed to a surge of divorces beginning in the mid-1960s. Ever-rising notions of a middle-class standard of living combined with women's growing expectations of self-fulfillment to propel many mothers into the paid labor force. Above all, youth was becoming a group more distinct from children and adults. A large proportion of teens developed a separate existence, relatively free from the demands of adulthood and more independent of parental supervision. For longer and longer periods of their lives, young people were spending their time in the company of other young people within specialized youth-oriented institutions. New occupations sprouted up to serve this new and growing market, including disk jockeys, adolescent psychologists, and orthodontists. As the youth market grew, it became the target of marketers. With the average adolescent in the mid-1950s spending $555 annually "for goods and services, not including the necessities normally supplied by their families," manufacturers of record albums, cosmetics, and training bras aimed at the young consumer. Even young children were being defined and targeted by their interests and needs. They had their own television shows, like *The Wonderful World of Disney,* and their own heroes, like the coonskin-hatted Davy Crockett. The effect of the consumer culture was to peel young people away from their families into a world of peers.

Many adults, convinced that the youth culture posed a serious threat to traditional values, sought to break down the barriers it erected between parents and their offspring. *Look* magazine in 1957 hired a research company to define words commonly used by teenagers, such as *blast, bread,* and *raunchy.* San Antonio high schools banned tight jeans and duck-tail haircuts on the grounds that undisciplined dress encouraged undisciplined behavior. The city of Houston prohibited young people under eighteen from owning a car unless it was used exclusively for transportation to and from work. But these efforts to hold back the tides of change proved futile. During the next decade the youth culture flourished as never before.[83]

chapter fifteen

Youthquake

HER PARENTS tried to shield her from the humiliation of Birmingham, Alabama's, segregation laws. When the family shopped at a local department store, Carolyn McKinstry's mother told her that she didn't need to try on the clothes. "This is fine," she said. "This'll fit." Nor was she allowed to ride on the city's segregated bus system. A special bus drove the family's six children to school, "because they didn't want us to have bad feelings about ourselves on the city buses." But it proved impossible to screen out the realities of segregation. Carolyn's textbooks, passed down from white schools, were filled with obscenities "that seemed written to us." She knew that her father, who waited on tables at the Birmingham Country Club, was not allowed to enter the club as a visitor.[1]

Her parents didn't want her to take part in civil rights protests, but she became involved anyway. At the 16th Street Baptist Church, she heard the Reverend Dr. Martin Luther King Jr. say words to which she could relate: "We want the right to sit down in a restaurant and eat a hot dog after we shop . . . We want the right to use the water fountain because all water is water, and it's God's water." At church she took classes in nonviolent protest, and on May 2, 1963, fourteen-year-old Carolyn was one of nearly 1,000 schoolchildren who marched through Birmingham's streets to end segregation at downtown businesses. Six hundred young people were arrested that day. The next day she and 400 other students marched downtown, only to be met by police wielding firehoses and water cannons. Later she recalled the hoses' power: "It felt like the side of my face was being slapped really hard. It hurt so bad I tried to hold on to a building so it wouldn't push me down the sidewalk, and it just flattened me against the building." The hair on the right side of her head was ripped away.[2]

She was in church on Youth Day in September 1963. At 10:25 A.M., fifteen sticks of dynamite, set by segregationists, exploded next to the church's stone staircase. The bombing killed eleven-year-old Addie Mae Collins and fourteen-year-old Denise McNair, Carole Robertson, and Cynthia Wesley, and injured twenty-three others. A day planned to celebrate the church's young people instead became a day to mourn them. The brutality of racism manifest in the deaths of these children would mobilize the civil rights struggle as never before.

Carolyn McKinstry was one of many young people who stood on the front lines of the social upheavals of the 1960s. Young people were at the cutting edge of social and cultural change, whether this involved racially integrating schools, protesting against the Vietnam war, or participating in the burgeoning youth culture. Their protests and actions transformed not only their sense of self, but the very character of American culture.

In the spring of 1960, students around the world were making their voices heard on political issues. Thousands of South Korean students, many still in high school, staged massive demonstrations against suspected rigged elections in the hope of toppling the authoritarian government of Syngman Rhee. In Japan masses of students protested their government's support for a U.S.-Japanese defense treaty that they feared would lead to Japan's remilitarization. In Britain student groups demonstrated against racial oppression in South Africa and their country's nuclear policies.[3]

In the United States student political activity in 1960 was at a higher pitch than at any time since the 1930s. For many, John F. Kennedy's election as president, with the youngest president succeeding the oldest, signified a new spirit of youth at the very top of the nation. In San Francisco 200 college students were clubbed, firehosed, and dragged down the steps of San Francisco's City Hall when they protested a House Un-American Activities Committee hearing. At the 1960 White House Conference on Children and Youth, 1,400 youth delegates organized demonstrations against racial discrimination. Yet nothing could match the electrifying effect of the sit-in movement that began in Greensboro, North Carolina, on February 1, 1960, when four well-dressed black college freshmen walked into a dime store and sat down at the whites-only lunch counter. Within weeks 70,000 young people were participating in the sit-in movement that swept across the segregated South, teaching adults a lesson in the power of nonviolent direct action.[4]

During the 1950s young people were tarred with the epithet "fat, dumb and happy." But by early 1961 journalists detected a new mood. "Youth everywhere is exploding into action," reported *Look* magazine in a special issue on "The Explosive Generation." "Apathy has given way to action." A survey of high school principals reported that students were more serious about education, harder working, and more intellectually curious. A poll of high school students also suggested a shift. An overwhelming majority said that "someone who does not believe in our present form of government should be allowed to make a speech," and only 13 percent admitted to "any bad feelings" about members of other races. A majority agreed with the social critic Paul Goodman that the main trouble with growing up today was finding productive and meaningful goals in a mass consumer society. This, said *Look* magazine, was a generation that feared not change, but stagnation. Said one student: "What I fear about most is the most terrible of all curses, found in the book of Isaiah: 'Make the heart of this people fat, make their ears heavy, and shut their eyes.'"[5]

The term *the sixties* instantly evokes images of bell-bottom jeans, sandals, and clenched fists; of countercultural experimentation, underground newspapers, and militant protest. It is a decade synonymous with campus unrest, urban rioting, psychedelic art, hallucinogenic drugs, and political assassination. Although the word *revolution* strikes many as hyperbolic, the 1960s is a period in which the word seems apt. The young lived through turbulent times, including a sexual revolution, a cultural revolution, a student revolution, and a rights revolution. For the 1960s generation, a new and promising world was unfolding.[6]

During the 1960s widely held presuppositions about authority, family life, gender, race relations, sexuality, and proper behavior were contested. At first many of the emerging values and behavior patterns were widely rejected, even by a majority of the young. But in the 1970s they were rapidly embraced. At the start of the 1960s a "cult of security" seemed firmly entrenched in family life. Half of all women married between the ages of sixteen and nineteen and then bore three or four children in rapid succession. Almost all of these women remained outside the paid workforce until their children reached school age. Meanwhile their husbands, generally a year or two older than their wives, entered the adult workforce at an early age. Securing a wife, children, and job were primary goals for the male breadwinner. During the decade, however, this desire for early marriage, family, and employment broke down. Prolonged schooling, delayed marriage, and postponed entry into a full-time adult career in an affluent economy created a period of youth extending far beyond adolescence. College attendance soared, and as it did, the age of marriage climbed

sharply. The doubling of the divorce rate between 1960 and 1970 indicated a new willingness to risk the security of marriage and family for
greater individual fulfillment. At the same time, the number of men and
women living together outside of marriage—or what used to be called
"living in sin"—increased sixfold. When the winds of change in family life
subsided, men and women married six years later than their 1960 counterparts, and men entered the adult workforce half a decade or even a decade later. Over half of married women with children under five were in
the labor force, and a growing proportion of adolescents began sexual relations in their mid-teens. A sea change had taken place in behavior and
attitudes.[7]

An activist generation was coming of age. During the 1960s youth
loomed larger than any other social group in making public their needs
and desires. As a result of depressed birthrates during the 1930s and the
postwar baby boom, the number of teenagers exploded. Unlike their parents, whose values and expectations had been shaped by the Depression
and World War II, young people grew up in a period of unprecedented
prosperity, security, and ease, when the gross national product expanded
at an average rate of 3.9 percent a year and real income doubled. Their
parents' concern for their well-being became translated into their own
search for personal fulfillment.[8]

Several times in the course of American history, generations have been
the country's most salient social division. The Revolutionary generation
dominated national politics through the presidency of Andrew Jackson.
Generational consciousness was intense among the disillusioned youth of
the Lost Generation of the 1920s and the World War II generation. Almost from birth, the baby-boom children constituted a cohesive generation. During the 1960s they were envisioned as intensely idealistic and rebellious; in later years they were caricatured as uniquely self-absorbed,
materialistic, and narcissistic.

It is easy to dismiss talk of generations as overly simplistic. After all, the
same period that gave rise to the radical Students for a Democratic Society
also produced the conservative Young Americans for Freedom. Although
the 1960s generation is usually associated with the baby boom, many of
the figures most closely linked with the youth culture of the decade were
born before the postwar boom. Abby Hoffman, Jerry Rubin, and Tom
Hayden were not baby boomers. Nor were H. Rap Brown, Stokely
Carmichael, Janis Joplin, or Angela Davis. The formative influence on
their lives had been the democratic idealism of the New Deal and World
War II. But their activism found a ready following among many baby
boomers. No previous generation in American history developed the baby

A teenage girl smokes marijuana in Leakey, Texas, in 1973. Courtesy of the National Archives, Washington, D.C.

boomers' intense generational self-consciousness. Nor had any previous generation felt such an intense sense of responsibility for promoting social and moral change. Purveyors of consumer products had targeted the young as a conspicuous market who had followed a common path of consumption through childhood, sharing the same fads, television shows, music, and many of the same experiences in school. It was ultimately, however, the events of the tumultuous 1960s that defined them as members of a common generation: all were shaped, to one degree or another, by the struggle for civil rights, the counterculture, the rebirth of feminism, and the Vietnam war. More than a common frame of reference, these events forced young people to confront choices about dress, hairstyle, drug use, sex, the military draft, and the politics of the war. The most significant issues involved a questioning of authority in schools and the family.[9]

By 1960 a new genre of books, with titles like *Parents on the Run* and *Suburbia's Coddled Kids,* criticized permissive childrearing, defiant children, and parents who let their offspring bully them. An issue of *Newsweek* titled "Are We Trapped in a Child-Centered World?" depicted a child manipulating mother and father dolls. After a decade of sentimentality and anxiety about children, a rash of articles in popular magazines, such as "Is the Younger Generation Soft and Spoiled?" and "Child Monarchy in America?," harshly criticized the young. When 251 teenagers and young adults were caught smoking marijuana in wealthy suburban Westchester County, New York, in the fall of 1960, parents were shocked. The causes, according to the *New York Times,* were peer pressure, defiance of conformist parents, and an effort to escape the emotional poverty that existed amid material plenty.[10]

Meanwhile maverick social critics advanced the argument that growing up in America was becoming more problematic, and that the most sensitive young people were growing deeply alienated from their society. In 1959 Edgar Z. Friedenberg published *The Vanishing Adolescent,* which argued that the period of growth and exploration known as adolescence was disappearing from American life. Earlier in the century, adolescence had been a vital period when a young person "learns who he is . . . what he really feels . . . [and] differentiates himself from his culture." But the stifling postwar emphasis on conformity and material possessions had made it more difficult for young people to find themselves.[11]

The Vanishing Adolescent was one of a number of books that argued that postwar society interfered with central developmental tasks. In 1960 the poet Paul Goodman published *Growing Up Absurd,* a provocative critique of how Americans had failed their children. The postwar young, he claimed, were growing up in a world of contradictions. Middle-class society valued independence but made the young dependent on adults to fulfill their needs; it stressed achievement but gave the young few avenues in which to achieve. Schools educated young people to be callow and stupid and denied them meaningful opportunities to explore, experiment, and express their deepest instincts. "It is hard," he wrote, "to grow up in a society in which one's important problems are treated as nonexistent." Goodman contended that the smothering love and hovering attention of postwar parenting made it more difficult for the young to assert their independence or to establish a unique identity.[12]

Jules Henry's 1963 study *Culture against Man* painted a nightmarish picture of youth obsessed with popularity and consumption. "In contemporary America," he wrote, children were "trained to insatiable consumption of impulsive choice and infinite variety." Family life, Henry believed, was characterized by insensitivity and an ethos emphasizing competition. He described an incident in which a mother vacuumed a rug for twenty minutes while her daughter cried miserably. Finally, the mother told the baby, "O.K., you're the winner." The mother's neglect stemmed from the values of competition (in which giving in to the child's demand for attention represents a loss of control); materialism (a concern for cleanliness takes precedence over the child's needs); individualism (placing the mother's desires above the infant's); and toughness and independence (by not spoiling the baby and leaving her to fend for herself). Henry's point was that the overly intense child-centered postwar family produced children who found it difficult to break the umbilical cord during adolescence.[13]

Psychologist Kenneth Keniston's 1965 book *The Uncommitted* examined why many bright, affluent young people, who had all of American society's material advantages and opportunities, despised their society. He attributed youthful alienation to a family configuration in which the father was emotionally withdrawn and the mother frustrated, unfulfilled, and overly invested in her children; and an educational system that cultivated cognitive skills at the expense of feelings and moral sensitivities. The result was that morally sensitive young people adopted an anti-intellectual posture and rejected adulthood. "Adulthood," to them, "means accepting an adult self-definition which entails limitation of awareness, openness, and genuineness; it involves materialism, boring work, being controlled by the demands of others." Encumbered by an excessive moral sensitivity, these youths found it impossible to identify with their society's goals and aspirations. The books of Friedenberg, Goodman, Henry, and Keniston identified a deep current of alienation and disaffection among the young, despite the attention and nurture they had received as children. Soon that estrangement had a name: the generation gap.[14]

At a time when Americans worried about gaps of all kinds, including the missile gap and the "credibility" gap, the generation gap was the most distressing. It signaled a growing sense of solidarity among young people and a belief that their peers could understand their passions and ideals in a way their parents could not. In 1967 *Time* magazine observed: "The young have already staked out their own mini society, a congruent culture that has both alarmed their elders and, stylistically at least, left an irresistible impression on them." The generation gap was easily exaggerated and romanticized. Social scientists, such as Joseph Adelson, Albert Banduras, and Elizabeth Douvan, assured adults that the generation gap was an unfounded myth. They reported that there was very little divergence of ideas between teens and their parents on moral and social issues, and that most young people turned to parents for advice. The biggest cultural division, they argued, was not between young people and their parents, but among youth themselves, especially between white middle-class and white working-class adolescents. Yet the generation gap was real nonetheless. It was readily apparent in dress, style, music, and the "jive" language adopted from the hipsters and beats of the 1950s. Blue jeans, overalls, work shirts, tie-dyed T-shirts, and long hair symbolized the distance separating middle-class youth from the world of conventional adulthood.[15]

Music became a defining symbol of generational difference. S. I. Hayakawa, the semanticist and president of San Francisco State University during its most turbulent years, referred to a youthful rebellion against songs that tended "toward wishful thinking, dreamy and ineffectual nostalgia, unrealistic fantasy, self pity and sentimental clichés masquerading as emotion." Instead, folk music, with its concern for the downtrodden and oppressed, struck a responsive chord, as did the rhythms and beats of world music. With its protest themes, passion, and vitality, the youth music of the 1960s created a shared sense of identity and fostered a vision of a utopian world unlike that created by adults.[16]

The social and cultural upheavals of the 1960s had demographic, economic, institutional, and political roots. These included the postwar baby boom, which reduced the median age by a decade, to less than twenty; unprecedented postwar prosperity, which freed many young people from the need to join the workforce at an early age; and the rapid expansion of higher education, which increased the campus population from just two million in 1946 to nearly eight million by 1970. At the same time the great postwar migration of nearly four million African Americans from the rural South to urban areas had yielded protests and struggles against job and housing discrimination in northern cities, and the diminishing intensity of the Cold War permitted a questioning of the direction of American foreign policy. Conditions were ripe for young idealists to participate in creating a new and counter culture.

For black youth, the time of waiting was coming to an end. When Franklin McCain was thirteen, the black Washingtonian considered killing himself. "I was brought up with a major myth," he later explained. "I was told that if I worked hard, believed in the Constitution, the 10 Commandments and the Bill of Rights, and got a good education, I would be successful." And he knew it wasn't true. What did blacks like his father or grandfather get? "No respect, no manhood, not even a modicum of decency for obeying all the rules and doing the right stuff," he said. A college friend, Joseph McNeil, also knew about prejudice. When his dog was hit by a car, he later remembered, a veterinarian refused to treat it because "it was a black['s] dog." On February 1, 1960, McNeil, then seventeen, and eighteen-year-old McCain and two friends—Ezell Blair Jr. and David Richmond—sat down at an F. W. Woolworth's "whites only" lunch counter in Greensboro, North Carolina, to protest racial segregation. They were refused service, but remained even after threats from the manager and the local police. By sitting-in, they risked a six-year prison term and expulsion from college, but the time had come to act. The Woolworth's was chosen after some consideration. The store was part of a national chain. The students weren't hoping for much sympathy from the Greensboro business community, but they thought shareholders in New York might have something to say about the segregated lunch counters. None anticipated that the protest would become a national phenomenon.[17]

On the first day, when they didn't know whether they would be beaten, arrested, or both, an older white woman walked up to them and said, "Boys, I'm disappointed in you." She hesitated a second and added, "You should have done this sooner." The four freshmen returned with more friends the next day. By the fifth day, more than 200 supporters entered the store. During the protests, white toughs burned black protesters' clothing with cigarettes and dumped soda and coffee on their heads, not to mention mouthing obscenities and threats. Six months later, however, Woolworth's and other Greensboro stores desegregated their counters. "From my perspective, it was a down payment on manhood," said Joseph McNeil, who later became a brigadier general. The spark struck by the four students in Greensboro ignited student-led protests across the nation.[18]

Critics of 1960s radicalism adopted crude forms of psychologizing to explain the decade's rebelliousness. Vice President Spiro Agnew and the Reverend Norman Vincent Peale blamed permissive childrearing, arguing that it had produced a generation of "demanding little tyrants," who had grown up to be "unkempt, irresponsible, destructive, anarchical, drug-oriented" hedonists. Student protests and drug use, they claimed, were little more than Oedipal rebellions or puberty rites in which coddled youth sought to assert adulthood and autonomy. In fact the primary sources of unrest were not psychological but political. Youth activists were appalled by racial inequities, impersonal and unresponsive educational bureaucracies, irrelevant school curricula, and a foreign policy perceived as immoral. For many young African Americans, the reason seemed self-evident: they were stepchildren of the American dream.[19]

Anne Moody's childhood home was anything but a haven in a heartless world. A sharecropper's daughter, born in Wilkerson County, Mississippi, in 1940, she grew up surrounded by violence and desperate poverty. Years later she vividly recalled the hunger pangs she felt while living in a succession of shacks. Her upbringing was colored by violence—violence inflicted on her neighbors and relatives and violence within her own family, including beatings inflicted by a cousin. Her mother fed her family on leftovers from her domestic job or on beans and bread. Work came early in a family with nine children. She had to clean houses for white families to help her family afford food and clothing.[20]

Her family was riven by tensions rooted in Mississippi's racial system. Her father, unable to cope with the humiliations of a sharecropper's life, abandoned his family. Her mother, exhausted and irritable, got angry whenever her daughter talked about race. Her relatives, who internalized the racist emphasis on skin color, were bitterly divided between those with lighter and darker skin. From a young age, however, Moody was determined not to accommodate herself to injustice. When she was fourteen, she refused to enter a white woman's house, which she cleaned, through the back door. Every day she came to the front door, until the woman relented and let her in.

The themes Moody developed in *Coming of Age in Mississippi,* the memoir of her youth, were echoed in other writings by young black participants in the civil rights struggle. They, too, choked on memories of violence and humiliation and sought to direct their rage outward. Frustrated by the passivity and submissiveness of their parents' generation, they sought to confront the Jim Crow system with direct action. Like their white counterparts, they shared in the educational and recreational possibilities of the era as well as the rebellion. All shared an impulse to assert their dignity.[21]

Before the 1960s, influential studies of black children had revealed low levels of self-esteem and racial pride. By the end of the decade, however, attitudes among children had measurably shifted. When researchers replicated studies in which black children were asked whether a white or a black doll was "nice" or "pretty," 70 percent of black second- and third-graders chose the black doll, and 79 percent said that the white doll "looks bad." Young blacks were also significantly less likely than their parents to say that skin color would be a factor in the choice of a spouse. A growing number felt that blacks had a special spiritual quality— "soul"—setting them apart from whites. A new pride-filled generation of African Americans was emerging, apparent in Afro hairstyles, the promotion of the holiday of Kwanzaa, and a new emphasis on African history and culture.[22]

A large number of white radicals were ministers' children. Others were "red diaper babies," the sons and daughters of members of the Old Left, like Mary Travers of Peter, Paul, and Mary. A disproportionate number of the early white radicals were of liberal Protestant and, especially, of Jewish background. The central role of Jews in the early New Left, which resembled their parents' role in the student organizations of the 1930s, reflected the socialist tradition that their families had carried from the ghettoes of eastern Europe, a distrust of authority fed by historical memories of centuries of persecution, and an upbringing in which their parents had been respectful of progressive ideas.[23]

Many 1960s activists—including Students for a Democratic Society leaders Al Haber, Tom Hayden, Paul Potter, and Rennie Davis; the feminist Gloria Steinem; the future football union leader Ed Garvey; Representative Barney Frank; and editors Willie Morris and Ronnie Dugger—had participated in the National Student Association, the nation's largest student group. Growing out of a convention held at the University of Wisconsin in the summer of 1947, NSA delegates had drafted a Student Bill of Rights calling for stronger student government and expanded access to higher education. From its founding, the organization had an activist thrust, electing an African American, Ted Harris, as its president in 1948. Three years later the organization condemned McCarthyism, and in 1959 it opened a civil rights office in Atlanta, which provided funds and logistical support for the Student Non-Violent Coordinating Committee (SNCC) after its founding in 1960.[24]

While some critics claimed that young radicals were driven by self-hatred, sexual inadequacies, narcissism, conflict with their fathers, alienation or guilt over their middle-class origins, and envy of the sexual potency of blacks, more careful studies showed that the early student activists were generally close to their parents and no more neurotic than nonprotesters. Far from rebelling against their parents, many were fulfilling their parents' political aspirations. Reared in relatively permissive and egalitarian families, however, the young radicals naïvely expected authority figures other than their parents to be responsive to their concerns. Facing few career or financial pressures, impatient, and often inspired by religious idealism, they were prepared to risk violence or jail to bring about the social change that their peaceful protests did not seem to achieve.[25]

Their deepening antipathy and anger toward American society—its inequitable treatment of racial minorities, its unequal distribution of power and resources, and its interventionist foreign policy—was fueled by experiences with insensitive school administrators and by a mounting belief that fundamental reforms could not take place without threats of disruption. Above all, the Vietnam war and the military draft radicalized many students. As the Harvard sociologist Nathan Glazer observed in 1969, the war placed youth in a morally untenable position: "The poor and the black were disproportionately subjected to the draft. The well-favored, as long as they stayed in school, and even out of it, were freed from it. The fortunate middle-class youth . . . undoubtedly felt guilty because those with whom they wanted to be allied, whom they hoped to help, had to go and fight in Vietnam."[26]

Racial injustice also animated student radicalism and ignited the most far-reaching efforts in American history to address racial and economic inequality. Much of Lyndon B. Johnson's Great Society focused on children in poverty. In 1965 Daniel Patrick Moynihan, then an assistant secretary of labor, touched off a storm of controversy with a report calling "the breakup of the black family . . . the single most important social fact of the United States today." Twenty-five percent of black families were single-parent and female-headed, and broken homes, he contended, bred school failure, delinquency, and welfare dependency. Moynihan noted that the black failure rate on the Armed Forces Qualification Test, which measured the ability to perform at an eighth-grade level, was 56 percent, four times the rate for whites. Meanwhile black children made up a third of all the youths in juvenile institutions, and half of all African-Americans received welfare benefits at some point during childhood, compared with 8 percent of white children.[27]

The Moynihan report attributed worsening rates of illegitimacy, divorce, and separation to the effects of slavery, discrimination in employment and education, and thirty-five years of Depression-level joblessness. Three centuries of injustice had created a "tangle of pathology," producing matriarchal family patterns that led young men to overcompensate in asserting their masculinity and made it more difficult to seize opportunities opened up by civil rights legislation. To address the poverty, joblessness, and crime plaguing the African-American community, Moynihan called for a concerted national effort to enhance the "stability and resources of the Negro American family." The civil rights strategist Bayard Rustin accused Moynihan of trying to impose middle-class norms upon the urban poor, while the Reverend Dr. Martin Luther King Jr. feared that the report's bleak picture of black family life would be used to justify an argument for "innate Negro weakness." But whatever its flaws, the report's strength lay in its focus on the needs of the African-American family. It declared that only by mobilizing social, economic, and political forces could the country achieve true racial equality.[28]

President Lyndon B. Johnson drew on the Moynihan report in his commencement address at Howard University in 1965. The first stage in the struggle for equal rights, the president said, involved securing legal rights. "But freedom is not enough . . . You do not take a person who, for years, has been hobbled by chains and liberate him . . . and then say, 'you are free to compete with all the others,' and still justly believe that you have been completely fair." The next task was to ensure "equality as a fact and as a result." To break the cycle of poverty and disadvantage, the Johnson administration proposed a variety of new government programs, including job training, urban redevelopment, affirmative action in hiring and contracting, and expanded medical and nutritional programs, including prenatal and postnatal care. But the centerpiece of the War on Poverty involved targeting educational resources at disadvantaged youngsters through preschool, reading readiness, and other compensatory educational programs designed to give minority students a "head start" and to counteract inequalities in social and economic conditions.[29]

The 1965 Elementary and Secondary Education Act marked the first time that the federal government had provided ongoing funding for public education and sought to advance educational equity. Instead of providing aid to all school districts, the act allocated $1 billion a year to schools with high concentrations of low-income students. It funded counseling services, health and nutrition programs, and enrichment programs in reading and mathematics. The act also provided the first federal grants targeted at children with low English-language proficiency and those with disabilities. In addition it allocated $150 million for a preschool program for disadvantaged children, based on an experiment in Ypsilanti, Michigan, that offered a holistic approach to child development, providing health care, nutritious meals, socialization, and a chance to learn through play. Launched in 1965, Head Start initially offered preschool children from low-income families an eight-week summer program to meet their emotional, social, health, nutritional, and psychological needs. Key program goals were to foster disadvantaged children's physical well-being, social skills, self-image, and school readiness. A defining feature of Head Start was an emphasis on parental participation. Rather than being passive recipients of services, parents would be participants in developing skills to nurture and teach their children. For the children who participated in the project, Head Start offered a sense of government concern with social and racial justice.

Head Start met the needs of a small portion of disadvantaged children. To assist larger numbers of children, policymakers and private foundations looked to television. Middle-class preschoolers with affluent, educated parents already knew the alphabet and how to count when they got to kindergarten, but poor, inner-city children did not. In 1967 Joan Ganz Cooney, a documentary producer, chaired a study of children's television habits. The study found that Saturday morning cartoons had an average of twenty violent episodes an hour, and that preschool children watched about thirty hours of TV each week. Cooney assumed the challenge of creating a television show designed specifically to prepare poor children for school. With $8 million in grants from foundations and the federal government, Cooney's Children's Television Workshop developed a show to teach preschool kids the alphabet and how to count to ten. Ironically, the show took its direction from TV commercials: the segments—covering everything from the letter *W* to natural disasters—were short and repetitious, so that the lessons sunk in. The format included games, music, short films, cartoons, and catchy jingles.[30]

As a test, the first five programs were aired on a Philadelphia television station, and 100 families were paid to ensure that their children watched the show. The children's reactions were muted. The one thing that they liked were two puppets, Bert and Ernie, much as previous generations had adored Charlie McCarthy and Mortimer Snerd; Kukla, Fran, and Ollie; and Howdy Doody. The producers decided to redesign the show, showcasing the "Muppets," including Big Bird, Miss Piggy, and Kermit the Frog. To attract an inner-city audience, the show, which first aired in November 1969, was set on an urban street and featured a multiethnic and racially diverse cast. During its first six months, half of the nation's twelve million preschoolers watched the show. The program evoked intense controversy; critics denounced its TV-commercial style pacing and expressed concern that it would negatively affect children's expectations of school. But children loved *Sesame Street,* and it became an integral part of preschoolers' lives. It marked a radical expansion in the public commitment to meeting the educational needs of disadvantaged children.

In addition to providing children in poverty with preschool experience and educational television, children's advocates sought to help children who were disadvantaged by an inability to speak English through bilingual education. In New York City, where about 60 percent of the Puerto Rican students dropped out, public schools awarded academic diplomas to 331 Puerto Rican high school graduates in 1963—or about one percent of the total Puerto Rican enrollment. Only 28 Puerto Rican graduates went on to college.[31]

In 1959, following the Cuban Revolution and a massive influx of Cuban children into south Florida, Miami's public schools introduced the first bilingual education programs. In 1968 the Great Society inaugurated the first federally mandated programs for bilingual education. The Bilingual Education Act of 1968 (Title VII) provided supplemental funding for school districts that established programs to meet the needs of children with limited English proficiency. Title VII funded seventy-six bilingual programs its first year, serving students who spoke 14 different languages. In 1974, in *Lau v. Nichols,* the Supreme Court ruled that any school district with students who spoke a language other than English, not just those that received Title VII funds, had to provide English-language instruction. Lawyers for Chinese-speaking students in San Francisco successfully argued that the city's schools failed to provide English language instruction to some 1,800 students who spoke no English.[32]

For the first time, students with disabilities also received federal support. Among the most radical innovations of the era was the establishment of a legal right to special education. Until the mid-1970s, most states allowed school districts to refuse to enroll students they considered "ineducable," while physically disabled students of normal intelligence were routinely grouped with mentally retarded students. A 1949 Pennsylvania law was typical: a school district could refuse to enroll or retain any student who did not have a mental age of at least five years. Such children were considered ineducable, "unable mentally or physically to profit from school attendance." In Washington, D.C., eight-year old George Liddell Jr., who was mentally retarded, was denied admission to an elementary school because he would have required a special class. Sixteen-year-old Michael Williams, who suffered from epilepsy, was expelled from a Washington school because of frequent absences due to health problems. Altogether, an estimated 12,340 children with disabilities were excluded from school in the nation's capital during the 1971–72 school year.[33]

Not until 1966 did the federal government provide grants to school districts to provide services to students with disabilities. Two landmark 1971 court cases—*Pennsylvania Association for Retarded Children v. Commonwealth of Pennsylvania* and *Mills v. Board of Education*—established the principle that states had a constitutional duty to provide a free public education to children with mental or behavioral disabilities. Yet despite more than thirty federal court decisions upholding the principle that states had to provide these children with an education appropriate to their learning capacities, as late as 1975 almost a million children with disabilities received no education at all, and only seventeen states provided an education to even half of the known physically or mentally disabled children. In 1973 Congress enacted legislation prohibiting any recipient of federal aid from discriminating in offering services to people with disabilities, and empowering individuals to bring lawsuits to end discriminatory practices. Two years later it passed the Education for All Handicapped Children Act, which required that students with disabilities receive a free public education appropriate to their unique needs. The law required that students be educated in regular classrooms, whenever appropriate, and mandated parental involvement in all decisions regarding students with special needs.

A new sense of agency and entitlement arose among students during the 1960s. Unwilling to passively accept conditions as they were, students transformed schools into arenas of cultural and political conflict. In Chicago, public school enrollment increased by 146,000 during the 1950s, almost exclusively in African-American schools. To meet the demand, many Chicago schools operated on double shifts. But by 1961 the only schools with double shifts were located in black areas. African-American schools also had more pupils per teacher and twice as many noncertified teachers. In October 1963 and again in February 1964, black school children in Chicago staged massive school boycotts to protest the gerrymandering of school attendance boundaries and inequitable conditions in the black schools.[34]

At the same time that African-American students in Chicago, Detroit, and many other cities protested inequities in public education, Latinos in the Southwest staged "blowouts," spontaneous boycotts of school classes on behalf of Brown Power. The first took place in March 1968, in Eastside Los Angeles, when at least 1,000 students left classes. Student demonstrators demanded remedies for soaring dropout rates, overcrowded, dilapidated schools, incompetent teachers, and counselors who steered Latino students into auto shop instead of college-track courses. They were angry that Latino students—classified as white—were used to integrate public schools, while non-Latino whites remained in their own racially segregated schools They also wanted bilingual education, Mexican-American principals, culturally relevant courses, and cafeteria food prepared by mothers from the barrios. At the time, the average dropout rate in Eastside high schools was 44 percent, three times higher than in schools on the Westside or in the San Fernando Valley. In 1968 Latinos, then predominantly Mexican Americans, accounted for 20 percent of the enrollment but for fewer than 3 percent of teachers and 1 percent of administrators. The initial walkout, which lasted several days, quickly spread to fifteen high schools, where 20,000 students left their classes.[35]

Title VII of the 1964 Civil Rights Act called for a sweeping survey of "the lack of . . . equal educational opportunities" due to race, religion, or national origin. In the space of just three months James S. Coleman, a social scientist at Johns Hopkins, surveyed 600,000 students, 60,000 teachers, and 4,000 schools—the largest social science project ever conducted. Coleman concluded that the social and educational backgrounds of students and teachers, not the quality of school facilities or class size, were the key factors in children's academic success. Regardless of the quality of teachers, facilities, or curricula, inner-city schools failed to overcome the problems of a disadvantaged home environment. His report described

Teenage Mexican Americans demonstrate on behalf of Chicano power in Denver, Colorado, in 1970. Courtesy of the Denver Public Library.

gains in educational motivation for disadvantaged children who mixed with middle-income students in school, as well as higher scores on standardized tests, and found no educational harm to middle-income students. The report concluded that integration was more effective than compensatory programs for low-income students. The Coleman report was invoked to support busing to achieve racial balance in public schools. It was taken to mean that high expenditures on teachers, curricula, facilities, or compensatory education had only a modest impact on student achievement. Floyd McKissick, the national director of the Congress on Racial Equality (CORE), angrily denounced the report for implying: "Mix Negroes with Negroes and you get stupidity."[36]

In 1968—fourteen years after the *Brown v. Board of Education* decision—federal courts began to order busing as a way to deal with de facto segregation brought about by housing patterns. In April 1971, in the case of *Swann v. Charlotte-Mecklenburg Board of Education*, the Supreme Court upheld "bus transportation as a tool of school desegregation." Busing proved to be extraordinarily divisive. Many white working-class families viewed schools as centers of local pride and bitterly resisted intrusions on "their" schools. Meanwhile, because the privileged lived outside central cities, the burden of busing fell upon the inner-city poor. In 1974, by a five-to-four vote in *Bradley v. Milliken*, the Supreme Court rejected a school desegregation plan that would have involved busing across school district boundaries.[37]

The most ferocious conflict over busing occurred in Boston. Ruling that the Boston School Committee had "intentionally brought about and maintained a dual school system," Judge W. Arthur Garrity ordered a busing plan that initially involved eighty schools. The most controversial element involved mixing students from Roxbury, a predominantly poor black neighborhood, and South Boston, a poor Irish enclave. Most schools integrated quietly, but protesters in South Boston screamed epithets and hurled stones, eggs, and rotten tomatoes at school buses. Nine black students were injured, and Theodore C. Landsmark, a black lawyer, was struck by a white youth wielding a flagpole topped by the American flag. During the second phase of integration, obscene taunts, racial tensions, and fights were particularly pronounced in Charlestown, a predominantly Irish neighborhood in the northern part of Boston. In 1973, before Judge Garrity issued his order, Boston had 94,000 public school students, 57 percent of them white. By 1984 the total had fallen to 57,000 students, only 27 percent white. In a study published in 1975, James S. Coleman declared busing a failure because it had prompted a massive departure of whites from public schools. For some children, especially in large and mid-sized cities, court-ordered school busing meant that they attended more diverse schools than in the past. But for millions of others, busing spurred their parents to enroll their children in private schools or to move to the suburbs, where they attended predominantly white public schools.[38]

During the 1960s a platoon of books—including Nat Hentoff's *Our Children Are Dying* and Jonathan Kozol's *Death at an Early Age*—lambasted American public education as racist, mind deadening, and soul destroying. Educational critic John Holt called children a "subject people." "School for them is a kind of jail," he wrote. "Do they not, to some extent, escape and frustrate the relentless, insatiable pressure of their elders by withdrawing the most intelligent and creative parts of their minds from the scene?" Part of the broader critique of American society's inequalities, the attack on education was prompted by glaring inequities in school funding, rigid systems of tracking and ability grouping, and arbitrary discipline policies. It carried far-reaching implications for children's schooling, including court-ordered changes in school funding mechanisms, institution of more elective courses, due-process protections for students accused of violating school policies, and adoption of laws prohibiting discrimination against female students. Meanwhile student radicals conceived of youth as a new proletariat and a potentially revolutionary class, who, alongside African Americans and other marginalized and disaffected groups, would overturn the social order. According to John and Margaret Rowntree in a 1968 pamphlet, youth was confined in school in order to prevent adolescents from disrupting the labor market. Used exclusively in part-time minimum-wage jobs, young people were alienated and increasingly conscious of their exploitation. Such arguments reflected a new cynicism and suspicion of authority.[39]

Ferocious debates erupted about whether education was breaking free of the rigidities of the 1950s to focus on the aspirations of children and to encourage the development of free, balanced individuals with a fair place in society, or whether the 1960s was a disastrous period of declining standards and weakening authority. In New York City a teacher named Elliot Shapiro tried out a curriculum organized around the release of hostility. Drawing on Frantz Fanon's notion that colonized people must vent their hate against imperialists in order to recover their unique identities, Shapiro had the students give talks, write compositions, and act out why and how they hated their parents, their siblings, the police, the neighborhood, the school, and the school's principal.[40]

Others, like John Holt and Ivan Illich, advocated "unschooling"—allowing children to learn through their interactions with the adult world rather than through formal instruction. At A. S. Neill's experimental school Summerhill, in the small town of Leiston, England, the forty students were free to do whatever they pleased as long as they did not violate the rights of others. "As it is practiced in other schools," Neill claimed, education "invariably means cramming a child full of generally useless information, forcing him to forgo completely whatever spontaneity, inclination and creativity he might have." At Summerhill no effort was made to train students to accept authority over their own judgments.[41]

Of all the changes that took place in education in the 1960s, perhaps the most lasting development involved the emergence of a concept of student rights. Six weeks after the bodies of civil rights workers James Chaney, Andrew Goodman, and Michael Schwerner were discovered in Philadelphia, Mississippi, students in the town's all-black Booker T. Washington High School began to wear "freedom buttons" bearing the words "One Man One Vote" and the initials "SNCC." The school's principal prohibited the buttons, claiming that they would "cause a commotion" and "didn't have any bearing" on the children's education. When fifty students disregardèd his order, he suspended them. Forty-seven students eventually backed down, but three went to court. When asked in court why she wore the button, one student replied, because she wanted people "to go to the courthouse and register to vote." "What people?" her lawyer asked. "The colored people in our community." "Do they vote in Philadelphia?" "No, sir," she replied. The federal district court refused to allow the students to wear the buttons, but the Fifth Circuit Court disagreed. The "freedom button," the judges held, communicated "a matter of vital public concern." The case of *Burnside v. Byars* served as a crucial precedent for a 1969 Supreme Court decision that upheld students' free-expression rights in a case known as *Tinker v. Des Moines*.[42]

In mid-December 1965 four children in the Tinker family in Des Moines, Iowa, decided to protest the government's policies in Vietnam by wearing black armbands, emblazoned with a peace symbol. A sixteen-year-old friend, Christopher Eckhardt, joined their protest. The Tinkers' father was a Methodist minister who was engaged in protests against the war; Christopher's mother was an official in the Women's League for Peace and Freedom. A few days before they began their protests, school authorities announced that any student wearing an armband to school would have to remove it or face suspension. The Tinker family filed suit, charging that a suspension violated their First Amendment right to freedom of speech. A lower court ruled against the Tinker children, concluding that schools could prohibit the wearing of armbands because this might disrupt the educational process. But in February 1969 the Supreme Court ruled on the Tinkers' behalf, declaring: "In our system, undifferentiated fear or apprehension of disturbance is not enough to overcome the right to freedom of expression." Holding that freedom of expression does not vanish at the school gate, the Court announced that "school officials do not possess absolute authority over their students. Students in school as well as out of school are 'persons' under our Constitution." For the first time, the Court ruled that First Amendment rights applied to students.

Tinker was part of a broader children's rights revolution. In 1964 Gerald Gault, a fifteen-year-old in Globe, Arizona, was accused of making an obscene telephone call to a neighbor. The judge found him guilty and ordered him placed in a reformatory until he turned twenty-one. Because he was a juvenile, Gault's rights were severely limited. His parents were not notified that he was under arrest, and he was not allowed to consult a lawyer. Nor, when he appeared before the juvenile judge, was he given a chance to prove his innocence. No evidence was presented at his hearing, no witnesses testified, and no record was made of the proceedings. Had he been an adult, Gault would have been able to present a defense, and would have faced a maximum punishment of a $50 fine or two months in jail. In a landmark 1967 ruling in the case of *in re Gault,* the U.S. Supreme Court declared that juveniles charged with criminal offenses were entitled to many of the procedural protections in juvenile courts that adults enjoyed in criminal courts, including the right to have legal counsel, to cross-examine witnesses, and to remain silent. "Neither the 14th Amendment nor the Bill of Rights is for adults only," Justice Abe Fortas wrote for the seven-to-two majority. "Under our Constitution, the condition of being a boy does not justify a kangaroo court."

The concept of children's rights was one of the most significant outgrowths of the liberation struggles of the 1960s. The idea itself was not new. As early as 1905, the Progressive-era reformer Florence Kelley asserted a right to childhood. During the late 1940s a number of books invoking the term appeared, enumerating children's needs, such as a right to an education, a right to play, and a right to be loved and cared for. These early defenses of children's rights emphasized children's vulnerable status and their need for a nurturing environment, and sought to encourage the state to assume a broader role in intervening in families in cases of need. Advocates of children's rights during the 1960s and 1970s had a more radical goal in mind. They wanted to award minors many of the same legal rights as adults, including the right to make certain medical or educational decisions on their own and a right to have their voice heard in decisions over adoption, custody, divorce, termination of parental rights, or child abuse. Traditionally children had been considered incompetent under the law. Children's rights advocates favored a presumption of competence, especially for older children, in decisions about motherhood, abortion, schooling, cosmetic surgery, treatment of venereal disease, sexuality, or any decision that would significantly affect the child's future.

One battlefield in the contest over children's rights involved the treatment of juvenile crime. Children's rights advocates looked skeptically at the claim that the juvenile court system operated in children's best interests. Proponents of the juvenile court argued that a minor's interests were best served by a system that removed the formalities and rules of evidence required in adult criminal trials and emphasized treatment and rehabilitation rather than punishment. Advocates of children's rights denounced this argument as a myth. They noted that many of the cases that juvenile courts heard—about 15 percent—involved status offenses, such as truancy or incorrigibility, which were not crimes if committed by adults.

Children's rights reformers stressed that juveniles were denied basic due-process protections, even after the high court's decision in *Gault*. While *Gault* gave minors the right to written notice of charges, the right to a lawyer, the privilege against self-incrimination, and the right to cross-examine witnesses, it denied them other rights, such as indictment by a grand jury, release on bail, and a right to a public trial and a trial before a jury.[43]

Another arena of legal conflict involved teenage sexuality. The most controversial issue was whether minors could obtain contraceptives or abortions without parental consent. In a 1977 case, *Carey v. Population Services International,* the Supreme Court invalidated a New York law prohibiting the sale of condoms to adolescents under sixteen, concluding that the "right to privacy in connection with decisions affecting procreation extends to minors as well as adults." The Court held that the state interest in discouraging adolescents' sexual activity was not furthered by withholding the means to protect themselves. As Justice John Paul Stevens explained in a concurring opinion, to deny teenagers access to contraception in an effort to impress upon them the evils of underage sex was as irrational as if "a State decided to dramatize its disapproval of motorcycles by forbidding the use of safety helmets." The Constitution forbade this kind of "government-mandated harm."

In subsequent cases courts struck down state laws requiring parental notice or consent if their children sought contraceptives. In *Planned Parenthood Association v. Matheson* (D. Utah 1983), a federal district court recognized that teenagers' "decisions whether to accomplish or prevent conception are among the most private and sensitive," and concluded that "the state may not impose a blanket parental notification requirement on minors seeking to exercise their constitutionally protected right to decide whether to bear or beget a child by using contraceptives." The two most important sources of federal family planning funds in the nation—Title X of the Public Health Service Act of 1970 and Medicaid (Title XIX of the Social Security Act of 1965)—required the confidential provision of contraceptive services to eligible recipients, regardless of their age or marital status. By 1995 condom distribution programs were operating in at least 431 public schools.

In the majority opinion in the *Tinker* case, Associate Justice Abe Fortas wrote that schools were special places, and that civil liberties had to be balanced against "the need for affirming the comprehensive authority of the states and of school officials, to prescribe and control conduct." In subsequent cases the court sought to define this balance. In the 1975 case of *Goss v. Lopez,* the Court granted students the right to due process when threatened with a suspension of more than ten days, and declared that a punishment could not be more serious than the misconduct. But the justices, fearful of disrupting principals' and teachers' authority, announced that schools needed only to provide informal hearings, not elaborate judicial proceedings. Students did not have a right, the Court ruled, to a hearing for a minor punishment, such as a detention, or if they posed a danger to other students or school property. In other cases the justices held that school officials might search student lockers, but only when they had grounds for believing that a specific locker contained dangerous or illegal items, and that they might impose random drug tests, but only on students engaging in extracurricular activities. The Court allowed school authorities to censor school newspapers only when they were sponsored by the school itself.

Gender equity offered yet another front in the battle for children's rights. In recent years, much of the attention on the issue of gender equity has focused on athletics, but equal access to academic opportunity prompted the initial concern. In the late 1960s, high schools typically segregated vocational education classes by sex: girls took home economics, boys took shop. Pregnant students were expelled from school and not welcomed back after they gave birth. Those schools that did allow pregnant girls and teen mothers to remain in school forced them into special programs that emphasized a nonacademic curriculum. The basic legal tool for attaining gender equity was Title IX of the Educational Amendments of 1972, which prohibited sex discrimination in any educational program or activity. Athletics quickly became the most visible field of contention. In 1971, 3.7 million boys and just 294,015 girls participated in high school sports. By 2000, boys' participation had risen to 3.9 million and girls' to 2.7 million, a nearly tenfold increase. Girls increasingly participated in such sports as lacrosse, wrestling, soccer, rugby, and ice hockey.[44]

Federal regulations adopted in 1975 prohibited sex discrimination in athletics, and policies adopted three years later required substantially equal expenditures for male and female athletes and expansion of opportunities and participation for women. Even before those rules were adopted, however, girls and young women had gone to court to seek equal treatment, arguing that a denial of access to sports violated the Fourteenth Amendment. In a series of 1973 cases, girls won the right to compete against boys in noncontact sports, such as tennis, cross-country skiing, and track, when no similar program for female students existed. In a 1974 case a twelve-year-old Ohio girl sued for the right to play on a high school football team. In *Clinton v. Nagy* a federal court found that the school district had failed to show that girls were more prone to injury than boys and that it violated the Constitution to deny a girl the right to compete solely on the basis of her sex.[45]

One other important area in the struggle for children's rights involved erasing the "stain" of illegitimacy. As recently as the early 1960s, children born outside of marriage were called "bastards" and had the word "illegitimate" stamped on their birth certificate. In 1968, in the landmark case of *Levy v. Louisiana,* the Supreme Court ruled that the Fourteenth Amendment's guarantee of equal protection extended to the children of unwed parents. After Louise Levy died in a charity hospital in New Orleans, her children, who had been born out of wedlock, attempted to sue her doctor and the hospital for negligence and wrongful death. The Louisiana courts threw out the lawsuit, claiming that out-of-wedlock children had no cause of action for a parent's wrongful death. The Supreme Court reversed this decision. In subsequent rulings the high court declared that states could not set an "unrealistically short time limitation" on a child's right to sue a father for financial support; nor could they deny children born outside of marriage a share of the inheritance. In addition, the justices held that states could not withhold welfare benefits from the children of unwed parents. Once paternity was established, children had a right to their parents' social security payments, health insurance, and child support. Despite these decisions, many legal distinctions still exist between children born within and outside of marriage. Although most states require an unwed father to support his offspring financially, children of married parents have broader rights to the level and duration of support. In addition, children born outside of marriage do not have a clear right to their father's name or his physical company.[46]

A repeated complaint voiced during the massive student protests against the Vietnam war was that if young people were old enough to be drafted by, and possibly to die for, their government, they had a right to have a voice in that government's affairs and to participate in the political process. When it extended the Voting Rights Act of 1965, Congress included a provision lowering the voting age to eighteen. In a 1970 decision the Supreme Court ruled that although Congress had the power to reduce the voting age in federal elections, it did not have the authority to alter the age in state elections. To end the possibility that states might be required to keep separate voter registration lists and hold separate elections, the Twenty-sixth Amendment to the Constitution, extending the vote to eighteen- to twenty-year-olds, was ratified in 1971. Contrary to some predictions, granting the vote to eighteen- to twenty-year-olds had little effect on American politics. Young voters did not prove to be as cohesive or as motivated as some hoped and others feared. Voters in their teens and early twenties had a much lower rate of registration and voting than the middle-aged or the elderly, and little influence on the political agenda.

It became part of the conventional wisdom that the student radicalism of the 1960s was largely a by-product of the military draft and that when the draft was replaced by a lottery and later a volunteer army, student militancy quickly dissipated. There can be no doubt that ending military conscription, combined with a stagnating economy and a conservative backlash against student radicalism and the rights revolution, did produce a decline in overt student activism. But eras of reform and social upheaval do not conform to neat chronological divisions, and many of the most far-reaching changes in values and behavior that we associate with the 1960s actually took place in the 1970s, including increased use of drugs in secondary schools and a sharp drop in the age at which many adolescents became sexually active. Major social issues such as minors' access to contraception and abortion emerged as contentious social issues only during the 1970s. Most of the important reforms related to special education, bilingual education, and equal rights for female students also took place in that decade "when nothing happened." Studies of young people's opinions indicate that during the 1960s most students, including most college students, did not consider themselves radicals. In 1970 only 8.5 percent of students identified themselves with the New Left. It was in the 1970s, not the 1960s, that a broad cross-section of young people adopted more favorable attitudes toward drugs and freer sexual expression.[47]

In the mid-1970s several trends converged to mark the start of a new phase in childhood's history. One was demographic, as a rapid increase in the divorce rate, unmarried parenthood, single-parent households, and working mothers that had begun in the mid-1960s produced new configurations of family life. A second trend was attitudinal, as a series of public panics over children's well-being erupted—over teen pregnancy, stranger abductions, child abuse, illicit drugs, juvenile crime, and flagging academic performance—and intensified parental anxieties, harshened the juvenile justice system, and provoked a sharp reaction against the children's rights revolution. A key third trend was economic, as the wages of noncollege graduates fell sharply in real terms, leading many young people to postpone marriage and making it more essential for the young to complete high school and enroll in college. These trends combined to produce a mounting concern that young people's well-being was declining and that only drastic measures could help.

chapter sixteen

Parental Panics and the Reshaping of Childhood

IN AUGUST 1983 a mother, later diagnosed as mentally ill, complained to police that her two-year-old son had been molested at the McMartin Preschool in Manhattan Beach, California. To gather evidence, the local police chief distributed a letter to about 200 parents of present or past students, informing them that a school employee might have forced the children to "engage in oral sex, fondling of genitals, buttocks or chest area, and sodomy." He urged the parents to question their children and to come forward if they had any information to offer.[1]

This letter, combined with a local television report about possible links between the preschool and a pornography ring in nearby Los Angeles, touched off a panic. The police referred anxious parents to the Children's Institute International, a private, nonprofit organization specializing in the treatment and prevention of child abuse, where about 400 children who had attended the preschool were interviewed. Initially most children denied having been molested. But after they were shown puppets and told that it was "all right to tell their yucky secrets," some 360 described incidents of abuse.[2]

The children said that their teachers had stuck silverware in their anuses, butchered rabbits on a church altar, and murdered a horse with a baseball bat. The children also described being flushed down toilets into sewers where they had been sexually abused. On the basis of testimony from eighteen children and from doctors about physical evidence of abuse, Virginia McMartin, her son and daughter, and six other daycare workers were indicted for sexually abusing children over a ten-year period. The McMartin Preschool charges resulted in the longest and costliest criminal case in American history, involving two trials that lasted seven years, cost at least $15 million, and concluded with no convictions. Initially these trials were seen as examples of ordinary citizens exposing horrible abuses in their midst. Over time, however, the public grew convinced that overzealous prosecutors and poorly trained social workers had bribed and badgered the children until they said they had been abused.

The McMartin Preschool case was the most sensational of forty cases involving charges of mass molestation in daycare centers. At least 100 daycare workers were convicted of abuse, but in virtually every case the prosecution claims were eventually overturned. A 1994 federal investigation of more than 12,000 accusations of ritual abuse of children at daycare centers did not find a single charge that could be physically substantiated. Why did seemingly far-fetched charges of animal mutilation, infant sacrifice, and satanic ritual provoke a wave of criminal prosecutions? In retrospect, one can see how terrified parents displaced their own anxieties and guilt feelings about leaving children with strangers onto daycare workers. Convinced that children would never lie about sexual abuse, psychologists and social workers underestimated children's suggestibility, their susceptibility to adult pressure, and their desire for adult approval. A sensationalist media and opportunistic and ambitious politicians and law enforcement officials stoked public anxiety into a frenzy. The convergence of these and other factors created parental panic.

Since the 1970s the United States has experienced a series of widely publicized panics over children's well-being. In addition to panics over abuse at daycare centers, there was widespread alarm over stranger abductions of children, adult sexual predators preying on teenage girls, and madmen inserting razor blades and poison into Halloween candies. The result was to convince many parents that their children were in deep danger. For a quarter-century adults have used the language of crisis to discuss the young. In her 1996 book *It Takes a Village,* then First Lady Hillary Rodham Clinton wrote: "Everywhere we look, children are under assault: from violence and neglect, from the breakup of families, from the temptations of alcohol, sex, and drug abuse, from greed, materialism and spiritual emptiness. These problems are not new, but in our time they have skyrocketed." In 1996 the bipartisan Council on Families in America claimed that children were worse off "psychologically, socially, economically, and morally—than their parents were at the same age." A grossly inflated and misplaced sense of crisis became widespread in the last quarter of the twentieth century, reflecting genuine worries—for example, over children's well-being in a hypersexualized society—and more generalized anxieties—over street crime, family instability, and shifts in women's roles.[3]

In the mid-1970s newspaper and magazine headlines began to trumpet a series of crises involving the young. There was a widespread impression that by most measures, young people were faring worse than in the past. On closer examination, however, much of the evidence cited to prove that children were in crisis proved to be exaggerated, misleading, or simply incorrect. An early panic followed the 1976 announcement by the Alan Guttmacher Institute, then a division of Planned Parenthood, that the country was experiencing an "epidemic" of teenage pregnancy. The report that nearly a million teenagers became pregnant each year provoked alarm that this epidemic would ruin the mother's life prospects and impose a heavy financial burden on society as a whole, raising costs for welfare, Medicaid, and food stamps. When looked at more closely, the phenomenon of teen pregnancy was far more complicated than usually portrayed. The overwhelming majority of teen births were among eighteen- and nineteen-year-olds, not the thirteen-, fourteen-, or fifteen-year-olds featured in the press. The teenage pregnancy rate had peaked in 1957 and was declining in the last quarter of the century. There were grounds for public concern, especially because a growing proportion of teen births was occurring out of wedlock. But the explanations commonly cited to explain teenage childbearing—immorality, ignorance, or ineptness in the use of contraceptives—were misleading. Teen pregnancy was connected to limited opportunity, poverty, and low self-esteem, as well as an association of childbearing with maturity and love.[4]

Soon afterward a panic over stranger abductions of young children was touched off by the mysterious disappearance of six-year-old Etan Patz in New York's SoHo district in 1979, and the murder of Adam Walsh, also six, in Florida in 1981. Published reports claimed that half a million children were kidnapped each year and as many as 50,000 were murdered annually. Soon pictures of missing children appeared on billboards and milk cartons, and the federal government established a National Center for Missing and Exploited Children. A federal investigation subsequently revealed that the actual number of children under twelve abducted by strangers was between 500 and 600 a year and the number murdered by strangers around 50. The overwhelming majority of missing children were runaways or were in the hands of noncustodial parents. It turned out that the gravest threat to children came not from strangers, but from family members or neighbors. About 2,000 children a year were murdered by their parents—400 times as many as were killed by strangers.[5]

Another panic, over youth gangs, erupted in the early 1990s, sparked by claims that gangs, armed with military-style assault weapons, were the primary agents in a crack cocaine epidemic plaguing the nation's inner cities. It was certainly the case that in particular cities during the 1980s and early 1990s, gangs accounted for a growing proportion of youth violence and that some gang members were actively involved in drug trafficking. It was also true that the easy availability of automatic and semiautomatic weapons made gang violence more lethal than in the past. But the popular image of youth gangs dominating the drug trade and spreading their tentacles across the country was grossly exaggerated. For the most part, drug trafficking was dominated by adults.[6]

Also during the 1990s a panic arose over youthful superpredators who killed without remorse. An incident in New York in 1989 and another in Chicago in 1998 seemed to confirm the existence of "kids without a conscience." In the New York case, five youths, between fourteen and sixteen years old, were accused of attacking joggers and bicyclists in Central Park and were convicted of beating a white female investment banker so badly that she was not expected to survive, but did. In 2002 their convictions were reversed after a prison inmate confessed to being the jogger's sole attacker and DNA evidence proved that he had raped the woman. In the Chicago incident, two boys, ages seven and eight, confessed to murdering eleven-year-old Ryan Harris. Further investigation revealed semen on the victim, and police eventually charged a thirty-year-old man with the crime. In both cases, confessions from the accused juveniles had been obtained by the police after prolonged interrogation.[7]

During the last quarter of the twentieth century there was a tendency to generalize about young people's well-being on the basis of certain horrific but isolated events. The literary term synecdoche—confusing a part for a whole—is helpful in understanding how late twentieth-century Americans constructed an image of youth in crisis, as shocking episodes reinforced an impression that childhood was disintegrating. Two cases from the 1990s seemed symptomatic of moral decay. In 1993, in Lakewood, California, near Los Angeles, a group of current and former high school students, known as the "Spur Posse," gained notoriety when members were arrested in connection with a "sex for points" competition. The winner had had intercourse with sixty-six girls, some as young as ten. In 1997 a New Jersey eighteen-year-old, attending her high school prom, gave birth to a baby boy in a bathroom stall, left the newborn in a garbage can, and returned to the dance floor.

These incidents were easily integrated into a popular narrative of moral decline, but in fact the lessons were more complex. The Spur Posse was connected to the downward economic mobility among families previously employed in southern California's defense industry. These circumstances contributed to unstable family lives, frequent divorces, a lack of adult supervision, and declining economic prospects for Lakewood youth. In the case of the young New Jersey woman, child psychologists spoke about the denial that some teens feel after discovering they are pregnant, their fear of disappointing their parents, and the difficulties they encounter in trying to obtain an abortion. Her decision to return to the prom and act as if nothing had happened is as pathetic as it is tragic.[8]

The late twentieth-century panics left a lasting imprint on public policy. In 1993, after twelve-year-old Polly Klaas was kidnapped during a slumber party and strangled by a California state prison parolee, states across the country enacted "three strikes" laws under which repeat offenders convicted of three felonies were sentenced to prison without possibility of parole. After the 1994 rape and murder of seven-year-old Megan Nicole Kanka of Hamilton, New Jersey, by a paroled sex offender, many states adopted "Megan's Laws," requiring the police to notify a community when a convicted sex offender lived nearby. Reports that men over the age of twenty-one were responsible for two-thirds of teen pregnancies led states to revive dormant statutory rape laws. A spate of murders by youths in their early teens led every state to make it easier to try juveniles as adults and commit them to adult prisons.[9]

Over the past quarter-century, the trumpeting of a dire crisis among the young proved to be a highly effective way to gain public attention. Whenever adults sensed that their children were in danger, they responded with passion. Sociologists use the term *moral panic* to describe the highly exaggerated and misplaced public fears that periodically arise within a society. Eras of ethical conflict and confusion are especially prone to outbreaks of moral panic as particular incidents crystallize generalized anxieties and provoke moral crusades. In recent decades, panics have arisen about Internet pornography; pedophiles; and the purported link between grunge, hip hop, and youth violence. These panics arose from legitimate worries for the safety of the young in a violent and hypersexualized society, but they were also fueled by interest groups that exploit parental fears, well-meaning social service providers, child advocacy groups, national commissions, and government agencies desperate to sustain funding and influence. If panics arise out of a genuine desire to arouse an apathetic public to serious problems, the effect of scare stories is not benign. They frighten parents, intensify generational estrangement, and encourage schools and legislatures to impose regulations to protect young people from themselves.[10]

When panics drive public policy, society tends to fixate on exaggerated problems rather than on more serious issues. During the late twentieth century there was a widespread impression that children's well-being was declining precipitously and that many of society's worst problems could be attributed to the young. According to surveys in the 1990s, adults believed that young people accounted for 40 percent of the nation's violent crime, three times the actual rate. Adults wrongly assumed that young people were more violent than their parents' generation had been and were more likely to smoke, abuse drugs and alcohol, commit suicide, become pregnant, and bear a child out of wedlock. In fact by most measures young people were healthier and more responsible than their baby-boom parents' generation.[11]

Alarmist myths about youth violence, adolescent sexuality, and declining academic performance led adults to project a variety of moral failings onto the young and bred a mistaken impression that contemporary youth were the worst generation ever. A 1997 poll reported that most adults believed that the young were in steep "moral breakdown." Today many adults assume that smoking, binge drinking, illicit drug use, obesity, and irresponsible sexual behavior are normative among the young and that adolescents are responsible for most crime in American society. Not surprisingly, such mistaken views discourage adults from supporting school bond issues and other public programs for the young.[12]

Children have long served as a lightning rod for America's anxieties about society as a whole. During the late 1940s and early 1950s, as anxiety about the Cold War deepened, many Americans doubted that the young had the moral fiber, intellectual acumen, and physical skills necessary to stand up to Communism. During the 1960s, as the nation underwent unsettling moral and cultural transformations, public worries again centered on the young, around such issues as permissive childrearing, youthful drug and sexual experimentation, and young people's scraggly hair and unkempt clothing. It is not surprising that cultural anxieties are often displaced on the young; unable to control the world around them, adults shift their attention to that which they think they can control: the next generation.

Toward the end of the twentieth century there was widespread fear that the country had entered a period of moral and economic decline as Americans worried about the country's international competitiveness, budget deficits and the national debt, and street crime. As in the past, larger social and economic concerns colored adult perceptions of children. Anxieties about unsafe streets translated into fears about youth gangs and teenage toughs. Anxieties about welfare dependency were reflected in images of teenage mothers and high school dropouts. Many adults worried that American children lagged far behind their foreign counterparts in their knowledge of science, mathematics, and technology and lacked the discipline and drive necessary to meet the challenges of the twenty-first century. Frightening media portraits of youthful nihilism supplanted earlier images of childhood innocence and teenage rambunctiousness. Kids provided society's most vivid images of urban disintegration. There was a fixation on crack babies, urban wolf packs, and teenage mothers. Bart Simpson, the irreverent, undisciplined scamp, "an underachiever and proud of it," supplanted Haley Mills as a popular symbol of childhood.

Familial, economic, and cultural shifts contributed to an upsurge in parental anxiety and to a hovering, emotionally intense style of parenting that made it more difficult for children to forge an independent identity and assert their growing maturity and competence. During the 1970s a growing number of Americans came to believe that the "breakdown of the family"—evident in an increasing divorce rate and a growing number of single-parent households and working mothers—had devastating consequences for young people's well-being, manifested in rapidly rising rates of juvenile crime, teen suicide, and substance abuse. In fact family fragility was not nearly as novel as moralists assumed, nor was the impact of changes in family structure on children's well-being as negative as many assumed.

In evaluating familial change, there is a tendency to exaggerate evidence of decline and to ignore conflicting data. Yet any accurate assessment must balance gains against costs. On the positive side of the ledger, families grew smaller, allowing parents to devote more attention and resources to each child. Attendance in preschools shot up, providing young people with opportunities for play and better preparing them for school. While fewer young children could count on a full-time mother than in the 1950s, working mothers are less likely to be depressed than stay-at-home mothers and more likely to provide valuable role models, especially for their daughters.

Divorce was a major source of concern. The number of divorces doubled between the mid-1960s and the late-1970s, before leveling off. Today nearly half of all children witness the breakup of their parents' marriage, and close to half of these children experience the breakup of a parent's second marriage. But rising divorce rates have not had the profoundly negative consequences that many feared. A substantial body of evidence suggests that conflict-laden, tension-filled marriages have at least as many adverse effects on children as divorce. Children from discordant homes permeated by tension and instability are actually more likely to suffer psychosomatic illnesses, suicide attempts, delinquency, and other social maladjustments than children whose parents divorce. Empirical evidence does not indicate that children from "broken" homes suffer more health or mental problems, personality disorders, or lower school grades than children from "intact" homes.[13]

Without a doubt, divorce is severely disruptive, at least initially, for a majority of children, and a minority continue to suffer from its psychological and economic repercussions for years after the breakup of their parents' marriage. Boys seem to have a harder time coping than girls, and younger children appear to have more trouble adjusting than older children, partly because they have excessive fears of abandonment and exaggerated hopes for reconciliation. Yet most children support their parents' decision to divorce and show resilience and increased maturity and independence in the months following the breakup.[14]

Many of the family-related problems that children confront reflect the country's failure to adjust institutionally to the fact that divorce, unmarried cohabitation, and residence, at least temporarily, in a single-parent household have become the normative experience for a near majority of American children. The American legal system has not built in sufficient safeguards to ensure children's economic well-being or to moderate the disruptions that follow divorce. Divorce is often accompanied by instability in living arrangements, less parental supervision, and loss of contact with the father's network of connections. Frequent movement between residences is a particular source of strain for children, since it complicates the problem of maintaining friendships and adjusting to school. Income decline is a major problem, resulting from the inadequacy of court-ordered child support payments, fathers' failure to pay support, and the fact that many mothers bargain away support payments in exchange for sole custody of children. But despite the stresses and upheavals that accompany divorce, a substantial majority of the young experience the breakup of their parents' marriage without suffering serious problems.[15]

Economics was a driving force behind changing family patterns. During the 1970s, in a period of prolonged inflation and economic stagnation, the maintenance of a middle-class standard of living required mothers to work and to limit births. The influx of married women into the workforce made daycare a necessity, and job opportunities meant that fewer women felt forced to remain in loveless or abusive marriages for economic reasons. Economics also contributed to the rapid increase in the proportion of births to unmarried women as self-supporting single women decided to become mothers. Meanwhile the real wages of young men in their twenties who lacked a college education fell steeply, making them less attractive as marriage partners and less willing to commit to marriage. The result was a return to a pattern common in preindustrial times, in which formal marriage was concentrated among financially secure partners and poorer families had less formal arrangements.[16]

The rising costs of childcare and college contributed to a sharp reduction in the birthrate as many parents chose to have just one child. But the trend to smaller families allowed parents and grandparents to devote more money to each child. Toygiving, which had largely been confined to birthdays and Christmas, became a year-round phenomenon. Meanwhile the service economy became increasingly dependent on part-time teenage labor, and as afterschool jobs became more common, teens had more disposable income than in the past. This income rarely went to pay for family necessities; instead it represented discretionary income that could be used to pay for a car or to purchase clothes, CDs, and snacks.

Parental anxieties greatly increased in scope and intensity after 1970 as many parents worried more than in the past about their children's safety, their vulnerability to drugs, and their academic achievement. Middle-class parents, in particular, sought to protect children from harm by baby-proofing their homes, using car seats, and requiring bicycle helmets. At the same time, the market for childrearing advice books became more crowded and confused, and these manuals conveyed a sense of urgency absent in earlier childcare books. Authorities such as Dr. Lee Salk rejected the easygoing approach championed by Dr. Spock and warned that "taking parenthood for granted can have disastrous results." The new childrearing manuals reflected a sharp rise in parents' aspirations for their children. Unlike the parents of the baby boomers, who had wanted their children to be "average," ambitious late twentieth-century parents sought to provide their children with every possible opportunity. The impulse to give children a leg up contributed to the rapid growth of educationally oriented preschools, which not only provided childcare but also sought to enhance children's cognitive, motor, language, and social skills. Meanwhile many middle-class parents filled up older children's afterschool time with lessons, enrichment activities, and organized sports. This led experts such as David Elkind to decry a tendency toward "hyperparenting," in which parents overscheduled and overprogrammed their children's free time, placing excessive pressure on their offspring and depriving them of the opportunity for free play and hanging out.[17]

In the 1970s many parents turned away from an older ideal of a "protected" childhood and began to emphasize a "prepared" childhood. Fearful that their children were surrounded by risks and dangers, parents rejected the notion that it was best to shelter children from adult realities in order to preserve their innocence. Convinced that a naïve child was a vulnerable child, a growing number supported drug abuse education programs and sex education courses that would inform their children about the risks of drugs and of sexually transmitted diseases and AIDS. Independence and resourcefulness became more highly prized values in children as a growing number of children had to learn how to unlock the side door, call their mother after school, and prepare their own snack and sometimes their own dinner.[18]

Romanticized portraits of the normality of childhood during the "golden years" earlier in the twentieth century do not hold up under scrutiny. Take the example of teen drinking. In 1954 *Better Homes and Gardens* magazine surveyed 1,000 New York high school students and found that nearly half of all the students between thirteen and eighteen reported drinking alcohol in the previous week; one in six started drinking before the age of eleven and 79 percent by fourteen. Continuity, not discontinuity, has characterized teen drinking habits. In contrast, the historical trend in teen smoking has been sharply downward, and teen smoking has declined far faster than smoking among adults. Adolescent smoking peaked in 1963, and the proportion of adolescents twelve to seventeen who smoke today is half the rate in 1974. Nor is drug use among juveniles as unprecedented as we sometimes assume. In 1953 a U.S. Senate subcommittee claimed that teenage drug abuse was an "epidemic." Adolescent drug use rose sharply between the early 1970s and early 1980s, but since then the trend has been downward. In 1983, 31 percent of high school seniors reported using an illegal drug in the past month; in 2001 the figure was 22 percent.[19]

Another widespread misimpression is that teen sexuality and delinquent behavior have increased sharply. In 2002 *U.S. News & World Report* announced in sensationalist language: "At younger ages and with greater frequency, teens are having sex—and catching more diseases." In fact the most rapid increase in adolescent sexuality took place in the 1970s, among the parents of today's high schoolers. During the 1990s teen pregnancy and abortion rates fell sharply, and sexual activity among teens declined, especially among boys. Meanwhile violent youth crime has fluctuated over the past four decades, and stands today at low levels unseen since the mid-1960s. Over the past three decades there have been surges in youthful smoking, drug use, and crime rates, but the general trend has been downward. Yet if history can be reassuring, it can also heighten awareness of troubling realities. The child poverty rate in the United States is higher today than it was three decades ago. In 2002 the official child poverty rate stood at 16 percent, about 14 percent above the lows of the early 1970s.[20]

Other problems have also persisted. Half a century ago, sex researcher

Alfred Kinsey reported that one in four women had been "approached sexually" before adolescence. About half the approaches involved exhibitionism, 31 percent involved fondling without genital contact, 29 percent involved genital fondling, and 3 percent involved rape or incest. The overall figures today remain about the same, although exhibitionism has declined and unwanted touching has increased. Yet while the sexual abuse of children has remained fairly constant, public concern has fluctuated widely. In 1986 nearly a third of adults identified abuse as one of the most serious problems facing children and youth; in a survey a decade later abuse went unmentioned.[21]

By most measures, the well-being of the young improved markedly between the early 1970s and the late 1990s, despite the sharp increase in divorce rates, working mothers, and out-of-wedlock births. Binge drinking among teenagers dropped 25 percent; smoking declined between 20 and 50 percent, depending on the measure; youth homicide and crime rates are now at their lowest level in thirty years. Today's teenagers miss fewer days of school, do about as well on aptitude and achievement tests as did their baby-boom counterparts, and are much more likely to graduate from high school and enroll in college. Surveys suggest that young people today feel far less alienation and anomie than their counterparts a quarter-century earlier. Far fewer report that they have seriously considered suicide or participated in a fight.[22]

Our society tends to treat young people's problems separately from those of adults, as if they were not interconnected phenomena. We hold youth to perfectionist standards that adults are not expected to meet. In fact young people's behavior tends to parallel that of adults. Over the last quarter of the twentieth century, trends in child obesity, teenage drug use, smoking, drinking, out-of-wedlock births, crime, and violence track closely with adults'. This result should not be surprising. Young people tend to behave much like the adults around them, and if those adults smoke or drink to excess or behave violently, their children are likely to do the same.[23]

In the late twentieth century, American society projected its fears and anxieties onto the young and instituted desperate measures to protect them from exaggerated menaces. The effect of these restrictive policies was to delay the transition to adult behavior and make that transition much more abrupt than in the past. Thus it seems likely that the problem with binge drinking among college students is related to the fact that the young did not learn to drink responsibly before college. Efforts to protect the young from the consequences of misbehavior tend to create problems of their own.

Media images of the young proliferated wildly in the last quarter of the century. There were "stoners," like Bill and Ted, whose *Excellent Adventures* mocked schooling and academic authority; bright but mischievous rebels like Ferris Bueller; and girls with special powers like Sabrina the teenage witch, a popular symbol of girls' empowerment. There were precocious miniadults, wiser than their parents, modeled on Michael J. Fox in the situation comedy *Family Ties;* symbols of juvenile self-sufficiency like Macauley Caulkin in the *Home Alone* films; and comic nerds like the Steve Erkel character played by Jaleel White. But one image of childhood that didn't conform to the media's penchant for the lighthearted comedy was an image of deeply alienated and disconnected youth.

Many of the most influential cinematic portraits of youth during the 1980s and 1990s painted a bleak picture of young people's lives, depicting them as "a tribe apart." Teen angst, youthful alienation, and generational estrangement have been common themes in film since *The Wild One* (1954), but more recent movies offered a grimmer vision. The 1987 film *River's Edge* was based loosely on a 1981 murder in Milpitas, California, where a sixteen-year-old raped and murdered his fourteen-year-old girlfriend, bragged about the killing to his friends, and took them to see the corpse. As in *Lord of the Flies,* the kids were presented as zombielike in the face of a blood-chilling crime. A depressing portrait of youthful nihilism in the Reagan era, the film depicts the teens' emotional numbness as a product of drugs, alcohol, television violence, deafening rock music, violent video games, and neglectful parents.

The 1995 film *Kids* followed a group of vacuous New York street children over a twenty-four-hour period, hanging out, skateboarding, stealing, brawling, gay-baiting, and getting high. Like *River's Edge,* it presented a picture of young people turning to drugs and sex not as a form of rebellion, but as a way to fill a void in otherwise empty and meaningless lives. *Kids* depicted young people living in a world of insecurity and risk from unprotected sex, sexually transmitted diseases, and violence. *Basketball Diaries,* also from 1995, based loosely on poet and musician Jim Carroll's cult memoir, chronicled the descent of a Catholic high school basketball star into a heroin addict who turns tricks for drugs. With its stark portraits of a sadistic priest and a sexually predatory basketball coach, this film stressed the allure of drugs and sex and the absence of supportive adults. Crude, stereotyped, and exploitative, these films reinforced a variety of caricatures about young people's lives. They supported the popular impression that young people were caught between two trends: an increasingly risky, violent, sex-saturated, drug-infested social environment, and a lack of adult guidance and support.

What, then, has changed in young people's lives? How did childhood in the late twentieth century differ from that in earlier years? Books with such titles as *The Disappearance of Childhood, The Hurried Child: Growing Up Too Fast Too Soon,* and *Ready or Not: Why Treating Children as Small Adults Endangers Their Future—and Ours* argued that an earlier ideal of childhood as a protected state, in which children were sheltered from the realities of the adult world, had given way to a very different ideal. We have returned, they contended, to the pre-industrial, premodern conception of children as "little adults." There is some truth to this argument. Young people, even before they enter their teens, are increasingly knowledgeable about adult realities. Through the instruments of mass culture, the young are exposed from an early age to overt sexuality, violence, and death. They have also become independent consumers at an earlier age. A precocious adulthood is apparent in young people's dress, their earlier initiation into sexuality, and the large number of students who hold jobs while going to school. Like their preindustrial counterparts, young people linger longer on the threshold of adulthood, delaying marriage and, in many cases, living off and on with their parents well into their twenties. Yet despite some superficial similarities, we have not returned to the premodern world of childhood and youth. We are much more self-conscious about the process of childrearing. Like our nineteenth-century ancestors, we continue to think of young people as fundamentally different from adults. Above all, we have institutionalized youth as a separate stage of life. Young people spend an increasing number of years in the company of other people their same age, colonized in specialized "age-graded" institutions. Young people's interactions with adults are largely limited to parents, teachers, and service providers.[24]

One defining feature of young people's lives today is that they spend more time alone than their predecessors. They grow up in smaller families, and nearly half have no siblings. They are more likely to have a room of their own and to spend more time in electronically mediated activities, playing video games, surfing the Internet, or watching television on their own set. Because fewer children attend neighborhood schools within walking distance, most children live farther from their friends and play with them less frequently, experiencing a greater sense of isolation.[25]

Meanwhile unstructured, unsupervised free play outside the home drastically declined for middle-class children. As more mothers joined the labor force, parents arranged more structured, supervised activities for their children. Unstructured play and outdoor activities for children three to eleven declined nearly 40 percent between the early 1980s and late 1990s. Because of parental fear of criminals and bad drivers, middle-class children rarely got the freedom to investigate and master their home turf in ways that once proved a rehearsal for the real world. Older children, too, had less free time as they spent more time in school, completing homework, performing household chores, and working for wages. The psychiatrist Bruno Bettelheim estimated that the span of a middle-class childhood, defined in terms of freedom from household responsibilities, declined from eleven years in the 1950s to between five and eight years toward the end of the century.[26]

The period of childhood innocence has grown briefer. Originally Barbie was aimed at six- to ten-year-old girls. Today her popularity peaks with three- to five-year-olds. By the time girls are eight, frilly dresses have given way to midriff tops, off-shoulder T-shirts, and low-slung jeans. Marketers coined the word *tween* to describe the demographic group from eight to twelve, which has not yet reached the teen years but aspires to teenage sophistication. In an era of niche marketing, the tweens—whose average weekly income rose from $6 to $22 a week during the 1990s—became one of the most popular markets for clothing manufacturers and record companies.[27]

The geography of young people's lives has been reshaped. Much of the "free space" available to youth in the past, from empty lots to nearby woods, has disappeared as a result of development and legal liability concerns. Public playgrounds continue to exist; but as they were childproofed to improve safety, they inadvertently reduced the opportunities for the young to take part in forms of fantasy, sensory and exploratory play, and construction activities apart from adults. Safety and maintenance concerns led to the removal of sandboxes and swings, metal jungle gyms, and firepoles. Fear of child abductions and sexual abuse resulted in the elimination of playgrounds with obstructed views. Meanwhile many traditional teen hangouts also vanished. McDonald's pioneered the practice of discouraging teens from hanging out at their restaurants, and this practice has since been mimicked by other fast-food outlets, pizza parlors, ice cream shops, and other traditional teen havens. Lacking spaces to call their own, adolescents engaged in frequent battles with adults as they sought space at shopping malls, fast-food restaurants, and public streets.[28]

One of the most striking developments was a sharp increase in part-time teenage employment during the school years. Today about 44 percent of sixteen- and seventeen-year-old males and 42 percent of females hold jobs, compared with 29 percent of boys and 18 percent of girls in 1953. In the past, teen employment was concentrated among the working class; it has since become predominantly a middle-class phenomenon. Most teens work in sales and service jobs requiring no special training or skills and spend most of their time working with other adolescents, without much adult supervision.[29]

Meanwhile a ritual that defined teen life in the past—dating—largely disappeared, replaced by hanging out at malls, participation in crowd activities, group dating, partying, and hooking up. Older symbols of commitment—like pinning or going steady—evaporated, mirroring the desire to postpone marriage to a later age as well as the general decline of marriage among adults. But of all the changes that took place in young people's lives, the most striking involved a marked increase in diversity—ethnic, economic, and familial. Ethnic diversity became a defining characteristic of childhood. Sixteen percent of young people are black (compared with 14 percent in 1972), 15 percent Hispanic (up from 6 percent), and 5 percent Asian (up from 1 percent). Diversity extends to family life. Between a quarter and a third of the children born during the baby boomlet of the late 1980s and 1990s were born to unmarried mothers, and about half of all children will spend at least part of their childhood in a single-parent home. This familial shift was accompanied by a deepening economic divide. Children born in recent years are the most affluent in

Children at play in Brooklyn's Bedford-Stuyvesant neighborhood in 1974. Courtesy of the National Archives, Washington, D.C.

American history—yet one in six lives in poverty. Reinforcing the sense of diversity is the fact that the generation of young today has not had the binding social or economic experiences that fostered an intense generational consciousness among the baby boomers or Depression kids.

The most popular children's names provide an index to society's increasing diversity. While the Roberts and Susans of earlier generations persisted, new names were added to the cultural stew. There was a sharp increase in gender-neutral names, such as Alex and Leslie, and feminized versions of boys' names, such as Sydney and Kari; in unusual and original names stressing children's uniqueness and individuality, such as Beyonce and LeToya; and in Waspy names with overtones of wealth and glamor, such as Kendall and Taylor. The most striking development was a proliferation of names exhibiting pride in ethnic heritage, including a surge in biblical names like Samuel and Rebecca, and, especially among African Americans, traditional African and Islamic names such as Jamail and Yasmin, as well as newly coined names that draw upon African patterns, such as Makayla and Nyasia.

Youth in America has never been a homogeneous or monolithic group. It has always been divided along lines of class, ethnicity, and gender. But as the twentieth century ended, these divisions, which appeared, at least superficially, to be declining, reasserted themselves. Two of the most crucial divides involved the children of the urban poor and the children of immigrants. Both demand closer examination.

Growing up in the ghetto has never been easy, but for two brothers caught in the crossfire of the crack epidemic of the late 1980s it was especially bleak. Eleven-year-old Lafeyette and nine-year-old Pharoah Rivers lived in the Henry Horner housing project on Chicago's near west side, a mile from the Sears Tower. Consisting of sixteen high-rise buildings on thirty-four acres of concrete eight city blocks long, the complex housed 6,000 residents; 4,000 were under eighteen. Grim and dilapidated, Henry Horner Homes was plagued by violence. One person was beaten, shot at, or stabbed at the project every three days during the summer of 1987. Kids played basketball by shooting the ball through an opening in a jungle gym.[30]

Children in the Chicago projects, observed a teenager, were "like M & M's—all hard on the outside and sweet on the inside." Tough, swaggering, and ruthless on the outside, because "if they see you're soft in the projects it's like a shark seeing blood," and on the inside, vulnerable, frightened, and lost. The Rivers family subsisted on a $931 monthly welfare check, supplemented by odd jobs the boys picked up. Their apartment, infested with cockroaches, had iron bars on the windows, rusted-out metal cabinets, and a faucet that leaked scalding water into the bath-tub for two years before the housing authority finally repaired it. The boys' father, an unemployed bus driver, was addicted to heroin and alcohol. An older sister was also a drug addict. One brother was in jail, and another had been arrested forty-six times before his eighteenth birthday. In a single year, the boys' mother was mugged, the family lost its welfare benefits, and Lafeyette was arrested for breaking into a truck and stealing cassettes. Speaking of his future, Lafeyette said: "If I grow up, I would like to be a bus driver." "If," not "when."[31]

Inner-city Chicago was not the only place where American children were exposed to poverty and violence. Even at the height of the economic boom of the late 1990s, a sixth of young people (and 30 percent of black children and 28 percent of Hispanic children) lived in poverty; children were almost twice as likely to live in poverty as any other age group. Navigating the road to adulthood has never been easy, but it is particularly difficult in the "other America," where children grow up amid the blight of joblessness and discrimination. Imprisoned by stereotypes, minimal expectations in school, and inadequate resources, children in the nation's ghettos quickly learn that society perceives them as potential criminals or welfare recipients. Constituting about 13 percent of the urban population, the residents of the neighborhoods where poverty is concentrated loom far larger in the public imagination, in part because these areas produce more than half of all those arrested for murder, rape, and nonnegligent manslaughter.[32]

In his classic study of St. Louis's now-demolished Pruitt-Igoe housing project, the Harvard sociologist Lee Rainwater argued that poverty and racism produced a very different world of childhood from that found in middle-class communities. Crowded ghetto conditions as well as the small size of slum apartments made it impossible to create a child-centered home or to insulate young children from adult activities. Children in Pruitt-Igoe grew up in a highly stimulating environment where they frequently interacted with other adults, including many nonfamily members, and were expected to become socially assertive and socially self-confident at an early age. Mothers in Pruitt-Igoe did not worry about when their children began to crawl or walk or talk; their concerns were more immediate: to ensure that their children were safe and adequately fed.[33]

Girls were expected to take part in household activities such as cooking, cleaning, and caring for babies, and therefore quickly assumed a recognized and valued family identity. As children grew older, it often proved difficult to protect them from the troublemaking possibilities of the outside world. Lacking the resources to insulate children from trouble, adults made greater use of physical punishment and cautionary horror stories as control mechanisms than their middle-class counterparts. Childrearing methods that might appear harsh by middle-class standards sought to prepare children for a more dangerous environment. As children reached adolescence, some parents stopped closely monitoring their children to protect themselves from what they might discover. In other instances, extended relatives formed supportive networks and offered close supervision to help adolescents negotiate a dangerous passage to adulthood. An overriding problem facing Pruitt-Igoe's youth was the hostility that they received from the outside world: the stares, the suspicion, the repeated reminders that authority figures neither trusted nor respected them.

What, then, is it like to grow up in America's poorest neighborhoods? All the challenges of growing up are compounded by poverty and unstable kinship structures. Temptations and dangers—from alcohol, drugs, gangs, and casual violence—lurk around young people. Isolated from mainstream society, many lack successful role models to guide them through the minefields of youth and instill a sense of their potential. When they are young, many mothers forbid them to go out to play, considering it too dangerous. They grow up with a sense of confinement, unfamiliar to suburban children. They inhabit a world where childhood mischief can lead to arrest or worse. They learn, from an early age, that they must be careful never to say or do anything that older youths might take as an insult. They quickly find out that there are places where they cannot go without provoking hostile stares and nervous glances.[34]

Their lives do not conform to the script of television mythology. Their kinship relationships are much more expansive, with an extended family of aunts, uncles, cousins, and grandparents who feel responsible for them. Ties between children and their mothers tend to be exceptionally strong; relationships with fathers are often complicated and conflicted. Contrary to the stereotype of uncaring, absent fathers, numerous fathers spend significant time with their offspring in infancy and early childhood, but many become disconnected after a few years.[35]

By middle-class standards, children in inner-city neighborhoods have to grow up fast. From an early age, boys and girls are expected to be housekeepers, nannies, protectors, and providers. The money they contribute, however little, offers a crucial margin of difference for their families. Some, convinced that they have no future, give in to immediacy, seeing no reason to resist the lure and profit of gangs or early pregnancy. Gangs offer some boys a missing source of employment, respect, and identity. Motherhood offers some girls the same. While overall school dropout rates have dropped sharply, 40 to 50 percent of youth drop out in the nation's most distressed inner-city neighborhoods. Youth unemployment rates in such areas stand at 40 to 60 percent, three times the rate in 1960. While labor force participation of white men and women under twenty-four has risen, the rate for poor black and Hispanic teenagers has fallen. Altogether, half of all inner-city youth have never held a regular job by their twenty-fifth birthday. Joblessness and school failure, in turn, contribute to rates of teen pregnancy and juvenile delinquency that are the nation's highest. The strongest predictors of teenage motherhood are poverty, poor reading skills, and school failure. Similarly, poor academic performance and a lack of job prospects have produced the nation's highest juvenile crime rate. By the age of thirty, over a third of all inner-city males have been in a youth facility or a jail or placed on probation.[36]

But despite popular stereotypes of ghetto pathology, most inner-city residents resist the temptations of crime, drug abuse, or teenage pregnancy. Indeed, inner-city youth drink less, smoke less, and use drugs less than their suburban middle-class counterparts. One factor that has contributed to this pattern is the strength of black mothers, who serve as models and nurturers of strong and independent behavior. Socialization among African Americans historically has not emphasized sex-role dichotomies in the way found among white families, and as a result many young black women, even in the poorest neighborhoods, have higher aspirations for education and a career than many of their white counterparts.[37]

Like their inner-city counterparts, the children of immigrants experience intense challenges as they find their way toward adulthood. Like earlier immigrant children, Esmeralda Santiago faced daunting and painful cultural adjustments. But unlike previous immigrants, her desire to assimilate clashed with an equally intense desire to maintain her cultural identity. Her family called her Negi, short for Negrita, "our dear little dark one." Born in a Puerto Rican barrio in 1948, the eldest of eleven children, she moved at the age of four to the town of Macun, where her family crowded into a one-room corrugated metal house on stilts. Each morning she awoke to a radio program that celebrated traditional *jibaro* music and poetry. She later wrote poignant descriptions of incidents in her life in rural Puerto Rico, including a custom in which she had to close a dead infant's eyelids to let the deceased child rest peacefully.[38]

In 1961 she, her mother, and six siblings arrived in Brooklyn. Her mother, seeking medical help for a son who had injured his foot, was also trying to escape an unhappy marriage, and supported the family by sewing bras. In Brooklyn Esmeralda's family struggled with a difficult and sometimes frightening social environment. None spoke a word of English, and Esmeralda encountered many instances of discrimination.

Taxi drivers refused to pick her up, people of a variety of ethnic groups treated her as a foreigner, and even Puerto Ricans born in New York kept their distance. When she enrolled in public school, the principal wanted to move her back a grade, and when she refused, he placed her in a class for learning-disabled students.

Compared with turn-of-the-century immigrant children, Esmeralda felt much more ambivalence about becoming American. She vividly recalled going to the Bushwick branch of the Brooklyn Public Library, seeking any book written by an author with a Spanish name. The closest she came was to a volume of poetry by William Carlos Williams. "The more I read, the more I realized that people like me didn't exist in English language literature," she said. "The feeling was that I wasn't wanted here. Otherwise, I would be reflected in the culture." She discovered that assimilation involved much more than learning the English language. She studied Archie comic books to understand the way American girls dressed and talked, and envied Veronica, who had fancy clothes and a car.[39]

Like earlier immigrant children, she had to assume adult responsibilities at an early age. Barely able to speak English, she translated for her mother at meetings with a welfare agent. Every few months her family moved, in search of lower rent or larger rooms. She received conflicting and confusing messages from her family. She was told to strive to get ahead, but not to leave other family members behind. Her mother warned her to be wary of men, and did not allow her to have male friends. At the High School for the Performing Arts in Manhattan, however, Esmeralda encountered a diverse, multicultural environment. She performed classical Indian dance and portrayed Cleopatra in a play. When she returned to Puerto Rico after thirteen years of living in the United States, Puerto Ricans told her that she wasn't Puerto Rican "because I was, according to them, Americanized." But she continued to feel a deep sense of uncertainty about whether she was black or white, rural or urban, Puerto Rican or American. Her experience was shared by innumerable other immigrant children caught between two cultures, neither of which they can identify fully as their own.

Today the number of immigrant children is at an all-time high. A fifth of all young people in the United States are the children of immigrants—either immigrants themselves or the U.S.-born children of immigrant parents. In New York City and Los Angeles, about half of all school children are the children of immigrants. Nationwide about four million children have limited English proficiency. The current surge in immigration followed enactment of the Hart-Cellar Immigration Reform Act of 1965, which ended a quota system that severely restricted immigration from

A young Cuban refugee enters the United States in 1961 following the Cuban Revolution. Under Operation Pedro Pan, the largest child refugee program in the history of the Western Hemisphere, more than 7,000 children arrived in the United States unaccompanied by their parents. Courtesy of the Florida Photographic Collection, Florida State Archives, Tallahassee.

outside northern and western Europe, and instead emphasized the principle of family reunification. Today's immigrant children are predominantly Asian, Caribbean, and Hispanic, and face racial barriers that did not exist for their European predecessors, as well as economic barriers that limit their economic prospects. A century ago the children of European immigrants joined an expanding American industrial workforce; today's second generation finds a stagnating job market with limited prospects for advancement for those without a college degree.[40]

For many children, the immigrant journey exacted a high cost. Many immigrants fled economic or political upheavals in their country of birth, and immigration entailed family separation, either because parents migrated ahead of the children or because the children were sent to the United States first. Altogether, only about 20 percent of immigrant children arrived in the United States with their entire immediate family. Family reunification often proved to be a prolonged, tension-filled experience, complicated by the fact that many immigrant parents hold multiple jobs, and thus have less time to interact with their children.[41]

In certain respects the experiences of immigrant children at the end of the twentieth century mirrored those at the century's start. Many immigrant fathers suffer a sharp loss in status following migration, as they have to take on low-prestige jobs to support their families, diminishing their authority over their children. Role reversal remains quite common, as children must serve as cultural and linguistic interpreters, but also very unsettling. Lan Cao, a Vietnamese immigrant who arrived in the United States at the age of thirteen, explained: "I was the one who would help my mother through the hard scrutiny of ordinary life." She, like other children of immigrants, had to assume adult responsibilities quickly: "I would have to forgo the luxury of adolescent experiments and temper tantrums, so that I could scoop my mother out of harm's way." As in earlier generations of immigrant families, the experiences of boys and girls diverged. Girls assumed greater domestic responsibilities as translators, as intermediaries in financial, legal, and medical transactions, and as babysitters, and were more likely to face restrictions on dating and other activities outside the home. One unexpected consequence of those restrictions was that immigrant girls viewed school as a liberation, unlike many nonimmigrants, who considered school a form of detention.[42]

Unlike early twentieth-century immigrants' children, who felt they had to reject the Old World to get ahead in the new, many contemporary immigrant children feel less eager to assimilate and less pressure to reject their cultural traditions. Foreign-language television shows, newspapers, magazines, radio talk shows, and the Internet allow immigrant children to maintain regular contact with family and friends in their country of birth. Some groups are able to sustain their native language at high rates, including about 70 percent of Haitian-American and Filipino-American children. Nevertheless, like second-generation immigrants of a century ago, immigrant children encounter the humbling experiences of learning English and of generational tensions with elders who find American culture profoundly alienating. For today's immigrant children, the process of adjustment is made all the more difficult by a sense of a profound gap with American-born children, who seem preoccupied with boyfriends, clothes, and the latest fads.

The lives of children of immigrants involve a paradox. On the one hand, they are healthier than nonimmigrant children, even though more than a quarter do not have a regular source of health care. Immigrant children also work harder in school than do nonimmigrant children, and are overrepresented as high school valedictorians. Yet the more Americanized these children become, the more likely they are to engage in risky behavior, such as smoking, drinking, using illegal drugs, engaging in unprotected sex, joining gangs, or committing crime. This trend seems to be related not only to the impoverished neighborhoods that many immigrant children live in, but also to the social expectations that children of immigrants encounter, especially the preconception that they are of lower intelligence or are dangerous. Some immigrant children who feel themselves marginalized and disparaged respond by embracing an adversarial identity, hostile to authority and school achievement. At the same time, many find themselves forced into preexisting American racial and ethnic categories, required to choose between being white, black, Asian, or Hispanic.[43]

During the last quarter of the twentieth century, many of the most divisive domestic policy issues, from gun control to the Internet, were debated in terms of their impact upon children. Images of fragile and vulnerable children, unable to assert their needs or defend their interests, gave legislative proposals a moral weight that they would otherwise have lacked. During the 1970s, liberals and conservatives discovered that child endangerment was a highly effective way to mobilize political support. It was a liberal, Marian Wright Edelman, the first black woman admitted to the Mississippi bar, who pioneered the politics of child advocacy by founding the Children's Defense Fund in 1973. Recognizing that support for programs identified with racial minorities and the poor was dwindling, she concluded that "new ways had to be found to articulate and respond to the continuing problems of poverty and race, ways that appealed to the self-interest as well as the conscience of the American people." By shifting the focus from poverty to children, she sought to generate support for childcare, child nutrition, and child health programs during a period of conservative ascendancy. Among the successes that can be attributed to lobbying by the Children's Defense Fund were an expansion of Head Start, prekindergarten, and afterschool programs; the Earned Income Tax Credit (a refundable federal income tax credit for low-income families enacted in 1975 to offset social security taxes and provide an incentive to work); the 1993 Family and Medical Leave Act, providing unpaid parental leaves; and the 1997 Children's Health Insurance Program, which furnishes health insurance to children in families with incomes too high to qualify for Medicaid but too low to afford private insurance.[44]

Social conservatives and political moderates quickly discovered that they could use the politics of childhood for their own purposes. Many policies they proposed in children's name proved to be highly restrictive. Convinced that it was politically counterproductive to regulate adult behavior, legislators imposed regulations on the young, including curfews, curbs on smoking and drinking, competency testing in schools, and more restrictive policies on teenage driving. Meanwhile school boards instituted dress codes, especially in middle schools, and zero-tolerance policies on drug use and school violence. A few mandated random drug tests for students engaged in extracurricular activities.

One of the most contentious issues was whether to fund daycare for the children of working mothers. The issue of how to care for children when their mothers worked burst onto the political agenda in 1964, when a Department of Labor study counted almost a million "latchkey" children who were unsupervised for large portions of the day. Over the years, their numbers skyrocketed. From the mid-1960s to the mid-1970s, the number of working mothers with children five or under who worked outside the home tripled. Today two-thirds of all children under the age of six have a mother who works, more than three out of every five children under the age of four are in a regularly scheduled childcare program, and nearly half of all one-year-olds spend part of their day in nonparental care. As the number of working mothers grew, many family experts advocated organized daycare programs as a necessary response.[45]

Liberals, led by Democratic Senator Walter Mondale, called for a national system of comprehensive child development and daycare centers. Building on the model of Head Start, Mondale proposed in 1971 that the federal government establish a care system that would include daycare, nutritional aid for pregnant mothers, and afterschool programs for teens. President Richard Nixon vetoed the bill in a stinging message that called the proposal fiscally irresponsible, administratively unworkable, and a threat to "diminish both parental authority and parental involvement with children." Tapping into the widespread view that childcare was a parental responsibility, the president warned against committing "the vast authority of the national government to the side of communal approaches to child rearing over against the family-centered approach."[46]

Following the presidential veto, congressional support for a comprehensive system of federally funded centers evaporated. Nevertheless, a fragmentary patchwork emerged, consisting of ad-hoc, makeshift arrangements by individual parents; informal, family-style care in private homes; and a wide variety of nonprofit and for-profit centers. This crazy-quilt included regulated and unregulated and custodial and educationally oriented programs. In the United States, childcare is thought of primarily as a family responsibility, whereas in Europe it is regarded as a public responsibility. Yet despite ingrained hostility toward state intervention in the family, public involvement in childcare gradually increased. Direct federal funding was restricted almost exclusively to the poor and to military personnel, but the federal government also indirectly subsidized childcare through grants to organizations that operate daycare centers as well as through tax incentives and credits to individual families. In contrast, corporate support for childcare for their employees has remained negligible, with about 5 percent of employees eligible for corporate childcare benefits. In 2000, forty-three states provided part-time prekindergarten programs, usually targeted at four-year-olds.

While most parents say that they are satisfied with the care that their children receive, expert studies have concluded that the care is of poor or mediocre quality for half of children in childcare arrangements. The most significant problem is inequality of access to educationally oriented programs, with 75 percent of the three- to five-year-olds of wealthier parents and only 45 percent of those of low-income parents in such programs. Other problems include the low status and pay of childcare workers, minimal standards for training, high staff turnover, prohibitive fees, and widely varied, loosely enforced regulations..

The politics of childhood has focused less on practical policies like childcare than on regulating children's lives. In 1970 Dr. Arnold Hutschnecker, who had once served as Richard M. Nixon's personal physician, recommended that the president order psychological testing for all seven- and eight-year-olds in order to determine whether they had "violent and homicidal tendencies." Disturbed, angry, rebellious, undisciplined, and disruptive children were to receive therapy from counselors and psychologists in afterschool programs and special camps. Dr. Hutschnecker's proposal was greeted with horror; critics labeled the treatment centers "concentration camps." While nothing like Dr. Hutschnecker's proposal for universal psychological testing has been implemented, there have been expanded efforts over the past three decades to intervene in children's behavior at an early age. These included greatly expanded use of psychotropic drugs such as Ritalin, not only among older children but also among preschoolers. There is also increased use of "sex-offense-specific" therapies directed at "children with sexual behavior problems," under which children as young as two have been diagnosed and treated for inappropriate behavior such as fondling or masturbating compulsively. The most pronounced trend was toward imposing new kinds of restraints and controls on the young.[47]

More than forty years ago, social critic Edgar Z. Friedenberg wrote that adults' hostility toward youth—"rooted in fear of disorder, and loss of control; fear of aging, and envy of life not yet squandered"—was often disguised as efforts to help the young. Friedenberg's comment provides an insight into the way society has addressed children's welfare since the early 1970s. Convinced that adult behaviors were deeply entrenched and not susceptible to change, persuaded that most problem behaviors take root in the early years of life, policymakers and advocacy groups focused on changing young people's behavior. This approach allowed authorities to address pervasive social problems without alienating adult voters. More disturbingly, focusing on youth provided a thinly veiled way to target minority and lower-income youths without provoking widespread outcries of racism or class bias. This "tough love" approached seemed to offer a commonsense solution to social problems. But if the ostensible goal was to ensure young people's safety and well-being, zero-tolerance policies also sent the message that young people's needs were subordinate to those of adults.[48]

In 1994 two boys, aged ten and eleven, attacked five-year-old Eric Morse in a Chicago public housing project because he had refused to steal candy for them from a local supermarket. The boys stabbed him, sprayed him with Mace, and pushed him downstairs before dangling him out a fourteenth-floor window and dropping him to his death. At the time the two boys were the youngest people in American history to be jailed for murder, but they were not isolated examples of "kids killing kids." At least ten youths, twelve or younger, were charged with murder in Chicago in 1993 and 1994. In the weeks following the boys' arrest, additional facts came to light that helped explain the factors that predisposed them to violence, including troubled families, neglectful schools, and law enforcement authorities who had failed to do their job. Both had fathers in prison, and one boy's mother was a drug addict. Both grew up surrounded by violence. Although one boy had skipped classes for much of the year and had failed all his courses, he had been promoted to the next grade. Finally, in the six months before Eric's murder, one of the boys had been arrested eight times, including once for possession of ammunition, but was released each time, even though Chicago police guidelines mandated a referral to a juvenile court after three arrests.[49]

The murder of Eric Morse raised troubling questions. Should ten- and eleven-year-olds be held culpable for serious crimes? What should be done about children who are deeply troubled and are at risk of growing into violent adults? In the wake of the Morse murder and a 1996 case in which a six-year-old Richmond, California, boy pulled a one-month-old baby from his crib and kicked, punched, and beat the infant with a broomstick, every state moved to prosecute as adults juveniles who committed serious crimes, such as murder, armed robbery, and burglary. By being placed in the adult justice system, juveniles would receive stiffer sentences and be jailed under harsher conditions. Some jurisdictions adopted laws preventing juvenile court records from being expunged and requiring that schools be notified whenever a juvenile was taken into custody for a crime of violence or when a deadly weapon was used. Meanwhile, many increased minimum sentences for juvenile offenders, and at least three states automatically tried delinquents with three previous convictions as adults.[50]

During the 1996 presidential campaign, President Bill Clinton urged cities to enact curfew laws to keep teenagers off the streets at night to reduce youth violence. "We simply cannot go into the 21st century with children having children, children killing children, children being raised by other children or raising themselves on the streets alone," he told 10,000 African-American church women. Curfews, he maintained, "give parents a tool to impart discipline, respect and rules at an awkward and difficult time in children's lives." At the time he made this speech, 146 of the 200 largest cities had curfews to keep youths off the street after dark.[51]

Clinton also called for other measures to reassert discipline and increase adults' authority. These included requiring school uniforms in elementary and middle schools; establishing a television rating system that used letters like *V* for violence and *S* for sex; preventing the movie, music, and video-game industries from marketing violent, sexually explicit products to children; requiring libraries to install filtering software on Internet-accessible computers; and placing "V-chips" in television sets to allow parents to block offensive programming. He also urged school districts to adopt "zero-tolerance" policies on illicit drug use, smoking, and violence to restore "order in our children's lives." The president portrayed these ideas as neither too coercive nor too strict. Young people needed to know that "these rules are being set by people who love them and care about them and desperately want them to have good lives." Like other measures that President Clinton took on behalf of parents and children—such as unpaid leave for teacher conferences and doctors' appointments, minimum hospital stays for childbearing, and a ban on tobacco ads aimed at the young—these had an activist flavor but required no new federal government spending. For a president accused of a pot-smoking, draft-evading, womanizing past, talking tough on values provided some rhetorical insulation from conservative attacks.[52]

In 1985 an elementary school in Oakland, California, launched an antidrug, antialcohol campaign with a simple message: "Just Say No." This campaign, which drew national attention after it gained vocal support from First Lady Nancy Reagan, was one of a number of efforts to alter youthful behavior through education. D.A.R.E., Drug Abuse Resistance Education, founded in Los Angeles in 1983 by then Police Chief Darryl Gates, was another. In nearly 70 percent of the nation's school districts, police officers lead classroom lessons on ways to resist peer pressure and live drug and violence-free lives. Usually in the fifth grade, students are asked to sign a pledge that they will keep their bodies drug free, despite the fact that no scientific study has uncovered any statistically significant difference in drug usage rates between students who had taken D.A.R.E. and those who had not.[53]

Similar efforts urged young people to say no to sex. The 1996 Welfare Reform Act earmarked $50 million a year in federal funds for states implementing programs that had as their "exclusive purpose, teaching the social, psychological and health gains" of sexual abstinence. In order to receive funding, the "exclusive purpose" of sex education must be to teach "that a mutually faithful monogamous relationship in the context of marriage is the expected standard of human sexual activity" and "that sexual activity outside of the context of marriage is likely to have harmful psychological and physical effects." Schools that received these grants had to teach abstinence as the only reliable way to prevent pregnancy and sexually transmitted diseases. Grant recipients were not to discuss contraception except in the context of failure rates of condoms. Supporters claimed that abstinence education helped youngsters develop the skills to "say no to sex." Critics noted that in a society in which half of high school students and three-fifths of high school seniors report having had intercourse, the abstinence-only approach failed to provide them with the information they needed about sexually transmitted diseases and contraception. By 1999 nearly a quarter of all sex education teachers taught abstinence as the only way of preventing pregnancy and sexually transmitted diseases, compared with just 2 percent in 1988.[54]

To buttress the "just say no" programs, many schools implemented zero-tolerance rules that mandated expulsion, denial of a diploma, or loss of a driver's license if a high school student smoked, drank, or used drugs. In North Carolina, teen smokers could be fined up to $1,000, and in Florida, Minnesota, and Texas, teen smokers could lose their driver's licenses. No empirical evidence has shown these programs to be effective in inoculating the young against substance abuse or premature sex. For a significant number of adolescents, risky behavior is a way to assert their individuality, define an identity, rebel against authority and conventionality, and symbolize their initiation into adulthood. Given that our society offers few positive, socially valued ways for the young to demonstrate their growing competence and independence, it is not surprising that many embrace these symbols of maturity.[55]

In the spring of 1993 national media focused on first-grader Jonathan Previte, who kissed a girl on the cheek at his North Carolina school. The principal, upon being informed of Jonathan's kiss, decided that he should be punished under the school's sexual harassment policy. The school subsequently retreated from the sexual harassment label, yet its initial response generated a media frenzy citing "political correctness" run amok. That same year, LaShonda Davis, a fifth-grader in Monroe County, Georgia, was harassed for five months by a boy who rubbed up against her, repeatedly grabbed her breasts and genital area, and asked her for sex. She and her mother complained to school officials to no avail. It took three months of daily requests before the boy was moved to another desk, and LaShonda was so depressed that she wrote a suicide note. The harassment ended only after she and her mother swore out a criminal warrant against the boy, who pleaded guilty to sexual battery. The family then sued the school district, claiming that its failure to take any action to stop the pervasive and damaging harassment violated Title IX, the federal law that prohibits schools from discriminating on the basis of sex. In 1999 the Supreme Court ruled in LaShonda's behalf, holding that when a school is deliberately indifferent to "severe, pervasive, and objectively offensive" harassment, a student has the right to compensation.[56]

Jonathan and LaShonda served as proxies in a broader culture war, a struggle over gender roles, abortion, homosexuality, and censorship that raged from the early 1970s to the late 1990s. School vouchers, charter schools, Internet filtering software, and abstinence-only sex education served as battlegrounds. Even potty training could become fodder in this *Kulturkampf*. John Rosemond, a North Carolina psychologist and a popular conservative writer on childrearing, attacked the pediatrician T. Berry Brazelton, whom he accused of adopting a "laissez-faire" approach to toilet training. Rosemond insisted that properly disciplined children needed to be toilet trained by the age of two.[57]

Child discipline was a central arena of conflict. At one pole were experts who echoed concerns first voiced by then Vice President Spiro T. Agnew: that too much coddling of children and overresponsiveness to their demands resulted in adolescents who were disrespectful, rebellious, and undisciplined. An extreme example of this viewpoint was James Dobson's *Dare to Discipline*, first published in 1970, which called on parents to exercise firm control of their children through the use of corporal punishment. At the other pole was Thomas Gordon's 1970 million-plus seller, *Parent Effectiveness Training*, which advised parents to stop punishing children and start treating them "much as we treat a friend or a spouse."[58]

The acceptability of spanking became a point of contention as definitions of what constituted "enlightened" childrearing underwent a dramatic transformation. In 1998 the American Academy of Pediatrics called on parents to reject spanking, saying that the practice taught children that "aggressive behavior is a solution to conflict." Murray A. Straus, an expert on abuse, called spanking a "major psychological and social problem" that could doom a child to a lifetime of difficulties ranging from juvenile delinquency to depression, sexual hangups, limited job prospects, and lowered earnings. Defenders of the practice included Dobson and Rosemond, whose *To Spank or Not to Spank* advocated the light swat on the bottom as "a relatively dramatic form of nonverbal communication."[59]

The issue of corporal punishment extended to the schools. As recently as the 1940s, corporal punishment in schools was legal in all but one state. By the end of the century, twenty-seven states and many municipalities had banned the practice. Increasingly, corporal punishment was concentrated in the South, where proponents argued that they were seeking "a return to accountability, authority, and increased order in schools." On the other side were those who wanted "to make schools a sanctuary from social violence," and who believed that corporal punishment contributed to disruptive student behavior. Despite four decades of efforts to ban the practice, corporal punishment remains a reality in many school districts.[60]

The gender wars were repeatedly played out in the juvenile arena. During the 1980s and 1990s a number of influential studies argued that girls were "underserved" and "shortchanged": that gender-biased teachers overlooked girls in class; that girls were less likely to participate in school sports; and that female students were discouraged from pursuing mathematics, science, and technology. Such popular writers as Peggy Orenstein and Mary Pipher reported that many adolescent girls had poor self-esteem, an obsession with body image, and encounters with sexual harassment. Their adversaries, such as Christina Hoff Sommers, claimed that boys had it worse. High school boys lagged three years behind girls in writing, one and a half years behind in reading, and were 50 percent more likely to be held back a grade. Boys were also three times more likely to be enrolled in special education programs, four times more likely to be diagnosed with attention deficit disorders, five times more likely to be involved in drugs and alcohol, and eight times more likely to commit suicide.[61]

During the last decades of the twentieth century, arguments over gender were often fought over how best to socialize girls and boys. One side saw the traditional virtues of boyhood as threatened by psychologists who "medicalized" and "pathologized" everyday boyhood behavior, treating physicality, mischief, rough-and-tumble play, and confrontation as psychological disorders. Their opponents argued that boys needed to have more of the nurturing, expressive qualities associated with girls, while girls needed to be more "boylike": tougher, less preoccupied with popularity and appearance, and more analytical, athletic, and competitive. Such authorities as William Pollack and James Garbarino believed that boys were programmed at an early age to be little men, to refrain from crying, to keep their feelings inside, and never to display vulnerability, and therefore found it difficult to express their emotions without feeling effeminate or to manage their anger and frustration in a way that did not involve violence.[62]

In fact both sexes face significant problems that need to be addressed and have unique voices that need to be heard. Neither boys nor girls find it easy to navigate the path to maturity, and both sexes suffer from gender stereotyping. Thanks in large part to the battles fought by feminists, girls are now better able to synthesize disparate worlds, such as the world of sports, academics, and relationships. But anorexia and bulimia have increased in frequency, and girls must still navigate a social landscape that urges them to define themselves in terms of physical appearance. Both the academic and social problems faced by boys and the inequities and cultural expectations about appearance and proper behavior that girls confront need to be remedied.[63]

Neither the Democratic nor the Republican political party has been consistent on issues relating to children. Generally Republican conservatives favored parents' authority to raise their families without government interference. But in two of the highest-profile public controversies of the 1980s and 1990s—involving twelve-year-old Ukrainian immigrant Walter Polovchak and six-year-old Cuban Elian Gonzalez—conservatives took the lead in arguing that children should be allowed to decide where to live, even if this conflicted with their parents' wishes. Conversely, liberal Democrats, who generally emphasized the ideals of free expression, choice, and questioning authority, took the lead in advocating school dress codes, curfews, and other restrictions on youthful behavior. Clearly, political ideology does not always determine policy.[64]

One of the most explosive issues in the culture war involved introducing children to the reality of gay parents. Leslea Newman's *Heather Has Two Mommies* was the first picture book depicting a young child living with two lesbian parents. Published in 1989, it presented the story of Heather, a preschooler, who discovers that her friends have very different sorts of families. Juan has a mommy and a daddy and a big brother named Carlos. Miriam has a mommy and a baby sister. And Joshua has a mommy, a daddy, and a stepdaddy. Their teacher encourages the children to draw pictures of their families, and reassures them that "each family is special" and that "the most important thing about a family is that all the people in it love each other." This book produced a firestorm of controversy.

A curriculum guide in New York City, which urged first-grade teachers to acknowledge "the positive aspects of each type of household," including those headed by gays and lesbians, placed *Heather Has Two Mommies* on a list of recommended books. School boards in Brooklyn, the Bronx, and Queens banned the guide, calling it inappropriate for first-graders. Critics termed it a document designed to help recruit gays and lesbians, and in 1993 it headed the list of books that people sought to ban from public library shelves. The next year, after Republican Senator Jesse Helms branded the book an example of the "disgusting, obscene materials that's laid out before school children in this country every day," the U.S. Senate voted sixty-three to thirty-six to deny federal funds to schools that "implement or carry out a program that has either the purpose or effect of encouraging or supporting homosexuality as a positive lifestyle alternative."[65]

Heather Has Two Mommies was the product of a trend in children's literature in which writers dealt much more openly than in the past with such topics as divorce, death, domestic abuse, and the psychological complexity of childhood and adolescence. Joanne Greenberg's *I Never Promised You a Rose Garden* (1964) charted a new direction in adolescent literature by treating an openly sexual relationship as a symbol of growing up. John Donovan's 1969 novel, *I'll Get There, It Better Be Worth the Trip,* introduced homosexuality as a theme. Alice Childress' *A Hero Ain't Nothing but a Sandwich* (1973), which described a thirteen-year-old heroin addict, depicted drug abuse as an escape from an intolerable environment and inept parenting. Books for younger children also underwent a radical shift in tone and content. In 1963, *Where the Wild Things Are* by Maurice Sendak aroused controversy because of its depiction of a child's temper tantrum. To be sure, works of fantasy and adventure, like the Harry Potter series, persist, but many of the escapist elements of earlier children's books were disputed.[66]

Of all the battlefields in the culture war involving children, the most hotly contested involved education. There were bitter controversies over Ebonics—the concept that vernacular black English is different enough from standard English to be considered a separate language—whole-language versus phonics in reading instruction, school vouchers, and accountability testing. At the heart of these battles was a conflict between traditional pedagogy, with its emphasis on the importance of memorization, discipline, and a traditional canon, and progressive pedagogy, with its stress on active learning, relevance, and skills-building. Five devastating critiques of public schools in the late 1970s and early 1980s touched off a wave of breast-beating over the state of American education. The most influential, *A Nation at Risk,* argued that there had been no measurable increase in student achievement despite sharp increases in school spending. In its most memorable passage, the report warned: "The educational foundations of our society are presently being eroded by a rising tide of mediocrity that threatens our very future as a Nation and a people . . . If an unfriendly foreign power had attempted to impose on America the mediocre educational performance that exists today, we might well have viewed it as an act of war." Other studies reported that American students ranked near the bottom in scores on international mathematics and science tests.[67]

Critics challenged the contention that student achievement was eroding, arguing that the proportion of poor students and those with limited English proficiency had sharply increased and that much of the increase in educational expenditures went to remedial tutoring, special education, guidance counselors, and social workers. Their arguments were rejected. Two movements to revitalize education arose. A back-to-basics movement called on schools to emphasize traditional reading, grammar, and arithmetic skills, while a movement for academic excellence sought to improve student achievement by raising requirements for graduation and imposing exit exams. In response to fears that students were not learning enough, that expectations were too low, and that a stronger curriculum was needed for all students, every state increased its graduation requirements, and many imposed "minimum competency tests" to ensure that children were learning basic skills. In 2002 the No Child Left Behind act required the states to create standards in math, reading, and science and to test every student's progress toward those standards. As a result of these campaigns, school curricula became more test driven and more tightly focused on reading, mathematics, and science.[68]

Not surprisingly, these years also saw a succession of movies and books that depicted schools in harshly negative terms. Unlike the more idealistic movies of the mid-1960s, like *To Sir with Love, Back to School, Bill and Ted's Excellent Adventure, Ferris Bueller's Day Off,* and *Porky's* presented a depressing picture of schools as little more than detention camps populated by rigid, uncaring teachers and lackadaisical, disconnected students. While some books, like Jonathan Kozol's *Amazing Grace,* discussed inequities in educational spending on the rich and the poor, others like *Dumbing Down Our Kids: Why American Children Feel Good about Themselves but Can't Read, Write or Add* expressed a fear that schools, in their preoccupation with educational fads and instilling self-esteem, had allowed student achievement to decline; that textbooks had decreased in difficulty by two grade levels over the last quarter-century; and that children were not encouraged to work hard or to master rigorous or complex material. The schools became politicized, and as a result legislatures increasingly dictated curricula and graduation standards.[69]

The culture wars played out in the courtroom as well, as a series of legal cases functioned as moral theater, gripping the public's attention and allowing it to debate its beliefs and values. In the mid-1980s the *Baby M* case, the first high-profile court case involving surrogate mothering, generated intense controversy about the meaning of the "best interests of the child" standard. William and Elizabeth Stern agreed to pay Mary Beth Whitehead $10,000 and medical expenses to be artificially inseminated by the father's sperm and carry the child to term. After the birth, Whitehead refused to turn over the baby to the Sterns. A lower court awarded custody to William Stern, the biological father, and gave Elizabeth Stern the right to adopt the infant, partly on the ground that their higher income would allow them to better provide for the child. This decision was overturned in 1988 by the New Jersey Supreme Court, which awarded custody to William Stern, banned the practice of bearing children for money, prohibited Elizabeth Stern from adopting the baby, and granted Mary Beth Whitehead visitation rights.

The case of "Baby Jessica" dramatized the conflicting rights of biological and adoptive parents. In 1991, two days after giving birth, Cara Clausen signed papers giving up the child for adoption. Two weeks later she filed papers to revoke the decision. The child's biological father, who had not previously been informed that the child had been put up for adoption, sued for custody. The adoptive parents, Jan and Roberta DeBoer, contested the case in court and, after a protracted legal battle, were ordered in 1993 to give Baby Jessica to the child's biological father. The case of Gregory Kinsley, a twelve-year-old Nintendo-playing Florida boy, involved the conflicting rights of parents and children. In 1992 he became the first minor to successfully sue his parents for a "divorce." In the preceding eight years his mother had spent only one year with him, and he asked to be placed with his foster parents, an upper-middle-class Mormon family. His biological mother argued that the boy was seeking more affluent parents and, as a Catholic, should not be placed with Mormons. The judge ultimately ruled that in cases involving overwhelming abuse or neglect, children had a right to sue to terminate their parents' rights.

In cases involving children, the courts had to balance three competing claims: young people's independent rights, including the right to make decisions about medical treatment and to decide where and with whom to live; the right of parents, in the absence of abuse or neglect, to raise their child as they saw fit; and government's authority to regulate children's behavior. A majority on a bitterly divided Supreme Court took the position that earlier court decisions had fostered legalistic and adversarial relations within homes and schools, undercut adult authority, and undermined the nurturing environments young people needed to grow up. The conservative majority also expressed concern that federal and state governments were intruding on parents' right to raise their children as they wished.

In one area, young people's health, the Court extended children's rights. In three landmark decisions—*Planned Parenthood of Missouri v. Danforth* (1976), *Carey v. Population Services International* (1977), and *Belloti v. Baird* (1979)—the Court declared that juveniles had a right to obtain birth control information, contraceptives, and abortions even over their parents' objections. The Court's majority held that pregnancy had such significant implications for young people's future life that they had to be empowered to make this decision for themselves. In a 1981 case, *H. L. v. Matheson et al.*, the Court upheld the constitutionality of a Utah statute that required parental notice in cases of unemancipated minors seeking abortions, while affirming juveniles' right to an abortion. But the high court also required states with parental notification laws to provide a "judicial bypass" process allowing judges to drop the notification requirement.

While the Court extended juvenile rights in the area of reproductive health, the justices gave greater deference to the authority of parents and government in other realms. In a 1979 decision, *Parham v. J. R.*, the Supreme Court affirmed the right of parents to institutionalize their children without due process. The Court also granted school officials leeway in disciplining students and regulating their behavior. It ruled in 1977 that states could allow children to be paddled in school without parental consent or a hearing; in 1986, that a principal could suspend a student for making an obscene speech; and in 1988, that principals could censor school newspapers. The courts also held that school dress codes and restrictions on hairstyle were permissible so long as they were not unreasonable or discriminatory; and that school administrators could search lockers without demonstrating probable cause.

In 1995 the high court ruled that schools could test entire teams of student athletes, even if individual team members were not suspected of using drugs, on the grounds that athletes were important role models. In 2002 the Court went further and upheld the random drug testing of students in all extracurricular activities, not just athletics. The Court's conservative majority summed up its new attitude in a 1985 decision that upheld the right of school officials to search a New Jersey girl's purse after she was caught smoking in a lavatory. "Maintaining order in the classroom has never been easy, and drug use and violent crimes in the schools have been a major problem," declared Justice Byron R. White. "Accordingly we have recognized that maintaining security and order in the schools requires a certain degree of flexibility in school disciplinary procedures." A commitment to child protection trumped the principle of children's rights.

Early in 2000, six-year-old Dedrick Owens shot and killed a six-year-old classmate, Kayla Rolland, at their elementary school in Mount Morris Township, Michigan. Under a revision of the state's juvenile justice law in 1997, generally considered the nation's toughest, Dedrick, despite his age, could be tried as an adult for murder. After the initial shock gave way, the complexities of treating juveniles as adults became apparent. Dedrick's classmates considered him a bully, and he had already been suspended for stabbing a classmate with a pencil. But there was also a sense in which Dedrick was himself a victim. His father was in jail. He, his mother, and his brother, lived with an uncle in a boardinghouse that local authorities called a crack house. His uncle, his closest male adult role model, exchanged drugs for stolen guns, one of which Dedrick brought to school to show off. After he shot Kayla and was taken into police custody, he drew pictures and asked whether he would see Kayla the next day. Ultimately he was deemed too young to be held criminally responsible and was placed in a private institution for children who have emotional problems.

For the past three decades, the overarching narrative of childhood has consisted of a discourse of crisis: a story of unstable families, neglectful parents, juvenile oversophistication, and teenage immorality. Individual children served as potent symbols in this morality tale. There was Jessica Dubroff, the would-be Amelia Earhart, who died because her father wanted her to become the youngest person to fly across the United States. Or JonBenet Ramsey, the six-year-old whose mother sought to make her a beauty queen. Rather than treasuring these children for their own sake, their parents treated them as pint-sized extensions of their own egos. These girls served as symbols of a society that professed to prize children, but in fact viewed them as means to their parents' fulfillment.

Americans are usually considered believers in progress, but the narrative of childhood turns the theme of progress on its head. However, this emphasis on decline is deeply flawed. It treats all children as if they were alike, while ignoring the crucial variables of gender and class. If the lives of suburban, middle-class white boys have grown riskier, middle-class girls and minority children have more opportunities and role models than ever before. Equally important, the discourse of decline exaggerates the impact of family structure on children's well-being even as it distracts our attention from the genuine stresses that afflict the lives of the young, tensions that came glaringly to light in the youthful rampage at Columbine High School in Littleton, Colorado, in 1999.

chapter seventeen

The Unfinished Century of the Child

In 1900 the Swedish reformer Ellen Key predicted that the twentieth century would be the century of the child. Just as the nineteenth century had brought recognition of women's rights, the twentieth century would bring acceptance of children's rights. She argued on behalf of a childhood free from toil in factories and fields, devoted to play and education, and buttressed by legislation guaranteeing children's well-being. She also called for a child-centered pedagogy tailored to children's abilities and interests.[1]

During the twentieth century the United States moved a long way toward fulfilling Key's noble vision. During the Progressive era a loose coalition of child psychologists, educators, jurists, physicians, and settlement-house workers, supported by thousands of middle-class women, took the crucial first steps toward universalizing the middle-class ideal of a protected childhood, through the establishment of playgrounds and kindergartens, the expansion of high schooling, and enactment of mothers' pensions and a separate system of juvenile justice emphasizing rehabilitation rather than punishment. The 1920s saw a proliferation of childrearing advice based on the most up-to-date understanding of children's psychological and developmental needs. The New Deal marked another significant advance as the most exploitative forms of child labor were outlawed, an economic safety net for dependent children was established, and high school education became a normative experience, irrespective of class, region, and race. The late 1960s and early 1970s marked the culmination of Key's century of the child as fundamental legal rights—to due process,

Within sixteen minutes Eric Harris and Dylan Klebold killed thirteen people at Columbine High School in Littleton, Colorado, and wounded twenty-one others in the deadliest school shooting in American history. Over an eighteen-month period in 1998 and 1999, there were six multiple-victim school shootings. Courtesy of the Jefferson County Sheriff's Office, Golden, Colorado.

freedom of expression, gender and racial equity, and contraception and abortion—were established.

But the century of the child ended with a bang, not a whimper. On April 20, 1999, eighteen-year-old Eric Harris and seventeen-year-old Dylan Klebold, clad in long black coats, stormed into Columbine High School in Littleton, Colorado, a suburb south of Denver. The high school seniors were armed with two sawed-off 12-gauge shotguns, a 9-millimeter semiautomatic rifle, and a 9-millimeter semiautomatic pistol. They also carried fifty-one bombs, including an explosive fashioned from two twenty-pound propane tanks and a gasoline-filled canister that they placed in the school cafeteria. The bomb—filled with nails, BB's, and broken glass—contained enough propane and gasoline to kill a majority of the 500 students in the school's lunchroom. The two youths apparently timed the attack to coincide with the anniversary of Adolf Hitler's birth. Within sixteen minutes they had gunned down twelve classmates and a teacher and wounded twenty-three others. Less than an hour after their rampage began, each committed suicide by shooting himself in the head.[2]

Before the rampage, no one noticed anything unusual about their behavior, even though the boys had left numerous warning signs. Klebold walked down his school's halls making aggressively racist remarks and wore black clothing lettered with German phrases. Police testified that the youths had left a sawed-off shotgun barrel and bombmaking materials in plain sight in one of the boys' rooms. In the weeks preceding the assault, the shooters exploded pipe bombs and fired automatic weapons in the mountains near Denver. The boys were arrested for breaking into a van and stealing $400 worth of electronic equipment. In a class in video production, they made a videotape showing trench-coat-clad students walking down the hallways of Columbine High School shooting athletes dead. Meanwhile Harris, who had been suspended for hacking into the school computing system, posted on a website drawings of shotgun-toting monsters and skulls and instructions for making pipe bombs like those he brought to Columbine. Eight times, a classmate's parents contacted the local sheriff's office with allegations that Harris had threatened their son. The complaints were ignored. Because the boys came from affluent, intact two-parent families, those danger signs were disregarded. Their mood swings and infatuation with violence and death were dismissed as if they represented typical examples of adolescent alienation and resentment. The Columbine massacre produced an unsettling picture of a suburb where adults had only the most superficial insight into the lives and mentality of the young.[3]

Why would two boys from stable, affluent homes try to massacre their classmates? Police investigators concluded that Harris and Klebold were angry and alienated and were seeking revenge for years of perceived slights from peers. "You've been giving us shit for years," Klebold had written. "You're fucking going to pay for all the shit." According to police officials, the shooters were also motivated by a desire to become cult heroes. Like Leopold and Loeb, the pair felt superior to their peers. "We're the only two who have self-awareness," wrote one. In a flagrant attempt to gain publicity, the boys left a diary and videotapes for the police to find. One thread was an expectation of notoriety. "Directors will be fighting over this story," wrote Klebold.[4]

The Columbine shooting was partly the grotesque outcome of a long-running feud with the more popular cliques at the school. The "preps" and "jocks" who dominated the school apparently taunted the pair by referring to them with derogatory homosexual terms. But unlike high school misfits of an earlier generation, Klebold and Harris were willing to offend, antagonize, and ultimately kill their tormentors. Nor were they alone in expressing their resentments with violence. The Columbine massacre was the sixth multiple-victim school shooting over an eighteen-month span in 1998 and 1999. During the 1990s the number of school shootings with multiple victims climbed from an average of two a year to an average of five. In West Paducah, Kentucky, fourteen-year-old Michael Carneal told schoolmates that "it would be cool" to shoot into a student prayer group. He did as promised, killing three girls and wounding five other students who were praying in a school hallway. In Edinboro, Pennsylvania, Andrew Wurst, also fourteen, started shooting at his eighth-grade prom, killing a teacher and injuring three others. In Jonesboro, Arkansas, eleven-year-old Andrew Golden and thirteen-year-old Mitchell Johnson activated a fire alarm and shot four girls and a teacher to death and wounded ten others as they evacuated the school. In Springfield, Oregon, fifteen-year-old Kipland Kinkel killed his parents, then shot twenty-four people in his school cafeteria, killing two students. In Pearl, Mississippi, a suburb of Jackson, sixteen-year-old Luke Woodham stabbed his

At a makeshift memorial to the Columbine High School shooting victims, the public left stuffed animals, crosses, angels, candles, bouquets, and ribbons. Because the Columbine rampage could not be blamed on broken homes, poverty, or a rural gun culture, it provoked disturbing questions about how American society raises children, especially boys. Courtesy of the Jefferson County Sheriff's Office, Golden, Colorado.

mother to death before shooting nine students, killing two, at his high school. In Bethel, Alaska, sixteen-year-old Evan Ramsey murdered a popular athlete and then tracked and killed the school principal.[5]

Some commentators argued that media coverage of these shootings was overblown, since multiple-victim school shootings were extremely rare. Not only was school violence not a new phenomenon; it had actually peaked during the 1992–93 school year, when nearly fifty young people and adults were killed in school-related violence. Yet what made these school shootings especially shocking was that violence had spread from urban to rural and suburban areas and involved multiple victims. The schoolyard killings in 1998 and 1999 were not gang related, nor were they fights over money or girlfriends. The victims were chosen randomly, and the motives for the killings were obscure.[6]

In general, explanations of juvenile violence stress a process of brutalization, involving abuse, exposure to violence, and emotional numbing; but in none of the schoolyard shootings of 1998 and 1999 was there evidence of a history of physical abuse, severe corporal punishment, or family violence. Nor could the shootings be blamed on such suspects as urban poverty, broken families, or single parenthood. The Columbine rampage was particularly unsettling, since unlike the earlier school attacks, it could not be explained as the product of southern or rural gun culture. The killings seemed to embody two characteristics: gestural suicide, intended to provoke widespread attention; and revenge fantasies, modeled on the indiscriminate violence featured on television and video games, in which the victims provide an audience for the killers to work out their needs.[7]

Adolescent revenge fantasies were not new. They first became a recognized part of popular culture's image of adolescence in *Carrie*, the 1976 film version of the Stephen King novel, in which a tormented teen unleashed her occult force to incinerate her high school. Even earlier, toward the end of his own tortured teenage years, King had written a novel called *Rage* (under the pseudonym Richard Bachman). In those days he remembered the feeling of "rejection, of being an outsider, what it was like to be teased relentlessly, and to entertain visions, fantasies of revenge on the people who'd done it to you—the system that had done it to you." In the book, a boy took his class hostage and murdered his teacher. In the school shootings, life appeared to imitate art. In 1993 in Grayson, Kentucky, Scott Pennington took his senior English class hostage and killed his teacher and a custodian. Three years later fourteen-year-old Barry Loukaitis of Moses Lake, Washington, took over his junior high algebra class, killed two students and a teacher, and wounded another student.[8]

Images of student-inflicted violence proliferated during the final years of the twentieth century. Influential songs and movies depicted schools as rife with fierce social tensions and fantasies of violent retaliation. The 1989 film *Heathers* featured a character wearing a dark trench coat who carried a revolver, which he pulled out when two athletes teased him in the cafeteria. Later he tried to blow up the school during a pep rally. In the 1995 movie *The Basketball Diaries,* a character played by Leonardo DiCaprio fantasized about pulling a shotgun from beneath his trench coat and killing his classmates. Although the links between media imagery and actual behavior are complex, there is little doubt that the revenge fantasies in film and literature gave expression to some young people's feelings of powerlessness and resentment.[9]

Popular explanations of the violence that took place in Littleton, West Paducah, and Pearl emphasized such factors as young people's easy access to semiautomatic weapons, capable of firing off dozens of rounds of ammunition in less than a minute; their exposure to video games that involved the graphic killing of human targets; a popular culture in which people settle scores violently; and a lack of an adult presence in their lives. Many commentators attributed the school rampages to school status hierarchies, suburban alienation, and inadequate parental supervision. Social contagion and copycat killing, with one rampage feeding on another, certainly played a role.

Several threads linked the rampages. Each case involved a child or youths who felt unpopular, rejected, or picked upon. Many student killers exhibited signs of serious depression. Most were suicidal, writing notes before the killings that assumed they would die. For many, the attack offered a way to end a life of torment in a blaze of terror. To varying degrees, the attackers were obsessed with violent popular culture and preoccupied with guns, death, and killing. For many school killers, the boundaries between reality and fantasy had eroded, and many of the shootings had a gamelike quality. In the Jonesboro, Arkansas, killings, an eleven-year-old and a thirteen-year-old dressed up in fatigues and hid in the bushes like snipers and killed four girls and a teacher in the crossfire. There was frequently a misogynist element in the shootings, with girls, mothers, and female teachers constituting a majority of the victims. Like Harris and Klebold, most of the shooters left a road map of warning signs pointing toward the violence to come, often in detailed writings at school. In case after case, friends and acquaintances heard boasts and muttered plans for mayhem. Many of the student killers had a history of violent behavior. Kip Kinkel set off firecrackers in cats' mouths, threw rocks at cars from an overpass, and gave a talk in speech class about how to build a bomb. But the clues were missed by parents who were unable to face the evidence of serious mental turmoil and by teachers who failed to take threats seriously.[10]

Were the schoolhouse shootings aberrations or were they symptoms of unacknowledged failings in the ways that Americans raise children, especially boys? Precisely because the Littleton rampage could not be attributed to "broken homes," to a violent or abusive family life, or to declining job prospects in decaying working-class communities, it focused public attention on the stresses besetting the lives of privileged youths. It led commentators to focus on the social dynamics of secondary schools, where social ostracism, marginalization, and alienation are commonplace; a boyhood "culture of cruelty," where bullying, taunting, and insults are everyday occurrences; and the psychological impact of movies that feature casual cruelty and gratuitous violence, music that is fixated on death and features the abuse of women, and video games that involve the graphic killing of opponents.[11]

During the twentieth century, high schools had become the primary arena where American adolescents tried out new styles, trends, and identities. But high schools also mimicked some of the most disconcerting aspects of adult society, including clearly defined ladders of status and prestige. At the end of the twentieth century, popular culture reexamined these status hierarchies from a much more critical perspective. No longer was the ideal simply to "fit in" or join the "in crowd." Such teen films as *Clueless* (1995), *Jawbreaker* (1998), and *Varsity Blues* (1999) portrayed high schools as brutal, Darwinian environments that were status-obsessed, materialistic, hierarchical, and savagely competitive. In real life, too, secondary schools were roiling emotional cauldrons, filled with bullying and snobbery. Middle and high schools had their own social pecking order, with a status hierarchy defined largely by looks, athletic prowess, and money.[12]

In recent years the cliques found in middle schools and high schools have proliferated. Alongside the strutting jocks, cheerleaders, and preppies of the past, there were now skateboarders, freaks, Goths, stoners, and other outcast cliques as geeky loners banded together. Unlike yesteryear's high schools, where the nerds, wallflowers, and other outcasts felt truly powerless, their contemporary counterparts were less willing to suppress their hostilities and resentments. The social dynamics of secondary schools, where kids engage in various forms of social ostracism and casual sadism, lurked behind many of the schoolhouse shootings. It is clear that the killers felt disrespected and unnoticed and desperately wanted power and attention. While secondary schools address young people's intellectual needs, they do not do an effective job of meeting their psychological and emotional needs. They are filled with social as well as academic stresses, and many students feel a deep sense of isolation and estrangement. A recent survey of 100,000 students found that only 1 in 4 said they went to a school where adults and other students cared for them.[13]

Gender hostility was another thread running through the school shootings. All the schoolhouse assailants were male, and over half of their victims were female. Rage or resentment against female teachers and students helped generate violence. Gender hostility was not new. Younger boys have long pulled girls' pony tails, and adolescent male culture has long treated girls as sex objects. One boys' rhyme from the 1970s went:

> Tra ra ra boom de ay!
> Have you had yours today?
> I had mine yesterday
> from the girl across the way.
> I laid her on the couch
> and all she said was "Ouch!"
> Tra ra ra boom de ay!
> Tra ra ra boom de ay![14]

Yet even as an antifeminist backlash against female assertiveness spread within the adult male culture, it appeared in the youth culture, too, especially among deeply disaffected middle-class adolescent males. Anger and rage at women became part of the background noise of their world. One of the harshest complaints against rap music, which found its largest and most enthusiastic audience among white suburban teenaged boys, was that it glorified sexist, misogynist, patriarchal ways of thinking and behaving. Rap lyrics frequently associated blunt sexist language and graphic descriptions of rape and violence against women with manliness and rebelliousness.[15]

There can be no doubt that youth violence in the United States is highly gendered. During the 1990s, 96 percent of youths committing serious acts of violence were male. Most school killers showed signs of clinical depression, and responses to depression vary by gender. Depressed girls are more likely than boys to cry openly or talk about their problems; they are also more prone than boys to self-mutilate or attempt suicide. Boys, in contrast, have fewer socially acceptable outlets to express depression or frustration and rage. Depressed boys tend to withdraw socially or group together with others who feel outcast, to act out aggressive impulses, and to succeed in committing suicide.[16]

Sometimes isolated incidents, like bolts of lightning that suddenly illuminate a darkened landscape, can reveal stresses and contradictions otherwise difficult to discern. The school shootings point to contradictions that lie at the very heart of the contemporary conception of childhood. By most measures, the young were better off than ever. They were bigger, richer, better educated, and healthier than at any other time in history. In many ways they were uniquely privileged. They had grown up in a period of sustained prosperity, had access to unprecedented amounts of information and education, and had more private space in their homes than ever before. Girls and racial and ethnic minorities had unparalleled opportunities and role models to emulate. Yet despite genuine gains, 60 percent of all adult Americans and 77 percent of African Americans said that their children were worse off than when they were children.[17]

Certainly, some of this anxiety reflects nostalgia for a lost world of childhood innocence, when six-year-old girls didn't wear slinky dresses, lycra, and glitter nail polish, and preteen boys didn't wear earrings or dye their hair purple. Partly, adults' concern involves the problems facing poor children. Even at the height of the economic boom of the 1990s, child poverty remained a severe problem, with 13.5 million children living in poverty and 12 million lacking health insurance. Still, when the public expressed alarm about the young, it reflected their sense that for all young people, not simply the poorest, childhood and adolescence had grown riskier and more stressful. Adults worried that children were growing up too quickly and faced pressures, risks, and choices far greater than those that they experienced at a similar age. Drugs, alcohol, unstable families, sexual pressures, and the risks of sexually transmitted diseases were only a few of the perils the young faced. They also confronted school stresses greater than those their parents encountered. There was a widespread impression that the number of young people with serious emotional and behavioral problems, especially depression, had rapidly increased over the preceding decades, and that the age of onset was occurring earlier. Young people, too, worried that something was wrong. A 1999 survey found that a majority of teens agreed with the statement that young people were powerless, that they would make little difference to the country, or would make things worse. Other surveys reported that many felt lonely and isolated, overwhelmed by stress, pressure, and responsibilities.[18]

Contemporary childhood is characterized by a host of contradictions. Numerically, today's children are the largest generation of young people ever, even bigger than the baby boom at its peak in 1964. Nevertheless, with the average age of Americans over thirty-three, the United States is a more adult-centered society, deeply ambivalent toward the young. Adults mimic the styles of the young and envy their appearance, energy, and virility, but intergenerational contact is increasingly confined to relationships between children and parents, teachers, and service providers. More fully integrated into the consumer economy than ever before, and at a much earlier age, the young are, at the same time, more segregated than ever in a peer culture. Kids have more space than ever inside their homes, but less space outside to call their own.

American society romanticizes childhood and adolescence as carefree periods of exploration, a time of freedom and irresponsibility, and young people do have more autonomy than ever before in their leisure activities, grooming, and spending. Yet there has simultaneously been a counter-trend toward the systematic overorganization of young people's lives, a trend especially noticeable in schools, where student behavior is much more closely monitored than it was three or four decades ago, and where many nonacademic and extracurricular activities have been eliminated. As anxiety intensified over whether the young were prepared to compete in the global economy, many schools curtailed recess (which has been eliminated in about 40 percent of school districts), cut programs in art and music, expanded summer school programs, imposed competency testing, eliminated many extracurricular activities and assemblies, and reemphasized drill and repetition as part of a "back to basics" movement. Not surprisingly, fewer students found school intellectually stimulating or fulfilling. Instead, they found it stressful and pressured.

The underlying contradiction in youthful lives is the most disturbing. Young people mature physiologically earlier than ever before. The media prey on children and adolescents with wiles of persuasion and sexual innuendo once reserved for adult consumers. The young have become more knowledgeable sexually and in many other ways. They face adultlike choices earlier. Yet contemporary American society isolates and juvenilizes young people more than ever before. Contemporary society provides the young with few positive ways to express their growing maturity and gives them few opportunities to participate in socially valued activities. American society sends young people many mixed and confusing messages. The young are told to work hard and value school, but also to enjoy themselves. They are to be innocent but also sexually alluring. They are to be respectful and obedient, but also independent consumers beholden to no one. They are to be youthful but not childish. The basic contradiction is that the young are told to grow up fast, but also that they needn't grow up at all, at least not until they reach their late twenties or early thirties.

History offers no easy solutions to the problems of disconnection, stress, and role contradictions that today's children face, but it does provide certain insights that might be helpful as we seek solutions. The first is that nostalgia for the past offers no solutions to the problems of the present. It is not possible to recreate a "walled garden" of childhood innocence, no matter how hard we might try. No V-chip, Internet filtering software, or CD-rating system will immunize children from the influence of contemporary culture. Since we cannot insulate children from all malign influences, it is essential that we prepare them to deal responsibly with the pressures and choices they face. That task requires knowledge, not sheltering. In a risk-filled world, naïveté is vulnerability.

Second, we must recognize that the solutions to young people's problems cannot simply come from individual parents, nor should they; effective solutions will necessarily be communal. Today's parents are beset with economic stresses, time pressures, and emotional upheavals of their own. American society could not put children's needs first to the exclusion of adults', even if it wanted to. What Americans can do seems so obvious that it is hard to understand the reluctance to take the necessary steps. Government can ensure that all young people grow up with their basic needs for food, clothing, schooling, and health care met. It can guarantee that children have access to high-quality preschool and afterschool care. It can moderate the economic disruptions of divorce on children's lives. It can encourage family-friendly workplace policies to allow parents to spend more time with their children. Above all, our society can provide the young with meaningful opportunities to contribute to their communities, and provide the young with adult mentoring relationships. Young Huck needs Jim as he and his little raft brave a raging Mississippi.

A little more than a century ago, the American ideal of childhood as a world apart, a period of freedom and self-discovery, received its most influential and lasting embodiment in *The Adventures of Huckleberry Finn*. In superficial ways, that ideal was realized. Emancipated from traditional forms of child labor, youth has become a prolonged period of education and leisure. More than ever before, youth has come to occupy a separate and autonomous realm, free from its traditional familial obligations. Yet in a deeper sense, the world we created is the polar opposite of the ideal embodied by Twain's novel. Over the past century and a half, the timing, sequencing, and stages of growing up have become ever more precise, uniform, and prescriptive, purportedly to better meet children's developmental needs, but in practice often failing them. In *Tom Sawyer* and *Huckleberry Finn*, many ties connected the young to a host of adults, some of whom were family members, but many of whom, like the fugitive slave Jim, were not. Today, connections that linked the young to the world of adults have grown attenuated. The young spend most of their day in an adult-run institution, the school, or consuming a mass culture produced by adults, but have few ties to actual adults apart from their parents and teachers.

Huckleberry Finn represented a rejection of the idea that childhood was a period of life that was important merely as preparation for adulthood. Like Jean-Jacques Rousseau, Mark Twain considered childhood valuable in and of itself. We may cling to that idea in the abstract, but in practice American culture—oriented toward mastery and control—views childhood as a "project," in which the young must develop the skills, knowledge, and character traits necessary for adulthood success, which is increasingly defined in terms of academic skills, knowledge, and competencies—and the forms of discipline those require. We expect even very young children to exhibit a degree of self-control that few adults had 200 or more years ago. Meanwhile, forms of behavior that previous generations considered normal are now defined as disabilities. American society is unique in its assumption that all young people should follow a single, unitary path to adulthood. Those who cannot adjust are cast adrift, to float aimlessly in a river that threatens to sink their lonely raft.

Contemporary American childhood is characterized by a fundamental paradox. More than ever before, children are segregated in a separate world of youth. We live at the tail end of a protracted process in which childhood was redefined as a special and vulnerable period of life that required affection, freedom from work, and separation from the adult world. In response, childhood was prolonged and sentimentalized, and new institutions were created to ensure that children's upbringing took place in carefully calibrated steps that corresponded with their developing capacities. Yet at the same time, children became more tightly integrated into the consumer society and more knowledgeable about adult realities at an earlier age. The result is a deepening contradiction between the child as dependent juvenile and the child as incipient adult.

In recent years, the psychological costs of this contradiction have grown more apparent. Hovering parents make it more difficult for children to separate; schools, preoccupied with testing and discipline, monitor students more closely and make education an increasingly stressful experience; demanding peer groups enforce conformity and ostracize those who fail to fit in. Our challenge is to reverse the process of age segmentation, to provide the young with challenging alternatives to a world of malls, instant messaging, music videos, and play dates. Huck Finn was an abused child, whose father, the town drunk, beat him for going to school and learning to read. Who would envy Huck's battered childhood? Yet he enjoyed something too many children are denied and which adults can provide: opportunities to undertake odysseys of self-discovery outside the goal-driven, overstructured realities of contemporary childhood.

Notes

Index

Notes

Preface

1. William Bradford, *Of Plymouth Plantation,* ed. Samuel Eliot Morison (New York: Modern Library, 1952), 25.

Prologue

1. Ron Powers, *Dangerous Water: A Biography of the Boy Who Became Mark Twain* (New York: Da Capo, 1999); idem, *Tom and Huck Don't Live Here Anymore: Childhood and Murder in the Heart of America* (New York: St. Martin's, 2001), 2, 32–34, 40, 131; Shelley Fisher Fishkin, *Lighting Out for the Territories: Reflections on Mark Twain and American Culture* (New York: Oxford University Press, 1997).
2. Powers, *Dangerous Water,* 26, 84, 167; idem, *Huck and Tom,* 78.
3. Richard Weissbourd, *The Vulnerable Child: What Really Hurts America's Children and What We Can Do about It* (Reading, Mass.: Addison-Wesley, 1996), 48.
4. On changes in the onset of sexual maturation, see Marcia E. Herman-Giddens et al., "Secondary Sexual Characteristics and Menses in Young Girls Seen in Office Practice," *Pediatrics* 99 (April 1997), 505–512. In 1890 the average age of menarche in the United States was estimated to be 14.8 years; by the 1990s, the average age had fallen to 12.5; 15 percent of white girls and 48 percent of African-American girls showed signs of breast development or pubic hair by age eight.
5. Stephen Robertson, "The Disappearance of Childhood," http://teaching.arts.usyd.edu.au/history/2044/.
6. James A. Schultz, *The Knowledge of Childhood in the German Middle Ages, 1100–1350* (Philadelphia: University of Pennsylvania Press, 1995), 11.

7. Leslie Fielder, "Come Back to the Raft Ag'in, Huck Honey," *Partisan Review* 25 (June 1948), 664–671; Shelley Fisher Fishkin, *Was Huck Black? Mark Twain and African-American Voices* (New York: Oxford University Press, 1993).

1. Children of the Covenant

1. John Demos, *The Unredeemed Captive: A Family Story from Early America* (New York: Knopf, 1964).
2. Quoted in Rosalie Murphy Baum and Elizabeth Maddock Dillon, "John Williams," in *Heath Anthology of American Literature*, ed. Paul Lauter, 4th ed., vol. 1 (Boston: Houghton Mifflin, 2002), 521–523.
3. Titus King, *Narrative of Titus King* (Hartford: Connecticut Historical Society, 1938), 17.
4. Demos, *Unredeemed Captive*, 144–146; James Axtell, "The White Indians of Colonial America," *William and Mary Quarterly*, 3d ser., 32 (1975), 55–88, 57, 62–63, 68, 85.
5. Anne S. Lombard, *Making Manhood: Growing Up Male in Colonial New England* (Cambridge, Mass.: Harvard University Press, 2003), 43, 52–53; C. John Sommerville, *The Discovery of Childhood in Puritan England* (Athens: University of Georgia Press, 1992).
6. James Axtell, *The School upon a Hill: Education and Society in Colonial New England* (New Haven: Yale University Press, 1974), 4; David Hall, *Worlds of Wonder, Days of Judgment: Popular Religious Belief in Early New England* (New York: Knopf, 1989), 154.
7. Gerald F. Moran and Maris A. Vinovskis, *Religion, Family, and the Life Course: Explorations in the Social History of Early America* (Ann Arbor: University of Michigan Press, 1992), 116, 144, 146–148; Gerald F. Moran, "Adolescence in Colonial America," in *Encyclopedia of Adolescence,* ed. Richard Lerner, Anne C. Petersen, and Jeanne Brooks-Gunn, vol. 1 (New York: Garland, 1991), 157–164.
8. Leah S. Marcus, *Childhood and Cultural Despair: A Theme and Variations in Seventeenth-Century Literature* (Pittsburgh: University of Pittsburgh Press, 1978).
9. Ibid.; Moran and Vinovskis, *Religion, Family, and Life Course,* 116; Sandford Fleming, *Children and Puritanism* (1933; reprint, New York: Arno, 1969), 96; David E. Stannard, *The Puritan Way of Death* (New York: Oxford University Press, 1977), 50.
10. Sommerville, *Discovery of Childhood,* 21–68.
11. Michael Zuckerman, *Friends and Neighbors: Group Life in America's First Plural Society* (Philadelphia: Temple University Press, 1982), 42; Barry Levy, *Quakers and the American Family: British Settlement in the Delaware Valley, 1650–1765* (New York: Oxford University Press, 1988), 100; Richard Archer, "New England Mosaic: A Demographic Analysis for the Seventeenth Century," *William and Mary Quarterly,* 3d ser., 47 (October 1990), 477–502.

12. Richard L. Bushman, *From Puritan to Yankee: Character and the Social Order in Connecticut, 1690–1765* (Cambridge, Mass.: Harvard University Press, 1967), 14; Roger Thompson, *Sex in Middlesex: Popular Mores in a Massachusetts County, 1649–1699* (Amherst: University of Massachusetts Press, 1986), 34; Lombard, *Making Manhood,* 35.

13. Carole Shammas, "Anglo-American Household Government in Comparative Perspective," *William and Mary Quarterly,* 3d ser., 52 (January 1995), 117. Axtell, *School upon a Hill,* 22–23.

14. Lombard, *Making Manhood,* 15–16, 74, 80.

15. Edward Shorter, *A History of Women's Bodies* (New York: Basic Books, 1982); Catherine M. Scholten, *Childbearing in American Society, 1650–1850* (New York: New York University Press, 1985); Charles R. King, *Children's Health in America* (New York: Twayne, 1993), 11; Moran and Vinovskis, *Religion, Family, and Life Course,* 106, 215; Peter Gregg Slater, *Children in the New England Mind* (Hamden, Conn.: Archon Books, 1977).

16. Moran and Vinovskis, *Religion, Family, and Life Course,* 110–111.

17. Axtel, *School upon a Hill,* 6, 13; Daniel Scott Smith, "Continuity and Discontinuity in Puritan Naming: Massachusetts, 1771," *William and Mary Quarterly,* 3d ser., 51 (January 1994), 67–91; Joseph Illick, "Childrearing in Seventeenth-Century England and America," in *The History of Childhood,* ed. Lloyd DeMause (New York: Psychohistory Press, 1974), 325; Hall, *Worlds of Wonder,* 153.

18. Smith, "Continuity and Discontinuity in Puritan Naming," 67.

19. Valerie Fildes, *Wet Nursing* (Oxford: Basil Blackwell, 1988), 81, 86, 136; Ernest Caulfield, "Infant Feeding in Colonial America," *Journal of Pediatrics* 41 (1952), 676.

20. Valerie A. Fildes, *Breasts, Bottles, and Babies: A History of Infant Feeding* (Edinburgh: Edinburgh University Press, 1986), 351, 379. According to Fildes, *Wet Nursing,* 130, breast milk was the most commonly advertised commodity in colonial newspapers.

21. Monica M. Kiefer, *American Children through Their Books* (Philadelphia: University of Pennsylvania Press, 1948), 182; Elizabeth Wirth Marvick, "Nature versus Nurture: Patterns and Trends in Seventeenth Century French Child-Rearing," in DeMause, *The History of Childhood,* 269; Karin Lee Fishbeck Calvert, "To Be a Child: An Analysis of the Artifacts of Childhood" (Ph.D. diss., University of Delaware, 1984) 32, 36, 108.

22. Calvert, "To Be a Child," 42.

23. Moran and Vinovskis, *Religion, Family, and Life Course,* 121; Colonial Society of New England, ed., *Seventeenth-Century New England* (Charlottesville: University Press of Virginia, 1984), 168; Axtell, *School upon a Hill,* 22–23.

24. John Morgan, *Godly Learning: Puritan Attitudes towards Reason, Learning, and Education, 1560–1640* (Cambridge: Cambridge University Press, 1986), 123, 143; Illick, "Childrearing in Seventeenth-Century England and America," 316; Moran and Vinovskis, *Religion, Family, and Life Course,* 117, 120.

25. Constance B. Schultz, "Children and Childhood in the Eighteenth Century,"

in *American Childhood: A Research Guide and Historical Handbook,* ed. Joseph M. Hawes and N. Ray Hiner (Westport, Conn.: Greenwood, 1985), 71; Kiefer, *American Children through Their Books,* 191.

26. Illick, "Childrearing in Seventeenth-Century England and America," 316, 349 n. 123.

27. John Norris, *Spiritual Counsel, or, The Father's Advice to his Children* (London: S. Manship, 1694).

28. Hall, *Worlds of Wonder,* 230; Moran and Vinovskis. *Religion, Family, and Life Course,* 5, 225; Stannard, *Puritan Way of Death,* 66; Larzer Ziff, *Puritanism in America* (New York: Viking Press, 1973), 278; Lombard, *Making Manhood,* 23.

29. Rose Ann Lockwood, "Birth, Illness, and Death in 18th Century New England," *Journal of Social History* 12 (1978), 118, 119; King, *Children's Health in America,* 9–11; Gordon E. Geddes, *Welcome Joy: Death in Puritan New England* (Ann Arbor: UMI Research Press, 1981), 48; Hall, *Worlds of Wonder,* 167.

30. Hall, *Worlds of Wonder,* 34, 35, 37, 47; Axtell, *School upon a Hill,* 12.

31. Axtell, *School upon a Hill,* 29; Moran and Vinovskis, *Religion, Family, and Life Course,* 124; Hall, *Worlds of Wonder,* 34; Morgan, *Godly Learning,* 160.

32. Moran and Vinovskis, *Religion, Family, and Life Course,* 125, 127; Hall, *Worlds of Wonder,* 34; Morgan, *Godly Learning,* 160; Lombard, *Making Manhood,* 32.

33. On Salem witchcraft, see Paul Boyer and Stephen Nissenbaum, *Salem Possessed: The Social Origins of Witchcraft* (Cambridge, Mass.: Harvard University Press, 1974); Elaine G. Breslaw, *Tituba, Reluctant Witch of Salem: Devilish Indians and Puritan Fantasies* (New York: New York University Press, 1996); John Putnam Demos, *Entertaining Satan: Witchcraft and the Culture of Early New England* (New York: Oxford University Press, 1982); Richard Godbeer, *The Devil's Dominion: Magic and Religion in Early New England* (New York: Cambridge University Press, 1992); David D. Hall, *Witch-Hunting in Seventeenth-Century New England: A Documentary History, 1638–1692* (Boston: Northeastern University Press, 1991); Peter Charles Hoffer, *The Devil's Disciples: The Makers of the Salem Witchcraft Trials* (Baltimore: Johns Hopkins Press, 1996); Carol F. Karlsen, *The Devil in the Shape of a Woman: Witchcraft in Colonial New England* (New York: W. W. Norton, 1987); Mary Beth Norton, *In the Devil's Snare: The Salem Witchcraft Crisis of 1692* (New York: Knopf, 2002).

34. On age and gender and the witchcraft scare, see Karlsen, *Devil in Shape of a Woman;* Merry E. Wiesner, *Women and Gender in Early Modern Europe,* 2d ed. (Cambridge: Cambridge University Press, 2000); W. de Blécourt, "The Making of the Female Witch: Reflections on Witchcraft and Gender in the Early Modern Period," *Gender & History,* 12 (2000), 287–309.

35. Young boys, unlike girls, did not wear head coverings; Lombard, *Making Manhood,* 22, 31.

36. Thompson, *Sex in Middlesex,* 92.
37. Illick, "Childrearing in Seventeenth-Century England and America," 258, 330; Ross W. Beales Jr., "In Search of the Historical Child: Miniature Adulthood and Youth in Colonial New England," *American Quarterly* 27 (1975), 384; Lombard, *Making Manhood,* 21.
38. Morgan, *Godly Learning,* 146–147; Illick, "Childrearing in Seventeenth-Century England and America," 330; Christine Leigh Heyrman, *Commerce and Culture: The Maritime Communities of Colonial Massachusetts, 1690–1750* (New York: W. W. Norton, 1984), 255; Beales, "In Search of the Historical Child," 33; *The Autobiography of Benjamin Franklin,* ed. John Bigelow (Philadelphia: Lippincott, 1868), 85–86, 90–93, 103–107, 114.
39. Fleming, *Children and Puritanism,* 154–55; Stannard, *Puritan Way of Death.*
40. N. Ray Hiner, "Adolescence in Eighteenth-Century America," *History of Childhood Quarterly* 3 (1975), 259.
41. Ross W. Beales Jr., "The Child in Seventeenth-Century America," in Hawes and Hiner, *American Childhood,* 36; Axtell, *School upon a Hill,* 28; Hiner, "Adolescence in Eighteenth-Century America," 261; Thompson, *Sex in Middlesex,* 72.
42. Moran and Vinovskis, *Religion, Family, and Life Course,* 92.
43. Ibid., 64, 69, 92; Axtell, *School upon a Hill,* 7.
44. Moran and Vinovskis, *Religion, Family, and Life Course,* 31, 95, 100.
45. Maris A. Vinovskis, "Family and Schooling in Colonial and Nineteenth-Century America," *Journal of Family History* 12 (1987), 19–37; Moran and Vinovskis, *Religion, Family, and Life Course* 4–5, 99, 101.
46. Bushman, *From Puritan to Yankee,* 42.
47. Thompson, *Sex in Middlesex,* 92; Daniel Blake Smith, *Inside the Great House: Planter Family Life in Eighteenth-Century Chesapeake Society* (Ithaca: Cornell University Press, 1980), 287–288.
48. Hall, *Worlds of Wonder,* 4, 5, 10, 210–11, 258.
49. Thompson, *Sex in Middlesex,* 95.
50. Steven Mintz, "Regulating the American Family," *Journal of Family History* 14 (1989), 387–408; Thompson, *Sex in Middlesex,* 67, 91, 93; Beales, "The Child in Seventeenth-Century America," 37.
51. Thompson, *Sex in Middlesex,* 105; Moran and Vinovskis, *Religion, Family, and Life Course,* 153–154.
52. Moran and Vinovskis, *Religion, Family, and Life Course,* 102, 154.
53. Axtell, *School upon a Hill,* 45; Moran and Vinovskis, *Religion, Family, and Life Course,* 154, 199.
54. Fleming, *Children and Puritanism,* 60; Moran and Vinovskis, *Religion, Family, and Life Course,* 152–153.
55. Moran and Vinovskis, *Religion, Family, and Life Course,* 151.
56. Glenn Wallach, *Obedient Sons: The Discourse of Youth and Generations in American Culture* (Amherst: University of Massachusetts Press, 1997), 17; Moran and Vinovskis, *Religion, Family, and Life Course,* 151.

2. Red, White, and Black in Colonial America

1. John Van Der Zee, *Bound Over: Indentured Servitude and American Conscience* (New York: Simon and Schuster, 1985); Peter Williamson, *Authentic Narrative of the Life and Surprising Adventures of Peter Williamson* (Albany, N.Y.: H. C. Southwick, 1813), 43–47.

2. Memorial for Poor Peter Williamson . . . against Alexander Cushnie . . . 1762, CS29/10/3: 1762, National Archives of Scotland, Edinburgh; Printed signet letters at instance of Peter Williamson . . . v. bailie William Fordyce of Aquhorties, April 9, 1762, GD248/590/4, ibid.

3. Van Der Zee, *Bound Over,* 209–211.

4. Elizabeth Sprigs, "We Unfortunate English People Suffer Here," http://www.historymatters.gmu.edu/d/5796/.

5. Van Der Zee, *Bound Over,* 160–161, 164.

6. Kenneth Morgan, *Slavery and Servitude in North America, 1607–1800* (Edinburgh University Press: Edinburgh, 2000), 44; Van Der Zee, *Bound Over,* 12–13.

7. Zeisberger quoted in James Axtell, *The Indian Peoples of Eastern America: A Documentary History of the Sexes* (New York: Oxford University Press, 1981), 23–25. Joseph E. Illick, *American Childhoods* (Philadelphia: University of Pennsylvania Press, 2002), 8.

8. Quoted in Axtell, *Indian Peoples,* 42; Adriaen Van der Donck (1655) quoted in Steven Mintz, ed., *Native American Voices,* 2d ed. (St. James, N.Y.: Brandywine, 2000), 60; John Long (1791) quoted in ibid., 61.

9. Illick, *American Childhoods,* 9; Axtell, *Indian Peoples,* 41–42.

10. Axtell, *Indian Peoples,* 42; Adriaen Van der Donck (1655) quoted in Mintz, *Native American Voices,* 60.

11. Axtell, *Indian Peoples,* 42–43, 52, 60.

12. Ibid., 44, 46, 50–51.

13. Gerald F. Moran, "Adolescence in Colonial America," in *Encyclopedia of Adolescence,* ed. Richard Lerner, Anne C. Petersen, and Jeanne Brooks-Gunn, vol. 1 (New York: Garland, 1991), 157, 164–167.

14. Daniel Blake Smith, *Inside the Great House: Planter Family Life in Eighteenth-Century Chesapeake Society* (Ithaca: Cornell University Press, 1980), 26, 35, 79, 149, 176, 243–44, 265.

15. Ibid., 80, 124, 265; Gerald F. Moran and Maris A. Vinovskis, *Religion, Family, and the Life Course: Explorations in the Social History of Early America* (Ann Arbor: University of Michigan Press, 1992), 149.

16. Frethorne quoted in "The Experiences of an Indentured Servant, 1623," *Virtual Jamestown,* http://www.iath.virginia.edu/vcdh/jamestown/frethorne.html.

17. Moran, "Adolescence in Colonial America," 164–167.

18. Smith, *Inside the Great House,* 21–22; Moran and Vinovskis, *Religion, Family, and Life Course,* 171, 176.

19. Moran, "Adolescence in Colonial America," 166; Smith, *Inside the Great House,* 25, 286.

20. Smith, *Inside the Great House,* 25, 139, 191, 286; Moran, "Adolescence in Colonial America," 166–167.
21. Smith, *Inside the Great House,* 151, 161, 245–246; Anne S. Lombard, *Making Manhood: Growing Up Male in Colonial New England* (Cambridge, Mass.: Harvard University Press, 2003), 37.
22. Moran and Vinovskis, *Religion, Family, and Life Course,* 150.
23. Jan Lewis, *The Pursuit of Happiness: Family and Values in Jefferson's Virginia* (New York: Cambridge University Press, 1983); Moran, "Adolescence in Colonial America," 167.
24. Alan Taylor, "The Exceptionalist," *New Republic,* June 9, 2003, 36.
25. *San Diego Union-Tribune,* September 15, 1999, E-1; *New York Daily News,* July 20, 1997, 22; ibid., December 7, 1997, 8.
26. Joyce Hansen and Gary McGowan, *Breaking Ground, Breaking Silence: The Story of New York's African Burial Ground* (New York: Henry Holt, 1998); *New York Daily News,* July 20, 1997, 22; ibid., December 7, 1997, 8.
27. Ottobah Cugoano, *Narrative of the Enslavement of Ottobah Cugoano, a Native of Africa; Published by Himself, in the Year 1787* (London: Hatchard, 1825), 123–124.
28. George Francis Dow, *Slave Ships and Slaving* (Westport: Negro Universities Press, 1970), 172–173; John Warner Barber, *History of the Amistad Captives* (New York: Arno, 1969), 9–15. See Sylviane A. Diouf, *Growing Up in Slavery* (Brookfield, Conn.: Millbrook, 2001), 12, 17.
29. Park quoted in Colin A. Palmer, "The Middle Passage," in *Captive Passage: The Transatlantic Slave Trade and the Making of the Americas,* ed. Beverly C. McMillan (Washington, D.C.: Smithsonian Institution Press, 2002), 56.
30. Samuel Moore, *Biography of Mahommah G. Baquaqua* (Detroit: Geo. E. Pomeroy, 1854), 41; Diouf, *Growing Up in Slavery,* 18; Palmer, *Captive Passage,* 60.
31. Elizabeth Donnan, *Documents Illustrative of the History of the Slave Trade to America,* vol. 3 (New York: Octagon Books, 1969), 45; Palmer, *Captive Passage,* 54; Diouf, *Growing Up in Slavery,* 21.
32. Steven Mintz, ed., *African American Voices,* 3d ed. (St. James, N.Y.: Brandywine, 2004), 16–18, 27–28.
33. Philip Morgan, *Slave Counterpoint: Black Culture in the Eighteenth-century Chesapeake and Lowcountry* (Chapel Hill: University of North Carolina Press, 1998), 501–502, 507, 509.
34. Ibid., 508.
35. Ibid., 499–501, 518.
36. Ibid., 510, 512.
37. Ibid., 540–541; Mintz, *African American Voices,* 110.
38. Morgan, *Slave Counterpoint,* 528–529, 537, 545–547.
39. Michael Zuckerman, ed., *Friends and Neighbors: Group Life in America's First Plural Society* (Philadelphia: Temple University Press, 1982), 5, 13.
40. Gottlieb Mittelberger, *Journey to Pennsylvania* (Cambridge, Mass.: Belknap Press of Harvard University Press, 1960).

41. Smith, *Inside the Great House*, 289; Rhys Isaac, *The Transformation of Virginia, 1740–1790* (Chapel Hill: University of North Carolina Press, 1982), 136, 309; Stephanie Grauman Wolf, *As Various as Their Land: the Everyday Lives of Eighteenth-Century Americans* (New York: HarperCollins, 1993), 30; Roger Thompson, *Sex in Middlesex: Popular Mores in a Massachusetts County, 1649–1699* (Amherst: University of Massachusetts Press, 1986), 157.
42. Wolf, *As Various as Their Land*, 42–46; Isaac, *Transformation of Virginia*, 294–95, 305.
43. Wolf, *As Various as Their Land*, 42.
44. Billy G. Smith, *The "Lower Sort": Philadelphia's Laboring People, 1750–1800* (Ithaca: Cornell University Press, 1990), 177, 183.
45. Smith, *Inside the Great House*, 288; Barry Levy, "The Birth of the 'Modern Family' in Early America: Quaker and Anglican Families in the Delaware Valley, Pennsylvania, 1681–1750," in Zuckerman, *Friends and Neighbors*, 26–64.
46. Winthrop D. Jordan, "Familial Politics: Thomas Paine and the Killing of the King, 1776," *Journal of American History* 60 (1973), 294, 295; Moran, "Adolescence in Colonial America," 167–168.
47. Moran, "Adolescence in Colonial America," 168; Harold E. Selesky, *War and Society in Colonial Connecticut* (New Haven: Yale University Press, 1990).
48. Jay Fliegelman, *Prodigals and Pilgrims: The American Revolution against Patriarchal Authority* (Cambridge: Cambridge University Press, 1982), esp. chap. 2; Steven Mintz and Susan Kellogg, *Domestic Revolutions: A Social History of American Family Life* (New York: Free Press, 1988), 45–46.
49. Paine quoted in Wolf, *As Various as Their Lands*, 135.

3. Sons and Daughters of Liberty

1. V. T. Dacquino, *Sybil Ludington: The Call to Arms* (Fleischmanns, N.Y.: Purple Mountain, 2000).
2. James Kirby Martin, *Ordinary Courage: The Revolutionary War Adventures of Joseph Plumb Martin* (St. James, N.Y.: Brandywine, 1999); Joseph Plumb Martin, *Private Yankee Doodle*, ed. George F. Scheer (Boston: Little, Brown, 1962), 186–187.
3. Julie Winch, *A Gentleman of Color: The Life of James Forten* (New York: Oxford University Press, 2002). Forten quoted in Neil J. William Smelser, William Julius Wilson, and Faith Mitchell, eds., *America Becoming: Racial Trends and Their Consequences* (Washington, D.C.: National Academy Press, 2001), 175.
4. Hannah More quoted in Steven J. Novak, *The Rights of Youth: American Colleges and Student Revolt, 1798–1815* (Cambridge, Mass.: Harvard University Press, 1977), v.
5. Gerald F. Moran, "Adolescence in Colonial America," in *Encyclopedia of Adolescence*, ed. Richard Lerner, Anne C. Petersen, and Jeanne Brooks-Gunn, vol. 1 (New York: Garland, 1991), 168–169.

6. Edwin Burrows and Michael Wallace, "The American Revolution: The Ideology and Psychology of National Liberation," *Perspectives in American History* 6 (1972), 193; Melvin Yazawa, *From Colonies to Commonwealth: Familial Ideology and the Beginnings of the American Republic* (Baltimore: Johns Hopkins University Press, 1985), 85.

7. Winthrop D. Jordan, "Familial Politics: Thomas Paine and the Killing of the King, 1776," *Journal of American History* 60 (1973–74), 304–305; Burrows and Wallace, "American Revolution," 168, 177, 186, 212, 232.

8. Burrows and Wallace, "American Revolution," 168, 177, 193, 204, 215; Yazawa, *From Colonies to Commonwealth*, 96, 221, 295.

9. Yazawa, *From Colonies to Commonwealth*, 260.

10. Ibid., 167–306.

11. Burrows and Wallace, "American Revolution," 186; Yazawa, *From Colonies to Commonwealth*, 47, 261; Francis Hutcheson, *A System of Moral Philosophy*, vol. 2 (Glasgow: R. and A. Foulis, 1755), 192.

12. Mary Beth Norton, *Liberty's Daughters: The Revolutionary Experience of American Women, 1750–1800* (Boston: Little, Brown, 1980), 85–86, 88.

13. Yazawa, *From Colonies to Commonwealth*, 61–63, 65–68, 72.

14. Novak, *Rights of Youth*, 2–3.

15. Ibid., 2, 4; Thomas Hine, *Rise and Fall of the American Teenager* (New York: Bard, 1999), 89.

16. Charity Clarke Moore and Clement Clarke Moore papers, 1767–1863, Columbia University; George DeWan, "A Woman Ready to Fight," *Newsday*, December 22, 1997, A17.

17. Robert Leckie, *George Washington's War* (New York: HarperCollins, 1990) 48, 49; Todd Alan Kreamer, "Sons of Liberty," http://earlyamerica.com/review/fall96/sons.html.

18. *Diary of Anna Green Winslow: A Boston school Girl of 1771*, ed. Alice Morse Earle (Boston: Houghton Mifflin, 1894); Ray Raphael, *A People's History of the American Revolution* (New York: New Press, 2001), 112, 117.

19. "Captain Prescott's Account of the Boston Massacre," Boston Massacre Historical Society, http://www.bostonmassacre.net/trial/acct-preston2.htm.

20. Raphael, *People's History of American Revolution*, 112, 117.

21. Ebenezer Fox, *The Adventures of Ebenezer Fox in the Revolutionary War* (Boston: Charles Fox, 1847).

22. Raphael, *People's History of American Revolution*, 64–65; M. M. Quaife, ed., "Documents—A Boy Soldier under Washington: The Memoir of Daniel Granger," *Mississippi Valley Historical Review* 16 (1930), 538–560.

23. Martin, *Ordinary Courage*, xv.

24. Quoted in Jeanne Winston Adler, "In the Path of War," *Appleseeds*, October 2000, 21–22.

25. Norton, *Liberty's Daughters*, 157; Elisabeth O'Kane Lipartito, "The Misfortunes and Calamities of War: The Impact of the Revolutionary War on Civilian Society, 1775–1781" (Ph.D., University of Houston, 1990), 1–2, 112, 175, 326.

26. Lipartito, "Misfortunes and Calamities of War," 24, 43–44, 47–48, 50, 65; "Depositions of Elisabeth Cain and Abigail Palmer" (Philadelphia: Continental Congress, March 22, 1777).

27. Lipartito, "Misfortunes and Calamities of War," 70, 79, 91, 97; Mary Beth Norton, *The British-Americans: The Loyalist Exiles in England* (Boston: Little, Brown, 1972), 32.

28. Lipartito, "Misfortunes and Calamities of War," 273, 273, 283, 293, 303, 330.

29. Ibid., 308, 310–11, 319, 322.

30. Stanley Elkins and Eric McKitrick, "The Founding Fathers: Young Men of the Revolution," *Political Science Quarterly* 76 (1961), 799–816.

31. Douglas Adair, *Fame and the Founding Fathers* (New York: Norton, 1974), 7, 10.

32. Lawrence A. Cremin, *American Education: The Colonial Experience 1607–1782* (New York: Harper and Row, 1970); Donald George Tewksbury, *The Founding of American Colleges and Universities before the Civil War* (New York: Teacher's College, Columbia University, 1932).

33. Raphael, *People's History of American Revolution*, 15. The historian Pauline Maier draws a useful distinction between the older and younger revolutionaries, suggesting that the older leaders took pride in the British constitution and were reluctant to make a final break with the British empire. See Pauline Maier, *The Old Revolutionaries: Political Lives in the Age of Samuel Adams* (New York: Knopf, 1980). Stanley Elkins and Eric McKitrick argued that supporters of the Constitution were on average ten to twelve years younger than their opponents. They contended that the Federalists were young men who had partly taken on national political office because the older Anti-Federalists had already monopolized the best state offices. In contrast, Jackson T. Main found no significant age difference between supporters and opponents of the Constitution; *The Antifederalists: Critics of the Constitution* (Chapel Hill: University of North Carolina Press, 1961), 259.

34. Main, *The Antifederalists*, 288.

35. Nancy F. Cott, "Notes toward an Interpretation of Antebellum Childrearing," *Psychohistory Review* 7, no. 4 (1973), 8; Yazuka, *From Colonies to Commonwealth*, 191.

36. Yazuka, *From Colonies to Commonwealth*, 144, 168, 192.

37. See *Nancy Shippen: Her Journal Book, The International Romance of a Young Lady of Fashion of Colonial Philadelphia*, ed. Ethel Ames (Philadelphia: J. B. Lippincott, 1935); Randolph Shipley Klein, *Portrait of an Early American Family: The Shippens Of Pennsylvania across Five Generations* (Philadelphia: University of Pennsylvania Press, 1975); Norton, *Liberty's Daughters*, 48, 236.

38. Penny Colman, *Girls: A History of Growing Up Female in America* (New York: Scholastic, 2000), 59.

39. Ibid., 59–60, 62.

40. Norton, *Liberty's Daughters*, 236.

4. Inventing the Middle-Class Child

1. Increases in the uniformity of the life course are examined in Howard Chudacoff, *How Old Are You? Age Consciousness in American Culture* (Princeton: Princeton University Press, 1989); Joseph F. Kett, *Rites of Passage: Adolescence in America, 1790 to the Present* (New York: Basic Books, 1977).
2. Kett, *Rites of Passage.*
3. James Holt McGavran, *Literature and the Child: Romantic Continuations, Postmodern Contestations* (Iowa City: University of Iowa Press, 1999), 128, 137; Judith Plotz, "Perpetual Messiah," in *Regulated Children/Liberated Children,* ed. Barbara Finkelstein (New York: Psychohistory Press, 1979), 67; James Holt McGavran, *Romanticism and Children's Literature in Nineteenth-Century England* (Athens: University of Georgia Press, 1991); Kett, *Rites of Passage,* 286–287.
4. McGavran, *Literature and the Child,* 25.
5. Peter Coveney, *The Image of Childhood, the Individual and Society: A Study of the Theme in English Literature,* rev. ed. (Baltimore: Penguin, 1967), 291; Kett, *Rites of Passage,* 129.
6. Kett, *Rites of Passage,* 115.
7. Jacqueline S. Reinier, *From Virtue to Character: American Childhood, 1775–1850* (New York: Twayne, 1996), 61, 90; Chudacoff, *How Old Are You?* 93–4, 97.
8. See Karin Lee Fishbeck Calvert, "To Be a Child" (Ph.D. diss., University of Delaware, 1984), 32.
9. Nancy F. Cott, "Notes toward an Interpretation of Antebellum Childrearing," *Psychohistory Review* 7, no. 4 (1973), 8.
10. John Demos and Virginia Demos, "Adolescence in Historical Perspective," *Journal of Marriage and the Family* 31 (1969), 633; Kett, *Rites of Passage,* 44; Cott, "Notes toward Interpretation of Antebellum Childrearing," 5.
11. Cott, "Notes toward Interpretation of Antebellum Childrearing," 6.
12. Reinier, *From Virtue to Character,* 10, 48.
13. Anne Scott MacLeod, "Children's Literature in America from the Puritan Beginnings to 1870," in *Children's Literature: An Illustrated History,* ed. Peter Hunt (New York: Oxford University Press, 1995), 111.
14. Gillian Avery, *Behold the Child: American Children and Their Books, 1621–1922* (Baltimore: Johns Hopkins University Press, 1994), 61–62; Anne Scott MacLeod, *A Moral Tale: Children's Fiction and American Culture, 1820–1860* (Hamden, Conn.: Archon Books, 1975), 37–39; idem, "Children's Literature in America," 110–112.
15. Annette Atkins, *We Grew Up Together: Brothers and Sisters in Nineteenth-Century America* (Urbana: University of Illinois Press, 2001), 155.
16. David J. Rothman, "Documents in Search of a Historian: Toward a History of Children and Youth in America," in *Growing Up in America,* ed. Harvey J. Graff (Detroit: Wayne State University Press, 1987), 78.
17. E. Anthony Rotundo, *American Manhood: Transformation in Masculinity*

from the Revolution to the Modern Era (New York: Basic Books, 1993), 32, 52, 58.

18. Ibid., 32, 53–54.

19. Barbara Welter, *Dimity Convictions: The American Woman in the Nineteenth Century* (Athens: Ohio University Press, 1976), 9.

20. Joseph F. Kett, "Growing Up in Rural New England, 1800–1840," in Graff, *Growing Up in America,* 175–184; Nancy F. Cott, "Young Women in the Second Great Awakening," in ibid., 187.

21. Karin Lee Fishbeck Calvert, *Children in the House: The Material Culture of Early Childhood, 1600–1900* (Boston: Northeastern University Press, 1992), 100, 111, 113; Monica Mary Kiefer, *American Children through Their Books, 1700–1835* (Philadelphia: University of Pennsylvania Press, 1948), 111, 113, 217.

22. Lynne Vallone, *Disciplines of Virtue: Girls' Culture in the Eighteenth and Nineteenth Centuries* (New Haven: Yale University Press, 1995), 114; Penny Colman, *Girls: A History of Growing Up Female* (New York: Scholastic, 2000), 12.

23. Vallone, *Disciplines of Virtue,* 124, 131; Welter, *Dimity Convictions,* 13, 61; Colman, *Girls,* 21.

24. Carol Dyhouse, *Girls Growing Up in Late Victorian and Edwardian England* (Boston: Routledge and Kegan Paul, 1981), 20–23; Welter, *Dimity Convictions,* 27, 60.

25. *To Read My Heart: The Journal of Rachel Van Dyke, 1810–1811,* ed. Lucia McMahon and Deborah Schriver (Philadelphia: University of Pennsylvania Press, 2000).

26. Welter, *Dimity Convictions,* 7; Atkins, *We Grew Up Together,* 138, 166.

27. Reinier, *From Virtue to Character,* 40; Kett, *Rites of Passage,* 36–37.

28. Harvey J. Graff, *Conflicting Paths: Growing Up in America* (Cambridge, Mass.: Harvard University Press, 1995).

29. Welter, *Dimity Convictions,* 17; Cott, "Young Women in Second Great Awakening," 187–188.

30. Rotundo, *American Manhood,* 21, 251; Glenn Wallach, *Obedient Sons: The Discourse of Youth and Generations in American Culture, 1630–1860* (Amherst: University of Massachusetts, 1997), 59; Mary P. Ryan, "Privacy and the Making of the Self-Made Man: Family Strategies of the Middle Class at Midcentury," in Graff, *Growing Up in America,* 251.

31. Wallach, *Obedient Sons,* 61, 67–68.

32. Ibid., 81.

33. Peter N. Stearns, *Anxious Parents: A History of Modern American Childrearing* (New York: New York University Press, 2003).

34. Steven Mintz, *Moralists and Modernizers: America's Pre–Civil War Reformers* (Baltimore: Johns Hopkins University Press, 1995), 58–59.

35. Horace Mann quoted in "Children Everywhere: Schooling," Old Sturbridge Village, http://www.osv.org/education/ChildrenEverywhere/Schooling.html.

36. Chudacoff, *How Old Are You?* 3.

37. Carl F. Kaestle and Maris A. Vinovskis, *Education and Social Change in Nineteenth-Century Massachusetts* (New York: Cambridge University Press, 1980), 149, 153.

38. Joseph M. Rice, *The Public School System of the United States* (1893), in David B. Tyack, ed., *Turning Points in American Educational History* (Waltham, Mass.: Blaisdell, 1967), 330.

39. Ibid., 37.

40. Elizabeth Pleck, *Domestic Tyranny: The Making of Social Policy against Family Violence from Colonial Times to the Present* (New York: Oxford University Press, 1987).

5. Growing Up in Bondage

1. Melton A. McLaurin, *Celia, A Slave* (Athens: University of Georgia Press, 1991), 20.

2. Ibid., 21, 125 n. 8.

3. Douglass quoted in Christine Stansell, "The Pages of Eros," *New Republic,* March 6, 2000, 33. Wilma King, *Stolen Childhood* (Bloomington: Indiana University Press, 1995), xix–xx; Thomas L. Webber, *Deep like the Rivers: Education in the Slave Quarter Community, 1831–1865* (New York: Norton, 1978), 136–137.

4. Sylviane A. Diouf, *Growing Up in Slavery* (Brookfield, Conn.: Millbrook, 2001), 25.

5. King, *Stolen Childhood,* xxi, 1, 90; Thomas H. Jones, *The Experience of Thomas H. Jones, Who Was a Slave for Forty-three Years* (Boston: Bazin and Chandler, 1862), 6.

6. Diouf, *Growing Up in Slavery,* 37.

7. King, *Stolen Childhood,* 5; Marie Jenkins Schwartz, *Born in Bondage* (Cambridge, Mass.: Harvard University Press, 2000), 27.

8. King, *Stolen Childhood,* 9–11; Schwartz, *Born in Bondage,* 64, 68; Steven Mintz and Susan Kellogg, *Domestic Revolutions: A Social History of American Family Life* (New York: Free Press, 1988), 73.

9. Mintz and Kellogg, *Domestic Revolutions,* 73.

10. Steven Mintz, *African American Voices* (St. James, N.Y.: Brandywine, 2000), 103–104; Diouf, *Growing Up in Slavery,* 29.

11. Mintz and Kellogg, *Domestic Revolutions,* 70.

12. Schwartz, *Born in Bondage,* 85, 87–88, 126; Peter Bardaglio, "The Children of Jubilee: African American Childhood in Wartime," in *Divided Houses: Gender and the Civil War,* ed. Catherine Clinton and Nina Silber (New York: Oxford University Press, 1992), 216; Mintz, *African American Voices,* 90–92.

13. Schwartz, *Born in Bondage,* 91, 102, 105; King, *Stolen Childhood,* 24, 105; David K. Wiggins, "The Play of Slave Children in the Plantation Communities of the Old South, 1820–60," in *Growing Up in America,* ed. N. Ray Hiner and Joseph M. Hawes (Urbana: University of Illinois, 1985), 175; King, *Stolen Childhood,* 45, 48; Webber, *Deep like the Rivers,* 95; Albert J.

Raboteau, *Slave Religion: The "Invisible Institution" in the Antebellum South* (New York: Oxford University Press, 1978), 282; Stephen C. Crawford, "Quantified Memory" (Ph.D. diss., University of Chicago, 1980), 169–170.

14. King, *Stolen Childhood*, 7; Cheryll Ann Cody, "Naming, Kinship, and Estate Dispersal: Notes on Slave Family Life on a South Carolina Plantation, 1786 to 1833," *William and Mary Quarterly*, 3d ser., 39 (January 1982), 192–211; idem, "There Was No 'Absalom' on the Ball Plantations: Slave-Naming Practices in the South Carolina Low Country, 1720–1865," *American Historical Review* 92 (1987), 563–596; John C. Inscoe, "Carolina Slave Names: An Index to Acculturation," *Journal of Southern History* 49 (1983), 527–554; John Thornton, "Central African Names and African-American Naming Patterns," *William and Mary Quarterly*, 3d ser., 50 (October 1993), 727–742.

15. Only rarely were daughters named for mothers; Cody, "There Was No 'Absalom,'" 573–576, 591, 594.

16. Schwartz, *Born in Bondage*, 71, 86; King, *Stolen Childhood*, 14.

17. Schwartz, *Born in Bondage*, 83, 140–41; King, *Stolen Childhood*, 15, 17, 30.

18. Octavia George in *Remembering Slavery*, ed. Ira Berlin, Marc Favreau, and Steven F. Miller (New York: New Press, 1998), 40, 43.

19. Michael P. Johnson, "Upward in Slavery," *New York Review of Books*, December 21, 1989, 53–54.

20. Diouf, *Growing Up in Slavery*, 44.

21. King, *Stolen Childhood*, 21–22.

22. Ibid., 27, 29–30.

23. Ibid., 24, 29–30, 34–35; Schwartz, *Born in Bondage*, 108, 145.

24. Webber, *Deep like the Rivers*, 21; Schwartz, *Born in Bondage*, 26, 108, 123, 133–4, 136, 139, 146, 149; King, *Stolen Childhood*, 38–39.

25. Stephanie J. Shaw, "Mothering under Slavery in the Antebellum South," in *Mothering: Ideology, Experience, and Agency*, ed. Evelyn Nakano Glenn, Grace Chang, and Linda Rennie Forcey (New York: Routledge, 1994), 237–38; King, *Stolen Childhood*, 98; Webber, *Deep like the Rivers*, 20.

26. Mintz, *African American Voices*, 87–89; Bardaglio, "Children of Jubilee," 215.

27. Francis Black, First Series, Library of Congress Rare Book Room Collection, Texas Narratives, vol. 4, 87 ff.

28. Webber, *Deep like the Rivers*, 33, 42; Schwartz, *Born in Bondage*, 91–92.

29. King, *Stolen Childhood*, 53; Webber, *Deep like the Rivers*, 20; Wiggins, "Play of Slave Children," 185.

30. Stephanie Coontz, "United States," in *International Encyclopedia of Marriage and Family*, ed. James J. Ponzetti Jr. (New York: Macmillan Reference, 2003), 1683; Schwartz, *Born in Bondage*, 95.

31. Schwartz, *Born in Bondage*, 9; Diouf, *Growing Up in Slavery*, 26; Webber, *Deep like the Rivers*, 68.

32. Diouf, *Growing Up in Slavery*, 65; Leon F. Litwack, *Trouble in Mind: Black Southerners in the Age of Jim Crow* (New York: Knopf, 1998), 38, 39.

33. Wiggins, "Play of Slave Children," 188; Schwartz, *Born in Bondage*, 45–46, 97, 99–100, 125.

34. Schwartz, *Born in Bondage*, 80, 167; King, *Stolen Childhood*, 56.

35. King, *Stolen Childhood*, 53; Webber, *Deep like the Rivers*, 20; Wiggins, "Play of Slave Children," 185.

36. Wiggins, "Play of Slave Children," 175; King, *Stolen Childhood*, 45, 48; Webber, *Deep like the Rivers*, 95; Raboteau, *Slave Religion*, 282.

37. King, *Stolen Childhood*, 48; Wiggins, "Play of Slave Children," 177.

38. Wiggins, "Play of Slave Children," 180, 187; Webber, *Deep like the Rivers*, 95; King, *Stolen Childhood*, 48.

39. Wiggins, "Play of Slave Children," 181.

40. Douglass quoted in Stansell, "The Pages of Eros," 33. King, *Stolen Childhood*, xix–xx; Webber, *Deep like the Rivers*, 136–137.

41. Leon F. Litwack, *Been in the Storm So Long: The Aftermath of Slavery* (New York: Knopf, 1979), 25, 29, 53.

42. Webber, *Deep like the Rivers*, 66, 134.

43. Ibid., 66, 134. Douglass is quoted in Janet Duitsman Cornelius, *"When I Can Read My Title Clear": Literacy, Slavery, and Religion in the Antebellum South* (Columbia: University of South Carolina Press, 1991), 1.

44. Cornelius, *"When I Can Read My Title Clear,"* 61, 69; Diouf, *Growing Up in Slavery*, 70; Webber, *Deep like the Rivers*, 66, 134.

45. Diouf, *Growing Up in Slavery*, 73.

46. King, *Stolen Childhood*, 60; Schwartz, *Born in Bondage*, 156, 158, 179.

47. Crawford, "Quantified Memory," 162; Drew Gilpin Faust, *James Henry Hammond and the Old South* (Baton Rouge: Louisiana State University Press, 1982); John B. Edmunds Jr., *Francis W. Pickens and the Politics of Destruction* (Chapel Hill: University of North Carolina Press, 1986); Charles C. Osborne, *Jubal: The Life and Times of General Jubal A. Early* (Chapel Hill, N.C.: Algonquin Books of Chapel Hill, 1992).

48. Raboteau, *Slave Religion*, 177, 267; Webber, *Deep like the Rivers*, 129.

49. Raboteau, *Slave Religion*, 266, 268, 270, 275, 279.

50. Bardaglio, "Children of Jubilee," 218–219; Wiggins, "Play of Slave Children," 184.

51. Bardaglio, "Children of Jubilee," 222, 224.

52. Ira Berlin and Leslie S. Rowland, *Families and Freedom: A Documentary History of African-American Kinship in the Civil War Era* (New York: New Press, 1997), 97, 99, 100; Bardaglio, "Children of Jubilee," 221.

53. David Brion Davis and Steven Mintz, *Boisterous Sea of Liberty* (New York: Oxford University Press, 1998), 538; Berlin and Rowland, *Families and Freedom*, 77, 103, 112.

54. Rebecca J. Scott, "The Battle over the Child: Child Apprenticeship and the Freedmen's Bureau in North Carolina," in Hiner and Hawes, *Growing Up in America*, 204.

55. Ibid., 195; Berlin and Rowland, *Families and Freedom*, 211, 221.

56. Scott, "Battle over the Child," 196; Berlin and Rowland, *Families and Freedom*, 242.

57. Scott, "Battle over the Child," 194, 197, 206.

58. Litwack, *Trouble in Mind*, 62, 64, 67, 79.

59. Ibid., 10.
60. Ibid., 11–13, 16, 24.
61. Ibid., 4, 7, 9, 28, 34, 41.
62. Ibid., 9, 16, 20.
63. Ibid., 13, 19, 34, 44.

6. Childhood Battles of the Civil War

1. Susie King Taylor, *Reminiscences of My Life in Camp with the 33d United States Colored Troops Late 1st S. C. Volunteers* (Boston: Privately printed, 1902), 5.
2. Emmy E. Werner, *Reluctant Witnesses: Children's Voices from the Civil War* (Boulder: Westview Press, 1998), 43.
3. James Marten, *The Children's Civil War* (Chapel Hill: University of North Carolina Press, 1998).
4. Joseph T. Glatthaar, *American Civil War: The War in the West, 1863–1865* (Oxford: Osprey, 2001), 75–76.
5. G. Clifton Wisler, *When Johnny Went Marching: Young Americans Fight the Civil War* (New York: HarperCollins, 2001), 1–2; Patricia Polacco, *Pink and Say* (New York: Putnam, 1994); William B. Styple, *The Little Bugle: The True Story of a Twelve-Year-Old Boy in the Civil War* (Kearney, N.J.: Belle Grove, 1998); Wisler, *When Johnny Went Marching*, 10–13; S. Emma E. Edmonds, *Nurse and Spy in the Union Army* (Hartford: W. S. Williams; Philadelphia: Jones Bros., 1865); Sylvia G. L. Dannett, *She Rode with the Generals: The True and Incredible Story of Sarah Emma Seelye, Alias Franklin Thompson* (Edinburgh: T. Nelson, 1960); "Why Did Women Fight in the Civil War?" Smithsonian Associates, http://civilwarstudies.org/features/women.htm; Gail Skroback Hennessey, "Uncommon Soldiers: Women during the Civil War," http://teacher.scholastic.com/lessonrepro/lessonplans/womcivwar.htm.
6. Werner, *Reluctant Witnesses*, 9; Jim Murphy, *The Boys' War: Confederate and Union Soldiers Talk about the Civil War* (New York: Clarion Books, 1990), 8.
7. Murphy, *Boys' War*, 11, 13.
8. Werner, *Reluctant Witnesses*, 12; Murphy, *Boys' War*, 27.
9. Murphy, *Boys' War*, 27–28, 48–49, 55.
10. William Bircher, *A Drummer-Boy's Diary: Comprising Four Years of Service with the Second Regiment Minnesota* (St. Paul: St. Paul Book and Stationery, 1889).
11. Murphy, *Boys' War*, 84.
12. Werner, *Reluctant Witnesses*, 25; Murphy, *Boys' War*, 70, 78.
13. Murphy, *Boys' War*, 63, 86; Werner, *Reluctant Witnesses*, 32–34, 23–24.
14. Ibid., 93–94.
15. Ibid., 105, 113.
16. Marten, *Children's Civil War*, 101; Werner, *Reluctant Witnesses*, 15, 28, 51.
17. Werner, *Reluctant Witnesses*, 59–60, 64, 72, 154.
18. Ibid., 52, 82.

19. Anne Scott MacLeod, *American Childhood* (Athens: University of Georgia Press, 1994), 107; Marten, *Children's Civil War*, 155.

20. George M. Fredrickson, *The Inner Civil War: Northern Intellectuals and the Crisis of the Union* (New York: Harper and Row, 1965), 226; Werner, *Reluctant Witnesses*, 58.

21. Werner, *Reluctant Witnesses*, 53–54; Marten, *Children's Civil War*, 152.

22. Marten, *Children's Civil War*, 157.

23. Werner, *Reluctant Witnesses*, 8; Marten, *Children's Civil War*, 118, 165, 177, 179.

24. Glatthaar, *American Civil War*, 85; Werner, *Reluctant Witnesses*, 127, 141.

25. Reid Mitchell, *The Vacant Chair: The Northern Soldier Leaves Home* (New York: Oxford University Press, 1993); Marten, *Children's Civil War*, 76; Stephen M. Frank, *Life with Father: Parenthood and Masculinity in the Nineteenth-Century American North* (Baltimore: Johns Hopkins University Press, 1998), 180; David Brion Davis and Steven Mintz, *Boisterous Sea of Liberty* (New York: Oxford University Press, 1998), 523.

26. James M. McPherson, *For Cause and Comrade: What They Fought For, 1861–1865* (New York: Oxford University Press, 1997); Davis and Mintz, *Boisterous Sea of Liberty*, 544; Marten, *Children's Civil War*, 116; Werner, *Reluctant Witnesses*, 20.

27. Fredrickson, *Inner Civil War*, 219; James M. McPherson, *The Abolitionist Legacy: From Reconstruction to the NAACP* (Princeton: Princeton University Press, 1975).

28. Werner, *Reluctant Witnesses*, 5; Davis and Mintz, *Boisterous Sea of Liberty*, 555–556.

29. David Blight, *Race and Reunion: The Civil War in American Memory* (Cambridge, Mass.: Harvard University Press, 2001); Leon F. Litwack, *Trouble in Mind: Black Southerners in the Age of Jim Crow* (New York: Knopf, 1998).

30. LeRoy Ashby, *Endangered Children: Dependency, Neglect, and Abuse in American History* (New York: Twayne, 1997) 34, 63.

31. Marten, *Children's Civil War*, 205–206.

32. Richard Sennett, *Families against the City: Middle Class Homes of Industrial Chicago, 1872–1890* (Cambridge, Mass.: Harvard University Press, 1970).

7. Laboring Children

1. Lucy Larcom, *A New England Girlhood* (Boston: Houghton Mifflin, 1889), 42–45, 120–121, 152–157.

2. Ibid., 42–45, 120–121, 152–157; Shirley Marchalonis, *The Worlds of Lucy Larcom, 1824–1893* (Athens: University of Georgia Press, 1989); Daniel Dulany Addison, ed., *Lucy Larcom: Life, Letters, and Diary* (Boston: Houghton Mifflin, 1895); Bernice Selden, *The Mill Girls: Lucy Larcom, Harriet Hanson Robinson, Sarah G. Bagley* (New York: Atheneum, 1983).

3. Linda S. Peavy and Ursula Smith, *Frontier Children* (Norman: University of Oklahoma Press, 1999), 37; Frances Cavanah, ed., *We Came to America*

(Philadelphia: Macrae Smith, 1954), 136–143; Mary Goble Pay, "Death Strikes the Handcart Company," in *A Believing People: Literature of the Latter-Day Saints*, ed. Richard H. Cracroft and Neal E. Lambert (Provo: Brigham Young University Press, 1974), 143–150; Priscilla Ferguson Clement, *Growing Pains: Children in the Industrial Age, 1850–1890* (New York: Twayne, 1997), 7, 225.

4. Clement, *Growing Pains,* 7, 225.

5. Ibid., 37, 62, 78, 86, 120; Elliott West, *Growing Up with the Country: Childhood on the Far Western Frontier* (Albuquerque: University of New Mexico Press, 1989), 253–254.

6. Nan Wolverton Franklin, "Toying with 1830s Childhood," Old Sturbridge Village, http://www.osv.org/education/OSVisitor/Toying.html.

7. Barbara M. Tucker, *Samuel Slater and the Origins of the American Textile Industry, 1790–1860* (Ithaca: Cornell University Press, 1984).

8. Anthony F. C. Wallace, "The World of Work in a Nineteenth-Century Mill Town," in *Family Life in America, 1620–2000,* ed. Mel Albin and Dominick Cavallo (St. James, N.Y.: Revisionary, 1981), 174–175.

9. Thomas Dublin, "Women and Outwork in a Nineteenth-Century New England Town," in *The Countryside in the Age of Capitalist Transformation,* ed. Steven Hahn and Jonathan Prude (Chapel Hill: University of North Carolina Press, 1985), 51–69.

10. W. J. Rorabaugh, *The Craft Apprentice: From Franklin to the Machine Age in America* (New York: Oxford University Press, 1986), 16, 130.

11. Joseph F. Kett, *Rites of Passage: Adolescence in America, 1790 to the Present* (New York: Basic Books, 1977), 144–172.

12. Howard P. Chudacoff, *How Old Are You?: Age Consciousness in American Culture* (Princeton: Princeton University Press, 1989), 19.

13. Glenn Wallach, *Obedient Sons: The Discourse of Youth and Generations in American Culture, 1630–1860* (Amherst: University of Massachusetts Press, 1997), 55–88.

14. Rorabaugh, *Craft Apprentice,* 27–29, 37, 41, 69, 83, 97–101, 161, 190–194.

15. Ibid., 165, 170–171.

16. Ibid., 164–165, 167; Iver Bernstein, *The New York City Draft Riots: Their Significance for American Society and Politics in the Age of the Civil War* (New York : Oxford University Press, 1990).

17. Rorabaugh, *Craft Apprentice,* 130, 133, 166.

18. Thomas Dublin, *Women at Work: The Transformation of Work and Community in Lowell, Massachusetts* (New York: Columbia University Press, 1979).

19. Penny Colman, *Girls: A History of Growing Up Female in America* (New York: Scholastic, 2000), 76.

20. Christine Stansell, *City of Women: Sex and Class in New York, 1789–1860* (New York: Knopf, 1986), 158.

21. Jacqueline S. Reinier, *From Virtue to Character: American Childhood, 1775–1850* (New York: Twayne, 1996), 126; Stansell, *City of Women,* 50–51, 53, 116, 204.

22. Stansell, *City of Women,* 50, 53–54; Barbara M. Brenzel, *Daughters of the*

State: A Social Portrait of the First Reform School for Girls in North America (Cambridge, Mass.: MIT Press, 1983); Wallace, "World of Work," 179.

23. Susan Campbell Bartoletti, *Black Potatoes: The Story of the Great Irish Famine, 1845–1850* (Boston: Houghton Mifflin, 2001), 53, 121, 168–169; "Famine and Starvation in the County of Cork," *Illustrated London News, January 16, 1847, http://vassun.vassar.edu/?sttaylor/FAMINE/ILN/CorkFamine/CorkFamine.html.*

24. Peter Collier and David Horowitz, *The Kennedys* (New York: Summit Books, 1984), 21–22; Cecil Woodham Smith, *The Great Hunger* (New York: H. Hamilton, 1962).

25. Kerby A. Miller, *Emigrants and Exiles: Ireland and the Irish Exodus to North America* (New York: Oxford University Press, 1985), 282; Kerby A. Miller and Paul Wagner, *Out of Ireland* (Niwot, Colo.: Robert Rinehart Publishers, 1997), 27, 31; Collier and Horowitz, *The Kennedys,* 21–22; Robert Whyte, *Robert Whyte's 1847 Famine Ship Diary: The Journey of an Irish Coffin Ship,* ed. James J. Mangan (Cork: Mercier, 1994), 13–22; David Brion Davis and Steven Mintz, *Boisterous Sea of Liberty* (New York: Oxford University Press, 1998), 449–451.

26. Miller, *Emigrants and Exiles,* 319.

27. Hasia R. Diner, *Erin's Daughters in America: Irish Immigrant Women in the Nineteenth Century* (Baltimore: Johns Hopkins University Press, 1983), 31–32; Mathew Carey, "Appeal to the Wealthy of the Land," in *The Irish in America, 550–1972,* ed. William D. Griffen (New York: Oceana, 1973), 46.

28. Diner, *Erin's Daughters,* 45–46, 55, 59–61, 132–133, 140–141.

29. Ibid., 109.

30. Phillip Hoose, *We Were There, Too! Young People in U.S. History* (New York: Farrar Straus Giroux, 2001), 168–171.

31. Steven Mintz and Susan Kellogg, *Domestic Revolutions: A Social History of American Family Life* (New York: Free Press, 1988), 102; Susan Campbell Bartoletti, *Growing Up in Coal Country* (Boston: Houghton Mifflin, 1996), 13–16.

32. Mintz and Kellogg, *Domestic Revolutions,* 103–104.

33. James Kirby Martin et al., *America and Its Peoples,* 5th ed. (New York: Pearson Longman, 2003), 339.

34. Emmy E. Werner, *Pioneer Children on the Journey West* (Boulder: Westview, 1995), 46.

35. Pay, "Death Strikes the Handcart Company."

36. Mintz and Kellogg, *Domestic Revolutions,* 96–97; John Faragher, *Women and Men on the Overland Trail* (New Haven: Yale University Press, 1979), 66, 69, 71–84, 106, 136–143.

37. Donald Zochert, *Laura: The Life of Laura Ingalls Wilder* (Chicago: Contemporary Books, 1976); Dwight M. Miller, ed., *Laura Ingalls Wilder and the American Frontier: Five Perspectives* (Lanham, Md.: University Press of America, 2002); Ann Romines, *Constructing the Little House: Gender, Culture, and Laura Ingalls Wilder* (Amherst: University of Massachusetts Press, 1997).

38. Clement, *Growing Pains*, 124; West, *Growing Up with the Country*, 75–76, 88, 246.

39. West, *Growing Up with the Country*, 91, 192; Elliott West, "Heathens and Angels: Childhood in the Rocky Mountain Mining Towns," in *Growing Up in America: Historical Experiences*, ed. Harvey J. Graff (Detroit: Wayne State University Press, 1987), 370.

40. West, "Heathens and Angels," 372; West, *Growing Up with the Country*, 76, 77, 88.

41. West, "Heathens and Angels," 374, 379.

42. West, *Growing Up with the Country*, 91, 192; West, "Heathens and Angels," 370.

43. West, *Growing Up with the Country*, 254, 255; *Columbus Dispatch*, May 3, 1998, 7G; *New York Times*, August 10, 1980, sec. 3, 1; Elizabeth Hampsten, *Settlers' Children: Growing Up on the Great Plains* (Norman: University of Oklahoma Press, 1991), 234.

44. Clements, *Growing Pains*, 130; West, *Growing Up with the Country*, 168.

45. Gilbert C. Fite, "Daydreams and Nightmares: The Late Nineteenth-Century Agricultural Frontiers," *Agricultural History* 40 (1966), 285–291.

46. On the useful and the invaluable but economically useless childhood, see Viviana A. Zelizer, *Pricing the Priceless Child: The Changing Social Value of Children* (New York: Basic Books, 1985).

8. Save the Child

1. Christine Stansell, *City of Women: Sex and Class in New York, 1789–1860* (New York: Knopf, 1986), 194, 202, 205; Robert H. Bremner, ed., *Children and Youth in America: A Documentary History* (Cambridge, Mass.: Harvard University Press, 1970), 755, quoted in Ken Libertoff, "The Runaway Child in America," in *Family Life in America, 1620–2000,* ed Mel Albin and Dominick Cavallo (St. James, N.Y.: Revisionary, 1981), 272.

2. Seth Rockman, *Welfare Reform in the Early Republic* (Boston: Bedford/St. Martin's, 2003), 87–88, 90.

3. In the early nineteenth century, poor relief typically represented more than half of towns' budgets; LeRoy Ashby, *Endangered Children: Dependency, Neglect, and Abuse in American History* (New York: Twayne, 1997), 34; "Howard," *Baltimore American*, February 2, 1820, quoted in Rockman, *Welfare Reform in Early Republic*, 17.

4. Michael Grossberg, *Governing the Hearth: Law and the Family in Nineteenth-Century America* (Chapel Hill: University of North Carolina Press, 1985), 10, 298.

5. Between 1820 and 1890 the ratio of whites under age fifteen to those over fifteen fell from 96 per 100 to 53 per 100; U.S. Bureau of the Census, *The Statistical History of the United States from Colonial Times to the Present* (Stamford, Conn.: Fairfield, 1965), 10.

6. Michael Grossberg, "Changing Conceptions of Child Welfare in the United States, 1820–1935," in *A Century of Juvenile Justice*, ed. Margaret K.

Rosenheim, Franklin E. Zimring, David S. Tanenhaus, and Bernardine Dohrn (Chicago: University of Chicago Press, 2002), 22–27; Lela B. Costin, Howard Jacob Karger, and David Stoesz, *The Politics of Child Abuse in America* (New York: Oxford University Press, 1996), 47, 50.

7. Annette Atkins, *We Grew Up Together: Brothers and Sisters in Nineteenth-Century America* (Urbana: University of Illinois Press, 2001), 105–106; E. Wayne Carp, *Family Matters: Secrecy and Disclosure in the History of Adoption* (Cambridge, Mass.: Harvard University Press, 1998), 7; David J. Rothman, *Discovery of the Asylum: Social Order and Disorder in the New Republic* (Boston: Little, Brown, 1971); Kenneth Cmiel, *A Home of Another Kind: One Chicago Orphanage and the Tangle of Child Welfare* (Chicago: University of Chicago Press, 1995); Judith A. Dulberger, *"Mother Donit fore the Best": Correspondence of a Nineteenth-Century Orphan Asylum* (Syracuse: Syracuse University Press, 1996); Nurith Zmora, *Orphanages Reconsidered: Child Care Institutions in Progressive Era Baltimore* (Philadelphia: Temple University Press, 1994).

8. Ashby, *Endangered Children*, 27–34; Dulberger, *"Mother Donit fore the Best,"* 9.

9. Dulberger, *"Mother Donit fore the Best,"* 111.

10. Ashby, *Endangered Children*, 90.

11. Quoted in Nina Bernstein, "Don't Bring Back the Bad Old Days," *Newsday,* November 30, 1994, A35.

12. Ashby, *Endangered Children*, 101–110, 120.

13. John E. Yang, "The Speaker Comes to Boys Town," *Washington Post,* October 24, 1995, A3; Bernstein, "Don't Bring Back the Bad Old Days."

14. John R. Sutton, *Stubborn Children: Controlling Delinquency in the United States, 1640–1981* (Berkeley: University of California Press, 1988), 74; Robert Mennel, "Juvenile Delinquency in Perspective," *History of Education Quarterly* 13 (fall 1973), 275; Robert S. Pickett, *House of Refuge: Origins of Juvenile Reform in New York State, 1815–1857* (Syracuse: Syracuse University Press, 1969); Rockman, *Welfare Reform in Early Republic,* 85–86, 87–88, 95–96.

15. Sutton, *Stubborn Children,* 77, 81; Steven Mintz, *Moralists and Modernizers: America's Pre–Civil War Reformers* (Baltimore: Johns Hopkins University Press, 1995), 90–92.

16. Mintz, *Moralists and Modernizers,* 90–92.

17. Ibid., 92.

18. Barbara M. Brenzel, *Daughters of the State: A Social Portrait of the First Reform School for Girls in North America* (Cambridge, Mass.: MIT Press, 1983), 354, 357–359.

19. Ashby, *Endangered Children*, 18.

20. Ibid., 236.

21. Grossberg, *Governing the Hearth,* 241.

22. Ibid., 238, 247.

23. Jacob Krason, "A Grave Threat to the Family: American Law and Public Policy on Child Abuse and Neglect," in *Defending the Family: A Sourcebook,* ed.

Paul C. Vitz and Stephen M. Krason (Steubenville, Ohio: Catholic Social Science Press, 1998), 235–267.

24. Lee E. Teitelbaum, "Family History and Family Law," *Wisconsin Law Review,* 1985, 1158–59.

25. Carp, *Family Matters,* 4–7, 11–12; Grossberg, *Governing the Hearth,* 196.

26. Stephen O'Connor, *Orphan Trains: The Story of Charles Loring Brace and the Children He Saved and Failed* (Boston: Houghton Mifflin, 2001); Miriam Z. Langsam, *Children West: A History of the Placing-Out System of the New York Children's Aid Society, 1853–1890* (Madison: State Historical Society of Wisconsin, 1964).

27. Carp, *Family Matters,* 10.

28. Quoted in *San Diego Union-Tribune,* August 16, 2000, B-7.

29. Clay Gish, "Rescuing the 'Waifs and Strays' of the City: The Western Emigration Program of the Children's Aid Society," *Journal of Social History* 33 (1999), 121–141.

30. Ibid., 133, 136.

31. *New York Times,* December 15, 1990, 26; Marilyn Irvin Holt, *The Orphan Trains: Placing Out in America* (Lincoln: University of Nebraska, 1992), 156–87.

32. Paula S. Fass, *Kidnapped: Child Abduction in America* (New York: Oxford University Press, 1997), 21–56.

33. Ashby, *Endangered Children,* 55–59; Costin, Karger, and Stoesz, *Politics of Child Abuse,* 52–61.

34. Costin, Karger, and Stoesz, *Politics of Child Abuse,* 74; Ashby, *Endangered Children,* 57.

35. Costin, Karger, and Stoesz, *Politics of Child Abuse,* 63; Linda Gordon, *Heroes of Their Own Lives: The Politics and History of Family Violence: Boston, 1880–1960* (New York: Viking, 1988); Elizabeth Pleck, *Domestic Tyranny: The Making of American Social Policy against Family Violence* (New York: Oxford University Press, 1987), 69–87.

36. Costin, Karger, and Stoesz, *Politics of Child Abuse,* 65.

37. Gordon, *Heroes in Their Own Lives;* Costin, Karger, and Stoesz, *Politics of Child Abuse,* 89; Pleck, *Domestic Tyranny,* 205–216.

38. Jacob Riis, *How the Other Half Lives: Studies among the Tenements of New York,* ed. Sam Bass Warner (Cambridge, Mass.: Belknap Press of Harvard University Press, 1970), 124–129; Viviana A. Zeliser, *Pricing the Priceless Child: The Changing Social Value of Children* (New York: Basic Books, 1985).

39. Nicola Kay Beisel, *Imperiled Innocents: Anthony Comstock and Family Reproduction in Victorian America* (Princeton: Princeton University Press, 1997), 37, 65, 91.

40. Bessie V. Cushman, "Another Maiden Tribute," *Union Signal,* February 17, 1887, 8–9; Timothy J. Gilfoyle, *City of Eros: New York City, Prostitution, and the Commercialization of Sex, 1790–1920* (New York: Norton, 1992); Marilynn Wood Hill, *Their Sisters' Keepers: Prostitution in New York City, 1830–1870* (Berkeley: University of California Press, 1993); Mary E. Odem,

Delinquent Daughters: Protecting and Policing Adolescent Female Sexuality in the United States, 1885–1920 (Chapel Hill: University of North Carolina Press, 1995).

41. Katherine G. Aiken, *Harnessing the Power of Motherhood: The National Florence Crittenton Mission* (Knoxville: University of Tennessee, 1998).

42. Quoted in *Columbus Dispatch,* August 23, 1995, 1E.

43. Peavy and Smith, *Frontier Children,* 120; Lisa May, "An Indian School Is Remembered," *Newsday,* May 28, 2000, A29.

44. Peavy and Smith, *Frontier Children,* 120; May, "An Indian School Is Remembered."

45. During the twentieth century at least 50,000 Indian children were adopted by non-Indians, prompting Congress in 1978 to pass the Indian Child Welfare Act, which gave tribes preference in adopting children of Indian heritage; Tim Vanderpool, "Lesson No. 1: Shed Your Indian Identity," *Christian Science Monitor,* April 2, 2002, 14.

46. Michael Willrich, *City of Courts: Socializing Justice in Progressive Era Chicago* (Cambridge: Cambridge University Press, 2003).

47. Jack Holl, *Juvenile Reform in the Progressive Era: William R. George and the Junior Republic Movement* (Ithaca: Cornell University Press, 1971), 1–34, 302–309.

48. Ibid., 307.

49. Michael Katz, "Child-Saving," *History of Education Quarterly* 26 (1986), 413–424.

50. LeRoy Ashby, *Saving the Waifs: Reformers and Dependent Children, 1890–1917* (Philadelphia: Temple University Press, 1984), 13, 84; Katz, "Child-Saving," 418–421; Sutton, *Stubborn Children,* 134.

51. Joseph Mayer Rice, "The Absurdity of Primary Education," in *The Annals of America,* vol. 2: *1884–1894, Agrarianism and Urbanization* (Chicago: Encyclopedia Britannica, 1976), 396–403; Michael B. Katz, "The New Departure in Quincy, 1873–1881: The Nature of Nineteenth-Century Educational Reform," *New England Quarterly* 40 (1967), 3–30.

52. Alexander W. Siegel and Sheldon H. White, "The Child Study Movement: Early Growth and Development of the Symbolized Child," in *Advances in Child Development and Behavior,* vol. 17, ed. Hayne W. Reese (New York: Academic, 1982), 244; Ashby, *Endangered Children,* 99; Selma Cantor Berrol, *Immigrants at School: New York City, 1898–1914* (1967; reprint, New York: Arno, 1978), 115.

53. Dominick Covallo, "The Politics of Latency," in *Regulated Children/ Liberated Children,* ed. Barbara Finkelstein (New York: Psychohistory Press, 1979), 158–83; David I. Macleod, *The Age of the Child: Children in America, 1890–1920* (New York: Twayne, 1998), 72; Berrol, *Immigrants at School,* 130.

54. "A Faithful Mirror: Standards," College Board, http://www.collegeboard.com/faithfulmirror/standards/who.html.

55. Henry L. Minton, *Lewis M. Terman: Pioneer in Psychological Testing* (New York: New York University Press, 1988); Paul Davis Chapman, *Schools as*

Sorters: Lewis M. Terman, Applied Psychology, and the Intelligence Testing Movement (New York: New York University Press, 1988).

56. Daniel Eli Burnstein, "Clean Streets and the Pursuit of Progress: Urban Reform in New York City in the Progressive Era" (Ph.D. diss., Rutgers University, 1992), 307, 312, 323.

57. Richard A. Meckel, *Save the Babies: American Public Health Reform and the Prevention of Infant Mortality, 1850–1929* (Ann Arbor: University of Michigan Press, 1998).

58. Victoria Gettis, *The Juvenile Court and the Progressives* (Urbana: University of Illinois Press, 2000); Anne Meis Knupfer, *Reform and Resistance: Gender, Delinquency, and America's First Juvenile Court* (New York: Routledge, 2001).

59. Mennel, "Juvenile Delinquency in Perspective," 280; Sutton, *Stubborn Children*, 135.

60. Macleod, *Age of the Child*, 142.

61. Mennel, "Juvenile Delinquency in Perspective," 280; Sutton, *Stubborn Children*, 135.

62. Thomas V. DiBacco, "Kids and Crime," *USA Today,* May 3, 1989, 10A; Sutton, *Stubborn Children*, 147, 173.

63. In Chicago, overburdened juvenile court judges hear an average of sixty cases a day; *New York Times,* July 21, 1997, A1; *USA Today,* December 16, 1999, 3A; Jeffrey A. Butts and Daniel P. Mears, "Reviving Juvenile Justice in a Get Tough Era," *Youth & Society,* December 2001, 169–198.

64. Willrich, *City of Courts,* 241–259.

65. Dominick Cavallo, *Muscles and Morals: Organized Playgrounds and Urban Reform, 1880–1920* (Philadelphia: University of Pennsylvania Press, 1981).

66. Costin, Karger, and Stoesz, *Politics of Child Abuse,* 68; Clement, *Growing Pains,* 108; Sonya Michel, *Children's Interests/Mothers' Rights: The Shaping of America's Child Care Policy* (New Haven: Yale University Press, 1999).

67. Ashby, *Endangered Children,* 79–80, 112–114.

68. Kriste Lindenmeyer, *"A Right to Childhood": The U.S. Children's Bureau and Child Welfare, 1912–46* (Urbana: University of Illinois Press, 1997), 37, 41, 52, 108, 119–138.

69. More than 60,000 mentally retarded or mentally ill women were involuntarily sterilized; Philip R. Reilly, *Surgical Solution: A History of Involuntary Sterilization in the United States* (Baltimore: Johns Hopkins University Press, 1991); Charles R. King, *Children's Health in America* (New York: Twayne, 1993), 140.

70. Costin, Karger, and Stoesz, *Politics of Child Abuse,* 68.

71. Leon Stein, Triangle Fire (Ithaca: Cornell University Press, 2001).

72. "Newsboys Act and Talk," *New York Times,* July 25, 1899, 3; David Nasaw, *Children of the City: At Work and at Play* (Garden City, N.Y.: Doubleday/Anchor, 1985), 168–177.

73. Newsstands and home delivery eliminated the need for "newsies," while pneumatic tubes reduced the need for "runners" in department stores; Macleod, *Age of the Child,* 117.

74. Walter I. Trattner, *Crusade for the Children: A History of the National Child*

Labor Committee and Child Labor Reform in America (Chicago: Quadrangle Books, 1970); Macleod, *Age of the Child*, 115–116.

75. Macleod, *Age of the Child*, 116.

76. Ibid.; *Hammer v. Dagenhart*, 247 U.S. 251 (1918); *NLRB v. Jones & Laughlin Steel Corp.*, 301 U.S. 1 (1937).

77. *Scribner's*, August 1892, 244; Costin, Karger, and Stoesz, *Politics of Child Abuse*, 63.

78. Macleod, *Age of the Child*.

9. Children under the Magnifying Glass

1. Gillian Avery, *Behold the Child: American Children and Their Books, 1621–1922* (Baltimore: Johns Hopkins University Press, 1994), 61–62; Anne Scott MacLeod, *A Moral Tale: Children's Fiction and American Culture, 1820–1860* (Hamden: Archon Books, 1975), 37–39; idem, "Children's Literature in America from the Puritan Beginnings to 1870," in *Children's Literature*, ed. Peter Hunt (New York: Oxford University Press, 1995), 110–112.

2. *Atlantic Monthly*, December 1865, 724.

3. Jerry Griswold, *Audacious Kids* (New York: Oxford University Press, 1992), 36, 47, 95; Priscilla Clement, *Growing Pains: Children in the Industrial Age, 1850–1890* (New York: Twayne, 1997), 164: A. S. Byatt, "Harry Potter and the Childish Adult," *New York Times*, July 7, 2003.

4. Ann Hulbert, *Raising America: Experts, Parents, and a Century of Advice about Children* (New York: Knopf, 2003); G. Stanley Hall, *Adolescence* (New York: D. Appleton, 1904), x–xi.

5. Charles R. King, *Children's Health* (New York: Twayne, 1993), 65, 85, 91; Richard A. Meckel, *Save the Babies: American Public Health Reform and the Prevention of Infant Mortality, 1850–1929* (Baltimore: Johns Hopkins University Press, 1990), 1.

6. Charles Darwin, "A Biographical Sketch of an Infant," *Mind* 2 (1877), 285–294; Ann Hulbert, "The Century of the Child," *Wilson Quarterly*, winter 1999, 20.

7. Alexander W. Siegel and Sheldon H. White, "The Child Study Movement," in *Advances in Child Development and Behavior*, vol. 17, ed. Hayne W. Reese (New York: Academic Press, 1982), 251.

8. Ibid., 249; Dorothy Ross, *G. Stanley Hall: The Psychologist as Prophet* (Chicago: University of Chicago Press, 1972), 287, 290–291.

9. Ibid., 293–294, 340 n. 57.

10. Ibid., 300, 304–06, 307.

11. Hulbert, "Century of the Child," 14–29.

12. Hulbert, *Raising America*, 63–93.

13. Peter N. Stearns, *Anxious Parents: A History of Modern American Childrearing* (New York: New York University Press, 2003), 42.

14. Barbara Ehrenreich, "What It's Like to Be a Child," *New York Times*, May 24, 1987, sec. 7, 3; Margaret Mead and Martha Wolfenstein, eds., *Childhood in Contemporary Cultures* (Chicago: University of Chicago Press, 1955).

15. Michael Kimmel, *Manhood in America* (New York: Free Press, 1996), 181–

188; Mark Gerson, *A Choice of Heroes: The Changing Faces of American Manhood* (Boston: Houghton Mifflin, 1992), 51; David I. MacLeod, "Act Your Age: Boyhood, Adolescence, and the Rise of the Boy Scouts of America," *Journal of Social History* 16 (1982), 5.

16. David I. MacLeod, *Building Character in the American Boy: The Boy Scouts, the YMCA, and Their Forerunners, 1870–1920* (Madison: University of Wisconsin, 1983), 285.

17. Ibid., 2, 50–51, 110, 119, 123.

18. Nan Enstad, *Ladies of Labor, Girls of Adventure: Working Women, Popular Culture, and Labor Politics at the Turn of the Twentieth Century* (New York: Columbia University Press, 1999).

19. Griswold, *Audacious Kids*, 21; Sally Mitchell, *The New Girl: Girls' Culture in England, 1880–1915* (New York: Columbia University Press, 1995), 149.

20. Fairfax Downey, *Portrait of an Era as Drawn by C. D. Gibson* (New York: Charles Scriber's Sons, 1936).

21. Mitchell, *New Girl*, 173, 183, 188; idem, "Girls and Their Ways," *American Literary History* 10 (1998), 350–359.

22. Ross, *G. Stanley Hall*, 327.

23. James A. Schultz, "Medieval Adolescence: The Claims of History and the Silence of German Narrative," *Speculum* 66 (1991), 519–539; John Demos and Virginia Demos, "Adolescence in Historical Perspective," *Journal of Marriage and the Family* 31 (1969), 632–638.

24. Ibid., 333, 335, 337.

25. Joseph F. Kett, *Rites of Passage: Adolescence in America, 1790 to the Present* (New York: Basic Books, 1977), 215–244.

26. Ibid., 319.

27. Ibid., 320.

28. Ibid., 183–184.

29. Ibid., 183–186; Stephen Hardy, *How Boston Played: Sport, Recreation, and Community, 1865–1915* (Boston: Northeastern University Press, 1982).

30. Kett, *Rites of Passage*, 243–244.

10. New to the Promised Land

1. Mary Antin, *The Promised Land* (Boston: Houghton Mifflin, 1912), 187–188; Magdalena J. Zaborowska, *How We Found America: Reading Gender through East-European Immigrant Narratives* (Chapel Hill: University of North Carolina Press, 1995).

2. Antin, *Promised Land*, 187–188.

3. Melvyn Dubofsky, "Some of Our Mothers and Grandmothers: The Making of the 'New' Jewish Woman," *Reviews in American History* 19 (1991), 385–386; Arthur Hertzberg, *The Jews in America* (New York: Simon and Schuster, 1989); Elizabeth Ewen, *Immigrant Women in the Land of Dollars: Life and Culture on the Lower East Side, 1890–1925* (New York: Monthly Review Press, 1985), 230.

4. Ewen, *Immigrant Women in the Land of Dollars*, 13.

5. Virginia Yans-McLaughlin, *Family and Community: Italian Immigrants in Buffalo, 1880–1930* (Ithaca: Cornell University Press, 1977), 106, 167; Selma Cantor Berrol, *Growing Up American: Immigrant Children in America, Then and Now* (New York: Tawyne, 1995), 16–17, 22.

6. Ewen, *Immigrant Women in the Land of Dollars*, 20–21.

7. Berrol, *Growing Up American*, 44, 52; Selma Cantor Berrol, *Immigrants at School: New York City, 1898–1914* (1967; reprint, New York: Arno, 1978), 55, 86, 115.

8. Berroll, *Growing Up American*, 31, 43; Berroll, *Immigrants at School*, 122, 127, 228–229.

9. Berrol, *Growing Up American*, 34–35, 55.

10. Yans-McLaughlin, *Family and Community*; Jerome Karabel, "The Reasons Why," *New York Review of Books*, February 8, 1979, 8; Berrol, *Growing Up American*, 35, 37; Selma Cantor Berrol, review of Stephan A. Brumberg, *Going to America, Going to School, History of Education Quarterly* 26 (1986), 646.

11. Michael R. Olneck and Marvin Lazerson, "The School Achievement of Immigrant Children: 1900–1930," *History of Education Quarterly* 14 (1974), 453–482; James W. Sanders, *The Education of an Urban Minority: Catholics in Chicago, 1833–1965* (New York: Oxford University Press, 1977).

12. Berrol, *Growing Up American*, 44, 45, 49, 52–53; Selma Cantor Berrol, "Immigrant Children at School," in *The Social Fabric: American Life from the Civil War to the Present*, ed. John H. Cary, Thomas L. Hartshorne, and Robert Anthony Wheeler, 8th ed., vol. 2 (New York: Longman, 1999), 111.

13. Ruth Hutchinson Crocker, "The Settlements: Social Work, Culture, and Ideology in the Progressive Era," *History of Education Quarterly* 31 (1991), 253.

14. Ewen, *Immigrant Women*, 77–79, 85, 89, 91, 135–136, 138–139.

15. Rose Cohen, *Out of the Shadow: A Russian Jewish Girlhood on the Lower East Side* (Ithaca: Cornell University Press, 1995), 108–112, 123–127.

16. Stephen Cole, "Heaven Will Protect the Working Girl," *American Historical Review* 99 (1994), 1265; Cohen, *Out of the Shadow*, 108–12, 123–27, http://womhist.binghamton.edu/shirt/doc1.htm.

17. Berrol, *Growing Up American*, 60, 63, 68, 80.

18. Ewen, *Immigrant Women*, 122, 125, 153; Berrol, *Growing Up American*, 65.

19. Ewen, *Immigrant Women*, 98, 101.

20. Paula S. Fass and Mary Ann Mason, *Childhood in America* (New York: New York University Press, 2000), 631.

21. Cohen, *Out of the Shadow*, 119–135.

22. Beverly Gordon, "'They Don't Wear Wigs Here': Issues and Complexities in the Development of an Exhibition," *American Quarterly* 47 (1995), 117–119, 123–125, 127, 136; Andrew R. Heinze, *Adapting to Abundance: Jewish Immigrants, Mass Consumption, and the Search for American Identity* (New York: Columbia University Press, 1990); Ewen, *Immigrant Women*, 25, 71.

23. Gordon, "'They Don't Wear Wigs Here,'" 124–125, 127, 129–131, 136; Ewen, *Immigrant Women*, 71–72.

24. Ewen, *Immigrant Women,* 71–72, 88.
25. Ibid., 72–73.
26. Hilda Satt Polacheck, *I Came a Stranger: The Story of a Hull-House Girl* (Urbana: University of Illinois Press, 1989).
27. Cole, "Heaven Will Protect the Working Girl," 1265; Berrol, *Growing Up American,* 92; Ewen, *Immigrant Women,* 98, 104, 106, 197–198.
28. Ewen, *Immigrant Women,* 195; Bernard J. Weiss, "The World of Our Mothers: The Lives of Jewish Immigrant Women," *History of Education Quarterly* 29 (1989), 163.
29. Dubofsky, "Some of Our Mothers and Grandmothers," 388; Ewen, *Immigrant Women,* 190; Mary E. Odem, *Delinquent Daughters: Protecting and Policing Adolescent Female Sexuality in the United States, 1885–1920* (Chapel Hill: University of North Carolina Press, 1995).
30. Beverly Gordon, "'They Don't Wear Wigs Here,'" 116; Susan Sachs, "American Dreams, No Illusions," *New York Times,* January 9, 2000, sec. 1, 21; Meri Nana-Ama Danquah, ed., *Becoming American: Personal Essays by First-Generation Immigrant Women* (New York: Hyperion, 2000).

11. Revolt of Modern Youth

1. Gilbert Geis and Leigh B. Bienen, *Crimes of the Century* (Boston: Northeastern University Press, 1998); Paula S. Fass, *Kidnapped: Child Abduction in America* (New York: Oxford University Press, 1997), 57–93; Armand Deutsch, "The First Crime of the Century," *Pittsburgh Post-Gazette,* September 10, 1996, B1; Dianne Zuckerman, "Inside the Leopold, Loeb Case," *Denver Post,* October 22, 2001, EE2; "'Intellectual' Murder in Chicago," *Literary Digest* 82 (July 15, 1924), 40.
2. Fass, *Kidnapped,* 76–83; Douglas O. Linder, "The Leopold and Loeb Trial," http://www.law.umkc.edu/faculty/projects/ftrials/leoploeb/Accountoftrial.htm.
3. Judge Ben Lindsey quoted in Fass, *Kidnapped,* 67.
4. E. Anthony Rotundo, *American Manhood: Transformations in Masculinity from the Revolution to the Modern Era* (New York: Basic Books, 1993), 259; Linda W. Rosenzweig, *Anchor of My Life: Middle-Class American Mothers and Daughters, 1880–1920* (New York: New York University Press, 1993), 170–171; Kathleen W. Jones, *Taming the Troublesome Child: American Families, Child Guidance, and the Limits of Psychiatric Authority* (Cambridge, Mass.: Harvard University Press, 1999), 128.
5. Rosenzweig, *Anchor of My Life,* 170–171; Robert S. Lynd and Helen Merrell Lynd, *Middletown: A Study in Contemporary American Culture* (New York: Harcourt, Brace, 1929); Ben Wattenberg, "Middletown I," The First Measured Century, http://www.pbs.org/fmc/timeline/dmiddletown.htm.
6. Theodore Caplow and Howard M. Bahr, "Half a Century of Change in Adolescent Attitudes: Replication of a Middletown Survey by the Lynds," *Public Opinion Quarterly* 43 (1979), 1–17.

7. Quoted in Paula S. Fass, *The Damned and the Beautiful: American Youth in the 1920s* (New York: Oxford University Press, 1977), 53, 382 n. 22.

8. Fass, *The Damned and the Beautiful,* 90–91, 93–95; James R. McGovern, "The American Woman's Pre–World War I Freedom in Manners and Morals," *Journal of American History* 55 (1968), 319 nn. 25, 26.

9. Gary Cross, *Kids' Stuff: Toys and the Changing World of American Childhood* (Cambridge, Mass.: Harvard University Press, 1997); *San Antonio Express-News,* November 15, 2002, F1; Peter N. Stearns, *Anxious Parents: A History of Modern Childrearing in America* (New York: New York University Press, 2003), 82; *Washington Post,* November 14, 20002, B1.

10. Nan Wolverton Franklin, "Toying with 1830s Childhood," *Old Sturbridge Visitor,* spring 1998, 4–5, http://www.osv.org/education/OSVisitor/Toying.html; Miriam Formanek-Brunell, *Made to Play House: Dolls and the Commercialization of American Girlhood, 1830–1930* (Baltimore: Johns Hopkins University Press, 1993).

11. Cross, *Kid's Stuff.*

12. On Stratemeyer, see Deidre Johnson, *Edward Stratemeyer and the Stratemeyer Syndicate* (New York: Maxwell Macmillan International, 1993); Carol Billman, *The Secret of the Stratemeyer Syndicate* (New York: Ungar, 1986); John T. Dizer Jr., *Tom Swift & Company* (Jefferson, N.C.: McFarland, 1982); Carolyn Stewart Dyer and Nancy Tillman Romalov, eds., *Rediscovering Nancy Drew* (Iowa City: University of Iowa, 1995).

13. Sally Squires, "She Learned to See the World through the Eyes of a Child," *Washington Post,* November 28, 1989, Z17; Fass, *The Damned and the Beautiful,* 87.

14. Joseph M. Hawes, *Children between the Wars: American Childhood, 1920–1940* (New York: Twayne, 1997), 82.

15. Stearns, *Anxious Parents,* 42; Margo Horn, *Before It's Too Late: The Child Guidance Movement in the United States, 1922–1945* (Philadelphia: Temple University Press, 1989), 142–144.

16. Jones, *Taming the Troublesome Child,* 121, 123–128, 132.

17. Ibid., 8, 47, 67–68, 80–81, 84, 174.

18. Ibid., 14, 94, 124–25, 137–138.

19. Joan Jacobs Brumberg, *Body Project: An Intimate History of American Girls* (New York: Random House, 1997), 15; Rosenzweig, *Anchor of My Life,* 78, 81.

20. James H. Jones, *Alfred Kinsey: A Public/Private Life* (New York: Norton, 1997), 67, 69.

21. Ibid., 33, 40, 49, 52.

22. Ibid., 57, 64, 75; David I. Macleod, *Building Character in the American Boy: The Boy Scouts, the YMCA, and Their Forerunners, 1870–1920* (Madison: University of Wisconsin, 1983).

23. Helen Mayer Hacker, "The New Burdens of Masculinity," *Marriage and Family Living* 19 (1957), 230; David Tyack and Elisabeth Hanson, *Learning Together: A History of Coeducation in American Schools* (New York: Russell

Sage Foundation, 1990), 227–242; *Christian Science Monitor,* January 5, 1996, 11; Michael Kimmel, *Manhood in America* (New York: Free Press, 1996), 160; Peter N. Stearns, "Girls, Boys, and Emotions: Redefinitions and Historical Change," *Journal of American History* 80 (1993), 48; *Ottawa Citizen,* March 5, 2001, A11.

24. Jones, *Taming the Troublesome Child,* 133, 159–160, 180–181, 183.

25. Ibid., 73; Rosenzweig, *Anchor of My Life,* 73, 77.

26. Roberta J. Park, "Physiology and Anatomy Are Destiny," *Journal of Sport History* 18 (1991), 37, 38, 39, 60.

27. Shelley Stamp, *Movie-Struck Girls: Women and Motion Picture Culture after the Nickelodeon* (Princeton: Princeton University Press, 2000), 125; Birgitte Søland, *Becoming Modern: Young Women and the Reconstruction of Womanhood in the 1920s* (Princeton: Princeton University Press, 2000), 22, 25–26; John Modell, "Dating Becomes the Way of American Youth," in *Essays on the Family and Historical Change,* ed. Leslie Page Moch and Gary D. Stark (College Station: Texas A&M Press, 1983), 107, 112–113.

28. Søland, *Becoming Modern,* 41; Beth Brophy, "Dear Diary: A History," *U.S. News & World Report,* October 23, 1995, 89; Brumberg, *Body Project,* 60–61; Kevin White, *The First Sexual Revolution* (New York: New York University Press, 1993), 22.

29. Søland, *Becoming Modern,* 14, 21, 54–55, 70; McGovern, "American Woman's Pre–World War I Freedom," 320; Rosenzweig, *Anchor of My Life,* 41.

30. Randolph S. Bourne, "The Handicapped—by One of Them," *Atlantic Monthly,* 1911; Daniel Aaron, "American Prophet," *New York Review of Books,* November 23, 1978, 136–140; Casey Nelson Blake, *Beloved Community: The Cultural Criticism of Randolph Bourne, Van Wyck Brooks, Waldo Frank, and Lewis Mumford* (Chapel Hill: University of North Carolina Press, 1990), 64; Randolph S. Bourne, *Youth and Life* (New York: B. Franklin, 1971), 20.

31. Richard Wightman Fox, "Apostle of Personality," *New York Times,* January 13, 1985, sec. 7, 12; Blake, *Beloved Community,* 63–64; Randolph S. Bourne, "Youth," *Atlantic Monthly,* April 1912, 436–437, reprinted in Lillian Schlissel, ed., *The World of Randolph Bourne* (New York: E. P. Dutton, 1965), 9–11, 15.

32. Michael Gordon, "Was Waller Ever Right? The Rating and Dating Complex Reconsidered," *Journal of Marriage and the Family* 43 (1981), 67–76; White, *First Sexual Revolution,* 14.

33. Brumberg, *Body Project,* xxviii.

34. Quoted in Modell, "Dating Becomes Way of American Youth," 119.

35. Ibid., 95; White, *First Sexual Revolution,* 167; D. C. Thom, *Guiding the Adolescent,* quoted in Modell, "Dating Becomes Way of American Youth," 94.

36. Modell, "Dating Becomes Way of American Youth," 121–122.

37. Ibid., 101, 108–109, 114; Fass, *The Damned and the Beautiful,* 262–263, 324–335.

38. Mary P. Ryan, "The Movie Moderns in the 1920s," in *Decades of Discontent,*

ed. Lois Scharf And Joan M. Jensen (Westport, Conn.: Greenwood, 1983), 118–119.

39. Steven Mintz and Randy Roberts, *Hollywood's America,* 3d ed. (St. James, N.Y.: Brandywine, 2001), 13–14.

40. Kimball Young, "Children's Sleep," *American Journal of Sociology* 41 (1935), 255; Henry James Foreman, "What Our Children Learn When They Go to the Movies," *New York Times Book Review,* December 24, 1933, 3; idem, *Our Movie-Made Children* (New York: Macmillan, 1933).

41. Foreman, "What Our Children Learn," 3.

42. Ibid.

43. Cornelia A. P. Comer, "A Letter to the Rising Generation," *Atlantic Monthly,* February 1911, 145.

44. Randolph S. Bourne, "The Two Generations," *Atlantic Monthly,* May 1911, 591.

45. Leslie J. Vaughan, *Randolph Bourne and the Politics of Cultural Radicalism* (Lawrence: University Press of Kansas, 1997), 62–64; Bourne, "Youth."

12. Coming of Age in the Great Depression

1. In 1998 the Ontario government awarded Yvonne, Annette, and Cecile $4 million (Canadian) in compensation for separating them from their parents and placing them on public display; Cleo Paskal, "Curiosity and the Canadian Quints," *St. Petersburg Times,* July 28, 2002, 1E; Saila K. Dewan, "Yvonne Dionne Dies at 67," *Montreal Gazette,* June 25, 2001, A3; Ian Parker, "Dark Side of the Famous Five," *The Independent* (London), November 5, 1995, 4.

2. Steven Mintz and Susan Kellogg, *Domestic Revolutions: A Social History of American Family Life* (New York: Free Press, 1988), 140; Robert Cohen, *Dear Mrs. Roosevelt: Letters from Children of the Great Depression* (Chapel Hill: University of North Carolina Press, 2002), 7.

3. Grace Palladino, *Teenagers* (New York: Basic Books, 1996), 37; Caroline Bird, *Invisible Scar* (New York: D. McKay, 1966); Glen H. Elder Jr., *Children of the Great Depression* (Chicago: University of Chicago Press, 1974); Cohen, *Dear Mrs. Roosevelt,* 7–9, 146.

4. Russell Baker, *Growing Up* (New York: Congdon and Weed, 1982), 21–22, 80, 84; Mintz and Kellogg, *Domestic Revolutions,* 133.

5. Mintz and Kellogg, *Domestic Revolutions,* 136.

6. Cohen, *Dear Mrs. Roosevelt,* 19, 75–76; Mintz and Kellogg, *Domestic Revolutions,* 136–137.

7. Mintz and Kellogg, *Domestic Revolutions,* 133–134.

8. Ibid., 138–140.

9. Glen H. Elder Jr., John Modell, and Ross D. Parke, eds., *Children in Time and Place* (New York: Cambridge University Press, 1993), 7, 16.

10. Cohen, *Dear Mrs. Roosevelt,* 46, 61, 106, 156, 162–163, 176–177, 206–208.

11. Mintz and Kellogg, *Domestic Revolutions,* 140; Errol Lincoln Uys, *Riding the Rails: Teenagers on the Move during the Great Depression* (New York: TV Books, 1999), 11, 22; Cohen, *Dear Mrs. Roosevelt,* 92.

12. Betty and Ernest K. Lindley, *A New Deal for Youth: The Story of the National Youth Administration* (1938; reprint, New York: Da Capo, 1972), 184; Richard A. Reiman, *The New Deal and American Youth* (Athens: University of Georgia Press, 1992); Carol A. Weisenberger, *Dollars and Dreams: The National Youth Administration in Texas* (New York: P. Lang, 1994); Palladino, *Teenagers*, 45.

13. Lindley, *New Deal for Youth*, 194; Palladino, *Teenagers*, 13.

14. James H. Jones, *Bad Blood: The Tuskegee Syphilis Experiment* (New York: Free Press, 1981), 61–65, 85–86, 218–219; Mintz and Kellogg, *Domestic Revolutions*, 141; Charles S. Johnson, *Shadow of the Plantation* (Chicago: University of Chicago Press, 1934).

15. Mintz and Kellogg, *Domestic Revolutions*, 142.

16. I am deeply grateful to Wilma King for permission to quote from "What a Life This Is: An African American Girl Comes of Age during the Great Depression," a chapter in her book *African American Childhoods in Historical Perspective, 1600–2000* (New York: Palgrave Macmillan, forthcoming).

17. Mintz and Kellogg, *Domestic Revolutions*, 141; Cohen, *Dear Mrs. Roosevelt*, 196.

18. Steven Mintz, *Mexican American Voices* (St. James, N.Y.: Brandywine, 2000), 165.

19. Mintz and Kellogg, *Domestic Revolutions*, 143–144; Mintz, *Mexican American Voices*, 160, 164–165.

20. Dan T. Carter, *Scottsboro* (Baton Rouge: Louisiana State University Press, 1969); James Goodman, *Stories of Scottsboro* (New York: Pantheon, 1994).

21. Uys, *Riding the Rails*, 13, 15–16, 29.

22. Ibid., 28.

23. Thomas Minehan, *Boy and Girl Tramps of America* (New York: Farrar and Rinehart, 1934); Gail Pennington, "Teen Hobos," *St. Louis Post-Dispatch*, April 13, 1998, E6.

24. "Tough Guy Mitchum Dies," *Toronto Star*, July 2, 1997, C1; Uys, *Riding the Rails*, 30, 38, 145, 154–155, 220–230; Walter Goodman, "The Depression's Victims, Hopping the Freights," *New York Times*, April 13, 1998, E5.

25. Cohen, *Dear Mrs. Roosevelt*, 6–9, 13, 91–92; Lindley, *New Deal for Youth*, 11.

26. Linda Gordon, *Pitied but Not Entitled: Single Mothers and the History of Welfare, 1890–1935* (New York: Free Press, 1994).

27. Palladino, *Teenagers*, 39; Cohen, *Dear Mrs. Roosevelt*, 8, 91–92; Lindley, *New Deal for Youth*, 66.

28. Palladino, *Teenagers*, 39–42.

29. Lindley, *New Deal for Youth*, 14–15, 18, 66; Cohen, *Dear Mrs. Roosevelt*, 8, 91–92; Palladino, *Teenagers*, 41; Uys, *Riding the Rails*, 41–42.

30. Uys, *Riding the Rails*, 42.

31. Theodore H. Draper, "The Life of the Party," *New York Review of Books*, January 13, 1994.

32. Robert Cohen, *When the Old Left Was Young* (New York: Oxford University Press, 1993).

33. Robert Cohen, "Activist Impulses: Campus Radicalism in the 1930s," New Deal Network, http://newdeal.feri.org/students/essay02.htm.

34. Cohen, *When the Old Left Was Young.*

35. Cohen, "Activist Impulses"; Eunice Fuller Barnard, "The Class of '36: The Graduate Is Socially Minded, Soberer than His Predecessor," *New York Times,* June 21, 1936, 3.

36. Bradford W. Wright, *Comic Book Nation: The Transformation of Youth Culture in America* (Baltimore: Johns Hopkins University Press, 2001).

37. Quoted in Martha Sherrill, "Dimply the Best," *Washington Post,* July 16, 1995, G1; Robert Coles, "The Gloom and the Glory," *New York Times,* June 18, 1989, sec. 8, 1.

38. Palladino, *Teenagers,* 45.

39. Ibid., 52.

40. Stephen Holden, "After the War, the Time of the Teen-Ager," *New York Times,* May 7, 1995, sec. 4, 6; John Lyttle, "They Don't Make Them like They Used To," *The Independent,* September 13, 1994, 24.

13. *Mobilizing Children for World War II*

1. Dorinda Makanaonalani Nicholson, *Pearl Harbor Child* (Honolulu: Arizona Memorial Museum Association, 1993), 15–20; Emmy E. Werner, *Through the Eyes of Innocents: Children Witness World War II* (Boulder: Westview, 2000), 61–67.

2. Jane Fishman, "I Could See Their Goggles," *Savannah Morning News,* June 13, 2001.

3. William M. Tuttle Jr., "Kansas in World War II," http://ktwu.wuacc.edu/journeys/scripts/905b.html.

4. Jonathan Yardley, "On the Home Front," *Washington Post,* September 12, 1993, sec. 10, 3; Steven Mintz and Susan Kellogg, *Domestic Revolutions: A Social History of American Family Life* (New York: Free Press, 1988), 152–153; William M. Tuttle Jr., *Daddy's Gone to War: The Second World War in the Lives of America's Children* (New York: Oxford University Press, 1993).

5. Deborah Gorham, "They Use Real Bullets: An American Family's Experience of the Second World War: A Fragment of Memoir," *Women's History Review* 6 (1997), 22.

6. Yardley, "On the Home Front"; Tuttle, *Daddy's Gone to War,* 14.

7. Tuttle, *Daddy's Gone to War,* 3, 6, 8; Mintz and Kellogg, *Domestic Revolutions,* 167.

8. Mintz and Kellogg, *Domestic Revolutions,* 153–154.

9. Ibid., 155–156.

10. Ibid., 156, 162–163.

11. Ibid., 157.

12. Werner, *Through the Eyes of Innocents,* 68–69, 72; Mintz and Kellogg, *Domestic Revolutions,* 160.

13. William M. Tuttle Jr., "America's Home Front Children in World War II," in *Children in Time and Place,* ed. Glen H. Elder Jr., John Modell, and Ross D.

Parke (New York: Cambridge University Press, 1993), 29; idem, *Daddy's Gone to War*, 124; Yardley, "On the Home Front."

14. Mintz and Kellogg, *Domestic Revolutions*, 165–166.
15. Ibid., 166.
16. Ibid.
17. Ibid., 165.
18. Ibid., 161–162.
19. Ibid., 161–163; Tuttle, *Daddy's Gone to War*, 81–82.
20. Mintz and Kellogg, *Domestic Revolutions*, 163; Tuttle, "Kansas in World War II."
21. Tuttle, *Daddy's Gone to War*, 26.
22. Mintz and Kellogg, *Domestic Revolutions*, 164.
23. Ibid.
24. 319 U.S. 624, 628.
25. Tuttle, "Home Front Children in World War II," 29; idem, *Daddy's Gone to War*, 119–122, 187; idem, "Kansas in World War II."
26. Bradford W. Wright, *Comic Book Nation: The Transformation of Youth Culture in America* (Baltimore: Johns Hopkins University Press, 2001), chap. 3.
27. Tuttle, *Daddy's Gone to War*, vii.
28. Werner, *Through the Eyes of Innocents*, 66.
29. David Hinckley, "Blue Eyes Sinatra at the Paramount," *New York Daily News*, June 11, 1998, 67.
30. Quoted in Jim Auchmutey, "Sinatra: An Appreciation," *Atlanta Journal and Constitution*, May 17, 1998, G1.
31. Mintz and Kellogg, *Domestic Revolutions*, 167.
32. Ibid.
33. Grace Palladino, *Teenagers* (New York: Basic Books, 1996), 64, 86, 106.
34. Ibid., 104, 109–110; Thomas Hine, *The Rise and Fall of the American Teenager* (New York: Bard, 1999), 237.
35. *Washington Post*, April 5, 1998, C1.
36. Tuttle, *Daddy's Gone to War*, 166, 174, 184.
37. Cary Quan Gelerntner, "Artifacts of Internment," *Seattle Times*, November 24, 1991, A1, K1.
38. Werner, *Through the Eyes of Innocents*, 84.
39. Fred Barbash, "Internment: The 'Enemy' 40 Years Ago," *Washington Post*, December 5, 1982, A1.
40. Mintz and Kellogg, *Domestic Revolutions*, 169.
41. Werner, *Through the Eyes of Innocents*, 83, 87–88.
42. Gelerntner, "Artifacts of Internment," K1; Werner, *Through the Eyes of Innocents*, 84; Mintz and Kellogg, *Domestic Revolutions*, 168–170.
43. Steven Mintz, *Mexican American Voices* (St. James, N.Y.: Brandywine, 1998), 175–176.
44. Palladino, *Teenagers*, 58; Hine, *Rise and Fall of American Teenager*, 239.
45. Mintz, *Mexican American Voices*, 175–178.
46. Quoted in ibid., 178–181.
47. Gorham, "They Use Real Bullets," 5–28; Tuttle, *Daddy's Gone to War*, 218, 220.

48. Tuttle, *Daddy's Gone to War,* 171.
49. Ibid., 44, 241.

14. In Pursuit of the Perfect Childhood

1. Douglas T. Miller and Marion Nowak, *The Fifties: The Way We Really Were* (Garden City, N.Y.: Doubleday, 1977).
2. Carole Kismaric and Marvin Heiferman, *Growing up with Dick and Jane: Learning and Living the American Dream* (San Francisco: Harper, 1996), 59.
3. Only three other countries—Canada, Australia, and New Zealand—experienced a prolonged baby boom; Landon Y. Jones, *Great Expectations: America and the Baby Boom Generation* (New York: Coward, McCann and Geoghegan, 1980), 21.
4. Approximately 22 percent of the women born in 1908 bore no children; ibid., 15, 28. Only 8 percent of the married women born in the early 1930s were childless; Charles E. Strickland and Andrew M. Ambrose, "The Baby Boom, Prosperity, and the Changing Worlds of Children, 1945–1963," in *American Childhood: A Research Guide and Historical Handbook,* ed. Joseph M. Hawes and N. Ray Hiner (Westport, Conn.: Greenwood, 1985), 535–536; Wini Breines, *Young, White, and Miserable: Growing Up Female in the Fifties* (Boston: Beacon, 1992), 59.
5. *Tampa Tribune,* August 8, 1995, 1; Doug Owram, *Born at the Right Time: A History of the Baby-Boom Generation* (Toronto: University of Toronto Press, 1996), 59, 60, 85.
6. Kismaric and Heiferman, *Growing Up with Dick and Jane,* 15, 64; Jones, *Great Expectations,* 39; Strickland and Ambrose, "Baby Boom, Prosperity, and Changing Worlds," 542–543.
7. Owram, *Born at the Right Time,* 81–82.
8. Kismaric and Heiferman, *Growing Up with Dick and Jane,* 38.
9. "Goodbye to Barbie's Maker," *New York Times,* April 30, 2002, A28; Ginia Bellafante, "It Was Fashion That Set Barbie Free," *New York Times,* April 30, 2002, B8.
10. A "live" virus vaccine, which was based on a weakened virus and developed by Albert Sabin, was approved in 1960. It required no shots and was originally taken on a sugar cube.
11. Claudia Ann Miner, "What about the Children? Americans' Attitudes toward Children and Childhood in the 1950s" (Ph.D. diss., Washington State University, 1986), 77, 78; Strickland and Ambrose, "Baby Boom, Prosperity, and Changing Worlds," 533.
12. Nicholas Stowell Sammond, "The Uses of Childhood: The Making of Walt Disney and the Generic American Child, 1930–1960" (Ph.D. diss., University of California at San Diego, 1999), 414, 417.
13. Julia Grant, *Raising Baby by the Book: The Education of American Mothers* (New Haven: Yale University Press, 1998).
14. Ibid.; Owram, *Born at the Right Time,* 256, 259; Ferdinand Lundberg And Marynia F. Farnham, *Modern Woman: The Lost Sex* (New York: Grosset and Dunlap, 1947) 402–403.

15. Daniel Gomes, "'Sissy' Boys and 'Unhappy' Girls: Childrearing during the Cold War," in *Thresholds: Viewing Culture*, vol. 9 (University of California at Santa Barbara, 1995), http://proxy.arts.uci.edu/~nideffer/Tvc/section1/05.Tvc.v9.sect1.Gomes.html; Miner, "What about the Children?" 6, 37–38.

16. Jones, *Great Expectations*, 49; Breines, *Young, White, and Miserable*, 47, 64–65; John R. Seeley, R. Alexander Sim, and Elizabeth W. Loosley, *Crestwood Heights: A Study of the Culture of Suburban Life* (New York: Basic Books, 1956).

17. Seeley, Sim, and Loosley, *Crestwood Heights*; Breines, *Young, White, and Miserable*, 64.

18. Breines, *Young, White, and Miserable*, 69.

19. "Ah, she eats him alive and he takes it," James Dean says about his father. "If he had guts to knock Mom cold one time then maybe she'd be happy and stop picking on him." Owram, *Born at the Right Time*, 256, 259.

20. W. E. Blatz quoted in Owram, *Born at the Right Time*, 41–42; Breines, *Young, White, and Miserable*, 8, 41.

21. Owram, *Born at the Right Time*, 87.

22. Jones, *Great Expectations*, 56; Owram, *Born at the Right Time*, 105, 107–108.

23. Susan J. Douglas, *Where the Girls Are: Growing up Female with the Mass Media* (New York: Times Books, 1994), 43; William Graebner, *Coming of Age in Buffalo: Youth and Authority in the Postwar Era* (Philadelphia: Temple University Press, 1990), 69.

24. Douglas, *Where the Girls Are*.

25. Breines, *Young, White, and Miserable*, 74, 107, 111, 234; Michael Barson and Steven Heller, *Teenage Confidential: An Illustrated History of the American Teen* (San Francisco: Chronicle Books, 1998), 108.

26. Barson and Heller, *Teenage Confidential*, 26.

27. Breines, *Young, White, and Miserable*, 78.

28. Ibid., , 50, 78.

29. Ibid., 92–93, 108.

30. Owram, *Born at the Right Time*, 141, 145; Frank Furstenberg, "The Sociology of Adolescence and Youth in the 1990s," *Journal of Marriage and the Family* 62 (2000), 896–910; Gerald Grant, *The World We Created at Hamilton High* (Cambridge, Mass.: Harvard University Press, 1988), 16; Breines, *Young, White, and Miserable*, 132–133.

31. Barson and Heller, *Teenage Confidential*, 96.

32. Beth L. Bailey, *From Front Porch to Back Seat: Courtship in Twentieth-century America* (Baltimore: Johns Hopkins University Press, 1988), 81; Owram, *Born at the Right Time*, 256–257.

33. Barson and Heller, *Teenage Confidential*, 101.

34. Owram, *Born at the Right Time*, 147; Bailey, *From Front Porch to Back Seat*, 50; Graebner, *Coming of Age in Buffalo*, 98.

35. Owram, *Born at the Right Time*, 50; Kismaric and Heiferman, *Growing Up with Dick and Jane*, 30; Paul Dickson, *Sputnik: The Shock of the Century* (New York: Walker, 2001), 117; Robert A. Divine, *The Sputnik Challenge*

(New York: Oxford University Press, 1993). The Associated Press announcement can be found at http://wire.ap.org/APpackages/20thcentury/57sputnik.html; Bennett quoted in www.hq.nasa.gov/office/pao/History/sputnik/chap11.html; Teller quoted in http://more.abcnews.go.com/sections/scitech/sputnik_race/.

36. Dickson, *Sputnik*.

37. Educational Policies Commission, *Education for All American Youth* (Washington, D.C.: Educational Policies Commission, National Education Association of the United States and the American Association of School Administrators, 1944); Thomas R. McCambridge, "Liberal Education and American Schooling" (Ph.D. diss., University of California at Los Angeles, 1997), http://www.realuofc.org/libed/mcam/ch3.html.

38. Arendt quoted in Richard Rothstein, *The Way We Were: The Myths and Realities of America's Student Achievement* (New York: Century Foundation Press, 1998), 11–13.

39. Ibid.; Floyd M. Hammack, "Current Prospects for the Comprehensive High School," paper presented at the annual meeting of the American Educational Research Association, New Orleans, April, 2000, http://pages.nyu.edu/~fmh1/AERA_2000.htm; William G. Wraga, "The Comprehensive High School and Educational Reform in the United States, Retrospect and Prospect," *High School Journal* 88, no. 3 (February/March 1998), 121–133; Christopher Jencks, "Hard Marker," *New York Review of Books,* January 9, 1964.

40. James Bryant Conant, *The American High School Today: A First Report to Interested Citizens* (New York: McGraw-Hill, 1959), xi.

41. Nicholas Lemann, *The Big Test: The Secret History of the American Meritocracy* (New York: Farrar, Straus and Giroux, 1999).

42. Fred M. Hechinger, "The Middle School is 20 Years Old," *New York Times,* March 17, 1981, C1.

43. Miner, "What About the Children?" 152, 159, 162, 164; Robert Lindner quoted in Steve Rubio, "The Kids Are Alright," *Bad Subjects,* no. 47 (January 2000), http://eserver.org/bs/47/rubio.html.

44. John M. McGuire, "Comic Books as a Corrupting Influence," *St. Louis Post-Dispatch,* October 16, 2000, F3; James Burkhart Gilbert, *A Cycle of Outrage: America's Reaction to the Juvenile Delinquent in the 1950s* (New York: Oxford University Press, 1986), 97.

45. Gilbert, *Cycle of Outrage,* 101.

46. Walter Goodman, "Seducing the Innocent," *New York Times,* October 8, 2000, sec. 4, 2; Jay Maeder, "No Harm in Horror," *New York Daily News,* September 17, 1998, 41; Gilbert, *Cycle of Outrage,* 92, 101; Miner, "What about the Children?" 147. *Mad* magazine satirized Frederic Wertham with an article titled "Baseball Is Ruining Our Children" supposedly written by "Frederick Werthless, M.D."

47. Barson and Heller, *Teenage Confidential,* 52; Thomas Patrick Doherty, *Teenagers and Teenpics: The Juvenilization of American Movies in the 1950s* (Boston: Unwin Hyman, 1988), 109.

48. Miner, "What about the Children?" 136–137, 141–142.

49. Gilbert, *Cycle of Outrage*, 71, 79; Graebner, *Coming of Age in Buffalo*, 52.

50. "How Gangs Started and Got Those Names," *New York Times*, October 3, 1999, sec. 14, 5; Eric C. Schneider, *Vampires, Dragons, and Egyptian Kings: Youth Gangs in Postwar New York* (Princeton: Princeton University Press, 1999), 52

51. Gilbert, *Cycle of Outrage*, xix, 53, 71, 184.

52. Ibid., 75; Schneider, *Vampires, Dragons, and Egyptian Kings*, 75 and passim; Claude Brown, *Manchild in the Promised Land* (New York: Macmillan, 1965), 37.

53. Strickland and Ambrose, "Baby Boom, Prosperity, and Changing Worlds," 566.

54. Schneider, *Vampires, Dragons, and Egyptian Kings*, 138.

55. Allan Luke, *Literacy, Textbooks and Ideology: Postwar Literacy and the Mythology of Dick and Jane* (London: Falmer Press, 1988); "Dick and Jane's Lost Dad," *University of Chicago Magazine*, December 1998, http://magazine.uchicago.edu/9812/html/enquirer2.htm.

56. Rudolf Franz Flesch, *Why Johnny Can't Read—And What You Can Do about It* (New York: Harper, 1955).

57. Jim Davies, "What Mad, Worry?" *The Guardian*, October 5, 1992, 25.

58. W. Tasker Witham, *The Adolescent in the American Novel, 1920–1960* (New York: Frederick Ungar, 1964), 214.

59. Ibid., 12, 22, 25, 41–43.

60. Lynn Spigel, "Seducing the Innocent: Childhood and Television in Postwar America," in *The Children's Culture Reader*, ed. Henry Jenkins (New York: New York University Press, 1998), 117; Sammond, "The Uses of Childhood," 508.

61. Spigel, "Seducing the Innocent," 128; Sammond, "The Uses of Childhood," 509.

62. It is perhaps not a coincidence that in an era when many social critics argued that Americans were becoming conformist puppets, and childrearing experts feared that children were tied to their mothers' apron strings, children's shows featured marionettes, hand puppets, and dummies; Susan Vaughn, "Welcome to the 'Good Old Days,'" *Los Angeles Times*, August 11, 1997, 14; W. T. Lhamon, *Deliberate Speed: The Origins of a Cultural Style in the American 1950s* (Washington, D.C.: Smithsonian Institution Press, 1990).

63. Doherty, *Teenagers and Teenpics*, 113.

64. Owram, *Born at the Right Time*, 142; Gilbert, *Cycle of Outrage*, 64, 187; Barson and Heller, *Teenage Confidential*, 61; Doherty, *Teenagers and Teenpics*, 146–147, 180.

65. Doherty, *Teenagers and Teenpics*, 188, 193, 196.

66. James M. Curtis, *Rock Eras: Interpretations of Music and Society, 1954–1984* (Bowling Green: Bowling Green State University Popular Press, 1987), 37; Deena Weinstein, "Rock: Youth, and Its Music," in *Adolescents and Their Music: If It's Too Loud, You're Too Old*, ed. Jonathon S. Epstein (New York: Garland, 1994), 13.

67. Joseph A. Kotarba, "The Postmodernization of Rock and Roll Music: The Case of Metallica," in Epstein, *Adolescents and Their Music,* 141–164; Deena Weinstein, "Expendable Youth: The Rise and Fall of Youth Culture," in ibid., 68; Curtis, *Rock Eras,* 46.

68. Curtis, *Rock Eras,* 41, 43–44.

69. Doherty, *Teenagers and Teenpics,* 81; Curtis, *Rock Eras,* 41–46.

70. Curtis, *Rock Eras,* 37–38.

71. Weinstein, "Rock," 20.

72. Breines, *Young, White, and Miserable,* 15.

73. Stephen J. Whitfield, *A Death in the Delta: The Story of Emmett Till* (New York: Free Press, 1988); Christopher Metress, *The Lynching of Emmett Till* (Charlottesville: University Press of Virginia, 2002).

74. William Faulkner wrote, "If we in America have reached that point in our desperate culture when we must murder children, no matter for what reason or what color, we don't deserve to survive"; quoted in David Hinckley, "Till's Story Lives On in Song," *New York Daily News,* August 24, 1995, 50.

75. Anne Moody, *Coming of Age in Mississippi* (New York: Dial, 1968), 125.

76. Richard Kluger, *Simple Justice* (New York: Knopf, 1976), 75–77; Morris quoted in U.S. Department of the Interior, National Park Service, "School Desegregation in Public Education in the U.S.," 7, http://www.cr.nps.gov/history/school.pdf.

77. Quoted in *Washington Post,* June 23, 1987, B3.

78. Quoted in "She Would Not Be Moved," *The Guardian* (London), December 16, 2000, 8.

79. Quoted in Bob Baker, "Complex Legacy of Little Rock," *Los Angeles Times,* September 4, 1987, sec. 1, 3.

80. Heather Greewood, "Pioneering Black Student at Little Rock," *Toronto Star,* March 30, 1997, E1; *Ottawa Citizen,* November 30, 1997, D3.

81. Quoted in Phillip Hoose, *We Were There, Too! Young People in U.S. History* (New York: Farrar Straus Giroux, 2001), 218–220.

82. Robert Coles, *The Story of Ruby Bridges* (New York: Scholastic, 1995); Grant, *World We Created at Hamilton High,* 214.

83. Steven Mintz and Susan Kellogg, *Domestic Revolutions: A Social History of American Family Life* (New York: Free Press, 1988), 200–201.

15. Youthquake

1. Phillip Hoose, *We Were There, Too! Young People in U.S. History* (New York: Farrar, Straus and Giroux, 2001), 220–224.

2. Ibid., 222–223.

3. *Look,* January 3, 1961, 17.

4. Ibid.

5. Ibid., 19–20.

6. See Gertrude Himmelfarb, "Everybody Look What's Going Down," *Washington Post,* November 29, 1998, X5.

7. David Chalmers, *And the Crooked Places Made Straight: The Struggle for So-*

cial Change in the 1960s, 2d ed. (Baltimore: Johns Hopkins University Press, 1996), 81; Patricia Cohen, "New Slant on the 60's: The Past Made New; Experts Are Reassessing a Tumultuous Decade," *New York Times,* June 13, 1998, B7.

8. The number of those cohabitating outside of marriage increased sixfold between 1970 and 1998. Today, about half of those getting married have lived in a cohabitating relationship.

9. Edward K. Spann, *Democracy's Children: The Young Rebels of the 1960s and the Power of Ideals* (Wilmington, Del.: Scholarly Resources, 2003).

10. Claudia Ann Miner, "What about the Children? Americans' Attitudes toward Children and Childhood during the 1950s" (Ph.D. diss., Washington State University, 1986), 83–84.

11. Edgar Z. Friedenberg, *The Vanishing Adolescent* (Boston: Beacon, 1959).

12. Paul Goodman, *Growing Up Absurd: Problems of Youth in the Organized System* (New York: Random House, 1960).

13. Wini Breines, *Young, White, and Miserable: Growing Up Female in the Fifties* (Boston: Beacon, 1992), 29; Jules Henry, *Culture against Man* (New York: Random House, 1963), 70; Carl Ratner, "Contributions of Sociohistorical Psychology and Phenomenology to Research Methodology," in *Recent Trends in Theoretical Psychology,* ed. Henderikus J. Stam, Leendert P. Mos, Warren Thorngate, and Bernie Kaplan, vol. 3 (New York: Springer Verlag, 1993), 503–510.0

14. Kenneth Keniston, *Uncommitted: Alienated Youth in American Society* (New York: Harcourt, Brace and World, 1965); Edgar C. Friedenberg, "Kids without a Country," *New York Review of Books,* January 6, 1966, http://www.nybooks.com/articles/12626; Henry, *Culture against Man,* 70.

15. "Man of the Year: The Inheritor," *Time,* January 6, 1967, 18–23; Joseph Adelson, "The Myth of the Generation Gap," *New York Times,* January 18, 1970, sec. 6, 10.

16. George Lipsitz, *Time Passages: Collective Memory and American Popular Culture* (Minneapolis: University of Minnesota Press, 1990); Emily D. Edwards, "Does Love Really Stink: The 'Mean World' of Love and Sex in Popular Music of the 1980s," in *Adolescents and Their Music,* ed. Jonathon S. Epstein (New York: Garland, 1994), 229; *Look,* January 3, 1961, 60; Lawrence Grossberg, "The Political Status of Youth and Youth Culture," in Epstein, *Adolescents and Their Music,* 38.

17. Kim Masters, "Lunch Counter Revolution; 35 Years Ago, They Took Their Seats and Found a Place in History," *Washington Post,* January 16, 1995, B1; Peggy Brown, "When Lunch Could Change the World," *Toronto Star,* February 3, 1993, A15.

18. Jim Schlosser, "The Story of the Greensboro Sit-ins," (Greensboro, N.C.) *News and Record,* February 1, 1998, A1.

19. Henry Jenkins, "'The All-American Handful': Dennis the Menace, Permissive Childrearing and the Bad Boy Tradition," in *The Revolution Wasn't Televised: Sixties Television and Social Conflict,* ed. Lynn Spigel and Mike Curtin (New York: Routledge, 1997), 119–135.

20. Anne Moody, *Coming of Age in Mississippi* (New York: Dial, 1968).

21. Tamara K. Hareven, "Step-Children of the Dream," *History of Education Quarterly* 9 (winter 1969), 505–514.

22. Harrell R. Rodgers Jr. and Charles S. Bullock III, "Political and Racial Attitudes: Black versus White," *Journal of Black Studies* 4 (1974), 471–472.

23. At least a third of the activists in the Free Speech movement at the University of California, Berkeley, in 1964 were of Jewish descent; Allen J. Matusow, *The Unraveling of America: A History of Liberalism in the 1960s* (New York: Harper and Row, 1984), 309.

24. Peter T. Jones, *History of U.S. National Student Association Relations with the International Union of Students, 1945–1956* (Philadelphia: Foreign Policy Research Institute, University of Pennsylvania).

25. Stanley Rothman and S. Robert Licter, *Roots of Radicalism: Jews, Christians, and the New Left* (New York: Oxford University Press, 1982); Dominick Cavallo, *A Fiction of the Past: The Sixties in American History* (New York: St. Martin's, 1999).

26. Nathan Glazer, "Anger against the State," *Atlantic Monthly* 224 (July 1969), 43–53.

27. Steven Mintz and Susan Kellogg, *Domestic Revolutions: A Social History of American Family Life* (New York: Free Press, 1988), 210–213.

28. Quoted by Mary McGrory, "Moynihan Was Right 21 Years Ago," *Washington Post*, January 26, 1986, B1.

29. "Freedom Is Not Enough," *Washington Post*, May 6, 1992, A29.

30. Shalom M. Fisch and Rosemarie T. Truglio, eds., *"G" Is for "Growing": Thirty Years of Research on Children and Sesame Street* (Mahwah, N.J.: Erlbaum, 2000); Peter B. Mann, ed., *Sesame Street Research* (New York: Children's Television Workshop; Princeton, N.J.: Educational Testing Service, 1990); Joan Ganz Cooney, *The First Year of Sesame Street* (New York: Children's Television Workshop, 1970).

31. James Crawford, Bilingual Education: History, Politics, Theory, and Practice, 4th ed. (Los Angeles: Bilingual Educational Services, 1999).

32. Josué M. González, *Towards Quality in Bilingual Education: Bilingual Education in the Integrated School* (Rosslyn, Va.: National Clearinghouse for Bilingual Education, 1979). In 1981, in *Casteñeda v. Pickard*, the Supreme Court adopted a three-pronged test for whether bilingual educational programs adequately met the needs of non-English-speaking students. The Court required a pedagogically sound plan, with sufficient qualified teachers to implement the program, and a system to evaluate the programs' effectiveness.

33. *Mills v. Board of Education, DC,* 348 F.Supp. 866 (D. D.C. 1972).

34. Matusow, *Unraveling of America,* 199–200.

35. Dolores Delgado Bernal, "Chicana School Resistance and Grassroots Leadership: Providing an Alternative History of the 1968 East Los Angeles Blowouts" (Ph.D. diss., University of California at Los Angeles, 1997).

36. U.S. Office of Education, *Equality of Educational Opportunity* (Washington, D.C.: U.S. Department of Health, Education, and Welfare, 1966). McKissick quoted in *Baltimore Sun*, April 4, 1995, B2.

37. By the 1970s the South had the nation's most integrated schools. In 1976, 45.1 percent of the South's African-American students were attending major-

ity white schools, compared with just 27.5 percent in the Northeast and 29.7 percent in the Midwest. As early as 1971 only 18 percent of the public, according to a Gallup poll, supported busing; blacks also opposed it, though by a very slight margin. Thomas Byrne Edsall with Mary D. Edsall, *Chain Reaction: The Impact of Race Rights and Taxes on American Politics* (New York: Norton, 1991), 89–90.

38. In 1989 the federal courts withdrew their oversight of the Boston public schools.

39. Quoted in "Tough Times in Education Call for Tough Teachers," *St. Petersburg Times,* August 10, 1991, 2; Grossberg, "Political Status of Youth and Youth Culture," 31.

40. Paul Goodman, "What Rights Should Children Have?" *New York Review of Books,* September 23, 1971, 20–22.

41. Holt argued that learning was a natural, organic function, and therefore didn't need to be managed by adults; *Look,* November 19, 1963, 30.

42. Nat Hentoff, "Philadelphia, Miss., Revisited," *Washington Post,* July 9, 1988, A23.

43. In 1971 the Supreme Court ruled that constitutional due process did not require states to provide a jury trial in juvenile court.

44. As late as 1970, many public universities did not admit women. It was not until 1970 that a court ordered the College of Arts and Sciences at the University of Virginia to admit its first woman student.

45. *Morris v. Michigan State Bd. of Educ.,* 472 F.2d 1207 (6th Cir. 1973); *Gilpin v. Kansas High Sch. Activities Assn.,* 377 F.Supp. 1233 (D. Kan. 1973); *Clinton v. Nagy,* 411 F. Supp. 1396 (N.D. Ohio 1974). Federal regulations issued in 1979 stated that when there is no comparable sport for girls, girls must be allowed to try out in all sports except contact sports. Under federal regulations adopted during the 1970s, school districts cannot let outside supporters provide perquisites to boy athletes that are denied to girl athletes. To comply with Title IX, a school district must show that the ratio of girls to boys in the sports program is "substantially similar" to that in the student population; or that it is continually expanding athletic opportunities for girls; or that it is meeting female athletes' interests and abilities fully.

46. *Weber v. Aetna Casualty & Surety Co.,* 406 U.S. 164 (1972); *New Jersey Welfare Rights Org. v. Cahill,* 411 U.S. 619 (1973).

47. Alan Lawson, "The New Left and New Values," *American Quarterly* 28 (1976), 107–123.

16. Parental Panics and the Reshaping of Childhood

1. Debbie Nathan and Michael Snedeker, *Satan's Silence: Ritual Abuse and the Making of a Modern American Witch Hunt* (New York: Basic Books, 1995); Paul and Shirley Eberle, *The Abuse of Innocence: The McMartin Preschool Trial* (Buffalo: Prometheus, 1993); Cynthia Gorney, "The Terrible Puzzle of McMartin Preschool," *Washington Post,* May 17, 1988, B1.

2. Robert Reinhold, "The Longest Trial—A Post-Mortem," *New York Times,* January 24, 1990, A1; Jay Mathews, "Child Molestation Case a Long Way

from Trial," *Washington Post*, May 10, 1985, E1; Anne C. Roark, "Sex Case Spotlighted Problem of Proving Children Tell Truth," *Toronto Star*, January 31, 1990, A23.

3. Philip Jenkins, *Moral Panic: Changing Concepts of the Child Molester in Modern America* (New Haven: Yale University Press, 1998); Hillary Rodham Clinton, *It Takes a Village and Other Lessons Children Teach Us* (New York: Simon and Schuster, 1996); Mike A. Males, *Scapegoat Generation: America's War on Adolescents* (Monroe, Maine: Common Courage, 1996), 30.

4. Alan Guttmacher Institute, *11 Million Teenagers: What Can Be Done about the Epidemic of Adolescent Pregnancies in the United States* (New York, 1976); Kristin Luker, *Dubious Conceptions: The Politics of Teenage Pregnancy* (Cambridge, Mass.: Harvard University Press, 1996); Maris A. Vinovskis, *An "Epidemic" of Adolescent Pregnancy?* (New York: Oxford University Press, 1988).

5. National Center for Missing and Exploited Children, "Frequently Asked Questions and Statistics," http://www.missingkids.org/.

6. James C. Howell, *Juvenile Justice and Youth Violence* (Thousand Oaks, Calif.: Sage, 1997), 115. A 1989 congressional study claimed that two Los Angeles gangs, the Crips and Bloods, controlled 30 percent of the crack cocaine market in the United States; ibid., 116, 131.

7. Ken Armstrong, Steve Mills, and Maurice Possley, "Coercive and Illegal Tactics Torpedo Scores of Cook County Murder Cases," *Chicago Tribune*, December 16, 2001, 1.

8. William Finnegan, *Cold New World: Growing Up in a Harder Country* (New York: Random House, 1998).

9. In most cases, these men were only a year or two older than the mother.

10. Philip Jenkins, *Moral Panic: Changing Concepts of the Child Molester in Modern America* (New Haven: Yale University Press, 1998).

11. Males, *Scapegoat Generation*, 274–275.

12. Mike A. Males, *Framing Youth: Ten Myths about the Next Generation* (Monroe, Maine: Common Courage, 1999), 338.

13. Divorce rates certainly increased, but the rise was much more gradual and less disjunctive than many assumed and in part reflected a sharp decrease in marital separations; Karen S. Peterson, "Kids of Divorced Parents Straddle a Divided World," *USA Today*, July 13, 2003.

14. One comprehensive study found that after six years, a quarter of the ex-spouses had severe conflicts, a quarter of children saw their noncustodial father once a year or less, and a significant number of stepfathers no longer attempted to deal with resisting stepchildren after two years. Twenty years following the divorce, about two-thirds of sons and three-quarters of daughters had poor relationships with their biological fathers, compared with 30 percent of children from intact marriages. E. Mavis Hetherington found that up to 25 percent of children with divorced parents "have serious social, emotional or psychological problems" in the long term, compared with 10 percent of children from intact families. See E. Mavis Hetherington and John Kelly, *For Better or for Worse: Divorce Reconsidered* (New York: Norton, 2002).

15. How well children cope with the stresses of divorce is closely related to the

bitterness of the divorce proceedings. About a quarter of divorcing parents resort to litigation, and up to 70 percent of these parents are unable to build a cooperative relationship after the divorce is finalized. More than 350,000 children are kidnapped each year by disgruntled family members, usually noncustodial fathers. Typically such kidnappings last only a few days but leave a lasting legacy of distrust.

16. Nuclear families enjoy a median annual income of $48,000; stepfamilies average an income of $45,900; cohabiting couples $25,000; divorced or separated families, $18,500; and never-married, single-parent families, $15,000; John E. Murray Jr., "The Current State of Marriage and Family," http://www .dufi.duq.edu/family/csmf/children.html.

17. Timothy J. Owens and Sandra L. Hofferth, eds., *Children at the Millennium* (Greenwich, Conn.: JAI Press, 2001); Steven Mintz and Susan Kellogg, *Domestic Revolutions: A Social History of American Family Life* (New York: Free Press, 1988), 220; David Elkind, *The Hurried Child* (Reading, Mass.: Addison-Wesley, 1981).

18. Karin Lee Fishbeck Calvert, *Children in the House: The Material Culture of Early Childhood, 1600–1900* (Boston: Northeastern University Press, 1992), 153; Marie Winn, *Children without Childhood* (New York: Pantheon, 1983).

19. Males, *Scapegoat Generation*, 186. In the 1960s the average age of initiation into drinking was thirteen and a quarter of high school students reported getting "high" from drinking at least once a week; Males, *Scapegoat Generation*, 193. The legal treatment of teen drinking has changed much more than the incidence of drinking. In the late 1960s and early and mid-1970s, many states liberalized their laws to allow older teens to drink. By 1978, twenty-eight states allowed eighteen-year-olds to drink beer, and many allowed them to drink hard liquor. Another twenty states enacted a nineteen- or twenty-year-old drinking age. Between 1978 and 1989 all states raised the drinking age to twenty-one. Males, *Framing Youth*, 146–147, 167; Males, *Scapegoat Generation*, 152, 177–178; National Center for Health Statistics, "Illegal Drug Use," http://www.cdc.gov/nchs/fastats/druguse.htm.

20. "Juveniles Account for 1 in 8 Violent Crimes Cleared," http://www.ncjrs.org/ txtfiles/fs-9415.txt; Office of Juvenile Justice and Delinquency Prevention, *Statistical Briefing Book*, http://ojjdp.ncjrs.org/ojstatbb/html/OFFENDERS .html; Jeff Madrick, "A Rise in Child Poverty Rates Is at Risk in U.S.," *New York Times*, June 13, 2002, C2.

21. William Feldman et al., "Is Childhood Sexual Abuse Really Increasing in Prevalence?" *Pediatrics* 88 (July 1991), 29–34; Males, *Framing Youth*, 257. In 1998 government agencies substantiated over a million cases of child maltreatment, including approximately 101,000 cases of sexual abuse. About 51 percent of lifetime rapes occur before age eighteen, and 29 percent of lifetime rapes occur before age twelve; Coordinating Council on Juvenile Justice and Delinquency Prevention, *Combating Violence And Delinquency: The National Juvenile Justice Action Plan: Report* (Washington, D.C., 1996), 75; National Criminal Justice Reference Service, http://www.ncjrs.org/html/ojjdp/ action_plan_2001_10/page1.html. The 1994 Sex in America study of the sex

lives of 3,400 men and women reported that 17 percent of the women and 12 percent of the men reported childhood sexual abuse; Males, *Scapegoat Generation*, 74.

22. Males, *Framing Youth*; idem, *Scapegoat Generation*.

23. Males, *Framing Youth*, 275.

24. Stephen Robertson, "The Disappearance of Childhood," http://teaching .arts.usyd.edu.au/history/2044/.

25. Eighty-one percent of teens have their own bedrooms and 63 percent their own television set.

26. Bill Maxwell, "Child's Play: A Thing of the Past?" *St. Petersburg Times*, November 15, 1998, D1.

27. *Christian Science Monitor*, May 6, 2002, 1.

28. Tracey Skelton and Gill Valentine, eds., *Cool Places: Geographies of Youth Cultures* (London: Routledge, 1998); Herb Childress, *Landscapes of Betrayal, Landscapes of Joy* (Albany: State University of New York Press, 2000).

29. Low-wage, low-skill adolescent employment can result in cynical attitudes toward work, school absences, and increased alcohol and marijuana use, but these negative effects disappear among those who work for fewer hours. Especially for girls and minority youth, work contributes to higher levels of self-esteem and gains in skills and contacts that prove useful in later life. See Ellen Greenberger and Laurence Steinberg, *When Teenagers Work: The Psychological and Social Costs of Adolescent Employment* (New York: Basic Books, 1986).

30. Alex Kotlowitz, *There Are No Children Here: The Story of Two Boys Growing Up in the Other America* (New York: Doubleday, 1991).

31. Ibid.; Michiko Kakutani, "Children without Childhood," *New York Times*, July 11, 1997, C27.

32. "Children of the Shadows," *New York Times*, April 4 (sec. 1, 21), 6 (A1), 8 (A1), 11 (sec. 1, 1), 13 (A1), 15 (A1), 18 (sec. 1, 1), 20 (A1), 22 (A1), 25 (sec. 1, 46), 1993.

33. Lee Rainwater, *Behind Ghetto Walls: Black Families in a Federal Slum* (Chicago: Aldine, 1970).

34. "Children of the Shadows."

35. Ibid.

36. Ibid.; Andrew Sum and Joe McLaughlin, "The National Economic Recession and Its Impact on Employment among the Nation's Young Adults," Center for Labor Markets, Northeastern University, 2002, http://www.nupr.neu.edu/ 02-02/youth.pdf.

37. National Institute of Drug Abuse, "Epidemiology of Youth Drug Abuse—Research Findings," May 2001, http://www.drugabuse.gov/ICAW/epidemiology/ epidemiologyfindings501.html; J. M. Wallace Jr. et al., "Gender and Ethnic Differences in Smoking, Drinking and Illicit Drug Use among American 8th, 10th and 12th grade students, 1976–2000," *Addiction* 98 (2003), 225–234.

38. Esmeralda Santiago, *When I Was Puerto Rican* (Reading, Mass.: Addison-Wesley, 1993).

39. Irina Langer, "A Lesson in Turning Memories into Memoirs," *New York Times,* April 2, 2000, WC15.

40. During the 1990s about a million documented immigrants entered the United States each year, along with perhaps another 250,000 to 500,000 undocumented immigrants; Carola Suarez-Orozco and Marcelo M. Suarez-Orozco, *Children of Immigration* (Cambridge, Mass.: Harvard University Press, 2001), 31–32, 56.

41. Ibid., 6, 19, 66, 75.

42. Ibid., 73, 75–76, 79–81.

43. Ibid., 1, 2, 5, 46, 99, 107, 120.

44. Robert Pear, "Greasy Kid Stuff; Washington Kidnaps Dick and Jane," *New York Times,* June 15, 1997, sec. 4, 1.

45. "Record Share of New Mothers in Labor Force," http://www.census.gov/Press-Release/www/2000/cb00–175; Mintz and Kellogg, *Domestic Revolutions,* 222.

46. Mintz and Kellogg, *Domestic Revolutions,* 223.

47. Arnold A. Hutschnecker, "Nixon-Era Plan for Children Didn't Include Concentration Camps," *New York Times,* October 15, 1988, sec. 1, 30; "A Fair Chance, Even before School," ibid., September 28, 1988, A26. Between 1991 and 1995 there was a 50 percent increase in prescriptions to treat ADHD and other behavioral and psychiatric disorders, including depression, in children aged two to four. On sex-offense-specific therapy, see Judith Levine, *Harmful to Minors: The Perils of Protecting Children from Sex* (Minneapolis: University of Minnesota Press, 2002).

48. Males, *Scapegoat Generation,* 149, 223.

49. Kevin Johnson, "2 Boys Held in Death of 5-Year-Old," *USA Today,* October 17, 1994, A3.

50. Office of Juvenile Justice and Delinquency Prevention, "Trying Juveniles as Adults in Criminal Court: An Analysis of State Transfer Provisions," December 1998, http://ojjdp.ncjrs.org/pubs/tryingjuvasadult/intro.html.

51. Maureen Dowd, "Liberties," *New York Times,* June 2, 1994, sec. 4, 15.

52. "Clinton Pledges New Measures to Restore Discipline in Schools," *Toronto Star,* July 21, 1998, A11. Five years after the V-Chip was required in all new TV sets, a survey found that half of the purchasers didn't know that TVs included the chips and of those who did, only a third ever used them; David Broder, "Politics Collides with Culture Wars," *Newsday,* July 29, 2001, B6.

53. Earl Wysong, Richard Aniskiewicz, and David Wright, "Truth and DARE: Tracking Drug Education to Graduation and as Symbolic Politics," *Social Problems* 41 (August 1994), 448–472.

54. "Sex Education: Politicians, Parents, Teachers, and Teens," *Guttmacher Report* 4 (February 2001), 9–12.

55. Males, *Framing Youth,* 155, 172.

56. *Davis v. Monroe County Board of Education,* 526 U.S. 629.

57. Shawn Hubler, "Our Next Moral Battleground: Potty Training," *Los Angeles Times,* January 25, 1999, B1. Cultural conflict has a long lineage in the na-

tion's history, as "provincials" and "progressives" have battled over such issues as immigration, alcohol, and evolution. See James Davison Hunter, *Culture Wars: The Struggle to Define America* (New York: Basic Books, 1992).

58. Lynn Rosellini, "When to Spank," *U.S. News & World Report,* April 13, 1998, 52–53.

59. There does not appear to have been much change in attitudes among parents, 65 percent of whom approved of spanking in 1997, only modestly less than the 74 percent who did so in 1946. But this aggregate figure obscures class differences. In a 1997 poll, 41 percent of college-educated Americans disapproved of spanking children, compared with only 20 percent of those who hadn't completed high school. Rosellini, "When to Spank."

60. Rosellini, "When to Spank"; Ronald Hyman and Charles Rathbone, *Corporal Punishment in Schools: Reading the Law* (Dayton: Education Law Association, 1993); American Academy of Pediatrics, "Corporal Punishment in Schools (RE9754)," http://www.aap.org/policy/re9754.html. In the United Kingdom, a European court ruling led Parliament to ban corporal punishment in schools by one vote in 1986.

61. Peggy Orenstein, *School Girls: Young Women, Self-Esteem, and the Confidence Gap* (New York: Anchor, 1995); Mary Pipher, *Reviving Ophelia: Saving the Selves of Adolescent Girls* (New York: Putnam Book, 1994); Christina Hoff Sommers, *The War against Boys: How Misguided Feminism Is Harming Our Young Men* (New York: Simon and Schuster, 2000).

62. William Pollack, *Real Boys: Rescuing Our Sons from the Myths of Boyhood* (New York: Random House, 1998); James Garbarino, *Lost Boys: Why Our Sons Turn Violent and How We Can Save Them* (New York: Free Press, 1999).

63. Anthony Rotundo, "The War against Boys," *Washington Post,* July 2, 2000, sec. 10, 1.

64. Eric Cohen, "A Cultural Stalemate," *Los Angeles Times,* February 4, 2001, M1.

65. "Senate Aims to Block Teaching about Gays," *Cleveland Plain Dealer,* August 2, 1994, A7.

66. Eden Ross Lipson, "Zena Sutherland," *New York Times,* June 15, 2002, B18.

67. In John Dewey's classic formulation in *Education and Experience* (New York: Macmillan, 1938), 5–6, progressive education is characterized by the "cultivation of individuality, free activity as opposed to external discipline, learning from experience rather than from texts and teachers, acquiring skills that are deemed relevant to the individual at the present time rather than preparing for some unknown future, and becoming acquainted with the world rather than learning through static aims and old materials."

68. National Commission on Excellence in Education, *A Nation at Risk.*

69. In Montgomery County, Maryland, students currently must take fifty hours of state testing each year, not including PSATs, SATs, or Advanced Placement tests; Jay Mathews, "Parents' Push Gives Students More SAT Time," *Washington Post,* May 8, 2001, B1.

17. The Unfinished Century of the Child

1. Ellen Karolina Sofia Key, *The Century of the Child* (New York: G. P. Putnam, 1909).

2. Detailed government reports on the shootings at Columbine High School are available online. The Jefferson County, Colorado, sheriff's report can be found at http://www.cnn.com/SPECIALS/2000/columbine.cd/frameset.exclude .html. The Colorado Governor's Columbine Review Commission Report of May 2001 is online at http://www.state.co.us/columbine/. Also see Sam Howe Verhovek, "2 Youths Wanted to 'Destroy the School,' Sheriff Says," *New York Times,* April 23, 1999, A1; Michael Janofsky, "Columbine Victims Were Killed Minutes into Siege at Colorado School, Report Reveals," ibid., May 16, 2000, A1.

3. Paul Schwartzman, "A Lot of Signs Were Given—but Ignored," *New York Daily News,* April 25, 1999, 4; Mitchell Zuckoff and Lynda Gorov, "Early Signs of Trouble Seen," *Boston Globe,* April 25, 1999, A1; James Brooke, "A New Hint of Missed Signals in Littleton," *New York Times,* May 5, 1999, A18; Jodi Wilgoren and Dirk Johnson, "Sketch of Killers: Contradictions and Confusion," ibid., April 23, 1999, A1; Pam Belluck and Jodi Willgoren, "Caring Parents, No Answers, in Columbine Killers' Pasts," ibid., June 29, 1999, A1; Jeff Kass, "Portrait of Two Teens Reveals a Lot of Gray," ibid., May 3, 1999, 3; James Brooke, "Little Was Done on Complaints in Littleton File," ibid., May 1, 1999, A1; James Brooke, "Attack at School Planned a Year, Authorities Say," ibid., April 25, 1999, sec. 1, 1; Jodi Wilgoren and Dirk Johnson, "Sketch of Killers: Contradictions and Confusion," ibid., April 23, 1999, A1.

4. Michael Janofsky, "The Columbine Killers' Tapes of Rage," *New York Times,* A22; James Barron, "Warnings from a Student Turned Killer," ibid., May 1, 1999, A12; Dave Cullen, "Kill Mankind. No One Should Survive," *Salon,* September 23, 1999, http://www.salon.com/news/feature/1999/09/23/journal/ index.html.

5. Bill Dedman, "Bullying, Tormenting Often Led to Revenge in Cases Studied," *Chicago Sun-Times,* October 15, 2000, 14; Gus Kelly, "Afterwards, No Tidy Explanations," *Rocky Mountain News,* April 25, 1999, A26.

6. Juvenile homicides declined 45 percent between 1994 and 1999; Sheryl Gay Stolberg, "By the Numbers; Science Looks at Littleton, and Shrugs," *New York Times,* May 9, 1999, sec. 4, 1.

7. *USA Today,* July 26, 2000, D9; Delbert S. Elliott, Beatrix A. Hamburg, and Kirk R. Williams, eds., *Violence in American Schools: A New Perspective* (Cambridge: Cambridge University Press, 1998); Seymour B. Sarason, *American Psychology and Schools: A Critique* (Washington, D.C.: American Psychological Association; New York: Teachers College Press, 2001); Gregory K. Moffatt, *Blind-Sided: Homicide Where It Is Least Expected* (Westport, Conn.: Praeger, 2000); Mohammad Shafii and Sharon Lee Shafii, eds., *School Violence: Assessment, Management, Prevention* (Washington, D.C.: American Psychiatric Publishing, 2001).

8. Alex Fryer, "School Violence Pervades Films, Books, and Music," *Seattle Times*, April 25, 1999, A1.

9. Ibid.

10. Erica Goode, "Terror in Littleton: The Psychology; Deeper Truths Sought in Violence by Youths," *New York Times*, May 4, 1999, A28; "The Gaming of Violence," ibid., April 30, 1999, A30.

11. John Ritter, "Nobody Took Him Seriously: Oregon Student 'Joked' He Would 'Get People," *USA Today*, May 22, 1998, A3; Carey Goldberg, "After Girls Get the Attention, Focus Shifts to Boys' Woes," *New York Times*, April 23, 1998, A1; Sherry Stripling, "Boy Trouble," *Seattle Times*, April 30, 1999, E1; Stephen S. Hall, "The Troubled Life of Boys," *New York Times*, VI, 31; Barbara F. Meltz, "Boys and a Culture of Cruelty," *Boston Globe*, October 19, 2000, H3; Walt Belcher, "Myths of Manhood Make It Tough for Boys," *Tampa Tribune*, June 11, 2001, 1.

12. Peter Applebome, "Alma Maters; Two Words behind the Massacre," *New York Times*, May 2, 1999, sec. 4, 1.

13. Donna Gaines, *Teenage Wasteland: Suburbia's Dead End Kids* (Chicago: University of Chicago Press, 1998); Applebome, "Alma Maters." In the 1950s a sizable proportion of high school students felt like outsiders. According to one survey, 22 percent of high school students felt out of things, 11 percent felt different, 44 percent seldom had dates, 13 percent felt they were not wanted, and 20 percent felt lonesome. See Wini Breines, *Young, White, and Miserable: Growing Up Female in the Fifties* (Boston: Beacon, 1992), 132–133.

14. Tom Mashburg, "Violence May Be Gender Issue," *Boston Herald*, May 23, 1999, 7; Carol Kreck, "Finding the Lost Boys: We Must Change the Way We Treat Sons, Experts Say," *Denver Post*, May 9, 1999, E4; Nancy McCabe, "Glory, Glory Hallelujah, Teacher Hit Me with a Ruler: Gender and Violence in Subversive Children's Songs," *Studies in Popular Culture* 20 (1998), 71–82.

15. bell hooks, "Sexism and Misogyny: Who Takes the Rap?" *Z Magazine*, February 1994, http://eserver.org/race/misogyny.html.

16. Mashburg, "Violence May Be Gender Issue."

17. Dale Russakoff, "Report Paints Brighter Picture of Children's Lives," *Washington Post*, July 14, 2000, A1; Peter Steinfels, "Formative Years; Seen, Heard, Even Worried About," *New York Times*, December 27, 1992, sec. 4, 1; Mintz, "The Century of the Child: An Assessment," paper presented at the Benton Foundation, Washington, D.C., June 2000; Linda Feldmann, "Surveys Paint Portrait of Strained American Family," *Christian Science Monitor*, November 22, 1991, 6; "All for One: American Family Not Unraveling, Polls Say," *St. Louis Post-Dispatch*, November 22, 1991, A16; R. A. Zaldivar and Gregory Spears, "Children Worse Off than in 1970," *Philadelphia Inquirer*, June 25, 1991, A3; National Commission on Children, *Beyond Rhetoric: A New American Agenda for Children and Families: Final Report of the National Commission on Children* (Washington, D.C., 1991).

18. U.S. Census Bureau, "Poverty: 1999 Highlights," http://www.census.gov/hhes/poverty/poverty99/pov99hi.html. One influential study reported that the

incidence of attention deficit disorder and hyperactivity increased from 1.4 percent to 9.2 percent of children, while emotional problems such as anxiety and depression increased from negligible amounts to 3.6 percent. See "Number of Troubled Children Increases," *Washington Post*, June 6, 2000, A11; Jordana Horn, "One Lesson from School: Survival of the Cruelest," *Philadelphia Inquirer*, April 24, 1999, A17.

Index